Crucial Needs, Weak Incentives

Crucial Needs, Weak Incentives

Social Sector Reform, Democratization, and Globalization in Latin America

Edited by

Robert R. Kaufman and Joan M. Nelson

Woodrow Wilson Center Press
Washington, D.C.

The Johns Hopkins University Press
Baltimore and London

Editorial Offices

Woodrow Wilson Center Press
Woodrow Wilson International Center for Scholars
One Woodrow Wilson Plaza
1300 Pennsylvania Avenue, N.W.
Washington, D.C. 20004-3027
Telephone: 202-691-4029
www.wilsoncenter.org

Order from

The Johns Hopkins University Press
Hampden Station
P.O. Box 50370
Baltimore, Maryland 21211
Telephone: 1-800-537-5487
www.press.jhu.edu/books

2 4 6 8 9 7 5 3 1

Library of Congress Cataloging-in-Publication Data

Crucial needs, weak incentives : social sector reform, democratization, and
globalization in Latin America / Robert R. Kaufman and Joan M. Nelson, editors.
    p. cm.
  Includes bibliographical references and index.
  ISBN 0-8018-8049-1 (cloth : alk. paper) — ISBN 0-8018-8082-3 (pbk. : alk. paper)
  1. Health care reform—Latin America—Cross-cultural studies. 2. Medical policy—
Latin America—Cross-cultural studies. 3. Educational change—Latin America—
Cross-cultural studies. 4. Education and state—Latin America—Cross-cultural
studies. I. Kaufman, Robert R. II. Nelson, Joan M.
  RA395.L3C78 2004
  362.1′098—dc22

                                                            2004011342

ABOUT THE CENTER

The Center is the living memorial of the United States of America to the nation's twenty-eighth president, Woodrow Wilson. Congress established the Woodrow Wilson Center in 1968 as an international institute for advanced study, "symbolizing and strengthening the fruitful relationship between the world of learning and the world of public affairs." The Center opened in 1970 under its own board of trustees.

In all its activities the Woodrow Wilson Center is a nonprofit, nonpartisan organization, supported financially by annual appropriations from the Congress, and by the contributions of foundations, corporations, and individuals. Conclusions or opinions expressed in Center publications and programs are those of the authors and speakers and do not necessarily reflect the views of the Center staff, fellows, trustees, advisory groups, or any individuals or organizations that provide financial support to the Center.

Contents

Tables and Figures

Figures

Acknowledgments

This book has grown out of two workshops on the politics of health and education reform, sponsored by the Latin American Program of the Woodrow Wilson International Center for Scholars in April 2002. We thank the Wilson Center for its financial support, and we are especially grateful to Joseph S. Tulchin, the director of its Latin American Program, for his encouragement and helpful advice throughout the project. Luis Guevara of the Latin American Program managed the logistics and made sure that the workshops ran smoothly. In the course of preparing the manuscript, we received helpful research assistance from Jennifer Curtis and Jing Chen.

Our second major debt is to our case-study authors and discussants. Both during and after the workshops, they have been lively collaborators in the search for parallels and contrasts and for underlying causal factors. Marta Arretche, Mary Clark, Javier Corrales, Christina Ewig, Merilee Grindle, Alejandra González, Pamela Lowden, and Patricia Ramírez provided thoughtful suggestions on some or all of chapters 1, 2, 9, and 16. Thomas Bossert, Deborah Brautigam, Varun Gauri, James Manor, James McGuire, Judith Tendler, and Kurt Weyland were invaluable discussants in the original workshops. In later stages of the project, Maria Victoria Murillo, Juan Carlos Navarro, Judith Tendler, and James McGuire were extremely generous in providing information, suggestions, and critiques, and Linda Larach offered useful insights regarding chapter 9. The manuscript also benefited greatly from the detailed and thoughtful critiques of Michael Reich and Kurt Weyland. We are grateful to them all.

Abbreviations and Acronyms

	Portuguese or Spanish	*English*
ASP	[Programa de] Escuelas Autonomos, Nicaragua	Nicaraguan Autonomous Schools Program
AVEC	Asociación Venezolana de Educación Católica	Venezuelan Association of Catholic Schools
CCSS	Caja Costarricense de Seguro Social	Costa Rican Social Security Fund
CLAS	Comités Locales de Administración en Salud, Peru	Local Health Administration Committees, Peru
COPRE	Comisión Presidencial para la Reforma del Estado, Venezuela	Presidential Commission for State Reform, Venezuela
CTERA	Confederación de Trabajadores de la Educación de la República Argentina	Confederation of Education Workers of the Argentine Republic
EBAIS	Equipos Básicos de Atención Integral de Salud, Costa Rica	Basic Health Teams, Costa Rica
FECODE	Federación Colombiana de Educadores	Federation of Colombian Teachers
FUNDEF	Fundo para o Desenvolvimento da Educação Fundamental e de Valorização do Magistério, Brazil	Elementary Education Development and Teacher Valorization Fund, Brazil
IDB	Banco Interamericano de Desarrollo	Inter-American Development Bank
IMSS	Instituto Mexicano del Seguro Social	Mexican Institute of Social Security
INAMPS	Instituto Nacional de Assistência Médica da Previdência Social, Brazil	National Institute for Medical Assistance in Social Insurance, Brazil

ISS	Instituto de Seguros Sociales, Colombia	Institute of Social Security, Colombia
NOBs	Normas Operacionais Básicas, Brazil	Basic Operational Norms [health sector], Brazil
PAMI	El Programa de Atención Médica Integral, Argentina	Program of Comprehensive Medical Care [for pensioners], Argentina
PMDE	Programa de Manutencao e Desenvolvimento do Ensino, Brazil	Program for the Maintenance and Development of Teaching, Brazil
PREAL	Programa de Promoción de la Reforma Educativa en America Latina	Partnership for Educational Revitalization in the Americas
PRESSAL	Programa para la Reforma de Servicios de Salud, Argentina	Health Sector Reform Program, Argentina
PRI	Partido Revolucionario Institutional, Mexico	Institutional Revolutionary Party, Mexico
PSBT	Programa de Salud Básica para Todos, Peru	Basic Health for All Program, Peru
PSDB	Partido da Social Democracia Brasileira	Social Democratic Party of Brazil
SEG	Seguro Escolar Gratuito, Peru	Free School Health Insurance, Peru
SISBEN	Sistema de Seleccíon de Beneficiarios de los Programas Sociales, Colombia	System of Selection of Beneficiaries of Social Programs, Colombia
SNTE	Sindicato Nacional de Trabajadores de la Educación, Mexico	National Teachers' Union, Mexico
SUS	Sistema Único de Saúde, Brazil	Unified Health System, Brazil

Crucial Needs, Weak Incentives

Chapter 1

Introduction: The Political Challenges of Social Sector Reform

Robert R. Kaufman and Joan M. Nelson

Throughout Latin America, the provision of more extensive and equitable access to education and health care constitutes one of the most pressing challenges of the twenty-first century. Virtually all aspects of social life will be affected by the kinds of social policies adopted in response to these challenges. Improvement in the health and education of the mass of the population is essential for reducing the profound inequalities of Latin American societies, for enhancing the prospects of sustained economic growth, and for raising the quality of democratic governance.

For the individual, access to a good-quality education is the most promising route out of poverty, and it becomes ever more important as jobs require more and more skills and less brawn. Establishing and maintaining good health is also crucial; research now provides extensive evidence that malnutrition and disease in early childhood can impair mental capacity, while good health is also crucial to enable schoolchildren to learn and to empower workers to be reliable and productive employees. Illness or accidents are often the main cause for low-income households sinking into deep poverty.

For the economy as a whole, recent research demonstrates that widespread poor health and short life expectancies are much more important drags on per capita growth than had been assumed earlier (Przeworski et al. 2000; World Health Organization 2001). And education has long been recognized as a major factor contributing to increased productivity, flexibility, and the capacity to compete in an integrated world economy (Rodrik 1999; IDB 1998; Birdsall and Londoño 1998).

Equally fundamental are the potential political effects of health and education policies. The prospects for a reasonably long and healthy life are arguably the most fundamental of rights (Sen 2001). Schools are key potential channels for encouraging a sense of national identity and citizenship, and for promoting values and attitudes important for democratic societies, such as independent judgment and tolerance of competing views. Conversely, the persistence of wide disparities in education and health reinforces de facto concentrations of socioeconomic power and undermines the quality of formal democracy. Social sector reforms directed at correcting these inequalities are thus of critical importance for increasing the capacity of citizens to exercise their democratic rights (O'Donnell 2001; Mendez, O'Donnell, and Pinheiro 1999).

The goals of improving equity and quality must be pursued, however, within the constraints of limited resources. As we discuss a little later in this introduction and in more detail in subsequent chapters, almost all Latin American health and education sectors have serious inefficiencies. Resources are often misallocated, favoring higher-level and high-technology kinds of services while starving more basic services that generate bigger gains in health and productivity. Moreover, specific parts of the systems often perform very poorly; for instance, high repetition rates in elementary schools double or triple the costs of getting a child through the first few grades. The economic crisis of the 1980s, and the increased emphasis on responsible fiscal management since that decade, have heightened the need to pursue increased efficiency jointly with the goals of equity and quality. The tensions among these goals are recurring themes in the stories of social service reforms in the 1990s.

Notwithstanding these problems, indicators of health and education have improved substantially since at least the 1960s. Even after taking into account the setbacks of the 1980s, Latin Americans are generally much more literate than they were a generation ago, and infant and child mortality rates have declined. These improvements, however, have not been sufficient to reduce pervasive social inequalities or to raise the millions of low-income people out of poverty. From a comparative perspective, moreover, ongoing efforts to reduce the deficits of "human capital" within the region aim at a moving target. Conditions in countries in other regions—especially in Asia—have generally improved at a faster rate; Latin America has fallen further behind, reducing its prospects for economic growth in an increasingly competitive global setting (Birdsall and Londoño 1998).

In this volume, we focus on the political factors that shaped reform initiatives aimed at correcting these problems during the late 1980s and the 1990s. Although the politics of reform has been examined extensively in the case of "first-phase" macroeconomic reforms (Nelson 1990; Haggard and Kaufman 1992; Haggard and Webb 1994; Bates and Krueger 1993; Williamson and Haggard 1994), it has only very recently begun to receive attention in the case of "second-phase" social sector policies (Corrales 1999; Gauri 1998; González and Bossert 2000; González 2001; Graham 1998; Grindle 2004; Murillo 1999; Navia and Velasco 2003; Reich 1994; Tendler and Freedheim 1994; Tulchin and Garland 2000; Weyland 1996).

For the most part, research and debate on health and education have focused instead on how these social sectors can be reorganized to deliver services more equitably and effectively. The World Bank, the Inter-American Development Bank, the specialized United Nations agencies, and the Organization for Economic Cooperation and Development, among other international organizations, have produced a great deal of research and policy analysis on education and health sector policies and programs. The World Bank's *World Development Report 1993* (World Bank 1993) and the Inter-American Development Bank's *Economic and Social Progress in Latin America* (IDB 1996) were particularly broad and influential analyses. Other major contributions to the analysis of health and education policies include Altenstetter and Bjorkman (1997); Berman (1995); Burki, Perry, and Dillinger (1999); Cruz-Saco and Mesa-Lago (1998); Filmer, Hammer, and Pritchett (2000); Glewwe (2002); Lloyd-Sherlock (2000); Navarro, Carnoy, and Castro (1999); Reimers (2000); Savedoff (1998); and Wolff and Castro (2003). This body of research is mainly concerned, however, with the design and impact of social sector reforms, rather than with the political processes through which such reforms are brought about, diluted, or blocked.

In this volume, we analyze this still underresearched set of issues. How, for example, have reforms in the delivery of health and education services been affected by "macrotransformations" related to democratization and integration of Latin America into the global economy? How have international financial institutions influenced this process, and what is the role of domestic politics and political institutions? To what extent have the politics of reform been shaped by more specific sets of reformers and stakeholders within the social sectors, and to what extent are these similar or different across the health and education systems? Our attempts to provide some answers to these questions are directed to political scientists and other academic specialists, but it is our hope that they will also be of interest to policymakers directly engaged in efforts to improve social services. A deeper and more nuanced understanding of the range of political forces shaping social service reform efforts cannot provide specific guidance on how best to promote those efforts, but it can suggest crucial considerations that must be taken into account in designing effective country-specific strategies and tactics.

We explore these issues both through case studies of reforms in specific Latin American countries and through comparative essays that examine the patterns of political interaction that cut across these cases. Collectively, we examine who the principal actors are in the "reform story," their preferences and power resources, and the way their choices and interactions are shaped by domestic and international institutions.

Especially in the case studies and our conclusions, we emphasize the dynamic character of social policymaking and implementation. Reform efforts constitute an ongoing process. Specific attempts begin with identifying and defining the nature of the issue, and move through successive phases: getting the issue onto the government agenda, designing a response, gaining authorization for that response, implementing it over a sustained period, and strengthening, modifying, or replacing it as its impact becomes clear. Each phase of the process poses different political challenges; each phase is influenced by the tactics and outcomes of earlier phases. Moreover, sector reform efforts are embedded in larger national political and economic settings that are likely to shift over time, altering the resources and roles of major players. As a whole, the process responds to both international and national political stimuli, but it is shaped most definitively by domestic incentive structures and their susceptibility to change.

Our conclusions about this process are complex and multifaceted. As the title of this volume suggests, there is a crucial need for sector reforms, but the incentives to put them into effect are surprisingly weak. Because measures to improve the equity, quality, and efficiency of education and health services are urgent, we might expect them to appeal to diverse constituencies. Yet despite this potential appeal, organized pressures for reform are limited, and decision makers have generally not faced strong political pressures to take action. Indeed, one of the key points to emerge from the studies is that major social sector reforms in health and education tend to be secondary to more pressing concerns on the political agenda, and they have often been set aside when they appear to come into conflict with these concerns. One consequence has been slower change than might have been expected in newly democratized political systems that are under competitive pressure to increase their stock of human capital.

Nevertheless, significant changes have been taking place within the region. Our case studies discuss at least two types of change. The more common and widespread takes the form of relatively small steps that slide under the radar screen of national politics: ministerial decrees, shifts in administrative practices, or local initiatives that may escape the attention of actors outside the sector. Such modest steps rarely challenge strong status quo interests within the sector, but potentially they can have an important cumulative effect on the way services are delivered. In some countries, moreover, "piecemeal" reforms that address specific problems in particular parts of the system can be undertaken with only minimal coordination with measures taken elsewhere in the sector. The greatest threat to this type of reform comes not from overt opposition, but from a loss of the momentum needed to sustain ongoing progress.

In a smaller number of countries, we see initiatives that have altered the structure and organization of delivery systems in quite extensive ways, despite strong stakeholder opposition. We argue that these typically go forward when they are linked to the broader objectives of powerful actors outside the social sectors themselves. A well-designed comprehensive approach potentially offers greater coherence and continuity for sector reform efforts. Such approaches, however, are not only less common but are also much more likely to provoke intense political opposition. Moreover, although linkage to higher-priority objectives offers significant opportunities for health or education reformers, it also carries significant risks that improvement in the sector will be stalled or even undermined by omissions or compromises in design, or by lapses in implementation that reflect the secondary status of the sector reforms.

Background and Analytic Objectives

To analyze the political challenges that have characterized contemporary efforts at reform, it is important to review some of the main features of the delivery systems as they evolved during previous decades. Access to education and health services did in fact increase considerably from the end of World War II until the debt crisis of the early 1980s, in part as a consequence of economic growth and urbanization. Table 1.1 provides basic data regarding population and income, and trends in health and education inputs and outcomes for the eight countries discussed in the case studies, and for Latin America as a whole.

Despite the improvements shown in the table, however, the education and health care delivery systems were generally marked by significant problems at the beginning of the 1990s. In many countries, they were dominated by highly centralized and unaccountable administrative structures that served as vast centers of patronage and political power for politicians and union leaders. Both social sectors mirrored and often reinforced profound inequities within the region, responding primarily to the concerns of middle-class and unionized blue-collar workers for higher education and curative health services (World Bank 1993; Birdsall and Londoño 1998). In many countries, inequities were exacerbated by tremendous inefficiencies, for instance, by extremely high repetition and dropout rates in primary schools (PREAL 2001; Puryear 1997).

The debt crisis of the 1980s and the onset of market reforms in the early 1990s constituted important, though quite different, turning points in this evolution. Many health care systems were already encountering severe fiscal strains even before the debt crisis (Mesa-Lago 1985). The inflation and austerity brought about by the crisis, however, had devastating effects on both sectors. Sharp contractions in most areas of public spending jeopardized funds devoted to maintaining and equipping schools and hospitals, as well as the salaries of teachers and health workers. In addition, social insurance health coverage declined with rising unemployment and the growth of the informal sector, swelling the already large numbers dependent on inferior public health services.[1]

---

1. These cuts are not fully apparent in tables 1.2 and 1.3, which show consolidated public spending on education and health at five-year intervals from 1980 to 2000, as a percentage of GDP. In those countries where GDP dropped faster than social spending during some years in the 1980s, education and health outlays may have risen relative to GDP despite a drop in absolute levels of spending. We chose to show spending as a

Table 1.1

Basic Indicators for the Eight Case-Study Countries and Latin America: Status and Trends in Population, Health, and Education

Indicator	Argentina	Brazil	Colombia	Costa Rica	Mexico	Nicaragua	Peru	Venezuela	Latin America
Population and income									
Population, 2000 (millions)[a]	37	170	42	4	98	5	26	24	514.7
Average annual population growth, 1990–2000 (percent)[a]	1.3	1.4	1.9	2.0	1.6	2.8	1.7	2.1	1.6
Population under 15 years, 1999 (percent)[b]	27.9	29.3	33.1	32.8	33.6	43.1	33.9	34.5	32.3
Population over 65 years, 1999 (percent)[b]	9.7	5.0	4.7	5.0	4.6	3.0	4.7	4.4	5.2
Income per capita, purchasing power parity, 2000 (dollars)[a]	12,090	7,320	5,890	8,250	8,810	2,100	4,720	5,750	7,030
Health									
Life expectancy at birth, 1970–75 (years)[c]	67	60	62	68	62	55	55	66	61
Life expectancy, 1999 (years)[a]	74	67	70	77	72	69	69	73	70
Under-5-year mortality per 1,000 live births, 1970[c]	71	135	113	77	110	65	178	61	125
Under-5-year mortality per 1,000 live births, 1999[c]	22	40	31	14	33	47	52	23	39

continued

Table 1.1
Continued

Indicator	Argentina	Brazil	Colombia	Costa Rica	Mexico	Nicaragua	Peru	Venezuela	Latin America
1-year-olds immunized for measles, 1990–91 (percent)[d]	99	83	75	n.a.	78	54	59	54	75
1-year-olds immunized for measles, 1997–99 (percent)[e]	97	96	77	86	98	71	92	78	n.a.
Doctors per 1,000 population, 1988–92[d]	2.99	1.46	0.87	n.a.	0.54	0.60	1.03	1.55	1.25
Nurse/doctor ratio, 1988–92[d]	0.2	0.1	0.6	n.a.	0.8	0.5	0.9	0.5	0.5
Education									
Adult illiteracy, 1999 (percent)[a]	3	15	9	5	9	32	10	8	12
Net primary enrollment, 1980 (percent)[f]	97	80	73	89	98	71	87	83	85
Net primary enrollment, 1997 (percent)[f]	100	97	89	89	100	79	94	83	94
Net secondary enrollment, 1980 (percent)[f]	59	46	60	39	67	51	80	24	55
Net secondary enrollment, 1997 (percent)[f]	77	66	76	40	66	51	84	49	66

Note: n.a. = not available.

[a]The data are from World Bank (2002, table 1, 232–33).
[b]The data are from UNDP (2001, table 5, 154–57).
[c]The data are from UNDP (2001, table 8, 166–69).
[d]The data are from World Bank (1993, appendix table A.8, 208–9).
[e]The data are from UNDP(2001, table 6, 158–61).
[f]The data are from World Bank (2000, table 6, 284–85).

As Latin America entered a phase of recovery during the 1990s, there was a reversal of these trends, at least in terms of fiscal effort. Despite the slowing of overall rates of public spending, expenditures in education and health increased substantially as a percentage of gross domestic product (GDP) throughout the region (ECLAC 2002; also see Wolff and Castro 2003, table 8.4).

As tables 1.2 and 1.3 show, the trends were somewhat mixed within the countries covered in this volume, but they were generally consistent with patterns in the region as a whole. Education spending relative to GDP was higher in 2000 than in the precrisis year of 1980 in Argentina, Brazil, Colombia, Mexico, and Nicaragua; stayed more or less level in Venezuela; and had failed to recover to 1980 levels in Costa Rica and Peru. Health spending had increased considerably by 2000, compared with 1980, in Argentina, Brazil, Colombia, Mexico, and Peru (where, however, outlays remained very low relative to GDP). In Venezuela, spending on health in the late 1990s was comparable, relative to GDP, to 1980 levels; in Nicaragua, there had been a modest increase; Costa Rican health outlays had dropped.[2] The econometric evidence suggests that the increases in spending were due not only to the economic recovery but also to the wave of redemocratization that swept most countries during that period. Even after controlling for such factors as growth, inflation, and trade and capital flows, democracies tended to spend more on health and education than authoritarian regimes (Kaufman and Segura-Ubiergo 2001).

A central premise of this volume, however, is that *how* money is spent is as important as *how much* (World Bank 2004). Given the inequities and

---

percent of GDP in tables 1.2 and 1.3, rather than absolute expenditures, because the latter entail complex and potentially still more misleading problems of correcting for rapid and variable inflation and (for cross-national comparisons) changing exchange rates.

2. Different standard sources of data on government spending vary significantly regarding the levels and even the direction of trends in spending on education and health in specific countries. We consulted the International Monetary Fund's *Government Financial Statistics,* the World Bank's *World Development Indicators,* and the *Statistical Yearbook for Latin America and the Caribbean* published by the Economic Commission for Latin America and the Caribbean. Despite differences among these sources, the broad trends are similar for most of the countries examined in this volume. Data from UNESCO's *Statistical Yearbook 2002,* cited in Wolff and Castro 2003, table 8.4, also confirm the trend in education expenditures. Data for Argentina, Brazil, and Nicaragua varied particularly sharply in different sources. Variation in data for Argentina and Brazil may reflect different ways of handling federal transfers to states for education and health spending.

Table 1.2

Education Spending by the Central Government Relative to Gross Domestic Product, Eight Case-Study Countries, 1980–2000

Country	1980	1985	1990	1995	2000
Argentina	1.9	1.6	3.3	3.9	3.8 (1997)
Brazil	0.7	2.7	3.7	4.5	5.1 (1997)
Colombia	2.5	2.7	3.7	4.4	4.5 (1997)
Costa Rica	6.2	5.1	4.5	4.4	4.7
Mexico	3.1	4.2	4.0	4.9	6.2
Nicaragua	3.5	6.6	4.0	4.1	4.5
Peru	2.5	3.0	2.5	2.3	2.0
Venezuela	4.1	4.7	2.5	4.4	n.a.

Note: n.a. = not available.
Source: ECLAC (2002, table 41); for the year 2000, ECLAC (2003, table 39).

inefficiencies briefly discussed above, there is little a priori reason to think that more money will translate into more equitable and effective delivery of services, rather than into patronage or increased benefits for politically influential white- and blue-collar workers. Thus, although fiscal politics is undoubtedly a crucial part of the contemporary reform story, an equally important component is an inherently political reorganization of roles, incentives, responsibility, and accountability within each of the sectors.

The chapters that follow focus on policy reforms that lead to significant changes in the structure, finance, management, and coverage of the health and education sectors. The stated goal of such reforms is to improve the *quality* of social services, their *efficiency* or cost-effectiveness, and the

Table 1.3

Health Spending by the Central Government Relative to Gross Domestic Product, Eight Case-Study Countries, 1980–2000

Country	1980	1985	1990	1995	2000
Argentina	1.6	1.6	4.4	4.8	4.0 (1997)
Brazil	1.3	2.1	2.9	3.6	3.0 (1997)
Colombia	1.2	1.1	1.3	4.7	n.a.
Costa Rica	7.2	5.0	7.2	7.1	5.0
Mexico	0.4	0.3	2.9	3.6	2.6
Nicaragua	4.4	5.0	5.1	4.7	5.7
Peru	0.8	1.0	1.0	1.0	1.2
Venezuela	1.3	1.8	1.5	1.0	1.4 (1997)

Note: n.a. = not available.
Source: ECLAC (2002, table 46); for the year 2000, ECLAC (2003, table 44).

equitable distribution of access across income, ethnic, and gender cate-gories and among regions. However, we confine our analysis to the policy reforms themselves; we do not attempt to assess the extent to which their long-term goals are actually achieved.

We have limited our focus in this way for several reasons. First, as is the case with any policy analysis, it is difficult to untangle the effects of policy from other factors that may also be influencing social outcomes. Moreover, whereas many health and education reforms have been enacted only very recently, it may take many more years before their effects become fully visible; and there is still considerable uncertainty among policy specialists about the kinds of reforms that are likely to "work" over the long term. Finally, there is a good deal of disagreement about the yardsticks that should be used to measure progress. Most reforms involve difficult trade-offs in the allocation of resources, and they raise many questions for which there are no clear answers. To what extent, for example, should preventive health care or primary education be strengthened at the expense of curative health care or higher education? How should the burdens for financing such measures be allocated?

In the long-term, of course, such outcome issues must be confronted in order to evaluate the policy reforms now under way. As an essential inter-mediate step, however, we also need to know why and how policy reforms were initiated in the first place, and the extent to which they actually have been implemented. We are also interested in explaining choices with re-spect to the dimensions, design, and specific objectives of the policy re-forms themselves. Reforms can vary in several dimensions—in their scope, ranging from comprehensive sector remodeling to quite narrow changes in the organization of the sector; in the substantive "design" choices regarding decentralization, targeting, community participation, and competition among service providers; and in the relative emphasis they place on such objectives as accountability, quality and equity of service, and fiscal efficiency.

The Politics of Reform: Some Preliminary Observations

In response to the debt crisis of the mid-1980s, many Latin American countries adopted far-reaching stabilization and structural adjustment mea-sures. Many of these measures were executive initiatives, enacted by de-cree or pushed through reluctant legislatures. Some, especially exchange-rate and interest-rate changes and deregulation, were "stroke-of-the-pen" actions that could be adopted by a small circle of high-level economic officials and became effective very rapidly. By the early 1990s, the need to strengthen the health and education sectors became a part of the ongoing reform agenda. Such second-wave or "late stage" reforms often involve changes in complex institutions as well as in policies; and for this reason, it was widely expected that they faced challenges that differed significantly from the political challenges of the earlier reforms (Naim 1995; Nelson 1999). This has led many observers to argue that it is necessary to adjust reform strategies and tactics in ways that make them less "top-down" and much more inclusive and consultative.

As we argue more extensively elsewhere in this volume, social sector reforms do share one important aspect in common with many of the earlier market reforms: Both have encountered substantial asymmetries between the intended beneficiaries from reforms and the groups that stand to lose. Although the general public favors efforts to improve health and education services in principle, they face significant problems of collective action in organizing and sustaining community involvement. Citizens are rarely organized to exert pressure on social service policies, nor are their concerns with these policies at the top of their political agendas. Moreover, much of the public is uninformed, bewildered, or suspicious of many of the reform proposals for restructuring social services and improving incentives for efficiency and quality. They do not believe the proposed means will serve the desired ends, or they fear that reforms will serve some goals (efficiency) at the expense of others (equity or quality).

Stakeholders in the status quo, in contrast, are often strongly organized. They are intensely opposed to some of the proposed reforms. Their influence frequently penetrates governments; Health and Education Ministries have typically been colonized by patronage-oriented politicians and union elites that resist reorganization. Especially in the health sector, private providers and insurers constitute another potential source of opposition.

These difficulties have been compounded further by three factors that are more specific to social sector reform (Nelson 2000). First, health and education reforms lack widely accepted international policy templates. The Chilean model of partially privatized health and education services has attracted wide attention and debate, but few imitators. Some more general reform principles have wider currency; for example, decentralization, stronger performance incentives, increased competition, and user choice. As we shall see, however, these terms can have very different, even contradictory, meanings to actors involved in the reform process, and even specialists argue bitterly about the merits of various options. In contrast, there was wider agreement among international policy elites about the goals of stabilization and structural adjustment policies and the means of getting there, even if the specificity of the "Washington consensus" was often exaggerated.

Second, whereas first-phase market reforms were often spurred by the threat of hyperinflation and financial crisis, those in health and education can rarely capitalize on a sense of urgency. Macroeconomic crises generate immediate, dramatic, and widespread losses of income, savings, and employment. They affect most people in a country, and their consequences are immediately perceived. In contrast, if education and health services are deteriorating, they tend to do so slowly; the impact is harder to perceive and is uneven across regions and classes. And where services have long been weak, most people do not regard the resulting problems as a crisis, or even as unusual. Therefore, the political costs of delaying improvements in health care delivery or education quality are far lower than the costs of failing to cope promptly with spiraling inflation or rapidly dwindling foreign exchange reserves. Indeed, fiscal pressures induced by macroeconomic crises often derail efforts at social sector reform.

Third, reforms of the health and education systems have raised a range of issues related to the redesign of complex administrative machinery, including new roles and lines of authority among service providers, changes in the relation between central and local governments, and increased community participation in oversight of services. As we shall discuss in chapter 2, important differences between the health and education sectors must be taken into account. However, both sectors are large employers—indeed, they usually employ the two largest categories of public employees in the nation. Those workers are physically dispersed throughout the country, and they interact with millions of students and patients. The quality of education and health services depends ultimately on the performance of teachers in the classroom and of doctors, nurses, and public health workers in clinics, hospitals, and communities. Both social sectors, therefore, face political challenges related to oversight, accountability, coordination across levels of government, and support from service providers—problems that were much less acute for earlier macroeconomic reforms.

Despite these daunting challenges, as was noted, there have been both incremental and large-scale reform initiatives throughout the region, and in some cases these have led to substantial changes in the way social sectors are organized. In all the countries covered in this volume, the broad regional and international trends of democratization and economic liberalization established the context in which reform proposals were propelled onto the political agenda. International organizations such as the World Bank and the Inter-American Development Bank did much to shape more specific discussion of policy alternatives. Nevertheless, as we shall see in more detail in subsequent chapters, the linkages between these external influences and sector policy outcomes were complex and indirect. Reforms themselves were largely domestic stories, nested in highly specific networks of political institutions and coalitional alignments.

The fate of large-scale reforms, as was noted, turned on whether they could be bundled with other objectives sought by actors that were not directly linked to the social sector itself. With some exceptions, however, the political alliances that emerged around these objectives were formed within and through the executive bureaucracy. Design was shaped to an important extent by reform teams within the relevant ministries, finance ministers, and presidents themselves, usually with only limited consultation with stakeholders and other groups. Legislatures and parties were important in some cases, but they generally played a less prominent role than executives, even in the authorization phase of the process. Implementation involved a broader set of actors over far longer periods of time, but this phase also depended crucially on the continued monitoring and involvement of central executive authorities.

The top-down character of many of these reform experiences challenges the widely accepted prescription about the greater need for consultation and inclusion in second-phase reforms. Conversely, it leaves open the question of how to enlist the active cooperation of service providers during the later phases of implementation.

Research Design and Approach of the Volume

Many factors have played a role in the degree and types of social sector reforms that are now under way in Latin America. However, an assessment of their relative causal weight and a refinement of causal arguments is impeded by a lack of information about the reform stories themselves. With the exception of Chile and perhaps one or two other cases, knowledge about "what has happened" and "how much" remains confined primarily to country and sector specialists, and it is only rarely integrated into a comparative analysis. For this reason, our efforts have emphasized informed induction, which seeks to map the scope, design, and objectives of specific countries' social sector reforms and address the causal questions and propositions discussed above.

The selection of country cases was motivated largely by this inductive approach. We sought countries with experiences that ranged from failed initiatives to rather substantial reforms, with the expectation that these could offer some preliminary insights into the analytic issues raised above. Our choices were also guided in part by the availability of specialists who could tell these stories in ways that combined deep knowledge of the sectors with a strong grasp of the underlying politics.

We present studies of both health and education reforms in four countries: Argentina, Brazil, Colombia, and Mexico. These four are among the largest countries of the region, and they frequently serve as bellwethers for other Latin American countries. Examining both health and education reforms in these countries, moreover, makes it easier to identify the similarities and differences in the politics of the two social sectors. The course of reform in the two sectors sometimes differed substantially within one country; among our cases, Colombia's experience of far-reaching health reforms and ineffective education policies offers the most clear-cut example. In addition, this volume presents case studies of education reform in Nicaragua and Venezuela, and of health reform in Costa Rica and Peru.

Taken together, these twelve case studies offer a perspective that includes a wide range of reform experiences in a variety of political settings. Both Brazil and Colombia underwent extensive social sector reforms during the 1990s, whereas those in Argentina and Mexico were much more limited. After the sharp break with the Sandinista regime, Nicaragua also undertook a relatively extensive reorganization of its educational sector, although this was of a different kind than the ones in the larger South American countries. Costa Rica is of interest because it provides Latin America's clearest instance of a consensual, democratic welfare state, while in Peru, incremental but significant health reform was initiated under the autocratic and highly personalistic rule of Alberto Fujimori. Finally, Venezuela provides an important case of "nonreform." There was little significant change in its educational sector during the 1990s, despite a succession of ambitious initiatives during the 1990s. Exploring why this was so will provide a clearer perspective on the factors that have contributed to reform in the other countries.

The comparative implications of these cases are discussed more explicitly in chapters 2 and 9, which respectively introduce the health and education parts of the book, and in the conclusion, chapter 16. Chapters 2 and 9 provide comparative "snapshots" of cross-national differences in the goals, scope, and implementation of the sectoral reform policies undertaken during the 1990s. They introduce readers to issues specific to each social sector, map the interests and resources of the relevant actors, and suggest some of the factors that account for the cross-national differences. Chapter 16 builds on these comparative chapters, but it focuses more directly on the *dynamics* of reform and discusses how political challenges and actors change as reforms move from initiation through design and authorization to implementation. Because the selection of cases is neither random nor complete, the conclusions drawn from them are inevitably preliminary. Given the fairly wide range of differences among them, however, they can provide the foundations for propositions that can be explored in other cases.

References

Altenstetter, C., and J. Bjorkman, eds. 1997. *Health Policy Reform, National Variations and Globalisation.* London: Macmillan.

Bates, Robert H., and Anne O. Krueger, eds. 1993. *Political and Economic Interactions in Economic Policy Reform: Evidence from Eight Countries.* Cambridge: Basil Blackwell.

Berman, Peter, ed. 1995. *Health Sector Reform in Developing Countries.* Cambridge, Mass.: Harvard University Press.

Birdsall, Nancy, and Juan Luis Londoño. 1998. No Tradeoff: Efficient Growth via More Equal Human Capital Accumulation. In *Beyond Tradeoffs: Market Reform and Equitable Growth in Latin America,* ed. Nancy Birdsall, Carol Graham, and Richard H. Sabot. Washington, D.C.: Inter-American Development Bank and Brookings Institution Press.

Burki, Shahid Javed, Guillermo Perry, and William Dillinger. 1999. *Beyond the Center: Decentralizing the State.* Washington, D.C.: World Bank.

Corrales, Javier. 1999. *The Politics of Education Reform Implementation: Bolstering Supply and Demand; Overcoming Institutional Blocks.* Washington, D.C.: World Bank.

Cruz-Saco, M., and C. Mesa-Lago, eds. 1998. *Do Options Exist? The Reform of Pension and Health Care Systems in Latin America.* Pittsburgh: University of Pittsburgh Press.

ECLAC (Economic Commission for Latin America and the Caribbean). 1999. *Social Panorama of Latin America 1998.* Santiago: ECLAC.

———. 2002. *Statistical Yearbook for Latin America and the Caribbean 2002.* Santiago: ECLAC.

————. 2003. *Statistical Yearbook for Latin America and the Caribbean 2003.* Santiago: ECLAC.

Filmer, Deon, Jeffrey Hammer, and Lant Pritchett. 2000. Weak Links in the Chain: A Diagnosis of Health Policy in Poor Countries. *World Bank Research Observer* 15, no. 2: 199–224.

Fiske, Edward B. 1996. *Decentralization of Education: Politics and Consensus.* Washington, D.C.: World Bank.

Gauri, Varun. 1998. *School Choice in Chile: Two Decades of Education Reform.* Pittsburgh: University of Pittsburgh Press.

Glewwe, Paul. 2002. Schools and Skills in Developing Countries: Education Policies and Socioeconomic Outcomes. *Journal of Economic Literature* 40, no. 2: 436–82.

González-Rossetti, Alejandra. 2001. The Political Dimension of Health Reform: The Case of Mexico and Colombia. Ph.D. dissertation, Department of Public Health Policy, London School of Hygiene and Tropical Medicine, University of London.

González-Rossetti, Alejandra, and Thomas J. Bossert. 2000. *Enhancing the Political Feasibility of Health Reform: A Comparative Analysis of Chile, Colombia and Mexico.* Cambridge, Mass.: School of Public Health, Harvard University.

Graham, Carol. 1998. *Private Markets for Public Goods: Raising the Stakes in Economic Reform.* Washington, D.C.: Brookings Institution Press.

Grindle, Merilee. 2000. *Audacious Reforms: Institutional Invention and Democracy in Latin America.* Baltimore: Johns Hopkins University Press.

————. 2004. *Despite the Odds: Contentious Politics and Education Reform.* Princeton, N.J.: Princeton University Press.

Haggard, Stephan, and Robert R. Kaufman, eds. 1992. *The Politics of Economic Adjustment.* Princeton, N.J.: Princeton University Press.

Haggard, Stephan, and Steven B. Webb, eds. 1994. *Voting for Reform: Democracy, Political Liberalization, and Economic Adjustment.* New York: Oxford University Press.

IDB (Inter-American Development Bank). 1996. *Economic and Social Progress in Latin America: Making Social Services Work.* Washington, D.C.: IDB.

————. 1998. *Facing Up to Inequality in Latin America 1998–1999: Economic and Social Progress Report.* Baltimore: Johns Hopkins University Press.

Kaufman, Robert R., and Alex Segura-Ubiergo. 2001. Globalization, Domestic Politics, and Social Spending in Latin America: A Cross-Sectional Time Series Analysis, 1973–1997. *World Politics* 53, no. 4: 553–87.

Koivusalo, M., and E. Ollila. 1997. *Making a Healthy World: Agencies, Actors, and Policies in International Health.* London: Zed Books.

Lloyd-Sherlock, Peter, ed. 2000. *Healthcare Reform and Poverty in Latin America.* London: Institute of Latin American Studies, University of London.

Mendex, Juan E., Guillermo O'Donnell, and Paulo Pinheiro, eds. 1999. *The (Un)Rule of Law and the Underprivileged in Latin America.* Notre Dame, Ind.: University of Notre Dame Press.

Mesa-Lago, Carmelo. 1985. The Crisis of Social Security and Healthcare: Latin American Experiences and Lessons. Center for Latin American Studies, University Center for International Studies, University of Pittsburgh, Pittsburgh (unpublished).

Murillo, Maria Victoria. 1999. Recovering Political Dynamics: Teachers' Unions and the Decentralization of Education in Argentina and Mexico. *Journal of Inter-American Studies and World Affairs* 41, no. 1: 31–57.

Naim, Moisés. 1995. Latin America: The Second Stage of Reform. In *Economic Reform and Democracy,* ed. Larry Diamond and Marc F. Plattner. Baltimore: Johns Hopkins University Press.

Navarro, Juan Carlos, Martin Carnoy, and Claudio de Moura Castro. 1999. Education Reform in Latin America: A Review of Issues, Components and Tools. Inter-American Development Bank, Washington, D.C. (unpublished).

Navio, Patricio, and Andres Velasco. 2003. The Politics of Second-Generation Reforms. In *After the Washington Consensus: Restarting Growth and Reform in Latin America,* ed. Pedro-Pablo Kuczynski and John Williamson. Washington, D.C.: Institute for International Economics,.

Nelson, Joan M., ed. 1990. *Economic Crisis and Policy Choice: The Politics of Adjustment in the Third World.* Princeton, N.J.: Princeton University Press.

———. 1999. *Reforming Health and Education: The World Bank, The IDB, and Complex Institutional Change.* Washington, D.C.: Overseas Development Council.

———. 2000. Reforming Social Sector Governance: A Political Perspective. In *Social Development in Latin America: The Politics of Reform,* ed. Joseph S. Tulchin and Allison M. Garland. Boulder, Colo.: Lynne Rienner Publishers for the Latin American Program of the Woodrow Wilson International Center for Scholars.

O'Donnell, Guillermo. 2001. Democracy, Law, and Comparative Politics. *Studies in Comparative International Development* 36, no. 1 (October): 7–36.

PREAL (Partnership for Educational Revitalization in the Americas). 2001. *Lagging Behind: A Report Card on Education in Latin America.* Report of the Task Force on Education, Equity, and Economic Competitiveness in the Americas. Santiago: PREAL.

Przeworski, Adam, Michael E. Alvarez, Jose Antonio Cheibub, and Fernando Limongi, 2000. *Democracy and Development: Political Institutions and Material Well-Being in the World, 1950–1990.* Cambridge: Cambridge University Press.

Puryear, Jeffrey. 1997, *La educacíon en América Latina: Problemas y desafios.* Working Paper 7. Santiago: PREAL (Partnership for Educational Revitalization in the Americas).

Reich, Michael. 1994. The Political Economy of Health Transitions in the Third World. In *Health and Social Change in International Perspective,* ed. Lincoln Chen, A. Kleinman, and N. C. Ware. Cambridge, Mass.: School of Public Health, Harvard University.

Reimers, Fernando, ed. 2000. *Unequal Schools, Unequal Chances: The Challenges to Equal Opportunity in the Americas.* Cambridge, Mass.: Harvard University Press.

Rodrik, Dani. 1999. Where Did All the Growth Go? External Shocks, Social Conflict, and Growth Collapses. *Journal of Economic Growth* 4, no. 4 (December): 385–412.

Savedoff, William D., ed. 1998. *Organization Matters: Agency Problems in Health and Education in Latin America.* Washington, D.C.: Inter-American Development Bank.

Sen, Amartya Kumar. 2001. *Development as Freedom.* New York: Oxford University Press.

Tendler, Judith, and Sara Freedheim. 1994. Trust in a Rent-Seeking World: Health and Government Transformed in Northeast Brazil. *World Development* 22, no. 12: 1771–91.

Tulchin, Joseph S., and Allison M. Garland, eds. 2000. *Social Development in Latin America: The Politics of Reform.* Boulder, Colo.: Lynne Rienner Publishers for the Latin American Program of the Woodrow Wilson International Center for Scholars.
UNDP (United Nations Development Program). 2001. Human Development Indicators. In *Human Development Report 2001.* New York: Oxford University Press.
Weyland, Kurt. 1996. *Democracy without Equity: Failures of Reform in Brazil.* Pittsburgh: University of Pittsburgh Press.
Williamson, John, and Stephan Haggard. 1994. The Political Conditions for Economic Reform. In *The Political Economy of Policy Reform,* ed. John Williamson. Washington, D.C.: Institute for International Economics.
Wolff, Laurence, and Claudio de Moura Castro. 2003. Education and Training: The Task Ahead. In *The Political Economy of Policy Reform,* ed. John Williamson. Washington, D.C.: Institute for International Economics.
World Bank. 1993. *World Development Report 1993: Investing in Health.* New York: Oxford University Press.
———. 2000. World Development Indicators. In *World Development Report 2000/ 2001: Attacking Poverty.* New York: Oxford University Press.
———. 2002. World Development Indicators. In *World Development Report 2002: Building Institutions for Markets.* New York: Oxford University Press.
———. 2004. *World Development Report 2004: Making Services Work for Poor People.* New York: Oxford University Press.
World Health Organization. 2001. *Macroeconomics and Health: Investing in Health for Economic Development.* Report of the Commission on Macroeconomics and Health. Geneva: World Health Organization.

Part One

The Politics of Health Sector Reform

Chapter 2

The Politics of Health Sector Reform: Cross-National Comparisons

Joan M. Nelson

General health status improved rapidly in most of Latin America in the decades following World War II. Between 1960 and 1990, average life expectancy increased from fifty-four to seventy years; child mortality dropped from 161 to 60 per 1,000 births (World Bank 1993, table A.3). Yet these and more detailed indicators varied tremendously, both among and within countries. In Haiti, infant mortality was still 156 per 1,000 births as the 1990s began; in Bolivia, the rate was 125; while Colombia had pushed infant deaths down to 21 and Cuba to 12. During the 1980s, 57 percent of children in Guatemala between the ages of two and five years were stunted as a result of inadequate nutrition; in Venezuela and Chile, the corresponding figures were 7 and 10 percent.

The author thanks Marta Arretche, Mary Clark, Christina Ewig, Alejandra González Rossetti, Robert Kaufman, James McGuire, and Patricia Ramírez for helpful comments on this chapter.

By 1990, the Southern Cone countries were well advanced in the demographic transition from high to low birthrates and death rates; substantial fractions of their populations were more than sixty years of age (16 percent in Uruguay, 13 percent in Argentina), and the pattern of health problems had shifted increasingly to noncommunicable diseases typical of wealthier countries. But parts of the region (including poor and remote areas within more advanced countries) were still characterized by sharply different patterns: an average of four or five children born to each woman, high infant and child mortality rates, relatively low life expectancy, and the continued prevalence of communicable diseases, parasites, and maternal and prenatal problems typical of poor countries (World Bank 1993, tables A.3 and A.6).

Health outcomes of course are determined not only by the amount and quality of health care but also—indeed, more importantly—by nutrition, housing, and related services (especially the supply of clean water), income and education, environmental factors, and an array of public health measures. The varied picture sketched above reflects differences in all these factors. But weaknesses in health care systems in much of the region contributed to health and life expectancy outcomes well below those achieved outside the region in countries with comparable per capita income. In the mid-1990s, more than 40 percent of the population in eight Latin American countries, and a third of Brazil's citizens, lacked access even to basic health services. The quality of public health care services was poor or declining in many countries, in part as a lingering result of budget pressures during the difficult 1980s, but more fundamentally as a result of weak structure, perverse incentives, and misallocated resources in the systems themselves. Those who could afford to do so increasingly relied on private insurance, especially in the middle-income countries of the region (IDB 1996, 301).

By the early 1990s, several international and national trends converged to highlight the need for reforms in the organization and incentives of health sector finance and delivery systems. But reforms faced formidable political obstacles; typically, a small set of reformers confronted a diverse array of opponents and indifferent groups. This chapter briefly sketches the trends promoting reform. It surveys the cast of characters in the political drama, examining each group's concerns and sources of influence. The chapter then reviews the scope and nature of reforms actually adopted in the countries discussed in this volume. Even among this limited set of six, there is a great deal of variation in what was attempted and in implementation experiences. The final sections of the chapter explore the political explanations for contrasts in different countries' efforts, and for varied rates of progress among different kinds of reforms.

The Scene in 1990

Most Latin American health systems are segmented. They generally include three subsystems: social security health care finance and delivery systems for formal-sector workers, funded by payroll contributions from employers and employees; public systems funded from general tax revenues, serving that part of the population not covered by social security; and diverse private systems for the wealthy and increasingly for middle and poor classes, financed by private insurance (for better-off people) and out-of-pocket expenditures. The segments overlap to varying degrees. In some countries, the social security segment operates its own clinics and hospitals, but workers covered by social security may also seek care from public or private providers; elsewhere the social security segment may operate by reimbursing public and private providers. Costa Rica, Cuba, Panama, and the English-speaking Caribbean countries have predominantly public systems.[1]

Private hospitals and clinics play a significant role in much of the region; pharmaceutical production and distribution is largely private in most cases.[2] Private health sector interests are much more intertwined with public-sector activities and agencies than is the case in the education sector. For example, doctors often have both public-sector positions and private practices. Private hospitals may be compensated for services provided from patients' personal insurance plans, their social security benefits, their out-of-pocket payments, and public funds. In Brazil, the social security segment of the system has long relied on contracts with private hospitals and clinics to provide health services for its members. After the social security and public segments of the system were unified in the early 1990s, private hospitals continued to provide a large portion of all services.

1. See IDB (1996, 309–19) for a more detailed classification and discussion of problems specific to different types of systems.

2. In 1990, Latin American and Caribbean countries spent an average (weighted by population) of 4 percent of gross domestic product on health; of this, 2.4 percent was public expenditure and 1.6 percent private. The ratio varied widely among countries; in three of those listed—Colombia, El Salvador, and Paraguay—private expenditures were greater than public (World Bank 1993, table A.9).

Although different combinations of public, private, and social security finance and provision generate somewhat different problems (see IDB 1996, 309–19), almost all Latin American systems share certain common weaknesses. Among the most obvious are these:

- There are striking inequalities in access to and quality of services, between wealthy and poor people, between urban and rural areas, and between more prosperous regions and those that are poor and remote. In Peru in the mid-1990s, infant mortality per 1,000 births varied between 52 in Callao to more than 100 in Inka (IDB 1996, 303).
- Funding systems are biased in favor of large and sophisticated providers, and they tend to neglect primary care and preventive services. Doctors' interests and preferences reinforce these biases.
- Funding arrangements and personnel and management systems do not create incentives for efficiency; on the contrary, they often perpetuate or encourage absenteeism, underutilization of some facilities and excessive demand on others, the use of more costly procedures where less expensive options are available, and other kinds of waste.
- In the public and sometimes the social security segments, wages and other key labor decisions tend to be highly centralized in the national ministry and/or social security institute; labor relations with a small number of large health workers' unions are sometimes acrimonious, whereas labor regulations are extremely rigid.

Parallels and Contrasts between Education and Health Sector Structure and Politics

As the introductory chapter briefly suggested, noting the similarities and contrasts between the education and health sectors can improve our understanding of the politics of each. Problems typically shared by the education and health sectors include inequalities in access and quality; a bias in the distribution of resources in favor of higher levels of the systems; a lack of incentives for efficiency; and centralized, rigid, and often acrimonious labor relations. The pattern of middle-class flight to private providers is an additional similarity in the two sectors. In both, middle-class exit (from public to private elementary and secondary schools, and from reliance on social security coverage to purchase of private supplementary health insurance) has the effect of reducing middle-class stakes in the improvement of the public or social security systems.

However, contrasts between the structure of the education and health sectors in most of the region generate differences in the politics of sector reform efforts. Two basic contrasts have important political implications:

- The segmented structure of most health care systems, and the extent to which private interests intertwine with public and semipublic segments of the sectors, have no real parallels in the region's education sectors. Underlying the segmentation of the health sector is a fundamental contrast in the predictability and uniformity of individual needs for education versus health services. Individual needs for health care (other than routine preventive services) are episodic, unpredictable, and highly variable. Therefore, health care lends itself to partial financing through insurance (private, or social security); modest sums can be collected on a regular schedule from many people, whereas only a fraction of them will require payment for health services in any one time period. In contrast, education does not lend itself to insurance.
- Private schools are important components of the education systems in many Latin American countries, though in the early 1990s in all but a very few countries they enrolled less than a fifth of primary students and less than a third of secondary students (IDB 1996, table 5). But whereas private, social security, and public doctors, hospitals and clinics are intertwined in a variety of ways, private schools in most countries operate almost entirely independently of public schools and teachers.

These structural contrasts generate several important implications for the politics of reforms in health as compared with education:

- Social security institutes are frequently important players in health sector reforms. Their relations with the ministries of health are often strained, and in some countries the institute is considerably more powerful than the ministry. Their autonomous status and independent finance permits them to resist change, but with rare exceptions they have not led change.
- Because a major segment of the health sector is linked through social security payments to pensions and payroll taxes, ministers of finance and other powerful politicians on the economic team are often interested in health sector reforms. No similar links focus their attention on education reforms.
- In some countries, the segmented character of the health sector creates pressure for a more unified system—an issue that does not come up in education.

- As a result of the insurance component of health systems, sector reforms often include restructuring financial arrangements to separate payers from providers—a reform component that has no parallel in the education sector.
- Because private and public components of health sectors are often tightly intertwined, private interests are likely to take more active roles in seeking to influence reforms than are their counterparts in education sectors.

In short, the different structures of the two sectors lead to differences in key actors and in the complexity and scope of reform efforts.

Reform Proposals: Sources, Content, and Motives

In most Latin American countries, health sector problems and shortcomings had long been recognized, among at least some public health specialists. Reform proposals at the beginning of the 1990s usually grew out of years or decades of debate and earlier initiatives. Among our cases, this was most obvious in Brazil, where the network of health officials known as the *sanitaristas* had emerged in the late 1970s, and continued throughout the 1980s and early 1990s to pursue its goals of a universal, public system and increased emphasis on preventive and primary care. The Constitutional Assembly of 1987–88 provided a unique opportunity for the *sanitaristas,* and they succeeded in enshrining in the new constitution the principle of a unified and universal health care system.[3] In Colombia in the late 1980s and early 1990s, health policy analysts in the universities, private think tanks, and the government actively debated ways to extend coverage and improve the health care system. The innovative and radical reform adopted in Law 100 of 1993 drew eclectically on Colombian and international ideas. In Costa Rica, the concept of the EBAIS teams offering integrated preventive and primary care to even the most remote communities grew from the experience of a key reformer as director of a successful primary care pilot clinic, but health specialists had long been seeking ways to improve the sector's service to poor people. Mexico had adopted measures in 1984 moving toward a more unified and less centralized system; union resistance and the economic crises of the 1980s hobbled implementation.

Reform proposals and initiatives were not new, but the momentum for reforms increased palpably in the early 1990s. In many countries, the

3. Such "issue networks" have played key reform roles in other countries as well, e.g., the Rural Doctors' Movement in Thailand in the 1970s (McGuire 2003, 27).

economic crisis of the 1980s had blocked reform efforts while deepening the problems of the sector. The improved economic climate of the early 1990s gave reformers somewhat greater leeway. At the same time, recently revived democracy in some countries and pressure for more open and responsive governments in others generated increased attention to social sectors. This push was particularly clear in the constitutional conventions in Brazil in 1988 and Colombia in 1991. The partially related trend toward decentralization in many countries also prompted fresh thinking about the structure and administration of the social sectors, and created incentives for governors and mayors—now directly elected, in a number of countries—to give more attention to services demanded by voters.

In international circles as well, the 1990s saw a surge of attention to health sector reforms. Like the domestic reform impetus, international pressure and support had long roots. The global conference held in 1978 in Alma Ata, USSR (now Almaty, Kazakhstan), asserted the goal of health care for all and emphasized the key importance of preventive and primary health care. These principles shaped the agendas of specialized international agencies (World Health Organization, Pan American Health Organization), global and regional development agencies (World Bank, Inter-American Development Bank), and the bilateral aid donors. Transnational associations and networks, within and beyond Latin America, also helped to spread these principles. By the early 1990s, these ideas were powerfully reinforced by an escalating general emphasis in international circles on reaching poor people.

At the same time, a new set of ideas and principles was emerging, rooted in the neoliberal economic philosophy that increasingly dominated thinking about macroeconomic management and structural reforms.[4] The World Bank (and, somewhat later and less emphatically, the Inter-American Development Bank) became prime proponents of these views. The new approach sought the same long-run goals of the older approach: increased equity, efficiency, and quality. But much more emphasis was placed on heightened efficiency and cost containment, to stretch the impact of limited resources. Altered incentives were seen as a major key to improved efficiency, and institutional and structural changes in turn were needed to alter

---

4. The degree to which neoliberal analysis, with its emphasis on market incentives, is relevant to issues of health care finance and delivery is hotly disputed. Many aspects of health services (especially preventive and primary care) have the characteristics of public goods with important positive externalities. For a discussion of the issues, see Barr (1998, 2001).

incentives in the sector. Although the older themes (increased emphasis on preventive and primary care; stronger maternal and child health care programs; etc.) continued, new themes appeared on the reform agenda. These included increased autonomy and accountability for hospitals and clinics and efforts to link resources more tightly to performance (both of individual doctors and other health care workers, and of hospitals and clinics).

To that end, reformers advocated a shift from budgets based on prior years' spending to payment systems based on actual services provided; heightened competition among insurers and health service providers, including wider scope for private insurance and care; and increased consumer choice. Older themes of decentralization of public responsibilities to subnational levels of government, and increased citizen participation were carried over into the "new" agenda, bolstered by broader democratization and by the hopes that bringing management closer to those being served would increase efficiency. These international trends in thinking strongly influenced reform proposals and debate in most Latin American countries.[5]

To what extent did economic pressures linked to globalization (other than neoliberal ideas) exert pressure and influence on health sector reforms in the 1990s? Contrary to widespread impressions, our cases give little support to the notion that health sector reforms were driven mainly by fiscal pressures and desire to reduce sector spending. Heightened emphasis on fiscal responsibility has certainly prompted increased concern for efficient use of funds, and reforms in most of our cases included measures aimed at efficiency. But most reform efforts have been accompanied by rising public outlays in the health sector, not by cuts (see table 1.3 in the present volume).

Macroeconomic policy issues spurred health sector reforms in some countries, via a different and indirect route. In large part in order to deepen domestic capital markets as well as to avoid fiscal pressures some years or decades in the future, many Latin American countries in the 1990s adopted reforms in their pension systems, replacing traditional pay-as-you-go models with mixed systems that allow or require younger workers to put their social security contributions into individual accounts. These accounts are managed by private firms and invested in securities, in the expectation that accumulated returns will permit larger pensions (Brooks 2001; Madrid 2003). Because a major segment of health care finance is linked to pensions through the social security system, the pension reforms created both need and opportunity for health care finance reforms in three of our six country

---

5. For a useful discussion of these trends, see Koivusalo and Ollila (1997).

cases: Brazil, Colombia, and Mexico. The linkage and the outcomes were quite different in each of the three cases. But the point here is that change in pension systems (itself reflecting both demographic shifts and pressures of globalization) often helped to trigger major health sector reforms.

The Cast of Characters: Reformers, Opponents, and the Uninvolved

Health is so basic to human welfare, and dissatisfaction with Latin American health care systems is so widespread, that one would think reformers would be able to mobilize substantial support.[6] However, our cases and other evidence make it clear that there are surprisingly few influential proponents of health care reforms in most Latin American countries, while there are many strong opponents, and quite a few fence-sitters and uninvolved. The pattern parallels that in the education sector.

Who Presses for Health Sector Reform?

Almost all reforms in health care finance and delivery require an executive branch initiative. Yet most kinds of health sector reforms offer politicians few incentives (some exceptions are noted later in the chapter). Time inconsistency problems are one major set of reasons for the lack of interest. Most reforms take years to produce results. Political rewards are delayed and uncertain, but political costs of reforms are prompt and clear. Politicians' hesitations are often reinforced by disagreement among the experts regarding desirable measures.

Public health specialists, rather than top-level political leaders, initiated most of the major reforms among our cases. In Brazil, the *sanitarista* network had long pressed for a universal public health system. The impetus for the EBAIS team approach in Costa Rica came from a handful of health officials in the social security agency (CCSS). In Peru, several very small groups within the Ministry of Health initiated reforms in primary health care delivery. In Colombia, major reforms were demanded by several key senators and largely designed by a small team in the Ministry of Health.

The Ministry of Finance and other high-level economic officials were

6. In this and later sections of this chapter, specific information regarding Argentina, Brazil, Colombia, Costa Rica, Mexico, and Peru is drawn from the case studies in this volume, unless otherwise noted.

the main instigators of several other reforms among our cases. In Mexico, the Ministry of Finance and the economic team more broadly took the lead in pressing for basic changes in the finance and structure of the social security–funded segment of the health system, made necessary by reforms in the pension system. The team placed their own nominees within the social security administration to design the reforms. In Colombia, the minister of health and his team had recently transferred from the Department of National Planning and had close ties to the government's economic team. In both Mexico and Colombia, the economic team's interest was driven by links between pension reform and health sector reform. In Argentina, the Ministry of the Economy supported the effort to introduce competition among (and thereby fundamentally restructure) Argentina's unusual system of monopolistic union-controlled *obras sociales* providing social security– funded health care.

More generally, high-level economic officials are likely to turn their attention to the health sector in the context of a concern with high payroll taxes and their impact on investment, and a broader interest in the modernization of the state. Among our cases, this concern was evident in Mexico and in Argentina (where total payroll taxes, for health and other purposes, amounted to 60 percent of base wages as of the early 1990s).

International organizations are a third source of initiative for health sector reforms. The World Bank pressed governments to pursue specific measures in several of our cases. Yet it is striking that external attempts to prompt specific actions had a rather limited impact, despite the substantial influence, mentioned above, of broader international intellectual currents on reform debate and government agendas. In Costa Rica, the World Bank insisted on including in the reform package a series of measures to increase hospital autonomy and accountability and to separate purchasing and service provision functions. The World Bank had doubts regarding the financial sustainability of the main thrust the Costa Ricans wished to pursue: the integrated community-level health teams (EBAIS). An agreement was finally reached to pursue both courses of action; the EBAIS initiative was rapidly implemented, while progress toward hospital autonomy and new budgeting mechanisms was glacial (and reflected a deliberate Costa Rican decision to pursue a gradual approach).

In Argentina, the World Bank pushed strongly for introducing competition and inducing greater efficiency in the union-run *obras sociales* providing medical services to roughly half the population. That goal appeared consistent with the agenda of the powerful Ministry of the Economy, and decrees establishing the necessary framework were indeed adopted. But implementation was repeatedly delayed, as the measures were used as bargaining chips in a broader set of tripartite negotiations regarding reform of labor relations. Little had been accomplished by the end of President Menem's second term, and (despite initially encouraging moves) the initiative was not revived under the successor government, before the economic and political collapse of 2001. World Bank initiatives to reform PAMI, the notoriously corrupt organization responsible for delivering health services to retirees, failed even more completely.

In other countries, policy and financial support from the World Bank, the Inter-American Development Bank, or other external agencies certainly helped to sustain specific reforms (e.g., the Peruvian program of community-run clinics, CLAS; or aspects of the implementation of Colombia's health reforms). But in these cases, external influence played a supporting role, rather than moving out in front of the governments.

Opponents and Fence-Sitters

In contrast to the short list of likely sources of health reform initiatives, many powerful groups and institutions are likely to oppose reforms, or at least to harbor serious doubts and withhold support. Throughout the world, doctors and other health service providers predictably oppose aspects of reform that seem to them to threaten their income, status, independence, and established working routine. Mechanisms that link pay to performance, both for individual hospital and clinic staff, and for clinics and hospitals as units, are perceived as threats on all these counts. Doctors also deeply dislike administrative and financial management systems that place them under the control of nondoctors, or give representatives of the community some voice in administration.

Doctors and their associations are also suspicious of efforts to shift the emphasis, and the allocation of resources, away from secondary and tertiary levels of health care to buttress primary and preventive care in poor urban and rural areas. Such measures imply lower salaries, less sophisticated equipment, pressures to serve where living conditions and career prospects are unattractive, and the substitution of less highly trained health workers (nurses, public health workers, midwives) for doctors in performing certain services. Moreover, doctors' training and the Hippocratic Oath focus their attention on individual patients' needs; reform proposals based on broader social benefits and costs often seem irrelevant or wrongheaded to them.

Health care workers other than doctors also often oppose many aspects of sector reforms. Where health workers' unions traditionally negotiate wages and working conditions at the national level (with the Ministry of Health and/or the social security institute), they bitterly contest reforms that shift some control over personnel matters to provincial or municipal governments or to hospitals and clinics. Nondoctor personnel and some doctors in the public sector also strongly resist measures that increase private participation in the sector, usually by contracting out specific services or by permitting large firms to "opt out" of the public system and provide their own health care arrangements.

These patterns applied without exception in the cases reviewed in this volume. Even in Costa Rica—and despite that country's proud record of social integration and concern for poor people—some doctors complained that the new system of integrated community medical teams would convert them into public health officials, "dragging the medical profession back into the days of fighting parasitic diseases" (*parasitismo;* see chapter 7 of this volume). Efforts to restructure payment mechanisms and modernize hospital administration in Colombia provoked bitter complaints. In none of our cases except Peru did reform measures significantly decentralize control over salary and personnel decisions (though in Brazil and Argentina those functions had long been largely under the control of subnational authorities for the public segments of the systems).

Although patterns of resistance were similar across all cases, the political influence and alliances of doctors' and other health care workers' associations and unions, and therefore their capacity to block reforms, varied substantially. Health care providers' unions are often organizationally weaker than teachers' unions, for several reasons. Doctors' associations are usually separate from those of nurses and other nondoctor health care workers. Doctors' associations are often further divided among different fields of specialization, and sometimes even by level and kind of training (domestic versus foreign). Unions among workers other than doctors may be discouraged in countries where private hospitals provide the bulk of services, in contrast to the predominantly public character of education in most Latin American countries (Murillo and Maceira 2002, 8–9). However, health workers gain leverage because of the nature of their work; the threat of strikes in even one or a few major hospitals prompts great concern. Moreover, doctors often have extensive elite contacts. Therefore, even where health workers' unions and doctors' associations are fragmented, other sources of influence often help them to resist reforms they view as undesirable, especially those that would erode established labor relations and wage arrangements.

Among the cases in this volume, health workers' leverage was least effective in the public segment of Peru's health sector. Peru's health care services had been decimated by the economic turmoil and mismanagement of the 1980s and by Shining Path attacks on clinics. Ministry of Health unions had virtually disappeared. There was no effective protest against the radically changed terms of employment in the new primary care programs (CLAS, and especially PSBT clinics), including short-term contracts for doctors and nurses with renewal based on productivity. Although unions continued to function within the social security segment of the system, and some opposed proposed reforms to this segment, they were also under considerable pressure during the Fujimori era.

In Brazil and Argentina, providers' associations were somewhat stronger but did not mount effective resistance to reforms. Unions were fragmented in part because responsibility for much health care delivery, including power to hire and fire personnel, had long been decentralized to the state or provincial level, and to some degree to municipalities. In Brazil, in addition to the federal structure, the fact that more than 60 percent of publicly financed health care is provided by private and philanthropic hospitals may have weakened union organization (see table 6.9 in the present volume). In Argentina, the unusual structure of social security–financed health care delivery, through *obras sociales* run by the country's many (nonhealth) labor unions, interfered with formation of strong providers' unions in this segment of the system.

In sharp contrast, providers' organizations were extremely powerful in Mexico, and quite strong as well in Colombia and Costa Rica. In each of these cases, major unions were linked to extremely strong social security institutes; in Colombia and Mexico, the social security institutes were in turn linked to political parties and were major providers of political patronage. Social security institutes also can usually count on the support of those covered by the system to resist any reforms that imply a reduction in their benefits. In Colombia, the Institute of Social Security (ISS) bitterly opposed the 1993 reforms from the outset, and for years refused to carry out changes imposed by the new system. In this, it had the backing of many (nonhealth) unions that feared dilution of their benefits.[7] However, the ISS failed to

7. It is worth noting that the powerful teachers' and petroleum workers' unions opposed provisions in the 1993 law that would alter their traditional generous health and pension provisions. In the end, they were exempted from these provisions.

block the reform, and by the late 1990s it was reluctantly moving to comply with its requirements.

In Mexico, the Social Security Institute (IMSS) and its associated union were still more formidable adversaries. The Social Security workers' union, the Sindicato Nacional de Trabajadores de la Seguridad Social (SNTSS), is the largest in the country. Unusually among health workers' unions, it includes doctors, nurses, and administrative personnel, and it controls virtually all appointments within the social security bureaucracy. During the era of Partido Revolucionario Institutional (PRI) domination, it also had a fixed quota of congressional seats. In exchange, the PRI indirectly controlled health sector job appointments and access to medical attention. By the early 1990s, as PRI dominance weakened, the SNTSS was threatening to turn toward the opposition, thereby enhancing its leverage. In this context, it is not surprising that even the Cabinet's powerful economic team sought to avoid a confrontation with the union, and it removed or greatly diluted almost all nonfinancial health provisions from key 1995 legislation.

In contrast to the Colombian and Mexican stories, the Costa Rican social security institute, the CCSS, initiated reforms in the 1990s, rather than opposing or constraining them. The CCSS already controlled most health care finance and delivery. However, the Ministry of Health operated a number of primary care clinics as well as public health programs. The reform package entailed shifting the medical staff (and associated budget) still under Ministry of Health control into the CCSS, to help finance the costly new program of integrated health teams for all communities. In this case, the opposing union represented the medical staff of the Ministry of Health. Extensive negotiations—and the fact that the CCSS pay scale was more generous than that of the Ministry of Health—won their acceptance.

In Brazil, reforms during the 1990s entailed the opposite pattern: the health component of the social security administration (INAMPS) was moved into the Ministry of Health. As was already noted, the Brazilian system did not include strong providers' unions at the national level linked to the social security system. Opposition to the shift in this case came primarily from the social security bureaucracy itself (defending its autonomy) and from its powerful allies in the private hospital sector, fearing the ministry would be less accommodating to their interests.

Among stakeholders within the health systems, hospital administrators might be expected to favor at least those aspects of reform packages that increase hospital autonomy. Indeed, in some of our cases, hospital administrators do report satisfaction with reforms such as increased authority to purchase supplies. Yet administrators have more often opposed than supported reforms. Shifts from annual budgets to fee-for-service arrangements and other measures designed to link funds to performance demand far-reaching changes in hospital routines and regulations.

Moreover, in many countries public hospital administrators' control over their personnel is extremely limited. They can neither hire nor fire, cannot set salaries, and cannot determine promotions. In some cases, their authority even to alter work schedules is restricted by union guidelines negotiated at the national or state level. Because personnel costs often absorb between 60 and 80 percent of total budgets, administrators are left with little room to maneuver. Furthermore, altered funding arrangements imply much greater uncertainty and risk. Directors are uncertain not only about their staff's capacity to deliver but also about the reliability of the new mechanisms to ensure payment for services on a timely basis. All these concerns are powerful counterweights to the attractions of increased autonomy.

Private health care providers and insurers predictably oppose reforms that tighten surveillance and regulation, and they tend to support measures that broaden their scope of action. Their influence varies with their share of the sector, and also with their political alliances. In Brazil, private hospitals had long been closely allied with INAMPS bureaucracy and provided a large share of health services funded through the system. Other than IN-AMPS itself, private hospitals and their associations offered the most intense resistance to the proposal, in Brazil's 1988 Constitutional Convention, to create a unified national health system under the control of the Ministry of Health, and they have continued to resist measures to increase regulation within the new system.

In Colombia, major components of Law 100 of 1993 were intended to increase private participation in purchasing and service provision. However, private insurers opposed aspects of Law 100 of 1993 that would heighten their competition, and private hospitals joined their public counterparts in complaints about the complexity of the payment system created by the reforms. In Argentina, private insurers were interested in access to the better-funded of the *obras sociales,* but they sought to avoid any obligation and increased regulation that might be part of the deal. In Peru, private insurers played no role in the development of separate payers' organizations in the social security segment of the sector, but once these were established, the private firms pressed for an increased share of workers' contributions. Only in Costa Rica, where private insurance barely exists and public clinics and hospitals are dominant, were private-sector interests essentially absent.

Moving beyond the health sector itself, decentralizing reforms directly involve state or provincial governors and local mayors. In several countries including Colombia and Venezuela, direct elections for governors and mayors had been introduced in the middle or late 1980s. If voters in local jurisdictions demanded better social services, elected local officials might be expected to increase attention and budget allocations to those services. This is precisely what happened in Venezuela in the early 1990s (Navarro 2000). Despite electoral incentives, however, local officials do not always welcome a shift to their jurisdiction of major education and health programs that had traditionally been run and funded by the national government. In many countries in and beyond Latin America, decentralization was introduced during the late 1980s and 1990s (or earlier partial decentralization was deepened) in a hasty and poorly thought through manner (e.g., see Rojas 1999). A key failing was that procedures and criteria for transfers of funds from center to state, and (directly or indirectly) to municipalities often were not clearly spelled out. In several countries, including Brazil and Colombia, confusion and delays were compounded by national economic crises a few years into the reforms. Governors and mayors (and their health departments) had little confidence that they would receive the funds they needed to carry out their new responsibilities promptly, or at all.

Moreover, in all our cases except Argentina (and Costa Rica, where no decentralization was attempted), central funds for state and local health activities were at least partly earmarked. The requirement that central funds be spent for specified activities enabled national ministries to determine the norms and standards to be met by state and local health programs. In Brazil, much of the politics of health sector reform after 1994 focused on the tug-of-war between state and local officials, on the one hand, and national ministry officials, on the other, regarding the precise ministry norms for centrally funded programs. State and local governments did not welcome closer monitoring by central officials. Nor were they eager to take more responsibility for dealing with assertive health care workers' unions.

National and local politicians' attitudes toward health sector reforms are also influenced by the extent to which patronage opportunities are destroyed or created. In Mexico and Colombia, the social security institutes provided massive political patronage—that is, individual politicians' or party influence over appointments to the bureaucracy or to health care jobs. Allocation of investments in new facilities, and of contracts for construction or maintenance work, also offered patronage possibilities. In Argentina, PAMI—the agency responsible for providing health services to pensioners—traditionally has been a large-scale patronage pool. In all three cases, important politicians quietly or openly opposed reforms.

Conversely, decentralizing reforms can create new patronage opportunities, or at least shift control over patronage to different levels of government. In Colombia, health outlays accounted for roughly 30 percent of municipal budgets by the late 1990s, while control over clinics and hospitals offered new sources of employment patronage. In addition, some municipal politicians manipulated to their advantage the SISBEN system for certifying those eligible for subsidized medical care. In Brazil, however, increasingly demanding norms for local health programs established by the Ministry of Health, accompanied by strengthened monitoring, may well have reduced the scope for patronage.

The Uninvolved

Pressures from the general public, from nongovernmental organizations (NGOs), and from social movements affected the course of national health sector reforms indirectly in three of the cases examined in this volume, and little or not at all in the other cases. In Colombia, many of the delegates at the 1991 Constitutional Assembly viewed universal access to adequate health care services as part of the more socially responsive political system they hoped to create. The same was true in Brazil's Assembly of 1987–88. In that case, the diffuse general demand for better social services including health care was given specific focus and content by the *sanitaristas,* who were strongly represented in the Assembly committee concerned with social policy.[8] In Costa Rica, once the EBAIS integrated primary health care teams were launched in some communities, others were quick to press for their teams.

Yet, considering the importance of adequate health services to the quality of life, it is somewhat surprising that pressures from public opinion or NGOs seem to have played fairly limited roles in prompting national re-

8. Weyland (1996, 168); he explicitly notes that pressures from the general public in Brazil in the 1980s played little role in promoting national health sector reforms. Social movements focused on local health care delivery problems, whereas "experts remained decisive in designing projects for redistributive health reform" (p. 158).

forms in these three countries, and still less in Argentina, Mexico, and Peru. One partial explanation may be the episodic nature of most people's concern with health care. When a family member or close friend is ill or injured, prompt access to good medical care is an extremely high priority. But in the normal course of life, health services may be viewed as a less urgent concern than other issues, including education. As is discussed in chapters 9 and 16, annual public opinion surveys show that whereas "education" was the first or second most frequently cited public policy problem in many countries, far smaller proportions of respondents—in most cases, only about 1 or 2 percent—named "health" as the most important problem (see tables 9.2, 9.3, and 9.4).

Moreover, those with most cause to be dissatisfied with the services available (or not available) to them are poor people, in urban and particularly in rural areas, who are often not organized or active in politics. More vocal formal-sector workers and the middle classes usually have social security and/or private insurance coverage, and therefore are little concerned with improving access to and the quality of the public segment of the sector. They are also better placed to dodge long waiting periods or choose the doctor they prefer by using private clinics; they choose exit over voice. Where popular pressures for better service do emerge (often channeled through local NGOs or parties), they are likely to focus on improved service from local facilities, not on major revisions of national policy. Furthermore, where national reforms are proposed, the relevance of the specific measures to better service may not be immediately obvious. For instance, increased hospital autonomy and changes in how hospitals and doctors are paid are not likely to excite much public interest. Beyond indifference, parts of the public often oppose certain kinds of reforms, especially those perceived as moving toward "privatization" (contracting out by public services of some functions), imposing financial or convenience costs on users (e.g., requiring that primary care physicians authorize visits to specialists), or diluting the quality of service (expanding nurses' or paramedics' authority to treat simple illnesses). Such "efficiency-oriented" measures are widely viewed either as intrinsically undesirable, or as dubious means toward better health services. All these considerations help to explain the limited public support for major health sector reforms at the national level.

Business and industrial interests (outside the health sector itself) also seem to play a less active role in promoting reform than one might expect. Private employers stand to gain if their employees are healthy (losing less time from illness, and performing better on the job). In many countries, employers pay hefty wage taxes for the health component of social security systems. Some employers (often of large and medium-sized enterprises) are so dissatisfied with the services of the national social security system that they purchase private health care plans for their employees, in effect paying twice. In some cases, business interests have pressed for wage tax reductions; in Argentina, this was one of the private sector's goals in tripartite negotiations to recast labor relations in the mid-1990s. Mexican business groups have also been quite interested in changing social security financial arrangements, and they financed a major analysis of health sector reform options in the early 1990s. In some other countries, widespread evasion may dilute business concern about payroll taxes. More generally, there seem to be few if any instances of significant organized business support for measures designed to increase the efficiency or improve the quality of the social security segment of health sectors.

Understanding the Record: Variation among Countries

Even among our small sample of six country cases, there are striking contrasts in the extent and character of health sector reform efforts. National patterns of reform varied with regard to three important dimensions: broad scope and vision versus narrower unconnected measures; relative emphasis on equity versus efficiency objectives; and effective versus ineffective implementation (see table 2.1, and also see table 2.2 later in the chapter).

Scope and Vision

Reforms in Brazil and Colombia were shaped by a broad vision of a future health sector quite different from the starting point. Reformers wanted to create health care finance and delivery systems that would provide at least basic services to the entire population and that would eventually close the gap between the health care available to citizens covered by social security and those (mainly poor people) without such coverage. They envisaged systems in which state and local governments would take on major responsibilities for administering health care delivery; agencies responsible for purchasing services were separated from providers (hospitals and clinics); and hospitals and clinics had both greater autonomy and greater accounta-

Table 2.1

Health Reform Initiatives in Six Countries: Scope, Focus, and Implementation

Country and Reforms	Scope	Focus	Implementation
Argentina 1. Transfer of federal hospitals 2. Reform of *obras sociales* 3. Hospital autonomy 4. PAMI reform	Narrow, piecemeal	Efficiency	Transfer: accomplished *Obras:* limited Hospital autonomy: limited PAMI reform: failed
Brazil 1. Unified but decentralized system 2. Central norms with fiscal incentives	Broad, comprehensive	Equity emphasis; efficiency also a concern	Unified system: achieved Central norms: variable but significant impact
Colombia 1. Expanded coverage 2. Revised and semi-unified funding, hospital autonomy and funding reforms 3. Decentralization	Broad, comprehensive	Equity and efficiency roughly equally balanced (and intended as reinforcing)	Coverage: big increase Funding: new payers' organizations in place, hospital autonomy reforms slow but moving Decentralization: substantial

Country / Reforms	Vision	Goals	Outcomes
Costa Rica 1. Primary care teams (EBAIS) 2. Hospital autonomy and funding reforms	Narrow, but part of comprehensive vision	Primary care reforms: equity Hospital autonomy: efficiency	Primary care reforms: achieved Hospital autonomy: limited and slow
Mexico 1. Changed funding for IMSS health program 2. Expanded coverage: IMSS 3. Opt-out, contract out, etc. (IMSS) 4. Expanded primary care coverage (Health Ministry)	Narrow, piecemeal	Funding: adjust to impact of pension reforms Coverage: equity Opt-out etc.: efficiency MOC primary coverage: equity	Funding change: achieved Expanded coverage: limited Opt-out, contract: no progress MOC primary coverage extended
Peru 1. Primary health care reforms (PSBT, CLAS) 2. Free health insurance for schoolchildren (SEG) 3. Social Security system reforms: EPSs	Moderate, piecemeal	Primary care reforms: equity and efficiency SEG: equity Social Security reforms: efficiency	PSBT: considerable progress CLAS: considerable progress despite controversy SEG in place Social Security reforms: delayed, but some progress

Note: CLAS = Local Health Administration Committees; EBAIS = Equipos Básicos de Atención Integral de Salud; EPSs = Entidades Prestadoras de Salud; IMSS = Mexican Institute of Social Security; PAMI = Programa de Atención Médica Integral; PSBT = Basic Health for All Program; SEG = Seguro Escolar Gratuito.

bility. In both countries, albeit in quite different ways, reform packages were designed to pursue this entire set of goals.[9]

In contrast, reform initiatives in the other cases considered in this volume were narrower, directed to specific problems and parts of the agenda. Often several programs were launched, independent of each other. In short, in Argentina, Costa Rica, Mexico, and Peru, reform efforts were in varying degrees "piecemeal." In Costa Rica, however, the vision of a unified system had been pursued from the late 1970s on; aspects of the primary health care reforms in the 1990s can be viewed as the completion of that vision.

Why did health reformers in Brazil and Colombia launch such ambitious programs? In both countries, constitutional assemblies had written mandates regarding the health sectors into new constitutions. The Colombian assembly was made up of delegates representing somewhat different, broader, and to some extent more left-oriented groups and interests than were usually present in the legislature. In Brazil, progressive groups were an influential though not controlling faction in the constituent assembly but dominated the committee responsible for social policies, and public hearings provided further opportunities for reform advocates (Weyland 1996, 168). The 1988 Brazilian Constitution explicitly mandates creation of a unified health system, with the Ministry of Health absorbing the health component of the social security system. The 1991 Colombian constitution mandates decentralization of social services, but it is less clear regarding other aspects of social sector reforms.

In each case, the specific constitutional mandate regarding the health sector is perhaps best viewed in a broader context, as part of a more general attempt to redefine relations between state and society. Both constitutional assemblies met at critical political junctures: in Brazil, as the vehicle for expressing and consolidating the recent return to democratic government; and in Colombia, as an urgent effort by progressive segments of the elite in alliance with previously excluded groups to restore democratic legitimacy and governability. In both countries, social sector reforms were understood as means for helping to restructure relations between the state and citizens and ultimately to remake the character of society. In contrast, social sector

9. It is worth noting that the Inter-American Development Bank's 1996 analysis of health care finance and delivery systems concluded that the "integrated [predominantly] public systems" of Costa Rica and the English-speaking Caribbean produced the best health outcomes in the region, at spending levels (relative to GDP) only a little higher than the regional average (IDB 1996, 303, 309). Cuba's integrated system has achieved still more impressive health outcomes.

reforms in Mexico in the 1990s were essentially mechanisms to help modernize the state, in order to preserve the broad outlines of the established political system.[10] In still sharper contrast, the redefining of relations between state and citizens was virtually entirely absent from government agendas in Argentina and Peru.

However, in both Brazil and Colombia, constitutional mandates offered only broad, vague principles. Spelling out more detailed measures proved intensely controversial. In Colombia, the Constituent Assembly charged a special commission with developing more specific guidelines; the commission agreed on several important principles later incorporated into Law 100, but it could not resolve disagreements on some key points. The constitutional requirements for decentralization were spelled out in Law 60 of 1993; the additional and radical reforms in Law 100 owe relatively little to constitutional guidance and were mainly the product of the initiative and creativity of reformers in the Ministry of Health and Senate. In Brazil, the health component of the social security bureaucracy was fairly promptly incorporated into the Ministry of Health in accord with the constitutional mandate for a unified system. But crucial questions of funding and the specific powers of the Ministry of Health vis-à-vis state and local governments were hotly debated in the legislature; many pieces of the resulting legislation were then vetoed by President Collor and only partially reinstated by the legislature. Moreover, the social security administration resisted and eventually (in 1993) stopped passing the health share of social security taxes to the Ministry of Health, while the Ministry of the Economy also diverted social security revenues from health to other purposes (Weyland 1996, 169–72).

Despite these difficult first years, the unification of Brazil's health system opened space for progressive changes. Such measures, affecting state and municipal governments, public and private hospitals, and geographic allocation of federal funds, were introduced gradually during the course of the 1990s, in the form of evolving Ministry of Health standards and regulations attached to transfers of federal funds. The pace of reforms quickened under the Cardoso governments in the second half of the 1990s. In Colom-

10. It is interesting to note that Mexico's General Health Law of 1984 had sought to increase integration between social security and public segments of the health care system, but key measures were never enforced or later eroded (Roemer 1991, 346–49). In 2001, the health minister of the new Fox government announced a National Health Program with the central objective of developing a universal and decentralized health care delivery system.

bia, the reforms introduced in 1993 by Laws 60 and 100 also faced formidable obstacles, including a change of government and appointment of a minister of health hostile to the radical structural changes incorporated in Law 100 only a few months after that law was passed. The reform was sustained in the face of strong opposition from many sources, in part because it rapidly created two new groups of stakeholders: the millions of Colombians who became eligible for subsidized health insurance, and the newly created health care purchasing agencies.

In sum, in both Brazil and Colombia, broad-gauged health sector reform grew out of specialists' vision in the context of a "critical juncture" and a larger political endeavor to restructure state–society relations. In each country, initial impetus was not itself sufficient for significant change. Determined health sector bureaucrats, backed to some extent by progressive presidents, played central roles in turning broad mandates into concrete measures and in designing content and tactics to wear down ongoing resistance. In Argentina and Mexico, in contrast, narrower health sector measures were driven in good part by national financial objectives, rather than by a vision of a fairer and more effective national health system, as is discussed in the next section.

Variation among Countries: Primary Objectives

Health sector reforms in all countries almost always seek improved equity, efficiency, and quality. Narrowing the gap in access to and the quality of health care services between rich and poor people and between urban and rural citizens, and better serving more remote and poorer regions, are virtually always among the stated goals of national health policies. So too is greater cost-effectiveness—that is, larger improvements in health status per unit of money spent. However, the relative emphasis on these different goals varies substantially.

Gauging relative emphasis on different goals is tricky, because specific programs and policies often serve more than one goal. To illustrate: Expanded coverage of health care insurance or delivery is clearly largely equity oriented. Yet there is an efficiency component to expanded coverage; people who have no health insurance and/or live far from even basic medical facilities delay seeking medical care until they are extremely sick, so that treatment is more costly and less effective than it might have been with earlier attention. For the nation as a whole, moreover, in the medium run, broader coverage is likely to mean more effective prevention of infectious diseases, lower incidence of easily corrected conditions like malnutrition due to lack of micronutrients, and a healthier and more productive population. Broadened coverage and increased emphasis on preventive and primary care therefore serve both equity and efficiency objectives.

Conversely, if typical reforms are arrayed from those most concerned with equity to those most focused on efficiency, then increased hospital autonomy and revised methods of paying providers (so that money follows patients) are probably the most efficiency-focused measures among those considered in this chapter. Yet these measures can also serve equity. For example, several of our case studies note the tendency for patients who have social security or private insurance to use public hospitals for complicated or expensive treatments. However, the hospitals find it very difficult to get paid for these services. Revised provider payment systems put pressure on hospitals and clinics to seek payment from their better-off patients' insurers—a measure that reduces free riding by the better-off, increases hospitals' revenues, and thereby permits expanded services for poor people.

Despite the fact that equity and efficiency goals are intertwined in most reforms, the relative emphasis of specific measures and national programs varies. Among our cases, Argentina and Mexico stand out for their strong focus on efficiency and fiscal considerations (see table 2.1). In both countries, basic political institutions—powerful executives with majority control of their legislatures—certainly facilitated this emphasis. Mexico and Argentina also had particularly dominant ministers of finance during much of the 1990s (though this was true as well in Brazil). But why did Mexico and especially Argentina give such limited attention to equity-oriented programs, rather than attempting to pursue equity jointly with efficiency?

In Argentina, institutions may have constrained reform options. The Argentine national government had only limited influence over provincial use of funds, and therefore little leverage on inequalities within provinces. Allocation of federal transfers among provinces was not earmarked by sector or function, and was largely determined by "high politics"—bargaining and negotiations between governors and the central government (Tommasi 2002). Some major health sector institutions did operate at the national level and could be addressed by reforms at the center: the *obras sociales* health care organizations associated with each union, and PAMI, the agency responsible for health care for the elderly. Reforming the *obras* and PAMI would have improved equity, but the dominant motives for attempted reforms of both were reductions in blatant inefficiencies and (particularly for PAMI) corruption—that is, efficiency motives.

The same explanations do not apply in Mexico, where many millions remained severely underserved or unserved, and where the national government continued to control most aspects of the segmented health system in the early 1990s. Nor did Mexican health initiatives during the decade focus as exclusively on efficiency as those in Argentina. From the late 1980s on, primary health care and nutrition programs were components of the countrywide poverty reduction programs known successively as Solidaridad and Progresa. In the second half of the decade, the Ministry of Health carried out a Program of Extended Coverage (PEC), with sizable World Bank funding. PEC aroused virtually no opposition, but it also generated little support; nor were there vigorous efforts to monitor the program. At best, the government's pursuit of equity-oriented reforms was halfhearted—undoubtedly reflecting the limited political influence of the groups that stood to gain from such reforms (Gomez-Dantes 2000, 138–41). In contrast, the efficiency-oriented measures to reform the social security segment of the health care system drew direct and sustained support from the powerful economic team.

Reforms in Brazil, Colombia, and Peru were driven by more balanced concerns for efficiency and equity (and in the first two cases, at least indirectly, by broader visions of redefined relations between the state and society). Among the six cases examined in this volume, equity objectives were most dominant in Costa Rica. Left to its own devices, Costa Rica would probably have focused its efforts entirely on the expansion of coverage and improvement in services for poor people that the EBAIS teams were designed to achieve. Efficiency-oriented measures to increase hospital autonomy and accountability were largely the product of persistent and strong persuasion from the World Bank. The preferred emphasis on equity reflects long-standing Costa Rican social and political traditions.

In cross-regional perspective, analyses of the post–World War II history of social policies in Western Europe suggest that pressures from left-leaning parties and unions played important roles (Huber and Stephens 2001). Among our Latin American cases, however, the picture is more complex. In Costa Rica, solidaristic values similar to those of European social democrats had long shaped social policies, but trade unions were not particularly strong. In Brazil, the *sanitarista* network was quite leftist in orientation, and later in the 1990s, impetus for accelerated sector reform came primarily from politicians and cabinet members associated with President Cardoso's social democratic party. However, the Brazilian Workers' Party was marginalized during most of Cardoso's two terms.[11]

More generally, many left-leaning groups in Latin America were ambivalent or divided regarding the social sector reform agenda of the 1990s—precisely because of its combination of goals. In the wake of the crises of the 1980s, and in the context of ongoing emphasis on conservative fiscal management, measures to expand coverage and improve quality were unavoidably intertwined with efforts to improve efficiency. Teachers' and health workers' unions, as well as many unions not directly connected with social services, were often leftist in orientation, but they opposed measures that seemed to threaten what they viewed as their prerogatives. For instance, in Mexico the powerful Social Security union adamantly and successfully opposed health sector reforms, threatening to leave the PRI and affiliate with the opposition Partido de la Revolución Democrática (PRD), while the PRD pursued a strategy of siding with unions that felt threatened by adjustment and opposed reforms.

Variation among Countries: Implementation

Our half-dozen country cases display a surprising range not only with regard to the scope and focus of reforms attempted but also in the degree to which reforms, once authorized, were in fact carried out. To a considerable extent, scope and focus themselves affected prospects for implementation, by shaping the kinds of support and opposition aroused. But other factors also played a role: the autonomy and dedication of the implementing agency; the instruments available to that agency, as shaped by political, legal, and bureaucratic institutions; the emergence of new stakeholders; and national political and economic trends.

What was accomplished depended partly on what was attempted. Ambitious programs, with complex and radical changes affecting much of the sector, inevitably encounter severe problems of implementation. Brazilian and Colombian reforms both remain far from complete. Yet they have made substantial progress toward fulfilling the intent of their designers. And because their reach was ambitious, partial progress is another way to describe quite major change.

11. The Workers' Party held roughly 10 percent of congressional seats during most of the Cardoso period, not enough to block even constitutional amendments requiring particularly large majorities. Nor was the Workers' Party candidacy for president regarded as a serious threat at this time.

Several of the narrower reform programs are fully or substantially in place as their designers intended. By the end of 2001, Costa Rica's EBAIS teams served about 80 percent of all communities. In the same year, Peru's two primary health care programs together covered about 98 percent of the nation. It is worth noting that these were new or "add-on" programs that required only modest changes in the modes of operation of established institutions. They were also equity oriented (despite important efficiency features); as we will discuss in more detail in the concluding chapter, in general equity-oriented reforms are somewhat easier to implement than measures focused mainly on efficiency.

In contrast, the fairly narrow measures undertaken in Argentina— introducing competition among the *obras sociales,* reducing corruption and increasing efficiency in PAMI, and increasing autonomy and accountability in public hospitals—made little headway or failed outright. These measures all were mainly focused on efficiency objectives. The first two entailed important losses for influential political actors (unions, politicians relying on patronage); and the hospital autonomy program demanded difficult changes in hospital modes of operation (as well as being perceived in many provincial legislatures as a possible threat to equity). The *obras sociales* reforms would give union members the right to choose their preferred health care provider; this was widely recognized, but the potential beneficiaries were not organized to press for the reform. Those who would benefit from cleaning up PAMI and increased hospital autonomy probably were not aware of the (abortive) reform efforts, or did not see much connection between the proposed reforms and improved service for themselves.

The autonomy, commitment, and capacity of the key implementing agencies, and the emergence of new stakeholders with an interest in reforms also powerfully affect implementation. In Costa Rica, the social security institute (CCSS) was particularly well endowed to pursue reforms. It had its own funding, had unique autonomy from executive branch (and therefore indirect party) control, and was widely regarded as highly competent and honest.

Brazil and Colombia are both more complex stories. Hostile presidents took office shortly after the attempts to authorize and launch major reforms. In Brazil, President Collor (1990–92) vetoed key provisions of the legislation intended to implement the constitutional mandate for a more decentralized and pro-poor-people system. In Colombia, President Samper (1994–88) initially appointed a minister of health who did his best to sabotage implementation of Law 100. Moreover, both ministries of health included many defenders of the old system. In Brazil, heel-draggers included many bureaucrats transferred from the former social security health agency. In Colombia, many Ministry of Health officials doubted the desirability of Law 100's complex provisions, and the Social Security Institute remained adamantly opposed. But neither ministry could be characterized as captive to stakeholders in the old system. And in both countries, persistent reform advocates within and outside of government kept pressing for the next steps needed to fulfill the mandates and the legislation. In Colombia, new stakeholders—the health service purchasing agencies and the millions of poor Colombians provided with subsidized health insurance under the new system—were crucial to maintaining the reform in the face of early opposition.

In contrast, Mexico's IMSS was virtually entirely controlled by the key union, with the exception of the director and the change team parachuted into the agency by the government's top economic officials to prepare for and guide the legislation of 1995. Nor did the law create new stakeholders. As a result, the agency made very little effort to implement even the very modest structural and policy reforms that had survived as part of the 1995 law. More generally, where the key agency charged with implementing reforms is reasonably autonomous, without extensive ties to unions or political parties (in provision of patronage), and when new beneficiaries are rapidly created, implementation is clearly facilitated.

Institutional arrangements also affect implementation. For example, where decentralization is an important aspect of reform, the rules and channels for fiscal federalism are crucial to the nature and degree of control central agencies can exert over key actors in the sector. Argentina's federal fiscal system channels most funds directly from the Treasury to provincial governments, and it lets the provinces determine how to allocate the transfers among sectors and functions. The federal Ministry of Health therefore has little financial leverage. Brazil's Ministry of Health has considerably greater voice in the use of funds transferred to the states and municipalities; "norms" and conditions attached to release of various funds provided substantial influence on decentralized health programs. Colombia's complex system of transfers, before the further reforms of 2001, was much closer to the Argentine than the Brazilian case, with the Ministry of Health exercising little control over allocation of funds to departments and municipalities.

Broad economic and political trends also of course influence sector performance, as we discuss in somewhat more detail in chapter 16. Two among many examples: Economic difficulties in Brazil in the years following creation of a unified health system joined with more specific resistance from within the sector to hamper implementation; and deepening economic and political problems during Colombian president Samper's term of office similarly contributed to slowing implementation of the health sector reforms adopted in 1993.

Understanding the Record: Variation among Types of Reforms

The contrasting records of the six countries with regard to the scope, orientation, and implementation of reforms provide insights into the impact of political factors. We can also look across the several country cases to compare the progress made by different types of reform measures. Different kinds of reforms entail different political challenges and dynamics, to some extent independently from their specific country settings. Most of the reform initiatives in our cases fit one of the following categories (see table 2.2):

- decentralization of responsibility for health care provision to state and local governments;
- extension and improvement of primary care, especially in poorer areas;
- allocation or reallocation of national funds to reduce bias in favor of better-off states and municipalities;
- creation of agencies to separate health service purchase from provision;
- increased hospital autonomy and accountability, usually entailing a shift from fixed annual budgets to reimbursement payment systems; and
- provision for elected community representatives to monitor or participate in hospital and clinic administration, and broader social representation in municipal, state, and national policymaking councils.

Broadly, extended primary health care and decentralization have moved furthest within our country cases. There has been some progress on geographic allocation of funds, and on separation of purchasing from service provision. Hospital autonomy and community participation have been very slow to take hold. To what extent do political factors help us to understand these patterns?

Decentralization

As in the education sector, decentralization of health care delivery links to broader goals. The resurgence of democracy in Latin America in the 1980s

Table 2.2

A Profile of Health Reforms in Six Countries, 1990s

Reform	Argentina	Brazil	Colombia	Mexico	Costa Rica	Peru
Unification		Social Security and public systems unified	Social Security and public systems unified		Health care functions of Health Ministry transferred to CCSS, completing system unification	
Decentralization	Nineteen federal hospitals transferred to Buenos Aires and two provinces	Already decentralized. During 1990s, transferred progressively broader responsibilities to states, cities	Major responsibilities transferred to departments and municipalities under Law 60 of 1993	Modest administrative change in IMSS structure approved but not implemented. Substantial decentralization of Health Ministry system for uninsured		
Improve quality and coverage of primary and preventive care		Federal fiscal incentives encourage action by states and cities. Formula for allocating federal funds changed in favor of poorer states	Expanded (universal) insurance coverage key goal of reform; big increase achieved	Basic health care package introduced for those without access to public clinics as part of larger antipoverty program	Improved quality a central goal of EBAIS program; almost fully implemented	Central focus of PSBT and CLAS programs. Coverage also expanded through insurance program for all public school students
Reallocate central funds among subnational units	(Fiscal pact renegotiating all central transfers—not only in health—in 1993)	Per capita component for municipal primary health care introduced in 1998	Laws 60 of 1993 and 715 of 2001 altered allocation formulas	Zedillo government introduced new allocation criteria, but used only to top up traditional budgets		

continued

Table 2.2
Continued

Reform	Argentina	Brazil	Colombia	Mexico	Costa Rica	Peru
New provider payment and purchasing systems	Attempt to permit workers to transfer (with their Social Security contributions) among *obras sociales* largely stymied	(States and municipalities reimburse hospitals for services)	Central aspect of reform. Purchasing entities created; most operating	Effort to authorize opt-out provision for workers defeated		Purchasing entities introduced in social security segment of sector
Hospital or clinic autonomy and funding reforms	Federal law established framework for public hospital autonomy. Provinces control; most took little action	(*Note:* Many hospitals private, already largely autonomous)	Major changes in funding process intended to increase efficiency. Introduced slowly, inconsistently, but spreading		Changes in funding process to increase efficiency and autonomy implemented extremely slowly	Major reforms in organization and funding process for two main types of primary care clinics
Citizen participation			Included in reform law (100) but limited implementation		Built into reform provisions but almost no effective implementation	Active citizen councils administer CLAS clincs (about a fifth of all health centers and posts)
Miscellaneous	Attempted reform of PAMI (serving elderly) failed			Central element of reform major increase in direct budget funding for Social Security health care		

Note: A blank cell does not necessarily mean no activity, but does indicate that the topic was not an important feature of reform efforts in that country during the 1990s. CLAS = Local Health Administration Committees; EBAIS = Basic Health Teams; IMSS = Mexican Institute of Social Security; PAMI = Program of Comprehensive Medical Care; PSBT = Basic Health for All Program.

brought widespread interest in decentralization of many services and programs, as a means of bringing government closer to the people. Advocates of modernization of the state in the 1990s viewed decentralization as a means to improve both responsiveness and efficiency.

Decentralization was a major reform theme in four of our six health sector cases: Argentina, Brazil, Colombia, and Mexico. But the scope and nature of the efforts varied widely, as did success in implementation. In Argentina, health care services were almost wholly decentralized to the provinces and municipalities by the end of the 1970s. The transfer in 1991 of nineteen federal hospitals to Buenos Aires and two provinces simply completed this process. Health care services in Brazil were also substantially decentralized before 1990. But during the 1990s, major additional responsibilities were transferred, while new regulations and monitoring increased federal influence on state and local policies and programs, seeking to reduce cross-regional inequities and to encourage pro-poor-people and preventive measures.

By the end of the decade, there was considerable progress towards these goals. Colombia's health system was considerably more centralized than Argentina's or Brazil's in 1990; its 1993 reforms sought a radical transfer of authority and responsibility to departments and municipalities. Though some subnational governments took up the challenge fairly quickly, implementation lagged in many others, due to mismatched incentives, complex and confusing funding mechanisms, and the simultaneous introduction of drastic additional health sector changes, as well as the deepening economic and security crises of the late 1990s. Mexico had attempted to decentralize substantial health care responsibilities in the 1980s, but states were often reluctant to take on new functions, fearing both additional fiscal burdens and potential conflict with the IMSS and its union. In the 1990s, a new effort to deconcentrate administration of social security health services was again opposed by the union, and confined to a few pilot projects. However, the Ministry of Health did decentralize many of its functions, completing a process initiated in the 1980s.

Effective implementation of decentralizing reforms of course requires action not only by the central government but also, and on a continuing basis, by local governments. Local technical and administrative capacities vary tremendously, and are usually weakest in the poorest regions and cities. State and municipal systems may also be deeply penetrated by clientelism and patronage networks linking local bureaucracies to unions and parties. More subtly, local (often informal) political and social structure and relationships color the provision of health services. In the Brazilian Northeast state of Ceará, for instance, decentralized responsibility for health care delivery was interpreted in quite different ways by local health professionals in three different communities (peri-urban, small town, and rural) and was shaped in different ways by highly local patterns of clientelism and politics (Atkinson 2000, 78–93; Gallardo, Beeharry, and Pancorvo 2001).

Governors' and mayors' commitment to and priority for improved health services is also a key factor explaining differences among states and localities in responses to decentralization. We have argued that national political leaders rarely view improved health and education services as urgent goals, unless those sectors are linked to broader objectives. State and local governments are not automatically more committed than the national government to either equity or efficiency in the health sector, and our cases suggest a great deal of variation on this dimension. However, social services increasingly comprise a very large share of state and local governments' portfolios. We noted above that citizen demands for health sector reforms are weak at the national level; NGOs and other groups are more likely to focus on problems at the local level. A growing number of governors and mayors may come to view improved social services as important to their prospects for reelection, and thus they will assign a higher priority to reform. In Venezuela, for instance, the introduction of direct elections for governors and mayors in the early 1990s was followed in short order by increased financial and other support for social services, before increases in central government transfers to the subnational governments went into effect (Navarro 2000, 211 and passim).

A different set of factors may interact with state and local leadership: Decentralization may tend to generate different kinds of responses from richer and poorer states and cities. Wealthier states and cities are likely to be better endowed with skilled technical and administrative personnel, and to have an array of well-developed local institutions. They may well use increased authority to develop and pursue autonomous policies and programs. Poorer, smaller, and more remote states and cities may find that decentralization increases not only their responsibilities but also their dependence on the central government for resource transfers, and the guidance and constraints that often accompany those transfers (Tommasi 2002).

More generally, support and pressure from the central government are important factors shaping subnational responses to decentralization. To play their changed roles well, national ministries of health must reorient their efforts and strengthen information systems, monitoring efforts, and incentives for desired behavior by state and local governments. Ministry bureaucracies predictably resist reorientation. Health ministers committed to reform often must first introduce far-reaching changes in their own agencies.

Increased Hospital Autonomy and Accountability

Along with the decentralization of health responsibilities to state and local governments, increased autonomy and accountability at the level of hospitals and clinics is widely viewed among health policy analysts as a way to increase efficiency and client responsiveness. But the political cards are stacked against this approach. National ministries and state or local health authorities are normally reluctant to reduce their own authority by shifting decision-making power to operating units. Less obviously, hospital and clinic directors are often ambivalent or skeptical about increased authority. Such measures are virtually always packaged with requirements for upgraded information systems, more detailed record keeping, and monitoring by national or state authorities. Those requirements are always viewed as burdensome. Moreover, under the status quo, weak information and poor monitoring by those authorities often give hospitals—especially large and influential ones—a great deal of actual autonomy. Better information and more vigorous monitoring might have the paradoxical effect of reducing their freedom of action.

Reforms aimed at increased autonomy are also sometimes paired with changed financing mechanisms of the kinds described in the next subsection, leading to increased insecurity and pressure. Health care workers often view hospital autonomy and altered payment mechanisms as the veiled equivalent of partial privatization—and therefore, they argue, a threat to equity. They also fear that increased hospital and clinic directors' control over personnel policies and actions will erode their labor rights.

Among our cases, measures to promote hospital autonomy and accountability and create incentives for efficiency were major reform themes in Argentina, Costa Rica, and Colombia, though not in Brazil (where most hospitals remain private) or Mexico. (Peru introduced substantial autonomy for some primary care facilities, linked to community participation, as described later in this chapter.) In Argentina, federal legislation established a framework authorizing increased public hospitals' autonomy, including authority to seek repayment from insured patients' *obras sociales* or private insurers. But Argentine hospitals are under the jurisdiction of the provinces, and each province could decide whether, and how, to move in this new direction. Provincial responses varied widely. Two provinces chose not to implement hospital autonomy, because they were concerned about lack of coordination and inefficiencies, as well as potential discrimination against the uninsured. At the other extreme, one province opted for radical autonomy. Actual change has been minimal even in the provinces that authorized increased autonomy (Castenada, Beeharry, and Griffin 1999, 262).

In Costa Rica, as was noted above, hospital directors and staff mostly did not welcome increased autonomy and associated increases in accountability, and the CCSS adopted a deliberate policy of very gradual implementation. In Colombia, Law 100 of 1993 envisaged increased operating authority for public hospitals, linked to a shift from up-front budgets based on past performance to reimbursement for services provided. That shift, and associated changes in hospital management and information systems, has proven slow and difficult. Nonetheless, by the decade's end most public hospitals had been converted to "social state enterprises" with a directorate and director who can manage aspects of labor contracts and time schedules, and contract out services (Castenada, Beeharry, and Griffin 1999, 254). In all three countries, hospital management changes are hampered by tight restrictions on their control over personnel.

New Provider Payment and Purchasing Systems

In Latin America, public hospitals (as well as Social Security hospitals in some cases) typically rely on operating budgets that cover anticipated costs for the coming year. Budgets usually reflect the previous year's expenditures, rather than the amount and kind of services actually provided. Such budgets create no incentives to provide care efficiently or well. International health circles increasingly favor alternative payment systems such as capitation, diagnostic-related group payments, or performance contracts.[12] Different systems are appropriate for different circumstances and kinds of services. Health policy analysts also often favor a related but distinct principle: separation of responsibility for purchasing services from service provision. Purchasing organizations, like those established as part of Colombia's comprehensive sector reform, can encourage providers to take cost considerations more seriously. Among our cases, Peru also established purchasing agencies to serve those covered by the social security system. The initial

12. For a useful discussion of these alternative systems, see IDB (1996, 257 ff.).

design for the IMSS reforms in Mexico included measures to separate purchase from provision, but union opposition blocked the effort.

Doctors and hospital and clinic administrators usually resist new payment and purchasing systems. The new arrangements require elaborate service records and cost accounting. They introduce varying degrees of uncertainty and competition into the flow of revenues. The new mechanisms also increase the authority of nonmedical administrators, a trend deeply resented by doctors and nurses. Public opinion often sides with the care providers. Support for such measures comes mainly from the small circles of health policy analysts, sometimes backed by planning, economics, or finance ministers. If purchasing agencies are created, however, they rapidly become new stakeholders.

Extending and Improving Primary Health Care

Extending and improving primary health care is attractive to political leaders because it may bolster electoral support, in an era of growing electoral competition. Moreover, programs like Costa Rica's EBAIS teams or Peru's PSBT clinics arouse little opposition. They may somewhat disrupt the operations of existing clinics but do not demand major changes in the organization or procedures of hospitals or the health sector bureaucracy. To the extent that the new programs are staffed with new or young recruits, resistance to responsibilities or personnel policies different from those in old establishments is minimized. In short, primary health care innovations often have the characteristics of add-on programs. If external donors fund much of the cost, as for instance with Mexico's Program of Extended Coverage (PEC) in the second half of the 1990s, potential opposition is further reduced. Where state and local governments have primary responsibility for introducing such programs, increased federal funding can have a similar effect; for instance, Brazil's Ministry of Health offers special funds for municipalities that establish family and community health teams.

Reallocation of Central Funding

In several of the countries surveyed, inequalities in health care funding and provision among richer and poorer regions were addressed to some extent through fiscal equalization mechanisms. In Brazil since 1998, federal transfers for municipal primary health care include a per capita component. However, federal funds for complex, hospital-based services continue to be

paid to reimburse services actually provided, a formula that favors municipalities with well-developed hospital facilities.[13] In Mexico, the Zedillo
government introduced a formula for resource allocation that took into
account states' poverty levels, health needs, and demographic profiles.
However, the initiative had only a modest impact, because it was used to
top up budgets allocated on the basis of historical levels.

Community Participation

As with decentralization and increased autonomy for hospitals and clinics,
user and citizen participation in management at all levels of the system is a
virtually universal theme in the rhetoric of health sector reform. But with a
few exceptions, efforts to put principles of participation into practice are
weak, particularly at the level of provider institutions. Not only doctors but
also hospital administrators are deeply skeptical that nonmedical citizens
can provide informed inputs into decision making and management. And
citizens themselves usually are diffident regarding their grasp of medical
matters. Health sector experience on this point differs from education sector reforms, which have made parent and community participation in
school administration a major and effective theme in a number of cases.

Among our health sector cases, the CLAS clinics in Peru are the only
examples of seriously applied and effectively functioning participation. By
the end of 1997, three and a half years after the program was introduced on
a low-key pilot basis, roughly 10 percent of primary health care clinics
were being administered by community councils; by 2001 the proportion
expanded to 19 percent (1,244 out of a total of 6,485 public primary-level
establishments). The program has been highly controversial and was almost disbanded in 1998. But it has produced some outstanding clinics. It
seems to work better in less-poor urban settlements than in rural areas
(Altobelli and Pancorvo 2001, 192–99).

Reform design in Costa Rica calls for elected citizen councils for each
hospital and clinic. Indeed, much of the 1998 law on deconcentration and
hospital autonomy concerns these committees. However, in the first two

13. Political acceptance of pro-poor-people reallocations in Brazil may have been
facilitated, indirectly, by the fact that expenditures on private health insurance are tax-
deductible (see chapter 6 of this volume)—thus facilitating (at broad public expense)
measures by better-off people to ensure high-quality care for themselves and their
family. The better-off people are concentrated in wealthier states and regions—the same
regions that were somewhat negatively affected by fiscal reallocations.

elections for the councils (held in alternate years), only 14,000 of a million eligible voters bothered to vote. Moreover, local CCSS authorities were reluctant to let the councils take any meaningful role in administration of the hospitals and clinics. In Argentina as well, there are legal provisions for citizen hospital councils, but few have been established. In Colombia and Brazil, reform guidelines call for councils with community representatives for all hospitals and clinics. Some have been established and play an active role, but many exist in name only or not at all (regarding Brazil, see Atkinson 2000, 79).[14] Brazil's constitution and the National Health Law of 1992 further require every state and municipality to establish a council in order to receive transfers of federal funds. Colombia's Law 100 also created a broadly representative National Health Council, attached to the Ministry of Health and charged with reviewing ministry policies and programs regarding the social security system. Although the council is not problem free, it has gradually taken on an active role. In short, rhetoric and legal provisions regarding citizen participation in health care administration are not empty, but reality lags far behind the laws.

Neglected Issues

The political incentives and disincentives intrinsic to different kinds of reforms are useful in explaining not only what reforms were undertaken but also issues that were not addressed. As in the education sector, one such set of issues is personnel policy for the health sector. In most of the cases examined here, attempts to introduce changes that affected health workers' pay or the arrangements for hiring, firing, promotion, transfer, and discipline provoked bitter resistance, and those reform provisions were diluted or deleted. The main exception in our cases, the radically altered terms of employment in Peru's primary health care clinics in the PSBT program, reflected exceptionally weak unions.

A second set of issues that received little or no attention in most of the countries we reviewed was regulation of private health sector interests—hospitals and clinics, suppliers of pharmaceuticals and equipment, and insurance firms. These interests predictably oppose laws and regulations designed to establish quality controls, restrict adverse selection by insurance firms, or otherwise constrain their activities. Efforts to regulate the

14. An earlier effort to promote community health councils in Brazil, in the late 1980s, generated only 118 councils in more than 4,000 municipalities (Weyland 1996, 167).

private hospitals were a major ongoing theme in Brazil's health sector reform story from the 1980s on; bitter resistance, often channeled through the legislature, limited but did not block some progress (Weyland 1996, chap. 7 passim).

Conclusions

The 1990s saw a wide array of reforms intended to address the weaknesses of Latin America's health care systems. Regional and international economic, political, and intellectual trends and influences encouraged these reforms, but domestic forces largely determined their scope and focus, and the degree to which they were effectively carried out. A few countries adopted particularly broad-gauged and ambitious programs; most launched narrower, more piecemeal efforts. The most ambitious programs were driven by a combination of democratic impetus, expressed most clearly in mandates in new constitutions, and the vision of dedicated and technically sophisticated networks, change teams, and key legislators. Variation across countries also reflected differences in institutional features, such as channels for transferring central government funds to lower-level authorities.

Political factors at all levels—from the goals and priorities of national political leaders to the bureaucratic concerns of municipal health authorities or the fears of clinic staff—were strong determinants of the kinds of reforms that moved ahead, as well as those that barely budged or were simply not attempted. Top-level support was most likely for reforms that served not only sector but also broader goals. Programs that created new stakeholders or addressed obvious equity goals, and that did not seriously disrupt established institutions and interests, were more sustainable and made more progress than those that made new demands and altered operating procedures in bureaucracies and hospitals; thus, programs to extend and upgrade primary health care facilities moved forward faster than measures to increase hospital autonomy and accountability.

Decentralization, a common theme in much of the region, does not fit this formula: almost by definition, it requires a great deal of restructuring of responsibilities, working relationships, and procedures. But in the health sector, as in education, broader goals and assumptions about the structure of government and state—citizen relations drove the decentralization initiatives so widespread in the region in the 1990s. And in health as well as education, powerful unions and, in many cases, ties of patronage and clientelism between unions and parties or politicians, were formidable obstacles to reforms affecting labor relations and rights of health service workers.

References

Altobelli, Laura C., and Jorge Pancorvo. 2001. Shared Administration Program and Local Health Administration Associations (CLAS) in Peru. In *Challenges of Health Reform: Reaching the Poor,* ed. Magdalene Rosenmoller. Barcelona: Estudios y Ediciones IESE.

Atkinson, Sarah. 2000. Decentralisation in Practice: Tales from the North-East of Brazil. In *Healthcare Reform and Poverty in Latin America,* ed. Peter Lloyd-Sherlock. London: Institute of Latin American Studies, School of Advanced Study, University of London.

Barr, Nicholas. 1998. *The Economics of the Welfare State,* 3rd ed. Oxford: Oxford University Press.

———. 2001. *The Welfare State as Piggy Bank: Information, Risk, Uncertainty and the Role of the State.* Oxford: Oxford University Press.

Brooks, Sarah M. 2001. Social Protection and Economic Integration: The Politics of Pension Reform in an Era of Capital Mobility. *Comparative Political Studies* 35, no. 5: 491–525.

Burki, Shahid Javed, Guillermo E. Perry, and William R. Dillinger. 1999. Empowering Mayors, Hospital Directors, or Patients? The Decentralization of Health Care. In *Beyond the Center: Decentralizing the State,* ed. Shahid Javed Burki, William R. Dillinger, and Guillermo E. Perry. Washington, D.C.: World Bank.

Castaneda, Tarsicio, Girindre Beeharry, and Charles Griffin. 1999. Decentralization of Health Services in Latin American Countries: Issues and Some Lessons. In *Decentralization and Accountability of the Public Sector: Proceedings of the Annual World Bank Conference on Development in Latin America and the Caribbean 1999,* ed. S. Javed Burki and G. Perry. Washington, D.C.: World Bank.

Gallardo, Henry M., Girindre Beeharry, and Jorge Pancorvo. 2001. Public Hospital Self-Government and Competitiveness in the Santa Fe de Bogotá Health Services Market. In *Challenges of Health Reform: Reaching the Poor,* ed. Magdalene Rosenmoller. Barcelona: Estudios y Ediciones IESE.

Gomez-Dantes, Octavio. 2000. Health Reform and Policies for the Poor in Mexico. In *Healthcare Reform and Poverty in Latin America,* ed. Peter Lloyd-Sherlock. London: Institute of Latin American Studies, School of Advanced Study, University of London.

Huber, Evelyne, and John Stephens. 2001. *Development and Crisis of the Welfare State: Parties and Policies in Global Markets.* Chicago: University of Chicago Press.

IDB (Inter-American Development Bank). 1996. *Economic and Social Progress in Latin America: Making Social Services Work.* Washington, D.C.: IDB.

Koivusalo, M., and E. Ollila. 1997. *Making a Healthy World: Agencies, Actors, and Policies in International Health.* London: Zed Books.

Madrid, Raul 2003. *Retiring the State: The Politics of Pension Privatization in Latin America and Abroad.* Stanford, Calif.: Stanford University Press.

McGuire, James. 2003. Democracy, Social Policy, and Mortality Decline in Thailand. Paper prepared for 2003 Annual Meeting of the American Political Science Association, Philadelphia, August 28–31.

Murillo, M. Victoria, and Daniel Maceira. 2002. Markets, Organizations and Politics: Social Sectors Reforms and Labor in Latin America. Yale University, New Haven, Conn. (unpublished).

Navarro, Juan Carlos. 2000. The Social Consequences of Political Reforms: Decentralization and Social Policy in Venezuela. In *Social Development in Latin America: The Politics of Reform,* ed. Joseph S. Tulchin and Allison M. Garland. Boulder, Colo.: Lynne Rienner Publishers for the Latin American Program of the Woodrow Wilson International Center for Scholars.

Rojas, Fernando. 1999. Political Context of Decentralization in Latin America. In *Decentralization and Accountability of the Public Sector: Proceedings of the Annual World Bank Conference on Development in Latin America and the Caribbean 1999,* ed. S. Javed Burki and G. Perry. Washington, D.C.: World Bank.

Roemer, Milton. 1991. *National Health Systems of the World,* vol. 1. New York: Oxford University Press.

Tommasi, Mariano. 2002. Federalism in Argentina and the Reforms of the 1990s. Center for Research on Economic Development and Policy Reform, Stanford University, Stanford, Calif. (unpublished).

Weyland, Kurt. 1996. *Democracy without Equity: Failures of Reform in Brazil.* Pittsburgh: University of Pittsburgh Press.

World Bank. 1993. *World Development Report 1993: Investing in Health.* New York: Oxford University Press.

Chapter 3

Change Teams and Vested Interests: Social Security Health Reform in Mexico

Alejandra González Rossetti

This chapter analyzes the politics of health reform during the 1980s and particularly the 1990s. It focuses primarily on a key segment of Mexico's system of health care finance and delivery: the social security system managed by the Instituto Mexicano del Seguro Social (IMSS, Mexican Institute of Social Security). For more than a half-century, IMSS played an important role in Mexico's corporatist political arrangement formed around the ruling party, the Partido Revolucionario Institutional (PRI, Institutional Revolutionary Party). The stage for attempts to reform the IMSS was set by economic pressures from the early 1980s, the decline of the corporatist arrangement, and the increasing predominance of neoliberal policymakers in the PRI and the government. By the mid-1990s, technocratic change teams at the Cabinet level and within IMSS pursued a reform agenda that sought to privatize its pensions scheme and restructure its health care services. The formation of these teams was a strategy choice inherited from the technocratic governments that implemented structural adjustment reforms during the mid-1980s and the 1990s (Waterbury 1989).

Although the pension reform was thoroughly implemented, the reform of IMSS's health service provision encountered effective opposition from the IMSS union. Faced with this opposition, and in the midst of recurrent economic crisis and diminishing political capital, the change teams trimmed down their reform agenda. They reengineered some financing aspects of health services, but they left unresolved the policy and organizational changes that affected the union's interests.

The complexities of implementing reform in the social sector are a challenge not to be underestimated (Grindle 2000); however, this chapter argues that political factors play a major role in limiting the accomplishment of health reforms. In the Mexican health reforms of the 1980s and 1990s discussed here, the political context, the resources and interplay of the different actors involved, and the strategies of the reformers all played key roles in shaping the content and process of the reforms, and ultimately their outcome.

The chapter is divided into four sections. The first presents the political and economic context in which the reform efforts took place. The second presents a brief overview of Mexico's health care system. The third presents a political-economy account of the health reform processes of the 1980s and 1990s. The fourth presents concluding remarks.

The Political and Economic Context

The Mexican political system that emerged in the late 1920s, and that lasted until the early 1980s, was organized around a corporatist model.[1] State–society relations were structured around a dominant party (PRI), which incorporated organized groups representing key interests in the state, the economy, and society (Stevens 1977). Through this political arrangement, the state secured the support of these groups in exchange for giving them privileged access to public goods and services. Several aspects of this system are relevant to this case study.

1. A corporatist arrangement is "a system of representation of interests in which societal groups are organized in a limited number of categories: unique, obligatory, not competitive, hierarchically ordered and functionally differentiated, recognized or authorized (even created) by the state. These categories are granted a deliberate representative monopoly in exchange for accepting certain controls in the selection of their leaders and limiting their demands" (Schmitter 1981, 179).

First, the stability of the Mexican political system was built around this corporatist coalition, which was constantly buttressed and renewed by the political use of public policy. Policymakers resorted to a combination of concessions and impositions in the distribution of public goods and services (Purcell and Kaufman 1980). In official discourse, social benefits were distributed according to the state's commitment to improving the living conditions of the population. But in reality, access to benefits reflected each group's bargaining capacity in state–society relations. As a result, societal groups that were not organized and were not relevant in the maintenance of political support did not share equal access to public goods and services, in spite of having equal needs (Ward 1994).

As the following section discusses, the health care system clearly reflected these cleavages and provided services of varying funding and quality to distinct segments of the population according to their economic activity, political mobilization, and income level (Hernández Llamas 1982; González Rossetti, Soberón, et al. 1995). In this segmented system, IMSS played a central role as a key political mediator in state–society relations. Its employees became a powerful interest group as political intermediaries distributing access to social benefits and services—as well as contracts and jobs—in exchange for organized political support.

The structuring of state–society relations around the single corporatist party also implied that groups that did not have formal employment or did not belong to a state-sponsored organization faced significant barriers to political participation and were excluded from policy decision making. The PRI was essentially an instrument of executive-branch power, and interest-group representation and participation in policy decision making was channeled through the party and the state bureaucracy. Congress was reduced to rubber-stamping the executive's bills (Bizberg 1990). This system also converted the senior-level bureaucracy into the single most important veto point in the political system. Senior bureaucrats controlled the prospects of a policy reform and its final content through the selective granting of access of different actors interested in influencing it.

However, the groups that were incorporated within the limited and very structured spaces of the official party and the executive branch did not share the same ideology, and they competed to have their respective ideological stands and policy agendas prevail. This explains why in spite of the fact that the PRI remained in power for seventy-one consecutive years, Mexico's policy agenda followed a "pendulum pattern," oscillating between prostate and promarket ideologies with different governments, similar to that in democracies with party alternation (Cornelius and Craig 1988). This ideological competition within the limits of the dominant party system was also reflected in policy formulation and policy change, with health reform agendas being no exception. During a single administration, competing policy proposals were prepared and presented by different government agencies. However, the power concentrated in the president and in the Finance and the Interior Ministries gave them the last word in policy direction. This avoided institutional fragmentation and ensured policy homogeneity in spite of ideological diversity.

The mechanism of selective political inclusion of a corporatist coalition went hand-in-hand with the development model that prevailed until the late 1970s, which assigned the state a central role in allocating public goods and services. Until that time, public resources were sufficient to sustain this strategy, but the economic crisis of the early 1980s curtailed the state's capacity to maintain political stability through these means (Meyer 1992). This process crystallized in two phenomena that defined the 1980s in Mexico: the debt crisis, followed by the arrival in power of the first technocratic government under President Miguel de la Madrid. The magnitude of the economic crisis undermined the legitimacy of the economic model in force until the early 1980s, and severely damaged the credibility of the politicians and policymakers in power who promoted it. Thus, the crisis opened a window of opportunity for this technocratic group of policymakers to seize power, promote structural adjustment, and redefine the role of the state, the market, and state–society relations (Grindle 1996).

However, the de la Madrid government (1982–88), and the two technocratic administrations that were to follow, faced what has been labeled the *orthodox paradox*—"the attempt to use the agencies and personnel of the state to diminish or dismantle their own power" (Nelson, Waterbury, et al. 1989, 10). The structural adjustment measures alienated the interest groups that had thus far formed the core of the political support of PRI governments. In the case of the social sectors, the structural adjustment agenda—diminishing the size of the state and freezing wage increases— hampered the means to implement policy change, because the teachers and doctors whose salaries and job security were put at stake were expected to bring about change following the new rules of the game. Furthermore, the reformers depended on the corporatist apparatus they were seeking to dismantle to impose painful economic measures, distribute the costs of structural adjustment, and ensure the compliance of the economic actors involved.

In response to this dilemma, the administration of Carlos Salinas (1988–94) sought the support of new societal groups that had been marginalized by the old corporatist arrangement, improving their access to public goods and services in order to form a new political coalition that would compensate for the corporatist groups' resistance to change (Cavarozzi 1994). In light of this new political strategy, technocrats perceived the state bureaucracy in charge of social service provision—notably IMSS—more as an obstacle than an asset. In their view, it was a self-serving interest group that was hampering the renewal of state–society relations by diverting the bulk of public resources into wages, providing inefficient services, and maintaining the old corporatist criteria in determining who had access to them (Ward 1994).

But these new societal groups lacked a level of political organization comparable to that of the resilient corporatist groups. Furthermore, the new state–society relations envisioned by the technocratic governments could not coalesce around them, because the structural adjustment measures did not yield tangible benefits in a systematic manner (Cornelius, Craig, and Fox 1994). In view of this failure, the Salinas administration took a step back and reshaped its reform agenda. It sought to reestablish a relation of mutual support with segments of the ailing corporatist apparatus and the ruling party. It therefore limited the number of sectors to be reformed to those that were key for the transformation of the economy, and it retreated from those areas where reform was not essential for economic adjustment and yet was politically contentious. Such was the case of IMSS.

In spite of this attempt at realigning the political coalition, by the mid-1990s, the negative impact of the economic crises and the technocrats' structural adjustment agenda had placed great pressure on the political system. The technocrats' vulnerability became more evident with the political crisis resulting from the assassination of the PRI's (and the technocrats') preferred presidential candidate and from the economic crisis that erupted a few weeks after President Ernesto Zedillo (1994–2000) took office.

Faced with very little political capital to introduce major reforms and with the need to tighten the budget in order to limit the damage of the 1994 economic crisis, the Zedillo administration chose to minimize its reform agenda and to concentrate on stabilizing the economy. As the next section explains, this meant that the original plans for ambitious IMSS reform were reduced to the privatization of pensions and the financial reengineering of the agency, while all other reform components were confined to a pilot phase.

An Overview of the Health Sector

Before discussing the health reform processes of the 1980s and 1990s, this section presents a brief overview of Mexico's health care sector. Mexico's health system was administered through the Ministry of Health (MOH, established 1937) and the Mexican Social Security Institute (IMSS, established 1943). The MOH provided public health care services aimed at the general population, while IMSS offered a parallel system for formal workers as a component of the Social Security services financed by tripartite contributions from the government, employers, and employees. Currently, the Mexican health care system continues to be a complex combination of subsystems providing health care to different population groups, each owning their own facilities (see Frenk et al. 1994; González Rossetti et al. 1996). Figure 3.1 shows Mexico's health care system as it was depicted in the health reform program presented by the Zedillo administration in 1995.

The MOH officially provided health services to 26 million persons. Of the health subsystems, IMSS's health services covered the most numerous segment of the population under a single compulsory insurance scheme. At

Coverage	Insured		Uninsured		
Institutions	Private insurance	Social Security	Ministry of Health	IMSS-Solidaridad	No access to health services
Population (millions)	2	45[a]	26	9	10

Stratification →

High-income   Low-income

Figure 3.1. Mexico's Health Care System, 1995

[a]Includes Mexican Institute of Social Security (42 million), Instituto de Seguridad y Servicios Sociales de los Trabajadores del Estado, Petróleos Mexicanos, state-level employee schemes, navy, military, etc.
Source: Poder Ejecutivo Federal (1995).

the time of the reform, IMSS had 8.5 million enrollees (IMSS 1997); and because enrollees' families were also covered, the system reached an estimated 42 million beneficiaries, or approximately 46 percent of the country's population (IMSS 1996).

IMSS also had a special program called IMSS-Solidaridad that was entirely funded by federal resources and, according to official data, provided primary health care for 9 million people in the lowest income group, mostly in rural areas.[2] Other subsystems included Social Security and health services for special groups such as state workers (ISSSTE), oil workers (PEMEX), the military, and the navy. A small and fragmented private sector offered high-quality services for the higher income groups, who paid for them through private insurance and out-of-pocket payments, and low-quality care for lower-income groups who paid out-of-pocket. It was estimated that approximately 10 million persons, mostly indigenous communities in rural areas, had no access to public health services at all.

The simultaneous creation of a health subsystem for the general population and another for the workers in the formal economy, and the concentration of resources in urban and industrialised regions—responding to the political and economic leverage of these social groups—has led to serious inefficiencies and inequity in health care delivery. Among the most pressing challenges to the goal of achieving universal coverage are regional disparities in the allocation of resources and infrastructure,[3] as well as inequities in the allocation of public resources among the different health subsystems and the different social groups to which they cater.[4]

As the following section discusses, the technocratic governments of the 1980s and 1990s addressed these challenges as part of a broader state reform agenda. However, among all the health sector institutions in need of

2. IMSS-Solidaridad is the sole program offered by IMSS that caters for a population group that is uninsured. The fact that it is IMSS and not the MOH that provides services to this low income and mostly rural population group is the result of competing views about which of the two agencies should be the main provider in the health care system—in this case, the IMSS-centered view prevailed at the time of its launching in the late 1970s, under the name of IMSS-COPLAMAR. This interagency turf dispute for preeminence in the sector, and in particular for control of this program has resurfaced constantly since then; and was a determinant issue in the two agencies' cleavages during the 1980s health system reform attempt described below. For a more thorough analysis of these issues, see González Rossetti, Soberón, et al. (1995).

3. For instance, in 1993, while the national average of hospital beds per 1,000 inhabitants was 1.2, hospital beds averaged 0.6 per 1,000 inhabitants in the southern states of Chiapas, Guerrero, and Oaxaca. See González Rossetti et al. (1996).

4. In 1993, public resources allocated to IMSS via government quotas amounted to 57 percent of the MOH's total budget; see Frenk et al. (1994).

reform, IMSS ranked particularly high on the technocrats' policy agenda because of its impact on the equilibrium of public finances. The economic team were especially concerned about IMSS's inefficient performance and increasing deficits. The depletion of the pension fund, they feared, would eventually force the government to bail out the institution's two main components: pensions and health services.

At the same time, of all segments of the health system, IMSS was particularly visible in the political sphere because of its key role in state–society relations under the corporatist arrangement that the technocratic governments sought to dismantle.[5] The "IMSS problem" was therefore addressed within several government agencies, including the Ministry of Finance, the President's Office, and the Interior Ministry. It was perceived as a major state enterprise that had to be made more efficient, possibly with the participation of the private sector. In stark contrast, the MOH did not represent a financial or political threat; and as a result its reform was defined and implemented mostly within the ministry itself.

The Health Reforms

We now turn directly to a discussion of the health reforms themselves. We examine the initiatives undertaken by the technocrats in charge of the reforms, how the initiatives were linked to the government's broader economic agenda, and the political constraints that were encountered.

Reform in the 1980s

The first attempt at a health sector reform involving both the MOH and IMSS was initiated in the 1980s, as part of the state reform effort that

5. Along these lines, the relevance of IMSS as a centerpiece of the corporatist arrangement with politically organized societal groups was clear from the start. Per capita public resource allocations favored IMSS affiliates disproportionately until the mid-1990s. Since its foundation, different administrations turned to IMSS to maintain and expand health care coverage, and also protected its financial equilibrium in times of economic crisis by injecting fresh resources from the federal budget. As it will be discussed below, the health reform of the 1990s was no exception to this. Yet the MOH suffered a series of important budget cuts and remained underfunded until the 1990s. With its funds, and the use of pensions funds, IMSS built an important health infrastructure in urban and industrial areas. This infrastructure, plus its financial autonomy vis-à-vis the government—due to employer-employee mandatory contributions—helped it maintain its predominant role in Mexico's health sector.

accompanied structural adjustment. The de la Madrid administration (1982–88) sought to increase the efficiency and quality of services, and to improve equity in access to them. The reform agenda was based on the decentralization of the MOH's facilities and the formation—via the merging of IMSS-Solidaridad and MOH facilities at state level—of autonomous state-level health systems.

The reform also sought to increase the power of the MOH as head of the health sector vis-à-vis the other health institutions—including IMSS. A health cabinet chaired personally by President de la Madrid was created by decree to endow the reform with the political backing needed to ensure the compliance of all the stakeholders during implementation. A National Health System was created as an institutional framework, giving the MOH responsibility for national health policy formulation and coordination. The National Health System included the National Health Council, which was formed as a venue for representation and policy dialogue between federal and state authorities (Soberón, Kumate, and Laguna 1988).

These institutional arrangements implied a change in the balance of power between the MOH and IMSS. Formally, the MOH was in charge of the health sector, but historically IMSS outweighed it financially, organizationally, and politically at both federal and state levels. The IMSS bureaucracy and its leadership also perceived a threat in the designation of the MOH as head of the sector and the creation of the health cabinet, because this severed its direct link to the president for policy decision making. Furthermore, the creation of the decentralized state-level health systems forced IMSS to forsake the IMSS-Solidaridad infrastructure and health labor power, which had given it a key role and political visibility as a health provider among population groups that were not part of its formal sector affiliates throughout the country.

Although the direct political backing of the president forced IMSS to comply, this did not stop it from quietly organizing resistance. This came from state governors who were reluctant to assume possible new fiscal responsibilities and reluctant to cross swords with IMSS, from IMSS employees unwilling to be transferred to the MOH, and even from beneficiaries who were organized to protest the implementation of the reform.[6] Within two years of the reform's launching, IMSS managed to consolidate a strong coalition against change, and therefore to increase the political cost of its implementation.

---

6. Author's interview with former health-sector official. Mexico City, October 11, 1994.

These events coincided with growing public discontent triggered by the worsening of the economic crisis and harsh economic adjustment measures. Opposition to the health reforms became a part of the more general and increasing resistance of the ruling party and its corporatist sectors—particularly labor—whose interests were being directly affected. Political unrest and a damaging earthquake that hit the capital city in 1985 forced the government to downsize its reform agenda. The president and his economic team concentrated their efforts and decaying political capital on limiting the impact of the economic crisis at the macroeconomic level, and accelerating structural adjustment in key areas such as the privatization of state enterprises and trade liberalization. President de la Madrid ordered the health decentralization to a halt, with only fourteen of the thirty-two states having completed the process.[7]

President Salinas came to power amid great discontent and as a result of the most contested elections in Mexico's history. The corporatist coalition that formed the base of the PRI governments felt threatened by a second technocratic government with a structural adjustment agenda. In view of this, Salinas followed the same political strategy as his predecessor: He focused his scarce political resources on priority areas of the economic system, while leaving key areas of the old corporatist system untouched. Along these lines, he made it clear to his team and key politicians that IMSS was not to be touched. At the same time, the leaders of the oil workers' and teachers' unions, who had threatened his authority, were jailed and replaced by union members who were more amenable to the government. The combination of these approaches sent a clear signal to other corporatist unions and groups who were considering whether to confront or cooperate with this technocratic government. In the case of the teachers' union, it helped pave the way for the education sector reform analyzed in chapter 10 of this volume.

In the case of the health sector, the steps toward decentralization during the previous administration were reversed. The law mandating the decentralization of the health care system was not amended, but the budget was managed in the old centralized manner, making no distinction between the decentralized and nondecentralized state-level health services. The transformation of the health sector was thus brought to a complete halt by the late 1980s.

---

7. Given the strained relations with organized labor, the government decided to leave MOH's federal collective labor contracts untouched, even in those states whose health systems were decentralized, thus preserving the negotiation power of the MOH union at the national level.

The Reforms of 1995–2000

Health sector reform quietly reentered the policy agenda in the early 1990s, in the form of policy studies prepared by the government's economic team, and in 1995 a reform initiative was formally presented as part of the Zedillo administration's National Development Plan. It was a very ambitious program that addressed the health sector as a whole, including IMSS, and it embraced a long-term horizon extending beyond the administration's six years.

In the long run, the goal of the reform was to reshape the health system in such a manner that those social groups with purchasing power, regardless of their occupation, would be incorporated into an expanded social security system to which they would contribute. The rest of the population would be entitled to services from the tax-funded, decentralized state-level health systems. Under the new scheme, both systems would be able to resort to a mix of public and private health service providers to cater to their target groups (Poder Ejecutivo Federal 1995).

In the short run, IMSS's health services were to be made more efficient through the introduction of market competition, and the MOH's decentralization process was to be reactivated and consolidated.[8] However, in contrast to the reform in the 1980s, this new effort to decentralize the MOH did not entail merging IMSS-Solidaridad facilities into the new state-level health systems. Instead, IMSS implemented an internal decentralization process as part of its reform agenda, as will be discussed below.

Problem definition and reform formulation, 1992–94. The reform of IMSS's health services was officially considered as part of the sectorwide Health Reform Program (Programa de Reforma del Sector Salud, PRSS) under the leadership of the MOH. However, the IMSS's autonomous status and its political and organizational leverage relative to the rest of the sector gave it enough leeway to define and implement its own reform agenda independent of the MOH's influence. Thus, while formally the IMSS was required to discuss policy guidelines with the minister of health, in reality it negotiated its policy agenda directly with the core ministries—notably with the economic team at the Finance Ministry and the Office of the Presidency.[9]

---

8. This new attempt at health-sector decentralization needs to be analyzed in the context of the Zedillo administration's "new federalism" strategy, which was based on reallocating social expenditures to local levels through direct transfers, representing a significant part of total health expenditure; see Torres Ruiz (1997).

9. It also managed its own direct contacts with other actors in society, particularly

Two elements moved the locus of decision making about the IMSS reform away from the MOH and closer to the Finance Ministry. First, the economic team considered reform of the IMSS pension system a part of the economic agenda, given its impact on public finances. Second, the economic team hoped to restructure the financing of the IMSS by reducing employer and employee contributions and increasing those of the government, with the expectation that this would provide a major stimulus to employment in the formal sector and to Mexico's economic competitiveness in world markets (Dávila 1997).

It can be argued that the proposed reform of IMSS constituted a bridge between the economic and social aspects of the government's reform agenda. It included key elements related to economic policy, but it also addressed challenges in health service provision that were similar to those of the rest of the social sphere, such as inefficient and inequitable health care delivery, increasing demand, and spiraling costs (IMSS 1995).

Aside from the serious inefficiencies and the inertial increase in demand due to the affiliates' increase in number and age, IMSS presented an acute financial challenge. The original employer-employee-government quotas (contributions) had been calculated to finance services to workers alone, and they did not include family members. But benefits had been extended to family members (averaging four dependents per affiliate), without corresponding increases in contributions. Over time, the package of health services was also increased without adjusting the quotas, furthering IMSS's financial imbalance. This was aggravated by the fact that quotas were indexed to wages and not to costs, which spiraled due to increasing technical complexity (IMSS 1995). The financial gap had been covered with cross-subsidies from the pensions fund. As a result, by the mid-1990s, the pensions fund's reserves had been depleted by successive transfers to pay for IMSS's investment in its infrastructure and to meet the running costs of the defaulting health services. Patronage and corruption were also factors.

The economic team's neoliberal orientation and its focus on the financial aspect of policy reform permeated the government's proposal for reforming IMSS's pensions and health services. The proposal sought to reduce the state's monopolistic position in the provision of health and pension ser-

---

with organized business and labor, which—being affiliated with social security—were part of the Institute's board. IMSS also conducted its own public opinion strategy around its reform, in which it presented itself as an actor independent of the rest of the health sector.

vices, to encourage competition among providers, and to open the door for an increased role for the private sector. This, of course, reflected the more general assumption that a larger role for market forces would encourage a more efficient use of public resources. It was reinforced as well by the World Bank's policy recommendations, which at that time also encouraged the dominant neoliberal trend within the global health policy community (World Bank 1993).

The resulting pension reform proposal consisted of replacing the government's pay-as-you-go pensions scheme with a private system of fully funded individual retirement accounts. The comprehensive IMSS reform package also included five key health service elements to be streamlined: IMSS financial reengineering; health service decentralization; doctor eligibility and performance incentives; family health insurance; and last, the opt-out option policy and contracting-out of services (IMSS 1996).

Financial reengineering. With the privatization of the pensions scheme, the need to make IMSS health service provision financially viable became urgent. Cross-subsidies were to be eliminated, and modern actuarial systems were to be introduced to redress expenditure imbalances and ensure more transparency, thus limiting discretionary resource management and patronage. Most significantly, a new scheme of government-employer-employee quotas was designed to decrease employer and employee contributions, and increase the government's. This increase in government outlays was to be of such magnitude that it would not only compensate for the decrease in the amount of employer-employee quotas, but would inject fresh public resources to the IMSS, thus correcting its negative financial balance.

Health service decentralization. The reform package created a new administrative unit—called Áreas Médicas de Gestión Desconcentrada (AMGD, Medical Area Units)—to mediate between IMSS local services and the existing IMSS regional directions, operating as a "purchaser" of equipment and supplies on behalf of the local units. This was a first step toward dividing the purchasing from the provision functions within IMSS and thus generating an internal market mechanism.

Doctor eligibility and performance incentives. As a first step in introducing internal market mechanisms in the provision of health care, the reform envisioned allowing patients to choose the doctor they preferred at the primary health care level. The assumption was that this would endow patients with a certain degree of consumer power and, as is the case in the market, generate incentives for doctors to increase their quality of care.

This was to be accompanied by a first attempt at rewarding doctors according to their performance: doctors would receive an extra payment on top of their base salaries as an incentive for better performance.

Family health insurance. Because it had become clear that the inertial expansion of IMSS's coverage through the creation of new formal jobs would be very slow due to the country's sluggish economic growth, incorporating nonformal workers on a systematic basis through a voluntary insurance scheme was considered. This initiative ran in tandem with the government's policy goal of increasing overall health care coverage, as stated in the health reform program.

Opt-out option policy and contracting-out of services. The opt-out option allowed employers to provide health services directly to their employees through providers other than IMSS. Through this mechanism, if employers proved that the services they provided to their employees were of equal nature as those offered by IMSS, they would be allowed by IMSS to "opt-out" and forgo paying their quota or have it reimbursed. Because at the time of its creation IMSS provision of services could not meet the demand of the formal sector, the original IMSS Law (1943) provides for the opt-out option (Article 89), albeit in a vague manner. Its wording has never been modified, but the secondary law needed for its systematic implementation was never published. As a result, its application has been discretionary and only 2.5 percent of IMSS enrollees are under the opt-out option scheme. The IMSS reform proposal contained an amendment to Article 89 specifying the criteria under which employers were entitled to opt-out. It was expected that this would enable its systematic implementation, and would therefore break IMSS's monopoly on health service delivery. And given the size of its current market share, its dismemberment was expected to increase market competition in the health sector, generating incentives for better performance and cost containment.

The contracting-out of services followed the same logic: introducing market competition by allowing for services currently provided inefficiently by IMSS to be contracted-out to private providers who offered better value for money. The reform envisioned a first step in which nonmedical services currently provided by IMSS would be contracted out. But in the long run, it was expected that health service provision would also be purchased through contracts with other public and private providers offering competitive services. Reformers hoped this would also diminish the need to build more IMSS infrastructure to keep up with the increase in demand (Funsalud 2000).

Privatization of the pension fund was the most contentious component of the reform, but the opt-out option and the contracting-out of services were almost as controversial. The IMSS bureaucracy, and particularly its union, saw in these initiatives the first steps toward dismantling IMSS's health services. They perceived the market competition generated by both components as a threat, and they argued that implementation of the opt-out option would trigger a walk-out of high-income enrollees seeking private care, thereby deepening IMSS's financial crisis.

When the reform proposal took shape at the end of the Salinas administration, some of the junior members of the economic team were seconded to positions within IMSS to form a change team and to work on its technical details in preparation for its implementation during the incoming Zedillo administration. At that point, in addition to the reform proposal being prepared by this team, which was to prevail eventually, two other groups were preparing in-depth policy reform proposals for IMSS. One of them was Centro de Desarrollo Estratégico para la Seguridad Social (CEDESS), the IMSS think tank created by the IMSS director to provide policy analysis. The other was a heterogeneous group formed by a private think tank (Funsalud), representing the interests of the business community and the staff of the MOH. Its proposal helped articulate discussions of policy options for the reform of the health sector as a whole, and it significantly influenced president Zedillo's health reform program (PRSS).

The incorporation into the IMSS of this change team of nondoctors stemming from the economic team, and the government's negotiation of an important loan with the World Bank,[10] were seen as signals of incoming president Zedillo's resolution to implement the IMSS reform. However, in spite of these preparations and the existence of a virtually complete reform proposal at the outset of his administration, the economic crisis in which the country was engulfed within weeks of his mandate, and the legitimacy crisis that followed, forced him to revise his reform agenda, including the comprehensive IMSS reform.

10. The change team secured a $300 million loan from the World Bank, out of which $275 million was going to be allocated to cover infrastructure investments in the northern part of the country. The remaining $25 million was to fund the background research, design, and pilot implementation of some reform components related to IMSS health service provision—such as decentralization. As has been stated, the change team's reform agenda ran in tandem with World Bank's policy guidelines on health reform reflected in *World Development Report 1993*. However, difficulties stemmed from the union's successful bid to have a say on these reform projects—it had one of its members appointed as head of the World Bank–funded Reform Unit.

The urgent need to bring public finances back to equilibrium reinforced the new economic team's perception of the priority of pensions reform. The reengineering of IMSS finances was also perceived as indispensable, because the decrease in employer-employee quotas—due to the drop in formal employment—was increasing the strain on them.[11] But the remaining health service reform elements described above did not present an equally urgent challenge. Moreover, resources to cover their implementation were not at hand.[12]

Thus, as an outcome of the December 1994 economic crisis, reform of the social security's pension scheme gained priority status on the public agenda, but the impetus to pursue a comprehensive reform involving the transformation of IMSS's health services as well was lost. All five reform components described above—IMSS financial reengineering, health service decentralization, doctor eligibility and performance incentives, family health insurance, and the opt-out option policy and contracting-out of services—were included in the first draft of the law amendment, but the executive branch concentrated its lobbying efforts only on gaining approval for pensions and IMSS financial reengineering.

In view of this setback, during the months that followed, both the IMSS director and the change team explored other ways to pursue the four remaining components directed at reforming IMSS's health services, including the possibility of using the existing law and introducing policy change through a secondary law, administrative acts, and regulation. But, though this approach avoided blockage in Congress, it still faced the union's resistance within IMSS.[13]

Opening the Process? A Forum for Consultation, Late 1995

Once the content of the reform was agreed upon within the executive branch, labor and business leaders, together with public officials, were invited to participate in a forum (Comisión Tripartita para el Fortalecimiento del Instituto Mexicano del Seguro Social, or Tripartite Commission for the Strengthening of the Mexican Institute of Social Security) to discuss the reform as part of the formal reform process.

11. Author's interview with President's Office official, Mexico City, April 13, 1999.
12. Author's interview with Finance Ministry official, Mexico City, April 22, 1999.
13. The sole exception was the Family Health Insurance, which, being an expansion program, and not a transformation one, did not lead to an open confrontation with the union and IMSS bureaucracy—and therefore reached the implementation stage.

Although the formal objectives of this forum were to analyze IMSS's policy problems and to study different options to solve them, the exercise was directed toward what had already been decided within the executive branch.[14] In October 1995, the forum presented its final proposal to President Zedillo. Although it was a joint labor–business–government document, it clearly reflected the government's policy priorities: financial restructuring, decentralization, doctor eligibility and performance incentives, and the implementation of the opt-out option. It also recommended an increase in the government's quota share.

The formulation of the reform proposal was formally attributed to this forum, but its capacity to influence the reform agenda was limited. Rather than a real negotiation and consensus building, forum discussion was an exercise with which the government fulfilled the requirements of the sectors' participation in the process.[15] Presenting the document as a joint business–labor proposal was also expected to weaken the IMSS union's possible arguments against the reform.[16] Once the president gave his approval to the reform proposal, the process was opened to participation by a wider group of actors. Negotiations within the executive branch were brought to an end, and lobbying in Congress started in preparation for submitting the law's amendment.

Legislation, Late 1995

The informal institutional features of the Mexican political system enabled the president to establish a clear division of labor between the technocratic groups within the executive branch, entrusting them with policy formulation, and party officials who were put in charge of brokering it within the party and in Congress, even though they had not been included in the formulation of the policy and had no ownership over the reform agenda. Such was the case of the IMSS director, who tried to counterbalance the influence of the change team, lobbied for a more comprehensive IMSS reform, and was concerned about the political impact of the technocrat's strategies and their reform proposal. His attempts to participate in the formulation of the IMSS reform by presenting policy alternatives prepared by CEDESS had not progressed; but he had nonetheless been given the task

14. Author's interview with former adviser to IMSS, Mexico City, April 15, 1999.

15. Although this was not a formal requirement, given that IMSS is an autonomous agency with a governing body composed of government, labor, and business members, this forum was a means to present the proposal as a shared policy.

16. Author's interview with IMSS official, Mexico City, May 5, 1999.

of negotiating the change team's reform initiative with labor, business, and the IMSS union in early 1995. When the change team was ready to submit its reform package to Congress, he was once again put in charge. His political brokerage experience and network as former PRI president, former governor, and former PRI senator helped to increase the political feasibility of the technocratic reform proposal prepared within the executive branch.

At the time the government submitted its bill, it enjoyed an absolute majority in Congress, so the major political challenge did not stem from the opposition but from PRI's rank and file. As a result, following the historical pattern explained in previous sections, the promarket and prostate groups (technocrats and corporatist groups respectively) found themselves bargaining about the IMSS reform within the ruling party itself. Political operators coordinated by the IMSS director were assigned to lobby the party's "sectors" represented in Congress.[17] The union, which was the main actor lobbying against the reform proposal, was able to exert a significant degree of veto power through its influence on union members who held legislative positions, and other members of Congress—from both the PRI and opposition parties—who were unwilling to put themselves at odds with a key corporatist group.[18]

Although the union recognized and approved the increase of fresh resources that was to result from the reform, it starkly opposed the privatization of the pension fund and the opt-out option policy, because it saw both as threats to IMSS's integrity.[19] The union's power proved insufficient to veto the pension reform, which was a priority for the executive branch and was directly backed by the president and the Interior Ministry. However, it was successful in forcing a retreat regarding the opt-out proposal. The government found itself with too little political capital to pursue that option in addition to pension reform. In order not to jeopardize congressional

17. While the PRI peasant sector did not take issue with the reform because it did not touch its interests, the labor and "popular" sectors, which included most of the reform's stakeholders, presented adamant resistance both to the pension reform and to the opt-out option.

18. President Zedillo approached the right-wing opposition party PAN—which approved of the reform agenda but was not willing to pay the political cost of voting for it—as a means to obtain the necessary votes in case PRI legislators defaulted, which was unprecedented. The left-wing opposition party (PRD) opposed it from the start.

19. It also rejected the introduction of doctor eligibility and performance incentives, because it would incorporate control mechanisms to the daily practice of health labor power, and would impinge on the union's control on personnel incentives.

approval of pension reform, the Zedillo administration changed strategy: It struck from its bill the modification of the existing article that allowed for the opt-out option, and it presented this as a concession to PRI legislators opposing the bill before it was submitted to Congress. It then prepared to pursue the opt-out option policy by formulating and publishing a new secondary law based on this old article that would have allowed its systematic implementation.[20] With this strategy, the bargaining on this issue was transferred away from the legislative arena, where it would have been exposed to further politicization, and back into IMSS's internal arena, where the change team would be in charge of formulating the secondary law package.

In November 1995, President Zedillo submitted the New Social Security Law initiative to Congress. Of the original components related to IMSS health reform, it included only the creation of Family Health Insurance and the financial reengineering proposal. The reform was approved with 289 PRI votes in favor and 160 against—including those of the opposition parties, Partido de la Revolución Democrática and Partido Acción Nacional—in the Lower House in December 1995, and it was ratified in the Upper House by the PRI majority less than a week later. Through the law's initiative, the tripartite quota was modified significantly, increasing the government's participation and reducing that of employers and employees.[21] As a result, fresh resources stemming from the federal government were to increase seven times (from 998 million pesos in the first quarter of 1997 to 7,121.4 million pesos in the second quarter of 1997), and IMSS closed the 1997 fiscal year with a positive balance.

Implementation, 1997–2000

After the new Social Security Law was approved by Congress in late 1995, the pension reform component was put into effect immediately, whereas a transitory article mandated that the rest of the reform, related to IMSS's finances and health services, would be implemented in 1997 to allow IMSS to prepare for policy change. Thus the health reform process gravitated back to the IMSS arena. Here, following the economic team's strategy choice, the change team working at IMSS's Finance Division was to trigger the implementation of IMSS health service transformation through finan-

20. Author's interview with IMSS official, Mexico City, April 16, 1999.
21. With the reform, the government's contribution went from 5 to 39 percent, while the employers' went from 70 to 52 percent, and the employees' from 25 to 9 percent.

cial resource reallocation, administrative acts, and, in the case of the opt-out option, the formulation and publication of the necessary secondary law.

However, because the economic team had lost interest in the reform of IMSS's health services, the change team at IMSS lacked the political support to insulate itself and the reform from interest-group pressure resisting change from within IMSS.[22] Though the technocrats had some control over the financial reengineering because the complexity of resource reallocation made resistance to it difficult, the team was forced to negotiate and look for consensus within IMSS's apparatus in all aspects related to the implementation of changes to the health services.

The principal obstacle to policy change once the reform had gravitated back to IMSS was its union.[23] Although its influence during reform formulation was scant, and it had only a modest impact on the legislation, the union regained control over the reform once it entered the implementation stage, because policy change could only happen through the active involvement of its membership. It is not clear whether the union made any serious attempts at letting itself into the decision-making room during reform formulation. It exerted its veto power during legislation and succeeded in limiting the scope and depth of the reform, but it could not derail the process completely. It can therefore be argued that the union strategically chose to wait for the reform to gravitate back to IMSS during its implementation stage, when it had enough power to influence policy change.

The union's political strength was based on a series of factors, including its size and its average education level—because it incorporates doctors—which allowed it to influence IMSS activities at every level and to develop a sophisticated alternative policy agenda. Furthermore, the union's political base had expanded and diversified. Its leadership maintained a close interaction with the PRI's leadership, who still perceived it as a key intermediary in state–society relations, and thus an important political player to accommodate, but it also maintained close contacts with other groups with

22. In the competition for control over the reform's implementation within IMSS, the change team did not count on the support of the IMSS director either. Not only had both been rivals since the reform's early formulation stages, but the latter perceived the former as an extension of the economic team, and thus as foreign to IMSS. Furthermore, the IMSS director saw as a threat the change team's orthodoxy in using exclusively technical criteria in policy decision making without considering the political factors because it risked putting the institute's relations with business, labor, and particularly IMSS's union—still strained by the recent approval of the reform—in jeopardy (interview, June 9, 1999).

23. Author's interview with IMSS official, Mexico City, May 5, 1999.

high political mobilization capacity, such as the independent labor movement and left-wing parties.[24]

The expansion of IMSS as the single most important state provider of health services had consolidated the union's presence at the national, state, and local levels, where it had daily contact with the population, and thus the opportunity to generate a base of support. Although the union did not make any open threat to mobilize its membership or this base of support against the implementation of the reform, the fact that it had done so in the 1980s worked as an important deterrent for reformers.

The union focused its leverage on resisting change in health service provision. Its resistance to the opt-out option, as well as the economic team's dwindling interest on reforming IMSS's health services, effectively stopped any attempt by the change team to publish the needed secondary law to implement it. The union also stopped any additional contracts to private providers in nonessential areas, thus effectively undermining the contracting-out component of the change team's reform agenda. Regarding the remaining components of the IMSS reform, it used a strategy of no concessions, ensuring their implementation would not move beyond pilot phase. Such was the case of decentralization through the AMGDs, which were created on paper and officially assigned functions, but with few exceptions did not operate. Finally, the union was also successful in impeding any modifications to its collective labor contract, which were needed to implement the remaining elements of the IMSS reform: doctor eligibility and the introduction of performance incentives.

Reform Consolidation? 1998–2002

As the Zedillo administration came to an end, IMSS financial restructuring was well on its way. The significant increase in the government's quota participation, a result of the new 1995 Social Security Law, restored IMSS's financial equilibrium, at least in the short run. The IMSS change team leader had become the Financial Division's director. The Family Health Insurance scheme had been operating since 1997 and had affiliated 300,000 families, but it still needed to expand more aggressively if it was to

24. Since it joined the independent labor movement, IMSS's union had made a veiled threat to juggle alliances between the PRI and the PRD, a matter of concern for the former—and of interest for the latter—given the size and level of organization of its membership. The union itself has an ample ideological spectrum within its rank and file. The union's senior cadres had even had close relatives join key positions in the Zapatista movement in Chiapas.

meet the government's stated goal of increasing access to IMSS health services for all families with purchasing power that had members working in the informal economy. All the other elements in the original IMSS reform related to health service provision—decentralization (AMGDs),[25] family doctor eligibility, the use of performance incentives, and the contracting out of services—were still in pilot phase under the close scrutiny of IMSS's union leaders. The opt-out option and quota reimbursement policy still lacked secondary laws needed for systematic implementation.

In the meantime, the Zedillo administration made substantive progress in the decentralization of the MOH system catering to the uninsured. It reactivated the process that had started in the mid-1980s and was brought to a halt in the early 1990s, and as a result, by 1999, 53 percent of the MOH's budget was directly allocated to the country's states, up from 21.6 percent in 1995 (Zurita 2001).

Concurrent with this process, two elements that are expected to trigger policy change in the long run were introduced: One was to start using health needs as criteria for budget allocation at the national and state levels, rather than using historical expenditure levels. The other innovation was a formula for determining Treasury budget allocations to the different states that took into account their demographic and epidemiological profiles and their different health needs, as opposed to using previous budget allocations as a basis. The formula was only applied to a marginal fraction of state budgets, but it was the first attempt at redressing regional equity imbalances and stopping a budget allocation cycle that favors the high-income states (Zurita 2001; Secretaría de Salud 2000; Torres Ruiz 1997; Flamand Gómez 1997). Finally, to expand health care coverage to the 10 million people with no access to public health care, a package of basic health care was provided in rural areas of poor states in coordination with the government's poverty alleviation program.

A Word on Change Teams and Bureaucratic Politics in Health Reform

The strategy used by the economic team to pursue pension reform followed the same pattern as the ones used by previous economic teams in first-

25. The IMSS union contested this initiative on the grounds that it had not been given enough time to adjust its own organizational chart to that proposed by the institute, and slowed its implementation to a virtual halt. The Fox administration has abandoned the AMDG model (consisting of 139 such figures) and is currently considering 34 geo-demographic areas; see Fink (2002).

generation, macroeconomic reform. A small change team of highly technical policymakers, whose training and professional experience had been
outside IMSS, was placed in formal positions within IMSS; the team's
coordination was assigned to a junior member of the executive branch's
economic team. In this way, the team in charge of implementing IMSS's
financial reengineering was an extension of the economic team, linked by a
vertical network that included the direct support of the finance minister at
the outset of the Zedillo administration.

However, with the finance minister's resignation, this vertical link was
to be broken, and the change team in IMSS was left without the political
support of the core ministries. This event considerably narrowed its scope
of action, slowing the pace of IMSS reform. This fact was further aggravated by President Zedillo's decision to halt his support for any policy
reform that was not directly related to solving the economic crisis that had
ensued following his arrival to power.

However, during their work as junior members of the economic team,
the change team now at IMSS had developed close links with their colleagues at the Finance Ministry. These horizontal networks among like-
minded technocrats allowed the change team at IMSS to continue to have
access to information, knowledge and policy advice from the Finance
Ministry. If not political support, these networks allowed for policy coordination and opened spaces for the IMSS change team to make its point to
policymakers who were close to the economic team—a chance neither the
IMSS bureaucracy nor its director had. In this manner, the IMSS change
team was able to salvage enough room for maneuvering to pursue the
financial reengineering of IMSS in spite of the union's resistance and the
active competition of the IMSS director.

The IMSS director also attempted to create a change team similar in
nature and modus operandi to that used by the economic team. In view of
the technocrats' arrival to power, the IMSS director created CEDESS as a
political strategy. He hoped that CEDESS would establish working links
with the economic team, by providing a decision-making space outside the
realm of IMSS bureaucracy and its interest groups, in particular the IMSS
union. He staffed CEDESS with nondoctors, highly technical professionals
who had no direct link to IMSS, and he assigned them the task of formulating a comprehensive plan for IMSS reform with a solid economic and
actuarial base.

However, in contrast to the economic team, he was not successful in
transforming CEDESS from a think tank into a change team. The CEDESS
group lacked traits that are indispensable for the formation of a change

team, including ideological cohesiveness and a common reform agenda. But most significantly, it lacked vertical and horizontal networks of support stemming from the core ministries, and so it remained isolated. The economic team did not recognize the CEDESS group as a technocratic group of policymakers with the credentials to become a partner in IMSS reform.

Beyond and above these two teams, the executive branch maintained control over Social Security reform and put particular emphasis on its pension component. Instead of delegating full control over decision making to either the change team at IMSS or CEDESS, it created ad hoc interagency groups within the executive, under the leadership of the economic team, to study the reform proposals presented by CEDESS and the IMSS change team and to decide on the reform's final policy content. These interagency groups formally served as arenas for the representation of the core ministries and other government agencies involved, but this was not their main role. The interagency groups' members were like-minded policymakers who shared a common ideology and similar views on the reform agenda, and who therefore worked more as a homogeneous task force.

The use of these change teams and ad hoc interagency groups bears a strong resemblance to the strategy used for economic reform during the Salinas administration. In pursuing social sector reform, the Zedillo administration opted for a strategy of insulation, whereby the participation of societal groups and governmental agencies was restricted and entirely controlled by the core ministries, which, regardless of the policy issue, determined both the degree of participation and the composition of the group that was assigned the different tasks related to the reform process. Also, due to the executive branch's concentration of power, and the secondary role played by other arenas—Congress notwithstanding—these technocratic groups found an ample space for policy definition, limited only by the economic team's support and interest in the issue. However, as opposed to the economic reforms, Social Security reform was dependent on the state bureaucracy—in this case the IMSS union—to be implemented. As a consequence, the high degree of insulation during policy formulation did not enable the economic team to undermine the formidable veto power of the IMSS union during implementation.

Concluding Remarks

During the Zedillo administration, the economic team formed and empowered a change team as a strategy to reform part of the health sector.

Because it was the change team's principal source of power, the economic team delimited the former's margin for maneuvering by revising how much political backing to give it at each stage of the reform process. This had a direct effect on the political feasibility of the reform overall, and on the possibilities of pursuing its different components in particular, because change teams were dependent on the leverage with which they were endowed to pursue their reform agenda.

This means that the decision to implement a comprehensive or more limited reform of IMSS was not in the control of the change team but remained controlled by senior members of the economic team and, ultimately, by the president. As has been stressed, these officials were concerned with preserving the minimum level of political capital that would allow them to pursue as many as possible of the components of their policy agenda. This was particularly evident in the relation between health sector reform and pension reform, which were competing items on the government's policy agenda.

In particular, the direct transformation of an old provider institution such as IMSS in the short run entailed affecting the interests of large organized provider groups. As part of the state bureaucracy, these provider groups and their union had a significant political role as intermediaries in state–society relations, because they interacted with society constantly at the national level through their activities in health service delivery. They had historically exchanged their compliance and political backing for governments in office, in return for job security and employment and salary benefits. Thus, the economic teams that were pondering how far to back the IMSS change team and its reform agenda were facing the *orthodox paradox* described at the outset of this chapter: These groups resisted the reform and, more important, were not prepared to implement it, because it put their interests at risk.

The findings in this case study bring to the fore the centrality of the political dimension in health reform efforts. They have shown that the economic team failed to give its political backing to the consolidation of IMSS's health reform initiative because this ran against a powerful segment of the state bureaucracy. The transformation of old health provider institutions such as IMSS will remain the critical pending issue for the consolidation of health reforms, and their transformation will remain political, as governments confront the need to sit at the negotiation table with state health labor power and work out what needs to change if policy reform is to be implemented. In this political choice lies the key to consolidating more efficient and quality-oriented health care systems.

In December 2000, an opposition party took office for the first time in Mexico's modern political history, ending seventy years of a dominant party system. The new administration's National Development Plan (2001–6) presented the health policy agenda as the "democratization of health." Although no direct reference was made to health sector reform as such, the National Health Program (2001–6) put as its main objective the development of a universal health system (Frenk 2001). To achieve this end, Julio Frenk Mora,[26] the new minister of health, is relying on the approval of the state's fiscal reform to generate the resources to increase overall health expenditure, and on the continuation of the health sector's reform efforts—particularly the decentralization process. Notably, the MOH is piloting a targeted demand subsidy—an insurance scheme consisting of subsidized prepayments—called Seguro Popular de Salud. The MOH sees this initiative as a first step in a major financial reform of the health care system geared at increasing access to services for very poor people and at limiting their financial vulnerability to health risks.[27]

References

Bizberg, I. 1990. La crisis del corporativismo Mexicano. *Foro internacional* 30, no. 4: 695–735.

Cavarozzi, M. 1994. Politics: A Key for the Long Term in South America. In *Latin American Political Economy in the Age of Neoliberal Reform: Theoretical and Comparative Perspectives for the 1990s,* ed. W. Smith, C. Acuña, et al. Boulder, Colo.: Lynne Rienner.

Cornelius, W., and A. Craig. 1988. *Politics in Mexico: An Introduction and Overview.* San Diego: Center for U.S.–Mexican Studies, University of California.

Cornelius, W., A. Craig, and J. Fox, eds. 1994. *Transforming State Society Relations in Mexico: The National Solidarity Strategy.* San Diego: Center for U.S.–Mexican Studies, University of California.

Dávila, E. 1997. México: The Evolution and Reform of the Labor Market. In *Labor Markets in Latin America,* ed. S. Edwards and N. Lusting. Washington, D.C.: Brookings Institution Press.

Fink, K. 2002. Mexican Social Security Institute: Recent Reforms. Presentation, Mexican Social Security Institute, Mexico City.

---

26. Frenk had been the leader of Funsalud's health reform proposal mentioned earlier in the chapter. This proposal had influenced policy debate around health systems reform since its publication in 1994 in Mexico and elsewhere in the region. His arrival at the MOH in 2000 brought the opportunity to put its ideas into practice. For more on these issues, see Frenk et al. (1994).

27. *Milenio,* December 12, 2001.

Flamand Gómez, L. 1997. Las perspectivas del nuevo federalismo: El sector salud—las experiencias en Aguascalientes, Guanajuato y San Luis Potosí. División de la Administración Pública, Cuaderno 55, Centro de Investigación y Docencia Económicas, Mexico City (unpublished).

Frenk, J. 2001. Desempeño del sistema nacional de salud. In *La reforma de la salud en México*. Economía y salud, documentos para el análisis y la convergencia 18. Mexico City: Funsalud.

Frenk, J., et al. 1994. *Economía y salud: Propuestas para el avance del sistema de salud en México*. Mexico City: Funsalud.

Funsalud. 2000. Hacia un México más saludable: Una visión del sector privado. White paper, Funsalud, Mexico City (unpublished).

González Rosetti, A., et al. 1996. The Health Care System in Mexico. Working paper, Organization for Economic Cooperation and Development, Paris (unpublished).

González Rossetti, A., G. Soberón, et al. 1995. *La dimensión política en los procesos de reforma del sistema de salud*. Economía y salud, documentos para el análisis y la convergencia 13. Mexico City: Funsalud.

Grindle, M. 1996. *Challenging the State: Crisis and Innovation in Latin America and Africa*. Cambridge: Cambridge University Press,.

————. 2000. Designing Reforms: Problems, Solutions, and Politics. Harvard University, Cambridge, Mass. (unpublished).

Hernández Llamas, H. 1982. Historía de la participación del estado en las instituciones de atención medica en México 1935–1980. In *Vida y muerte de los Mexicanos,* ed. F. Ortiz Quesada. Mexico City: Folios Ediciones.

IMSS (Mexican Institute of Social Security). 1995. *Diagnóstico*. Mexico City: IMSS.

————. 1996. *Memoria institucional Enero—Diciembre 1995*. Mexico City: IMSS.

————. 1997. *Memoria institucional Enero—Diciembre 1996*. Mexico City: IMSS.

Koivusalo, M., and E. Ollila. 1997. *Making a Healthy World: Agencies, Actors and Policies in International Health*. London: Zed Books.

Levy, S. 2001. La modernización del Instituto Mexicano del Seguro Social. In *La reforma de la salud en México*. Economía y salud, documentos para el análisis y la convergencia 18. Mexico City: Funsalud.

Meyer, L. 1992. *La segunda muerte de la revolución Mexicana*. Mexico City: Cal y Arena.

Nelson, J., J. Waterbury, et al. 1989. *Fragile Coalitions: The Politics of Economic Adjustment*. New Brunswick, N.J.: Transaction Books.

Poder Ejecutivo Federal. 1995. *Programa de reforma del sector salud 1995–2000*. Mexico City: Poder Ejecutivo Federal.

————. 2001a. *Plan nacional de desarrollo 2001–2006*. Mexico City: Poder Ejecutivo Federal.

————. 2001b. *Programa nacional de salud 2001–2006*. Mexico City: Poder Ejecutivo Federal.

Purcell, J., and S. Kaufman. 1980. State and Society in Mexico: Must a Stable Polity be Institutionalised? *World Politics* 32, no. 2: 194–227.

Schmitter, P. 1981. Interest Representation and Regime Governability in Contemporary Western Europe and North America. In *Organising Interests in Western Europe: Pluralism, Corporatism, and the Transformation of Politics,* ed. S. Berger. Cambridge: Cambridge University Press.

Secretaría de Salud. 2000. Descentralización de los servícios de salud a las entidades federativas. Secretaría de Salud, Mexico City (unpublished).

Soberón, G., J. Kumate, and J. Laguna, eds. 1988. *La salud en México: Testimónios 1988.* Mexico City: Fondo de Cultura Económica.

Stevens, E. 1977. Mexico's PRI: The Institutionalisation of Corporatism? In *Authoritarianism and Corporatism in Latin America,* ed. J. Malloy. Pittsburgh: University Pittsburgh Press.

Torres Ruiz, A. 1997. *Descentralización en la salud: Algunas consideraciones para el caso de México.* Documento de Trabajo 69. Mexico City: CIDE.

Ward, P. 1994. Social Welfare Policy and Political Opening in Mexico. In *Transforming State–Society Relations in Mexico: The National Solidarity Strategy,* ed. W. Cornelius et al. San Diego: Center for U.S.–Mexican Studies, University of California.

Waterbury, J. 1989. The Political Management of Economic Adjustment and Reform. In *Fragile Coalitions: The Politics of Economic Adjustment,* ed. J. Nelson, J. Waterbury, et al. New Brunswick, N.J.: Transaction Books.

World Bank. 1993. *World Development Report 1993: Investing in Health.* New York: Oxford University Press.

Zurita, B. 2001. Gasto en salud y búsqueda de equidad en los servícios de salud. Presentación, Secretaría de Salud, Mexico City.

Chapter 4

Ambitious Plans, Modest Outcomes: The Politics of Health Care Reform in Argentina

Peter Lloyd-Sherlock

Argentina experienced a wide range of health sector reforms in the 1990s, and it is sometimes put forward as a regional model for successful reform (World Bank 1999). This chapter questions this view, arguing that many aspects of the reforms are of debatable value, and that key problems facing the health sector have been left untouched. These failings are linked to wider problems of governance, which are reflected in the processes of health sector reform. Rather than follow an open and transparent course, agenda setting has been dominated by a narrow set of interests closely aligned to the administrations of Carlos Menem. These have come into conflict with a range of vested interests, including labor unions, which have impeded the implementation of the Menemist agenda. The outcome has been an incomplete and incoherent set of reforms, which have considerably weakened the capacity of the health sector to meet the population's health needs equitably and efficiently.

The chapter begins with a brief description of economic and political

developments in Argentina during the 1990s. It is not possible to understand the nature of health reforms in the country without reference to these
processes, particularly the implementation of a wider neoliberal economic
and social agenda. Some general information is given about the health
sector, and this is followed by analysis of four areas of health policy: social
insurance reform, hospital decentralization, user fees, and the health fund
for pensioners. As will be seen, the nature of policy and the processes
through which it emerged were very different in each of these areas. A final
section considers health sector reforms as a whole, identifying common
threads and general policy process issues.

From Crisis to Crisis: Economic and Political Developments between 1989–1990 and 2001–2002

The year 1989 marked a watershed in Argentine economic and political
development. On one hand, it saw a macroeconomic crisis of unprecedented proportions, which coincided with the collapse and premature
capitulation of Raúl Alfonsín's Radical Party administration. Conversely,
the relatively smooth handover of power between elected civilian governments testified to the strength of Argentina's newly restored democracy,
and saw the victory of Menem's particular brand of Peronism, which would
dominate political and economic life through the 1990s.

The Menem administration quickly adopted a package of economic
measures that bore little relation to those of past Peronist regimes. Although
radical economic steps were in part driven by a need to "fire-fight" the acute
hyperinflationary episodes of 1989 and 1990, it was clear that the administration's commitment to economic restructuring was more than a short-
term contingency. Throughout the 1990s, but particularly in the first half of
the decade, Argentina's adoption of a radical neoliberal macroeconomic
doctrine rivaled that of Chile under Augusto Pinochet. The lynchpin of
economic policy was the introduction of peso convertibility in 1991. Other
key developments included a rapid liberalisation of trade, wholesale privatization of state enterprises (including the transfer of pension funds to
private administrators), and a series of labor reforms.

Menem was initially in a strong position to implement a radical reform
agenda, enjoying a strong popular mandate and a large majority in the
Congress. Nevertheless, many of these reforms were forced through by
presidential decree, and it is unlikely that most would have been ratified had

Table 4.1

Key Economic Indicators, Argentina, 1990–99

Indicator	1990	1993	1994	1995	1996	1997	1998	1999
Open urban unemployment	7.4	9.6	11.5	17.5	17.2	14.9	12.9	14.5
Growth of gross domestic product at constant market prices	(2.0)	5.9	5.8	(2.9)	5.5	8.0	3.8	(3.4)
Variations in the consumer price index	2,314.0	10.6	4.2	3.4	0.2	0.5	0.9	(1.2)

Note: Numbers in parentheses indicate negative values. The very large variations in the consumer price index in 1990 reflect hyperinflationary conditions.
Source: ECLAC (2000).

they gone through the usual channels of the Congress and Senate.[1] The Congress was only able to mount effective resistance to *decretismo* in small components of the reform agenda, mainly involving aspects of labor legislation. Its most notable success was in substantially modifying the Menem administration's initial proposal for pension reform, by ensuring that the public sector would retain a significant role (Isuani and San Martino 1993). The new economic measures reaped immediate dividends, including the virtual elimination of inflation and economic reactivation (table 4.1).

The measures received strong political support, as a consensus emerged that they were the only alternative to deal with Argentina's long tradition of economic instability and underperformance (Navarro 1995). The social benefits of the new economic model were less obvious, particularly beyond the financial sector and outside Buenos Aires (Lo Vuolo 1995; Lloyd-Sherlock 1997b). By 1992, urban unemployment rates were rising sharply, despite continued economic growth. However, there were no signs of a significant challenge to the neoliberal consensus, and it was widely felt that was anything was better than a return to the previous period of economic upheaval. Moreover, there were no obvious political channels for opposition. The union movement had been weakened by long-term falls in industrial employment, and it was hamstrung by its new, ambivalent relationship with the Peronist government and by multiple concerns about labor reform.

Consensus around the economic model survived to the mid-1990s, when Menem was reelected for a further four-year term. However, from 1994 the

1. During his first presidential tenure of 1989–93, Menem enacted 308 decrees. This compares with a total of 35 decrees for the period 1853–1989 (Peruzzotti 2001).

performance of the economy began to deteriorate, and the social fallout of the new economic model became more apparent. There were growing popular concerns about failures of governance, and the high concentration of power in the executive branch (Llanos 2001). A poor performance in midterm elections and increasingly effective resistance in the Congress foreshadowed the ouster of the Peronists in 1999.

By the late 1990s, there was more widespread recognition of the shortcomings of the new economic model, but there remained a strong consensus that the approach should be modified, rather than abandoned. In particular, there remained almost universal support for maintaining peso convertibility. The new coalition government promised that it would improve governance (making particular reference to the notorious pensioners' health fund) and would address the country's deepening social exclusion (Tedesco 2002). The coalition quickly failed to live up to these promises, and following the resignation of Carlos Alvarez, became a delegitimized, lame-duck administration incapable of heading off impending economic crisis. Increasingly frantic negotiations with Washington belied domestic policy inertia and were unable to prevent political and economic collapse in December 2001.

Argentina's Health Care System in the 1990s

As in other Latin American countries, Argentina's health system is highly fragmented, with three main subsystems: the publicly funded sector, social insurance funds (known as *obras sociales*), and private health care. The relationships between these are shown in figure 4.1. Estimates for coverage and financial flows are given in tables 4.2 and 4.3.

By common consent, Argentina's publicly funded health sector has suffered from decades of underfunding (World Bank 1987; EIU 1998). The 1940s and 1950s had seen the development of an impressive national network of hospitals and, to a lesser extent, other public health facilities. Since then, financing has been undermined by a series of fiscal crises and by a reorientation of the health sector away from universal services to insurance schemes. As a result, there has been a significant deterioration of the quality of provision in this sector, evidenced by poorly maintained buildings and equipment, and very low salaries (Stillwaggon 1998; Lloyd-Sherlock and Novick 2001). The publicly funded sector has become increasingly decentralized, and recent reform initiatives have encouraged

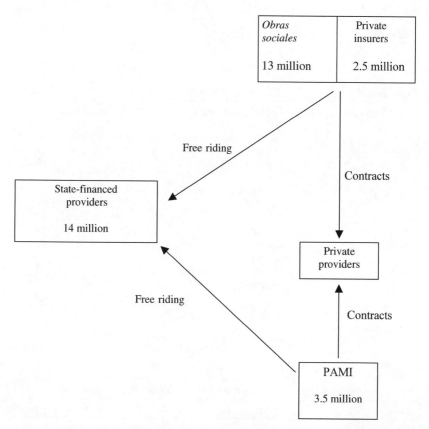

Figure 4.1. A Simplified Model of Argentina's Health Sector in the 1990s (with Estimated Coverage in Late 1990s)

Note: PAMI = Programa de Atención Médica Integral.

hospitals to become financially autonomous. The weak and decentralised nature of this sector has meant that the federal Ministry of Health has become an increasingly marginal figure in national health policy.

Until recently, the *obra social* sector consisted of almost 300 different funds, most of which are administered by trade unions and are autonomous of the state. *Obras sociales* are the principal source of funding for many unions in Argentina, and thus they represent a key resource that the labor movement would be loath to surrender. *Obras sociales* contract out to private-sector providers and mainly serve urban formal-sector workers (Belmartino and Bloch 1998). With rising unemployment, social insurance

Table 4.2
Estimated Health Expenditures in Argentina by Source and Channel, 1993

Expenditure Source	Channel of Expenditures	Total Expenditures (millions of pesos)	Percentage of Total Health Spending
General tax revenues	Federal government	357	2
	Provincial government	3,022	16
	Municipal government	639	4
	Subtotal	3,988	22
Earmarked social security taxes	National *obras sociales*	2,787	15
	Provincial *obras sociales*	1,311	7
	PAMI	2,211	12
	Other	367	2
	Subtotal	6,677	36
Private payments	Contributions to private insurance	3,539	19
	Out-of-pocket spending	4,161	23
	Subtotal	(7,700)	(42)
Total		18,374	100

Note: PAMI = Programa de Atención Médica Integral.
Source: World Bank (1997).

Table 4.3
Estimated Health Insurance Status of the Argentine Population, 1997

Status	Percentage of Population
Only *obra social*	54.4
Only private insurer	6.4
Obra social and private insurer	3.9
Uninsured	35.3

Source: Vassallo and Sellanes (2001).

coverage fell from about 15 million to 13 million between 1990 and 1995.[2] During the 1990s, the *obras sociales* were subject to a major reform attempt, which began to open them up to competition with private insurers.

The 1990s saw rapid growth of private health insurance, responding to market opening, income growth among richer groups, and mounting dissatisfaction with the quality of services provided by the public sector and *obras sociales* (Ahuad, Paganelli, and Palmeyro 1999). Private insurance is

2. More recent comparable data are not available, but the trend since 1995 has continued to be downward.

completely unregulated; recent proposals to change this state of affairs were strongly resisted by the insurance industry. Overseas firms, particularly health care maintenance organizations (HMOs) from Chile and the United States, have become important players in this market (Stocker, Waitzkin, and Iriart 1999).

Public hospitals do not only provide services to uninsured groups. Both the *obras sociales* and private insurers are permitted to send their affiliates to public sector hospitals, but in principle must pay for these services. Large numbers of affiliates use the public sector, particularly for more expensive and complex treatments, but hospitals are rarely reimbursed. Consequently, there is a large free-rider effect as seen in figure 4.1.

The Programa de Atención Médica Integral (PAMI) is a health insurance fund for pensioners, and officially it forms part of the *obra social* sector. However, it is more helpful to consider PAMI as a separate element of the health care financing system. Until recently, *obras sociales* were exempt from providing protection to members once they had retired. PAMI was designed to fill this gap. As with other *obras sociales,* PAMI mainly contracts out to private providers, although there is also "leakage" of affiliates to the public sector.

Until the recent economic collapse, overall health expenditures in Argentina had been relatively high. Throughout the 1990s, per capita spending was consistently more than $500—roughly double the regional average. Estimates for total health spending are notoriously difficult to capture, especially when financial reporting outside the state sector is weak. There are no reliable time-series for Argentina, but different estimates for the 1980s found spending accounted for between 8 and 9 percent of gross domestic product. By the 1990s, estimates fluctuated between 6.3 and 7.5 percent.[3]

These relatively generous levels of health spending should have been sufficient for the maintenance of an effective and embracing health care delivery system, even given the relatively high cost of living in the 1990s. However, Argentina's performance in terms of health indicators has been disappointing (McGuire 2001b). For example, infant mortality rates have been persistently high, standing at around 23 per 1,000 live births during the 1980s and early 1990s. During the mid-1990s, there was some improvement, with rates falling to 21 per 1,000 by 1996. Nevertheless, Argentine infant mortality rates remain significantly higher than those of Chile, Costa

3. These estimates are taken from González García and Tobar (1997) and Diéguez, Llach, and Petrecolla (1990).

Rica, and Venezuela. The fact that about two-thirds of infant deaths in Argentina are officially classified as "avoidable" suggests that the health care system is largely responsible for this poor performance. Also, the gap in regional disparities in infant mortality widened during the 1990s, ranging from 13 per 1,000 in Buenos Aires to 34 per 1,000 in the poor north, with significant rises in some provinces (INDEC 1998).

Many of the reasons for Argentina's poor performance will become apparent in the following sections. However, it is useful to make some initial observations about structural problems, as it might be hoped that these key issues could frame reform agendas. Two interrelated problems that cut across the health sector as a whole are, first, systemic fragmentation and lack of accountability, and, second, an extreme curative bias.

Each of the three main subsectors suffers from fragmentation and a lack of regulation. As can be seen in table 4.2, the public sector was already highly decentralized in the early 1990s, with the federal level accounting for only 2 percent of spending. In 1997, per capita public health spending in the richest provinces was roughly a quarter higher than in the poorest ones, but overall levels of spending in poor provinces were still reasonably high (e.g., $327 per person in Salta in 1997). However, allocative and technical efficiency vary widely across provinces, with some spending more than 95 percent of their budgets on personnel (Brissón et al. 2001). There has been little effort to oversee the performance of provincial health ministries, and it would seem that, as with other areas of provincial government, their role as employment generators sometimes takes precedence over their formally stated functions. As will be seen below, the insurance sectors constitute complex networks of service providers and financing agencies, which operate in a framework of minimal supervision or regulation. Fragmented, incoherent institutional structures have been identified as a serious problem for the *obra social* sector, but not for the health system as a whole.

Almost all parts of the country's health system suffer from a heavy bias toward high-cost specialist curative services, and they tend to overlook more basic interventions and therapies. This tendency is deeply entrenched and is reflected in the allocation of personnel across the system; by the late 1980s, the public sector employed almost five working doctors for every qualified nurse. Overreliance on high-technology interventions and expensive imported drugs and equipment was exacerbated by the overvaluation of the peso during the 1990s. The problem has been particularly acute in the largely unregulated insurance sectors. Basic public health services, including prevention, education, and promotion, are mainly the responsibility of provincial health ministries. With some notable exceptions (e.g., Neuquén Province), primary health care services are more weakly developed than in other countries in the region (McGuire 2001a, 2001b). Although it is claimed that access to basic services is near universal, the quality of services is often woeful. Stillwaggon (1998) provides firsthand accounts of public health centers in Buenos Aires that lack access to running water.

Health Sector Reforms in the 1990s

Unlike Brazil or Colombia, which are discussed elsewhere in this volume, no plans were put forward to reform and unify the health system in general. In part, this may have been because a plan along these lines had been actively pursed by the Alfonsín administration, and it was resisted with equal energy by the Peronists when in opposition.[4] This reflected the close ties in the 1980s between the Peronists and the unions, who feared that any reform would threaten their monopolistic status as *obra social* administrators. The piecemeal reform approach that was adopted in the 1990s also fit well with the new economic model, and it was actively encouraged by international institutions such as the World Bank, Inter-American Development Bank, and United Nations Development Program (Lloyd-Sherlock 2000).[5]

It therefore makes sense to look at health reforms as a collection of separate components. The following sections briefly outline policy in four key areas: social insurance, public hospital decentralization, cost recovery, and the pensioners' health fund. The first two of these sought to introduce radical changes, and initially appeared to have been implemented with some measure of success, although this later became questionable. As such, they have received considerable attention both inside and outside Argen-

4. The proposal was for a universal national health insurance scheme, in which unprotected sections of the population would be incorporated into the main social insurance system. The management of the new system was to be shifted from the unions to a single semipublic agency (World Bank 1987). The proposal was put forward by the federal MOH and was supported by the MOF. However, not surprisingly, it was strongly resisted by the unions.

5. E.g., the World Bank has taken a very cautious approach to the possibility of unified health care financing and provision in Argentina, arguing that "the problems of transition to a full demand subsidy, giving the poor the same choice of insurer and provider as the already insured, are formidable" (World Bank 1997, 44). However, the Bank does not explain why such a reform was less feasible than in countries such as Colombia and Brazil.

tina. Cost recovery (more specifically user fees) has involved a different reform process, which has largely gone unnoticed. The story of the pensioners' health fund is one of a series of failed reform initiatives. It provides a useful contrast with the other examples, and points to the political limits of the reform agenda.

Reforming Health Insurance

Argentina's health insurance system has its roots in the late 19th century, and several key features can be traced from that time through to the 1990s (Katz and Muñoz 1988; Lloyd-Sherlock 2000). There were a large number of separate funds, most of which were administered by unions. These funds had monopolistic rights over demarcated sectors of the labor force, as workers were not entitled to choose which fund they affiliated to. Within the *obra social* sector, it is useful to distinguish between insurance funds for rank-and-file workers, and a minority of wealthier funds that provide a more generous array of higher quality services to managers and executives ("*obras sociales de gestión*"). As will be seen, this distinction had an important bearing on the reform process.

Given the fragmentation of the social insurance sector, most funds were too small to provide services, and so they contracted out to private clinics and hospitals, creating a large private provision sector. This purchaser/ provider split was unusual in Latin American social insurance, but rather than promote efficiency and competition, it gave rise to a chaotic and unaccountable system of contracting and subcontracting. In large measure, this was due to a virtual absence of state regulation. A further problem was that the income of different funds varied by a wide margin (reflecting the numbers of workers and average pay in different industries), and this contributed to large disparities in the quality of the services they provided.

Private health insurance first emerged in Argentina in the late 1960s, but it did not become significant until the mid-1980s. The industry consists of two sectors, organized on a for-profit and nonprofit basis (*pre-pagas* and *mutuales*). These provide voluntary schemes mainly for high-income groups, supplementing the cover they are obliged to take with *obras sociales*. Private insurers are extremely varied in terms of size and the degree to which they rely on third-party providers. There is no regulatory framework, and *pre-pagas* have been criticized for high operating costs and a lack of transparency (EIU 1998).

Before the 1990s, attempts by successive governments to reform health insurance had proved unsuccessful in the face of powerful opposition lobbies (Belmartino and Bloch 1994). A further obstacle was the division of responsibilities and rivalry between the Ministry of Health (which oversaw most of the health system) and the Labor Ministry (which was responsible for social insurance). However, industrial decline and several years of neoliberal adjustment weakened the influence of unions and public-sector workers, and called into question traditional principles of corporatism and social insurance.

Social insurance reform emerged as an important area of policy in 1991, when the Ministry of Finance (MOF) produced a comprehensive set of proposals to introduce competition into the *obra social* sector, and thus (so the argument went) promote efficiency and equity. The proposed reform sought to introduce competition for members among *obras sociales,* and between the *obras* and private funds, all within a new regulatory framework in which a basic package of services for all comers would be guaranteed by internal cross-subsidization. This would mean that workers would no longer be compelled to stay with the *obra social* of the union to which they were affiliated. Instead, they would be able to freely choose the fund they preferred, be it an *obra social* or a private one, and transfer their membership and financial contributions to it.

The main instigator of the reform was the MOF, which was concerned about the burden of high payroll taxes on businesses seeking to compete in international markets. Dissatisfaction with the quality of care provided by the *obras sociales* led workers (and sometimes employers) to take out additional private cover, increasing pressure on wages. Outside the MOF, support for the reform was less evident, with neither the Ministry of Health nor the Ministry of Labor and Social Security taking obvious positions. It was expected that private insurers and other commercial interests would lend their weight to the reform. However, it soon became apparent that the proposals held few attractions for private insurers, which were primarily interested in the *obras sociales de gestión* and were reluctant to submit themselves to regulation and other obligations (Montoya and Colina 1998). By contrast, labor unions were naturally concerned about their loss of monopoly rights and associated funding, and therefore they strongly resisted the proposals. The situation was complex, because conflict between the labor unions and the MOF's reform agenda was taking place on a number of fronts, including the ongoing pension privatization process.

Despite the lack of political support, two decree laws passed in 1993 recognized the freedom of individuals to choose their *obras sociales*. However, this legislation was never implemented because of what has been described as "collusion among *obras sociales*, which aimed to keep the *status quo* by misinforming beneficiaries" (Montoya and Colina 1998, 29). A key factor was that the state agency responsible for overseeing the *obras sociales* and implementing the legislation was in the hands of traditional unions.[6] No government agency, not even the MOF, took significant steps to force through the implementation, which suggests that health insurance reform was not a priority concern for them. Although there is no proof, it is possible that the MOF may have used the threat of health reform to increase its leverage in other areas of labor negotiation (Acuña and Chudnovsky 2002).

This failure to follow through with the reform contrasts with the immediate enforcement of a 1994 decree law centralizing the collection of insurance contributions. This responsibility was moved from individual *obras sociales* to the National Social Security Administration. Though it was claimed that this was done on grounds of efficiency, the reform also served to reduce the unions' financial grip on health insurance.

In early 1995, the MOF put forward a set of proposals very similar to those of 1991, but there were few indications that the political conditions for success had significantly improved. However, these proposals were quickly followed by a comprehensive reform plan from the World Bank, along with offers of advice, logistical support, and a loan of $230 million (conditional upon the MOF providing an additional $270 million to the reform project). The World Bank's proposed reforms were more far-reaching than those of the MOF, including the creation of a new regulatory entity, the development of a mechanism for progressive cross-subsidization between funds, and reforms to PAMI (see below). It was planned that the reform would be implemented by the end of 1995. Given the strong commitments made by the World Bank, health insurance quickly rose to the top of the policy agenda.[7]

During the following year, the reform project made a number of important advances. For the first time, the *obras sociales* recognized that even

6. This is the Administración Nacional del Seguro de Salud (ANSSAL).

7. The reasons why the World Bank became in involved in 1995 are not immediately evident. However, it coincided with a general upsurge in World Bank interest in health sector reform, following the publication of *World Development Report 1993: Investing in Health.*

the poorest funds would offer a basic package of services (at an estimated cost of $40 a person per month). If an *obra social* were unable to meet this financial commitment, its resources would be topped up from a newly revamped redistribution fund. Perhaps more significantly, there was a reduction in employer contributions from 6 to 5 percent of the wage bill. It has been estimated that this represented a loss of $3.8 billion for the *obras sociales* for the period 1995–99 (Ventura 2000). Not surprisingly, the cut was strongly resisted by labor unions, and it was only possible to authorize it through presidential decree.[8] Whether the change in contribution rates was done at the behest of the World Bank remains unclear. It is evident that the reform reflected the bank's concerns about the relatively high level of wage taxes compared to other Latin American countries, and the consequent effects on international competitiveness (World Bank 1997, 17).

The reform process kept its momentum. In January 1997, the *obras sociales* recognized the rights of workers to select their funds, and an effective mechanism was put in place. Union resistance was largely overcome through a policy of divide and rule. A large part of the reform funding provided by the World Bank and MOF was devoted to supporting *obras sociales'* steps to develop their "commercial capability," thus preparing them for the new competitive environment. *Obras sociales* were invited to submit proposals for improving their own capacity and efficiency to the reform team, and only those which met various quality criteria were given money.[9] This proved an ideal tool to reward those unions that accepted the reform and that were prepared to go along with other proposals from the MOF. Some unions, such as the commercial workers' union, saw deregulation as an opportunity to attract members from their rivals. An additional factor was that the MOF was simultaneously pressing the union federation to abandon industry-wide collective bargaining and accept instead bargaining at the level of individual firms, and therefore the labor movement was engaged in more than one battle.

However, the unions were able to introduce a number of additional measures that greatly reduced the impact of competition. Workers were only entitled to switch between funds during biannual three month "win-

8. The World Bank directly encouraged the use of decree laws, recognizing that going through Congress would delay and dilute the proposals (Montoya and Colina 1998).

9. By mid-1998, the total number that had received funding was only 29 (out of 220 potentially eligible) *obras sociales.*

dows." No transfers would be allowed between *obras sociales de gestión* and rank-and-file funds. Also, newly employed workers would be obliged to remain in the *obra social* corresponding to their occupation at least one year. Most important, the unions were able to block the proposals that private insurers would compete in the sector. In 1998, unions were given the power to veto individual workers' requests to change their *obra social,* effectively ending the practice.

Thus, though some progress was made, the reforms still fell a long way short of the MOF and World Bank's original proposals. Many measures had been diluted or subverted in complex political bargaining processes and through what the bank viewed as "selective reinterpretation" of its proposals (Montoya and Colina 1998). A clear example of this was when the old *obra social* regulator was replaced with what was intended to be a more independent (i.e., not union controlled) regulatory entity. Yet the director of this new agency and almost all its staff were the selfsame individuals who had run the previous one.

It is possible that the World Bank had overestimated the capacity of the government (essentially the MOF) to push through the reform and had underestimated resistance to it. A poor Peronist performance in midterm elections had increased the weight of political opposition. Private insurers were no more attracted to the World Bank's plan than to previous ones. Indeed, some *prepagas* had already been able to penetrate the *obra social de gestión* sector without submitting to regulatory constraints.[10] In a Trojan horse strategy known as "triangulation," *obras sociales* started to contract out their administrative functions and, in some cases, effectively served as fronts for private health insurers.

During the 1999 election campaign, future members of the coalition made much of changing the Menemist "neoliberal" approach to social policy, although few specific references were made to health insurance. Yet within months of taking office, the new administration ratified the implementation of competition between private insurers and *obras sociales.* Full competition was officially allowed to commence from May 2000. At first sight, this represented the completion of the Menemist health insurance project, and this was done without significant input or pressure from the World Bank. It was expected that the reform would generate widespread popular support from key coalition constituencies.

10. An incentive for private insurers to operate through *obras sociales* is the possibility of escaping a 22 percent value-added tax levy on *Pre-pagas* introduced in early 1999.

By the late 1990s, private health insurance had extended its reach to a significant number of middle-class Argentines. Most of these were also obliged to pay *obra social* contributions, and so it was expected that the new system would reduce their overall monthly payments. The coalition's strategy may also have reflected a recognition that mergers between private and *obra social* funds were already occurring on an informal basis, and that this process would be difficult to stop. Moreover, the new administration was in a better position to push through the reform than the Peronists had been in the run-up to the election. At this stage, the coalition had a strong popular mandate and had fewer historical ties with trade unions.

In fact, competition between *obras sociales* and private insurers never occurred. Private insurers were not obliged to come into the *obra social* sector, and most were happy to remain outside it. The labor movement mounted increasingly effective resistance to the "privatization of social insurance." They were able to link this issue to wider concerns about the rapidly deteriorating economic and political situation, and the imposition of adjustment and austerity measures. Toward the end of the coalition administration, the World Bank and International Monetary Fund became increasingly influential, and they strongly urged that private insurers be obliged to enter the new arrangement. However, in a situation of deepening crisis, the capacity of the government to act decisively was extremely limited. In March 2002, the new Peronist administration of Eduardo Duhalde rescinded the coalition's legislation. This was an opportunity for Duhalde to placate labor unions, in the knowledge that he was merely recognizing the actual state of affairs.

The health insurance reform project has been a complex and tortuous process, running from 1991 up to the present day. Although the current situation remains a long way short of that envisaged by the World Bank, it is clear that some important changes did occur. Indeed, these changes have been more significant than at any time since the sector was created in the 1940s. Some of these changes were planned; others were unintentional or were by-products of other processes. Key planned changes include the introduction of limited competition between *obras sociales*. Despite the strict conditions placed on this, significant numbers of workers were able to switch health care providers (362,000 in 1997). However, since 1998 this has mainly been restricted to the *obras sociales de gestión*. Agreement on a basic service package supported by cross-funding might have represented another advance, but it was undermined by the failed reform of the *obra social* regulator, which still controlled the redistribution fund.

The failure of the new arrangement became apparent in 1997 when the fund for rural workers suspended its activities because of a financial crisis. Perhaps the most important change, the reduction in employer contributions, occurred in an almost incidental fashion. The swift use of a decree law outflanked the unions, whose main concern was to avoid the complete dismantling of their *obra social* empire. Unplanned change included the rapid growth of private insurance, fueled by dissatisfaction with the union funds. This considerably reduced the overall significance of the *obras sociales* in the Argentine health system.

On the surface, the conditions for a radical reform were excellent. The project received significant backing from the World Bank and had the support of the MOF. Outside the unions, there was a widespread perception that the old *obra social* system was highly inefficient, and was out of kilter with the country's increasingly fluid and precarious labor market. There was growing middle-class resistance to the need to pay insurance contributions as well as premiums to their private insurers of preference. Yet there were two key barriers to change. The first was the relative significance of the project to the unions and the government. For the unions, defending the *obras sociales* was of paramount importance; for the MOF, health insurance was one of several items on a long list of desired reforms. According to Acuña and Chudnovsky (2002, 35):

> The priority for the government was opening the labor market. Consequently, it used the threat of *obra social* reform as a bargaining chip in wider negotiations with unions.

Second, private insurers were not interested in merging with the *obras sociales,* and as the coalition discovered, "You can take a horse to water, but you can't make him drink."

Hospital Decentralization and Self-Management

Decentralization has involved two main elements: the transfer of responsibility for some public hospitals from the national to the provincial ambit, and the promotion of self-managed hospitals (SMHs). Both of these reforms followed on from a general decentralizing trend that went back as far as 1978, when the majority of hospitals were transferred from federal to provincial administration. However, the 1990s saw an acceleration in the decentralization process.

In 1992, a total of nineteen federal hospitals were transferred to three authorities: Buenos Aires City, Buenos Aires Province, and Entre Ríos. This reform followed provincial elections and the appointment of a new national minister of health. It was claimed that this transfer of responsibility would bring a number of benefits, including improved service quality, increased coverage and equity, wider participation, and greater technical and allocative efficiency. However, its principal impact has been a shift in funding responsibility from the nation to the provinces, which took over the entire budgets of the transferred hospitals (Repetto et al. 2001). This represented around a fifth of the national ministry of health's budget at the time.

The transfer of hospitals was closely linked to wider fiscal negotiations between the nation and the provinces, including efforts to agree on a nationwide fiscal pact (Bisang and Cetrángulo 1997). The pact sought to renegotiate a long-standing arrangement whereby tax revenue was transferred from the federal to the provincial levels of government. By the mid-1990s, these transfers accounted for about 40 percent of total provincial revenue. Whereas the provinces were responsible for the lion's share of public health spending, the federal transfers did not earmark specific funds for health. The three provinces involved hoped that they might receive favorable treatment in the pact in return for participating in the reform. They were also attracted by the prospect of using the hospitals as a source of public employment for their own political ends.

The legislative framework enabling hospitals to convert to SMHs was created in 1993. Subsequent legislative changes were introduced to facilitate the transfer process, as well as reducing the quality criteria for eligibility. By the end of 1999, 1,153 establishments had made the change, representing the great majority of public hospitals. However, because most hospitals were already under provincial control, the degree to which hospital autonomy has been promoted has been largely determined at this level. Although federal legislation merely provided a framework and general impetus for this shift, the implementation of the reform and the degree of actual independence granted to hospitals has varied considerably both within and between provinces. This has been influenced by the readiness of the different municipal and provincial authorities to give up powers to the hospitals (Repetto et al. 2001).

It would appear that increased hospital autonomy did not include authority over personnel.[11] As seen above, staffing accounted for almost the entire

11. Systematic information about the exact implementation of the program is not

health budget in some provinces, and ministries were not prepared to lose control of this key source of patronage. Retaining control over personnel meant that provincial government resistance to the reform was minimal, but it also meant that the reform itself was of scant significance. Most financial transfers from provinces to health care facilities remain historically based (Castañeda, Beeharry, and Griffin 1999). World Bank reform documents discuss specific aspects of hospital autonomy, such as controls over materials and supplies, but shy away from the thorny issue of personnel. The bank's reluctance to tackle this issue suggests that its commitment to achieving real improvements in provincial health services was weaker than its concern to push through a reform of whatever ilk.

According to official sources, the main motives for the reform were to improve hospital management capacity and culture, to increase local participation, and to facilitate the recovery of costs from the *obras sociales,* PAMI, and private insurers. Part of these recovered costs were to be passed on to a central redistribution agency, but the bulk were to be left in the hands of the hospitals themselves. Hospitals were entitled to use these funds to invest in equipment and infrastructure, and to provide productivity bonuses for staff.

The promotion of SMHs was attractive to the Menem administration for two main reasons. First, cost recovery offered the prospect of increasing resources for the already overstretched public hospitals. Second, it was strongly encouraged by the international community, including the World Bank. As with the social insurance reforms, it is possible to observe an axis of common interest between the World Bank and the MOF. The Ministry of Health obtained a loan of more than $100 million from the World Bank, with which it financed a Health Sector Reform Program (PRESSAL). The Ministry of Health was given considerable control over the design of the program and the disbursement of the funds, which ensured its support of the reform project.

PRESSAL ran from 1995 to 2001, starting with pilot schemes in Buenos Aires City, Buenos Aires Province, and Mendoza. Selected hospitals in these locations received funds for infrastructure, equipment and training. Other provinces received smaller disbursements, principally consultancy support for their reform efforts. PRESSAL funds strengthened the bargain-

---

available for all provinces. Where information is available (e.g., the province of Santa Fe), legislation ensured that human resource issues remained firmly in the control of the provincial ministry (Brissón et al. 2001).

ing power of the national Ministry of Health vis-à-vis its provincial counterparts. This was particularly important because no portion of federal transfers to provincial government was specifically earmarked for health. The possibilities of obtaining funds via PRESSAL and the prospects of increasing health resources via cost recovery were just as attractive to hospitals and local government as they were to the ministry of health, explaining the large numbers of hospitals that converted to SMH status.

There was initially some resistance to the SMH program from the labor unions and medical professionals.[12] The former were concerned that this process could entail a step toward hospital privatization, giving hospital managers increased powers to hire and fire, and creating incentive structures to deny treatment to non-fee-paying patients. These worries were quickly allayed, and the labor unions' main concerns shifted to the proportion of recovered costs that would be allocated to their respective memberships. Also, labor unions had greater concerns about other areas of the Menemist agenda, such as the pension reform, and therefore were prepared to play a less active role in this area. Likewise, medical professionals' concerns that the reform would leave them in a subordinate position to economists and managers were offset by the prospect of additional funds for investment in their hospitals and personal bonuses.

There have not been large-scale evaluations of the SMH reform or PRESSAL, but the limited available research suggests that neither has led to significant changes in hospital management or performance (Repetto et al. 2001). PRESSAL itself has admitted that some hospitals initially responded to the reforms by refusing to treat poor uninsured groups (for whom there was no likelihood of recovering costs), but claimed that new regulatory procedures would quickly stamp out this practice.[13] Information about the scale of cost recovery from *obras sociales* remains unclear. According to PRESSAL sources, this form of cost recovery grew from a negligible amount in 1994 to $23.4 million in the first quarter of 1999. This estimate has not been independently verified, and it would appear to contradict the findings of other surveys. These show that cost recovery had

12. It is important to distinguish between the role of labor unions in general and the role of unions representing workers employed in different parts of the health sector. On some issues, such as resistance to reform of the *obras sociales,* the interests of the two groups overlapped. Health worker unions had a particular stake in the reform of the public health system, but this was closely tied to wider union resistance to reform in other parts of the public sector, e.g., education.

13. Informal presentation by PRESSAL held at the Anglo-Argentine Chamber of Commerce, July 23, 1999.

already been taking place on a significant scale in at least some provinces well before the Menem reforms (Bisang and Cetrángulo 1997).

Studies of other provinces suggest that the initial surge in cost recovery quickly tailed off (Repetto et al. 2001). In some hospitals, cost recovery from *obras sociales* came into conflict with other forms of cost recovery that were already in place (see below). A general review of decentralization and deregulation of health care finance in Argentina as a whole suggested that funds recovered from the *obras sociales* rarely account for more than 2 or 3 percent of total hospital budgets, and that delays in repayments and the administrative efforts required are considerable (Belmartino and Bloch 1998).

User Fees (Passive Reform)

User fees are rarely discussed in policy debates but have become an important and established component of hospital financing in parts of Argentina (Lloyd-Sherlock and Novick 2001). Obligatory fees were first levied during the Proceso military regime in the 1970s, but they were discontinued shortly after redemocratization in 1984. However, the crisis of the late 1980s saw the reintroduction of emergency payments, which remained in place from 1989 to 1993. Fees could only be levied on a voluntary basis because the legislation was enacted at a lower level than the 1984 ruling that banned obligatory payments. The voluntary approach was also politically attractive, reducing comparisons with the unpopular Proceso dictatorship and, in theory, cushioning the poorest. Given that the contributions were meant to be voluntary, there was no apparent need for an explicit exemptions policy. However, a resolution the following year stipulated that "voluntary payments by pregnant women . . . and children aged under two years old will not be accepted" (Resolution 669,1992 of the Municipal Health Secretariat). This, on paper, represented a restriction of rights, rather than protection from obligations. More important, it raises doubts about the purportedly voluntary nature of the contributions.

Since 1993 there has been no official user fee policy nor legal provision for one. However, many hospitals still levy voluntary payments at the point of use. This is often done through independent fund-raising agencies known as *cooperadoras*.[14] Data for Buenos Aires in the late 1990s show

14. *Cooperadoras* consist of civil associations charged with the promotion of hospitals in their own neighborhoods. Their membership is usually drawn from key figures in

that these payments accounted for more than half the nonsalary budgets of some hospitals. *Cooperadoras* are permitted to make bonus payments and offer fringe benefits to senior hospital staff, ensuring their political support at the hospital level. Recent research in two hospitals casts doubt on the voluntary aspect of these payments, revealing widespread coercion and misinformation. It also found that *cooperadoras* were largely unregulated and unaccountable. Data about voluntary contributions are unreliable and difficult to obtain.

The lack of regulation of the *cooperadoras* is in part a reflection of the general weakness of governance in Argentina. As seen above, similar failings occur in the supervision of the *obras sociales* and the private health sector. However, turning a blind eye to the *cooperadoras* may also be a politically convenient strategy. In Argentina, as in many other countries, the implementation of user fees is a politically sensitive issue, particularly given associations with the previous military dictatorship. The response has been implementation by stealth; payments are notionally voluntary, and hospitals are free to interpret the policy as they feel fit. This has led to an ad hoc approach, with little concern for transparency or accountability. The low profile of the voluntary payments is apparent in an absence of reference to them in the national press, which focuses on other health policy issues. In this respect, it could be said that the implementation strategy has been a success.

PAMI (Reform Deadlock)

PAMI was originally designed to be a dedicated health insurance fund for pensioners, thus relieving the *obras sociales* of a potentially expensive set of responsibilities.[15] Health services were to be funded mainly through a combination of wage levies and a tax on pension benefits. Following its creation in 1971, PAMI grew rapidly, so that by the mid-1990s it had an annual budget of more than $2 billion and provided services to about 3.5 million people. The program's core medical services were complemented

---

the local community, particularly businesspeople. Activities are largely limited to generating additional hospital revenue, rather than developing community participation in hospital activities or vice versa.

15. PAMI was established during a period of democratic transition, which would culminate in the election of a civilian government in 1973. The incumbent military regime had hopes of regaining public support in order to promote its role in any future democracy. It was thought that transferring the cost of pensioner provision away from union-run *obras sociales* would reduce hostility from organized labor.

by a range of social services and transfers, including emergency food parcels, funeral costs, means-tested pension top-ups, and a national network of day centers. By this time PAMI was providing for more than a million people under sixty years of age, either as pensioners or as dependents. As such, it became misleading to think in terms of PAMI as purely a health fund for elderly pensioners (Lloyd-Sherlock 1997a).

The process of expansion accelerated in the late 1980s and early 1990s, responding to the general economic crisis and the retrenchment of other welfare programs. There was also a political logic to the expansion. Though PAMI was notionally an autonomous *obra social,* its director was usually a political appointment. Directors made use of PAMI's apparently limitless resources to further their own political careers.[16] PAMI remained almost entirely unaccountable to the general public, and it was not required to demonstrate where the funds for new commitments would come from.

PAMI did not appear to be affected by the financial problems facing other welfare agencies. In fact, the main source of its seemingly limitless funds was capital that had been accumulated during previous periods when the ratio of working-age contributors relative to retirees was rather higher. Also, there had been a large, one-off influx of funds generated by the partial privatization in 1992 of the main state oil company, Yacimientos Petrolíferos Fiscales. The end of the process of expansion and the emergence of a serious institutional crisis date from around 1994. By then, PAMI had depleted its capital stocks and was unable to finance the gap between income and expenditure that had reached $400 million a year. This shortfall was initially covered by emergency transfers from the Treasury. At the same time, the Menem government decided to reduce the level of the wage levy from 2 to 1 percent. Falling formal sector employment also reduced contributions to the program. Since then, PAMI has continued to receive substantial subsidies from the federal government, as well as loans from the National Social Security Administration.

The mid-1990s also saw the emergence of widespread claims of corruption and political patronage within PAMI. The scale of these problems was

16. The political nature of PAMI's directorship was reflected in the intervention of the national president to change the person in post on no fewer than eighteen occasions between 1971 and 1994. In newspaper reports, several ex-directors openly admitted the political nature of their roles. According to one: "PAMI has been fingered by everyone. . . . In PAMI there have been a lot of political appointments. . . . That's the nature of the Argentine system (Bramer Markovic in *Página 12,* November 25, 1996). Similar claims were made by Antonio Maldonado (*Página 12,* July 25, 1995).

exposed by the central government auditing body, the Auditoría General de la Nación, which was able to access PAMI's accounts for the first time in 1994. Media reports of malpractice have since proliferated, ranging from bribes and pilfering to corrupt contracts and the inclusion of large numbers of "ghost workers" on payrolls. One study identified twenty-six different categories of corruption in PAMI during the late 1990s (Bonvecchi et al. 1998).

Efforts to reform PAMI occurred in four areas: cutting staff, reducing services, restructuring contracts, and improving internal controls and regulation. These have received substantial inputs from the World Bank, in the form of both advice and loans. However, there is little sign that significant progress has been made in any of these areas. With the onset of the recent crisis, there have been mounting calls for a radical shakeup of the program, and its dismemberment into separate provincial funds looks increasingly likely.

A casual onlooker might get the impression that PAMI had been expressly designed with corruption and political patronage in mind. It is theoretically an independent organization, but in reality it is closely linked to the state. Until 1994, this had protected PAMI from the rigors of public-sector accountability but still left it wide open to political influence. Moreover, a labyrinthine system of contracts between PAMI and service providers creates widespread opportunities for malpractice. Not surprisingly, the data (to the degree that they exist and are in the public domain) suggest very low levels of technical efficiency, along with large gaps between services promised on paper and actual delivery of them.

Given the scale of these problems (and of PAMI's deficit), it is interesting to consider why efforts at reform have met with so little success, particularly when compared with other components of the health sector. By the end of 2000, estimates for PAMI's accumulated arrears varied between $1.8 billion and $4 billion, depending upon interpretations of existing contractual obligations and the degree to which creditors have written off outstanding debts. Whatever the figure, PAMI was responsible for a significant part of the total national debt of $20 billion that lay at the heart of the macroeconomic crisis of 2001. In this light, the inability of the MOF to effect reforms is striking. It is possible to identify two factors that, inter alia, contributed to this reform impasse: the lack of an obvious alternative and the impact of key interest groups.

There is little indication that any other component of the health sector— the public system, the *obras sociales,* or private insurers—would be willing or in a position to take over PAMI's services. By 1999, about 15 percent of persons more than sixty years of age living in Buenos Aires had taken out complementary private insurance (Vassallo and Sellanes 2001). However, a survey of insurers in the city found that the most firms refused to cover older people (Lloyd-Sherlock 2001). Those that did charged high premiums that rose sharply with age, and only individuals in good health were entitled to enroll. Given the continued absence of state regulation, the incentives for private insurers to take over PAMI's responsibilities are very weak.

Since 1995, PAMI affiliates have been permitted to re-register with their previous *obras sociales*. Half a million affiliates have taken this option, but this has mainly involved the richer *obras sociales*. There is little incentive for affiliates who belonged to one of the less privileged union funds to leave PAMI. The increased blurring between the *obra social* sector, and private insurance funds will do nothing to encourage the latter's exclusion of all but a minority of the richest elders.

Public hospitals are already the de facto providers of some services to PAMI affiliates. Transferring responsibilities and funds from PAMI might benefit public hospitals by reducing free riding. However, much of the public system is in a state of collapse, and it lacks the infrastructure to meet the additional demands that this would create. This policy would also be very unpopular with affiliates that perceive that the services offered by private providers contracted by PAMI are superior to those available in the public sector.

Taken as a whole, it is apparent that the possibilities for transferring PAMI's services to other parts of the health sector are very limited. This is largely due to the woeful state of public health services and to the emergence of a largely unregulated insurance sector. The lack of alternatives does much to explain the current reform impasse; were the program to be phased out, most pensioners would be left without effective health care. And pensioners account for about a fifth of voters in Argentina.

The second set of reasons for the reform impasse refers to the balance of power between actors whose interest lies in preserving the status quo and those who are in favor of change. The former include

- *Public-sector workers:* By all accounts, PAMI is grossly overstaffed, and most of its employees (including the director) are political appointments.[17] PAMI workers have strongly resisted efforts to cut jobs. As the

17. PAMI employs about 12,000 staff, compared with 4,000 employed by Medicare, which offers similar services to about 40 million affiliates in the United States.

formal sector contracted, secure jobs have become increasingly scarce, and PAMI's role as a quasi-public-sector safety net has become more important.

- *Political elites:* These have been able to use PAMI as a source of patronage (through job creation) and plunder, almost with impunity. This continued to occur after the onset of the program's financial crisis. As other public-sector agencies were cut back, PAMI's role in the machine politics of all Argentina's main parties became indispensable. This did not change, even after the coalition was elected on an anticorruption ticket and made specific promises to clean up PAMI.
- *Private drugs suppliers and clinics:* It is recognized that PAMI contracts often pay well above real market rates for private services. PAMI remains a major client for most private providers, offering expensive drugs and services more often on the basis of private profit than real need. As PAMI's finances have worsened, it has become increasingly tardy in paying providers. However, these concerns are outweighed by fears that a significant reform would mean the loss of a highly lucrative customer. Because many doctors are employed in private practice, they are likely to share this view.

Groups with a clear interest in reforming PAMI include

- *Pensioners:* Pensioners have become a high-profile political lobby and have campaigned for a radical improvement of PAMI services. However, mobilizations have been largely confined to a relatively small number of middle-class *porteños*. Many pensioners fear that reform could mean transferring PAMI services to the provincial ministries of health, and that this would further worsen the quality of provision. Richer pensioners are increasingly taking out private insurance and are less concerned with PAMI's shortcomings.
- *The World Bank:* The World Bank provided considerable support to the design of reform packages, along with offers of loans valued at $200 million. The bulk of these loan offers were withdrawn in 1998, when the bank concluded that there was a lack of political will to implement the reform package it had discussed. Given the close ties between the bank and the MOF, and given the Menem regime's general readiness to follow Washington's promptings, the World Bank's failure in pushing through the reform indicates the strength of vested interest in maintaining the status quo. It is also possible that the bank's influence in Argentina

dropped after about 1996, as Menem became distracted from reforms by his maneuvers for a third term, and as the political situation became much more volatile.

• *The Ministry of Finance:* Given the scale of PAMI's deficit, it is inconceivable that the MOF did not desire that PAMI put its house in order. Its failure to impose reform indicates the limits of the MOF's power when it came directly into conflict with the interests of political elites.

Policy Processes and Health Reform: An Overview

During the 1990s, Argentina experienced an unprecedented wave of reforms in different parts of the health sector. The Inter-American Development Bank, somewhat prematurely, described these as "the greatest transformation of a health care system in Latin America in the 1990s" (IDB 1998). Internationally, these have sometimes been portrayed as ambitious and largely successful. However, the nature and significance of these reforms is still a matter for debate.

According to the Inter-American Development Bank report just quoted, the reforms represent a radical break with the past and, taken together, constitute a coherent strategy for improving the performance of the health sector as a whole. This chapter questions this interpretation, for three reasons. First, it is possible to identify many areas of reform, such as decentralization, which were more incremental in nature, building on decades of change, and which were primarily driven by fiscal considerations. The apparently radical shift in social insurance belies the continuity of an opaque, poorly regulated system, albeit on a rather more competitive basis.

Second, the reforms have increased the overall fragmentation and complexity of Argentina's health sector. By deepening these divisions and by promoting a model of provision that is stratified by socioeconomic groups, the reforms have reduced the prospects for a more unified health system in the foreseeable future.

Third, some aspects of the different reforms are contradictory. Allowing hospitals to generate funds informally through ostensibly voluntary contributions undermines the objective of promoting cost recovery from *obras sociales*. Any possible gains through cost recovery are likely to be much smaller than the costs of allowing PAMI to continue free riding on public hospitals.

The failure to implement some parts of the reform agenda raises difficult issues about the underlying motivations of key actors. In particular, they raise questions about their real interest in achieving all aspects of the *purported* reform project. For example, decentralization has achieved few, if any, of its nonfiscal objectives, but it is doubtful that issues such as local participation were a key concern of key actors in the first place. Similar questions could be asked about the failure to regulate the private sector or to come to grips with PAMI's crisis.

Most important, the health sector reform agenda itself has been in-complete. When looking at any sector strategy, it is useful to identify areas where no reforms have been discussed, or what Walt (1994) calls "non–decision making." According to Ham and Hill (1986, 64), this occurs when

> the dominant values, the accepted rules of the game, the existing power relations among groups, and the instruments of force, singly or in com-bination, effectively prevent certain grievances from developing into full-fledged issues which call for decisions.

The case of "voluntary" user fees can be taken as an example of this. Other nondecisions (or nondebates) include the lack of discussion about the need to reallocate resources across the health sector as a whole. While total health spending in Argentina was relatively high until the recent crisis, the proportion devoted to public health programs, public hospitals and public clinics was a fraction of that devoted to other areas. Public provision has increasingly become an underfunded safety net of last resort, but there has been no discussion about the means to significantly improve its resource base.

More specifically, Argentina has the highest ratio of doctors to trained nurses in Latin America, but there has been no debate about the need to develop a more balanced and efficient personnel structure. Clearly, such a move would be resisted by the country's strong physicians' lobby. Instead, the 1990s saw a boom in new private sector medical schools, drawing on the aspirations of middle-class Argentine parents. The need to increase the number of trained nurses has scarcely figured in health sector reform agendas around Latin America.

In terms of creating an effective health system, the reforms cannot be understood as a coherent package. However, in terms of promoting key Menemist constituencies and priorities, there is a more obvious logic to what occurred. There have been a small number of key players in the health reform process. Most obviously, these involved a tight alliance of the national president, the MOF, and the World Bank. Each of these actors has perceived changes to the health sector to be part of a much wider social and economic restructuring agenda. The principal motive for hospital decentralization was to ease pressures on federal spending. Reforming the *obras sociales* was part of a wider package aimed at increasing the flexibility and international competitiveness of the labor force. As such, it might be argued that these were health sector reforms in which health considerations were actually of a secondary nature. Commercial interests (including private insurers, clinics, and drugs firms, as well as the plethora of private consultancies that sprang up in the wake of PRESSAL), have also played an important if less overt role in the health reforms. Although policy in previous periods was mainly driven by a corporatist alliance of state and organized labor, the 1990s saw a shift to a new configuration of state and commercial actors.

These leading players were able to realize part of their broad reform agenda. To a large extent, this was made possible by the unprecedented political mandate enjoyed by the Menem administrations before the late 1990s, and the willingness of the president to exploit this. The receipt of advice and substantial loans from the World Bank was another key factor, enabling the executive branch to reward "reform-friendly" provinces and unions. Limited progress in ending the *obras social* monopolies drew on the lessons of the earlier pension reforms, where union resistance had been relatively effective. By the late 1990s, the national government's policy mandate had weakened, and the World Bank money had been spent. As such, the window of opportunity for further reform was largely closed. The onset of the current crisis, and the declaration of a Health Sector Emergency in February 2002, are likely to lead to a range of short-term stopgap measures, but the long-run future of the system now remains very much in doubt.

References

Acuña, C., and M. Chudnovsky. 2002. *El sistema de salud en Argentina*. Buenos Aires: Centro de Estudios para el Desarrollo Institucional.
Ahuad, A., A. Paganelli, and A. Palmeyro. 1999. *Medicina prepaga: Historia y futuro*. Buenos Aires: Ediciones Isalud.
Barrientos, A., and P. Lloyd-Sherlock. 2000. Reforming Health Insurance in Argentina and Chile. *Health Policy and Planning* 15, no. 4: 417–23.

Belmartino, S., and C. Bloch. 1994. *El sector salud en Argentina: Actores, conflictos de intereses y modelos organizativos, 1960–1985.* Washington, D.C.: Pan American Health Organization.

———. 1998. Desregulación/privatización: la relación entre financiación y provisión de servicios en la reforma de la seguridad social médica en Argentina. *Cuadernos médico sociales* 73: 61–80.

Bisang, R., and O. Centrángulo. 1997. *Reformas de la política de salud en Argentina durante los años noventa, con especial referencia a la equidad.* Serie de Estudios 27. Buenos Aires: CECE.

Bonvecchi, A., H. Charosky, C. Garay, and D. Urribari. 1998. *Instituto Nacional de Servicios Sociales para Jubilados y Pensionados: Un análisis de sus condiciones de viabilidad organizacional, institucional y política.* Buenos Aires: Fundacíon Argentina para el Desarrollo con Equidad.

Brissón, B., C. Solis, C. Vassallo, and R. Falbo. 2001. *Políticas sanitarias, situación de salud en las provincias argentinas y su relación con la equidad.* Buenos Aires: Pan American Health Organization and Fundación Isalud.

Castañeda, T., G. Beeharry, and C. Griffin. 1999. Decentralization of Health Services in Latin American Countries: Issues and Some Lessons. In *Decentralization and Accountability of the Public Sector: Proceedings of the Annual World Bank Conference on Development in Latin America and the Caribbean 1999,* ed. S. Javed Burki and G. Perry. Washington, D.C.: World Bank.

Diéguez, H., J. Llach, and A. Petrecolla. 1990. *El gasto público social: Sector salud.* Buenos Aires: UN Development Program and World Bank.

ECLAC (Economic Commission for Latin America and the Caribbean). 2000. *Economic Yearbook for Latin America and the Caribbean 2000.* Santiago: ECLAC.

EIU (Economist Intelligence Unit). 1998. Profile: Changing Political Gears in Argentina's Healthcare System. In *EIU Healthcare International,* 2nd Quarter. London: EIU.

González García, G., and F. Tobar. 1997. *Más salud por el mismo dinero: La reforma de salud en Argentina.* Buenos Aires: Ediciones Isalud.

Ham, C., and M. Hill. 1986. *The Policy Process in the Modern Capitalist State.* London: Wheatsheaf.

IDB (Inter-American Development Bank). 1998. Argentina: Programa de modernización y reforma del sector salud. Available at www.iadb.org/exr/doc98/pro/uar0120.htm.

INDEC (Instituto Nacional de Estadística y Censos). 1998. *Statistical Yearbook of the Argentine Republic 1998.* Buenos Aires: INDEC.

Isuani, E., and J. San Martino. 1993. *La reforma previsional argentina: Opciones y riesgos.* Buenos Aires: Miño y Dávila.

Katz, J., and A. Muñoz. 1988. *Organización del sector salud: Puja distributiva y equidad.* Buenos Aires: Centro Editor de América Latina.

Llanos, M. 2001. Understanding Presidential Power in Argentina: A Study of the Policy of Privatisation in the 1990s. *Journal of Latin American Studies* 33, no. 1: 67–99.

Lloyd-Sherlock, P. 1997a. Healthcare Provision for Elderly People in Argentina: The Crisis of PAMI. *Social Policy and Administration* 31, no. 4: 371–89.

———. 1997b. Policy, Distribution and Poverty in Argentina since Redemocratisation. *Latin American Perspectives* 24, no. 6: 22–55.

———. 2000. Health Care Financing Reform and Equity in Argentina: Past and Present. In *Healthcare Reform and Poverty in Latin America,* ed. P. Lloyd-Sherlock. London: Institute of Latin American Studies.

———. 2002. Financing Health Services for Pensioners in Argentina: A Salutary Tale. *International Journal of Social Welfare* 12, no. 1: 24–30.

Lloyd-Sherlock, P., and D. Novick. 2001. "Voluntary" User Fees in Buenos Aires: Innovation or Imposition? *International Journal of Health Services* 31, no. 4: 709–28.

Lo Vuolo, R. 1995. Estabilización, ajuste estructural y política social: los inocentes y los culpables. In *Mas allá de la establidad: Argentina en la época de globalización y la regionalización,* ed. P. Bustos. Buenos Aires: Fundación Freidrich Ebert.

McGuire, J. 2001a. Health Policy and Mortality Decline in the Province of Neuquén, Argentina. Department of Government, Wesleyan University, Middletown, Conn. (unpublished).

———. 2001b. Politics, Policy and Mortality Decline: Argentina in Comparative Perspective. Paper presented at the 2001 Annual Meeting of the American Political Science Association, San Francisco, August 30–September 2.

Montoya, S., and J. Colina. 1998. *La reforma de obras sociales en Argentina: Avances y desafíos pendientes.* Centro Internacional de Investigaciones para el Desarrollo Report TC-93-04-39-6. Washington, D.C.: Inter-American Development Bank.

Navarro, M. 1995. Democracia y reforma estrucuturales: Explicaciones de la tolerancia popular al ajuste económico. *Desarrollo Económico* 35, no. 139: 443–65.

Peruzzotti, E. 2001. The Nature of the New Argentine Democracy: The Delegative Democracy Argument Revisited. *Journal of Latin American Studies* 33, no. 1: 133–55.

Repetto, F., K. Ansolabehere, G. Dufour, C. Lupicia, P. Potenza, and H. Rodríguez Larreta. 2001. *Decentralización de la salud pública en los noventa: Une reforma a mitad de camino.* Buenos Aires: Centro de Estudios para el Desarrollo Institucional, Fundación Grupo Sophia.

Stillwaggon, E. 1998. *Stunted Lives, Stagnant Economies. Poverty, Disease and Underdevelopment.* New Brunswick, N.J.: Rutgers University Press.

Stocker, K., H. Waitzkin, and C. Iriart. 1999. The Exportation of Managed Care to Latin America. *New England Journal of Medicine* 340, no. 14: 1131–36.

Tedesco, L. 2002. The 1999 Elections in Argentina: Change in Style or Substance? *European Review of Latin American and Caribbean Studies* 70, no. 11: 105–13.

Vassallo, C., and M. Sellanes. 2001. Salud y tercera edad. In *Informe sobre tercera edad en la Argentina,* ed. Secretaria de la Tercera Edad. Buenos Aires: Secretaria de la Tercera Edad.

Ventura, G. 2000. *Impacto de la reducción de los costos laborales sobre el sistema de salud.* Buenos Aires: Fundación Isalud.

Walt, G. 1994. *Health Policy: An Introduction to Process and Power.* London: Zed Books.

World Bank. 1987. *Argentina: Population, Health and Nutrition Sector Review.* Washington, D.C.: World Bank.

———. 1993. *World Development Report 1993: Investing in Health.* New York: Oxford University Press.

————. 1997. *Argentina: Facing the Challenge of Health Insurance Reform.* Washington, D.C.: World Bank.

————. 1999. Health Reform Project in Argentina Yields Results. In *World Development Report 1999/2000: Entering the 21st Century.* New York: Oxford University Press.

Chapter 5

A Sweeping Health Reform:
The Quest for Unification, Coverage, and
Efficiency in Colombia

Patricia Ramírez

In December 1993, the Colombian Congress approved the law on Social Security Reform (Law 100), which radically transformed the legal frameworks for Colombia's pension and health care systems (Congreso de Colombia 1994). The health reform, in particular, was the most comprehensive in Latin America in the 1990s. This chapter sketches the political context of Colombia's health sector reform and traces key points in the debates within the Constitutional Assembly of 1991, the executive branch, and the Congress that shaped Law 100. The chapter then follows the

This chapter is partially based on "Enhancing the Political Feasibility of Health Reform: The Colombia Case," by A. González and P. Ramírez, Data for Decision Making Project, School of Public Health, Harvard University, in collaboration with the Latin American and Caribbean Regional Health Sector Reform Initiative, June 2000. The author thanks Joan Nelson and Robert Kaufman for their comments, suggestions, and editing of the final version of the chapter. She also thanks Oscar Emilio Guerra, Ivan Jaramillo, Beatriz Londoño, Juan Luis Londoño, Nelcy Paredes, Mauricio Perfetti, and Teresa Toño for their informative interviews.

implementation process under the next two governments, describes the varied progress of different elements of the reform, and suggests reasons for its successes and disappointments.

Recent History

During the 1980s, Colombia was marked by sharply contrasting economic and political scenarios. On the one hand, despite the debt crisis in Latin America, the Colombian economy was doing moderately well. The growth of gross domestic product (GDP) remained positive throughout the period, and averaged 4.3 percent between 1987 and 1990, well above the growth rate for the region as a whole. Although inflation averaged around 25 percent at the end of the 1980s, it remained more or less under control. On the political side, however, Colombia was experiencing growing internal conflict and a sharp erosion of governability. At the same time, the illegal drug-trafficking industry flourished, creating one of the most violent scenarios since the 1950s.

The Virgilio Barco administration (1986–90) attempted to change the political rules and introduced major state and economic reforms. Although these reform efforts were not to be consolidated during Barco's term, they provided the basis for major economic and social reforms that followed in the 1990s (Cepeda 1994). Responsibility for many public goods and services was decentralized to local governments, accompanied by reallocation of intergovernmental financial transfers and an increase of the share of the value-added-tax to be transferred directly to municipal governments. The Constitution was amended to provide for direct election of mayors. In the health sector, Law 10 of 1990 assigned municipal governments responsibility for primary health care and primary-level hospitals and health centers; departmental governments became responsible for secondary-level hospitals as well as coordination of health campaigns.[1] The central government retained the responsibilities of formulating policy, establishing minimum health standards. and managing tertiary-level hospitals. The national Ministry of Health was reformed; the National Hospital Fund was dismantled. In the economic arena, the Barco administration launched reforms to modernize and internationalize the economy, setting the stage for more far-reaching measures in the early 1990s.

1. Since 1986, municipalities have had some responsibility for primary-level hospitals and health centers.

Barco also attempted a constitutional reform, but the initiative was rejected by the traditional parties. This failure, in the context of increasing violence and social and political crisis, finally mobilized popular demand. During the 1990 congressional elections, a student-led movement forced the insertion of an additional ballot asking voters whether or not they wanted a constitutional reform. The "yes" vote won an overwhelming majority. The mandate was repeated with a formal referendum organized to coincide with presidential elections two months later. The next government, under President Cesar Gaviria, convened a National Constituent Assembly.

The Political Context: The New Constitution

During President Gaviria's administration (1990–94), Colombia's governmental and economic institutions were radically transformed (Acosta and Fainboim 1994; Cepeda 1994; Gaviria 1994). The depth of the reforms was surprising; Colombian economic policy in the previous two decades had been characterized by continuity. Gaviria's approach to reforms was grounded on liberalization, privatization, modernization, and internationalization of the economy.[2] Government policies had three main goals, which eventually were all incorporated into the 1991 Constitution: first, improving competitiveness, deepening free-market economy and reducing trade barriers; second, increasing government efficiency, through the privatization of state-owned enterprises, decentralization of governmental functions, and allocation of resources according to competitive advantage; and third, boosting local government autonomy in the decision-making process, service delivery, and financial resources, to achieve greater efficiency (DNP 1991).

The 1991 National Constituent Assembly

In accord with the referendum of 1990, President Gaviria called for elections for a National Constituency Assembly (NCA, the Asamblea Nacional Constituyente). The election rules allowed for the participation of interests that had been underrepresented within the existing system. The NCA had seventy members, elected from nationwide constituencies (as distinct from congressional regional districts). Members of Congress or government executives were not eligible unless they had previously resigned. Moreover,

2. Colombia's economy was not in crisis, but there was some consensus on the need for economic liberalization.

Constituent Assembly members could not run for Congress until the second election after the NCA (Salazar 1997).

The character of the National Constituent Assembly radically departed from the coalition scheme that had characterized Congress during the previous three decades. It included several former guerrilla groups that had chosen to pursue their goals through political rather than violent means. The influence of more established interests was further weakened by the fact that the politicians from traditional parties decided to boycott the NCA election, on the grounds that the NCA would usurp the authority of the current Congress (Cepeda 1994). Although the boycott contributed to an unprecedented decline in turnout (less than 30 percent), the failure to deploy traditional clientelist and partisan machinery facilitated the election of political forces outside the traditional parties.

After much debate, the NCA approved a comprehensive new Constitution. Major political reforms affected the judicial branch, the composition of Congress, the democratic election of governors at the departmental level, new participatory measures, electoral reform, and other institutions (Constitución Política de la República de Colombia 1991). Decentralization was a major theme, setting the framework for the social reforms that followed, including both health and education. However, the reforms had very different outcomes in the two sectors, for reasons that will be outlined in the conclusions to this chapter.

The new constitution also established guiding principles for a wide array of social and economic reforms. The executive branch and Congress were granted a broad mandate for designing the details of these reforms, but the Constitution required that within a year the executive should prepare a bill on each topic and present it to Congress for consideration; the latter should discuss and approve those proposals within a single legislative period. It was in these circumstances that health sector reform was discussed and approved.

Main Features of the Health Sector before Reform

As in many Latin American countries, health conditions in Colombia improved substantially in the 1970s and 1980s. Life expectancy increased; infant mortality and malnutrition among small children fell substantially. The life expectancy of women rose from 52.3 years in 1959 to 63.5 in 1970 and 72.3 in 1990. The overall fertility rate dropped from 6.6 in 1969 to 2.6 in 1990. Infant mortality decreased from 132 per 1,000 in 1960 to 20 in 1994. The share of communicable diseases in mortality shrank from 60 percent in 1950 to 15 percent in 1990 (Londoño 1992, 3).

But the health care system was characterized by low coverage, high segmentation in access to care, high costs for the poorest people, and significant inefficiencies. In 1991, only 20 percent of the population was covered by Social Security, even though affiliation was formally mandatory. Although the Social Security Institute (Instituto de Seguros Sociales, ISS) was in principle supposed to have a monopoly, in practice it covered only 16 percent of the population (and 70 percent of those with Social Security). Parallel systems had proliferated, and by 1991 there were 1,040 social security agencies in the country. Some governmental agencies had developed their own health provider systems (covering 4 percent); the Cooperative Organizations (Cajas de Compensación Familiar) offered some health services for formal-sector workers and their families, and private insurance covered health care for the wealthiest people (4.5 percent). There were also experiments with cooperatives and mutual organizations. This spontaneous institutional development generated overlapping expenditure and affiliation, segregation, and few incentives to save. Most of the population relied for their health care on public facilities, which offered only limited access and low-quality services (Londoño 1996). Efforts under the Barco and earlier governments to decentralize and strengthen the public system had faced strong resistance and had never been fully implemented.

The Design of Health Sector Reform: Main Actors, Arenas, and Strategies

This section examines the evolution of the basic design of the health care reform. Although the market-oriented government played a highly influential role in this process, reformers found it necessary to compromise with actors holding a wide variety of views. The outcome was a design for a mixed health care system that combined elements of solidarity and equity with principles of efficiency and competition.

The Reform Proposal and the New Constitution

Two opposing positions regarding health services and social security clashed during the Constituent Assembly. The government, with the exception of the ISS, wanted to introduce competition to increase efficiency; the private sector, and some other delegates, supported this position. The ISS sought to promote solidarity, universality, and a nonsegmented system and to preserve a strong role for the state. These positions were never fully reconciled by the Assembly. In effect, both were combined in the provisions of the new Constitution, which defined social security as a compulsory public service under state control, guided by principles of solidarity, universality, efficiency, and scope for participation by the private sector (Constitución Política de la República de Colombia 1991; Jaramillo 1997).

Before it adjourned, the Assembly established a broadly representative commission to resolve the underlying differences over the organization of the social security and health sectors. During the last four months of 1991, three separate subcommissions discussed the topics of health, pensions, and workers' compensation. The government's representatives in the commission were again divided (Ministerio de Salud 1994; Molina and Trujillo 1992). The government's development plan, *La Revolucion Pacifica,* had been released in August 1991. It did not include proposals for comprehensive social security or health reforms but emphasized principles of efficiency and decentralization (DNP 1991). In the commission debates, the liberal technocrats in the National Planning Department (Departamento Nacional de Planeación, DNP) emphasized competition and a larger role for the private sector to promote efficiency.

In sharp contrast, the ISS wanted to maintain the social security monopoly for the state, introducing competition only in service provision. The Asociación de Médicos Sindicalizados (ASMEDAS, the doctors' union), was still more extreme, seeking to maintain the monopoly of the ISS in all respects including provision of services. The Ministry of Health adopted an intermediate position, pushing for a reform that would maintain solidarity but introduce competition as well. The ministry at that time was headed by members of the ex–guerrilla group Movimiento Revolucionario 19 de Abril (M-19), who had played an important role in the NCA. However, the ministry was not in a strong position within the executive branch, and ministers do not stay long.[3]

The Assembly and commission debates were paralleled by a much broader process of discussion among sector specialists and stakeholders. University forums, workshops, and international seminars were held not only in Bogotá but also in the regions; think tanks, universities, nongovernmental organizations, unions, and government representatives with their varied views took part. It was a process of learning and reflection for many, and during this time the proposals were gradually enriched, modified, and

3. During the Gaviria administration, there were four ministers (the presidential term is four years), and there were three ministers each during the Samper and Pastrana administrations.

made more concrete. Nonetheless, major technical and political disagreements persisted. In the end, the members of the commission were still unable to agree on the main issues of the reform. At this point, the president and his close advisers decided to abandon health sector reform and to focus their efforts on pension reform (González and Ramírez 2000).

How Reform Gained Backing within the Executive Branch

Pension reform was a high priority for the president; it was seen as an important component of the broader economic reforms and was part of a strategy to boost internal savings (Botero 1991). But important groups opposed pension reform. On the one hand, the unions feared that the reform would cut their benefits; on the other hand, there were those who did not disagree with the pension proposal, but wanted to include health. Some senators saw an opportunity to promote radical health reform; others were aware of the fact that pension reform was extremely controversial, but they thought that comprehensive health reform designed to increase services for poor people could attract wide support. Still another group of senators thought that including health would delay and probably stop the pension reform that the executive wanted. In any case, the Congressional Commission for Social Affairs, in a meeting with President Gaviria, suggested that health reform be included as part of a broader reform of Social Security.

In response, President Gaviria ordered the formation of a high-level technical team to develop the proposal (Jaramillo 1997). The team initially proposed fairly broad-gauge reforms. The president found the proposal too complex and feared that it could jeopardize the pension reform. For the second time, he decided to withdraw health reform from Social Security reform (González and Ramírez 2000).

At this point, M-19 decided to leave the government, providing Gaviria with the opportunity to reshuffle his Cabinet. In November 1992, Juan Luis Londoño, a liberal economist who had been deputy director of the DNP and had played a key role in the economic reforms, was appointed the new health minister. Gaviria had earlier replaced the minister of labor and the director of the ISS; for the first time, there was unity within the government regarding health reform (González and Ramírez 2000). Gaviria had probably decided that despite his doubts health was going to be a key component of Social Security reform, and he wanted to consolidate his team. From this time on, Londoño played a crucial role in the reform process, and became its clear leader, regaining control of the process for the executive branch.

Londoño promptly formed a small group to work on health reform, the "change team," which was recruited from outside the Ministry of Health, where he found strong opposition. The health reform group was technical and imbued with the broader ideology of the Gaviria reforms; it did not have political party connections (González and Ramírez 2000).

Londoño sought to build backing for reform throughout the executive bureaucracy. He established vertical networks with President Gaviria himself, the finance minister, and the director of the national planning department. He and his team also established horizontal networks, working closely with the group in charge of pension reform, particularly the minister of labor and his team, the deputy finance minister, the ISS under its new director, and sections of the Planning Department, including those developing the Sistema de Identificación de Beneficiarios de los Subsidios del Estado (SISBEN, a system for identifying citizens eligible for subsidized benefits). The health reform team also worked with several nongovernmental groups of health specialists, the Cooperative Organizations (Cajas de Compensacion Familiar), and the Asociación Colombiana de Entidades de Medicina Integral (ACEMI, the association of private prepaid medical plans). The change team played a crucial role in steering the reform through Congress and in drafting the decrees needed to put Law 100 into effect (González and Ramírez 2000).

The Politics of the Legislative Phase

In December 1992, the health reform team, with Gaviria's backing, proposed a limited program to the joint Social Affairs Commission of the Senate and the House of Representatives. In discussions with Londoño and his team early in 1993, the commission rejected this proposal and urged a more comprehensive approach. When Congress reconvened in April 1993, the executive branch presented an ambitious new plan in the form of an amendment to the initial bill. It finally incorporated an integral and comprehensive proposal for Social Security reform in both sectors, pensions and health (González and Ramírez 2000; Jaramillo 1997; Ministerio de Salud 1994).

The struggle to approve the legislation continued throughout 1993. A wide variety of groups participated in congressional hearings and in the broader public debate. The main actors involved in the congressional discussion were the Ministry of Health, government officials, territorial health authorities, private health institutions (e.g., prepaid medical plans, health providers, the pharmaceutical industry), the Colombian Medical School Association (Asociación Colombiana de Facultades de Medicina, ASCOFAME), the Colombian Medical Federation, the Colombian Hospital Association, and the National Academy of Medicine. Also active were the insurance sector; productive, industrial, and financial associations (Consejo Gremial, Andi, Asobancaria); workers' organizations and unions (Asmedas, Anea, SintraISS); Cooperative Organizations (Cajas de Compensación); nongovernmental organizations and foundations (Corona, Foundation FES de Liderazgo); think tanks (Fescol, Consenso, Fedesarrollo, and Metrosalud); and important independent opinion leaders (Ministerio de Salud 1994).

Doctors were consulted through their organizations, which were in favor of principles such as solidarity, equity, and universality. However, doctors' associations were fragmented, and generally they were not deeply involved in the discussions of the reform proposals; they probably did not anticipate the depth of the reforms. Later on, they felt they had not been sufficiently consulted during the process. Patients and civic groups had little influence over the reform; they were not well organized, lacked trust in the policy-making process, and saw no clear channels for participation. Some viewed the process of debate as democratic, giving procedural legitimacy to reform; others regarded it as a strategy of Congress to delay the process; and still others saw the process of public debate as a formality while the real decisions took place in private, within a small group of executive-branch actors with some participation by Congress (González and Ramírez 2000).

In spite of the consultation efforts, the reform did not progress during the first months of 1993. By May not a single article had been approved. This period was also marked by union movements and protests. In particular, the Federación Colombiana de Educadores (FECODE) and the Union Sindical Obrera (USO), the teacher's and petroleum workers' organizations, opposed the decentralization reform being discussed in Congress in a separate bill (Law 60, 1993) and the proposed social security reforms that could reduce their particularly generous pensions and health benefits. In the end, the teachers, the oil workers, and the armed forces were not included in the Social Security reform.

At this point of crisis, President Gaviria intervened, persuading the main leaders of the traditional parties to sign an agreement supporting the reform. As a result, the study of the proposals was speeded up. However, disagreements persisted as the bill moved into plenary sessions in the Senate and the

House; some were eventually resolved only in the conciliation commission charged with brokering differences introduced in the two chambers. The bill finally became law in December 1993.

Key Issues in the Debates

Key issues in the debates concerned both fundamental principles and technical and financial details.[4] A basic dispute focused on whether to continue separate health systems for those who could afford financial contributions and those who could not—that is, whether to extend or to merge the segmented social security and public subsystems. The final legislation provided for a unified system with two subsystems or "regimes," one financed by individual contributions (the "contributory regime"), and a second subsidized regime for low-income members. Each regime would offer a specific package of insured services (Plan Obligatorio de Salud, POS), with provision for a risk-adjusted per capita payment (Unidad de Pago por Capitación, UPC) to prevent adverse selection.

A second area of disagreement concerned the content of the POS for the subsidized regime. Doctors represented by ASMEDAS and the Medical Federation, unions, some liberal, left-wing, and independent members of Congress, and various research institutes supported a broad package of services. The Ministry of Health (heavily influenced by the World Bank), private-sector actors such as the prepaid medical plans, and the government economic team urged a package focused on prevention, promotion, birth attention, and basic services to reduce expenses and maximize cost-effectiveness. This was a key issue, because it was not financially viable for the subsidized regime to immediately offer the same services as the contributory one. In the end, the legislature approved an initial limited package for the subsidized regime, along with provisions that the package would be broadened during the next several years to approximate the services under the contributory regime; by 2001, the packages were to be identical.

A more technical debate concerned the definition of preexisting health conditions that affected insurance risks. ACEMI was particularly concerned with the high costs a liberal definition would imply. In the end, the Health Service Purchasers (Empresas Promotoras de Salud, EPS) were required to include insurance for high cost treatments.

Funding details were intensely controversial. Agreement was reached on two key aspects. The contributory regime would be financed by contribu-

4. The main source of information for this section, besides interviews, was Ministerio de Salud 1994.

tions of 11 percent of the salary or income of formal-sector workers and the better-off self-employed. The subsidized regime would be financed by a 1 percent wage tax on those in the contributory regime, plus support from national and local government revenues. Nevertheless, even inside the executive branch there were disagreements, based on fiscal, economic, and political issues; the economic team feared the reform's potential fiscal burden and were concerned about the increased wage tax that employers and employees would have to pay for both pensions and health.

Another key issue was the role and functions of the ISS under the new system. Some reformers urged that the ISS be decentralized or even dismantled. Some members of Congress, including some Liberal Party politicians, parties from the left and civil movements, unions and the group from the ISS-Consenso defended the institution, in large part because of ideological commitment to a dominant state role in public services. The final decisions left the ISS in a relatively strong position. However, it was no longer entitled to the compulsory affiliation of private-sector workers and had to compete with new institutions offering health insurance services. Yet public employees who chose to join the ISS program would be permitted to do so.

The reform plan called for replacing "supply subsidies," the old system of funding public hospitals and clinics by budget allocations for the coming year (usually based on their costs in the previous year) with a new payments mechanism of "demand subsidies," reimbursing private as well as public hospitals and clinics for each insured service they actually provide to patients, after the services are provided. Demand subsidies, it was argued, created incentives for hospitals and clinics to compete with each other and provide better service, and gave patients greater freedom to choose among providers. Those opposed to this shift wanted to preserve the public status quo and saw the transition from supply to demand as very difficult. Eventually, the new principle for reimbursing providers was approved.[5]

A dispute also developed regarding the definition of social security as an essential public service, and the classification of public-sector health workers as "public" rather than "official" employees. Some unions opposed this definition because it limited the right to strike; they preferred the "official" designation because it carried legal implications for more generous pensions. The executive branch, in contrast, sought to minimize the possibility of collective bargaining. In the end, the reformers' position was

5. The reports on health published by the World Bank and United Nations Development Program were sources consulted for information and comparison with other experiences, and they favored a move toward demand subsidies.

approved, but health workers won a sweetener: a commitment to significant wage increases between 1995 and 1998.

Still another issue concerned the composition of the new National Health Board (Consejo Nacional de Seguridad Social en Salud, CNSSS), which was to advise the Ministry of Health. All actors involved and affected by the reform wanted to be represented on the board. Eventually, a ten-member board was approved.

In December 1993, Congress finally approved Law 100, and on December 23 President Gaviria signed it. Law 100 fundamentally altered the existing segmented system for health care finance and delivery. It established a framework that would provide obligatory insurance to the entire population and would combine public and private payers' and providers' organizations in a coordinated and regulated fashion. In the new scheme (see figure 5.1), each individual must sign up with (become an affiliate of) a Health Service Purchaser (EPS in the contributory regime; Administradora de Régimen Subsidiado in the subsidized regime) of his or her choice, and must pay a social security contribution. This contribution[6] is paid jointly by the employee and the employer if the worker is salaried; the payment is made individually if the worker is self-employed; a state subsidy covers those individuals too poor to pay.[7] The money is collected in the Fondo de Solidaridad y Garantia (FOSYGA, National Health Fund), which pays the insurance and purchasing entities (the EPSs) a designated sum for each affiliate. This Social Security contribution entitles the affiliate and his or her family to a POS provided by either the contributory or subsidized regime. Each insuring and purchasing entity (EPS) contracts with hospitals and clinics, called Health Service Providers (Instituciones Prestadoras de Servicios, IPS) to provide medical attention to its affiliates and their families (Congreso de Colombia 1994; Fedesarrollo 2000).

Law 100 also created a National Council for Social Security in Health, with regulatory powers over the system, leaving management and technical assistance to the Ministry of Health. Provision of services was shifted from the ministry to local agencies and independent providers, and a supervisory agency was created to monitor the system. By creating the independent National Health Fund, the law separates financing from provision of health

6. This contribution is 12 percent of labor income in the case of the contributory regime, in which the employer pays two-thirds of the total portion.

7. Poor people are identified by municipalities through a survey which is part of the focus of the Sistema de Selección de Beneficiarios de los Programas Sociales (SISBEN).

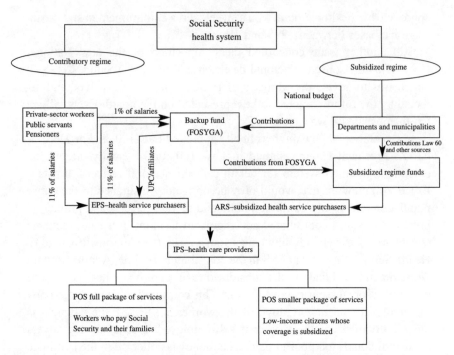

Figure 5.1. Colombia's Unified Social Security Health System

Note: ARS = Administradora de Régimen Subsididado; EPS = Empresas Promotoras de Salud;
FOSYGA = Fondo de Solidaridad y Garantía (National Health Fund); POS = Plan Obligatorio
de Salud; IPS = Instituciones Prestadoras de Servicios de Salud; UPC = Unidad de Pago por
Capitación.
Source: Based on Cuartas (1998).

care, while keeping financial control consolidated to avoid segmented markets and dispersion of services. Because patients can choose the clinic or hospital they prefer, the new system generates competition for the delivery of services.

Also in 1993, a separate law, Law 60, made its way through Congress. Law 60 carried out the mandate in the 1991 Constitution to decentralize a range of government functions including the public segment of the old health care delivery system—primary-level public hospitals and clinics, plus public health programs such as inoculations, health education, and sanitation. Departments and municipal governments were to take over responsibility for administering these functions. Law 60 also provided for increased transfers from central to local governments to fund these responsibilities, jointly with locally raised revenues. The focus and underlying assumptions of Law 60 differed somewhat from those of Law 100. Inconsistencies between the two laws and the sheer complexity of the two radical and simultaneous changes plagued implementation throughout the next two administrations.

Strategies Used during the Legislation Process

Reformers used a variety of tactics and strategies to win congressional approval. Perhaps the most fundamental strategy was to formulate and discuss health reform in Congress under the umbrella of a major social security reform project, where attention was focused on the highly controversial pension reform. In addition, the health reform team decided to approach each senator involved in the discussion, and to listen to each of his or her suggestions, even when they were not always included in the proposals. For the senators, it was important to be heard during the discussions. The team simultaneously appealed to President Gaviria to secure party votes for the reform. Both individual and party support were perceived as necessary (González and Ramírez 2000).

The team worked particularly intensively with a few key senators, some in favor and others against. The team relied on the like-minded senators to take the leadership in presenting certain issues in Congress. Various forms of clientelism were also necessary to gain the support of certain senators. For the most part, this was handled by the minister of labor, who was in charge of the political strategy for the entire bill. Nevertheless, as the time approached for a congressional vote, the Ministry of Health began to establish Health Solidarity Enterprises (Empresas Solidarias de Salud, ESS) in some senators' regions, giving them a political stake in this component of the reform (González and Ramírez 2000).

During this stage, and as a result of the congressional request to consult a wide range of groups, the reform team talked to every visible leader of the groups involved in the reform: unions, doctors, producers' associations, prepaid medicine organizations, academic forums, and so on. This was more a long and exhaustive process of information exchange than an arena for consensus building, because in general terms the team did not alter its proposal. The team also worked closely with the group in charge of Law 60, which was simultaneously before Congress, because the decentralization reform could help to reduce the financial difficulties of the proposed health care system.

Finally, the change team decided that to pass the law in Congress, it was necessary to make it as general as possible. This strategy, which proved useful during the legislative stage, also left wide room for maneuvering during the later stage of developing detailed regulations to implement the law. Therefore, broad aspects of the law were subsequently defined in greater detail by decree. However, later governments could also alter those regulations by decree, applying their own principles. Particularly at the beginning of Ernesto Samper's administration (1994–98), these were contrary to those of the change team (González and Ramírez 2000).

The Development of Detailed Regulation

As just noted, Law 100 left enormous flexibility regarding the detailed design of health reform. To set the law in motion, at least twenty-five regulatory decrees had to be issued. The main focus of the reform team during the seven months remaining before a new government took office (January–August 1994) was to develop the regulations as rapidly as possible. These decrees were designed by the Ministry of Health, in consultation with the new National Health Council (CNSS), and were eventually approved and signed by the president. During this process, the change team was more insulated than in earlier phases, and it did not have to consult or make concessions as in the legislative process. Indeed, the change team viewed consultation as less necessary, because—according to it—its main decision criteria were purely technical. In addition, the institutional context did not require the same consultation that was needed during the formulation and the legislative process.

The supporting decrees focused mainly on the creation of the National Health Council; the various new institutions for collecting and disbursing payments; the standard package of services; and reform in public institutions such as the Ministry of Health, public hospitals, and the supervisory agency. The team sought advice from national and international experts, who played a key role in this part of the reform. International organizations and international cooperation were very important in bringing these experts to the process. In addition, loans for the health reform were contracted with the Inter-American Development Bank and the World Bank, and the School of Public Health at Harvard University provided ongoing analytic and advisory services (Colombia Health Sector Reform Project 1996).

Seven months was not enough time to develop all the regulations needed to implement the reform. The reform team decided to give priority to developing detailed regulation for new health purchaser entities, regarding the creation of new stakeholders as a strategy that could help prevent reversal of the reforms. But key processes were not defined, including precise measures to reorganize existing institutions such as the public hospitals and the Social Security Institute, and to shift from supply to demand subsidies. Those points proved to be problematic during the implementation process (González and Ramírez 2000).

Although officials from the Ministry of Health and the DNP argued that there were no fundamental changes to the reform at this stage, others argued that the Ministry of Health defined elements that were vague in the law according to their principles, which favored efficiency, the role of the private sector, the introduction of competition, free choice, and financial sustainability (ASSALUD and FES 1997; Fedesarrollo 1995).

The Politics of Implementing Colombia's Reforms

In August 1994, when President Samper took office, a new team was appointed. Although they were also from the Liberal Party, they were critical of Gaviria's ideas regarding development and modernization. The group of people who had been at the ISS at the beginning of the Gaviria administration returned to power, and now they had been appointed to more powerful positions and had more capacity to influence decision making.

After 1995, a number of factors impeded the full implementation of the reforms initiated earlier in the decade, including those related to health. During the Samper administration, the severe crisis of governability, originating with accusations of campaign finances from drug cartels, led the government to dedicate much of its efforts to avoiding a greater loss of legitimacy. Moreover, in 1999, Colombia experienced its greatest economic crisis since the 1970s. GDP fell 4.3 percent. In macroeconomic terms, the deficit in the public sector increased from 2.3 percent in the mid-1990s to 5.8 percent by 1999. In social terms, the unemployment rate doubled between 1994 and 1999. Urban poverty in Colombia increased by 7 percentage points between 1995 and 1999, placing it at 59.7 percent, similar to the levels at the end of the 1980s. The economic crisis was accompanied by an intensification of internal conflict, displaced populations, and general increases in violence and insecurity; these became the central policy issues of the later administration of Andres Pastrana.

A Difficult Beginning

On November 8, 1994, shortly after President Samper replaced Gaviria and one year after Congress approved Law 100, Decree 2491 set in motion the transition from old to new health systems. Although the new minister of finance and the new director of the National Planning Department generally favored the reform, many in Samper's government opposed certain aspects: many technical aspects of the reform were still hotly debated. The new minister of health, Alonso Gomez, was among those against the reform.

Decree 2491 of 1994 authorized the transformation of department and municipal health authorities into Health Service Purchasers (EPS) in order to administer the subsidized part of the new system. However, the decree included no provisions to help develop EPS capacity to run the subsidized regime, to introduce competition, or to begin to change supply subsidies into demand subsidies, as the law envisaged. Rather than introducing demand-based payment for hospitals, it established a tariff system of payments to hospitals, ignoring Law 100's provision for UPC. The decree also made the departmental and municipal authorities responsible for insurance and funding as well as management of public health services, dropping Law 100's principle of separating these functions to enhance efficiency. In effect, the decree eliminated the concept of social security as it applied to the subsidized regime, delaying the transition and leading to higher costs and inefficient allocation of resources (Fedesarrollo 1995; Jaramillo 1997). The tensions surrounding the launching of the reform have continued throughout the implementation stage.

Law 100 included, as part of the compromises in the course of its passage, a provision that the salaries of public-sector health workers would be brought into line with those of other public-sector workers, at the beginning of the reform implementation. Accordingly, Minister of Health Gomez announced annual wage increments of 5 percent above inflation for health workers between 1995 and 1998, while other workers' wage increases were tied to inflation. The increases were difficult for the national and regional governments to finance. In addition, the wage increases absorbed funds that might have been used to help public hospitals strengthen their data systems and administrative capacity, thus furthering the reform. Furthermore, high union wages made it difficult for public hospitals and public Health Service Providers (IPS) to compete with private providers.

In July 1995, Samper appointed a new minister of health, Augusto Galán Sarmiento, and implementation began to move in a more positive direction. In December 1995, the minister announced Decree 2357, which corrected the problems generated by the earlier decree and authorized Cooperative Organizations (Cajas de Compensacion Familiar), the EPS, and Health Solidarity Enterprises (ESS) to manage the subsidized regime. The pace of reform picked up even more during the second semester of 1996, after

María Teresa Forero de Sade was appointed as the third minister of health. During her period as minister, the reform started to be implemented after two years of delay.

During the next government, under President Pastrana (1998–2002), there was consensus on the need to continue developing the reform, while addressing problems that had emerged during implementation of Law 60 (on decentralization) as well as Law 100. In 2001, Congress did modify the Constitution and passed new legislation (Law 715) aimed at correcting earlier problems of financing and accountability (see chapter 12 for more on Law 715). Revisions in Law 100, and perhaps a more far-reaching new reform of the pension system, were widely viewed as central to Colombia's economic adjustment. But attempts to reach a consensus among the government, unions, and the private sector regarding pension reform were unsuccessful.[8] Nor were there strong efforts to further develop the health reforms. In particular, the practice of funding public hospitals and clinics with annual budgets (supply subsidies) persisted, despite Law 100's mandate to shift to payments for services provided (demand subsidies). National and local bureaucracies, hospitals, and health workers remained strongly opposed to many aspects of the reform. Meanwhile, the deepening general economic crisis prevented expansion of coverage within the subsidized regime and contributed to a crisis in public hospitals, weakened public health measures, and shrinking social security contributions as workers were laid off.

The Politics of Implementing Various Aspects of the Reform

Different aspects of the reform generated different kinds of support and opposition; some were easier to implement than others. The subsidized regime is the most important aspect in terms of social policy, due to its impact on reducing poverty and inequity. It also is the most difficult to implement, because it implies greater transformations of old actors than the contributory regime (González and Ramírez 2000). National and local bureaucracies have passively resisted reforms, preferring to maintain the public-sector monopoly and to continue with a funding system based on supply subsidies. The contributory regime has had fewer problems, in good part because the new actors—the EPS and the new affiliates—support the system However, the ISS, which still covers 30 percent of all those enrolled in the contributory system, has not yet made a full transition to the new system.

8. In December 2002 a pension reform was finally approved and further changes are expected.

Many doctors and health workers are unhappy with the system. Although they complain about their incomes, there is no substantial evidence that their earnings have actually declined. Doctors' dissatisfaction seems to be more related to the increase in control of nonmedical personnel and organizations over their activities. The reform introduced many changes, particularly with the introduction of intermediaries between doctors and patients (Health Service Purchasers) and the need to consider efficiency and competition criteria.

Despite these problems, the reform has been sustained by a number of factors: the rapid expansion of access to Colombia's health services at the beginning of the reform implementation, a significant increase in new resources for health, the procedural legitimacy attached to the formulation of the reform and its approval in Congress, the creation of new stakeholders, and the ongoing support of the multilateral development banks and international organizations.

Expanded Coverage

Affiliation with the health component of the Social Security system increased dramatically between 1993 and 1997, from 20.6 to 57 percent of the population.[9] The reform also greatly expanded geographic coverage, primarily under the subsidized regime. Before the reform, social security in health was confined to the main cities, with low or nonexistent coverage in remote and rural areas. Today, there is coverage throughout the country, though it remains more concentrated in more advanced areas (Cuartas 1998). In rural areas, the affiliation rate increased from 7 percent in 1993 to 48 percent in 1997. Furthermore, increases in coverage were concentrated in the lower-income deciles; in the first decile, insurance coverage went from 4 percent in 1993 to 40 percent in 1997.[10] Coverage has also been extended to cover workers' families, greatly benefiting women and children.

In spite of these important achievements, the goal of universal affiliation by 2001 was not met. Indeed,, coverage decreased after 1997 (from 57 to 53 percent in December 2000).[11] The drop is entirely due to shrinking affiliation to the contributory regime (from almost 40 percent of those eligible in

9. According to Fedesarrollo data; Ministry of Health data report peak affiliation in 1998 of slightly more than 60 percent.

10. Escobar and Panapoulou (2003).

11. Fedessarrollo data; Ministry of Health data also indicate falling total coverage, to 56.1 percent at the end of 2001.

1998 to somewhat more than 30 percent in 2001),[12] while affiliation with the subsidized regime continued to rise steadily (from about 21 percent of those eligible in 1998 to almost 26 percent in 2001). The reform was slow to incorporate the self-employed into the system, in spite of the legal requirement for compulsory affiliation. In 1998, among all those affiliated with the contributory regime, only 5 percent were self-employed (Ministerio de Salud 1998). However, by March 2000, the self-employed made up almost 29 percent of those affiliated with the contributory regime, and almost 35 percent of affiliates in both regimes taken together (data from National Household Survey).

Efficiency and Equity

One of the reform's main mechanisms for encouraging efficiency was competition among Health Service Purchasing organizations (EPSs, and Administradora Régimen Subsidiado, ARS) for affiliates and among hospitals for provision of services. But several factors have limited competition, particularly within the subsidized regime. At the local level, particularly in small localities, there are often too few purchasing organizations and hospitals for competition. Laws passed in 1996 and 2001 require the Subsidized Health Service Purchasers to contract 40 percent of their services with public hospitals without taking into consideration efficiency measures.[13] Only 30 percent of affiliates of the subsidized regime report having chosen their Health Service Purchaser (ARS). Continuous changes in regulations and the slow increase in the per capita payment to hospitals (UPC) have discouraged many private hospitals and clinics from contracting or participating with the subsidized regime.

Finally, there is not enough competition among providers of complex health services. Private clinics and hospitals offering simple procedures have proliferated, but high-cost treatment remains a natural monopoly of specialized institutions, mainly public hospitals. Another obstacle to efficiency has been the failure to separate affiliation and service provision functions, particularly among old actors of the system such as the ISS and territorial authorities.

The reform has contributed to greater solidarity in access to social security and health services. Law 100 requires workers who pay social security taxes to contribute 1 percent of their salaries to a pooled fund that

12. This is the result of the country's economic problems and the rise in unemployment.
13. Public Expenditure Rationalization Law, 1996; Law 715, 2001.

helps to support the subsidized system. As was noted above, coverage has expanded greatly. However, inequity persists, because there are still different systems of health provided by different institutions and under different conditions, even though the law intended to abolish those privileges. Within the contributory regime, some Health Service Purchasers have specialized in affiliating higher-income groups, particularly in the biggest urban centers. There is also segmentation between private and public clinics and hospitals, because the latter are concentrating on high-cost interventions. And though the POS offered through the subsidized regime has expanded,[14] the goal of having the same basic package for both regimes by 2001 was not reached.

Changing the Funding Arrangements

Largely because of the requirements of Law 60, public expenditures on health have increased significantly. During the 1980s, health expenditures funded from general taxes (excluding social security contributions) were about 1.2 percent of GDP.[15] Between 1993 and 1996, health spending financed from general taxes grew 21.1 percent yearly. In 1998, it was 3.6 percent of GDP—of which 2.5 percent was spent by local governments and 1.1 percent by the central government. In addition, Social Security contributions from workers and employers for health insurance and other private health expenditures amounted to roughly 4.3 percent of GDP. In 2000, public plus private expenditures on health reached almost 8 percent of GDP (Fedesarrollo 2000).

Currently, the central government expenditures on health are higher in Colombia than the average for middle-income countries; within Latin America, Colombia and Paraguay have had the greatest increases in expenditures for health and education in recent years (Fedesarrollo 2000). Expenditures cannot keep growing at the same pace, especially given the current economic crisis. At the same time, however, much of the population is still not insured. To expand coverage and to broaden the range of insured services, efficiency must increase. In particular, the transition from supply to demand subsidies must be completed to eliminate the current double allocation of resources to providers (e.g., through annual budgets plus for-service payments).

14. As of 2003, the subsidized package of services covered about 60 percent of the services provided by the contributory regime.
15. Most of the resources were for hospitals, particularly those with greater specialization.

Contributory Regime

The contributory regime is funded with a payroll tax on each family's combined income. Those resources grew significantly as a result of the reform; workers' contributions increased from 8 to 12 percent of wage income, of which the employee pays 4 percent and the employer pays 8 percent. (The self-employed must pay the entire 12 percent.) This was done to cover the worker's family as well as himself or herself, and to broaden the package of services.

A major funding problem for this part of the system is evasion; many people do not enroll in the contributory regime or underreport their income when they do. Deteriorating economic conditions have also affected revenues for the system, as unemployment and evasion have increased and average wages have decreased. As a result, the central compensation account and the solidarity account have both dwindled.

Subsidized Regime

The subsidized regime relies on different sources of funding from that of the contributory regime, including the solidarity account of the National Health Fund (1 percent of wages from workers belonging to the contributory regime, plus a contribution from the national budget[16]), contributions from the cooperative organizations Cajas de Compensacion Familiar (10 to 15 percent of their resources), and income from export charges on international petroleum companies. Those resources are sent to departments and municipalities to cofund the subsidized regime, where they are supplemented with intergovernmental transfers allocated to municipalities under Law 60 and with local taxes (Paredes 1999). These resources have been diminishing as a result of the reduction in central government funding and dwindling local resources. Moreover, in both the contributory and the subsidized regimes, delays and confusion have plagued the transfer of funds from the national to local levels, and among agencies at local levels, creating financial problems for many hospitals and clinics (Duarte 1997).

Creating New Entities

Law 100 created a complex institutional network, including many new entities (Giedion, López, and Marulanda 2000). There are 29 Health Ser-

16. According to Law 100/1993, it should be 1 percent. However, there have been several attempts to reduce this contribution (Law 344, 1998), and currently it has been established at 0.25 percent (Law 715/2001).

vice Purchasers (EPSs) including the ISS, which had covered 70 percent of all social security affiliates before the new system was launched, and still covered about 29 percent by the end of 2001. However, the most important proliferation of new institutions has been in the subsidized regime. Initially, 276 Subsidized Health Service Purchasers (ARS) were organized; after the Health Superintendency put into effect new norms, the number was reduced to 43. However, 60 percent of the population live in regions with less than 3 EPSs, which means there is virtually no competition. Subsidized Health Service Purchasers experience more problems than the institutions that manage the contributory regime. Their most significant problem is financial feasibility due to the small number of affiliates and low levels of capital.

Law 100 also established the CNSSS, which is attached to the Ministry of Health. Although the CNSSS was rather passive initially due to its lack of technical capacity and its advisory role, it has gradually become stronger and is beginning to play an important role regarding health policies. The Constitutional Court has ruled that decisions made in the CNSSS are autonomous, giving them greater weight. However, the CNSSS is still dominated by the Ministry of Health, and some groups within the health system do not feel effectively represented.

Changing the Administration and Operational Procedures of Old Entities

The transformation of old institutions and use of resources have proved to be far more difficult than the creation of new organizations and the use of new resources (González and Ramírez 2000). Law 100 provided for a two-year period of adaptation for the ISS and health care institutions for contributing public workers. However, resistance to change within the ISS and public hospitals, as well as the complexity and comprehensiveness of the reform, has posed formidable obstacles to implementation.

The Social Security Institute

Law 100 called for administrative changes in the Social Security Institute, the ISS, converting it into an industrial and commercial state enterprise with autonomy and contracting rules along the lines of private firms, so that it would compete with private Health Service Purchasers and providers. It was authorized to become a Health Service Purchaser with national coverage, but with decentralized services and autonomy for its clinics and hospitals. However, administrative and financial problems, lack of political will, unions' resistance, and pervasive patronage practices within the ISS have made the transformation extremely difficult (Fedesarrollo 2000). The organization has again and again delayed putting key reforms into effect, failing to redefine the package of insured services, introduce copayments, revise compensation mechanisms, or separate the administration and provision of health services. Insurance and provision of health services are combined in the ISS, although Law 100 prohibits this.

The ISS also faces major financial difficulties. In 1997, a standard risk-adjusted per capita payment was established for all health care providers, at Col$174,989. However, the average cost of attending a person in the ISS was Col$225,000. ISS overhead costs were 26 percent of the total, while the new system established a maximum of 15 percent. High overhead, in turn, reflected inflated payroll costs due to unusually high salaries and generous pensions.[17] The ISS remains the largest insurer in the contributory system, and its financial difficulties cause repercussions in other health institutions, particularly the hospitals with which it contracts. Problems with solvency and quality of service led the Superintendency to forbid new affiliates to the ISS for almost three years (between 1998 and 2001). Discussion about the future of the ISS has been ongoing and is a primary issue for presidential candidates. No radical solution was adopted during the Pastrana government. Twice, under Pastrana and more recently under Alvaro Uribe, the government has had to cover sizable ISS deficits.

Public Hospitals

The inefficiency of public hospitals was one of the main reasons for the reform, but it has proven to be one of the biggest obstacles of transformation as well. The reform envisages public hospitals as self-financed autonomous enterprises; funding will depend on payments for services provided (demand subsidies), not on up-front budgets (supply subsidies). To free up resources from supply subsidies to pay for demand subsidies, hospitals must also become more efficient. This is a key component of the reform. During the transition period established by Law 100, it was decided to

17. The ISS workers receive pensions, equal to 100 percent of their final year's salary, which usually has been increased by extra pay for night shifts and overtime. However, they have preserved the "pension retroactivity," even though the new labor law derogated this.

continue providing hospitals with budgets for several years but on a declining basis, while phasing in the system of filing claims for reimbursement for patients. However, it has not been possible to eliminate this temporary mechanism as quickly as expected; in 2001, 53 percent of resources from the subsidized regime were still distributed directly to public hospitals. At the beginning of the implementation stage, hospitals received both supply and demand subsidies, giving the wrong signals and incentives for the transformation as they accumulated more resources than ever before.

Adjustment within hospitals has also been hampered by rigid personnel rules and wages set by negotiations between unions and the national Ministry of Health and by pervasive patronage interference with personnel. In addition, because the demand for services within the subsidized regime is low, resources do not flow smoothly from the Subsidized Health Service Purchasers (ARS) to the hospitals as expected. Hospitals also have to cover those citizens who are not poor enough to qualify for the subsidized regime, yet cannot afford to pay for treatment,[18] and for treatments for patients in the subsidized regime that go beyond the package of insured services in that regime. Small municipal hospitals often find that low utilization of capacity due to low demand for certain services makes it impossible to cover their fixed costs through ARS contracts. Departments and municipal governments are obliged to cover the deficits.

In spite of the problems, a significant proportion of the 800 public hospitals have improved their financial autonomy and management capacity. The Ministry of Health is now supporting the allocation of resources through demand subsidies. However, from time to time it has also financed hospital deficits, sending mixed incentives for the transformation of these institutions.

Decentralization

As was noted above, in compliance with the 1991 Constitution, Law 60 governing decentralization of responsibility for much of the operation of primary and secondary health care and education was passed at almost the same time as Law 100. Therefore, local and departmental governments have been key actors in health sector reform, particularly in the implementation of the subsidized regime. Local authorities are responsible for identifying those eligible for the subsidized system and encouraging them to

18. These are called *vinculados;* in principle, they must make copayments for treatment, but in practice they seldom do so.

register for services, as well as promoting affiliation to the contributory regime by those who can pay the wage tax. Municipalities are also responsible for public health measures, while departments have to coordinate, complement, and provide technical assistance to municipalities.

Law 60 established two stages in the decentralization process. Departments and municipalities were given immediate access to some resources and responsibilities over hospitals in their jurisdiction. They were also required to go through a process of "certification" (taking certain measures and demonstrating capacity) to qualify for broader authority and responsibilities. The two-step process applies both from the central governments to departments and from departments to municipalities. Law 60 provided a transition period of three years for this process (Vargas and Sarmiento 1997).

However, only half the departments and 10 percent of municipalities have been certified. There are political, financial, institutional, and regulatory obstacles, including problems in shifting from supply to demand systems of funding local hospitals and clinics. Pressure from local hospital managers and politicians, low coverage in the subsidized regime, and the slow flow of resources have delayed the transition.

Laws 60 and 100 guaranteed important new resources for health and decentralization. As a result, resources at the local level for the subsidized regime increased sharply. In many municipalities, health now accounts for 30 percent of the budget where it used to be 10 percent. Between 1993 and 1996, the resources transferred from the central government to territorial authorities increased from 0.6 percent of GDP to 1.2 percent, taking up 53 percent of all social sector resources. The increases were crucial in expanding coverage.

Although decentralization has given local governments more autonomy in the organization and provision of health services and responsibility for the health conditions of poor people, it has not created incentives for financial responsibility. Moreover, key aspects of human resources management remain in the control of the national Ministry of Health. It is difficult to push the decentralization process further, due to the lack of clarity and support from the national level, uncertainty over the future of resources, high turnover of local health authorities, the inflexibility and high cost of health sector workers, and the fear of union opposition (Vargas and Sarmiento 1997).

At the local level, there is no incentive to change the flow of resources, because territorial authorities do not want to lose power. They are not interested in promoting affiliation and providing health service through institutions that they do not control, and even less so when they are to a large extent financing those services. They do not have incentives to separate affiliation from provision and to promote competition, key elements of the reform. The politics of implementing health sector reform at the local level explain to an important extent why the transformation remains incomplete.

In late 2001, after a constitutional amendment, Law 60 was reformed through Law 715, revising the decentralization process. Law 715 diminished the rate of growth of financial transfers from the central government to territorial authorities, simplified the certification process, and redefined responsibilities. In the case of health, municipalities retained responsibility for identifying and enrolling people in the subsidized regime, and departments were made responsible for providing public health services. They were assisted in this task by a major national program, supported by the Inter-American Development Bank, to strengthen the public hospitals. However, Law 715 still failed to provide clear incentives for increasing the coverage of the subsidized regime or transforming supply subsidies into demand subsidies.

Targeting

Targeting is at the center of the reform, and particularly at the center of the subsidized regime. In fact, the subsidized regime is known simply as SISBEN (the name of the targeting *instrument*) by the majority of the population, the media, and some politicians. SISBEN has been accepted and adopted in every municipality. However, it has proved to be an imperfect mechanism; in spite of gains in the allocation of resources for the poorest people, about 30 percent of the beneficiaries selected through the SISBEN and affiliated with the subsidized regime are not poor.

In part, this is because SISBEN has been used for clientelist practices, particularly in small municipalities. To tackle this problem, steps are currently being taken to adjust the instrument, to diminish political pressure on the system. Yet more needs to be done to improve the political sustainability of the targeting system.[19] It is estimated that 10.5 million people are not so poor as to be eligible for the subsidized health regime but also do not

19. SISBEN does not establish eligibility for the subsidized regime on the basis of current income, but instead it assesses earnings capacity based on education and other factors. Therefore, many people who are currently unemployed may not be eligible.

earn enough to pay the Social Security contribution for the contributory regime (Fedesarrollo 2000).

Conclusions

Law 100 has brought about a significant transformation of the health care sector, in spite of many difficulties. The main achievements have been the increase in Social Security coverage from 20 to 53 percent; family coverage; the generation of dynamic institutions within the contributory and the subsidized regime contributing to the expansion of affiliation; and an important increase in resources for health, both fiscal (national and subnational) and para-fiscal. These achievements are reflected in improvements in access to health, greater equity, and somewhat greater efficiency within the contributory regime.

Colombia was able to undertake such a broad, radical, and comprehensive reform due to widespread and intense concern about social and political disintegration, leading to the formulation of a new Constitution that gave room to important reforms. In addition, health sector reform was part of a broader set of reforms promoted by the government of President Gaviria, which, even though it could not formulate a consensus proposal for health on its own, was capable of responding to pressures from Congress and seized the opportunity to promote health reform. The strategy of broad consultation and procedural legitimacy during the stages of reform design and approval gave it substantial legitimacy despite difficulties during the implementation process. This was reinforced with the rapid creation of new stakeholders.

In contrast to health sector reform, the story of the education reform in Colombia during the past decade seems to have been a story of reform failure, at least until 2001. There are at least four main reasons for this contrast. First, health sector reform was facilitated by its linkage with the pensions reform in which the economic team and President Gaviria himself were actively involved. Second, after a cabinet reshuffle, high levels of the executive branch were able to reach a consensus regarding health reform. Third, the health sector workers' unions and the medical associations did not take a strong and unified position, and theywere less active than the teachers' union. And fourth, the health reform proposal combined the quest for universality and equity and the principle of efficiency.

In the case of education, the story was different, for at least three reasons. First, the reform was not linked to economic measures; furthermore, the executive branch was distracted by simultaneous reforms in other sectors. Second, the executive was divided regarding education reform. As a matter of fact, there were two competing proposals for education reform before Congress, both of which had at least some endorsement by the government: what became known as Law 60 was supported by the National Planning Department and the Finance Ministry, and the General Law on Education was promoted by FECODE (the teachers' union) but also supported by the Ministry of Education. Third, FECODE was able to exercise a great deal of power in both the Ministry of Education and the legislature.

Nevertheless, many problems persist regarding the implementation of health sector reform. Despite important progress in achieving the reform's objectives, it has not been possible to achieve important goals within the time frame that was initially envisioned. The subsidized part of the system, which covers the poorest people (who are often also those with the most serious health problems), faces financial and institutional difficulties that are reflected in both incomplete coverage and less than adequate quality. Furthermore, the process of implementing the reform seems to be putting its present and future achievements at risk. The transition period of the reform remains unfinished, for both political and technical reasons (Montengro, 1995).

In particular, institutions established before the reform have found the transformation and the reallocation of resources very difficult. The ISS has had especially acute problems in applying new principles. Many of the fresh resources allocated to the sector as a result of the reform have failed to be directed toward expanding coverage or consolidating policy change. Instead, funds have been diverted toward wage increases, the bureaucracy, health managers, and corruption. It can be said that the important achievements of the reform have been made primarily with new resources and through new institutions, but what existed before the reform has been very difficult to change.

References

Acosta, O., and I. Fainboim, eds. 1994. *Las reformas económicas del gobierno del Presidente Gaviria: Una visión desde adentro.* Bogotá: Ministerio de Hacienda y Crédito Público.
ASSALUD and FES (Asociación Colombiana de Salud and Fundación para la Educación Superior). 1997. Implantación de la Ley 100: Un año de implementación. ASSALUD and FES, Bogotá (unpublished).
Botero, F. 1991. Es urgente reformar el sistema de seguridad social. In *Apertura y modernización: Las reformas de los noventa,* ed. E. Lora. Bogotá: Tercer Mundo Editores.

Cárdenas, M., and G. Olano, eds. 1992. *Reforma de la seguridad social en salud.* Bogotá: Fundación Friedrich Ebert de Colombia, Fundación para la Educación Superior, and Fundación Antonio Restrepo Barco.

Cepeda, F. 1994. *Dirección política de la reforma en Colombia.* Bogotá: Departamento Nacional de Planeación, Fondo Financiero de Proyectos de Desarrollo.

Colombia Health Sector Reform Project. 1996. *Report on Colombia Health Sector Reform and Proposed Master Implementation Plan.* Cambridge, Mass.: School of Public Health, Harvard University.

Congreso de Colombia. 1994. *Ley 100 de 1993.* Bogotá: Congreso de Colombia.

———. 2001. *Ley 715 de 2000.* Bogotá: Congreso de Colombia.

Constitución Política de la República de Colombia. 1991. Bogotá: Escuela Superior de Administración Pública.

Cuartas, Carlos. 1998. *El sistema de seguridad social en salud y el ISS.* Bogotá: Departamento Nacional de Planeación.

DNP (Departamento Nacional de Planeación). 1991. *La revolucion pacifica: Plan de desarrollo economico y social 1991–1994.* Bogotá: DNP.

Duarte, Jesús. 1997. Problemas del esquema actual de asignación de recursos en educación y salud. *Debate de coyuntura social,* no. 16, May.

Escobar, M.-L., and G. Panopoulou. 2003. Health. In *Colombia: The Economic Foundation of Peace,* ed. M. Giugale et al. Washington D.C.: World Bank.

Fedesarrollo, ed. 1995. Reglamentación de la Ley 100: Un retroceso? *Debate de coyuntura social,* no. 5, May.

———. 1998. Indicadores sociales, salud. *Debate de coyuntura social,* no. 18, May.

———. 2000. El sistema de seguridad social en salud: Logros y retos. *Debate de coyuntura social,* no. 23, November.

Gaviria, C. 1994. *Las bases de la nueva Colombia: El revolcón institucional 1990–1994.* Bogotá: Consejería Presidencial para la Modernización del Estado.

Giedion, U., R. López, and J. Marulanda. 2000. Desarrollo institucional del sector salud en Bogotá. *Debate de coyuntura social,* no. 23, November.

González, A., and P. Ramírez. 2000. *Enhancing the Political Feasibility of Health Reform: The Colombia Case.* Cambridge, Mass.: School of Public Health, Harvard University.

González, Jorge, and Francisco Pérez. 1998. Salud para los pobres en Colombia: De la planeación centralizada a la competencia estructurada. *Debate de coyuntura social,* no. 18, May.

Grindle, M. 2000. The Social Agenda and the Politics of Reform in Latin America. In *Social Development in Latin America: The Politics of Reform,* ed. Joseph S. Tulchin and Allison M. Garland. Boulder, Colo.: Lynne Rienner Publishers for the Latin American Program of the Woodrow Wilson International Center for Scholars.

Haggard, S., and R. Kaufman. 1994. Las instituciones y el ajuste económico. In *La Política de Ajuste Económico,* ed. S. Haggard and R. Kaufman. Bogotá: Cerec.

Hommes, R. 1994. Políticas que promueven el crecimiento económico Colombiano. In *Las reformas económicas del Presidente Gaviria: Una visión desde adentro,* ed. O. Acosta et al. Bogotá: Ministerio de Hacienda.

Hommes, R., A. Montengro, and P. Roda, eds. 1994. *Una apertura hacia el futuro: Balance económico 1990–1994.* Bogotá: Ministerio de Hacienda.

Jaramillo, I. 1997. *El futuro de la salud en Colombia: La puesta en marcha de la Ley 100.* Bogotá: FESCOL.

————. 1998. La seguridad social en salud: Análisis comparativo. *Revista salutad,* no. 3, Julio.

Karl, C. R. 2000. *Incidencia del gasto publico en salud 1990–1999.* Bogotá: Departamento Nacional de Planeación.

Londoño, Juan Luis. 1992. La infraestructura social en el plan de desarrollo. *Planeación y desarrollo* 23, no.1, May.

————. 1996. Managed Competition in the Tropics? Paper presented at International Health Economics Association Inaugural Conference, Vancouver, May.

Lora, E. 1991. Reformas para la modernización del estado. In *Apertura y modernización: Las reformas de los noventa,* ed. E. Lora. Bogotá: Tercer Mundo Editores.

Mina, L. 2001. Una evaluacíon de la Ley 100 como herramienta de cumplimiento del derecho a la salud. In *Informe de desarrollo humano para Colombia 2000,* ed. Departamento Nacional de Planeación. Bogotá: Departamento Nacional de Planeación.

Ministerio de Salud. 1993. La reforma de la seguridad social en salud: La Ley 100 de 1993. Ministerio de Salud, Bogotá (unpublished).

————. 1994. *Recuento del diseño y trámite de la reforma de seguridad social en salud.* Bogotá: Ministerio de Salud.

————. 1998. Informe de actividades 1997–1998, al honorable Congreso de la república. Bogotá: Ministerio de Salud.

Molina, C., and J. Trujillo. 1992. *La reforma del sistema de seguros de salud: Una comparación de tres propuestas.* Bogotá: Mejoramiento de la Gestión Hospitalaria.

Montenegro, A. 1997. Regulation and Deregulation: The Process of Reform in Colombia, 1990–1994. In *The Politics of Reforming the State,* ed. E. Posada-Carbó. London: Institute of Latin American Studies, University of London.

Montenegro, Armando. 1995. An Incomplete Case of Education Reform: The Case of Colombia. Human Capital Development and Operations Policy Working Paper 60. Washington, D.C.: World Bank.

Organizacion Panamericana de la Salud. 1999. *Colombia: Perfil del sistema de servicios de salud.* Bogotá: Organizacion Panamericana de la Salud.

Paredes, Nelcy. 1999. Qué está pasando con el régimen subsidiado? *Vía salud,* no. 9.

Presidencia de la República. 1994. *Evaluación de la política social.* Bogotá: Consejería Presidencial para la Política Social.

Roda, P., A. Montenegro, and R. Hommes. 1994. *Una apertura hacia el futuro: Balance económico 1990–1994.* Bogotá: Ministerio de Hacienda.

Salazar, M. 1997. Political Intervention in the Decentralisation Policy Implementation: The Case of the Colombian Grant System. In The Politics of Decentralisation in Colombia, Ph.D. dissertation, London School of Economics and Political Science, London.

Sánchez, F., and J. Nuñez. 1999. La Ley 100/1993 sí llegó a las personas de menores ingresos. *Vía salud,* no. 9.

Uribe-Vélez, A. 1991. Por qué la reforma laboral? In *Apertura y modernización: Las reformas de los noventa,* ed. E. Lora. Bogotá: Tercer Mundo Editores.

Urrutia, M. 1996. Colombia. In *The Political Economy of Policy Reform,* ed. J. Williamson. Washington, D.C.: Institute for International Economics.

Vargas, J. E., and A. Sarmiento. 1997. *La descentralizacion de los servicios de salud en Colombia.* Serie Reformas de Políticas Publicas 51. Santiago: Comisión Económica para América Latina y el Caribe.

Chapter 6

Toward a Unified and More Equitable System: Health Reform in Brazil

Marta Arretche

Brazilian health care has been provided through three different and somewhat independent mechanisms: (1) the Unified Health System (Sistema Único de Saúde, SUS), which is a comprehensive publicly financed system, with free and universal entitlement, involving all three levels of the federal system; (2) a supplementary health care system,[1] in which either individuals or enterprises have their own voluntary private health insurance plans; and (3) a private health care market, in which people pay directly for health care services.

The author is very grateful to the participants in the Woodrow Wilson Center Workshop on the Politics of Health Reform for their helpful comments on the earlier draft of this chapter. She owes particular thanks to Thomas Bossert, Robert Kaufman, Joan Nelson, and Kurt Weyland.

1. It is called supplementary because it is independent from—and not complementary to—the public health care system, which is supposed to be universal.

Many people who do not rely exclusively on SUS, but who cannot afford a private insurance plan, buy some medical services on their own. Moreover, neither SUS nor private insurance plans cover the costs of medicines. As a result, in 1998, 51 percent of the Brazilian population bought some health care services with their own income (IBGE 1998). The supplementary health care system has grown steadily since the late 1980s, reaching about 25 percent of the Brazilian population a decade later (IBGE 1998). More than 80 percent of Brazilian doctors have their own offices, and more than 50 percent of the Brazilian hospitals provide services to privately insured patients (Bahia 2001b).

In the late 1980s and 1990s, no important changes occurred in the supplementary health care subsector,[2] but the public component of the health care system was substantially restructured in two interrelated steps, namely, universalization and decentralization. The new Constitution adopted in 1988 mandated a single unified, universal health system under the control of the Ministry of Health, absorbing and expanding beyond the previous Social Security–funded system that covered only formal-sector workers. It also called for the decentralization of health care provision, within this unified system, to the states and especially the municipalities. Health sector politics during the 1990s revolved around the implementation of these mandates.

Proreform forces sought these changes in order to extend health services more equitably to the entire population; to permit more emphasis on primary and preventive services; and to reduce the influence of the large and well-organized private health care providers in health policies and provision. National health laws consistent with the 1988 Constitution were passed in 1990, and thereafter, the main arena for health sector reforms shifted from the legislature to the executive branch.

Until the late 1990s, the Ministry of Health had only limited political influence within government coalitions. Moreover, recurrent budget crises led state and local governments to doubt the ministry's capacity to meet its obligations to transfer federal resources for health programs. After 1998, however, Jose Serra, a much stronger minister of health, was appointed, and ministry transfers to municipalities increased, accelerating the progress of reforms.

Criteria and conditions attached to the transfer of federal funds were the main instruments by which the federal Ministry of Health encouraged local governments to take responsibility for health care provision (through a mix

2. The National Supplementary Health Agency was created only in 1998.

of direct public provision and contracts with private providers), and to introduce better preventive and public health measures. Much of the politics of health care reform during the 1990s focused on conflicts among health care reformers, local authorities, and the Health Ministry around both the rules of decentralization itself and the decision-making rules. In contrast to Argentina and Mexico, the World Bank and other international financial institutions played no significant role in Brazilian health sector reform.

By 2000, the reformers had succeeded in incorporating all of Brazil's municipalities into the unified health system and most municipalities had greatly expanded their responsibilities for health care administration. Local spending on health care had expanded within a context of increased federal transfers and local revenues. However, inequalities in service provision among and within states and regions remained sizable.

In analyzing the politics of Brazil's health care reforms, three themes emerge: the impact of shifting policy arenas, the importance of legacies from the earlier health care system, and the key roles of major actors' strategies in policy decisions and implementation. The politics of Brazilian health care reform can be divided into two phases. The first one established the reform objectives; its main arenas were the Constituent Assembly and the Congress.

In the second phase, these constitutional mandates were implemented, and the executive power replaced the parliament as the main decision-making arena. Policy legacies, inherited from the centralized previous model, played a role in both phases, shaping both actors' goals and their respective political resources, as well as the reform implementation path. Both phases tell a story of an ongoing struggle regarding the rules governing reform itself, and over the procedures for participation in the reform policymaking, although the position of the main actors within health reform arenas has sharply changed as reform has proceeded.

The Context for Health Care Reform

During the military period (1964–85), the state level health agencies were formally independent from the Federal Health Ministry and had their own state budgetary resources; but there were no significant conflicts between federal and local health care policies, because the selection of governors and most important cities' mayors was firmly controlled by the military authorities. For most of this period, in fact, there were only two legal parties and all governors, as well as the mayors of state capitals and medium-sized cities, belonged to the president's party. Central control over the appointment of governors, together with fiscal centralization, prevented most of the conflicts over policy formulation and implementation that are typical of most federal systems.

During the 1980s, the return to democratic rule substantially changed Brazilian political institutions and reshaped the political context in which health care reform took place. In 1982, the military authorities reintroduced direct elections for state governors and for mayors of state capitals and major cities, replacing the system of indirect election of governors and appointment of mayors established in the 1960s.

In 1988, the new federal Constitution established one of the most decentralized fiscal systems in the world (Shah 1991). Formula-driven transfers increased the amount of revenues automatically transferred to states and municipalities and also decreased federal government discretion over the allocation of tax revenues. Moreover, states and municipalities were entitled to levy their own revenues (Willis, Garman, and Haggard, 1999). Yet the new Constitution was unclear about the distribution of many public policy responsibilities; and the federal government continued to provide many of its traditional services.

Both fiscal federalism and local government political autonomy substantially changed the way intergovernmental relations have worked. Because tax power and revenue have been decentralized and public policy responsibilities have not, local governments cannot be held accountable for the delivery of social services. Federal institutional guarantees allow local governments to simply say "no" to any central initiative that implies sharing responsibility for public policies. This means that in Brazil's federal system, governors and mayors hold veto power over the implementation of public policies within their territories. Whether or not they agree to assume responsibility for a particular service depends on how they calculate the costs and benefits of doing so. The more costs a given policy imposes on local governments, the less successful it tends to be. The more benefits it offers to local governments, the greater its chances of getting support among governors and mayors.

The 1988 Constitution was drafted during the government of President José Sarney, within a context of great concern about the social debt inherited from the military government. The constituent assembly offered a political opportunity for health care reformers to incorporate their redistributive reform goals as constitutional mandates, thus increasing the political costs of letting them fall by the wayside.

In 1989, direct presidential elections were held for the first time since before the military dictatorship, amid recurring battles with inflation and growing concern with fiscal adjustment. The winner of the election, Fernando Collor (1990–92), was impeached two years later and replaced by the vice president, Itamar Franco, for the remainder of the term (1992–94).[3] The economic and political situation became somewhat calmer in 1994. The implementation of a new economic stabilization plan, Plano Real, brought a rapid reduction in inflation. Fernando Henrique Cardoso, the finance minister responsible for this success, was elected president in 1994 and reelected in 1998. Over the course of the entire decade, however, progress in implementing the constitutionally mandated health system reforms was constrained both by pressures for fiscal austerity, and—perhaps even more important—by a succession of governments with very different orientations toward the desirability and priority of health care reform.

The Health Care System before 1988

SUS, the universal and unified health system, replaced the health insurance system set up during the military regime. Some researchers (Draibe 1994; Mesa-Lago 1978) describe this previous system as Bismarckian, since it was financed from workers' and employers' contributions and was based on an insurance principle of entitlement. The Social Security system covered only workers in the formal sector of the labor market. It was administered by a single, highly centralized federal agency—the Instituto Nacional de Assistência Médica da Previdência Social (INAMPS), which managed finances and the selection, contracting, and payment of health care providers at the national level. Although federal civil servants and private-sector employees had different retirement benefit rights, the Social Security health insurance system provided the same services for both groups: free medical assistance, laboratory exams and diagnosis, and clinic and hospital services.

Health care services were provided either by INAMPS facilities or by private doctors or specialized hospitals, clinics, and laboratories under contract to INAMPS. Doctors with Social Security contracts were allowed to have their own offices, outside INAMPS facilities. The private and

3. President Itamar Franco took office in December 1992.

public specialized hospitals, clinics, and laboratories provided free services to insured clients and were paid by INAMPS according to the amount and kind of medical services delivered. This payment system implied strong incentives for providers to maximize the services delivered in order to enlarge their revenues.

Hospital and clinic facilities, as well as the pharmaceutical and hospital equipment industries, expanded impressively from the 1970s on (Furtado and Souza 2001; Queiroz and Velazquez 2001), mainly because the Social Security system guaranteed demand for private hospitals, without requiring them to deal exclusively within the system. That is, contracts with IN-AMPS allowed hospitals to accept whatever patients they wanted, insured under the Social Security system or not. Moreover, construction of private hospitals was subsidized by a federal policy adopted in the mid-1970s.

In the pre-1988 health care system, curative and preventive programs were managed by two independent federal agencies. While INAMPS managed the curative health care programs through the Social Security system, the Health Ministry was in charge of preventive health care programs, using federal budgetary resources. In the late 1980s, 78 percent of federal spending on health care was allocated to curative services; only 22 percent addressed preventive health care programs (Draibe, Castro, and Azeredo 1991, 28). In 1986, the combined total expenditures on health care at the federal, state, and municipal levels came to 2.34 percent of gross domestic product (estimated from data presented by Draibe 1994).

At the end of the 1980s, 98 percent of all primary health care establishments were public; of these, 93 percent were managed by state and local governments (see tables 6.1 and 6.2). These numbers were the result of a steady increase in state and local provision of primary health care services during the decade,[4] which in turn was a consequence both of pressures from local social movements for better medical services and decentralization measures taken before the creation of the Unified Health System.

Although virtually all primary clinics were public, about 80 percent of the specialized hospitals were private (see tables 6.1 and 6.2). Although we have no precise data on how many of them held contracts with INAMPS, it is certain that the provision of specialized hospital services financed by the Social Security system was absolutely dependent on private facilities, and the great majority of private hospitals held contracts with both INAMPS and private insurers.

    4. In 1981, only 22 percent of the total number of health care establishments were under the responsibility of municipalities, whereas 50 percent were states' responsibility and 28 percent were in federal hands (Costa 2001, 310).

Table 6.1

Active Health Establishments by Type, Brazil, 1988

Type	Public Number	Percent	Private Number	Percent	Total Number
Primary care	18,118	98.1	345	1.8	18,463
Secondary care	2,585	27.8	6,703	72.2	9,288
Emergency care	153	56.8	116	43.2	269
Hospital	1,243	18.9	5,336	81.1	6,579
Nonspecified	36	63.2	21	36.8	57
Total	22,099	63.7	12,500	36.1	34,656

Sources: Instituto Brasileiro de Geografia e Estatística and Pesquisa Assistência Médico-Sanitária no Brasil.

Within the public sector, the federal government was no longer an important health care provider by the late 1980s.[5] However, it remained by far the predominant source of financing for the system, far outpacing revenues from state and municipal sources. In 1987 and 1988, the federal government levied more than 80 percent of total health care revenues (see table 6.3) and allocated more than 60 percent of total health care spending (see table 6.4).

The regional distribution of health care services was quite uneven. Better and more specialized health services were concentrated in the richest regions (the Southeast and South), whereas public primary health care facilities were concentrated mainly in the poorest regions; the per capita number of primary care establishments was higher in the North and Northeast Regions than in the Southeast in 1988. In short, until 1988 the health care system was part of the Social Security system; it was insurance based and very centralized. Health care provision emphasized curative services and was strongly dependent on private health care providers for more specialized services. Private hospital facilities had expanded greatly, as a result of government-guaranteed demand and construction subsidies.

The Private Health Insurance Market

The current private health insurance market has been developing since the 1960s, and its main features have been decisively shaped by public policies. Social Security subsidies and federal regulations favored insurance

5. See in table 6.2 that only 5.5 percent of all health care establishments were federal in the late 1980s.

Table 6.2

Active Health Establishments by Level of Government and Type, Brazil, 1989

Type	Federal		State		Municipalities		Private		Total
	Number	Percent	Number	Percent	Number	Percent	Number	Percent	Number
Primary care	989	5.2	9,312	49.0	8,359	44.0	336	1.8	18,996
Secondary care	730	8.0	687	7.5	1,187	13.0	6,523	71.5	9,127
Emergency care	17	5.7	14	4.7	154	51.9	112	37.7	297
Hospital	187	2.9	491	7.7	579	9.0	5,154	80.4	6,411
Total	1,923	5.5	10,504	30.2	10,279	29.5	12,125	34.8	34,831

Sources: Instituto Brasileiro de Geografia e Estatística and Pesquisa Assistência Médico-Sanitária no Brasil.

Table 6.3
Public Sources of Health Service Funding by Level of Government, Brazil, 1985–96

Year	Source of Funds (millions of dollars)				Source of Funds (percent)			
	Federal	State	Municipal	Total	Federal	State	Municipal	Total
1985	10,573.8	2,523.1	1,343.9	14,440.8	73.2	17.5	9.3	100.0
1986	9,534.5	2,685.1	1,452.3	13,671.9	69.8	19.6	10.6	100.0
1987	14,743.7	1,325.0	1,435.9	17,508.2	84.2	7.6	8.2	100.0
1988	15,400.7	−95.4	2,482.3	17,787.6	86.6	−0.5	13.9	100.0
1989	19,172.4	2,067.8	2,676.2	23,916.4	80.2	8.6	11.2	100.0
1990	13,659.1	2,467.4	2,177.2	18,303.7	74.6	13.5	11.9	100.0
1991	11,344.1	2,000.8	1,575.6	14,920.5	76.0	13.4	10.6	100.0
1992	10,010.2	2,045.7	1,776.0	13,831.9	72.4	14.8	12.8	100.0
1993	10,294.6	—	—	—	—	—	—	—
1994	10,441.6	3,705.1	2,883.9	17,030.6	61.3	21.8	16.9	100.0
1995	14,500.3	4,275.0	3,969.8	22,745.1	63.8	18.8	17.4	100.0
1996	12,420.5	4,285.5	6,419.4	23,125.4	53.7	18.5	27.8	100.0

Note: A dash in a cell means that data are not available.
Sources: Medici (2002); the data are from Instituto de Economia do Setor Público/Fundação para o Desenvolvimento Administrativo and Diretoria de Política Social / Instituto de Planejamento e Economia Aplicada.

Table 6.4
Public Spending on Health by Level of Government, Brazil, 1985–96

Year	Public Spending on Health (millions of dollars)				Public Spending on Health (percent)			
	Federal	State	Municipal	Total	Federal	State	Municipal	Total
1985	9,677.6	3,382.3	1,380.9	14,440.8	67.0	23.4	9.6	100.0
1986	8,321.3	3,599.4	1,751.2	13,671.9	60.9	26.3	12.8	100.0
1987	11,179.6	4,314.1	2,010.9	17,508.2	63.9	24.6	11.5	100.0
1988	9,034.9	6,225.7	2,527.0	17,787.6	50.8	35.0	14.2	100.0
1989	12,943.8	8,011.8	2,960.8	23,916.4	54.1	33.5	12.4	100.0
1990	9,614.1	6,005.9	2,683.7	18,303.7	52.5	32.8	14.6	100.0
1991	7,809.9	5,414.7	2,695.9	14,920.5	52.3	29.8	18.1	100.0
1992	9,702.3	2,353.6	1,776.0	13,831.9	70.1	17.0	12.9	100.0
1993	9,301.6	—	—	—	—	—	—	—
1994	9,624.1	4,230.7	3,175.8	17,030.6	56.5	24.8	18.7	100.0
1995	13,005.4	4,854.1	4,885.6	22,745.1	57.2	21.5	21.3	100.0
1996	10,561.3	4,513.0	8,051.1	23,125.4	45.7	19.5	34.8	100.0

Note: A dash in a cell means that data are not available.
Sources: Medici (2002); the data are from Instituto de Economia do Setor Público/Fundação para o Desenvolvimento Administrativo and Diretoria de Política Social / Instituto de Planejamento e Economia Aplicada.

companies that also manage the provision of services—both hospital-based health maintenance organization–type organizations and medical cooperatives—as contrasted with insurers that only cover the financial costs of care. Consequently, the former became established earlier and have dominated the private health insurance market. The demand for private health insurance stemmed from the dissatisfaction of the middle class and the most strongly unionized workers with the public health care system, but private insurance was also stimulated by laws exempting all health expenses from taxation.

State-owned and large private enterprises developed their own self-managed health insurance programs, whereas financial institutions, medical cooperatives, and Medicina de Grupo (hospital-based, for-profit, health maintenance organization–type organizations) competed within the private health insurance market. From 1987 to 1997–98, private insurance clients almost doubled and the number of health care insurance enterprises tripled (see table 6.5). Currently, about 25 percent of the population (IBGE 1998)—mainly the middle and upper classes, and the best-organized workers as well—have their own private health insurance plans, although there is wide variation among them regarding prices and services provided.

Table 6.5

Private Health Insurance by Number of Enterprises and Clients, Brazil, 1977–98

Enterprises or Clients	1977	1987	1989	1994–95	1997–98
Number of enterprises					
Medicina de Grupo	200	300	—	555	730
Medical cooperatives	60	128	—	332	326
Enterprise's own insurance	—	50	—	150	300
Financial institutions	1	5	—	20	40
Total	—	483	—	1,057	1,396
Number of clients					
Medicina de Grupo	7,000,000	13,000,000	15,000,000	16,800,000	17,800,000
Medical cooperatives	—	3,500,000	7,300,000	8,500,000	10,671,000
Enterprise's own insurance	—	5,100,000	7,900,000	8,000,000	8,000,000
Financial institutions	—	800,000	940,000	5,000,000	5,000,000
Total	—	24,400,000	31,140,000	38,300,000	41,471,000

Note: A dash in a cell means that data are not available.
Source: Bahia (2001a).

Private health insurance remained almost entirely unregulated until the late 1990s. It was only in 1998 that a National Supplementary Health Agency (Agência Nacional de Saúde Suplementar, ANS) was established. The Finance and Health Ministries were sharply divided over which would have authority over this agency, but the health minister, Jose Serra, prevailed over the finance minister, Pedro Malan, and the ANS was established within the Health Ministry. The ministry proceeded to draft a presidential decree establishing minimum health care requirements for private health insurance plans; at present, however, implementation has been minimal. Among other things, private insurers have been able to frustrate regulatory controls by withholding information about their operation (Bahia 2001b).

The emergence of a sizable private medical insurance market has had important implications for the politics of health care reform. Because the middle class, the best organized workers, and state-owned enterprise employees are protected under their own private health insurance plans and are allowed to claim tax exemption for all their health expenses, they have no stake in reform of the public health care system. Rural workers and weaker blue-collar unions in the Social Security system, as well as the unemployed and the urban informal-sector workers who did not have health care rights before the creation of SUS,[6] have lacked the organizational resources to push for redistributive health care reform at the national level. Thus, although social movements all over the country began to press for better medical services from the late 1970s on, they focused mainly on problems of their local communities (Weyland 1996). As a result, state bureaucracies—whether led by politicians or civil servants—have been the most important actors in Brazilian health care reform.

The 1988 Constitution and the National Health Laws

Conflicts over decentralization, preventive versus curative health policies, and control over the private health providers were at the center of the health policy debate in Brazil throughout the 1980s, well before the 1987–88 Constitutional Assembly was convened. These debates pitted the INAMPS bureaucracy and private medical associations against a coalition of reformers, the *sanitarist* movement (the Movimento Sanitarista), which was formed in the late 1970s by medical professionals, local health authorities,

6. However, the universal right to emergency care was introduced in 1974.

and left-wing health experts. By the early 1980s, the *sanitaristas* had become highly influential advocates of a redistributive and comprehensive health care reform. For them, health care policy reform needed to address mistargeting, the rising costs of curative treatments, and the excessive reliance on private health care providers. They battled for an expansion of the public (Social Security) health care system to cover the entire population, the extension of preventive and primary health care programs to poor people, strengthened control over contracted private health care providers, and decentralization.

The then–highly centralized system of health care policymaking was viewed by the *sanitaristas* as an arrangement that favored private health care business interests. These were organized to lobby in federal agencies, and had been especially successful in capturing INAMPS. Thus, the reformers pressed for decentralization not only as a means to improve the efficiency of the health care system but also—and even more important—as a political strategy for weakening the policy influence of the for-profit providers.

The political context in 1987–88 favored the health care reformers. Public concern about the Social Security deficit had been aroused by reports that INAMPS had overspent on the purchase of private health care services and that it had diverted funds for construction of unrelated infrastructure.[7] Moreover, center-left politicians played a powerful role in Sarney's governing coalition, which opened the way for progressive health care experts to gain influence within the federal executive branch.

As a result of the reformers' pressures, the government took some steps toward decentralization in the years before the 1988 constitutional reforms, including the shift of some INAMPS resources and tasks to state governments. However, INAMPS kept authority over financing and private health providers' contracting (see NEPP 1989; Weyland 1996).[8] During the first years of the Sarney government (between 1985 and 1987), there were also some efforts to control the costs of contracts with for-profit health providers, although these were largely unsuccessful.

---

7. According to several sources, in the late 1970s, the Social Security deficit was partially brought about by its revenues deviation to build the country's infrastructure facilities, e.g., Rio-Niterói Bridge, Transmazônica Road, and Itaipu.

8. As we saw above, those decentralization measures, along with social-movement pressures for better medical services, implied an impressive increase in the number of primary care public facilities: They jumped from 13,071 in 1984 to 18,463 in 1988, and again to 19,839 in 1990 (IBGE 1998).

The 1987–88 Constitutional Assembly gave the *sanitarist* movement a political opportunity to establish its reform goals as constitutional mandates, and it succeeded in pushing through a significant part of its comprehensive health care reform proposals. The new Constitution mandated free and universal entitlement to all levels of health care; and it assigned responsibility to the state for health care provision, in place of the previous insurance-based model. It mandated a unified health care system at all levels of government, and it transferred control over federal policy (including over Social Security health insurance) to the Ministry of Health. Among other things, these provisions were intended to eliminate the previous split between curative and preventive programs in health care policy. Finally, the Constitution also defined decentralization as a health care reform goal, reversing a Brazilian pattern of centralized state building that began in the early 1930s. Together, these decisions provided the basis for the establishment of the Unified National Health System, the Sistema Único de Saúde.

The SUS project aimed at eliminating the INAMPS bureaucracy in two steps. In a transitional phase, INAMPS would be transferred from the jurisdiction of the Social Security Ministry to the Health Ministry. Later, the INAMPS bureaucracy would be absorbed into the ministry and lose its institutional autonomy. Despite these victories in the Constitutional Assembly, the *sanitarist* movement did lose one major battle. Its proposal for gradual nationalization of *all* health care provision was fiercely opposed and successfully defeated by for-profit private providers (see NEPP 1989; Weyland 1996). Thus, the establishment of the SUS did not displace the private providers from their long-established role in specialized health care services.

Once the 1988 Constitution was promulgated, its provisions had to be implemented through ordinary legislation. During the last year of Sarney's term (1989), the Health Ministry drafted a National Health Law, which was passed with the support of a broad political alliance during President Collor's first year in office (Carvalho 2001). Nevertheless, the progress and direction of the reform project were slowed by the orientation of the Collor government. Collor favored the introduction of market principles into health care policy. Instead of the automatic transfers of federal funds to municipalities, as desired by the reformers, he sought individually negotiated funding agreements (*convenios*) with the municipalities.

He used his constitutional powers to veto twenty-five articles of Law 8080/90, including key provisions regarding the closing of INAMPS, earmarking resources to finance the SUS, and automatic transfers to municipalities (Cordeiro 2001).

Under strong pressure from the *sanitarist* movement and local health authorities, the deadlock was resolved three months later with the approval of two National Health Laws (Laws 8080/90 and 8142/90). The progressive reformers were able to win legislative approval for obligatory regular and automatic transfers from the Ministry of Health to the municipalities, and a deadline for the closure of INAMPS.[9] However, the degree and nature of public control over private health sector activities remained vague. Moreover, medical business associations were given representation in the National Health Council, which allowed them to participate directly in health policy decision making.

The 1988 Constitution and the National Health Laws shaped the main features of the public health care system as it evolved in the 1990s. For the analytical purposes of this chapter, two of these features are crucial. First, the for-profit health care providers have maintained their role in public health care provision as well as their autonomy in the private health care market. Second, though municipalities were to be in charge of managing the local health care programs, the federal government retained responsibility for financing and coordination.[10] This distribution of functions within the federal system implied that the central government was entitled to decide the most important issues regarding national health care policy; the concentration of finance and coordination at the federal level means that local governments' policies depended heavily on federal rules and transfers.

From 1990 on, these arrangements established the Health Ministry both as the arena in which the most important health policy decisions are made and also as the most powerful actor in this arena. Throughout the 1990s, there was an ongoing struggle between the Health Ministry and local health authorities regarding the rules governing decentralization itself, and over the procedures for participation in policymaking at the federal level.

The rules governing decentralization define the mechanisms through which state and local governments assume responsibility for health care spending and management. Disputes over these rules involve how federal health care resources are transferred (automatically or through negotiations), to whom they are transferred (to health care providers or local health

9. INAMPS was transferred to Health Ministry in 1990 and ceased to exist in 1993.

10. State governments were to provide support for the municipal health care systems, but their responsibilities remained vague under the National Health Laws.

care authorities), and how their use is evaluated. Rules regarding policy-making procedures define institutional rights to participate in decisions on health policy. Disputes over these rules mainly involve which actors would have a say in health care policy reform.

Implementing Reform

Implementation of the constitutional mandates and new legislation creating the SUS shifted the main arena of reform from the parliament to the executive branch. Many additional, detailed regulations were essential to guide the decentralization process, and Basic Operational Norms (Normas Operacionais Básicas, NOBs) enacted by the Health Ministry became the main instrument for this purpose. Each successive government has drawn up new NOBs, and these evolving regulations have been the focus of intense dispute.

The Collor Government, 1990–1992

As noted above, President Collor (1990–92) opposed decentralization and sought instead to widen federal political control over the state and local governments. His choice for health minister was Alceni Guerra, a former official of INAMPS, whose strategy was to slow decentralization by establishing direct financial links between the ministry and the municipalities while widening federal government discretion over intergovernmental transfers (Lucchese 1996). Rules promulgated during Collor's term provided that health care providers, both public and private, would be paid directly by the ministry according to the amount of medical services delivered. Municipal governments would not receive health care transfers automatically. Rather, they would only receive funds on the basis of *convênios,* negotiated agreements with the Health Ministry. Investment in health care facilities would be restricted to maintenance of those already in existence (Levcovitz, Lima, and Machado 2001).

These rules were intended to trim the municipalities' autonomy and push them into accepting federal political requirements. Because money would go directly from the Health Ministry to the health care providers, and because local public providers would be paid the same way as private ones, municipalities would have no authority over funding. They would be constrained to accept federal requirements to receive the health care transfers.

On the other side, the constitutional and legal mandates served as a source of leverage for the *sanitarist* movement and local health authorities, making it difficult for the federal government to reverse the SUS principles. *Sanitaristas* and left-wing health experts denounced President Collor's decentralization rules, describing them as a tutelary decentralization model (*decentralização tutelada*) (Cordeiro 2001); indeed, they charged that they were illegal, because they were contrary to the National Health Law (Carvalho 2001).

Despite these protests, by 1993 about 22 percent of the 4,974 municipalities (Guimarães 2001, 50) had adhered to the Health Ministry decentralization norms. Even so, however, the ministry failed to meet its commitments. Between 1991 and 1994, it paid for medical services delivered by public and private health care providers, but did not transfer the health care resources stipulated by the agreements (*convenios*) negotiated with the states and the 1,090 municipalities that had signed them. (Lucchese 1196; Levcovitz 2001). In fact, the Collor government cut federal health spending sharply during its time in office (see the rows for 1990, 1991, and 1992 in table 6.3).

During the Collor period, health policy decisions regarding decentralization were closed to participation by progressive reformers and local health authorities. (Carvalho 2001). In fact, the Health Ministry tried to silence the progressive experts' voice by not convening the Ninth Health Conference,[11] which was scheduled to be held during Collor's term. The conference was eventually convened, but only under intense pressure from the *sanitarist* movement and local politicians, after Minister Alceni Guerra was accused of corruption and dismissed (Lucchese 1996).[12]

The Franco Government, 1992–1994

Progressive health care experts and local politicians learned during President Collor's term that the federal executive had institutional tools to exclude them from health care policy decision making. So, during President Franco's government (1992–94), their strategy was to push through de-

11. Since 1947, health care policy stakeholders have influenced federal health care policy formulation through national conferences called by the federal government. Since 1986, the *sanitarist* movement strategy to push forward its health care reform goals was to attend them massively and give them a strong policy formulation status.

12. The Ninth Health Conference was called by the health minister, Adib Jatene, at the very end of President Collor's administration.

centralization rules that would both deepen decentralization and establish their influence in federal health policy decision making.

President Franco's government was supported by a broad political coalition that had emerged after the civic mobilization that impeached President Collor. Franco nominated as health minister Jamil Haddad, who had ties to the *sanitarist* movement and local health care authorities. As a result, progressive reformers returned to key positions within the Health Ministry and the process of decision making was opened up. A special commission (the Special Decentralization Group, Grupo Especial de Descentralização, GED), was formed to rewrite the norms in force under Collor. The commission included state and local health authorities, as well as representatives of various bureaucratic groups within the ministry itself. Representatives of the municipalities were particularly active in GED meetings (Elias 2001; Goulart 2001).

The GED produced a report with a title that fully expresses the progressive health experts' evaluation of the Collor strategy: "Decentralization of health care: the courage to obey and enforce the law." The document was discussed for six months by the Health National Council and the Three-Level Government Commission (Comissão Intergestores Tripartite, CIT)[13] and provided the basis for a new 1993 Basic Operational Norm (1993 NOB).

One important aspect of the new regulations was a set of procedural rules aimed at insuring the participation of local government in ongoing decisions regarding health policy. Within each state, policy decisions were to be made by the Two-Level Government Commission (Comissão Intergestores Bipartite, CIB), composed of equal numbers of state and municipal representatives. At the federal level, decisions were to be approved by the CIT, which was composed of equal numbers of federal government delegates, representatives of the National Council of State–level Health Authorities (Conselho Nacional de Secretários Estaduais de Saúde, CONASS), and representatives of the National Council of Municipal-Level Health Authorities (Conselho Nacional de Secretários Municipais de Saúde, CONASEMS).

13. The Three-Level Government Commission (Comissão Intergestores Tripartite, CIT) was created in July 1991, under pressure from state and municipal health authorities. It is composed of an equal number of representatives from the Health Ministry, the state-level Health Authorities Council (Conselho Nacional de Secretários Estaduais de Saúde, CONASS), and the municipal-level Health Authorities Council (Conselho Nacional de Secretários Municipais de Saúde, CONASEMS) (Lucchese 1996). Yet, the inclusion of CIT in health policy decision making never happened during President Collor's administration (Goulart 2001).

From then on, representatives of the state and municipal health authorities were supposed to have an institutional voice regarding decisions about decentralization rules (Carvalho 2001).

The decentralization rules specified in the 1993 NOB allowed municipalities and states to choose the extent and nature of health care tasks for which they would take responsibility. They could select among three options offered by the Health Ministry. These three options were ranked according to their complexity, from primary health care provision to contracting with and payment of hospitals and clinics. Local governments were required to demonstrate their capacity to carry out whatever level of responsibility they selected. Federal funding transfers for health care would become full and automatic only at the most complex level, in which the municipality (or state) took over responsibility for the entire local health care system. At lower levels of responsibility, local governments assumed management of primary care and the Health Ministry continued to pay public and private providers of more complex health care services directly. In these lower-level cases, federal transfers to local governments were calculated according to the amount of medical services delivered.

The 1993 NOB incorporated a fine-grained strategy to discourage local government reluctance to accept the transfer of responsibility. On the one hand, under the new norm, local governments had discretion regarding whether and to what degree to adhere to federal health care policies; they could evaluate the costs and benefits attached to each option and choose the level of responsibility that best fit their management capacities and their political interests regarding health care accountability. On the other hand, failure to comply with the system entailed a price: No adhesion meant no money from the Health Ministry. The rule that full and automatic funding transfers would be attached only to the highest level of local responsibility provided local governments with a powerful incentive to take on more complex health care tasks.

Implementing these rules, however, turned out to be very difficult. The incentives described above required increased spending and encouraged more rapid and timely flows of funds to local governments (Carvalho 2001). Nevertheless, funding posed a continuing problem. From mid-1993 on, the Social Security minister, Antônio Britto, simply stopped the mandatory transfer of revenues (about 30 percent of the total) from payroll contributions to the Health Ministry. Since Britto was no longer responsible for health care policy, he had no incentive to implement the transfer (Weyland

1996); and he successfully argued that the revenues were required to solve his own shortfalls in covering pension payments. The 1988 Constitution had mandated new pension benefits for rural workers, and for those over 70 years of age who had never paid contributions.

Britto could thus justify his freeze on transfers by insisting that it was impossible for the payroll tax to cover both expanded pensions and health care funds. Britto's position prevailed within the government, and from that point on, the Health Ministry was dependent on the federal budget for its revenues. This posed additional difficulties, however, because the health minister in office at the time, Jamil Haddad, was politically weak relative to the Finance and Planning Ministries (Goulart 2001). For a time, the Health Ministry compensated for the withheld Social Security revenues by borrowing (Piola and Biasoto 2001), but it could not cover its commitments for financial transfers to the states and municipalities by this means (Lucchese 1996; Levcovitz 2001; Goulart 2001). Meanwhile, bureaucratic opposition within the Health Ministry from former officials of the now dismantled INAMPS slowed decentralization, mainly through excessive administrative and audit requirements regarding funds transfers (Goulart 2001).

Thus, although the 1993 NOB decentralization rules were much more acceptable to state and local governments than earlier rules, their uncertainty as to whether the Health Ministry could actually meet its financial commitments increased the risk of assuming new responsibilities, because these were likely to require additional spending on health facilities and personnel. In spite of this reluctance, by 1997, 3,127 municipalities out of 4,973—63 percent—had accepted the federal decentralization program. However, only 144 chose to undertake the highest level of health task responsibilities (Guimarães 2001, 52).

There was also wide variation across Brazilian states regarding the extent to which municipalities accepted new responsibilities. Some of this variation was attributable to differences in wealth and administrative capacity. But an even more important influence was the strategy of the state governors, and whether they were inclined to increase incentives for decentralization. In states where the governor favored municipalization, state secretaries of health encouraged municipalities to accept the federal norms by helping to cover the costs of installing the resources required to run health care programs. In states where governors opposed the norms, municipalities had to bear the costs of municipalization without state aid, and a much smaller proportion of municipalities accepted new responsibilities (Arretche 2000).

The Cardoso Government, 1995–2002

Until 1996, Health Ministry budget pressures and uncertainties continued to constrain progress in decentralization. In 1996, Cardoso's first health minister, Adib Jatene, won approval of a constitutional amendment creating a new revenue source earmarked for health care, a tax on checks written on banking accounts. Parliamentary approval of this constitutional amendment resulted from a personal two-year effort by the minister, along with *sanitaristas* and local health authorities, to build a broad cross-party alliance in support of health care financing. However, Jatene lacked support for his endeavor within the Cabinet, where the Finance Ministry opposed new taxes, especially ones earmarked for particular spending categories. For a short time after the passage of the amendment, Health Ministry revenues did increase sharply. But in the following year, the Finance and Planning Ministries reduced the funds allocated to the Health Ministry in the federal budget, offsetting the revenues from the new earmarked tax (see tables 6.3 and 6.6). At this point, it was clear to Jatene that his efforts to increase funding had failed, and he resigned from the Cardoso government.[14]

In the meantime, however, Minister Jatene did oversee the formulation of an important new NOB in 1996. The directive took almost a year to develop, and it involved state and municipal health authorities represented by CONASS and CONASEMS, as well as several health care policy stakeholders represented in the National Health Council.[15] A consensual decision rule and the broad representation of interests in the decision-making arena explain the length of the decision-making process (Levcovitz 2001).

From one perspective, the process seemed to show that state and local authorities had succeeded in establishing their voices in health care policy-making; their participation in the revision of NOBs had become a rule of the game. Nevertheless, CONASS and CONASEMS faced difficulties challenging the federal government's proposals for elaborating the 1996

14. Since 1998, the revenues of the Contribuição Provisória sobre as Movimentações Financeiras have not been exclusively devoted to health care.

15. There are two national councils with institutional authority over the formulation and execution of the health policy. The National Health Council has thirty-two members and includes representatives from civil society, state, health workers, and health providers. As representatives from state and municipal-level governments, CONASS and CONASEMS are represented on this council; each one has one seat. CIT, in turn, is a kind of federative arena, with fifteen members (five from each government level), and it is entitled to make decisions on decentralization measures.

Table 6.6
Health Ministry Spending, Per Capita and as Percentage of Gross Domestic Product, Brazil, 1993–99

Year	Millions of Reais (indexed, December 1998)	Index	Per Capita (reais, indexed, December 1998)	Percentage of Gross Domestic Product
1993	12,822	100	85.0	2.11
1994	13,021	102	85.2	2.15
1995	18,614	145	120.1	2.31
1996	16,154	126	102.8	1.85
1997	19,394	151	121.8	2.14
1998	17,665	138	109.5	1.94
1999	18,375	143	113.8	2.06

Sources: Piola and Biasotto (2001, 221); the data are from the Sistema Integrado de Administração Financeira.

NOB, because they were fundamentally dependent on the ministry. The councils' staff, offices, and operational resources are located within, and funded by, the ministry.

Moreover, the ministry has been able to go around some of the 1996 NOB provisions with unilateral administrative rulings. Although the 1996 NOB was published in November 1996, it did not go into effect until the beginning of 1998. In the interim, a new minister, Carlos Albuquerque, enacted a series of unilateral administrative norms that significantly changed the content of the NOB decree. This strategy was used again later by Cardoso's third health minister, Jose Serra (1998–2002) (Levcovitz 2001).

Thus, despite the formal incorporation of local representatives into policymaking bodies, in practice they were bypassed after the initial formulation of the 1996 NOB (Carvalho 2001). The fact that the Health Ministry is an actor that controls resources essential to the states and municipalities, including those going to their representatives in decision-making councils, enables it to dominate policymaking. The extent to which state and municipal demands and proposals are incorporated into federal policies is determined mainly by the will and political orientation of the minister of health.

One of the most important changes that the ministry unilaterally introduced in the 1996 NOB dealt with the procedures governing the transfer of funds to states and municipalities. The transfers were divided into several different programs, and local governments were obliged to meet the requirements of each program in order to receive the full amount of funding to which they were entitled[16] (Barros 2001; Levcovitz 2001). In addition, the Cardoso government instituted impressive improvements in health care evaluation and auditing, which allowed the Health Ministry to exercise more fine-grained oversight of the performance of state and municipal health care programs.

States and municipalities retained the option of selecting the level of responsibility for which they would qualify. However, after 1998 they had only two choices: to take over all primary health care tasks; or to be accountable for the whole local health care system, including contracting and paying specialized hospitals and clinics. The health transfers are automatic as long as municipalities satisfy the appropriate requirements, but the amount of the transfers varies according to the level of health care tasks taken over. In other words, although local governments were guaranteed autonomy within the federal system, they would have to pay a price in financial transfers for failing to adhere to the federal rules of health care decentralization.

This price in 2000 was higher than in the early 1990s, because all municipalities had already taken over at least some health care responsibilities. If a local government chose not to comply with 1996 NOB rules, it would have to bear the political costs of leaving the SUS project and the fiscal costs of providing health care on its own budget. Yet compliance with federal health care rules limited the control of local governments over their own health care programs.

The 1996 NOB also incorporated stronger incentives for preventive and public health programs. States and municipalities were entitled to receive additional funds if they introduced certain components, such as public health programs, into their local services. Hiring medical teams to practice home care and preventive health care activities also allowed municipalities to get additional resources, according to the number of medical teams installed. Attractive wages for practitioners were also an incentive for adopting preventive care programs (Levcovitz 2001). These programs, called the Health Community Agents Program (Programa de Agentes Comunitários de Saúde, PACS) and the Family Health Program (Programa de Saúde da Família, PSF), were governed by detailed ministry rules, so

16. The 1996 NOB introduced two different kinds of transfers to municipalities: a fixed and automatic one, calculated on a per capita basis, and a variable one, which is broken into different programs (preventive care, pharmaceutical supply, nutritional programs, and sanitary programs).

municipalities had little discretion regarding their implementation (Barros 2001; Carvalho 2001). Local governments that did not adopt these programs forfeited a large share of their federal health care transfers. As of May 2002, 99.6 percent—5,537 of 5,560—Brazilian municipalities had complied with the 1996 NOB rules;[17] 564 assumed responsibility for the entire system, and 4,973 chose the lower-level option.

The cumulative effects of the health care decentralization policies developed throughout the 1990s clearly played an important role in this result, but the specific incentives created by the 1996 NOBs' decentralization rules were very important as well. The new rules have given additional money to 66 percent of the Brazilian municipalities and were fiscally neutral in 22 percent of them (Costa, Silva, and Ribeiro 1999, 45). Because municipalities have discretion to comply or not, and because they calculate the costs and benefits of being accountable for public policies, the additional resources they received for meeting the Health Ministry requirements must have been regarded as an advantageous trade-off.

A stronger minister of health is an additional factor explaining these results. In comparison with his predecessors, Minister Jose Serra was much better able to defend his budget, probably due to his close relation to President Cardoso and to the expectation that he might run in the 2002 presidential elections (which he actually did). Thus, despite pressure for fiscal cutbacks coming from Finance Minister Pedro Malan, Serra was in a relatively good position to make ministry regulations credible to the municipalities.[18] From 1993 to 1998, the proportion of transfers to municipalities within the Ministry of Health's budget rose from 1.7 to 24 percent (Piola and Biasoto 2001, 223). In 1998, the Health Ministry's transfers to municipalities to finance primary health care were R$1.3 billion; in 1999,

17. The only important exception was São Paulo City, the biggest and richest city in the country, whose mayor, Paulo Maluf (1993–97), intended to run for president. He developed an alternative health care policy designed to be a sort of presidential marketing. Marta Suplicy, the mayor from the Partido dos Trabalhadores, who took office in 2001, nominated as local health secretary an SUS supporter, Eduardo Jorge, and quickly adhered to SUS.

18. Jose Serra was planning minister (1995–96) during the first term of President Cardoso and health minister in the second one (1999–2002), whereas Pedro Malan was the finance minister during President Cardoso's two terms. Conflicts between them went far beyond their respective institutional incentives, i.e., beyond the fact that the former had political incentives to spend and the latter, to cut down spending. In fact, they belonged to different groups within President Cardoso's governing coalition.

they jumped to R\$2.3 billion; in 2000, they went to R\$3 billion; and again in 2001, to R\$3.6 billion (extracted from Datasus). Therefore, they almost tripled in current values during Serra's term.

In short, the cumulative effects of long term health care decentralization policies, the incentives created by new ministry rules in the late 1990s, and the Health Ministry's increased capacity to make credible commitments explain the fact that in 2001 all Brazilian municipalities had qualified for the federal health care decentralization program, although they had the political autonomy to reject them.

The Health Ministry's capacity to control local policies in detail was also shown through two initiatives: the enactment of a new NOB in 2001 and the approval of a constitutional amendment in 2000 that obliges all government levels to spend specified proportions of their budgets on health care. The Health Ministry's new Operational Norm reassigns health care responsibilities according to their complexity, assigning the most complex tasks to federal or state management and removing responsibility for the payment of more complex health care services from local governments (Barros 2001). This change was motivated mainly by the fact that only 10 percent of the Brazilian municipalities had taken on responsibility for the entire system of local health care, and there were no hospitals in more than 2,000 municipalities. Regionalization of hospital services is viewed as a better way to organize their supply. However, as of 2002 the new norm had not been implemented.

The constitutional amendment provided that, as of 2001, states and municipalities would be obliged to spend at least 7 percent of their revenues on health care, and that by 2005 these shares would increase to 12 and 15 percent respectively. The federal government was also required to spend 5 percent more in 2001 than it did in 2000; and from 2002 to 2005 federal health spending is to increase in step with inflation and variation in gross domestic product (Piola and Biasoto 2001; Medici 2002).

Significantly, the initiative for the amendment came not from the Ministry of Health but from a Workers' Party representative, who gained support of the health policy community and from a broad alliance in the legislature. In fact, since his days as a constitutional deputy in 1988, Serra himself had been a long-standing opponent of earmarked spending. After several years as minister of health, however, Serra also came to support the amendment, with the expectation that constitutional guarantees for levels of health spending could serve as a defense against fiscal cutbacks advocated by the finance minister, Pedro Malan. In this respect, the constitutional amendment represented a victory for the Health Ministry over the Ministry of the Economy.

Health Care Reform Achievements and Shortcomings

In Brazil, the middle and upper classes as well as the best-organized workers get health care through private health insurance plans. According to the Instituto Brasileiro de Opinião Pública e Estatística, only 14 percent of people with college degrees use SUS exclusively or frequently, as compared with 74 percent of those that had not finished elementary school and 63 percent of those that did not complete high school (see table 6.7).

Thus, it seems that the SUS goal of universal entitlement to health care turned out to be a way to improve poor people's access to care. Even this goal has not been met completely, because 12 percent of those who did not finish elementary school still do not use SUS (see table 6.7). Nevertheless, the overall record shows significant improvements as well as continuing challenges.

As a result of increased access to health care, the proportion of pregnant women receiving assistance in delivery increased from 76 to 88 percent between 1986 and 1996 (Medici 2002). Infant mortality rates, for both males and females, dropped impressively from 1980 on throughout Brazil,[19] although present infant mortality rates reflect measures of health care reform initiated in early 1980s.

Yet these rates continue to be very uneven among and within the Brazilian regions. Infant mortality rates in the Northeast Region are still twice the rates in the Southern Region—58 deaths compared with 22 per 1,000 births in 1998. Moreover, some municipalities within the Northeast states (e.g., Maranhão, Alagoas, Paraíba, Rio Grande do Norte) have infant mortality rates similar to African countries (more than 100 deaths per 1,000 births), whereas in some municipalities in Rio Grande do Sul, infant mortality rates are similar to those in Chile and Costa Rica (15 deaths per 1,000

19. From 1975 to 1980, infant mortality rate dropped 17.2 percent: from 100 to 82.8 deaths per 1,000 births. In the period 1980–85, the reduction in the infant mortality rate was 24 percent (from 82.8 to 62.9 deaths per 1,000 births). In 1985–90, it dropped 23.7 percent (from 62.9 to 48 deaths per 1,000 births), and in 1990–95, another 23.9 percent (from 48 to 36.5 deaths per 1,000 births). In 1995–2000, the rate of reduction slowed down to 18.9 percent (from 36.5 to 29.6 deaths per 1,000 births). These data are from IBGE (1998).

Table 6.7

Access to Unified Health System (SUS) by Level of Education, Brazil, 1998 (percent of population)

Degree of SUS Use	Incomplete Elementary School	Elementary School Graduate to Incomplete High School	High School Graduate to Some Higher Education	Higher Education Graduate	Total
Exclusive	54	41	24	5	40
Frequent	20	22	22	9	21
Rare	14	23	35	38	23
Nonuser	12	14	19	48	16
Total	100	100	100	100	100

Source: Medici (2002); data are from the Instituto Brasileiro de Opinião Pública e Estatística.

births) (Medici 2002). Life expectancy indicators show similar trends; they have improved sharply from 1980 to 1999, but the unevenness among regions remains. The Northeast still presents the lowest life expectancy index among Brazilian regions; in 1999, it was 65.5 years in the Northeast, whereas Brazil's index was 68.4.

As was noted above, by 2000, the reformers had succeeded in incorporating all of Brazil's municipalities into the unified health system and most municipalities had greatly expanded their responsibilities for health care administration. In 2000, the municipalities delivered more than 80 percent of primary health services and managed more than 70 percent of the primary health care establishments in all Brazilian states—except for Roraima, Acre, and Amazonas, all in the North Region (Arretche and Marques 2001). Public spending on health care has also been decentralized; the federal government raised 73.2 percent of total public funds for health care in 1985, whereas this figure for 1996 was 53.7 percent (see table 6.3). Moreover, the federal government was responsible for 67 percent of total spending on health care in 1985, whereas it spent 45.7 percent in 1996 (see table 6.4).

There has also been some decentralization of specialized health care establishments. In 1992, SUS municipal hospitals accounted for 13.6 percent of all hospitals. The proportion increased to 25 percent in 2001, whereas federal hospitals decreased from 2.3 to 0.7 percent and state hospitals from 12.2 to 9.9 percent of all hospitals (see table 6.8). Health Ministry spending on investment—which includes building of new hospitals—remained below 1.5 percent of total Health Ministry spending from 1993 to 1998 (Piola and Biasoto 2001, 223). Due to recurrent Health Ministry

Table 6.8

Percent of Unified Health System Spending on Hospital Health Care by Hospital Type and Region, Brazil, 2001

Type	North	Northeast	Southeast	South	Center-West	Brazil
Federal	0.5	0.1	0.7	0.0	0.0	0.4
State	20.3	17.1	15.1	1.9	12.1	13.2
Municipal	17.8	15.9	8.3	4.1	10.1	10.0
Private	32.8	29.8	18.3	25.3	34.3	24.3
Philanthropic	22.8	21.9	38.1	35.0	21.4	31.6
University	5.5	15.1	19.5	33.7	22.0	20.5
Union	0.3	0.1	0.0	0.0	0.0	0.0
Region/Brazil	5.2	24.4	44.6	18.6	7.2	100

Source: Datasus.

financing crises throughout the 1990s, the ministry's price chart for medical services remained below market prices. Moreover, the ministry strengthened its audit and control procedures against frauds. As a result, many for-profit health care providers decided to discontinue their contracts with the SUS, and the proportion of private hospitals among all SUS hospitals dropped from 46.7 percent in 1992 to 35.2 percent in 2001 (see table 6.9).

The for-profit health care providers contracting-out movement has also brought about a slight change in the regional distribution of the SUS hospital supply. As private providers' participation sharply decreased from 1992 to 2001 in the Southeast and South Regions, the proportion of private hospitals among the Northeast Region's SUS hospitals increased (see table 6.9).

SUS spending on hospital health care is still heavily concentrated in the Southeast Region—which received 44.6 percent of total SUS spending on hospital health services in 2001 (see table 6.8). Yet Brazil's population is also concentrated in this region; 42.6 percent of Brazilians live there. In fact, spending on health care follows closely the population distribution in Brazil (see table 6.10).

SUS spending on hospital health care is also concentrated on private and philanthropic hospitals (most of them are classified as philanthropic but are in fact for-profit hospital establishments). Together, these categories received 56 percent of total SUS spending on all hospital care in 2001. This is because the best-equipped hospitals are either private or philanthropic and are mainly located in the Southeast Region (Barros 2001; Arretche and Marques 2001).

Table 6.9

Unified Health System Hospitals by Region and Type, Brazil, 1992 and 2001 (percent)

Type	North		Northeast		Southeast		South		Center-West		Brazil	
	1992	2001	1992	2001	1992	2001	1992	2001	1992	2001	1992	2001
Federal	9.6	2.9	2.7	0.4	2.3	1.0	0.5	0.1	0.2	0.0	2.3	0.7
State	44.8	29.6	21.6	14.0	5.7	7.1	1.9	2.1	3.9	3.2	12.2	9.9
Municipal	13.4	30.6	18.5	35.5	12.1	16.8	8.1	13.7	16.0	29.7	13.6	25.2
Private	26.1	28.0	37.8	31.7	46.7	29.1	56.8	43.3	67.2	53.8	46.7	35.2
Philanthropic	5.4	7.8	17.5	16.5	30.6	43.0	31.8	37.5	12.1	11.9	23.4	26.6
University	0.7	0.8	1.9	1.8	2.5	3.1	1.0	3.3	0.7	1.3	1.7	2.3
Union	0.0	0.2	0.0	0.1	0.1	0.0	0.0	0.0	0.0	0.0	0.0	0.0
Region/Brazil	7.1	7.8	29.7	34.4	32.8	29.0	20.6	17.3	9.9	11.4	100	100

Source: Datasus.

Marta Arretche

Table 6.10

Brazil's Population by Region, 2000

Region	Population	Percent
North	12,900,704	7.6
Northeast	47,741,711	28.1
Southeast	72,412,411	42.6
South	25,107,616	14.8
Center-West	11,636,728	6.9
Brazil	169,799,170	100

Source: IBGE. (2000), Demographic Census.

Conclusions

The politics of Brazilian health care reform can be divided into two phases. In the first phase, the health care reformers were able to incorporate their goals into constitutional and legal mandates. In this phase, the main arenas of policy reform were the Constituent Assembly and the Congress. The objective adopted was to replace the previous centralized, social insurance–based health care model by a free, universal, and decentralized system. In the second phase, these constitutional mandates were implemented, and the executive power replaced the parliament as the main decision-making arena.

Policy legacies played a role in both phases. The health care policies of the military regime provided guaranteed demand for for-profit providers of specialized health services. As a result, the private hospitals associations had been of great importance in shaping the health reform goals; in the Constituent Assembly, they fiercely fought changes that would reduce their privileged position within the public health care system. The negative evaluation of both the performance and decision-making rules of the previous health care model also shaped reformers' goals and strategies.

The legacy of earlier health care policies also strongly influenced the implementation of decentralization, because the consequence of the earlier centralized model was that many municipalities lacked bureaucratic capability, health facilities, and health management institutions to assume expanded responsibilities. It was mainly the federal branch that had installed skilled health care bureaucracies, which were able to formulate innovative policies to answer to reform challenges. The weaknesses of local level bureaucracies vis-à-vis the federal one contributed to the dominance of the Health Ministry in postreform policymaking.

The implementation phase also implied a switch of the main arena of decision making, because most decisions were to be made by the Health Ministry's bureaucracy. Moreover, because the National Health Laws stated that the Health Ministry would be in charge of the SUS's financing and coordination, the Health Ministry became not only the main arena of decision making but also the most powerful actor. Acknowledging this fact, state and local health authorities focused their attention on establishing decision-making rules that strengthened their institutional participation in health care decisions, whereas the Health Ministry attempted to bypass them.

The position of the main actors within the health reform arena has sharply changed as decentralization reform has proceeded. In the mid-1980s, the most important cleavage aligned left-wing health experts and local health authorities, on one side, against private health care providers and INAMPS (the federal Social Security agency), on the other. The decentralization policy and the termination of INAMPS (after merger into the Ministry of Health) was a successful strategy to weaken the influence of for-profit health providers in this policy arena. Thus, from 1990 on, bargaining between levels of government became the most important area of conflict, and the federal Health Ministry and local authorities moved to the center of the stage. There has also been a change in the political influence within the reform coalition; as states and municipalities have taken over health care responsibilities, they have replaced the left-wing experts' influence in policymaking. Moreover, the *sanitarist* movement has broken up into several groups that no longer have a unified strategy for health care reform.

The full decentralization of health care was achieved in 2001 with all Brazilian municipalities providing health care through a unified health care system coordinated by the Health Ministry. This outcome is the result of the cumulative effects of long-term health care decentralization efforts, the incentives built into the decentralization rules, and the increased capacity by the late 1990s for the Health Ministry to make credible commitments about the flow of funds to the states and municipalities. Altogether, these factors have been able to overcome local government resistance to assuming full health care responsibilities.

Brazilian health care reform has been implemented under intense austerity pressures. Yet the successive Health Ministry financial crises are better explained by conflicts within governmental coalitions and among ministries than as a direct result of the adjustment policies. In other words, though austerity pressures did constrain progress in implementing the health care system reforms mandated at the beginning of the 1990s, the Health Ministry's financial problems (and its resulting difficulties with implementing decentralizing reforms) also—and perhaps to a larger degree—reflected the varying attitudes of successive governments regarding the desirability and priority of reforming the health care system.

References

Arretche, Marta T. S. 2000. *Estado federativo e políticas sociais: Determinantes da descentralização.* Rio de Janeiro: Revan.

———. 2001. Federalismo, legado de políticas prévias e arenas decisórias: A reforma dos programas sociais. Paper presented at the Twenty-Sixth Meeting of the Associação Nacional de Pós-Graduação em Ciências Sociais, Caxambu, n.d.

Arretche, Marta, and Eduardo Marques. 2001. *La municipalización de la salud en Brasil: Diferencias regionales, poder do voto y estrategias del gobierno.* Série de relatórios técnicos 77. Washington, D.C.: Organização Pan-Americana da Saúde.

Bahia, Ligia. 2001a. O mercado de planos e seguros de saúde no Brasil: Tendências posregulamentação. In *Radiografia da saúde,* ed. Barjas Negri and Geraldo di Giovanni. Campinas: Instituto de Economia.

———. 2001b. Planos privados de saúde: Luzes e sombras no debate setorial dos anos 90. *Ciência e saúde coletiva* 6, no. 2: 14–25.

Banting, Keith, and Stan Corbett. 2003. Federalismo y politicas de atención a la salud. In *Federalismo y políticas de salud: Descentralización y relaciones intergubernamentales desde una perspectiva comparada,* ed. Fórum das Federações / Institucional Nacional para el Federalismo y el Desarrollo Municipal. Mexico City: Fórum das Federações / Institucional Nacional para el Federalismo y el Desarrollo Municipal.

Barros, Elizabeth. 2001. Implementação do SUS: Recentralizar será o caminho? *Ciência e saúde coletiva* 6, no. 2: 18–21.

Bodstein, Regina. 2001. Desafios na implementação do SUS nos anos 90. *Ciência e saúde coletiva* 6, no. 2: 26–29.

Carvalho, Gilson. 2001. A inconstitucional administração pós-constitucional do SUS através de normas operacionais. *Ciência e saúde coletiva* 6, no. 2: 1–10.

Cohn, Amélia. 2001. Questionando o consenso sanitário. *Ciência e saúde coletiva* 6, no. 2: 9–11.

Cordeiro, Hesio, 2001. Descentralização, universalidade e equidadenas reformas da saúde. *Ciência e saúde coletiva* 6, no. 2: 29–31.

Cordoni, Luiz, Jr. 2001. Política de saúde nos anos 90 e a reforma sanitária—considerações sobre o artigo "política de saúde nos anos 90: relações intergovernamentais e o papel das Normas Operacionais Básicas." *Ciência e saúde coletiva* 6, no. 2: 32–35.

Costa, Nilson do Rosário. 2001. A descentralização do sistema público de saúde no Brasil: Balanço e perspectiva. In *Radiografia da saúde,* ed. Barjas Negri and Geraldo di Giovanni. Campinas: Instituto de Economia.

Costa, N. R., P. L. B. Silva, and José Mendes Ribeiro. 1999. A descentralização do sistema de saúde no Brasil. *Revista do serviço público* 50, no. 3: 33–56.

Draibe, Sônia M. 1994. As políticas sociais do regime militar brasileiro. In *25 anos de regime militar*, ed. Gláucio Soares, A. Dillon, and Maria Celina D. Araújo. Rio de Janeiro: Fundação Getúlio Vargas.

———. 2001. A experiência brasileira recente de reforma dos programas sociais. *Socialis* 5: 131–58.

Draibe, S. M.; M. H. G. Castro, and B. Azeredo. 1991. O sistema de proteção social brasileiro. Research Report for the Social Policies for the Urban Poor in Southern Latin America project. Kellogg Institute, University of Notre Dame, Notre Dame, Ind. (unpublished).

Duarte, Cristina Maria Rabelais. 2001. A assistência médica suplementar no Brasil: História e características da coopertiva de trabalho médico Unimed. In *Radiografia da saúde*, ed. Barjas Negri and Geraldo di Giovanni. Campinas: Instituto de Economia.

Elias, Paulo Eduardo. 2001. Afinal, de que descentralização falamos. *Ciência e saúde coletiva* 6, no. 2: 21–24.

Esping-Andersen, Gosta. 1999. *Social Foundations of Postindustrial Economies.* Oxford: Oxford University Press.

Evans, P. B., D. Rueschemeyer, and T. Skocpol. 1985. *Bringing the State Back In.* Cambridge: Cambridge University Press.

Fagnani, Eduardo. 1996. Política social e pactos conservadores no Brasil 1964–92. *Desafios da gestão pública paulista* (Cadernos Fundap) 21: 59–102.

Furtado, A. T., and J. H. Souza. 2001. Evolução do setor de insumos e equipamentos médico-hospitalares, laboratoriais e odontológicos no Brasil: A década de 90. In *Radiografia da saúde*, ed. Barjas Negri and Geraldo di Giovanni. Campinas: Instituto de Economia.

Goulart, Flavio A. A. 2001. Esculpindo o SUS a golpes de portaria . . . considerações sobre o processo de formulação das NOBs. *Ciência e saúde coletiva* 6, no. 2: 1–7.

Guimarães, Luisa. 1995. Indução de novas práticas de gestão do sistema de saúde: Análise do componente normativo do Ministério da Saúde. Monografia de Conclusão de Curso de Especialização, Universidade de Brasília.

———. 2001. Arquitetura da cooperação intergovernamental: Os consorcios de saúde de Mato Grosso. Dissertação de Mestrado, Escola Naicional de Saúde Pública.

Hall, Peter. 1993. Policy Paradigms, Social Learning, and the State: The Case of Economic Policymaking in Britain. *Comparative Politics,* April, 275–96.

Héritier, Adrienne. 1999. *Policy-Making and Diversity in Europe.* Cambridge: Cambridge University Press.

IBGE (Instituto Brasileiro de Geografia e Estatística). 1998. *Pesquisa nacional por amostra de domicílios.* Rio de Janeiro: IBGE.

Immergut, Ellen M. 1996 As regras do jogo: A lógica da política de saúde na França, na Suíça e na Suécia. *Revista brasileira de ciências sociais* 30, no. 11: 139–63.

Kaufman, Robert R., and Alex Segura-Ubiergo. 2001. Globalização, política interna e gasto social na América Latina. *Dados* 44, no. 3: 435–79.

Levcovitz, Eduardo, Luciana Lima, and Cristiani Machado. 2001. Política de saúde nos anos 90: Relações intergovernamentais e o papel das Normas Operacionais Básicas. *Ciência e saúde coletiva* 6, no. 2: 40–59.

Lucchese, Patricia. 1996. Descentralização do financiamento e da gestão da Assistência saúde no Brasil: A implementação do sistema único de saúde. *Planejamento e políticas públicas,* no. 14: 75–156.

Medici, Andre. 2001. La asistencia sanitaria en el federalismo brasileño. Paper presented at a conference, Federalismo e Políticas de Saúde, São Paulo.

———. 2002. El desafío de la descentralización: Financiamiento público de la salud en Brasil. Washington, D.C.: Inter-American Development Bank.

Mesa-Lago, C. 1978. *Social Security in Latin America: Pressure Groups, Stratification and Inequality.* Pittsburgh: University of Pittsburgh Press.

NEPP (Núcleo de Estudos em Políticas Públicas). 1989. *Brasil 1987: Relatório sobre a situação social do país.* Campinas: UNICAMP.

Piola, Sergio Francisco, and Geraldo Biasoto Jr. 2001. Financiamento do SUS nos anos 90. In *Radiografia da saúde,* ed. Barjas Negri and Geraldo di Giovanni. Campinas: Instituto de Economia.

Pierson, P. 1994. *Dismantling the Welfare State? Reagan, Thatcher, and the Politics of Retrenchment.* Cambridge: Cambridge University Press.

———. 2000. Increasing Returns, Path Dependence, and the Study of Politics. *American Political Science Review* 94, no. 2: 251–67.

———, ed. 2001. *The New Politics of the Welfare State.* Oxford: Oxford University Press.

Queiroz, S., and Alexis Gonzales Velazquez. 2001. Mudanças recentes na estrutura produtiva da indústria farmacêutica. In *Radiografia da saúde,* ed. Barjas Negri and Geraldo di Giovanni. Campinas: Instituto de Economia.

Shah, Anwar. 1991. *The New Fiscal Federalism in Brazil.* World Bank Discussion Paper 124. Washington, D.C.: World Bank.

Skocpol, T. 1992. *Protecting Soldiers and Mothers.* Cambridge, Mass.: Harvard University Press.

Tsebelis, George. 1990. *Nested Games.* Berkeley: University of California Press.

Vianna, Maria Lúcia Teixeira Werneck. 1998. *A Americanização (perversa) da seguridade social no Brasil.* Rio de Janeiro: Revan.

Weyland, K. 1996. *Democracy without Equity.* Pittsburgh: University of Pittsburgh Press.

Willis, E., C. Garman, and S. Haggard. 1991. The Politics of Decentralization in Latin America. *Latin America Research Review* 34, no. 1: 7–56.

Chapter 7

Reinforcing a Public System: Health Sector Reform in Costa Rica

Mary A. Clark

The Costa Rican health sector is dominated by the state. A single public institution monopolizes health insurance and provides most of the curative and preventative services available in the country. The health sector reforms of the 1990s are unusual among Latin American cases because Costa Rican authorities rejected key aspects of the regional reform agenda, such as privatization and decentralization. The ideological orientation of the team that developed the reforms, the popularity of the national health system among all segments of society, and the autonomy of that public institution, the Caja Costarricense de Seguro Social, all contributed to this decision. Instead, Costa Rican health reforms have sought to improve the public system by completely overhauling the primary care network and deconcentrating administrative responsibility.

This chapter traces the political process of health sector reform in Costa Rica. After a summary of the history and organization of the sector as well as the major problems it faced on the eve of reform, the chapter maps the evolution of the health reforms begun in the 1990s. The description begins with the reform program's intellectual origins and negotiation with the World Bank and continues through two stages of implementation. Five important themes emerge from the Costa Rican "story."

First, the health reforms reflect a mix of priorities dating from the original negotiations between the Costa Rican government and the World Bank. Whereas the Costa Ricans were concerned to restructure primary care and steer more resources toward that level, the World Bank representatives pushed for the separation of the purchasing and providing functions within the public system as well as other institutional modifications. Second, we can see the importance of "change teams" in directing the health reforms toward particular goals. The turnover of political appointments resulting from the change of government in 1998 led to the substitution of one change team and its priorities by another. Third, the reforms that focused on expanding and improving primary health care moved rapidly, while those aimed at deconcentration and efficiency progressed very slowly. Fourth, the actual degree of independent decision making for operating units under deconcentration has been quite limited. Fifth, consistent with Costa Rican political traditions, both sets of reforms entailed extensive consultation and negotiation with stakeholders, after the basic character of the reforms had been determined.

National Context

For the past half-century, a stable two-party system has dominated the Costa Rican political scene. Despite the rise in voter abstention and support for minor parties (Seligson 2002), political consensus and respect for human and civil rights are still strong in comparison with the rest of the region. Costa Rica also stands out because of the degree of consensus about the positive achievements of its welfare state and the desirability of continuing the public finance and delivery of its main benefits (health, education, and, for the most part, pensions). The public health system, arguably the best in Latin America, is the crown jewel of Costa Rica's welfare state. Despite its faults, the health system is extremely popular among the citizenry and business community.

The stability of the party system, the endurance of consensual politics, and the support for the welfare state are all the more impressive given that they survived the acute economic crisis of the early 1980s and a subsequent twenty years of fiscal austerity and structural adjustment. The economic crisis helped to motivate the health reforms of the 1990s by both reducing state spending on health and heightening concern about the efficiency of public services. Nevertheless, the initiative and focus of Costa Rica's health reforms were largely sectoral and were not explicitly linked to a broader agenda of state reform until the administration of President Miguel Angel Rodríguez (1998–2002).

Organization of the Costa Rican Health Sector

The state dominates health insurance, employment, and provision in Costa Rica. The Caja Costarricense de Seguro Social (CCSS, Costa Rican Social Security Fund), a public institution, virtually monopolizes the domestic health insurance market as well as administering the national pension system. The CCSS also provides most of the country's curative services via 240 clinics, 29 hospitals, and 5,924 beds (Ickis, Sevilla, and Iñiguez 1997, 83; CCSS 2001b, 56). Membership in and financing for the public health insurance system are employment based. For formal-sector employees, membership is mandatory and quotas are based on an individual's wages and paid by employers (9.25 percent), workers (5.5 percent), and the state (0.25 percent). Self-employed and informal-sector workers are encouraged to join the CCSS's voluntary plans. Such workers pay between 5.75 and 13.75 percent of their salaries for health insurance, depending on income. The CCSS's health insurance programs enroll 67 percent of the economically active population and 89 percent of the total population. The latter figure includes workers' dependents as well as indigent persons who are provided free care under special regimes. Thus slightly more than 10 percent of the population, composed of agricultural laborers, informal-sector workers, self-employed professionals, and business owners, lives without public health insurance (Piza Rocafort 2001, 83). Nevertheless, uninsured people do use public health facilities, especially hospitals.[1]

1. Cercone, Durán, and Briceño (2001, 47). Hospitals are supposed to charge uninsured people for services, but this is not always done, especially when the patient is a foreigner. In addition, uninsured people will sometimes begin to pay social security contributions the month before being admitted for hospital procedures in order to be fully covered, and then discontinue payments immediately afterward.

Although more than 90 percent of Costa Rican doctors work for the state, a third of them also have private practices and there are six small private hospitals with a total of 196 beds.[2] Payments for private health goods and services, mostly medicines, dentistry, and office visits, account for 26 percent of total health spending (Cercone, Durán, and Briceño 2001, 37). Hospitalization and insurance account for only 4 percent of private health expenditures.[3] A very small number of people, mostly executives and the professional staffs of multinational corporations, carry foreign insurance policies. In addition, the state insurance institute, the Instituto Nacional de Seguros, sells private domestic medical insurance policies; but these account for less than 1 percent of private health spending (Cercone, Durán, and Briceño 2001, 65). It is illegal for private domestic companies to directly sell medical insurance.

The CCSS is one of Costa Rica's many "semiautonomous" institutions, meaning that its budget is separate from that of the central government and its policies are determined by a tripartite board.[4] The CCSS employs than 31,000 people (CCSS 2001a, 68) and manages a budget equivalent to nearly one-quarter of that of the central government.[5] It is a highly centralized institution, with all finance, management, and personnel resources and decisions emanating from the San José headquarters. Although the president, division managers, and regional directors are political appointees and change with each incoming government, other CCSS positions are not subject to political patronage, and the institution is regarded as highly professional. The CCSS is also Costa Rica's most independent government institution. Constitutionally, its board of directors has complete autonomy from government interference in selecting institutional policies. And legal reforms passed in 2000 gave employer and worker organizations the power to choose their own representatives to

2. Trejos et al. (1994, 56); Ickis, Sevilla, and Iñiguez (1997, 108); and interview with Eduardo Flores, president, Colegio de Médicos y Cirujanos de Costa Rica, San José, December 8, 2001.

3. Cercone, Durán, and Briceño (2001, 37), based on the author's calculations from the data in table 5.5.

4. The CCSS board of directors has nine members: three government officials, three from the business chambers, and three representing workers (one from the labor unions, one from the *solidarista* employees' groups, and one from the cooperative sector). The executive president of the CCSS is a member and chair of the board.

5. This is based on the author's calculations of data from Contraloría General de la República (2001); the data refer to the 2000 budget.

the board, although the president's Cabinet still chooses the government representatives.

The Ministry of Health shares responsibility for public health with the CCSS. The ministry formulates policy for the sector, regulates medical markets, coordinates disease eradication efforts, monitors food and water quality, and conducts public health campaigns. In spite of the ministry's formal policy role, however, it has no real power over the CCSS. Until 1973, the Ministry of Health was more powerful in the realm of health policy than the CCSS, because it indirectly controlled almost all the public hospitals. With the exception of the CCSS's own four hospitals, all public hospitals were administered by individual *juntas de protección social,* quasi-public bodies overseen by the Ministry of Health and funded by proceeds from the national lottery and various taxes and transfers from the central government. But legislation passed in 1973 transferred all public hospitals to the CCSS, and the ministry was left without any control over their funding or administration. The ministry did maintain a position in the direct delivery of health services with the expansion of its health posts and mobile teams that was part of the drive toward universalization in the 1970s. But over time, CCSS clinics came to operate in many of the same areas as the ministry health posts, and one of the objects of reform, discussed below, has been to eliminate overlapping services. Tables 7.1 and 7.2 illustrate the long-term decline in the Ministry of Health's resources and direct involvement in health services.

Antecedents to the Current Reforms

In the decades after its inception, the public health system all but wiped out the infectious diseases and infant diarrhea once responsible for high mortality rates in a young population. As figure 7.1 shows, during the second half of the twentieth century, life expectancy lengthened while infant mortality rates dropped precipitously. The Costa Rican health system is also notable for its success in shrinking the gap between the quality of care afforded to urban and rural dwellers. And these achievements have been gained in a relatively cost-effective manner; currently, health expenditures per capita total $285.[6] In 1998, public health spending and private health

6. Pan American Health Organization, online data generator; www.paho.org/ English/SHA/CoreData/Tabulator/.

Table 7.1

Trends in the Provision of Inpatient Beds in Hospitals and Clinics, Costa Rica, 1970, 1990, and 2000

Provider of Beds	1970	1990	2000
Ministerio de Salud	5,659	197	0
CCSS	1,045	6,536	5,924
Private sector	300	124	196
Total	7,004	7,173	6,120

Note: CCSS = Caja Costarricense de Seguro Social.
Sources: Data for 1970 and 1990 are from Miranda Gutiérrez (1994, 133). Data for 2000 are from CCSS (2001b, 56) and an interview with Eduardo Flores, president, Colegio de Médicos y Cirujanos de Costa Rica, San José, December 8, 2001.

Table 7.2

Trends in the Responsibility for Public Health Spending, Costa Rica, 1967, 1980, 1990, and 1999 (percentage of total)

Responsible Agency	1976	1980	1990	1999
Ministerio de Salud	33.7	32.2	11.4	7.4
CCSS	50.9	50.7	77.1	80.2

Note: Percentages do not add to 100 because spending by other agencies on sewerage and water and insurance are omitted. CCSS = Caja Costarricense de Seguro Social.
Sources: Data for 1976, 1980, and 1990 are from Miranda Gutiérrez (1994, 232). Data for 1999 are from Cercone, Durán, and Briceño (2001, 35).

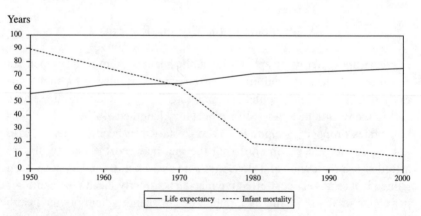

Figure 7.1 Trends in Life Expectancy and Infant Mortality, Costa Rica, 1950–2000 (years)

Sources: Miranda Gutiérrez (1994, 159); Pan American Health Organization data.

expenditure respectively represented 5.5 and 1.9 percent of gross domestic product (GDP).[7]

Despite these achievements, by the 1980s, the Costa Rican system showed the signs of trouble common to mature nation health plans: long waiting lists for diagnostic tests, surgery, and specialist care; deteriorated hospitals and medical equipment; and a demoralized physician corps. From the users' point of view, there is a problem of effective coverage because long waiting lists mean that many do not receive timely care for acute and potentially fatal conditions or reasonable attention for smaller maladies. This situation has given rise to growing inequities in access to medical care as wealthier citizens often bypass the queues by purchasing private services and some people use personal connections to arrange for *biombos* (illegal deals) to secure preferential treatment. There are several reasons for these problems.

One is that the cost of Costa Rican health care has risen dramatically (CCSS 1997, 20). Health care costs are being driven up, as in the rest of the world, by the increased use of sophisticated medical technologies and an aging population. Thanks to the success of the health system in treating and eliminating once-common infant diarrhea and infectious diseases and to declining birth rates, Costa Rica's population is now older, healthier, and living longer. But this older population presents a greater proportion of expensive, chronic, and degenerative diseases. The treatments for these maladies increase the cost of hospital stays, outpatient drug regimens, and physical therapies.

The second problem is that funding did not keep pace with rising costs, especially in the 1980s. The foreign debt crisis and its aftermath resulted in decreased real public spending on health care as a proportion of GDP and in per capita terms for most of the decade. In addition, the CCSS suffered from tax evasion by private employers, large arrears from unpaid state contributions (on behalf of its own employees), and overinvestment in low-yield government bonds throughout the same period (IDB 1992, 31). Insufficient funding contributed to deteriorating service in the regional hospitals, unmet demand in the national hospitals, delays in the acquisition of new technologies, and postponement of repair and replacement of the physical infrastructure. During the past twenty years, CCSS facilities have also felt the strain of serving undocumented Central American immigrants, mostly

7. Cercone, Durán, and Briceño (2001, 37). The last year of available data on the private sector is 1998.

Nicaraguans.[8] The CCSS estimates that the difference between what the immigrants contribute to the system via payroll taxes and the services they receive equals 3.5 percent of the health system's budget (Segnini 1999a).

Finally, this imbalance between costs and resources has been aggravated by internal inefficiencies and inequities. For example, hospital budgets have traditionally been determined at CCSS headquarters on the basis of the previous year's spending, leaving directors little incentive to worry about the quality or cost-effectiveness of their services. And the productivity of the health system's main human resource, doctors, is declining.[9] Doctors attest to feelings of demoralization and apathy as the rough quota system under which they labor lacks incentives that might reward superior work or updated skills. In addition, referrals are not tracked and hospitals do not bill clinics for them. This situation has created a perverse set of incentives for salaried doctors. Many fail to keep up in their fields. Others take shortcuts on CCSS consultations (e.g., by overusing referrals) in order to leave more time for lucrative private practices.[10]

Inequities have also crystallized within the system. Although the problem is not as bad in Costa Rica as in most other Latin American countries, health resources still tend to be concentrated in the capital and its environs, particularly because all the national-level hospitals are located in San José (CCSS 1997, 36). In addition to this imbalance between the capital and outlying areas, there are budgetary imbalances between regions resulting from past decisions. There have been cases where local demands for more spending were granted, leaving certain clinics better endowed than other, similarly situated, units. Inequities have also arisen because areas that were once fast growing received budget increases that were not reduced when they lost population, while others did not gain the extra budgets they should have when populations expanded.[11]

These problems were not fully developed or understood until the early 1990s. But in the 1980s, Costa Rican health officials were aware of overcrowding in the clinics and they began to experiment with alternative forms

8. Segnini (1999b). In 1999, conservative estimates put the number of Nicaraguans living in Costa Rica at 340,000–360,000, or 10 percent of Costa Rica's population.

9. The number of consultations per doctor dropped between 1983 and 1995 (Ickis, Sevilla, and Iñiguez 1997, 93).

10. Interview with Manuel Piza, director of medical administration, Colegio de Médicos y Cirujanos de Costa Rica, San José, July 31, 1997.

11. Interview with Rodolfo Piza, executive president, CCSS, San José, December 4, 2001.

of primary care delivery. The CCSS tried out several "mixed medicine" models involving mechanisms such as cost sharing with patients and employers and contracting out to private doctors' cooperatives. A combination of technical obstacles and bureaucratic politics meant that none of the models would serve as the basis for reform in the 1990s. But the concern with primary care continued to dominate the Costa Rican health agenda into the next decade.

The Reforms of the 1990s

This section describes the reforms of the 1990s. It first discusses their initial design, and then analyzes the two implementation stages and deconcentration in practice.

Initial Design

From the point of view of the Costa Ricans involved in the process, the reforms designed in the early 1990s were motivated by the need for sectoral improvement, specifically in the area of primary care. It was the shortcomings of primary health care toward which attention had been most focused in Costa Rica. Throughout the 1980s, there were media reports about issues such as the long waits for appointments and shortages of medicines in the clinics' pharmacies. The public health system's negative image hit a low point in the first half of Rafael Angel Calderón Fournier's administration (1990–94) with an outbreak of measles and employers threatening to withhold insurance quotas because they were having to pay for private doctor office visits on behalf of employees.[12] In this context, Ministry of Health and CCSS officials invited World Bank representatives to Costa Rica to begin discussions about health sector reform. While the Costa Ricans remained focused on reworking the model of primary care, the World Bank officials emphasized economic efficiency, the separation of purchaser and provider functions, and modernizing payment mechanisms.

In 1993, after two years of negotiations, the government signed a $22 million health sector loan package with the World Bank.[13] The package

12. Interview with Alvaro Salas, former executive president of the CCSS, San José, December 5, 2001.
13. The government signed a $42 million loan package with the Inter-American Development Bank the same year. Most of this loan was earmarked for the construction

contained three major components: (1) reorganization of the primary care model; (2) separation of the purchaser and provider roles, coupled with deconcentration of considerable authority and responsibility to operating units; and (3) modernization of payment mechanisms. This package effectively represented a compromise between Costa Rican officials and World Bank negotiators.[14] The Costa Ricans had no objections to upgrading payment collection technology. But they agreed to deconcentration only because the actual mechanisms to be used in formalizing purchasing relationships and creating an internal market were left vague in the loan document and because the final agreement represented a giant retreat from the World Bank's initial proposal of privatization.

During the negotiations, the World Bank had paid for Chilean consultants to offer recommendations about how to make the CCSS more efficient. Their proposals included creation of private health insurers, similar to the Chilean ISAPRES, and splitting up the CCSS into separate institutions for health financing, purchasing, and pensions. The Costa Ricans flatly rejected these proposals but did settle for the less radical idea of separating functions within the CCSS. Under this model, the central CCSS would purchase health services from its operational units. Competition among hospitals and clinics for provider contracts would breed efficiency within the system.

For its part, the World Bank finally agreed to accept the Costa Rican plan to overhaul the primary care system, an approach it has always opposed as overly expensive. This plan was largely the brainchild of Fernando Marín, the director of the first private cooperative clinic contracted by the CCSS in the 1980s. The problem was that the CCSS's primary care services were purely curative and were scattered around the country in a manner not necessarily corresponding to the distribution of the population. They were complemented in overlapping fashion by the Ministry of Health's preventative care and maternal-infant nutritional programs. Marín's idea was to

---

of a replacement hospital in Alajuela, the negotiations for which had been taking place over a period of nearly ten years. These negotiations were not related to health-sector reform discussions with the World Bank, although before the agreement was signed, support for repair and construction of public health buildings and redefining the role of the Ministry of Health was added.

14. Information on the positions of the World Bank and Costa Rican negotiators comes from interviews with Alvaro Salas; James Cercone, former World Bank official and former member of the Proyecto de Modernización de la CCSS, San José, December 10, 2001; and Norma Ayala, former member of the Proyecto de Modernización de la CCSS, San José, December 12, 2001.

replace this model with health care teams (Equipos Básicos de Atención Integral de Salud, EBAIS), which would provide integral care, that is, services attending to communities' physical, social, and psychological health needs.

These health care teams would be distributed on a capitation basis, and they would streamline public health services by taking over all direct medical functions provided by the Ministry of Health. The World Bank argued during the formulation stage and continues to believe that the EBAIS program may become financially unsustainable in the medium to long term. The bank contends that the great number of planned EBAIS, together with their nature as full-service primary care teams (including requisite equipment and the requirement that each be staffed by a physician) will make it difficult for the CCSS to contain expenditures as salaries and medical costs continue to rise.[15]

The reform program was agreed on with the World Bank in 1993; only then did Costa Rican officials begin consultations with stakeholders and the broader medical community. The CCSS team was focused on the EBAIS concept and very concerned about the opposition that might meet the plan of transferring all medical personnel from the Ministry of Health to the CCSS. The transfer was critical for supplying sufficient resources for the EBAIS to work, and, because the EBAIS were to be installed nationwide, had to be conducted fairly quickly. The Costa Rican team was led by Alvaro Salas, director of technical services for the CCSS, and he took the proposal to the Schools of Medicine and Public Health at the University of Costa Rica, to the Colleges of Physicians and Nurses, and to the largest of the many labor unions representing workers in the CCSS and Ministry of Health. Most of the discussion concerned the EBAIS rather than other institutional reforms because the latter were much less detailed at that point. Regarding the separation of functions, the unions principally sought and received assurance that the CCSS would not be split up or privatized. Concerning primary care, one union in particular, Asociación Nacional de Empleados Públicos, initially opposed the transfers because it would lose members as medical personnel migrated to the CCSS where they would be represented by other unions. The Colegio de Médicos also had reservations about the EBAIS because they saw the health teams as practicing public health, not medicine.

15. Telephone interview with Maria Luisa Escobar, project manager, World Bank, April 23, 2002. There are no recent studies of the EBAIS that might support or refute these viewpoints.

In Costa Rica, all foreign loans contracted by government entities must be approved by Congress, and so, at the outset, there existed the possibility that some of these objections might hold up approval, particularly because the legislative assembly would vote on the loan shortly before the 1994 elections. The loan had the approval of the President Calderón and his ministers, but would the opposition National Liberation Party (Partido Liberación Nacional, PLN) support it? In the end, the World Bank health sector loan received a unanimous vote of approval from the legislature. This outcome was facilitated in great part by the relationship between Alvaro Salas and PLN presidential candidate José Figueres. Costa Rica forbids the reelection of presidents or consecutive terms for legislators. Thus, as the PLN's presidential candidate, Figueres was the effective leader of the opposition in Congress, and his support was crucial in convincing the party to vote for health reform. Salas and his technical team had been working with Figueres to design his platform on health and convinced the candidate that he should support the loan package even though it had been developed under a different administration.

Implementation Stage 1, 1994–1998

After he won the presidential elections in February 1994, Figueres appointed key members of the team that had negotiated the health sector loan with the World Bank to important positions. Salas became the executive president of the CCSS. Hérman Weinstock became minister of health, and Fernando Marín became vice minister. Luis B. Saénz was appointed director of the CCSS–World Bank reform implementation unit, and Norma Ayala was made coordinator of the EBAIS program. In contrast to the Mexican case discussed in this volume, the health reform team was composed of public health specialists, and it controlled CCSS policy as opposed to outsiders from the Ministry of Finance. Together, this core group constituted a change team committed to implementing the proposals they had developed. Not surprisingly, they focused on that part of the program, the primary care model, that most powerfully motivated them. Plans for deconcentration developed much more slowly and would only gain center stage under the following administration.

The New Primary Care Model

Actual disbursement of the World Bank loan got off to a slow start, but the implementation team began restructuring primary care even before the external funding came in.[16] Before establishing the first EBAIS in February 1995, the minister and vice minister of health spent about six months negotiating terms with unions representing medical personnel to be transferred to the CCSS. As a result of these negotiations, transferred workers retained their seniority and the right to remain within the geographical area where they had always worked. Some felt the clash of organizational cultures as the public health–oriented Ministry of Health professionals joined the curative medical model of the CCSS, but the fact that CCSS pay scales were higher than those of the ministry must have helped ease the transition. And some of those eligible for pensions retired. In addition, reform team members traveled around the country educating ministry employees about working in the CCSS and talking to existing personnel about why and how primary care was changing. They also hired consultants to run workshops about the emotional aspects of change in the workplace. Approximately 1,600 health ministry workers were transferred to the CCSS between 1995 and 1998.

Each EBAIS consists, minimally, of a medical doctor, nurse, and a technician and is responsible for a geographical area consisting of about 4,000 people. Where necessary in rural areas, the EBAIS are mobile and travel around their territory. EBAIS are supported by personnel from the health area (*área de salud;* see below) to which they belong. Officially, the support personnel located in each health area include a family practitioner, nurse, laboratory technician, social worker, dentist, nutritionist, pharmacist, and medical records specialist. In reality, not all health areas have a family practitioner and nutritionist yet, but no EBAIS can be formed without a medical doctor.

The administration of the CCSS decided that it would reflect most positively on the government if they constructed the new primary care facilities in the poorest areas of the country first. This meant beginning in the rural areas, and the first EBAIS was established in one of the poorest areas of the Province of Puntarenas. Indeed, rural areas were served first, and, at this

16. General information on implementation in 1994–98 is based on interviews with Alvaro Salas, Cercone, Ayala, Luis B. Saénz, former director of the Proyecto de Modernización de la CCSS, San José, December 11, 2001; and Rigoberto Salas, president of SIPROCIMECA (Sindicato de Profesionales en Ciencias Médicas de la CCSS e Instituciones Afines) and coordinator of FOSS (Frente de Organizaciones Sindicales del Sector Salud), San José, December 14, 2001.
The team only carried out the steps necessary to make the project "effective," in World Bank terminology, in 1995. Then they discovered that the loan had not been included in the regular 1995 government budget and had to wait until the next special session to add it, meaning that loan disbursement did not start until early 1996.

writing, EBAIS exist in all counties of the country save some portions of
the Central Valley where the capital is located. The decision to serve rural
poor people first, even if partly motivated by electoral considerations,
reflects the CCSS authorities' commitment to equity and public health,
something that sets it apart from most regional counterparts.

As was mentioned above, there was some resistance to the EBAIS
concept from physicians because of the feeling that their orientation was
toward too much public health and that the doctors employed in them would
not be able to use their technical training. It was reported that surgeons at one
hospital even accused the CCSS of dragging the medical profession back
into the days of fighting parasitic diseases (*parasitismo*). But the reality is
that Costa Rican doctors do not have many alternatives to working for the
CCSS. In addition, because the CCSS had to hire many new doctors to staff
the EBAIS, they are composed mainly of new medical school graduates,
sparing the older physicians the need to change their attitudes.

Performance Contracts, the First Step toward Accountability and
Autonomy

During the administration of President Figueres, the EBAIS program expanded rapidly. By mid-1998, nearly 400 EBAIS, or about half the total
originally planned, had been formed (Clark 2001, 91). But the reform team
progressed more slowly in the area of deconcentration. Because the original
loan agreement offered few specifics in this regard, the reform team had to
first determine how it would work. They looked to foreign models for ideas,
particularly Spain and the United Kingdom, and they found the hospital
contracting system of the autonomous region of Catalunya to be the most
useful. Then they hired consultants from Spain and from Andersen Consulting to help design appropriate mechanisms for Costa Rica.

The central mechanism chosen was the *compromiso de gestión* (performance contract), an instrument that formalizes the relationship between
central authorities and operating units. It guarantees a budget in return for
the "production" of specified medical services and the achievement of
quality standards. Performance contracts were first applied to the seven
national hospitals in early 1997. In preparation, members of the CCSS
reform team held countless meetings with hospitals in the last six months of
1996 explaining the new system and essentially negotiating what the division of responsibilities between the "purchaser" and "providers" would
really look like.

At first, the CCSS floated a more radical plan, whereby hospitals would be quite autonomous, carry out their own personnel decisions, purchasing, and planning and bill the central authority ex post facto for services provided. But this version was roundly rejected by hospital authorities, unions, and CCSS management and quickly scrapped. Particularly important is that labor unions have from the beginning managed to defeat all proposals that hiring and firing be carried out by operating units. The idea that hospitals bill for services provided rather than receive all or most of their budgets at the beginning of the year also died in these exploratory discussions. In fact, many hospital administrators and employees voiced rejection of any sort of performance contract.

Upon launching the performance contract system for the seven national hospitals in 1997, the reform team published *Hacia un nuevo sistema de asignación de recursos,* a document that explained the future system envisioned by planners. As a first step, hospitals would receive a budget, from which 10 percent would be withheld for use as performance incentives. The value of all hospital procedures would then be calculated and expressed as hospital production units (*unidades de producción hospitalaria,* UPHs). In later phases, these calculations would be refined to incorporate two additional variables: average hospital stays and standard costs per case mix. The performance contract would stipulate the expected production of the hospital in terms of UPHs and other outcomes related to quality (e.g., length of waiting lists, numbers of intra-hospital infections). Hospitals whose performance fell short of the actual UPH's promised would be deemed inefficient and intervened by the central administration. Those which met or exceeded the goals would be efficient and have access to the incentive funds at variable rates.

Health areas (*áreas de salud*), or the administrative units responsible for primary care, would also be put on performance contracts and experience a phased transition.[17] Ten percent of their budgets would also be withheld and then returned in full or in part depending on whether the actual production and quality of services met the stipulations of the performance contracts. Health areas' budgets would gradually shift from being determined according to previous levels to being assigned on a capitation basis cor-

17. Although there are more clinics than health areas in Costa Rica, there is generally one large clinic (combining primary care with some specialist services such as obstetrics and gynecology, dermatology, pediatrics, psychiatry, etc.) per area. Thus performance contracts are normally signed by the director of the clinic as the officer responsible for the entire health area, including all EBAIS assigned to the location.

rected for age, sex, and epidemiological factors. In addition, hospitals were to begin charging health areas for each patient referred to them, thereby providing an incentive to resolve cases on the primary level.

At the end of 1997, the CCSS evaluated the hospitals according to the criteria of the performance contracts and released full details to the media. The hospitals were angered by the release of so much information, but project managers promised to restrict further press releases to summary grades and hospital directors shifted their energies to improving scores. Before President Figueres left office in May 1998, the CCSS signed performance contracts with the rest of the hospitals in the system and with the health areas. As the next section will explain, however, the budgeting system never evolved as envisioned in *Hacia un nuevo sistema de asignación de recursos.*

Implementation Stage 2, 1998–2002

With the presidential elections of 1998, the government changed presidents and parties, and this brought significant modifications in the context and priorities of the health reform agenda. The impetus behind the formulation and initial implementation of the health reforms had been largely sectoral, as the changes were developed to address problems in public health administration and not explicitly linked to ongoing structural adjustment measures. The incoming administration of Rodríguez, however, saw the health reform package as one of several initiatives intended to improve the functioning of the social security system, which in turn was defined as a key aspect of state reform. The government's new change team directed both pension and health reform. In health, this group placed a much stronger emphasis on role division and other institutional changes than on the primary care system.

The handover of the health reform project between the Figueres and Rodriguez administrations was facilitated by meetings during which outgoing officials educated the newcomers in the details of the reforms. But key players left office or were sidelined by the new leadership. The president of the CCSS, the director of the reform project, and the managers of the EBAIS and budgeting (*asignación de recursos*) components left or were reassigned to other, unrelated positions within the institution. A new change team with different priorities took office. This team included the new executive president of the CCSS, his advisers, and the chief of the new modernization and development division that would now oversee the reform project.

The new team was more focused on administrative deconcentration and other institutional changes than on the primary care system.[18] In particular, the incoming president of the CCSS was a lawyer keen to anchor new policies in health and pensions in national law. But they could not discontinue the EBAIS concept, because the health teams had become popular and communities not yet covered were demanding theirs. So during the period 1998–2002, the reform project continued to transform the primary level of care by forming new EBAIS, but at a slower pace than previously. At the end of 2001, there were 736 EBAIS covering about 80 percent of the population.[19]

Financing for the EBAIS and their new personnel came from several sources. One source was the medical budget of the Ministry of Health, which was absorbed by the CCSS when it took on the ministry's employees. In addition, total real public spending on health rose about 45 percent between 1992 and 1999. Real public health expenditures were consistently over 5 percent of GDP during this period, while per capita real spending grew about 17 percent.[20] In particular, CCSS health outlays increased from 75 to 81 percent of total public health spending during the same period, a trend that CCSS officials claim intensified in 2000–1.[21] Finally, as table 7.3 shows, there was a shift in new spending within the CCSS's health budget away from the hospitals and toward primary care. Because the global budget was growing in real terms, CCSS officials were able to direct new resources toward primary care without impinging on the hospitals' historical levels of funding.

CCSS officials also completed several institutional reform efforts. One was to create a formal evaluation system with which to measure the quality of CCSS medical services and user satisfaction. To this end, the CCSS established the Superintendencia General de Servicios de Salud (SUGESS) in 1999. SUGESS monitors quality indicators such as waiting lists, performs surveys of user satisfaction, collects complaints via 124 offices around the country, and disseminates information to clients about their rights and responsibilities. Although it is an internal unit, SUGESS maintains substantial autonomy from political appointees because the superin-

18. Interview with Rigoberto Urbina, San José, December 3, 2001; interview with María Isabel Solís, Proyecto de Modernización de la CCSS, San José, December 6, 2001; and interview with Ayala.

19. Interview with Solís.

20. Cercone, Durán, and Briceño (2001, 35–36).

21. Interview with Rodolfo Piza.

Table 7.3

Health Spending by the Caja Costarricense de Seguro Social, by Level of Care, Costa Rica, 1997–2000 (percentage of total)

Type of Care	1997	1998	1999	2000
Primary care	19	19	20	26
Second- and third-level care (mostly hospital)	81	81	80	74
Total	100	100	100	100

Source: Cercone, Durán, and Briceño (2001, 60).

tendent and regional directors have permanent, lifetime employment rights (*propriedad de plaza*) and cannot be removed from their jobs.[22]

Another institutional reform brought to fruition during the Rodríguez administration was the installment of a new CCSS collection system, that is, the mechanism by which the institution collects monthly pension and health quotas from workers and employers. The commitment to modernize collections had, at the urging of the World Bank, been included in the original health sector loan agreement. But the new system, Sistema Centralizado de Recaudación (SICERE), was only implemented in 2001. SICERE is intended to make payment of social security taxes easier, faster, and more traceable, thereby reducing evasion. Before the new system, employers had to send someone to a CCSS office every month to pay the taxes, and the transaction was handled entirely by hand. SICERE makes this unnecessary because it can automatically deduct payments from employers' bank accounts or accept payments at bank locations. SICERE has greatly sped up the process of updating company payment records and now provides data about taxes paid for individual employees.[23]

Of course, SICERE improves the collection of social security taxes destined to the CCSS pension system as well as to health accounts, and because of this, the Rodríguez administration prioritized its completion. The connection is that the collection system needed to be automated so that the new complementary pension system, also put in place in 2001, could work. Thus the president of the CCSS was very involved in drafting and lobbying for the Ley de Protección al Trabajador, a law passed in early 2000 that mandated the creation of an obligatory, private pension scheme to complement the state system. The new law further aims to enhance the financial situation of the CCSS by mandating the full universalization of

22. Interview with Roberto Galvas, superintendent of SUGESS, San José, December 4, 2001.
23. Interview with Cercone.

health and pension systems, ordering the CCSS to begin collecting quotas for these programs from the entire economically active population, including informal-sector workers, by 2005.

The bulk of the second health reform team's energy, however, has gone to furthering and formalizing the deconcentration process. Nevertheless, only a small portion of the blueprint laid out in *Hacia un nuevo sistema de asignación de recursos* has been implemented.[24] Hospital production is measured in UPHs, but the calculations are mainly used to justify spending and the basis for budgeting remains historical. What is more, CCSS statisticians know that the cost of UPHs varies among hospitals, but so far the health authorities have not employed case mix methodology to take this into account. The movement toward capitation-based budgeting for health areas is also incomplete. Here reformers have used historical budgets as a base, but because the budget for primary care is growing more rapidly than that of hospitals, they are addressing inequalities by awarding extra amounts to underfunded areas. All area budgets are growing at least as fast as inflation, but some are increasing more rapidly than that. In addition, health units do receive a financial incentive for efficient production (i.e., scoring above 85 out of 100 on their annual review), but this has been reduced to an amount equaling 2 percent of the unit's budget. There are no penalties for inefficiency or scoring lower than 85 on the annual evaluation and, so far, no hospital or health area has lost any portion of its budget. Finally, virtually no progress has been made in advancing a direct billing system between hospitals and clinics for referrals.

The limitations in relating budgets to performance and the absence of penalties reflects the resistance of health units to these measures and the conscious restraint of CCSS officials. The reformers have tacitly agreed to accept a very slow pace of deconcentration, at least in part because they fear a backlash from administrators and labor unions if pushed harder. CCSS managers admit that it will take at least five more years to really make budgeting dependent on performance contracts.[25]

The current change team has met with much more success in translating deconcentration into national law. The president of the CCSS and his main

24. The information in this section is based on the author's interviews with Saénz, Solís, Flores, Rodolfo Piza, Fabio Durán, former director of the Actuarial Department, CCSS, San José, December 10, 2001, and Claudio Arce, proyecto de modernización de la CCSS, San José, December 10, 2001.

25. Interview with Rodolfo Piza and Juan Carlos Sánchez Arguedas, manager, Modernization and Development Division, CCSS, San José, December 7, 2001.

adviser, both lawyers, drafted the Ley de Desconcentración de los Hospitales y Clínicas de la Caja Costarricense de Seguro Social, which was passed by the legislative assembly in late 1998. The law passed Congress so easily that even its authors were surprised. There was virtually no opposition from labor unions or the PLN, probably because the law did not propose any type of privatization or use the words "competition" or "market" in any form. The CCSS administration presented the draft law to health sector labor organizations before taking it to Congress, and it obtained a letter of support signed by union leaders. In addition, the law is short and vague, for the detail would only be added later in the *reglamento* published by the CCSS. And the largest portion of the law discusses the creation of the *juntas de salud,* or the locally elected health committees, giving the legislation the appearance of promoting community participation more than anything else. Finally, the Social Issues Commission, the congressional committee that examined the law before recommending it to the plenary, held a public hearing at which several well-known doctors endorsed the idea.

Although the authors of the legislation were inspired by regional trends toward political decentralization, they settled for the limited concept of deconcentration as more appropriate for Costa Rica's still highly centralized state. Here deconcentration means only the redistribution of management power and responsibilities from the central administration toward the units directly providing medical services within the same national institution. The 1998 Ley de Desconcentración offers hospital and clinic directors independent legal status (*personalidad jurídica instrumental*), such that they can execute contracts with third parties and manage their own budgets and human resources as long as they abide by the terms of performance contracts, CCSS regulations, and national law. The new law also changes the conditions of employment for directors from lifetime appointments to five-year contracts.

The other important change brought about by the 1998 Ley de Desconcentración is the creation of the *juntas de salud,* seven-member bodies composed of three representatives elected by citizens directly insured by the CCSS, two chosen from employers organizations, and two from community organizations (these cannot be labor unions). The CCSS officials who drafted the 1998 law saw community involvement as an essential balance to the power of the central health administration. There are 124 *juntas de salud,* one for each of the hospitals and larger clinics in the country. *Juntas de salud* are elected every two years in November; the timetable for these elections was designed specifically not to coincide with political elections so as to avoid linkages to partisan competition.[26] Their purpose is to oversee and supply input into a diverse array of functions carried out by the hospitals and clinics including: execution of the budget, drafting performance contracts, selecting directors, and promoting community health projects. Thus far, there have been two elections for the *juntas de salud,* and for each only about 14,000 of 1 million eligible voters cast ballots.[27] A survey of the first *juntas* conducted by SUGESS found that three-quarters of them had not participated in the administration of their corresponding health unit and that the biggest obstacle they confronted was the local CCSS authorities' refusal to cooperate (SUGESS 2001). CCSS officials admit that there is a great deal of variation in the actual participation rates of individual *juntas* and that it will be years before they reach their potential.[28]

Hospitals and clinics were not automatically deconcentrated as a result of the 1998 law and subsequent *reglamento.* Rather, the CCSS board of directors retained the authority to set up a process of transition for the health units, as well as the right to withdraw deconcentrated status from any hospital or clinic that mismanaged its responsibilities. Hospitals and clinics are eligible to apply for deconcentrated status when they have a signed performance contract and composed a functioning *junta de salud.* The board of directors approved the first group of fourteen hospitals for deconcentrated status in 1999. Since then, twenty more hospitals and clinics have received deconcentrated status. These thirty-four units include all the national hospitals and represent more than 70 percent of CCSS health spending and services.[29] Health officials say that they are happy with the gradual, phased pace of deconcentration because it allows both the operating units and the central administration time to make what are often cultural changes in the organization of their work. These authorities report that it took some prodding to motivate the first group to ask for deconcentrated status, but that the pace of applications has since sped up. Officially, deconcentration is strictly voluntary. In reality, central health authorities have constructed a set of sticks and carrots that push health units toward independence. The carrot is the independence gained by hospital and clinic directors to govern their own institutions. The stick is the knowledge that until the institution

26. Interview with Urbina, December 3, 2001.
27. Ibid.
28. Ibid.
29. Interview with Rigoberto Urbina, San José, December 12, 2001.

gains deconcentrated status, it will continue to receive instructions from the central or regional administration and sacrifice control over purchasing and other managerial matters.

Deconcentration in Practice

Deconcentration has had a variable impact on intrabureaucratic relationships. On the one hand, hospital and clinic directors in place before the 1998 law were allowed to keep their permanent appointments. This has allowed preestablished patterns to continue in some areas. On the other hand, deconcentration is forcing rapid improvements in the notoriously difficult relationships between hospital directors and administrators. Hospital directors have always been doctors promoted from within their institution to a position of medical leadership. The actual management of the hospital's budget was usually left to its administrator, traditionally appointed by the CCSS central authorities. Rifts often developed between the director seeking to protect his or her own institution and the administrator, commonly viewed as a spy from headquarters. Now the directors of deconcentrated hospitals can choose their own administrator, and the two are forced to work together to meet performance contract goals. Finally, the deconcentration process has largely undercut the power of the regional directors. The directors of the seven national hospitals always negotiated directly with the CCSS central administration, but smaller hospitals and all clinics reported to one of eight regional directors, who passed on annual budget allotments to each unit and had substantial control over purchasing and human resource matters within their areas. With deconcentrated status comes independence from regional directors, something most hospitals and clinics are happy to have, although they often turn to their former superiors when problems arise.[30]

While the directors may have resisted performance contracts and deconcentration at first, they now jealously guard their new independence. Hospitals and clinics appreciate the transparency of the central administration's budgetary obligation toward them as spelled out in the performance contracts, whereas in the past the CCSS sometimes withheld promised funds because of financial problems. And hospital directors cherish their new-found independence in the area of procurement. By doing their own pur-

30. Interview with María Eugenia Villarta, director of the Central South Region, CCSS, San José, December 11, 2001.

chasing, hospitals have more control over what they are buying and can execute the process more rapidly.[31]

But there are numerous restrictions on the actual freedom exercised by deconcentrated units. For example, a number of factors constrain hospital directors' discretion over budgets. Payrolls typically account for more than 60 percent of hospital budgets, and without the power to reduce the number of employees or tamper with their wages, this puts a large portion of total expenditures outside the directors' control. In addition, directors must obtain permission from central authorities to transfer any significant amount of money (more than 5 percent of the total budget) from one purpose or department to another. Without user fees, hospitals have few opportunities to raise funds independently. The one clear exception is that they may accept donations from community fundraising activities. Only the children's hospital seems to benefit much from this because it receives money from an annual telethon. Although hospitals may generate profits by selling nonmedical services (e.g., parking lot fees), they are not allowed to keep them. The CCSS central authorities have also decided to retain control over some purchases, principally pharmaceuticals.

In addition, and much as in the case of the Mexican Social Security Institute, negotiations between the central CCSS authorities and labor unions representing employees in the health sector overshadow the possibilities for independent decision making by hospital and clinic directors in two key areas: human resources and private contracting. Deconcentrated units were to receive substantial autonomy in human resource decisions, but this area continues to be governed by negotiations between the central CCSS authorities and labor organizations. The central administration retains control over the creation of new positions, and directors must respect salary scales previously negotiated. The unions have steadfastly resisted any attempt to tie the salaries of medical personnel to performance indicators. They have agreed to allow deconcentrated units to transfer employees, but only within an eight-kilometer radius. In these cases, the employee's salary follows him or her to the new post, leaving directors little incentive to make transfers. Hospital and clinic directors are also not able to force changes in working conditions previously negotiated (i.e., schedules) and so rely on new hires to work unpopular shifts.

31. One director said that purchases made through the central CCSS took six to twelve months but that made independently, they take three months; interview with Rodolfo Hernández, director, Hospital de Niños, San José, December 13, 2001.

Other than protecting their salaries and working conditions, the main concern of the health sector unions is to limit or eliminate the contracting of private medical services by clinics and especially hospitals. Payments for private services account for only 2 percent of the CCSS budget.[32] They are concentrated in a few areas such as radiation therapy, where technology lags are most acute and the need to reduce waiting lists is most pressing. A private clinic also recently won a bid to administer several EBAIS in the San José metropolitan area. The World Bank–sponsored reforms did not explicitly promote the contracting out of private services, and health officials did not foresee that labor union opposition to this practice would become a focus of dispute between the two sides. But third-party contracting has grown in the past decade, been widely publicized by the media, and been attacked by labor unions as a plot by reformers to privatize the CCSS.

In addition, the question of third-party contracting by hospitals has been plagued by conflicts of interest wherein CCSS specialists have referred patients to their own private practices for treatment. Not only labor unions but also many of the individual doctors I interviewed are concerned that the deconcentration of purchasing will only lead to more such corrupt practices. The position of the labor and professional organizations representing health workers is that using small quantities of CCSS funds to purchase private diagnostic tests and treatments rather than better equipment for the public sector will result in the latter falling farther and farther behind as potential investment is effectively siphoned off to private clinics.[33] In an October 2001 agreement between the unions and the CCSS, the CCSS agreed to curb the growth of third-party contracting by increasing spending on the entire public health sector toward a target of 10 percent of GDP, place stricter limits on private contracting by deconcentrated units, and study the possibility of requiring newly hired health professionals to forgo private practice.[34]

It is difficult to know how committed the CCSS is to this agreement, particularly the new spending target. To the extent that the goal of increasing health expenditures to 10 percent of GDP is a goal for the *entire* public

32. Interview with Rodolfo Piza.
33. Interview with Rigoberto Salas.
34. Declaración conjunta CCSS–Organizaciones Sindicales y Sociales: Relativa al futuro de la seguridad social en las areas de autonomía institucional, financiamiento y reforma de servicios de salud y pensiones, San José, October 29, 2001. This agreement was concluded after nearly a year of negotiations mediated by the Catholic Church, but the largest and most radical labor union representing CCSS workers refused to endorse it.

health sector, and not just the CCSS, the institution could argue that it cannot be held responsible for the budgetary decisions of other government agencies.[35] The outlook for increased government spending on health looks particularly bleak, for recently elected President Abel Pacheco has announced his intention to impose austerity measures in 2003. In addition, the business community did a great deal of complaining throughout the 1990s about the impact of social welfare payroll taxes on Costa Rica's competitiveness.

In 2000, employers did acquiesce to an increase in pension quotas, as long as it was used to establish privately invested funds. But no one is suggesting that they or insured citizens themselves would accept additional charges for health. Nonetheless, the financial stability of the CCSS's health insurance side improved to the point where it was running a surplus at the end of the 1990s. The only study on this issue argues that the major reason for this unexpected but fortuitous state of affairs is that the average number of dependents per insured person dropped rapidly during the decade.[36] The study also cautions, however, that the health fund's financial stability will erode during the coming decades as the population ages.

Conclusion

The one clear success of the Costa Rican health reforms is the reorganization of primary care through the EBAIS. Before implementing the EBAIS, officials took care to negotiate the terms of employee transfer from the Ministry of Health to the CCSS. This concerted effort to diffuse potential opposition to the plan meant that the government reaped almost nothing but advantage from the new EBAIS. Rapid implementation on a national scale, beginning in the humblest *cantones* and moving in toward the capital, gave the impression that the government was moving quickly to help poor people and to modernize the health system. The CCSS counted the EBAIS and took photographs of their newly painted buildings as evidence of recent achievements in health reform. Communities that had gotten their own EBAIS arose quickly as new stakeholders, and this created demands from other communities for the same benefit.

Deconcentration has progressed much more slowly. The pace of change

35. And increased government spending seems very unlikely as it is already clear that austerity measures will affect public finances in 2003; see Leitón (2002).
36. Cercone, Durán, and Briceño (2001, 56).

from a system of historical budgeting and centralized decision making toward independent management and financial accountability has been incremental. In addition, the scope of deconcentration, both in terms of the proportion of health units involved and the range of rights and responsibilities transferred, has been only gradually expanded. This gradualism is part strategy, part compromise. We can identify proactive decisions made by the reform teams (e.g., the decisions to begin performance contracts with a pilot project in the seven national hospitals, make health units apply for deconcentrated status, and grandfather hospital directors with permanent appointments), which were clearly meant to promote gradual change from the old model to the new one. But, to be sure, health reformers have had to make many compromises on their original plans in the face of opposition from various sectors of the CCSS. For example, hospitals have successfully rejected original designs to penalize them for inefficiency, and labor unions have blocked efforts to deconcentrate human resource policy and curbed hospital directors' independence in purchasing decisions.

Costa Rican health authorities faced a much more positive mix of incentives for pushing forward the primary care reforms than for deconcentrating administration. The creation of the EBAIS fixed a long-standing problem of overlap between the Ministry of Health and the CCSS with a solution that favored the stronger institution. The public health orientation of the original change team lent them commitment to the new model. The shift to EBAIS did not require confrontation with CCSS employees or the medical profession. In contrast, the full deconcentration of hospitals and health areas would threaten the professional autonomy of hospital physicians, the authority of central administrators, and the gains won by labor unions.

Three considerations help explain health authorities' avoidance of full and rapid deconcentration and the level of conflict that might be expected to accompany it. First, this decision reflects the widely held values of compromise and consensus in Costa Rican politics. Second, it testifies to the absence, among major political contenders, of any agenda to privatize public services or challenge the power of labor unions and professional associations. Third, the lack of urgency demonstrated by CCSS officials may well be the result of the current comfortable financial situation of the institution.

There are a number of advantages and disadvantages to incremental deconcentration. On the positive side, given that the reforms require changes within the most complex units of the CCSS (hospitals and central administration), it seems justified to allow time for the corresponding shifts in organizational culture to develop. And in the meantime, the process of deconcentration is creating new stakeholders (hospital and clinic directors), who are pushing for more independent decision-making power. On the negative side, there may well be significant opportunity costs, in the form of forgone efficiency gains, for not holding hospitals accountable for their budgets sooner. The gradual nature of reform has also allowed labor unions the time to organize to limit the process. Finally, it is possible that the result of negotiating each step of the process is that the endpoint originally envisioned, the separation of purchasing and providing functions in some sort of quasi-market, will never be reached.

References

CCSS (Caja Costarricense de Seguro Social). 1997. *Hacia un nuevo sistema de asignación de recursos.* Proyecto Modernización. San José: CCSS.

————. 2001a. *Plan Anual Operativo Institucional: Año 2002.* San José: CCSS.

————. 2001b. *Plan de atención a la salud de las personas: 2001–2006.* San José: CCSS.

Cercone, James, Fabio Durán, and Rodrigo Briceño. 2001. El desempeño del sector social en Costa Rica durante la década de los noventa. Instituto Latinoamericano de Políticas Públicas and SANIGEST, San José (unpublished).

Clark, Mary A. 2001. *Gradual Economic Reform in Latin America: The Costa Rican Experience.* Albany: State University of New York Press.

Contraloría General de la República. 2001. *Memoria Anual 2000.* San José: Contraloría General de la República.

Ickis, John, Carlos Sevilla, and Miguel Iñiguez. 1997. *Estudio del sector salud de Costa Rica.* Alajuela, Costa Rica: Instituto Centroamericano de Administración de Negocios.

IDB (Inter-American Development Bank). 1992. Costa Rica: Health Services Improvement Program. Washington, D.C.: Inter-American Development Bank.

Leitón, Patricia. 2002. Nadie escapa a medidas de plan fiscal. *La Nación,* October 17; www.nacion.co.cr/ln_ee/2002/octubre/17/pais1.html.

Martínez, Juliana. 1999. Poder y alternativas: La disponibilidad de agendas internacionales en las reformas de la salud en Costa Rica, 1988–1998. *Anuario de estudios centroamericanos* 25, no. 1: 159–82.

Miranda Gutiérrez, Guido. 1994. *La seguridad social y el desarrollo in Costa Rica.* San José: Editorial Nacional de Salud y Seguridad Social.

Piza Rocafort, Rodolfo E. 2001. *Seguridad Social: Nova el vetera.* San José: Editorial Nacional de Salud y Seguridad Social.

Segnini, Giannina. 1999a. Nicaraguenses impactan salud. *La nación,* December 7; www.nacion.co.cr/ln_ee/1999/diciembre/07.

————. 1999b. Nicaraguenses no superan los 400 mil. *La nación,* December 5; www.nacion.co.cr/ln_ee/1999/diciembre/05.

Seligson, Mitchell. 2002. Trouble in Paradise? The Erosion of System Support in Costa Rica, 1978–1999. *Latin American Research Review* 37, no. 1: 160–85.

SUGESS (Superintendencia General de Servicios de Salud). 2001. *Informe sobre el funcionamiento de las juntas de salud.* San José: SUGESS; www.nacion.com/ln_ee/ESPECIALES/informes/caja/juntas.html.

Trejos, Juan Diego, Leonardo Garnier, Guillermo Monge, and Roberto Hidalgo. 1994. Enhancing Social Services in Costa Rica. In *Social Service Delivery Systems: An Agenda for Reform,* ed. Cristián Aedo and Osvaldo Larrañgo. Washington, D.C.: Inter-American Development Bank.

Chapter 8

Piecemeal but Innovative: Health Sector Reform in Peru

Christina Ewig

When Alberto Fujimori assumed the presidency of Peru in July 1990, he faced a nation crippled by economic crisis and civil war. As a result of the desperate economic situation and political instability, the nation's health system was also in shambles. President Fujimori's initial objectives were

This chapter has benefited from comments from Joan Nelson and Robert Kaufman, participants in the Woodrow Wilson Center Workshop on Health Reform, two anonymous reviewers, and those who attended a presentation of this research in Lima at the offices of the Department for International Development, United Kingdom, on July 25, 2000, which was organized by Victor Zamora. This chapter is partially drawn from Ewig (2001). The author is grateful to the Fulbright Foundation, the Institute for the Study of World Politics, the Ford Foundation, and the Duke University–University of North Carolina Program in Latin American Studies for financial support for the dissertation research. She is also grateful to those who offered interviews and resources during her research period, and to committee members and colleagues who have read or commented on this portion of her research in its previous versions.

economic stabilization and the control of the powerful Sendero Luminoso (Shining Path) rebel group.

By 1993, with successes on both counts, the government's attention moved toward modernization of the state, including the health sector. Government officials rebuilt and redesigned the health sector, implementing reforms that drew on international reform currents including decentralization, targeting, and the incorporation of market mechanisms. Access to primary health care expanded greatly. Incentives for primary health providers were altered to increase productivity and efficiency. And private competition was introduced into the social security health system.

Peru's health reform consisted of a series of piecemeal measures—a set of not very integrated policies that addressed different parts of the health system and that were developed by separate teams of policymakers. Peru's reform mode was similar to that of Argentina, but it stands in sharp contrast to the comprehensive restructuring undertaken in Colombia or to the creation of a unified health system Brazil.

Political and Economic Context

Peru's economy in the 1980s was inflationary and burdened by debt obligations.[1] Orthodox stabilization had been the accepted tool of economic adjustment in Peru and elsewhere since the 1950s, but in the early 1980s had failed to stabilize the economy (Thorp 1996). The government of President Alan García Pérez, of the populist Alianza Popular Revolucionaria Americana Party (APRA) that took office in 1985, attempted an alternative to orthodox stabilization programs. García implemented a combination of exchange rate stabilization, price freezes, and wage controls, and he declared that no more than 10 percent of export revenues would go toward debt repayment. In the short run, this heterodox policy met with success. But by the end of his term, the experiment had utterly failed. By 1990, the annual inflation rate was 7,650 percent (INEI 1992), and Peru had lost credibility in the eyes of international creditors as a result of its debt moratorium.

As Peru faced spiraling economic crisis, it also confronted a powerful political threat. A number of rebel groups had gained strength throughout

1. The annual inflation rate in 1985 was 163.4 percent (cited in Thorp 1996, 63).

the 1980s, in particular the violent Shining Path.[2] In the early 1980s, Shining Path had established strongholds in several provincial areas. By the late 1980s, the group began to rock Peru's capital, Lima, through acts of sabotage against banks and government buildings, car bombs, and political assassinations. By 1990, Peru had endured years of civil war and severe human rights abuses by both the military and the rebels.

Candidate Fujimori, a political unknown before the 1990 presidential elections, ran on a platform that stressed the ineffectiveness of traditional political parties and a desire to avoid economic shock. Less than a month after taking office, in August 1990, Fujimori reversed position and implemented a draconian economic stabilization program that stabilized the economy but did so with little to no safety net. Fujimori's shift also entailed a sudden change in government personnel. By 1991, he had exchanged many left or center-left political appointees for persons with more economically conservative outlooks. The shock therapy also raised the status of the Ministry of the Economy, which had worked closely with the president on stabilization. Economic shock was a success in the medium term, and Fujimori returned Peru to good credit standing by restarting debt payments.[3] Thus, in the 1990s international financial institutions renewed ties with Peru, first in economic and later in social policy reforms.

In addition to successful economic stabilization, in 1992 intelligence forces captured the leader of Shining Path and effectively controlled the threat of Shining Path thereafter. The twin achievements of economic and political stabilization gave Fujimori substantial popularity throughout much of the 1990s. However, a stable but stagnant economy and a lack of a clear constituency demanded that he take steps to ensure continued support. His rule became increasingly authoritarian. Early in his tenure (1992), he staged a military-backed self-coup and closed the Congress until international pressures forced him to restore formal democracy. Political parties became fragmented and weak as a result of legal reforms, and due to public dissatisfaction. The weakness of parties left few political challengers, and

2. The full name is the Partido Comunista del Perú por el Sendero Luminoso de José Carlos Mariátegui, or Communist Party of Peru in the Shining Path of José Carlos Mariátegui.

3. In the short term, the effects of the shocks were horrendous. Inflation in August 1990 hit an annual rate of 21,316.3 percent (Cuanto, Webb, and Baca 1991), and pushed the working and middle classes into poverty. Only a weak social safety net existed to ease these costs. In the medium term (one to five years later), inflation did drop and level off dramatically, to rates near 10 percent annually (INEI 1996).

many of the adversaries that did appear were either threatened or bought off, often by Fujimori's close adviser and intelligence chief, Vladimiro Montesinos.

By the end of his tenure, Fujimori's power rested in part on support from the military and in part on support he gleaned through "neopopulist" tactics of directly providing material benefits to those groups—primarily poor people—from whom he sought political support in return.[4] Both of these power resources were used in the campaign leading up to the April 2000 elections, when Fujimori ran for a constitutionally disputed third consecutive term. Fujimori and his military supporters effectively controlled the news media while courting popular sectors through populist giveaways of land titles and other benefits. Outside observers such as the Carter Center attributed dirty campaign tactics to Fujimori's slim electoral victory in April 2000. The opposition pushed for a runoff, which was granted, but the president prevailed in an election international observers refused to monitor.

In September 2000, a congressional representative leaked to the public a videotape showing an opposition congressional member being bribed by Montesinos to join Fujimori's party. The video release set off a chain of events that led to Fujimori's resignation and his flight to Japan in November 2000.[5] A transition government led by Valentín Paniagua followed Fujimori's resignation, until new elections were held in April 2001. The winner, Alejandro Toledo of Perú Posible, was sworn in as president on July 28, 2001.

The Health Sector before Reform

The Peruvian health sector before reform faced a number of problems typical of Latin American countries. Health spending was low and inequitably distributed. The sector was highly segmented, resulting in duplicate coverage and inefficiency. The public health system run by the Ministry of Health was hierarchical and organized around vertical single-disease programs. Finally, health indicators placed Peru in the low to middle range among Latin American countries.

4. Funding for these populist projects were derived from the privatization of state-owned industries that freed up cash that was in turn spent by the president. This unlikely combination of populism and neoliberalism has been dubbed "neopopulism" (see Roberts 1995; Weyland 1996).

5. For a review of the events leading to his resignation and the transition government, see Conaghan (2001).

Viewed over the long term, Peru spent the most on health care in the 1970s and early 1980s. Health budgets then dropped severely with economic crisis in the late 1980s, hitting a low point in 1990–91. Beginning in 1992, health spending began to recuperate, but by the end of the 1990s spending had not matched levels of the precrisis period. The per capita spending by the central government on health (calculated in December 1990 nuevo soles) was 19.4 soles in 1970s, 21 soles in 1980, 2.2 soles in 1990, and 7 soles in 1994 (MINSA 1996a, 26). Between the state public health system serving poor and uninsured people and the state social security health system serving formal-sector workers, the public system was hardest hit by the economic crisis, with a budget in 1990 of just 15 percent of that spent in 1980 (MINSA 1996a, 26).

While general health sector spending rose as a percentage of gross domestic product in the 1990s, Ministry of Health budget figures show a relative decline in spending in the public health system for the latter part of the decade (see table 8.1). The Ministry of Health's budget fell from 9.7 percent of the national budget in 1996 to 4.9 percent in 2000.[6] This tapering off indicated the limits of health spending based on nonrenewable funds gained from privatizations of state industries. National revenues from privatizations were very high in 1994 and 1996, ranging near or above $2 billion. Since 1997, revenues have been in the range of between $250 million and $500 million per year.[7] It also could be due to the slowing of the national economy and the low priority placed on health spending.

6. The 1996 figure is from MINSA (1996a, 20); the 2000 figure is my calculation based on budget information in MEF (2001).

7. Although I document here the direct contributions of privatizations to the Ministry of Health, one should also keep in mind that this relationship is not necessarily direct; monies from privatization spent in other sectors may have effectively freed more general revenues for the health sector in the mid-1990s. The Ministry of Health did not see the benefit of funds from privatizations until 1995, when it received relatively minor contributions. Funds from privatizations initially went largely to Fujimori's populist programs, like FONCODES, and to the Ministry of Defense. In 1998 and 1999, MINSA received a more significant share, 12 percent and 13 percent of all privatization revenues that were spent in those years; in 1999, it leapt to 23 percent. In 2000, its proportion declined to 7 percent. (Percentages calculated by the author from Ministry of Economy and Finance reports: MEF 1999a, 1999b, 2000, 2001, 2002c, 2002d.) Although the proportion of the MINSA budget from privatizations grew significantly in the middle to late 1990s, the budget itself only grew moderately. In 2000, a Fiscal Stabilization Fund was established, in which the majority of funds from privatizations are saved for poverty alleviation in low growth years, and the rest go toward debt payments (MEF 2002b). As a result, in 2001 no privatization funds went toward health.

Table 8.1

Social Expenditures and Health Expenditures, Peru, 1990, 1994, and 1999
(percentage of gross domestic product)

Total Expenditures	1990	1994	1999
Social	3.3	5.8	6.8
Public health	1.03	2.23	2.4

Sources: For social expenditures, CEPAL (2000, 140); CEPAL División de Desarrollo Social, base de datos sobre gasto social. For health expenditures, World Bank, World Development Indicators database, July 2001.

Similar to most Latin American countries, Peru's health system is highly segmented into separate systems that serve separate populations. In 1994, the population could be divided into three main groups, according to health coverage: those with no insurance, those with state-provided health insurance, and those with private insurance.[8] The large majority of the population (73.8 percent) had no insurance at all (MINSA 1996a, 18). The majority of these depended upon the network of public health posts, clinics, and hospitals overseen by the Ministry of Health and its decentralized regional authorities. About 21.8 percent of the population was covered by the state health insurance plan, at the time called the Instituto Peruano de Seguridad Social (IPSS, now ESSALUD). The private sector, the third major area after public and pay-as-you-go provision, in 1994 insured only 1.5 percent of the population (MINSA 1996a) (see figure 8.1). Segmentation has resulted in a duplication of health services and marked inefficiency across the sector as a whole.

Figure 8.1 outlines insurance patterns, not overall financing. Insurance patterns mask the significant numbers of people that utilized private-sector health services on an out-of-pocket basis. The proportion of financing of these three major areas is best observed through financial flows in each sector, as listed in table 8.2.

Table 8.2 shows that the private sector accounted for more than one-third of financial flows—much of this on an out-of-pocket basis. Also, despite the fact the public sector served a much larger portion of the population (74 percent, plus a good number of insured people who opted to use Ministry of Health public services over their assigned IPSS social security

8. Although initial reforms of the Fujimori administration date back to 1991, 1994 marks the beginning of major reform efforts in the sector. The Encuesta Nacional de Niveles de Vida (ENNIV) of 1994 also provides more extensive data than the ENNIV of 1991.

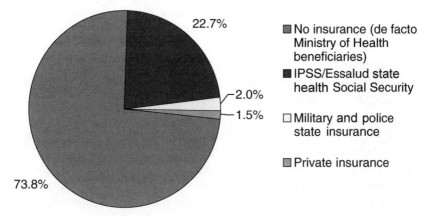

Figure 8.1. The Distribution of Health Coverage in Peru, 1994

Table 8.2
Peru's Sources of Health Care Finance (thousands of December 1995 nuevo soles)

Year	MINSA and Regions	IPSS/FFAA	Private Sector	Total
1992	888,097	1,256,471	1,406,084	3,550,652
Percent	25.01	35.39	39.60	100
1994	1,094,646	1,501,610	1,518,537	4,114,793
Percent	26.60	36.49	36.91	100

Note: IPSS = Instituto Peruano de Seguridad Social, the state social security system; FFAA = health system for the Police and Armed Forces; MINSA = Ministerio de Salud del Perú.
Source: Programa de Fortalecimiento de Servicios de Salud et al. (1997, 35–36).

security services),[9] it received disproportionately low financing. In short, the distribution of financial support for health services across the separate systems was highly inequitable.

Related to spending across sectors, there also existed severe regional inequities in spending patterns. Public-sector, state Social Security, and private spending were all concentrated in Lima, the area of Peru with the least incidence of poverty. In 1994, those areas with the greatest health needs and least ability to self-finance these needs (generally the poorest, most rural regions) received the lowest proportion of state health expenditures.[10] In addition, public spending has historically been disproportion-

9. Those persons who have health insurance use a MINSA public health facility 13.4 percent of the time that they require health care (MINSA 1996a, 24).
10. See Tamayo and Francke (1997, 38–39).

ately spent on more complex levels of care, to the detriment of primary level care. In 1994 nationally, 54 percent of public health expenditures went to hospitals, 33 percent to primary level care, and 13 percent to administration (Tamayo and Francke 1997, 64–65).[11]

The Ministry of Health itself has historically operated as a highly centralized and vertical institution. Initial efforts to decentralize began in the 1980s. Regional health authorities (Direcciones Regionales de Salud) linked to the ministry existed for some time prior to any reforms. In the 1980s, these authorities were given the responsibility for regional health programming, for administering personnel, and for financial and material resources on a regional level.[12] However, these served a largely bureaucratic function, not one of devolution of power (Becerra Hidalgo 1988, 46). These regional authorities later gained substantial power under the decentralization to regional governments begun by President García. Responsibilities for health care provision, including all material and fiscal resources, were devolved in this law directly to regional governments.[13] With regionalization, the Ministry of Health maintained the responsibility to develop national health policy—but essentially lost the power to implement it beyond Lima. Regionalization was implemented in the first years of the Fujimori administration.

In addition to its centralized form, the Ministry of Health was historically organized around "vertical" programs that focused on single health issues, such as tuberculosis and malaria.[14] Parallel vertical programs resulted in resource duplication and poor quality due to their focus on single health issues rather than integrated health services. Reforms of the sector in the 1990s tried to change these and other problems.

11. It is notable that these national proportions combine relatively high levels of hospital spending in Lima (at a rate of 70 percent) to low levels of hospital spending by the regions (46 percent). Lima also has much higher administrative costs, 21 percent of its spending, versus 8 percent of regional spending going to administration (1994 data in Tamayo and Francke 1997, 64–65).

12. These responsibilities are outlined in Ley de Organización del Sector Salud, Decreto Legislativo 70, Lima, April 1981.

13. The regional governments were dissolved under Fujimori. The regional health authorities—variously called Regiones, Sub-Regiones, and now Direcciones de Salud—have persisted. More recently, Toledo has reconstituted regional government.

14. Vertical programming is in part a result of historic collaboration with international agencies that were concerned with eradicating particular diseases, and thus initially funded these kinds of programs within Latin American health ministries. E.g., the Rockefeller Foundation provided substantial funding for eradicating malaria in Peru and elsewhere and thus influenced the early organization the health ministry (see Cueto n.d.).

Table 8.3

Basic Health Indicators for Peru, 1980–2000

Indicator	1980	1985	1990	1994	1995	2000
Life expectancy at birth	60	63	65.8	67.4	67.7	69.2
Men	58	61	63.5	65.0	65.3	66.8
Women	62	66	68.2	69.9	70.2	71.8
Infant mortality rate[a]	81	72	60.5	51.3	49.2	40.4
Under-five-year mortality rate[a]	126	—	75[b]	72.4	69.9	61.2 (1999)
Maternal mortality rate[c]	—	—	—	185	185	185
Fertility rate	4.5	4.0	3.7	3.2	3.2	2.8

Note: A dash in a cell means that the data are not available.
[a]Estimated figures, deaths per every 1,000 live births.
[b]World Bank data.
[c]Reported rate, deaths per every 100,000 live births.
Sources: For 1980 and 1985 data, World Bank, World Development Indicators, 2001. For 1990, 1994, 1995, and 2000 data, Pan American Health Organization, Special Program for Health Analysis, Regional Core Health Data Initiative, Technical Information System, 2001.

Peru's health indicators place it at the low to middle range among Latin American countries. Since 1980, these indicators have steadily improved, in spite of the difficulties faced by the public health system in the 1990s. Much of the improvement is likely due to rapid urbanization rather than to improvements in health services in this period.[15] The major indicators are given in table 8.3. The data for 1994 are provided as the baseline before major reforms were introduced that same year.

The major areas of health concern in Peru are infant mortality, under-five-year mortality, and maternal mortality. Each of these mortality indicators is much higher in rural than urban areas. Maternal mortality, for example, while at a rate of nearly 200 per 100,000 live births in the urban areas, rises to 448 per 100,000 in rural areas. Diseases that are most likely to lead to infant and under-five mortality are respiratory infections and intestinal infectious diseases. Also of concern for children is chronic malnutrition. In 1993, 58 percent of children age six to nine years suffered from chronic malnutrition. Among adults (age 15–59 years), infectious diseases are a leading cause of death, and diseases of the circulatory system are a primary cause of death for the population over sixty. Among communicable diseases, there are rising rates of malaria, leishmaniasis, dengue, and selvatic yellow fever, which in 1995 reached epidemic proportions. AIDs and tuberculosis rates also rose dramatically toward the end of the 1990s. On the

15. Thanks to Kurt Weyland and Deborah Brautigam, who brought this point to my attention. This hypothesis would need to be statistically tested with data on urbanization.

environmental front, of particular concern for Peru are deaths due to traffic accidents, and poor air and water quality.[16]

The Politics of Sector Reform, 1994–2000

The lack of vision for Peru's health sector reforms can be partly explained by looking at the broader national context at the time. The Fujimori administration was successful in so-called first-wave, or economic reforms, but (with the exception of pension reform) it stopped short of comprehensive second-wave reforms that would deepen economic reforms and reform social sectors—such as education, justice, housing, and health.[17] Health was a relatively low priority for Fujimori, except to the extent that it dovetailed with Fujimori's two social policy darlings: his Lucha Contra la Pobreza (Fight Against Poverty) and his promotion of education.[18] As a result, health reform largely remained the domain of Ministry of Health policy elites. These had the "green light" of the president, as one informant put it, but they worked within a political context in which there was little political opportunity for major reform.[19] Health reform will only progress to the extent that a larger state reform process is under way.

The piecemeal nature was also in part a result of the isolation within which reforms were developed—small groups of five to ten specialists were appointed by ministers to develop a particular reform. These groups generally eschewed interaction with members of civil society who might challenge their principles or their know-how. They worked apart from other professionals within the Ministry of Health—and even in isolation of other reform teams. The result was a potpourri of reforms that sometimes came into direct conflict with one another, and which were implemented to varying degrees.

When Fujimori first took office, his ministers of health largely focused

16. This paragraph is summarized from PAHO (1998, country chapter on Peru).

17. For a review of progress on state reform in the 1990s in Peru see Abusada et al. (2000).

18. For those readers interested in education reforms, it should be noted that Fujimori's interest in education stemmed primarily from his interest in using it as a tool of populism, not from an interest in education reform. E.g., he used school construction to bolster political support. There were reform efforts made in education, but as in health, these were only partially successful.

19. Interview by author with an anonymous member of the team that oversaw the overall health sector reform plan, Lima, March 11, 1998.

on continuing the process of the decentralization of Ministry of Health services begun under the García government. Ministers from 1991 to 1993 experimented with participatory forms of decentralization, following models outlined by the Pan American Health Organization. These experiments were short-lived. More lasting health reforms of the Fujimori administration began under the leadership of Minister Jaime Freundt-Thurne, whose team devised dual centralized and decentralized health delivery strategies in 1993, which began to be implemented in 1994. These were the targeted and centralized Programa de Salud Básica para Todos (Basic Health for All Program, PSBT) and the decentralized Programa de Administración Compartida (Shared Administration Program) that oversaw the Comités Locales de Administración en Salud (Local Health Administration Committees, CLAS).

This last program, which came to be known simply as CLAS, devolved administrative (and some fiscal) responsibility to community members elected or appointed to a board that jointly administered individual or networks of public health centers. In contrast to previous sector reforms, these reforms began to integrate neoliberal principles and strategies, such as the targeting of resources for greater efficiency and the use of employee incentives to generate higher productivity. The PSBT program was premised on the concept of targeting the poorest areas first. Both programs made a radical change in labor practices, contracting doctors, nurses, and other health professionals and renewing these contracts on the basis of performance rather than utilizing the traditional state labor system of permanent "named" positions.

All these programs emphasized increased access to primary care in poor communities. Although linked financially and later administratively within the ministry, the PSBT and CLAS programs, due to their opposing centralized and decentralized approaches and thus political implications, became competing and conflicting reforms within the overall public health system. Despite their contradictions, PSBT and CLAS were among the most successful reforms in that these were the backbone of the reconstruction and modernization of Peru's public health system, which had fallen into complete crisis in the previous decade. By 2001, CLAS and PSBT together accounted for 98 percent of all primary level health care establishments in the public system.

Much of the effort in the first years of reform (1993–96) was spent on PSBT and CLAS and the reconstruction of the dilapidated health care system. It was not until 1997 that other major reforms and reform proposals surfaced.[20] The first of these was the Ley de Modernización de la Seguridad Social en Salud (Modernization of Health Social Security Law), which allowed private health care providers to compete with the state health social security system. This reform was in many ways a completion of first-wave economic reforms. Efforts to pass the law began in 1991. Political obstacles, detailed below, slowed its progress until it passed in its final form in 1997. The next major health reform was introduced just a few months later, in July 1997. This was the Seguro Escolar Gratuito (SEG, Free School Health Insurance). SEG was a presidential initiative that grew out of Fujimori's personal interest in improving education; its impetus had little to do with health.

By the end of the decade, a number of additional reform proposals were put forward and piloted. These included contracts between the Health Ministry and some hospitals to promote greater efficiency through payment for service arrangements; the creation of health networks among differing levels of establishments to promote sharing of equipment and resources; and the development of a social insurance plan for infants and mothers (Seguro Materno-Infantil, SMI). The latter was the idea of outside lenders, and it was implemented by the outgoing Fujimori administration and the transitional Paniagua government. These reforms were implemented with only variable success. The hospital reforms were implemented in only a select number of hospitals; the networks did little to change existing inter-establishment relations (in many ways it amounted to a simple name change of intermediary administrative units); and the maternal-infant insurance program was implemented poorly. SMI was subsequently folded into the school health insurance program by the transition government, thus diluting much of its original focus.[21]

The International Financial Institutions and Health Sector Reform

The influence of the international financial institutions (IFIs) on the politics of Peru's health sector reform is understood best as agenda setting (Bachrach and Baratz 1962; Schattschneider 1960; Lukes 1974; Livingston 1992). Agenda setting is a process whereby certain issues or approaches are placed on the political agenda, while others are effectively closed out. In the

---

20. Elsewhere (Ewig 1999, 2001), I argue that the reform of the family planning program should be considered a reform. This reform began in 1996, but I will not include it in the present discussion.

21. I thank Alicia Yamín for her clarification on the status of the SMI reform.

case of Peru, IFIs first determined whether Peru's government could pursue social policy reforms at all, and second defined reform as based on neoliberal principles. Through loan agreements, IFIs approved of state spending on social policy, and later these also financially supported reform efforts, thus influencing the shape of these policies.

The major social policy strategies advocated by the IFIs—targeting, decentralization, private-sector competition, and the separation of the financing and provision of state services—were all evidenced in Peru's reforms. Via publications, conferences, training workshops, and person-to-person contact, the IFIs suggested that these were the appropriate and viable reform strategies. Though influential, the IFIs were not directly involved in the day-to-day development or implementation of reforms. The IFI representatives that I interviewed claimed a supportive role only, without intent to influence or condition health reform. Peruvian policymakers also guarded their autonomy from direct IFI interventions—often blocking the success of those reforms pushed hardest by the IFIs. Thus, though evidence of IFI influence is obvious at the level of the broad, neoliberal-inspired intellectual currents that informed the individuals on the various health reform teams, there existed some room for country-level innovation within the broader neoliberal paradigm.

In 1993, when Peru's economy was beginning to stabilize, the IFIs approved a social spending plan presented by the Peruvian government. Bureaucrats working in Peru's prime minister's office had outlined a plan for targeted spending in the areas of health, education, justice, and emergency food aid. Although skeletal, the plan marked a departure away from the safety-net approach to social spending that had been dominant in the first years of the decade, toward a longer-term social policy plan. In October 1993, the minister of economy and finance took this conceptual document to a meeting with the Paris Club creditors, who were enthusiastic about the plan. Their support was significant in two ways. First, it signaled a shift toward support of social policy spending by creditors that up until this point had advocated cuts in Peru's state expenditures. Second, this meeting was key in convincing the Ministry of the Economy and Finance to also support social spending.[22]

Although Paris Club approval allowed the Peruvian government to spend on social policy, the IFIs soon after began to play a more direct role in health reform. The most significant was the financial role of the Inter-

22. This is from an interview by the author with Luis Manrique, formerly affiliated with the national policy on targeting of social spending, Lima, February 18, 1998.

American Development Bank (IDB). The IDB cooperated with Japan to finance the Programa de Fortalecimiento de los Servicios de Salud, the Program to Strengthen Health Services. During the 1990s, this program funded the teams of Health Ministry consultants that spearheaded health reform from within the ministry.[23] The World Bank, the U.S. Agency for International Development (USAID), and the Department for International Development of the United Kingdom (DFID) also played supportive roles in the reform effort. The World Bank funded a major targeting project within the ministry, the Programa de Salud y Nutrición Básica, or the Basic Health and Nutrition Program. USAID personnel led workshops on health reform for ministry members, began pilot reform initiatives, and funded short studies of aspects of the health sector. DFID worked to build the technical capacity of Peruvians engaged in designing reforms. In comparison with the large sums of money lent by the IDB, these efforts were much smaller in scope.

When the loan for the Program to Strengthen Health Services expired at the end of 1998, it was not renewed. The IDB, which was unsatisfied with the progress made under this loan, sought other ways to support the reform process. In 1999 it teamed up with the World Bank to support two reforms that both institutions agreed held the most promise: CLAS and maternal-infant insurance.[24] CLAS was considered a success by most outside evaluators, and high rates of maternal mortality were a significant problem. Both of these programs also faced significant opposition within the Health Ministry. The reasons for opposition to CLAS will be detailed below. In the case of maternal-child insurance, the opposition stemmed at least in part from the fact that the program did not have strong advocates from within the ministry and had been introduced from the outside by the IDB.

Four Reform Initiatives

This section delves into the national dynamics of health reform, tracing the policymaking process of the major health reforms developed in the 1990s:

23. The funding consisted of a $68 million loan from the Inter-American Development Bank, a $20 million loan from the Overseas Economic Cooperation Fund of Japan, and a $10 million from the Peruvian national treasury.

24. This is from an interview by the author with an anonymous World Bank official, Washington, October 8, 1999, and from the World Bank's Public Information Center Operational Document on this structural adjustment loan, which is available at www.worldbank.org/pics/pid/pe64080.txt.

targeting through PSBT, decentralization to communities through CLAS, the introduction of private-sector competition into social security health care via EPSs, and free health insurance for children on public schools, SEG.[25]

Targeting Poor People: The Basic Health for All Program (PSBT)

Targeting was one of the first major and lasting reforms of the health sector of the 1990s. Targeting in the health sector stemmed from an overall national social policy orientation favoring targeting as a strategy, outlined in the above-mentioned document presented to the Paris Club. In the health sector, the major targeting initiative became the Basic Health for All Program, PSBT. The targeting policy was partly in reaction to the social deficit that Peru's population faced as a result of economic crisis and civil war. Thus, there was some urgency behind the reform, which was passed in December 1993 as one article of the extensive 1994 budget law. This article allowed the release of funds for a number of targeting initiatives, health being just one.

No other legislation was required, and thus PSBT was developed from that point on within the Ministry of Health by a team of five appointed by the then–minster of health, Freundt-Thurne. The reform targeted a basic package of primary health care services to the poorest Peruvian communities. It involved an inflow of resources to these communities, in terms of clinic construction, personnel who were attracted to poor and remote areas by competitive salaries, and medicines and medical supplies. Once implemented in 1994, the program expanded rapidly.

By emphasizing primary-level and preventative care, the program drew on policies advocated by public health experts. It also borrowed from neoliberal tenets by introducing private-sector models into public systems. In particular, PSBT health professionals were hired under a private-sector labor regimen. Unlike traditional state health workers who held "named" positions and were virtually immune to job loss (but also paid poorly), health professionals hired under the PSBT program were hired on short-term contracts, which would be renewed based upon productivity levels. Though the PSBT workers were paid competitive salaries, they forfeited job stability and benefits—they received no health, pension, vacation, or even sick day benefits.

25. The introduction of fees was another major reform that is still in force, but it is not discussed here. Fees were introduced during the economic crisis period as a way to help the public health establishments survive in a time of major budget slashes.

The new employment regimen was the most radical aspect of this reform, and it sets Peru apart from the other cases in this volume. The private-sector employment model was implemented in a number of program areas of the Health Ministry, including CLAS and among the reform consultants themselves. In PSBT, however, contracts were extremely short (three to six months, with no benefits, compared with the one-year contract of CLAS professionals with benefits) and productivity expectations were high—across the board. For example, persons working in rural areas with low population density had the same productivity requirements as those working in densely populated, high-demand urban areas.[26] With quotas to meet and jobs on the line, efficiency was successfully promoted, but there were no incentives to provide high-quality care.

The fact that such a radical change in employment practices was possible in Peru's health sector, but not in the other countries considered in this volume, is explained by national and sector-specific factors. The flexible labor contracts were part of a larger national process of labor reform that began in 1991, in which labor laws were radically revised from the most protective in the hemisphere to among the most flexible.[27] Major changes included easing of restrictions on terminating employees, the elimination of tripartite bargaining, and—significant for the health sector—the liberalization of the use of temporary contracts. The 1991 Ley de Fomento de Empleo allowed the use of temporary contracts for up to three years per employee, and in 1995 this was extended to a five-year period. PSBT used exclusively temporary contracts for its health staff.

A number of important changes were made regarding unions as well, two of which affected the health sector. One was a shift from sector-level bargaining to firm-level bargaining. This meant that with the above-mentioned regional decentralization of the health system in 1989-90, the ministry health care union, the Federación de Trabajadores del Ministerio de Salud (Federation of Ministry Workers), had to bargain with each regional director, not the ministry as a whole. The union of health professionals that worked for the ministry thus became ineffective and nearly dissolved. Second, strike days were no longer paid days, thus reducing the incentive to strike or to maintain a strike.

26. As a result, there were also high incentives in the rural areas to lie on productivity sheets.
27. The information in this paragraph on national labor reform is drawn largely from Saavedra (2000).

In the early 1990s, Peru also had an overabundance of young health professionals seeking work. These unemployed professionals, not affiliated with unions, welcomed the well-paid work opportunity that PSBT presented. The program effectively opened an alternative health labor market to the scarce "named" positions in IPSS and the Ministry of Health. The health care unions at the time, the above-mentioned Federation of Ministry Workers and the Asociación Nacional de Médicos del Ministerio de Salud (Association of Doctors of the Ministry of Health, ANMMS) did nothing to challenge the change. The ANMMS formed part of the national doctors guild, the Federación Médica (Medical Federation). The Medical Federation opposed reforms in the Social Security health system, but it ignored the new hiring regimen in the ministry and did not organize the workers hired under that system.

In addition to changing labor relations, PSBT changed health sector politics between the central and regional authorities. The PSBT program recentralized the financing of health services, because funding for this program came through the central ministry to the regional authorities rather than directly from the Ministry of the Economy and Finance to the regions as the rest of the health budget was channeled. Increased central funding changed the balance of power within the health sector, increasing the power of the ministry. Yet the resources that PSBT brought to the decentralized regional health authorities meant that these autonomous regional authorities also welcomed and supported the program; in 1995, PSBT accounted for 23 percent of the total budget spent by the regional authorities charged with delivering health care services.[28] The program was financed entirely by the national treasury, and central health authorities took pride in its independence from foreign financing.

The impact of PSBT on primary level public health care in Peru is notable when measured by its level of coverage—by the end of 1998, the program covered 89 percent of all primary level public health establishments. The percentage of centers covered by PSBT has since dropped, to 79 percent in 2001, owing to the fact that some of these centers converted to the CLAS model, an alternative form of health center administration discussed in the next section.[29]

28. This is from Francke (1998, 35).
29. These data were provided by the former director of the CLAS program, Ricardo Díaz Romero, February 19, 2001.

Decentralization: The Shared Administration Program (CLAS)

At about the same time that the Basic Health for All Program was developed in the Ministry of Health by one reform team, another small team was working on a policy called the Shared Administration Program. This program came to be known simply as CLAS, after the local health administration committees it created. The CLAS policy was created in the same context of urgency as PSBT. Yet it represents a different approach—the decentralization of resources and administration. The form of this decentralization is particular. Rather than decentralizing health care administration to municipal governments, as in the cases of Colombia and Brazil analyzed in this volume, CLAS involved decentralization of local health post administration to community representatives. Of the six representatives that sit on the CLAS board, the community elects three and the chief doctor of the local health post appoints the other three. Those selected by the doctor are drawn from health-related community organizations, such as mothers' clubs and soup kitchens.

Each health center that converted to the CLAS model legally became a private nongovernmental organization (termed *personería jurídica*). Though legally private and independent, each CLAS center was dependent on the Health Ministry (in the case of the Lima CLAS) or its regional health authority (in the case of provinces) for its main budget, primarily for salaries. CLAS's health center infrastructure also remains state property. CLAS centers were free to spend as they saw fit all the income they raised through fees for services, within basic ministry guidelines. This financial flexibility led many CLAS centers to improve their infrastructure and hire additional staff members. CLAS members were required to approve a local community health plan each year, a component that urged greater responsiveness of health services to community circumstances.

Finally, the health workers in the CLAS centers were hired directly by the CLAS members, who evaluated these workers on at least an annual basis. This provision in the policy effectively increased worker productivity and their responsiveness to the community, because their supervisors were local community members able to monitor their activities on a daily basis.[30] These workers, like PSBT workers, are contracted, but are generally contracted for a year rather than a few months at a time. In addition, CLAS workers, unlike PSBT workers, received regular benefits such as vacation

30. Altobelli (1998a) compared productivity levels in CLAS and non-CLAS centers, and she found CLAS productivity levels to be higher.

and pension contributions—though for this privilege their salary scale was lower than that of their PSBT counterparts.

The CLAS policy was developed entirely within the Ministry of Health by a small reform team appointed by the Minister Freundt-Thurne. The team at first consisted of eight people and was eventually reduced to three.[31] This three-person core team wrote the Supreme Decree signed by the president that created CLAS.[32] Freundt-Thurne supported the project within the ministry, and he successfully sought the support of the president, whose signature was required on the Supreme Decree to make the reform legal.[33]

CLAS was tied financially to PSBT, receiving its funds from the same budget line approved by Congress for targeting, as part of the same health sector restoration effort. As a result, it did not need to go to Congress for inclusion in the budget. Thus, many key state players, such as Congress and the Ministry of the Economy and Finance, played no role. Also, President Fujimori's interest in the policy was only improvement in health services; that this "was CLAS or not CLAS was not important."[34] In short, the formulation process proceeded simply from a minister-appointed reform team to the president for passage as a Supreme Decree.

There was no institutional point in this process that allowed for wider discussion of the policy, either with Congress and its political parties or with organized groups in civil society. At the time, the opposition to the government was fairly vocal and strong (e.g., Peru's new Constitution had barely passed in a referendum in 1993, and this low support was widely perceived to indicate a lack of public confidence in the Fujimori administration). Doctors' and health workers' associations initially viewed the CLAS policy as an attempt to privatize public health care, given the legally private status of each CLAS center. Opposition to the reform came from various associations of health professionals. The Colegio Médico, Peru's equivalent to the American Medical Association, issued a statement in opposi-

31. This is from an interview by the author with an anonymous member of the original CLAS formulation team, Lima, April 8, 1998.

32. This is from an interview by the author with Carlos Bendezú, a member of the three-person CLAS formulation team, Lima, March 17, 1998. The author also interviewed an anonymous member.

33. This is from an interview by the author with Juan José Vera del Carpio, director of Program of Shared Administration (CLAS), MINSA, Lima, April 23, 1998, and from an interview by the author with Jaime Freundt-Thurne, former minister of health, Lina, April 15, 1998.

34. Interview with Freundt-Thurne.

tion to CLAS after the Supreme Decree was first issued. This association and the Medical Federation opposed the reform due to its potential to privatize local health posts. As a member of the Medical Federation explained, when the policy was introduced, "we were not in agreement with giving the community the responsibility to finance health services, in other words the possible privatization of health services or self-administration."[35] In addition, the Federation of Ministry Workers, fearing the negative impact further decentralization would have on the unity and viability of their union, vocally opposed the measure.[36]

The formulators of the CLAS policy simply avoided discussion with opposition groups, and they did not let opposition stop or slow the reform. As one of the three central reform team members stated: "We never responded. We simply took a very low profile."[37] According to Freundt-Thurne however, taking a low-profile approach was not necessarily a strategy to avoid opposition—it was simply how the ministry reform teams worked.

The international arena played a support role in the development of the CLAS reform. The idea of community participation in health center administration came from publications by the World Bank and UNICEF. One policymaker involved in the formulation of the CLAS policy emphasized the importance of the World Bank's publication of *World Development Report 1993* on health care financing and UNICEF's 1990 book, *The Bamako Initiative,* on the experience of community participation in health administration in Africa.[38] The influence of these publications demonstrates the linkages between policy elites in Peru and international discourses on health reform.

In addition to these discursive influences, the reform team members were funded through international sources, specifically the above-mentioned Inter-American Development Bank loan. In addition, a small amount of international funding from USAID allowed the team to hire a foreign consultant in the development of the policy. Funding for the implementation of the CLAS program, like PSBT, came entirely from the public treasury, with no international financial support.

Upon implementation, rather than seeking national coverage as PSBT

35. Interview by the author with Ricardo Díaz Romero, a member of the board of directors of the Medical Federation (Federación Médica), Lima, February 14, 1998.
36. Interview with Vera.
37. This is from an interview by the author with Carlos Bendezú, consultant to the Program to Strengthen Health Services, MINSA, Lima, March 17, 1998.
38. Interview with Bendezú. See UNICEF 1990 on UNICEF's Bamako Initiative.

did, CLAS was piloted in a few regions. The expansion of CLAS depended upon the will of the autonomous regional health authorities. Some of these were enthusiastic and implemented the program widely, while others saw further decentralization as a political threat to their authority and refused to implement it either well, or at all. Thus, CLAS was implemented unevenly. By 1997, three years into the program, CLAS covered only 10 percent of all primary level health establishments connected to the Ministry of Health—a far cry from the 72 percent coverage of PSBT, which started at about the same time.[39] Positively, slow piloting allowed the reform to be tested and modified, responding to the needs of staff and community members, before expanding further.

As was noted above, CLAS and PSBT worked toward modernization of the public health system in two opposing forms—one via greater centralization and one via decentralization to community members. Although PSBT was accepted in part due to the substantial resources it provided, CLAS was rejected by many local doctors and regional directors who refused to give up their power to local community members whom they did not recognize as their peers.

When Freundt-Thurne left the minister's office, CLAS began to lose its high-level position in the ministry, and regional directors and policy elites within the ministry who opposed CLAS found ways to slow its progress. For example, the reform that proposed joining a number of establishments into a network that shared equipment and was supervised by a contracted manager was viewed as a reform incompatible with the independent nature of CLAS. Opponents of CLAS seized upon this inconsistency, and CLAS expansion was halted for much of 1998 and part of 1999.

The World Bank and Inter-American Development Bank, who viewed CLAS positively, coordinated parallel loans in 1999 that required CLAS to be expanded. Even with the strong support of the IFIs, CLAS still faced an uphill battle. In early 2000, CLAS had begun to expand once again as a result of the loan requirements. In mid-2000 however, the Fujimori government's minister of the economy and finance cut the CLAS program budget significantly, leading to the resignation of the director of CLAS. As of 2001, CLAS had grown from 10 percent of health centers and posts to 19 percent.[40] In the first year of the Toledo government, CLAS centers were

39. The data are from *Data Social* 4, no. 6 (Instituto Apoyo), and from MINSA (1996b).

40. The data were provided by the former director of the CLAS program, Ricardo Díaz Romero, February 19, 2001.

once again expanding, but they were not mentioned in that government's health sector reform plans. As of this writing, it is hard to gauge whether CLAS will survive the Toledo government's proposed decentralization of health care services to municipalities.

In sum, in the case of CLAS, we see significant support from IFIs. However, government officials used a number of tactics to thwart CLAS expansion and the intentions of the lenders. The chief issue in the case of CLAS was power—the program significantly democratized power relations within the health sector, and thus faced the most resistance.

Market Competition: Health Provider Entities (EPS)

Whereas the role of the state in health care provision expanded with the PSBT and CLAS programs aimed at poor people, the reform of the Social Security health system, serving the middle and working classes, reduced the role of the state as a provider. It did so by allowing private health care companies to offer health care provision to workers previously only covered by the state Social Security system.

In the early 1990s, Ministers Freundt-Thurne and Yong Motta made unsuccessful bids to create Health Service Organizations (Organizaciones de Servicios de Salud, OSS) on the heels of pension reform. In 1991, the OSS reform was passed by legislative decree, but it was never implemented due to strong opposition from organized labor, retired persons, and health care professionals.[41] The plan thus lay dormant until Marino Costa Bauer— a former insurance executive explicitly appointed to see the reform's passage—was appointed minister. In 1996, the president passed a second legislative decree, based on a modified version of the OSS policy developed by Costa Bauer's team, and titled Health Provider Entities (Entidades Prestadoras de Salud, EPS) rather than OSS. This time, opposition members of congress protested that this decree was unconstitutional, because it extended beyond the powers that Congress had granted the president for decree-making authority; they had authorized decrees related to privatization but not to reforming the Social Security system.

Ultimately, the proposal passed through Congress as the Modernization of Health Social Security Law in May of 1997 (Ley de Modernización de Seguridad Social en Salud). Peru's weak party system and presidential control of Congress at the time made passage of the law through Congress

41. Legislative Decrees are decrees made by the president within a specific policy area authorized by the Congress.

relatively trouble-free, and Congress made few changes to the 1996 decree. Neither the passage of the OSS bill by legislative decree nor the EPS bill, despite the fact that the latter finally passed Congress, allowed for more than a few hours of public debate on this reform.

The final reform allowed private networks of health clinics and hospitals, Health Provider Entities (EPS), to compete with the state Social Security health system for workers' health care coverage. Similar to the PSBT and CLAS reforms, the failed OSS and successful EPS proposals were devised by small reform teams appointed by the minister. The EPS team, furthermore, was funded through the IDB loan mentioned above.[42] As a result of resistance to all-out privatization (the route taken with pensions), the initial reform was substantially modified. First, it simply introduced competition to the state system, rather than privatization. Second, it allowed for "solidarity" among workers, in that workers as a whole in each company vote on which health provider will obtain a company health insurance contract. Company-by-company selection, rather than individual selection, avoids potentially different plans for different types of workers—management and labor, for example. In addition, as a cost-containment measure, EPS provide only primary and secondary care, while more expensive complex care is reserved for the state system. As a result of this final measure, of the paycheck contribution (9 percent of a worker's pay), 25 percent goes to EPS while 75 percent goes to the state system, ESSALUD.

This reform to the social security system faced much greater resistance than the public system reforms for a number of reasons. Although IPSS covered a smaller portion of the population (only 23 percent of the population, compared with the 74 percent covered by the Ministry of Health), it affected more organized sectors of society, including workers and Social Security health system workers, who remained better organized than public health sector workers. Second, because this reform initially mirrored the reform of the pension system privatized previously, the opposition was primed to oppose a reform of this type. Finally, whereas an important subgroup of health workers saw substantial benefit in the ministry reforms described above, and these reforms brought an increase in health services for the poor populations involved, the reform of the social security sector

42. This is from an interview by the author with Raúl Torres, head of the committee charged with monitoring the reform of health social security, Lima, February 25, 1998 (first interview). The author also interviewed an anonymous general on the MINSA reform team, Lima, February 23, 1998.

implied job and resource loss for the state Social Security system. The opposition to the reform failed to stop it, in part because many white-collar workers wanted a choice in health care options, and the improved health care quality that EPS reform promised. In large part, however, the reform progressed to implementation because the Fujimori administration used every political tactic possible to see it succeed despite opposition.

Targeted Insurance Schemes: Free School Health Insurance (SEG)

In July 1997, the Seguro Escolar Gratuito (again, SEG, Free School Health Insurance) reform was introduced. Unlike all the other health sector reforms, SEG fell outside both the neoliberal policy discourses and the traditional process of policy formulation by policy elites within the executive branch. SEG was clearly a presidential initiative motivated by populist presidential politics.

The SEG reform provided free health care coverage through Peru's public health system to all children, preschool through age seventeen years, enrolled in Peru's public school system. The insurance offered broad coverage that promised to increase economic access to health care. It was also targeted to the extent that primarily poor people and the lower classes attend Peru's public school systems. The major objectives of the reform, however, were not related to health but to education. Free health insurance for schoolchildren was to encourage parents to enroll their children in school and to act as a disincentive for children to drop out. From a public health perspective, by targeting an age group that is considered to be low risk compared with other age groups, the reform made little sense. If better health outcomes were the goal, this money would be better spent on children in the age range from birth to five years, who face the greatest health risks. For the president, however, it made political sense.

President Fujimori announced SEG in his July 1997 Independence Day address to the nation. SEG was an extension of his ongoing interest in education. (He had been using school construction in poor communities as a populist tool for some time.) His special consultants on education policy conceived of the concept, and his address was the first notice given to the Ministry of Health officials of the reform.[43] The ministry—charged with developing the specifics of the reform and launching it, all in the space of a

43. This is from an interview by the author with Ulisis Jorge Aguilar, director of Seguro Escolar Gratuito, Lima, January 19, 1999, and from a conversation with Victor Zamora of DFID, Lima, July 22, 2002.

month—assembled a small team of consultants to design and implement the program. Ulises Jorge Aguilar, a former head of a regional health authority, led the team.

According to Jorge, the process he led of formulating the SEG program "surged from his strong authority," where he "ordered things." Not only was input not invited from civil society but the advice of other reform teams and program administrators within the ministry was rejected.[44] As a result of the president's strong support for the reform and this authoritatively led reform team, the SEG reform proceeded from announcement to implementation rapidly—in less than a month—with no time for either support or opposition to the measure (though there were no clear "losers" in this case to protest). Nor did legal institutions pose barriers, as the program proceeded without any legal basis for the first two years of its existence.

SEG was also independent of international influence. The program's formulation and implementation was funded entirely through the national treasury. Only after over a year of implementation did one international agency, UNICEF, begin to take an interest in the program and support it in small ways.[45] The program was implemented at fairly low cost. Even after being combined with the maternal infant insurance in 2000, the two programs accounted for 5 percent of the budget of the Ministry of Health (MINSA 2002, 20). The closed policy formulation process however led to a lack of understanding of the reform by both parents and health care providers that bogged down health services delivery under the program for the first year. In subsequent years, the program did increase the health insurance coverage of children significantly.[46]

Conclusion

Peru's health care reform process during the 1990s was piecemeal. The lack of a vision for reform stems from the fact that, other than pension reform, second-wave state reforms were largely incomplete in Peru, and from the very insulated manner in which these policies developed. Health sector reform could only progress to the extent that a broader state reform process

44. Interview with Jorge.
45. Interview with Jorge.
46. In 2001, the combined Seguro Escolar and Seguro Materno covered 4,602,000 individuals. In February 2002, these programs were folded into the more comprehensive Seguro Integral de Salud (SIS, Integral Health Insurance) ("SIS Necesita S/.127 Milliones Más Para Brindar Mayor Cobertura," *Gestión Médica,* February 2003).

was under way. The two most dramatic reforms in the health sector, the employment and Social Security reforms, were either part of first wave reforms or strongly linked to these. The change in employment regimen, incorporated most vigorously in the PSBT program, from a public- to a private-sector model was made possible by a national level effort to make labor laws more flexible. The introduction of private-sector competition into the social security sector via EPS was also a significant reform, and one that was initially linked to the reform of pensions, a second-wave reform with strong ties to first-wave economic reforms due to the savings incentives built into private pension portfolios. The EPS reform was slowed by well-organized opposition for a remarkably long time, but it eventually did progress to implementation. In contrast to successful first-wave reforms, the reform of the social sectors, or second-wave reforms, were incomplete or incomprehensive under Fujimori—not only in health, but also in other social sector areas.

Another reason for the piecemeal character of health reform in Peru was its closed policy process—small groups of five to ten people worked on one reform, with little or no dialogue with groups concurrently working on separate reforms, or with those who had developed previous reforms. Moreover, political parties, civil society, and municipalities played a very minor, if any, part in the process. Greater democracy and dialogue may have led to a unified vision by forcing consideration of the underlying philosophy and how different reform ideas might coalesce or conflict—as occurred in Brazil and Colombia, where there were broad, encompassing reforms.

Despite the fact that the Fujimori regime is now widely recognized as having been authoritarian, the closed policy process is not unique to that period. Even outside the authoritarian Fujimori period, Peru's health politics has always been to some degree isolated—from the tactics of co-optation that led to the creation of the social security sector under President Óscar Raymundo Benavides Larrea in the 1930s, to the interventionist role played by the Rockefeller Foundation that influenced the fledgling public health sector in the 1920s and 1940s. The closed nature is reinforced by Peru's political institutions and legal system that do not require that all policies pass Congress and thus become open to greater public debate.

The implications of a closed process are rapid policy formulation that dodges opposition. But closed processes can result in conflicting policies, as the four cases detailed above noted—for example, between CLAS and PSBT, and CLAS and the networks. Top-down policymaking also risks a lack of consensus around reforms, or a misunderstanding of reforms. The CLAS program has faced both of these—a lack of political support and a severe lack of understanding of the way in which the reform works, its objectives, and its positive results. Thus, many oppose the reform not only due to the consequences it has for their own power but also due to faulty information. This lack of understanding and consensus contributed to the various stoppages in CLAS expansion.

Rather than a unified vision, policy elites seemed to share some common basic objectives for the sector—specifically modernization, efficiency, and equity. Modernization of the sector was in response to the crisis situation of the health system in the early 1990s. The PSBT and CLAS programs were designed to bring a basic level of health care to communities that had little or none. Funds for this modernization were available as a result of recent government sales of state industries. Modernization of the sector also helped to promote Fujimori's image as a leader who delivered. CLAS and PSBT incorporated some important strategies for increasing efficiency as well. The new employment regimen was a major reform; it gave strong incentives to PSBT staff in particular to achieve high productivity. CLAS staff were on a contracted regimen, but oversight by a community board was an innovative and effective mechanism for not only encouraging greater efficiency but also higher-quality work. Both were forms of targeting, a strategy of using health care resources more efficiently by offering them to those who need services most. The SEG reform, although derived from populism, was also a form of targeting—only children in public schools were eligible. Finally, the EPS reform intended to spur greater efficiency and quality in the social security sector by introducing market competition. Many policy elites also had the objective of increasing equity, but equity defined as a minimum standard of services for all (a basic needs approach), rather than a more egalitarian vision of a unified system or similar quality of care for all.[47]

References

Abusada, Roberto, Fritz Du Bois, Eduardo Morón, and Jose Valderrama, eds. 2000. *La reforma incompleta: Rescatando los noventa.* Lima: Centro de Investigación de la Universidad del Pacífico and Insitituto Peruano de Economía.

---

47. On competing definitions of equity in the field of health care, see Wagstaff and van Doorslaer (1993).

244   *Christina Ewig*

Altobelli, Laura C. 1998a. Comparative Analysis of Primary Health Care Facilities with Participation of Civil Society in Venezuela and Peru. Paper prepared for a seminar titled Social Programs, Poverty, and Citizen Participation, held by the State and Civil Society Division, Inter-American Development Bank, Cartagena, Colombia, March 12–13.

———. 1998b. *Salud, reforma, participación comunitaria e inclusión social: El programa de administración compartida.* Resumen Ejecutivo del Informe. Lima: UNICEF-Peru.

Bachrach, Peter, and Morton S. Baratz. 1962. Two Faces of Power. *American Political Science Review* 56, no. 4: 947–52.

Becerra Hidalgo, Armando A. 1988. *La salud en el Perú: Una etapa crítica 1979–1984.* Lima: Universidad Cayetano Heredia.

CEPAL (Comisión Económica para América Latina y el Caribe). 2000. *Panorama Social de América Latina 2000–2001.* Santiago: CEPAL.

Conaghan, Catherine M. 2001. *Making and Unmaking Authoritarian Peru: Reelection, Resistance, and Regime Transition.* North–South Agenda Paper 47. Miami: North–South Center, University of Miami.

Cortéz, Rafael. 1998. *Equidad y calidad de los servicios de salud: El caso de los CLAS.* Documento de Trabajo 33. Lima: Centro de Investigación de la Universidad del Pacífico.

Cúanto, S. A., Richard Webb, and Graciela Fernández Baca. 1991. *Perú en numeros 1991.* Lima: Cuanto S.A.

Cueto, Marcos. No date. Visiones de medicina y exclusión en los Andes y los Amazonas peruanos en la década de los cuarenta. Lima: Universidad Peruana Cayetano Heridia (unpublished).

Ewig, Christina. 1999. Democracia diferida: Un análisis del proceso de reformas en el sector salud peruano. In *Pobreza y políticas sociales en el Perú: Nuevos aportes,* ed. Felipe Portocarrero. Lima: Universidad del Pacífico.

———. 2000. Engineering Development: Family Planning Policy and Sterilization in Peru under Fujimori. Paper presented at the Twenty-First International Congress of the Latin American Studies Association, Miami, March 16–18.

———. 2001. Gender Equity and Neoliberal Social Policy: Health Sector Reform in Peru. Ph.D. dissertation, Political Science, University of North Carolina at Chapel Hill.

Francke, Pedro. 1998. *Focalización del gasto público en salud.* Lima: Ministerio de Salud.

Iguiñez Echeverría, Javier. 1998. The Economic Strategy of the Fujimori Government. In *Fujimori's Peru: The Political Economy,* ed. John Crabtree and Jim Thomas. London: Institute of Latin American Studies, University of London.

INEI (Instituto Nacional de Estadística e Informática). 1992. *Peru: Compendio estadistico 1991–1992.* Lima: INEI.

———. 1996. *Peru: Compendio Estadistico 1995–1996* Lima: INEI.

Livingston, Steven G. 1992. The Politics of International Agenda-Setting: Reagan and North–South Relations. *International Studies Quarterly* 36, no. 3: 313–29.

Lukes, Steven. 1974. *Power: A Radical View.* London: Macmillan.

MEF (Ministerio de Economía y Finanzas). 1999a. *Cierre del presupuesto del sector público para 1997.* Lima: Ministerio de Economía y Finanzas; www.mef.gob.pe/dnpp/index1.htm.

————. 1999b. *Cierre del presupuesto del sector público para 1998.* Lima: Ministerio de Economía y Finanzas. Available at www.mef.gob.pe/dnpp/index1.htm.

————. 2000. *Cierre del presupuesto del sector público para 1999.* Lima: Ministerio de Economía y Finanzas. Available at www.mef.gob.pe/dnpp/index1.htm.

————. 2001. *Cierre del presupuesto del sector público para 2000.* Lima: Ministerio de Economía y Finanzas. Available at www.mef.gob.pe/dnpp/index1.htm.

————. 2002a *Cierre del presupuesto del sector público para 2001.* Lima: Ministerio de Economía y Finanzas. Available at www.mef.gob.pe/dnpp/index1.htm.

————. 2002b. *Informe del monto acumulado en el Fondo de Estabilización Fiscal—FEF.* Lima: Ministerio de Economía y Finanzas.

————. 2002c. *Ingresos de recourses de la privatización de empresas del estado.* Tomos 1–24. Lima: Dirección General de Tesoro Público, Ministerio de Economía y Finanzas.

————. 2002d. *Uso de recursos de la privatización de empresas del estado.* Tomos 1–9. Lima: Dirección General del Tesoro Público, Ministerio de Economía y Finanzas.

MINSA (Ministerio de Salud del Perú). 1996a. *El desafío del cambio de milenio: Un sector salud con equidad, eficiencia y calidad—lineamientos de política de salud 1995–2000.* Lima: MINSA.

————. 1996b. *2ndo Censo de Infrastructura Sanitaria y Rescursos del Sector Salud 1996.* Lima: MINSA.

————. 2002. *Propuesta lineamientos de política sectorial para el período 2002–2012 y fundamentos para él plan estratégico sectorial del quinenio Agosto 2001–Julio 2006.* Lima: Ministerio de Salud del Perú.

PAHO (Pan American Health Organization). 1994. *Health Conditions in the Americas,* vol. 1. Washington, D.C.: PAHO.

————. 1998. *Health in the Americas.* Washington, D.C.: Pan American Health Organization.

Portocarrero Suarez, Felipe, and Mario Aguirre Guardia. 1992. *Informe de coyuntura: Evolución de la economía peruana.* Lima: Centro de Invesigaciones Universidad del Pacifico.

Programa de Fortalecimiento de Servicios de Salud y Consorcio ESAN-UPHA-SEVERS-FUNSALUD. 1997. *Análisis del financiamiento del sector salud.* Seminario modernización del sistema de financiamiento de salud. Lima: Ministerio de Salud del Perú.

Roberts, Kenneth. 1995. Neoliberalism and the Transformation of Populism in Latin America: The Peruvian Case. *World Politics* 48, no. 1: 82–116.

Saavedra, Jaime. 2000. La flexibilización el mercado laboral. In *La reforma incompleta: Rescatando los noventa,* ed. Roberto Abusada, Fritz Du Bois, Eduardo Morón, and Jose Valderrama. Lima: Centro de Investigación de la Universidad del Pacífico and Insitituto Peruano de Economía.

Schattschneider, Elmer Eric. 1960. *The Semi-Sovereign People: A Realist's View of Democracy in America.* New York: Holt, Rinehart, and Winston.

Tamayo, Gonzalo, and Pedro Francke. 1997. *Analysis del gasto público en salud.* Seminario modernización del sistema de financiamiento de salud. Lima: Ministerio de Salud del Perú.

Thorp, Rosemary. 1996. A Long-Run Perspective on Short-Run Stabilization: The Experience of Peru. In *The Peruvian Economy and Structural Adjustment: Past*

Present and Future, ed. Efraín Gonzales de Olarte. Miami: North–South Center Press, University of Miami.

UNICEF. 1990. Revitalizing Primary Health Care/Maternal and Child Health: The Bamako Initiative. Progress report presented to the UNICEF Executive Board 1990 Session. New York: UNICEF.

Wagstaff, Adam, and Eddy van Doorslaer. 1993. Equity in the Finance and Delivery of Health Care: Concepts and Definitions. In *Equity in the Finance and Delivery of Health Care: An International Perspective,* ed. Eddy Van Doorslaer, Adam Wagstaff, and Frans Rutten. Oxford: Oxford University Press.

Weyland, Kurt. 1996. Neopopulism and Neoliberalism in Latin America. *Studies in Comparative International Development* 31: 3–31.

Part Two

The Politics of Education Sector Reform

Chapter 9

The Politics of Education Sector Reform: Cross-National Comparisons

Robert R. Kaufman and Joan M. Nelson

The unequal coverage and low quality of public education in Latin America has long been viewed as a major cause of lagging economic growth and highly skewed distributions of income. After World War II, many governments did begin to recruit new teachers and build new schools; as a consequence, by the beginning of the 1980s, most children in the relevant age category were enrolled in the initial grades of primary school, and adult illiteracy rates had declined from about 34 to 13 percent (Puryear 1997, 4). Nevertheless, despite increased effort in these areas, the quality, efficiency, and equity of schooling remained low. Deficiencies in quality were reflected in a number of troubling patterns:

- Repetition and dropout rates were high relative to gross domestic product: As of the early 1990s, about one in every two students repeated first

The authors acknowledge the help of Javier Corrales, Merilee Grindle, Linda Larach, Maria Victoria Murillo, Juan Carlos Navarro, and Judith Tendler.

grade; and the urban workforce as a whole averaged just over five years
of schooling, well below levels of middle-income countries in other
regions (IDB 1998, 45; PREAL 2001, 8; Birdsall and Londoño 1998,
115).

- Although gender inequalities declined considerably during the 1960–90
period (PREAL 2001, 10), there were severe inequalities of other sorts.
Large disparities remained among urban and rural sectors of the population, across rich and poor regions within each country, and across income
categories. In the best cases (Argentina and Uruguay), the wealthiest 20
percent of the population had about twice as many years of schooling as
the poorest 20 percent; in the worst cases (Brazil and Mexico), the ratio
was about 4 to 1 (PREAL 2001, table A-12).
- Public spending priorities favored higher education, a pattern that reflected the preferences and influence of middle- and upper-income families in a position to send their children to private primary and secondary
schools (Birdsall, Londoño, and O'Connell 1998; Paul and Wolfe 1996).
In Chile, Costa Rica, the Dominican Republic, and Uruguay, the richest
fifth of the population received more than 50 percent of the higher
education subsidies, while the poorest fifth received only 10 percent
(World Bank 1990, 79).

By the early 1990s, a growing number of economists, policy specialists,
and international lending institutions began to focus increasingly on the
need to improve quality, equity, and efficiency in the provision of education. Such concerns reflected long-held convictions among market-oriented
economists concerning the importance of "human capital" investment, but
they were profoundly reinforced by the widening gap that opened between
Latin American and East Asian societies during the 1980s and 1990s
(World Bank 1993). The other chapters in this part of the book provide
accounts of efforts to address these challenges at the primary and secondary
levels within particular national settings. In this chapter, we draw comparisons across the cases and examine some of the factors that may account
for cross-national similarities and differences.

It needs to be emphasized that many of the shortcomings of Latin America's educational sectors are consequences of structural factors over which
reformers had little immediate control. The unequal distribution of assets
and income that characterized most Latin American societies was an underlying cause—as well as an effect—of many of the problems. Highly
skewed distributions of income increased the inclination of upper-income

families to resist taxes for public education and left families in low-income categories with fewer resources to shoulder the costs. The incentives of poor families to keep their children in school, moreover, were further weakened by the characteristics of regional labor markets. The primary product export sectors of Latin America did not require a large supply of skilled labor, and employment opportunities in import-substituting sectors were limited. The expectation of limited return to skills did much to account for high dropout rates at the primary school level (Birdsall and Londoño 1998).

Organizational and financing deficiencies on the supply side of education systems, however, also contributed to poor quality and performance. Much of the criticism that emerged during the 1980s and 1990s focused on the excessive centralization, organizational rigidities, and political penetration of the region's educational hierarchies. Not all school systems, to be sure, were fully centralized at the national level. Among the countries covered in this volume, state or provincial governments had acquired substantial responsibility for financing and management within the federal systems in Argentina, Brazil, and Colombia. Responsibilities were much more centralized in Mexico, Venezuela, and Nicaragua, although even in the first two countries, state-level systems did exist alongside much more extensive national ones.

Regardless of these differences, the central governments of all these countries retained substantial discretionary authority over funding transfers, textbooks and teaching materials, and curriculum; and politicians and union leaders typically controlled hiring and assignments of teachers and principals. School systems were characterized by a lack of accountability, by limited space for innovation or experimentation at the local level, and by a lack of incentives for local principals or teachers to improve pedagogical practices.

In this chapter, we compare efforts to correct these deficiencies, drawing on the case studies that follow. The first section sketches the emergence of the wide variety of reform proposals that came onto the political agenda during the 1980s and 1990s, and it maps the extent to which these were actually put into practice. In the next section, we outline the identity, preferences, and power resources of the major actors involved in these reform efforts. The "cast of characters," as we shall see, is similar to that discussed in chapter 2 above on health reform, and we group the actors in parallel categories: as proponents, opponents, and fence-sitters. The identity and resources of these actors changed during the course of the policy process; but as in the health sector, the power of status quo groups tended to predominate over actors whose primary goals were to improve the quality of education.

In the final section of the chapter, we assess the factors that propelled or impeded the initiation and implementation of reforms. Many countries undertook incremental and relatively noncontroversial initiatives, such as improved teacher training or curriculum modernization, that did not directly challenge stakeholder interests. Broader reforms, of course, were much more difficult. A relatively wide menu of more ambitious and controversial proposals for restructuring the education sector was also debated during the 1990s. For the most part, however, governments focused primarily on only one of these: the transfer of resources and responsibility to subnational units of government.

As we have already suggested in chapter 1, this aspect of education reform was emphasized mainly because it was a component of a broader political agenda supported by powerful actors whose primary interest lay outside the education sector. Reform proposals that could not be bundled in this way—for example, achievement testing, school autonomy, or community oversight—were given much lower priority.

The Context of Reform: How Much Has Happened?

The reforms discussed in the case-study chapters unfolded in a general context of sharply increasing international and domestic attention to the need to improve educational achievement throughout the region.[1] The centrality of education for development was underscored at a UNESCO-sponsored World Conference on Education, held in Thailand in 1990, in numerous regional conferences held in subsequent years, and in the 1998 meeting of American heads of state, in Santiago. In the course of the decade, investment in education became one of the highest priorities of the World Bank, the Inter-American Development Bank, and other international financial institutions. Conclaves, conferences, and studies in a number of individual countries replicated this ferment at the national level. In Argentina, for example, a National Education Congress convened in 1987 propelled "one of the most comprehensive debates about education reform ever witnessed in [that country]" (see chapter 11 of this volume). Our case

1. In this and later sections of this chapter, references to experience in specific countries are based on the case chapters in this volume, unless otherwise noted.

studies of Venezuela and Colombia, similarly, describe the organization of extensive discussions among education specialists and civic leaders over the need for education reform.

The evolving policy debate not only led to a heightened priority for education but also introduced new and highly controversial ideas regarding reforms. Reformers called not only for increased resources and measures to improve curriculum and pedagogy but also for broader changes in organization and financing aimed at strengthening performance incentives and accountability of teachers and school administrators. At the same time, in the general climate of concern about cautious macroeconomic management, the policy debate also focused on ways to make education systems more efficient. Ideas such as voucher and charter schools, contracting out of selected functions, merit pay and promotion, national tests and their use to assess performance of schools and teachers as well as students (and public access to test results), school autonomy, and parent and community participation took on much greater salience.

Two broad themes motivated both international and national ferment. One—emphasized especially by the World Bank and other international organizations—was the importance of education for development. Debates about education, it should be noted, were not closely tied to issues of fiscal savings. Indeed, in most of the countries discussed in this volume, education reform was linked to increased expenditures. Moreover, unlike several of the health reforms discussed in the second section, proposed reforms in education were not directly tied to other structural adjustment goals such as reducing payroll taxes or the partial privatization of pensions. Instead, the focus on education appeared to derive primarily from the broader conviction that investment in human capital was essential to modernization, poverty reduction, and economic competitiveness in increasingly integrated international markets.

Democratization in many countries also spurred the increasing interest in education. The inclusive civic discussions organized in Argentina, Colombia, and Venezuela all reflected a conviction that education was essential to deepening or consolidating democracy. Opinion surveys conducted by Latinobarómetro provide a useful picture of the extent to which the broader public viewed education as a major challenge facing their countries (the results are shown in tables 9.1 through 9.3). Not surprisingly, the highest proportion of respondents generally identified labor market issues as the most important problem, especially during the economic crisis of 2002. Nevertheless, in calmer periods, such as 2000, substantial proportions

Table 9.1

Survey Data on the Most Important Problem Facing the Country, 1998 (percent)

Problem	Argentina	Brazil	Colombia	Costa Rica	Mexico	Nicaragua	Peru	Venezuela
Education	**18.8**	**6.4**	**9.4**	**15.7**	**6.3**	**17.1**	**11.7**	**28.1**
Health	**1.7**	**8.9**	**2.7**	**0.6**	**2.4**	**2.0**	**1.4**	**8.1**
Labor market[a]	47.8	49.9	33.9	20.9	28.0	42.4	58.5	18.8
Crime and drugs[b]	8.6	15.9	2.6	19.5	11.5	9.0	4.4	8.8
Corruption[c]	9.8	5.5	6.9	13.5	8.7	8.3	3.3	14.3
Poverty	3.9	3.9	5.8	6.6	8.8	7.8	10.7	3.4
Inflation	0.8	0.9	3.3	7.7	21.1	5.8	2.5	9.0
Political violence	3.7	4.5	32.3	4.5	2.7	1.8	3.2	2.5
Other[c]	3.9	3.9	3.3	10.1	10.2	4.2	3.3	4.5
Do not know	0.4	0.2	0	0	0.3	0.7	0.9	0.5

[a]Combines questions on low salaries, conditions in the labor market, unemployment, and opportunities for the young.
[b]Combines separate questions on crime and drugs.
[c]Combines questions on environment and other.
Source: Data from Latinobarómetro, 1998; adapted from Grindle (2002, table 2.13).

Table 9.2

Survey Data on the Most Important Problem Facing the Country, 2000 (percent)

Problem	Argentina	Brazil	Colombia	Costa Rica	Mexico	Nicaragua	Peru	Venezuela	Total
Education	**17.5**	**9.5**	**14.6**	**16.4**	**12.7**	**21.7**	**17.0**	**31.3**	**21.2**
Health	**1.4**	**5.3**	**1.2**	**1.0**	**3.0**	**1.5**	**1.0**	**2.2**	**2.5**
Labor market[a]	46.5	47.0	29.0	18.9	29.4	37.4	60.0	28.5	36.1
Inflation and price rises	5.0	1.7	1.4	14.0	11.8	1.5	2.0	5.4	4.5
Poverty	3.4	3.7	4.6	8.3	9.9	9.5	6.0	5.4	7.1
Crime and drugs[b]	12.6	15.0	2.8	19.8	11.3	11.5	0	14.2	11.6
Corruption	12.5	9.6	8.6	14.3	11.1	13.7	3.0	5.0	9.1
Terrorism and political violence	2.9	5.3	35.5	1.0	4.1	0.9	4.0	3.2	4.7
Housing and environment[c]	1.1	1.0	1.2	4.7	4.3	0.9	0	3.1	2.0
Other	1.2	0.3	0.3	0.6	1.7	0.7	0	0.8	0.5
Do not know or no reply	0.4	1.0	0.5	1.1	0.8	0.8	0	1.0	0.7
Total									

[a]Combines questions on unemployment, instability in the labor market, low salaries, and opportunities for the young.
[b]Combines separate questions on crime and drugs.
[c]Combines questions on housing and the environment.
Source: Data from Latinobarómetro, 2000, in Graham and Sukhtnakar (2004).

Table 9.3

Survey Data on the Most Important Problem Facing the Country, 2002 (percent)

Problem	Argentina	Brazil	Colombia	Costa Rica	Mexico	Nicaragua	Peru	Venezuela	Total
Education	**6.3**	**2.8**	**3.0**	**1.8**	**7.9**	**1.1**	**5.0**	**5.9**	**3.8**
Health	**2.0**	**3.5**	**0.6**	**0.7**	**0.3**	**1.3**	**1.0**	**0.7**	**1.3**
Labor market[a]	44.8	42.0	36.3	29.8	41.2	49.6	60.0	47.3	46.4
Inflation and price rises	4.7	1.6	1.8	9.5	4.6	1.5	2.0	5.2	3.8
Poverty	10.5	5.9	4.1	11.4	11.8	9.8	13.0	6.2	10.3
Crime and drugs[b]	6.5	2.6	1.8	2.5	15.4	3.8	0	13.8	11.3
Corruption	17.9	6.2	4.8	11.5	10.7	27.3	6.0	6.0	11.4
Terrorism and political violence	2.0	5.7	43.3	1.2	2.6	1.3	3.0	6.3	5.7
Housing, transportation, and environment[c]	0.6	2.0	1.3	38.8	2.6	1.1	0	3.3	2.0
Human rights	3.3	1.9	1.7	1.7	2.0	0.5	1.0	2.1	1.7
Discrimination	0.1	1.4	0	0.8	0.7	0	0	0.2	0.3
Other or no response	1.3	0.4	0.6	0.9	0.7	1.6	0	1.7	0.9
Do not know or no reply	0.2	0.8	1.0	1.3	0.5	1.2	2.0	1.5	1.1

[a]Combines questions on unemployment, instability in the labor market, low salaries, and opportunities for the young.
[b]Combines separate questions on crime, drugs, and drug consumption.
[c]Combines questions on housing, transportation, and the environment.
Source: Data from Latinobarómetro, 2000, in Graham and Sukhtnakar (2004).

(between about 10 and 20 percent) also named education as an important problem. As table 9.3 shows, education ranked first in Venezuela, and second in Argentina, Mexico, Nicaragua, and Peru among the most important problems facing the country. Education also ranked first in 2000 in several countries not included in our tables: Bolivia, Costa Rica, Ecuador, Guatemala, Honduras, and Paraguay. In Colombia, education ranked third during this year, behind labor market issues and political violence. In all countries, mass publics consistently attached a far higher importance to education than to health issues, a concern that could conceivably be translated into electoral support for reform.

In light of this interest, how much education reform has actually taken place? As we shall see more clearly below, the extensive attention devoted to education did not translate directly into specific public policies. Although there is some statistical evidence that democratic transitions have led to increased spending on education (Kaufman and Segura-Ubiergo 2001), the connection to specific organizational reforms is much less clear. One reason is that—despite a flood of proposals and pilot plans—broad civic debates produced little in the way of a coherent reform agenda. Consensus within the policy community did not extend beyond commitments to broad principles of accountability, equity, and efficiency, and experts frequently disagreed about priorities among these goals or the types of measures that would achieve them. In addition, as we shall discuss in more detail below, there were potent political and institutional barriers to the implementation of broad structural changes in the sector. Nevertheless, by the early 1990s, educators and government reformers were presented with a broad menu of steps from which to choose (Gajardo 1999, 10).

The momentum provided by this increase in interest, moreover, did go beyond rhetoric. Many countries, as noted above, have undertaken a wide variety of relatively small-scale changes in the educational system. These have generally been pressed by policy specialists, educators, and other actors within the sector; and they have moved forward with the support—or at least without the strong opposition—of major stakeholders.

Among measures generally viewed within the sector as desirable were add-on programs expanding the coverage of preschool programs. Research during the 1990s offered growing evidence of the importance of early childhood education (and nutrition) for later performance. And the preschool programs did not threaten or inconvenience existing programs; indeed, in some cases they may have broadened patronage possibilities. Preschool enrollment increased more than fivefold in Colombia between

1980 and 1997, and it more than quadrupled in Brazil and Nicaragua during that period (Rama 2002, table 6). For the region as a whole, preschool enrollments increased from 44 to 54 percent of the relevant age category during the 1990s (Wolff and de Moura Castro 2003, 186).

Targeted pro-poor programs to provide materials, equipment, and better infrastructure for schools in neglected or poor regions were also part of reform efforts in Argentina, Brazil, and Colombia among our cases, as well as Bolivia, Chile, the Dominican Republic, Costa Rica, Guatemala, Paraguay, Peru, and Uruguay (PREAL 2001). For example, throughout the 1990s Chile's P900 program focused intensive efforts on the least-well-performing 900 schools, mainly in poor rural areas. The schools were given special supportive supervision, better materials and facilities, and teachers' aides; they were also challenged with mild competitive incentives (Angell 1996). The PREAL survey of education reforms mentions curricular reform in Argentina, Brazil, and Mexico, as well as in Chile, the Dominican Republic, Costa Rica, and Uruguay, and teacher training in Argentina, Brazil, Colombia, and Nicaragua, as well as in Chile, the Dominican Republic, Costa Rica, Guatemala, and Uruguay.

Some of these measures did involve vigorous technical debate; for instance, the use of teachers' aides in Chile provoked criticism from some union and professional groups. Expanded and improved teacher training, changes in pedagogic techniques, the use of testing, and curriculum and textbook modernization also had some potential for arousing vigorous argument in professional circles, but only the curriculum and textbook issues had much likelihood of erupting into broader political battles—as was the case with the nationalist and ideological reactions to proposed curriculum changes in Mexico. Often, however, the scope and intensity of these reforms were mainly determined by the commitment and capacity of education ministry leadership.

As in the health sector, incremental qualitative reforms were also accompanied, in many countries, by increased overall investment in buildings, equipment, and materials. For instance, Argentina adopted an objective of doubling investment in primary and secondary education over a period of five years. Though increased outlays are not themselves reforms, they could be an important supplement to reform efforts, especially where the fiscal pressures of the 1980s had virtually dried up investment in the sector.

Like the add-on programs in the health sector, these steps did not involve substantial reorganizations within the education sector and did not directly challenge strongly held stakeholder interests. They generally did not entail substantial restructuring of financing or lines of authority within the sector as a whole, and they did not touch the "entitlements" of teachers and other education specialists. Often, they could be carried out through ministerial decisions that do not require legislation or even a formal decree. In short, they could, and often did, fly "under the political radar screen."

Potentially, the cumulative effects of such measures may well produce a substantial improvement in educational achievement over time, and in some cases, a substantial political payoff for incumbent governments as well. Yet incremental policy reforms may also be vulnerable to reversal if they are not reinforced by changes in other parts of the system, or if a reshuffling of ministry personnel leads to a withdrawal of support. In chapter 16, we take up the question more generally of the circumstances in which the momentum for incremental reforms can be sustained.

Beyond incremental qualitative changes, a number of countries discussed in this volume also undertook more controversial reforms of core features of the education sector. As the case studies show, however, there was substantial variation both with respect to which of these items were initiated in the different countries and in the extent to which they were implemented. Table 9.4 below summarizes the major reform steps for each of our six cases. Several important features stand out.

As was noted in the introduction to this chapter, the most important theme was the decentralization of at least some components of the educational system to subnational governments. In at least four of the six cases (Argentina, Colombia, Mexico, and Venezuela) this was the most salient sector reform item on the political agenda, and it required legislative approval. Brazil is somewhat different, because much of the responsibility for operating the schools at the primary and secondary levels was already in the hands of governors and mayors. As in the other countries, however, a key issue of the Brazilian education reforms was how to adjust intergovernmental sharing of resources and responsibilities in ways that would change incentives within the educational system.

There were, of course, considerable differences in the goals and extent of decentralization in these countries. Motivations ranged from efforts to reduce central government expenditures (Argentina) to greater concern for making the system more efficient or equitable in the other cases. Results were also quite mixed. In Colombia, for example, vague constitutional mandates and poorly drawn legislative measures opened the way to considerable confusion of funding and lines of authority. In Venezuela, decentralization was authorized by legislation but never extensively

Table 9.4
A Profile of Education Reforms in Six Countries, 1990s

Reform	Colombia	Brazil	Argentina	Mexico	Venezuela	Nicaragua
Decentralization	Decentralized to departments and municipalities but works poorly	Already decentralized; used fiscal incentives to reduce inequities in funding, and encourage desired pro-poor and other programs	Secondary schools decentralized to provinces	Primary and some secondary schools decentralized to states, varied results	In Carlos Andres Pérez era, voluntary decentralization to states but almost no take-up	No decentralization (though much school autonomy, see below)
School autonomy	Not part of national reform, but important element in Bogotá program	Very limited national encouragement; big component in Minas Gerais	Not part of national program; big component in San Luis	Not part of program	Limited element in Escuelas Integrales program (Mérida) and Venezuelan Association of Catholic Schools	Major element in national Autonomous Schools Program
Parent and community participation	None	Major element in Minas Gerais program, but very limited elsewhere	Element (not major?) in San Luis program	Modest legal provision, but does not function	Very modest element in Mérida program	Major element in Autonomous Schools Program
Use of testing	None for purposes of school or policy evaluation	None for purposes of school or policy evaluation	None for purposes of school or policy evaluation	None for purposes of school or policy evaluation	None for purposes of school or policy evaluation	None for purposes of school or policy evaluation

implemented. Nevertheless, in all these cases, much of the "politics of education reform" revolved around issues of decentralization and fiscal federalism.

A second comparative point of interest is the contrasting emphasis in Nicaragua on school autonomy and community involvement rather than on decentralization to local government. In part because of the opportunities opened by the broader process of decentralization, such measures were also taken in several states and municipalities in the larger countries, such as in the state of Minas Gerais in Brazil. Nevertheless, Nicaragua was the only one of the six countries in which school autonomy was an integral part of the national reform program. As Gershberg stresses in chapter 14 of this volume, both the motives and the context for reforms focused on increased school autonomy are quite different from those driving a shift in responsibility for education from higher to lower levels of government.

Finally, table 9.4 also shows a number of important roads that were *not* taken. Notwithstanding the attention given in reform literature to the radical Chilean reforms in education (and health) services under Pinochet, school privatization and vouchers were generally "off the table"—although in Venezuela, unions raised the specter of privatization to block rather modest charter school proposals. Similarly, while many countries began to develop assessment testing during the 1990s, participation in standardized regional or international tests was very limited (Tiana Ferrer 2000), and the results of these and other tests were rarely used as policy tools to evaluate and reward the performance of schools or teachers (Gajardo 1999, 10). In Mexico and Brazil, governments backed down from initiatives to charge tuition or fees for higher education, and this was not even attempted in the other countries. Finally, and perhaps most important, initiatives to incorporate merit incentives into the statutes governing teacher pay and promotions were stillborn or blocked.

The Cast of Characters: Reformers, Opponents, and the Uninvolved

Many factors account for these cross-national parallels and differences in the type and extent of educational reform. An important first step in analyzing these patterns, however, is to identify the relevant actors, their resources, and their interests. As a number of chapters indicate, the identity, resources, and preferences of these actors may change considerably as policies move from the drawing board to implementation. Nevertheless, it is possible to identify players that are especially important at various points in the reform process, either as supporters or opponents of reform proposals. As in chapter 2, we also note actors that played a less active role than might have been expected.

Who Presses for Reform?

Notwithstanding the noticeable upsurge in civic interest in better education, the range of actors actively pressing for specific policy changes was relatively limited throughout the course of the 1990s. Typically, reform initiatives came from sector specialists within international and national organizations, officials concerned with macroeconomic reform, or in some instances from presidents and other top political leaders. In at least two of our cases—Nicaragua and Brazil—the main proponents of reform were ministers of education, specialists who ascended to that position after long careers as analysts of the educational system and advocates for measures intended to improve quality. In Venezuela, the minister of education appointed by President Rafael Caldera (1993–98) had also been a longtime advocate of education reform, although the main impetus for decentralization came from nonspecialists within the Presidential Commission for State Reform (COPRE) (Navarro 2000).

In some cases, key support for education reform also came from officials linked to finance ministries, whose careers had been in the macroeconomic policy area, rather than in education. Although such officials were generally concerned about efficiency, it is important to emphasize that decentralization was only rarely driven by the goal of relieving pressures on the federal budget. This goal was paramount only in Argentina; and even in that country, provincial governors and teachers' unions eventually forced the powerful finance minister to commit to significant funding increases in education expenditures. In Mexico, where macroeconomic officials also took the lead in initiating reform, President Salinas and then–minister of education Zedillo appeared to view decentralization less as a way to save public funds than as a necessary step toward making the Mexican economy more competitive; as Grindle points out in chapter 10 of this volume, educational expenditures rose during their period in power. Spending as a proportion of gross domestic product also rose significantly during the 1990s in Brazil and Colombia, and went up at least slightly in Venezuela (see table 1.2 in the present volume).

International financial institutions—especially the World Bank and the Inter-American Development Bank—have provided a third source of advocacy for education reforms. They have been important in focusing attention on education issues, and they have provided information and advice, especially about the experiences of other countries and regions. External funding has also provided important support in cases where local reformers have managed to gain political traction, and both the World Bank and Inter-American Development Bank have provided financial backing and technical advice in a number of cases. However, with the possible exception of Nicaragua, international financial institutions have not typically seized the initiative in launching and designing reform programs. Instead, in most instances, domestic actors have been pivotal in the initiative and design of reform programs.[2]

Stakeholders and Fence-Sitters

Teachers' unions were among the most visible and important stakeholders in the existing educational systems, and they generally wielded substantial political power in defense of their interests. During the 1950s, 1960s, and 1970s, teachers' unions had strongly supported the drive to expand primary schools and enrollments, which in turn contributed to substantial increases in union membership and political influence. In most countries, education workers constitute one of the two largest categories of public-sector employees. (The other large category is health.) Unlike health workers, moreover, teachers' career paths go almost entirely through the public sector; and in the absence of access to income from private markets, they are more likely to deploy political resources to press their demands (Maceira and Murillo 2001).

All the country case studies show that the unions were among the major opponents of the "quality reforms" that emerged on the political agenda during the 1990s. Their opposition, to be sure, was not always intransigent, as chapter 10 shows in the case of Mexico.[3] In general, though, they were powerful adversaries; and in most cases, they strongly objected to decentralization initiatives that would weaken bargaining leverage with polit-

2. Such conclusions are consistent with findings in large-N statistical studies that also show that the World Bank programs did not have a significant effect on pro-poor education policies (Hunter and Brown 2000).

3. In the Brazilian state of Minas Gerais, unions accepted an even more ambitious transfer of authority to local schools and parent communities.

ical authorities at the national level. Other measures that posed threats to core areas of union power—for example, efforts to strengthen incentives for teachers and schools by linking performance to rewards—were rarely attempted and vigorously resisted.

The capacity of the teachers' unions to block reforms, however, varied considerably, both across the countries and over time. Among the cases in this volume, the size, structure, and influence of the Colombian (FECODE) and Mexican (SNTE) unions gave them the greatest leverage over the course of the reform process. Both had grown rapidly during the expansion of the educational system in the 1970s. Both were highly centralized at the national level, and both exercised strong influence within their respective ministries of education.

Although these unions were unable to prevent changes in their respective educational systems, they did succeed in negotiating major compromises in the design of the reform and in defending their interests in the course of implementation. In both cases, they insisted successfully on the maintenance of centralized collective bargaining structures and personnel regulations; and they were able to extract a very high price in salary increases in return for concessions made with respect to decentralization. In Colombia's effort to decentralize education, union pressures significantly slowed attempts to increase municipal control and contributed to substantial confusion in the allocation of resources and responsibilities across levels of government. The union's demands for higher wages and increased hiring absorbed most of the dramatic constitutionally mandated increases in spending on education during the 1990s.

In other countries, the unions were weaker; and although this by no means guaranteed major changes in the educational system, it did provide reform proponents with greater room to maneuver. In Brazil's decentralized federal system, teachers' unions negotiated work contracts at the state level, and they were unable to coordinate an effective national response to restructuring initiatives discussed by Draibe in chapter 13. In Nicaragua, the main teachers' union was affiliated with the defeated Sandinista government, and it showed even less capacity to resist the school autonomy reforms described by Gershberg in chapter 14. In Venezuela, teachers were represented in seven different unions, and, as in Brazil, faced significant barriers to collective action. Decentralization reforms initiated during the 1990s failed to go forward in Venezuela, but the unions were not the major impediment. Implementation failed mainly because of the difficulty of negotiating educational funding transfers and the reluctance of local governments to take on new, potentially costly responsibilities (see chapter 15 by Bruni Celli in this volume; Navarro 2000).[4]

Although we have emphasized cross-national differences in this chapter, it is important to note that unions' political influence can also change over the course of reform. Argentine teachers' unions provide an interesting illustration of these dynamic possibilities. These unions were organized into both state-level and national confederations; and as in Brazil and Venezuela, they faced significant collective action problems. In 1991, when the minister of the economy, Cavallo, shifted responsibility for secondary education to the provinces, they were at first unable to respond. In subsequent years, however, the national teachers' confederation succeeded in mobilizing constituent units into a broad campaign for increased pay and federal financing. In this instance, paradoxically, the political rebound of the unions may well have had a positive effect, because it helped to soften an initiative originally aimed less at improving educational quality than at off-loading federal expenditures.[5]

Elected politicians were also important stakeholders, because of the opportunities for political patronage afforded by the educational bureaucracy. Like teachers' unions, politicians had gained politically from the "access reforms" of earlier decades. School-building programs were an important source of pork-barrel resources, and the benefits of new educational opportunities for their constituents' children were immediately apparent. Quality reforms of the sort debated in the 1990s, however, had less visible and popular payoffs within the broader electorate. As has been noted, the education sector was typically the largest source of public employment, and except under exceptional circumstances (democratic transitions, legitimacy crises, etc.), the gains of championing quality reforms were often outweighed by the costs of forgoing access to patronage resources within the educational system (Geddes 1994).

These factors weighed particularly heavily in the Colombian case, where legislators and party leaders successfully resisted efforts to reduce patronage control of hiring and promotion within the education sector. This was

4. Navarro (2000) argues that, despite the failure to transfer formal social sector responsibilities, the establishment of local elections for governors and mayors in 1989 created an important incentive for them to deliver social services, observing among other things a substantial increase in state and local expenditures. He suggests as well, however, that much of this effort went toward health services, rather than education.

5. New legislation established both mandatory and discretionary goals, including extending compulsory schooling from seven to ten years, guaranteed free attendance, and a doubling of federal investment in the sector during the next five years.

not uniformly true across all of the cases, however. Legislators were not significant actors in the reform stories in Mexico, Nicaragua, and Venezuela, and they played only a marginal role in the outcomes.

In other cases, circumstances led at least some party politicians to facilitate aspects of the reform process. In Brazil, significant backing for education reform came from leaders of Cardoso's PSDB (the Social Democratic Party), who had long-standing commitments to social sector reform. In Argentina, in the context of the union campaign mentioned above, Peronist moderates in the Chamber of Deputies helped to broker a compromise between the technocrats in the Finance Ministry and the representatives of the provincial governors over the issue of funding guarantees for the provinces (see chapter 11 by Corrales in this volume). Control over patronage was not directly at issue in this dispute, and the compromise defused a potentially explosive stalemate among the government, provincial authorities, and teachers' unions.

State or municipal officials were initially another source of opposition, or at least of ambivalence, about reform. In Argentina and Colombia, where education had already been federalized to some extent, governors were reluctant to pass authority on to municipalities. In Argentina, Mexico, and Venezuela, moreover, governors faced the difficult political challenge of how to merge pay scales and administration of the newly transferred school systems with those of existing state-level systems. Such problems slowed bilateral negotiations and implementation in Argentina and Mexico, and as noted, stalled decentralization more or less entirely in Venezuela.

At the same time, for many state and local officials who had previously lacked this authority, the federalization or municipalization of education posed considerable risk, as well as opportunities for political gains. In some localities (e.g., Minas Gerais in Brazil, San Luis in Argentina, and Bogotá), decentralization did provide enterprising governors and mayors with an opportunity for innovative programs of school accountability and parental participation at the local level. As in the health sector, however, local officials were generally reluctant to support modes of decentralization that, they felt, would leave them with responsibility but not adequate funding. Where teachers' unions had in the past dealt mainly with the national ministry, moreover, local authorities were not eager to take on the task of negotiating with the combative unions.

As with the teachers' unions, the power of governors and mayors vis-à-vis the national executive varied across the countries. In Mexico in the early 1990s, most governors were, de facto if not de jure, appointees of the president who had selected them as candidates of the PRI. As Grindle points out in chapter 10, governors played only a marginal role in negotiations over decentralization. In contrast, Argentine governors could generally count on the support of local constituencies and usually controlled sizable cliques within the Congress. Although they did not succeed in preventing the transfer of secondary schools from federal to provincial control in 1991, in the follow-up legislation of 1993, senators and deputies representing provincial interests pressed hard for steep increases and iron-clad guarantees of federal funding for education and won assurances that investment would be doubled over a five-year period.

To the extent that governments sought to shift funds away from tertiary education, the beneficiaries of "free" public universities were another significant source of opposition. In Brazil (and other countries), middle- and upper-income families pay the expense of a private primary and secondary education, in the expectation that their children will then have opportunities for entry into fully subsidized national universities. Efforts to reduce entitlements by shifting some of the costs to the students and their families have generated prolonged student and faculty strikes in a number of countries, including Argentina, Brazil, and Mexico, forcing governments to abandon initial proposals. Of course, if aggregate education expenditures increase, spending priorities can be changed without politically costly cutbacks in support for universities. Fiscal limits to this path, however, place a significant constraint on governments seeking to fund quality improvements at the primary and secondary levels.

As in the health sector, it is important to note the relatively limited role of business groups as significant actors in the reform process. International and government policy elites have frequently emphasized the need to upgrade the skills of the workforce as economies become more exposed to international market competition. However, our case studies show little evidence that business groups actually lobbied for such changes. The main exception was in Venezuela. Foro Educativo Venezuela, an advocacy group for education reform, received substantial financial support from the business community.[6] Business associations also provided support for an attempt in 1992 to launch a pilot program in selected public high schools. The program was dropped, however, in the face of violent opposition from teachers' unions who feared that it would open the door to nonunion hiring.

6. Juan Carlos Navarro, personal communication.

Elsewhere, business sectors did not appear to be key players. Indeed, recent research in Northeast Brazil (Tendler 2002) shows that some business and industrial groups are not merely passive, but more fundamentally skeptical about increased education. According to surveys conducted in that region, the owners and managers of large modern plants believe that in-plant training can ensure reasonable productivity by workers with little formal education. More schooling, they fear, would reduce labor docility, encourage out-migration to more advanced regions, and ultimately raise wages. Regional politicians and officials often share these concerns, and view cheap labor as their region's main comparative advantage.

Reform efforts also appeared to gain only limited support from the general public, notwithstanding the relatively high priority accorded to education in public opinion surveys. The Latinobarómetro surveys discussed above show that public interest in education is widespread, but perhaps not intense, and is likely to diminish considerably during periods of economic crisis. Many parents with children attending school take an active interest in the affairs of that school; but that interest does not usually translate into awareness, much less activity, regarding policies and programs even at the local level, much less the national level. Moreover, high proportions of the middle-class parents most likely to be informed and vocal send their children to private schools. It is also possible that less-well-educated and poorer parents are less likely to be critical of the quality of the schools—perhaps because their children are receiving more education than they themselves were offered.

On a few occasions, government reformers have found it possible to mobilize broad support. In 2001, for instance, a far-reaching correction of educational reform in Colombia was facilitated by public opposition to chronically striking teachers who, despite hard times, were demanding yet further pay increases.[7] Most of the time, however, the public at large has played little direct role in encouraging initiation of reforms, or even in supporting reformers once the process is under way.

What conclusions can we draw about the impact of these actors on the reform process? As Grindle (2004) has rightly argued, we cannot account for the extent of change in the education sector by mechanically weighing

---

7. Bolivia provides another example. In 1999, the Ministry of Education successfully faced down the powerful teachers' union for the first time; the context included public impatience, fanned by well-framed government publicity, regarding constantly recurring teacher strikes and escalating demands (Grindle 2004).

the relative strength of "pro- and anti-reform" forces, in part because alignments among these forces and their relative power resources can change
over the course of the reform process. Reformers seeking to move beyond
incremental changes, however, did face well-organized opponents with
considerable capacity to defend their stakes in the status quo. As we shall
discuss below, that does much to explain "roads not taken." Even relatively
weak unions such as those in Venezuela, for example, were able to deflect
serious attempts to link pay to performance, or adopt pilot programs in-
stituting charter schools.

Conversely, despite these challenges, certain reforms did move forward
in some countries. As we have argued, the capacity of political opponents to
block significant changes varied by issue area and by country. At times, as
in Mexico, even relatively powerful unions proved willing to negotiate
compromises that did not entirely vitiate the efforts of reformers to transfer
responsibilities for education to the states. Similarly, although governors
were typically reluctant to take up the responsibilities of decentralized
educational systems, some of them did undertake innovative state-level
reforms. By the same token, although government reformers could not
count on sustained support from business, nongovernmental organizations,
or the general public, the upsurge of international and domestic concern
about education did offer them a potential resource, especially in periods
where economies appeared to have recovered from macroeconomic crises
and the relative salience of "social issues" increased.

Policy Linkages and Coalition Building in the Politics of Education Reform

How did reformers utilize these political resources? Under what circumstances were they able to work around the political opposition? In this
section, we return more directly to an examination of the politics of the
decentralization initiatives and other reform proposals discussed in the first
part of this chapter. The cross-national comparisons outlined in that section
raise at least three important issues:

1. Why did decentralization to states or municipalities appear as a central
   theme of education reform in so many of the countries, and what explains differences in design and implementation?

2. Why was there so much less emphasis on a variety of other controversial measures on the "international reform menu"—such as school autonomy, testing, or restructuring of professional career tracks?
3. What accounts for the Nicaraguan exception among our cases?

At least part of the explanation lies with the "linkage" proposition advanced in the introduction: Because the education sector itself was dominated by stakeholders with strong status quo interests, the prospects of reform rested on the opportunities available to reformers to expand their base of support by linking education policies to a broader agenda of political objectives or policy goals.

The Politics of Education Sector Decentralization

We first explore this proposition as it applies to the politics of decentralization. We examine successive phases of the reform process—the initiation, design, and implementation of the reform.

Initiation: Motives for Reform

Among all of the varied items on the international reform menu, decentralization, despite or perhaps because of its many different meanings, appealed to a very wide range of actors, including many with only limited interest in education per se—international development institutions, nongovernmental organizations, economic technocrats, and grassroots activists, and national political leaders.

The transfer of financial resources and policy responsibility to provincial or municipal governments promised different possibilities for different sets of actors. Groups seeking to deepen democracy and lower the threshold of access for grassroots movements saw decentralization as a means to more accountable government. Such views were especially important, for example, in the constitutional conventions held in Brazil and Colombia during the late 1980s and early 1990s. Many international and domestic economists also expected decentralization to encourage more efficient and effective delivery of social services, by improving decision makers' information and adjusting services to local conditions, although by the early 1990s this view was contested by at least some policy specialists (Prawda 1993). Finally, more specific political or economic objectives served as an important motivation in countries such as Colombia, Mexico, and Venezuela; incumbent presidents and their allies viewed decentralization as a way to weaken rival elites within the party or union leadership that exercised power primarily at the national level. Although motives and expectations varied, decentralization was thus an important goal of actors across the political spectrum.

These general trends toward decentralization affected specific changes in the education sector in a variety of ways, depending on the specific combinations of interests that crystallized in each case. In some instances, education reform initiatives were directly incorporated as provisions of broader legislation. This occurred most clearly in Colombia's constitutional convention of 1991, which expanded opportunities for popularly based groups to challenge the political establishment. The new Constitution mandated decentralization of all but the highest levels of both education and health services to Colombia's departments (provinces) and municipalities, and it stipulated that growing shares of revenues were to be phased in for these purposes.

Even when broader decentralization measures did not deal directly with the education sector, moreover, they altered the institutional framework for sector reform. For example, in Colombia and Venezuela, laws providing for the direct election of governors and mayors were passed without specific references to the education sector, but they contained implicit assumptions that local units would eventually assume greater responsibility for the delivery of social services. In Brazil, broad constitutional reforms that followed the demise of military rule in the late 1980s reflected a sharp upsurge in the influence of popular-sector forces, and they provided for a significant increase in the financial resources and policy discretion available to governors and mayors. Although education reforms did not get under way in that country until the mid-1990s, they built on the federal "rules of the game" established in the previous decade. The most important of these later measures was a constitutional amendment (FUNDEF) that focused primarily on reducing funding inequities within and between states.

Finally, in several countries, initiatives in the education sector were tied to broad projects of political restructuring or economic reform. In Mexico, the impetus for decentralization of primary and secondary schools came directly from President Salinas, and was part of an ambitious agenda that included reducing the influence of corporatist unions within the ruling party, modernizing the state, and reasserting presidential authority. Although Salinas may have been motivated by genuine commitment to improved education, decentralization of education provided a way for him to rein in the powerful teachers' union, which had become increasingly unreliable politically and prone to disruptive protest. In Argentina, as noted, the transfer of secondary schools to provincial control was a component of the integral program of structural and institutional reforms designed to restructure the economy and reduce the size of the public sector.

Design

Decentralization initiatives varied cross-nationally in how they allocated funding and responsibilities across levels of government. Garman, Haggard, and Willis (2001) provide one potentially useful way to account for these differences. They argue that the organization of power within the major political parties is a key determinant of legislation that establishes the conditions for the transfer of funding and policy responsibility to local government. In systems where state-level political leaders control nominations for elective office, legislators will be inclined to grant subnational governments considerable discretion in the use of fiscal transfers. This was the case, they argue, in the broad federal rules established in Brazil, Colombia, and—to a lesser extent—Argentina. Conversely, in Mexico and Venezuela, where party elites controlled patronage and party lists at the national level, the federal government retained far greater control.

Garman, Haggard, and Willis, it should be noted, do not discuss educational decentralization per se; and our cases point to some important limitations in the applicability of their argument. First, it does not fully capture the dynamics of the reform process within the educational system. National and subnational actors constantly attempted to renegotiate the way responsibilities were to be allocated. The consequences varied from case to case, but initiatives such as Brazil's FUNDEF legislation, or Colombia's Law 715 of 2001, reflected significant efforts to correct problems of funding and accountability that had arisen from previous reforms. As we have already suggested, moreover, many of the all-important details of decentralization arrangements were influenced by individuals and groups acting outside the framework of the party system. In Argentina and Colombia, the teachers' unions were at least as important as the party politicians in shaping the distribution of resources and responsibilities, and in Mexico and Venezuela, neither party elites nor legislative politicians were major players.

Despite these caveats, however, the patterns of party organization emphasized by Garman, Haggard, and Willis (2001) do appear to account for at least some important differences among our cases. The wide spending latitude accorded to the states by Brazil's 1988 federal constitution was in part a reflection of the power that the governors wielded over their states' congressional delegations. A decentralized party system also contributed substantially to emphasis on decentralization in the Colombian Constitution of 1991; and in Argentina, backlash from powerful governors helped to stall Cavallo's initial attempt to force states to pay a greater share of the expenses for secondary education.

Predictably, federal authorities retained considerably more power in the more centralized systems of Mexico and Venezuela. In Mexico, decentralization legislation was negotiated between representatives of the president and the unions, and passed by a compliant legislature. Governors, who had been largely marginalized during the negotiations, were constrained to accept the transfers, despite having to deal with complex problems of integrating transferred schools with those already under their control. In Venezuela, the federal government retained considerable power over fiscal transfers in the general decentralization legislation of the late 1980s. Within the education sector itself, the implementation of decentralization foundered over issues of funding liabilities, and by the end of the 1990s, no transfers had been completed.

Implementation

Once decentralization measures were set into motion, the effects on the schools depended both on the interest and capacities of state or municipal governments, and on the extent of policy guidance, monitoring, and financial support of the central government. As Grindle shows in the case of Mexico, the interests, capacities, and political alignments of different state governors were major determinants of the varied state responses to the imposition of decentralization. In Venezuela, despite the failure of explicit transfers of education responsibility, the institution of direct election of governors and mayors increased their incentives to increase their budgets for social services and to experiment with new programs (Navarro 2000). Decentralization also opened the way to successful local education initiatives in the Argentine province of San Luis, and in a variety of Brazilian states, including most notably, Minas Gerais.

Larger effects of the decentralization process, however, depended heavily on a continued role for central governments in supporting and regulating the activities of subnational units (Angell, Lowden, and Thorp 2000). Among our cases, only Brazil (where the sector had long been decentralized) made a major effort to devise instruments and programs not only to encourage deeper decentralization (from states to municipalities) but also to increase the equity of funding among and within states and to promote additional qualitative reforms. These efforts benefited from the sustained leadership of a powerful minister of education, Paulo Renato, who enjoyed close political ties to and support from President Cardoso.

At the other extreme, Colombia's constitutionally mandated effort at educational decentralization was captured almost entirely by the teachers' union (FECODE) and patronage politicians.[8] The Gaviria government was primarily concerned with other policy issues, and in the absence of vigorous executive leadership, the legislature became the venue in which FECODE could reshape government proposals. Two inconsistent laws, one sponsored by the government and one by FECODE, were both passed by the legislature. The legislation did reduce the role of the central government in the management of the education system, but it did so at the cost of compromises that undermined the coherence of the program.

Legislative factions backed by FECODE succeeded in blocking any significant move toward municipalization, as had been sought by the government's National Planning Department. Deconcentrated units of the Ministry of Education were not assigned clear functions vis-à-vis departmental (provincial) authorities. The central government was obliged by law to unconditionally transfer increasing sums to the departments, and it quickly found itself under pressure to finance large departmental deficits. Soaring (and ultimately unsustainable) expenditures were virtually entirely absorbed by growing teachers' wage bills (see chapter 12 of this volume). The Ministry of Education was more concerned with avoiding teachers' strikes than with promoting reforms. Educational outcomes as measured by tests not only did not improve but actually deteriorated.

Central governments retained responsibility for policy guidance (including, in most cases, the crucial area of personnel policies) and monitoring and evaluation, as well as major financial support for the sector. But with the notable exception of Brazil, they typically did little to encourage further reforms, once substantial responsibilities were transferred; and misalignments between intergovernmental transfers of funding and responsibility

8. For a striking description of the extent of patronage practices in Colombia's education sector, see Duarte (1998).

continued to pose serious problems. In the absence of central guidance and incentives, further reforms depended almost entirely on the initiative and capacity of state and local leaders and governments. Predictably, the outcomes varied tremendously.

Other Reforms and Some Roads Not Taken: Privatization, Testing, School Autonomy, and Parental Participation

Few other proposals for changing the educational system could be linked as clearly as decentralization to broader and widely held sets of political and policy objectives. As a consequence, it was much more difficult for reformers to overcome stakeholder opposition. Unlike decentralization, for example, neither Chilean style privatization nor the use of testing to evaluate and reward schools and teachers could be readily tied to broader goals of democratization. On the contrary, publics were typically antagonistic toward the first and relatively uninterested in the second. Both remained nonstarters throughout most of the region.

Efforts to introduce greater school autonomy and community participation were also limited, but somewhat more frequent; and they served as the centerpiece of the reforms introduced in Nicaragua. As in the case of decentralization, however, the degree to which these reforms were implemented depended to a large extent on how closely they were tied to political objectives outside the education sector itself.

Opposition to school autonomy and community oversight came from predictable components of the sector. National and subnational education bureaucracies, as well as teachers' unions, usually viewed school autonomy as a threat to their own authority and control over resources. Though school principals might be expected to favor increased autonomy, most did not like parent—community councils that were typically set up to monitor their performance, especially because council members often had limited educational backgrounds. Often, parents and community members themselves were deferential, hesitating to assert their views. With limited public support and multiple sources of resistance, neither school autonomy nor participation was a serious aspect of national reform efforts in Argentina, Colombia, or Mexico (despite legal provisions in some cases, and with the exception of some notable local experiments, e.g., charter schools in Bogotá and in San Luis, Argentina).

In Brazil, the Ministry of Education team of the Cardoso government did include school autonomy and associated school councils as aspects of its broader reform program, and it backed the provision with incentives. A federal program of small grants distributed modest sums for operating and maintenance costs directly to school councils, and after two years of operation the program covered more than 90 percent of schools. In part, however, the political viability of the program rested on the fact that the resources being distributed were quite limited, reducing the potential for conflict within the sector. Mayors raised little objection, perhaps because the sums of money allotted to each school were small, while the schools were understandably enthusiastic.

The Brazilian political authorities were, however, more reluctant to give up control over funds for school lunches provided in the Decentralization of School Meals program (PNAE). This program involves larger sums, delivered very regularly, and it offers opportunities for mayors to allocate valuable suppliers' contracts. By 2001, it reached almost 95 percent of public schools and 80 percent of municipal school districts, but despite Ministry of Education efforts, funds were channeled directly to only a little more than a quarter of all elementary schools.

As we have noted several times above, an ambitious program of school autonomy and community control was launched in the Brazilian state of Minas Gerais during the early 1990s. Although it is not among the cases in this volume, that program is particularly interesting because it was successfully "sold" to most of the state education bureaucracy and the state legislature. Backed by a dedicated governor, reformers within the state ministry of education made extensive efforts to inform and persuade mayors, principals, teachers, and the media, and they managed to reach a partial agreement on central principles with the key teachers' union.

A key and radical provision of the Minas Gerais reform was the election of school principals for fixed terms by school councils, choosing from a short list of candidates who had passed a qualifying test and prepared statements of their plans for the school. By the second year of the reform, more than two-thirds of the state's schools had elected directors, and almost all communities had created the councils mandated by the 1991 law. Student test scores improved in the mid-1990s, and repetition rates decreased. However, the school directors' association was never reconciled to the reform, and it challenged its constitutionality in the courts; it won this case, and thereafter the elections of school directors depended on the support of the state governor. When a new governor came into power, he dropped or reversed important aspects of the reforms (Grindle 2004). The Minas Gerais experience was large scale and impressive; however, it also demonstrates the fragility of autonomy and participatory reforms in the face of determined stakeholder resistance.

Against this background, the record of the Autonomous Schools Program in Nicaragua discussed in chapter 14 of this volume by Gershberg is exceptional. As in the cases of decentralization discussed above, a major factor contributing to this outcome is the fact that, in contrast to most school autonomy initiatives, this reform was linked to high-priority objectives extending beyond the education sector itself.

As in Colombia and Brazil, education reform in Nicaragua was undertaken at a point widely understood as a "critical juncture," one that provided post-Sandinista governments with broad opportunities to restructure the existing political order. In Colombia and Brazil, constitutional assemblies pressed for decentralization of social services. In Nicaragua, in contrast, the government chose to promote school autonomy and community participation. One reason, of course, is that Nicaragua is a far smaller country in both population and in territory than the others discussed in this volume; political decentralization may thus have had less appeal. In fact, school autonomy has been a theme in education reform in several of the smaller Central American countries, most notably in El Salvador, where schools sponsored by the EDUCO program played the key role in restoring education services to rural areas where civil war had essentially destroyed civil administration. Moreover, Humberto Belli, who served as Nicaragua's minister of education during the first two post-Sandinista administrations, was a distinguished education specialist who had long advocated school autonomy.

Nevertheless, both the choice of the school autonomy program and the extent of its implementation, must be viewed in the context of the political cleavages of the post-Sandinista era. Although the FSLN had been displaced from top government positions in 1990, it continued to occupy strategic political positions within the national bureaucracy, the unions, and in local government. The fact that many mayors had been affiliated with the Sandinista regime was a strong incentive to avoid the municipalization of the educational system. Conversely, as Gershberg has detailed in his case study, pay incentives linked to the autonomy project helped authorities to go around Sandinista-oriented union leaders and appeal directly to the interests of teachers themselves. Other measures noted by Gershberg served a similar purpose—the purging of the Ministry of Education and the establishment of local representatives selected and trained by the reoriented ministry. In short, in Nicaragua, a quite radical and ambitious program of educational reform was linked to the larger objective of weakening the Sandinista foothold within the state apparatus.

Conclusion

In one way or another, the politics of education reform in all the countries covered in this volume bear the agenda-setting imprint of broad concerns with economic liberalization and political democracy that swept through Latin America during the 1980s and 1990s. Widespread convictions that education is important for economic competitiveness increased the political salience of reform among policymakers. Concerns about consolidating and legitimating democracy had similar effects, prompting widespread debate about education reform in Argentina, Brazil, Colombia, and Venezuela.

These broad trends, however, were only loosely linked to specific reform outcomes, and they did not appear to work through any uniform set of causal mechanisms. Democratic legitimation was an important goal of reform in Brazil and Colombia, for example, but much less so in Argentina or Mexico; and there was no clear evidence in any of the countries that education reformers were responding directly to electoral incentives. Despite the concerns about economic competitiveness, business groups played only a very limited role in reforms, if any. And although international development banks served as an important source of funding and technical assistance in some instances, their influence varied substantially across the countries and was not decisive in any of them.

Although regional trends toward economic liberalization and democratization were important contextual factors, the design and implementation of specific policy initiatives were shaped by more specific factors: coalition politics, the relative power of teachers' unions and other stakeholders, and the institutional context of bargaining between national and local politicians. As we argue as well with respect to the health sector, education reform had broad support in principle, but it was not widely regarded as a priority issue, relative to other concerns about growth, macroeconomic stability, or political order. Consequently, broad reforms in education tended to move forward to the extent that they were linked by powerful actors to broader goals going beyond the sector itself; this applied most clearly to the decentralization efforts and the school autonomy program in Nicaragua. Where such linkages were weak or absent, the progress of reform was more incremental and depended mainly on the stance of major stakeholders, particularly the teachers' unions.

What has been accomplished? In some respects, many of the accounts of reform presented here are consistent with the conventional wisdom concerning the political difficulties of "second-phase" sector reforms. Although weaker than in the past, teachers' unions and other stakeholders remain powerful adversaries, and many core features of the educational systems have not been changed significantly. In most countries, these include career and incentive structures, the role of testing in evaluating schools and personnel, control over patronage resources, and school autonomy and community control. There has (so far) been little incentive to touch these issues, because they put at risk the bedrock interests of the groups that are essential to the operation of the system. Measures of educational outcomes are also disappointing for the region as a whole. Dropout and repetition rates remained very high relative to comparable countries in other regions. And Chile and Colombia, the only two Latin American countries willing to administer standardized international tests, ranked near the bottom of more than forty countries in math and language scores in 1996 (PREAL 2001).

Notwithstanding the severity of these continuing challenges, however, there have been incremental efforts at improvement throughout the region, as well as the more ambitious initiatives discussed in this volume. The potential long-term effect of such measures should not be underestimated. The question—still largely without a clear answer—is whether the glass is half full or half empty. The changes described above may stall, if new or old stakeholders that gain leverage within the system resist further adjustments. Yet the "destabilizing" effects of both decentralization and other, more incremental reforms could also increase the chances of further reforms that cumulate in a more positive way.

Ironically, the linkage to broader goals that drove efforts to decentralize responsibility for primary and secondary schools also contributed to hasty and inadequate preparation for the shift. Among our cases, this was particularly clear in Colombia. The benefits of decentralization, in terms of improved education outcomes, remain unproven. Outcomes will surely vary widely among states and municipalities, reflecting differences in capabilities, commitment, and local politics. From the perspective of this volume, decentralization does not automatically ease the politics of education reform: It simply pushes much of the politics to local levels.

However, decentralization does weaken control by central ministries steeped in bureaucratic conservatism or captive to powerful unions or parties. It provides more space for local experimentation, and the past

decade has seen some exciting and apparently effective innovations. Moreover, Brazil's experience suggests that if and when new forces take control
of the central Ministry of Education, financial and other inducements can
be devised that can strongly encourage state and local reforms, though such
inducements may be constrained by the broader mechanisms of fiscal
federalism (see chapter 16). Improved communications and more active
national and international networks of education specialists are also likely
to promote the gradual spread of innovations. With rare exceptions, change
will not be rapid and dramatic. But the process is under way.

References

Angell, Alan. 1996. Improving the Quality and Equity of Education in Chile: The
    PROGRAMA 900 ESCUELAS and the MECE-BASICA. In *Implementing Policy
    Innovations in Latin America: Politics, Economics and Techniques,* ed. Antonia
    Silva. Washington, D.C.: Inter-American Development Bank.
Angell, Alan, Pamela Lowden, and Rosemary Thorp. 2000. *Decentralization Develop-
    ment: The Political Economy of Institutional Change in Colombia and Chile.* Lon-
    don: Macmillan.
Birdsall, Nancy, and Juan Luis Londoño. 1998. No Tradeoff: Efficient Growth via More
    Efficient Capital Accumulation. In *Beyond Tradeoffs: Market Reform and Equitable
    Growth in Latin America,* ed. Nancy Birdsall, Carol Graham, and Richard H. Sabot.
    Washington, D.C.: Inter-American Development Bank and Brookings Institution
    Press.
Birdsall, Nancy, Juan Luis Londoño, and Lesley O'Donnell. 1998. Education in Latin
    America: Demand and Distribution Are Factors That Matter. *CEPAL Review* 66
    (December): 39–52.
Brown, David S. 1999. Reading, Writing, and Regime Type: Democracy's Impact on
    Primary School Enrollment. *Political Research Quarterly* 52, no. 4: 681–707.
Corrales, Javier. 1999. *Aspectos politicos en la implementacion de las reformas edu-
    cativas.* Working Paper 14. Santiago: Programa de Promocíon de la Reforma Edu-
    cativa en América Latina.
Duarte, Jesus. 1998. State Weakness and Clientelism in Colombian Education. In *Co-
    lombia: The Politics of Reforming the State,* ed. Eduardo Posada-Carbo. New York:
    St. Martin's Press.
Gajardo, Marcela 1999. *Reformas educativas en América Latina: Balance de una
    década.* Working Paper 15. Santiago: Programa de Promocíon de la Reforma Edu-
    cativa en America Latina.
Garman, Christopher, Stephan Haggard, and Eliza Willis. 2001. Fiscal Decentralization:
    A Political Theory with Latin American Cases. *World Politics* 53, no. 2: 205–35.
Geddes, Barbara. 1994. *Politician's Dilemma: Building State Capacity in Latin Amer-
    ica.* Berkeley: University of California Press.
Graham, Carol, and Sandip Sukhtnakar. 2004. Does Economic Crisis Reduce Support

for Markets and Democracy in Latin America: Some Evidence from Surveys of Public Opinion and Well-Being. *Journal of Latin American Studies,* May.

Grindle, Merilee. 2004. *Against the Odds: Contentious Politics and Educational Reform.* Princeton, N.J.: Princeton University Press.

Haggard, Stephan. 1999. The Politics of Decentralization in Latin America In *Decentralization and Accountability of the Public Sector: Proceedings of the Annual World Bank Conference on Development in Latin America and the Caribbean 1999,* ed. S. Javed Burki and G. Perry. Washington, D.C.: World Bank.

Hunter, Wendy, and David S. Brown. 2000. World Bank Directives, Domestic Interests, and the Politics of Human Capital Investment in Latin America. *Comparative Political Studies* 33, no. 1: 113–43.

IDB (Inter-American Development Bank). 1998. *Facing Up to Inequality in Latin America: 1998–1999 Economic and Social Progress Report.* Baltimore: Johns Hopkins University Press.

Kaufman, Robert R., and Alex Segura-Ubiergo. 2001. Globalization, Domestic Politics, and Social Spending in Latin America: A Time-Series Cross-Section Analysis, 1973-1997. *World Politics* 53 (July): 553–87.

Maceira, Daniel, and Maria Victoria Murillo. 2001. *Social Sector Reform in Latin America and the Role of Unions.* Working Paper Series 456. Washington, D.C.: Inter-American Development Bank.

Montenegro, Armando. 1995. *An Incomplete Educational Reform: The Case of Colombia.* Human Capital Development and Operations Policy Working Paper 60. Washington, D.C.: World Bank.

Murillo, Maria Victoria. 1999. Recovering Political Dynamics: Teachers' Unions and the Decentralization of Education in Argentina and Mexico. *Journal of Inter-American Studies and World Affairs* 41, no. 1: 31–57.

Navarro, Juan Carlos. 2000. The Social Consequences of Political Reforms: Decentralization and Social Policy in Venezuela. In *Social Development in Latin America: The Politics of Reform,* ed. Joseph S. Tulchin and Allison M. Garland. Boulder, Colo.: Lynne Rienner Publishers for the Latin American Program of the Woodrow Wilson International Center for Scholars.

Paul, Jean-Jacques, and Laurence Wolff. 1996. The Economics of Higher Education. In *Opportunity Forgone: Education in Brazil,* ed. Nancy Birdsall and Richard Sabot. Washington, D.C. Inter-American Development Bank.

Prawda, Juan. 1993. Educational Decentralization in Latin America: Lessons Learned. *Educational Development* 13, no. 3: 253–64.

PREAL (Partnership for Educational Revitalization in the Americas). 2001. *Lagging Behind: A Report Card on Education in Latin America.* Report of the Task Force on Education, Equity, and Economic Competitiveness in the Americas. Santiago: PREAL.

Puryear, Jeffrey. 1997. *La educación en América Latina: Problemas y desafíos.* Working Paper 7. Santiago: Partnership for Educational Revitalization in the Americas.

Rama, German W. 2002. Relaciones entre sociedad y educacion inicial. Inter-American Development Bank, Washington, D.C. (unpublished).

Tendler, Judith. 2002. Fear of Education. Massachusetts Institute of Technology, Cambridge, Mass. (unpublished).

Tiana Ferrer, Alejandro. 2000. *Cooperación internacional en evaluación de la educa-*

ción en América Latina y el Caribe: Análisis de la situación y propuestas de actua- ción. Washington, D.C.: Inter-American Development Bank.

Wolff, Laurence, and Claudio de Moura Castro. 2003. Education and Training: The Task Ahead. In *After the Washington Consensus: Restarting Growth and Reform in Latin America,* ed. Pedro-Pablo Kuczynski and John Williamson. Washington, D.C.: Institute for International Economics.

World Bank. 1990. *World Development Report: Poverty.* New York: Oxford University Press.

———. 1993. *The East Asian Miracle: Economic Growth and Public Policy.* New York: Oxford University Press.

Chapter 10

Interests, Institutions, and Reformers:
The Politics of Education Decentralization
in Mexico

Merilee S. Grindle

The political cards were stacked against improving the quality of education
in most Latin American countries in the 1990s. The opponents of change—
generally unions of teachers and central government bureaucrats—were
highly organized, vocal, and politically important. In contrast, the potential
beneficiaries of change—parents, local communities, society at large—
were dispersed, usually unorganized, and lacking in focused political clout.
Moreover, ministries of education were weak when compared with teachers' unions and were frequently colonized by these organizations. The
leadership of such ministries was often short-lived and ineffective in the
pursuit of policy change. Few political parties were deeply committed to
the kinds of reforms that would significantly improve the quality of education. And throughout the decade, there was little evidence of organized

This chapter is based on material published in Merilee Grindle, *Despite the Odds: The
Contentious Politics of Education Reform* (2004).

pressure for educational change, although many citizens ranked education high as a public issue.

Despite these daunting political odds, a surprising number of countries introduced, approved, and at least partially implemented significant education reform policies during the 1990s.[1] This is a puzzling political result, but one that can be explained by analyzing the actions of policy reformers as they seek opportunities to reshape the political context for reform. This chapter indicates that the strategic actions of reform proponents can enlarge the possibilities for introducing change, even in contexts in which interest-based opposition to reform is strong and political institutions are biased against it.

Mexico provides a good case for exploring the introduction of reform in a political context hostile to altering the education system. In the spring of 1992, President Carlos Salinas and his minister of education, Ernesto Zedillo, sat down with the leadership of the Sindicato Nacional de Trabajadores de la Educación (SNTE) and the governors of the country's thirty-one states to sign the National Agreement for the Modernization of Basic and Normal Education.[2] This agreement restructured education decision making and implementation in the country. After it was signed, 630,000 teachers and administrators and more than 13 million children became the responsibility of the state governments (Murillo 1999, 39).

The reform agreement included a number of other changes in the education system—a new career system for teachers, redesigned textbooks, improved teacher training—but decentralization was a major structural change that clearly surpassed all other aspects in significance. It was certainly the most important reform in education undertaken in the 1990s. Moreover, though other aspects of the 1992 agreement had only a minor impact on the education system, the decentralization initiative fundamentally altered responsibilities and political dynamics in the sector.

As this chapter shows, before the 1992 agreement, those opposed to reform were well positioned to resist change. Several previous presidents

---

1. Argentina, Bolivia, Brazil, Chile, Colombia, Costa Rica, El Salvador, Mexico, Nicaragua, and Uruguay made substantial progress in promoting education reform by 2000. Venezuela and Guatemala were less successful reformers, but did manage to make some progress in implementing significant changes. Ecuador, Honduras, Paraguay, and Peru made little progress in adopting or implementing change-oriented policies in the decade. See Grindle (2004).

2. On the content of the reform, see Cominetti and Gropello (1998), Gershberg (1999), and Tatto (1999). In Mexico, basic education comprises preschool, primary, and secondary schooling.

and education ministers—in a system that granted its presidents extraordinary informal power—had tried to promote decentralization, but all had failed. These failures were laid squarely at the door of the teachers' union and its close alliance with the country's dominant political party, the Partido Revolucionario Institucional (PRI). Given the obstacles to change in education policy in Mexico, the 1992 accord would not have been predicted.

In Mexico, reformers acted strategically to alter the conflict equations that surrounded their proposals, and they found moments when it was possible to affect the strength or coherence of the opposition and to change the bias of existing institutions. Nevertheless, reform leadership is not a universal panacea for needed, flagging, or orphaned policy changes. Interests and institutions can constrain the action of reformers, who cannot always be successful in the pursuit of change, however strategic they are. As a case in point, the Mexican experience shows how the objectives of reformers were modified and constrained. While policy changes were being negotiated and then implemented, even the impressive array of political resources controlled by a Mexican president under the PRI regime was not enough to ensure that reformers could fully meet their objectives. There was considerable scope for agency, but at the same time, the space available was narrowed by existing constellations of interests and institutions.

More broadly, education reform in Mexico was the product of a political administration—and its reformist leaders—wedded to the modernization of the country's economy and its rapid insertion into a global system of trade and finance. The policy change was part of this neoliberal vision; reformers believed that improving education in the country would increase the potential to generate benefits from globalization. Yet the reform was not neoliberal in the sense that it introduced market-oriented ideas about the delivery of education—vouchers and fees, for example—or lessened the fiscal burden on the national state.[3] Its political roots were also not particularly democratic. Although it was undertaken at a time when the PRI was under attack from proponents of a more open and democratic system, in the absence of any mobilized pressure for better schooling, decentralization cannot be directly tied to the response of political leaders to a more demanding civil society or to current or past electoral contests. Market ideology, fiscal concerns, and democratic demands were thus less important in

3. These concerns were much more a part of 1990s education reforms in other countries, e.g., Argentina, Chile, and Peru.

explaining how the reform emerged than more specific concerns and strategic choices of reform leaders.

The Roots of Contention

In the 1950s, 1960s, and 1970s, many Latin American countries made major strides in increasing access to education, particularly at the primary level. These access type reforms were politically popular. They meant increased education budgets along with efforts to train and hire more teachers, build more schools, distribute more textbooks, and administer more programs. Although they cost money and required some administrative capacity, these reforms provided citizens with increased benefits and politicians with tangible resources to distribute to their constituencies. They created more jobs for teachers, administrators, service personnel, construction workers, and textbook and school equipment manufacturers. They increased the size and power of teachers' unions and central bureaucracies.

In contrast, the reforms of the 1990s focused primarily on improving educational quality. Quality enhancement meant addressing the problem of poor management and inefficient use of resources. These reforms often meant reassigning responsibilities for decision making and putting more pressure on teachers to perform better in the classroom. Not surprisingly, these quality-enhancing initiatives were far less politically popular than earlier access reforms. Teachers' unions charged that such reform policies destroyed long-existing rights and career tracts. They strongly resisted the new accountability structures. Bureaucrats charged that they gave authority to those who "know nothing about education." Politicians were sometimes reluctant to support them because of the opposition of powerful teachers' unions. Governors, mayors, and parents did not necessarily want the new responsibilities they were given. As a consequence, the politics of putting them in place and implementing them were contentious and difficult, a far cry from the situation faced by promoters of access-type reforms (see table 10.1).[4]

This kind of political contention characterized the situation Mexican reformers faced in the early 1990s. Like the cases of Colombia, Argentina, and Venezuela discussed elsewhere in this volume, Mexico had done rea-

---

4. Indeed, when reformers at times failed in efforts to introduce significant quality-enhancing reforms, they generally reverted to more popular access-type reforms, e.g., building more schools and improving infrastructure.

Table 10.1

The Politics of Access and Quality-Enhancing Reforms: A Comparison

Action, Implication, or Response	Access Reforms	Quality-Enhancing Reforms
Typical actions to carry out such reforms	Build infrastructure Expand bureaucracies Increase budgets Hire administrators Hire service providers Buy equipment	Improve management Increase efficiency Alter rules or behavior of personnel Improve accountability Improve performance Strengthen local control

Typical political implications of such reforms	Creation of benefits:
	  Jobs
	  Construction and provisioning contracts
	  Increased budgets
	  Increased power for ministries and managers
		Imposition of costs:
		  Loss of jobs
		  Loss of decision-making power for some
		  New demands, expectations, and responsibilities for others

Typical political response to such reforms	Unions of providers welcome reforms and collaborate with them Politicians welcome tangible benefits to distribute to constituencies Communities are pleased to receive benefits Voters support changes	Unions of providers resist reforms Administrators seek to ignore or sabotage change Many politicians wish to avoid promoting reforms Many voters are unaware of changes (at least in the short term)

sonably well in providing access to education to a large portion of the eligible age groups. Between 1950 and 1990, it had reduced its adult illiteracy rate from 43 to 12 percent (UNESCO 2000, 30). Its youth literacy rate was 96.8 percent (UNDP 2001, 175). The country reported a net primary enrollment ratio of 100 percent, the highest in Latin American, and its school life expectancy was 11.2 years.[5] Its secondary net enrollment rate continued to lag seriously behind, at 45 percent, but this rate that was increasing rapidly.[6]

5. I.e., the average number of years of formal schooling; UNESCO (2000,137, 141). Although Mexico regularly reports very high net enrollment rates at the primary level, many studies point to evidence that a significant number of children, particularly in poor rural and indigenous zones, do not attend school. See, e.g., Schmelkes (2000).

6. By 1996, the secondary net enrollment rate was 51 percent; UNESCO (2000, 149).

The much more serious problem in the system was not access to education, but its quality and equity. Although Mexico claimed to spend 3.7 percent of gross national product (GNP) on education in 1990 (12.8 percent of government expenditures), the internal efficiency of education was low. For primary education, 9 percent of students were repeating grades, and only 86 percent of enrollees were reaching fifth grade (UNESCO 2000, 145). Its third-grade students scored significantly below the Latin American average on tests of language and mathematics, and its fourth-grade students only slightly above it (Laboratorio Latinoamericano de Evaluación de la Calidad de la Educación 1998, 50–51). Some 15 percent of teachers in the system did not have officially defined qualifications for their jobs (Reimers 2000, 91).

Inequality in the system was high. Whereas 92 percent of the top decile income group completed primary education, this was true for only 63 percent of the bottom four deciles; 70 percent of the top income decile completed secondary school, whereas only 10 percent of the lowest four deciles did.[7] In 1994, 90.1 percent of urban children of ages fourteen and fifteen years had completed primary school; in rural areas, the rate was 67.5 percent.[8] Indigenous children and those living in poor rural areas were those most afflicted by poverty and low achievement in school (Muñiz M. 2000; also Schmelkes 2000).

Proposals to fix this state of affairs almost always included initiatives to decentralize or deconcentrate the system. The Constitution of 1917 assigned responsibility for primary education to the municipalities and for secondary and normal schools to the states, but the establishment of a national education ministry in 1921, under the leadership of the country's most revered educator, José Vasconcelos, initiated a long process of centralization. In 1928, 20 percent of students were in the national system; by the early 1990s, 76 percent of public school students and teachers and 79 percent of the public schools were part of the national system, and the federal government contributed about 80 percent of the total education budget (Merino Juárez 1999, 41; Murillo 1999, 38).

The curriculum and teaching materials were determined in Mexico City, as were decisions about hiring, promoting, and firing teachers, salaries of all personnel, the distribution of funds to local schools, and school location

7. These are Inter-American Development Bank household survey data, cited in Reimers (2000, 66).
8. These are data from the Comisión Económica para América Latina y el Caribe, cited in Reimers (2000, 73).

and building activities. Moreover, teacher training became a national concern, and a national system of free textbooks helped cement the central government's role in the curriculum.

One of the primary beneficiaries of the centralization was SNTE, which by 1990 had 1.1 million members and was the largest union of any kind in Latin America. The union had long been firmly in support of the ministry's efforts; with centralization, its own power increased. The 1960s and 1970s were also a period of extensive growth in the educational system, and a half-million new teachers entered it during the 1970s, each of them duly registered in the union. Thus, during this extended period, the national ministry and the union shared an interest in promoting centralization.

Among the country cases of economic reform discussed in this volume, Mexico's teachers' union was clearly the strongest, and it had a full monopoly on the representation of teacher interests. In contrast, Brazil's teachers had very little representation at the national level, Argentina's principal union varied considerably in its power over time, Nicaragua's union was challenged through the creation of new unions once the Sandinista government was no longer in power, and Venezuela's unions were extremely fragmented. Only in Colombia was the union in a strong position to significantly hinder the progress of education reform.

Mexico's SNTE concentrated enormous power in the hands of its national executive committee. Traditionally, this committee was an instrument wielded by a powerful boss, the secretary general of the union. Moreover, since its founding in 1943, SNTE had been closely linked with the PRI. As part of the National Confederation of Popular Organizations, one of the corporatist pillars of the PRI, the union was a powerful player in the country's politics and in the maintenance of labor peace. In the late 1980s, SNTE's leader was a national senator; the union controlled 16 seats in the chamber of deputies as well as 42 seats in state-level legislatures and more than 100 mayors (Larmer 1989, 4). The union was also rich, collecting 1 percent of teachers' salaries. It owned department stores, hospitals, hotels, funeral homes, and other businesses. Indeed, the union was of such size and presence that it had been able to halt government action on many fronts and had long dominated the Ministry of Education by naming people to the most important posts, including several vice ministerial positions (Ornelas 1988, 108–9).

Through an elaborate patronage system, the SNTE placed and transferred teachers based on their relationship to important people in the union and the party and was able to assist in the assignment of perquisites of office for favored teachers—leaves, loans, and attention from the ministry.[9] Characteristically, school principals, those who headed regional offices of the ministry, and school inspectors were the local arms of the union. Thus, as in other countries discussed in this volume, many officials owed their first loyalty to the union, not to the ministry. As a consequence, the ministry had lost the capacity to manage the teachers and its own affairs. The union and the education bureaucracy were thus the primary impediments to education reform, and particularly to efforts to decentralize the system.

Confronting a Legacy of Failed Reforms

Before 1990, the politics of education reform in Mexico conformed closely to a scenario of strong opposition paired with weak support and political institutions biased against change. Indeed, efforts by reformist ministers to decentralize the system were blocked by union opposition in 1958, 1969, and 1978 (Arnaut 1998, 245–75; Fiske 1996, 17–18). In 1982, President Miguel de la Madrid announced an initiative to transfer responsibilities from the national ministry to the states, but union and ministry opposition was so strong that the plan was never approved by the Congress.[10] Given the extraordinary presidentialism of Mexico's traditional PRI-dominated system, these failed initiatives were testimony to the power of SNTE and to its control over the ministry. Union intransigence was particularly notable in the 1980s. At the time, SNTE was controlled by a self-styled "leader for life and moral guide," Carlos Jonguitud Barrios, whose reign began in 1972, when his Revolutionary Vanguard movement took over control of the national executive committee at gunpoint (Cook 1996, 73–77).

Jonguitud Barrios—widely believed to use gangster-like tactics in managing the organization and expanding his power and wealth—was in a good position to do so, given the wealth of the SNTE and its links to the PRI. Government efforts to initiate change in the 1980s created significant

9. On this system, see Duarte (1999, 17), Martin (1993, 153), and Murillo (1999, 37–41). In the late 1980s, dissident teachers alleged that the going rate for a teaching position was as much as $600–$650. Teachers at the time were earning $150 a month (Larmer 1989, 4; Rohter 1989, 12).

10. In 1982, the national ministry was "composed of 7 undersecretariats, 44 director-generalships, 304 managerships, 6 councils, an international general administration and budgeting committee, a controller's office, a general co-ordinator, 31 state delegations and nearly 60 co-ordinated institutions" (Ornelas 1988, 107). To this could be added 800,000 employees and millions of students. It distributed some 100 million textbooks and managed school siting and building around the country.

tension with the union's leadership at a time when a severe economic crisis was cutting into teacher salaries and benefits. Angry primary teachers claimed their wages had declined by 63 percent between 1982 and 1989 (Cook 1996, 268 n. 2).

Thus, on December 1, 1988, when Salinas became president, he could anticipate that SNTE, the PRI, and the ministry would all be firmly opposed to any plan to alter the structure, administration, or standards of the education system. The president, however, had reason to pursue such changes. In no small part, his attention to education was due to ongoing conflict with the union, a concern sharpened shortly after he assumed power by massive and politically embarrassing protests from dissident teachers. He was very concerned about the lagging fortunes of the PRI and its ability to continue to count on the teachers' votes. In addition, the president was convinced that improved education would have an impact on the distribution of income in the country—with better education would come better opportunities for generating income.[11]

Indeed, Salinas's interest in education was derivative of his vision of modernizing the country's economy. The country needed to "reformulate content and methods, maintain a sense of open and modern nationalism, and provide a level of quality that would be competitive worldwide" (Salinas de Gortari 2002, 610). Moreover, as he admitted some years later, "My mother was a public school teacher," a factor he believed gave him some sympathy for the claims of the teachers.[12]

At the time, however, there was little reason to expect that he could confront the odds against reform and be successful. The president faced a significant political dilemma. Salinas's years in government and his prior position as minister of planning and budgeting (1982–88), where he was involved in annual negotiations with the union over teacher salaries and benefits, had given him a good understanding of the problems created by this organization. But the legacy of earlier reform initiatives was also a clear reminder of the importance of SNTE to the management of change. Moreover, without the union, there would be no structure to control the teachers and their demands, a situation inimical to a basic organizing principle of the PRI regime.

Such an assessment was based not only on the demonstrable power of SNTE and its allies in the ministry but also on the uncharacteristically weak position of the president. In 1988, he garnered a bare 50.7 percent of the

11. Personal communication, March 8, 2002.
12. Personal communication, March 8, 2002.

vote, the lowest percentage ever received by a PRI candidate; the party was widely accused of having stolen the election from the Partido de la Revolución Democrática (PRD) through fraud, coercion, and violence.[13] Although the PRI maintained its majority in the Congress, with 260 out of 500 seats, it did not have enough votes for passing important legislation and constitutional amendments. Indeed, the authority and legitimacy of the PRI-led government was at its lowest point in decades (Grindle 1996, 81–82).

Salinas's situation was not helped by the economic problems that had afflicted the country since 1982; the growth of gross domestic product (GDP) in 1988 was 1.2 percent. The public-sector deficit was 10.4 percent of GDP, and inflation was 114 percent. Real wages were down another 1.3 percent after years of even more significant declines. The external debt reached $100 billion.[14] To add to the difficulties, many of the party bosses of the PRI distrusted Salinas and resented his technocratic style. Large and important groups of citizens, including the teachers, were deeply angry with the government over declining wages. These were hardly propitious circumstances for undertaking reform.

Before he could tackle education reform, then, the president needed to reassert the traditional power of the Mexican presidency. He did so in short order. Within weeks of taking office, he ordered the arrest of the powerful and corrupt leader of the petroleum workers' union. The notorious and previously untouchable "La Quina" was jailed in a move that was widely seen as a successful flexing of presidential muscle (Grindle 1996, 93).

SNTE offered Salinas another opportunity to achieve a similar win. The Coordinadora Nacional de Trabajadores de la Educación (CNTE), a movement of teachers based in the country's southern states, had been formed within the union in 1979 to protest against general economic conditions, low teacher salaries, a lack of internal union democracy, and the close association of the union with the PRI (Alvarez Béjar 1991, 48–51; Cook 1996; de la Garza 1991, 179–81). Throughout the 1980s, CNTE challenged the government to improve teacher conditions and the union to increase its democratic accountability. Late in the decade, the dissident group claimed a membership of some 300,000 teachers. Just as Salinas took office, CNTE vociferously demanded changes in government policy and union practices.

13. The narrow and widely questioned victory even called into question the SNTE's ability to deliver the teachers' votes. It was likely that many voted for the PRD (Cook 1996, 267).
14. Data in this paragraph were taken from World Bank, *World Tables,* various years.

In the wake of these demands, SNTE's leadership held a national congress in February 1989 and virtually banished dissident voices within the union. In response, CNTE protested publicly.

In the following months, strikes, mass demonstrations, sit-ins, and marches punctuated the political scene (Murillo 1999, 41; Cook 1996, 269–70). CNTE strikers demanded a doubling of their salaries to make up for the bite that austerity and inflation had taken during the past seven years. In addition, they demanded that the government ensure greater internal democracy in SNTE, that union boss Jonguitud Barrios be deposed, and that the alliance with the PRI be severed. Ending the reign of Jonguitud Barrios, who was accused of masterminding the assassination of at least 150 dissident teachers, primarily in the southern states of Oaxaca and Chiapas, was central to CNTE demands.

As the confrontation between the teachers and the government escalated, a half million teachers participated in a twenty-six-day work stoppage in April; schoolchildren throughout the country had an unexpected holiday (Murillo 1999, 41; Rohter 1989, 12; Larmer 1989, 4). In an unusual demonstration of force, parents and university professors joined the teachers in a massive demonstration in Mexico City on April 17. Indeed, the period between February and May was a chaotic one, with CNTE deeply engaged in protest, SNTE leadership trying to control it, and the Ministry of Education condemning it (Cook 1996, 269–70). For the government, the scope of the protest was alarming. On April 1, the president reports having written, "The situation with the teachers is critical. We may go into a state of emergency" (Salinas de Gortari 2002, 607).

These events raised uncomfortable alternatives for Salinas. Giving in to the economic demands of the teachers would mean the destruction of the Pact for Economic Growth and Stabilization, his plan for overcoming inflation and introducing an array of economic reforms. Moreover, there was danger in succumbing to the demand to depose Jonguitud Barrios. Certainly a large and powerful union without a powerful boss could further threaten the already shaky PRI regime. From this perspective, the fact that CNTE dissidents favored the left-of-center PRD was cause for some alarm. Yet a large and powerful union in disarray and unable to stifle opposition to its boss was equally unsettling.

The president's next actions helped resolve this dilemma in a way that was propitious for future reform. On April 23, Jonguitud Barrios was called to a meeting with the president and given no alternative but to resign. His downfall was widely seen as a successful assertion of presidential power and a message to other unions that might defy Salinas's leadership. Two days later, with presidential blessing, a new secretary general was elected to head SNTE.[15] About three weeks after this, the government and the union were able to settle on a 25 percent increase in teacher salaries, which, with the ousting of Jonguitud Barrios, was sufficient to send the teachers back to the classroom with some gain, even if far short of what they were asking. Then, in October 1989, Salinas announced the plan for the modernization of the education system.

Before moving ahead with this initiative, however, the fractured union had to be brought along. The presidential backing given to Elba Ester Gordillo to be the new secretary general of SNTE was problematic for the newly powerful CNTE. Gordillo had long worked within the leadership group of the union as a close associate of Jonguitud Barrios, and, for the dissidents, represented the old guard. Moreover, she was emblematic of the kind of imposed leadership characterizing the presidentialist system that CNTE activists wanted to see reformed. Despite their preferences, however, and in the face of dissent and competition from other contenders, Salinas was clear in his support for Gordillo.

Gordillo's task was clear: She had to bring more order and coherence to the union by incorporating the dissidents and weakening the remnants of Jonguitud Barrios's machine (Cook 1996, 271). She was largely successful in achieving these objectives. At the union congress in early 1990, Gordillo was again affirmed as the secretary general of SNTE. In the following two years, she consolidated her position by appointing her followers to important positions, engineering elections of the fifty-six locals of the union, altering the makeup of the national executive committee to include dissident teachers and extending the tenure of its leadership by two years. These changes made the national committee more representative of SNTE's membership but also less agile in reaching agreements that could bind the secretary general. Gradually, her ability to be more flexible than Jonguitud Barrios and to respond to some of the demands of the dissidents worked to calm the storms within the union. Through such actions, Gordillo placed herself in a strong position to be useful to the president. She owed him a large political debt for his support after Jonguitud Barrios was deposed. At the same time, by becoming its undisputed leader, she was in a powerful position to protect some of SNTE's core interests in any negotiations with the government.

15. Cook (1996, 269–70). The election was convened by the interior minister.

The Politics of Education Decentralization in Mexico   295

There were still impediments to reform, however. Under Gordillo, tension between the government and the union lessened, but it did not disappear. Moreover, the Ministry of Education was still primarily a creature of SNTE, not the government. Manuel Bartlett, the minister of education and a veteran politician, was given the task of wresting control of the organization from the union. Bartlett took advantage of a period during which union leaders were focusing on internal conflicts to regain the right to select his own people to head important positions in the ministry, "doing the dirty work of reclaiming the ministry from the union," as one observer commented.[16] In addition, he appointed teams within the ministry to study the possibilities for altering the education system, consult with numerous experts, write reports, and design new systems (Pescador Osuna 1992, 4–5).

These activities proceeded without a decision about how to deal with the union.[17] Despite the difficult years leading up to 1992, SNTE was still formidable, its membership was intact, and its capacity to corral votes and mobilize labor actions was still largely in place. And, with congressional elections looming in 1991, the president and his allies were well advised not to insist on a change that would further annoy the union. Its votes were needed. In the event, the 1991 elections provided a considerable boost to the president. The PRI won 61.5 percent of the vote and, with 320 seats in the Congress, regained the two-thirds majority needed to pass important legislation.

To add to this improved environment, the economy had grown by 3.4 percent in 1989 and 4.5 percent in 1990, and growth continued into 1991.[18] Inflation was reduced to 20 percent in 1989, and capital began to flow back into the country. The president had also instituted a highly popular social fund program, PRONASOL, which was garnering him both popular and political support (Cornelius, Craig, and Fox 1994). In addition, teachers received significant wage increases between 1989 and 1991, and these helped defuse union demands for economic justice (Cook 1996, 280–81).

Thus, the president was at the peak of his power at the midpoint of his administration. In January 1992, Salinas appointed his minister of planning and budgeting, Zedillo, to the post of education minister, with the instruc-

16. Interview, June 26, 2001, Mexico City. Bartlett had been one of the contenders for the PRI nomination in 1988.

17. Bartlett wanted to confront and defeat the union, taking advantage of its moment of weakened leadership and internal dissent. This was not considered a viable option by Salinas.

18. Data in this paragraph are taken from World Bank, *World Tables,* various years.

tion to move the education project forward. Zedillo was well regarded for his decisiveness, closeness to Salinas, and affinity for the modernizing vision that infused the administration (Loyo 1992, 22). The stage was set for negotiations that could lead to the education reforms that had been announced more than two years earlier.

Negotiating Change

Ruefully, a lead government negotiator explained that negotiating with the union was viewed as a necessity. "If you had asked any of us where we wanted the union, we'd have said, three meters underground. But the reality was that we needed them."[19] Indeed, the decision to negotiate rather than to confront the union recognized the important political role of SNTE. Unlike the reformers in Argentina, Brazil, Nicaragua, and Venezuela (considered in subsequent chapters of the present volume), Mexico's reformers believed they could not proceed far without the acquiescence of the teachers' union. Moreover, the Salinas presidency, tied as it was to the PRI, could not easily turn its back on the largest union incorporated into the party. But the same was true of SNTE; a powerful president was difficult to oppose directly. The union was also willing to negotiate because of the political debt that Gordillo owed Salinas and the relationship of trust that had developed between them. Moreover, given successive salary increases since 1989, there was likely to be more to gain from negotiation than from confrontation.

These negotiations began almost immediately. Although the resulting agreement was a tripartite consensus document, from the beginning, the talks centered on the national government and SNTE. Most governors, given their preferences, would have actively resisted taking on responsibility for education for fiscal and political reasons. They feared increased political and administrative burdens with the transfer of responsibility for large numbers of new teachers, schools, and students. They also anticipated great risk in central government revenue-sharing formulas that could be altered at the whim of the president or the ministry of finance, a concern that was echoed in the decentralization initiatives in Argentina, Colombia, and Venezuela that are considered in subsequent chapters. But they were in a weak position. All but one of them from the PRI, there was little they could do to stop a determined president who had already deposed several governors in bids to emphasize his power.

19. Interview, July 4, 2001.

Indeed, according to one official in the ministry, "The agreement was signed [by the governors] because Salinas said 'Sign!' Many of the governors did not want to touch it."[20] More generally, the approach to pursuing education reform in Mexico echoed that found in most of the rest of the case studies explored in this volume—small groups of committed reformers designed and pursued the approval of policy change in the absence of broad consultations or public participation. Mexico's reform was, like most of the health and education policy changes considered, a top-down initiative.

At the outset of the negotiations, SNTE was already on record as firmly against decentralization. Governors' authority over teacher pay and employment conditions would hit at the heart of the national power of the union, replacing its central role with annual negotiations focused at the state level and on the governors and state-level ministries of education. But the government's decision to refer to the "federalization" of education was something that *could* be discussed without loss of face. Indeed, Gordillo had already begun to speak of the importance of "modernizing" the educational system, providing another platform on which both the union and the government could agree (Loyo 1992, 20). By joining the government in its quest for modernization, the secretary general could then focus her energies on maintaining a national salary and benefit scheme. It was also useful that during the course of the negotiations, the government was careful not to portray the union as an enemy of change; it was, instead, referred to as an important interlocutor for the teachers.[21]

Gordillo strengthened the union's position by establishing the Fundación SNTE para la Cultura del Maestro Mexicano, a think tank staffed with well-regarded academics, some of whom had held important positions in the Ministry of Education. The foundation gave greater technical credibility to the union's positions by bringing in people who were not identified with the movement in the past. It produced studies and reports that argued for the importance of modernizing education, provided alternatives to the government's proposals, and encouraged greater dialogue about the contents of the reform (Gordillo 1992, 13). According Gordillo, "The proposal of SNTE was focused on three points: the reorganization of the system, the redesign of educational contents and improved social and political respect for teachers and the teaching role" (Gordillo 1992, 13; translation by the author).

20. Interview, July 4, 2001, Mexico City.
21. Interview, June 26, 2001, Lomas de Santa Fe, Mexico.

Moreover, in a Declaration of Principles, SNTE announced it was no longer officially connected to the PRI. This move had little immediate practical impact because relations between the union and the party continued much as usual, but it served to increase the autonomy of the union to negotiate directly with the ministry (Cook 1996, 279–80).

A team of ministry negotiators, headed by the undersecretary of education, Esteban Moctezuma, along with Carlos Mancera and others, began meeting daily with groups designated by Gordillo to consider how the education initiative would go forward. For the government, the most important issue was to make decentralization happen and to end the stranglehold of the union and ministry bureaucrats over efforts to improve the system. The minister, given the expectations of the president, was focused on making sure the negotiations proceeded ahead. He was ready to step in and deal personally with SNTE's leadership when needed. Similarly, he could count on the support of the president. Indeed, according to one of the lead negotiators, "Zedillo had exceptional support and trust [*confianza*] from the president. This was so apparent that he had considerable autonomy to carry out the negotiations without oversight from the office of the presidency."[22] At the same time, the president was clearly and frequently on record in support of the ministry team. This was important for the negotiators. "The ministry had no base of support in the PRI and really didn't have political weight. It was the president who made it happen by signaling his strong commitment very frequently."[23]

Strategically, the government negotiators sought to make clear that the discussions were about a larger package of reforms, not just about decentralization. According to the chief negotiator for the government, "It was important that they realize that if they said no to federalization, they were saying no to a whole package of things, some of which they wanted."[24] Implicit throughout the discussions, of course, was the promise of an increase in salaries if agreement could be reached. In addition, there was the proposal for a status and salary enhancing *carrera magisterial,* a career ladder that would allow for greater mobility within the teacher corps and increases in salaries with movement on the ladder (Tatto 1999, 278).

From time to time, as issues arose, the minister and the president met personally with Gordillo to move the agreement forward. Throughout, the union leader maintained a good relationship with Minister Zedillo. More

22. Interview, June 26, 2001, Mexico City.
23. Interview, June 26, 2001, Lomas de Santa Fe, Mexico.
24. Interview, July 4, 2001, Mexico City.

important, however, was her relationship with Salinas. "The relationship of Salinas to Elba Ester was key to the ability to put through the reform. . . . He couldn't have succeeded if someone else had been [leader of the union]. And, of course, behind Elba Ester was the role of Salinas in the conflict with Jonguitud [Barrios]," according to one negotiator.[25] In brief, "He helped her in the leadership struggle in '89 with Jonguitud, and she paid him back three years later by backing the agreement of '92."[26] Thus, along side the formal negotiations, a set of informal understandings and meetings helped smooth the way toward agreement. According to Salinas,

> Secretary Zedillo had asked me to intervene directly with the leaders of the SNTE because, within the organization, there was great resistance to the agreement's proposal, in particular, to decentralization. I spoke first with the secretary-general Gordillo. I trusted in her and in her integrity as a leader. She explained clearly to me all the areas that concerned her: The SNTE leadership believed that decentralization would tear the union apart. The decision to decentralize could mask the federal government withdrawal from its obligations to educate the youth of the country. Teaching salaries at the federal level varied greatly compared to those at the state level, and this would generate tension at the time of decentralization. Many states had no administrative or political capacity to take over the process of decentralization and paying teachers. Finally, she noted, various leaders of union locals believed it was necessary for my administration to postpone the decision to decentralize . . . for the teachers' leaders themselves to explain to me those and other issues so that we could debate these matters openly. (Salinas de Gortari 2002, 215–16)

A subsequent meeting of SNTE union locals with the president, the minister of education, and the mayor of Mexico City resulted in a presidential promise to increase spending on education in the remaining years of his term of office (Salinas de Gortari 2002, 217).

Eventually, four months of difficult negotiation resulted in an agreement that allowed SNTE to continue the practice of annual discussions between the Ministry of Education over increments for the base salaries of teachers and the package of benefits that all teachers were entitled to. State governors would have the opportunity to increase salaries and provide improve-

25. Interview, June 27, 2001, Lomas Anáhuac, Mexico.
26. Interview, June 27, 2001, Mexico City.

ments in work conditions, and the teachers would be ensured of a national minimum set of rewards and conditions. As part of this settlement, the teachers were granted a large salary adjustment that boosted their average income to second highest for public-sector employees (Murillo 1999, 44). A sticking point in the negotiations over the *carrera magisterial* was a government-proposed proficiency examination for teachers.

The union was adamantly opposed to such a test, but it eventually agreed to it when a formula was worked out that assessed proficiency along with seniority (Tatto 1999, 272–74; Street 1998, 11). In addition, the agreement reaffirmed SNTE as the rightful representative of the teachers in labor matters, set the bases for curriculum and textbook reform, and promised improved training for teachers.[27]

Although sidelined during the negotiations, the governors were able to insist that the government be more specific about the terms of the fiscal transfers that would come their way in the aftermath of decentralization. They were also delighted to have the central government continue to be in charge of negotiating salaries with the union.

Some aspects of the existing system did not change. Technical education, a strong fiefdom within the Ministry of Education, was successful in resisting the decentralization initiative. In addition, teachers of the Federal District, a strong group within SNTE, refused to be part of the new plan. The national government remained in control of this large bureaucracy as well as curriculum, the national program of free textbooks, and the standards set for student performance. The agreement was ratified through a constitutional reform in 1992 and the 1993 Law for the Modernization of Education. With strong presidential backing and a PRI majority in the Congress, the legislation passed easily and with little discussion.

More generally, the negotiations and the resulting package of reforms were clearly a milestone in the relations between the government and the union. In the years following the agreement, SNTE continued to focus its attention on basic salaries and work conditions for teachers. From time to time, the teachers went on strike, and annually, protests and marches interrupted traffic around the Ministry of Education building in central Mexico City. Indeed, these actions became normal aspects of politics in the country, which was annoying for ministry officials and drivers but not threatening to the political system. Even after 2000, when control of the presidency

27. For a discussion of the contents of the National Agreement for the Modernization of Basic Education, see Pescador Osuna (1992).

passed from the PRI for the first time in seventy-one years, the basic relationship between SNTE and the ministry did not change much. The union maintained its demands for salaries, and the ministry maintained its relatively close working relationship with the union. Gradually, the new *carrera magisterial* became subject to the union's capacity to influence teacher appointments and promotions. More broadly, the union continued to guarantee a large measure of labor peace for the government, even while it found that some decisions now focused the attention of its locals on state level negotiations. Gordillo became secretary general of the PRI in 2002.

Decentralization in Practice

In the years after the 1992 agreement was signed, some claimed that Mexico continued to have one of the most centralized education systems in the world.[28] There was considerable truth in this charge. Central administrators maintained their role in financing, curriculum design, textbook design and selection, regulation of teaching credentials, base salary and benefits negotiations, testing, standards setting, and compensatory programs.

Yet the decentralization of 1992 fundamentally altered the structure of education in Mexico. In contrast to the gradual and negotiated efforts to decentralize education in Colombia (chapter 12) and Venezuela (chapter 15), the Mexico reform was put into effect immediately and across-the-board. After decentralization, Mexico's federal government was responsible for 15 percent or less of teachers, students, and schools (see table 10.2). The practical implications of these numbers were considerable; state governments would now make decisions and solve problems that used to be transferred to bureaucrats and politicians in the national capital—such as hiring, firing, and placement of teachers, salaries and benefits beyond the basics set at the national level, school management and oversight, noncore curricula, and relationships with the union locals (Ornelas n.d., 12). Central bureaucrats lost many of their functions to the new state-level administrations. Indeed, much changed in terms of the relationship of the states to the center, of the teachers' union to the states, and of the governors to their education system. Ministry of Education expenditures on basic education increased significantly after the reform; between 1992 and 1994, overall expenditures increased by 32 percent and per pupil expenditures by 27 percent (SEP 2000b, 175).

28. Cabrero Mendoza et al. (1997, 330). Indeed, the system is often compared to the highly centralized French system.

Table 10.2

Basic Education in Mexico: Enrollment, Teachers, and Schools by Source of Funding, 1991–92 and 1996–97 (percent)

Educational and Funding Category	Prereform, 1991–92	Postreform, 1996–97
Enrollment		
National	71	8
State	22	86
Private	7	7
Teachers		
National	70	10
State	22	81
Private	8	9
Schools		
National	75	15
State	19	78
Private	7	7

Note: Basic education includes preschool, primary, and secondary schools.
Source: Merino Juárez (1999, 41).

There was also a marked improvement in overall education spending as a percentage of GNP, even while state-level expenditures remained virtually the same (see figure 10.1). Thus, the 1992 agreement cannot easily be portrayed as an effort of the center to decrease its role in education funding. Equally, anticipating that states would step forward and increase their investment in education was not warranted, at least in the aggregate. Nevertheless, some states, notably those in the northern, more prosperous, and industrialized part of the country, significantly increased their contributions to education (Merino Juárez 1999, 95). Moreover, because the education reform was introduced with an increase in teacher salaries and because the new teachers' career included monetary incentives for improved training and performance, most of the increased funding reflected increases in real wages.[29]

Yet changes in funding do not necessarily imply improvements in educational outputs—increased student achievement, decreased dropout and repetition rates, or more relevant teaching in the classroom. Although reformers claimed that the principal objective of their initiative was to improve the quality of schooling, by the end of the decade, there was little evidence to suggest that significant advances had occurred. In part, this was an inevitable result of a paucity of information and data on what was

29. Merino (1999, 86). In 1995, 97.9 percent of total current federal education expenditures were destined for teacher salaries (UNESCO 1998, 161).

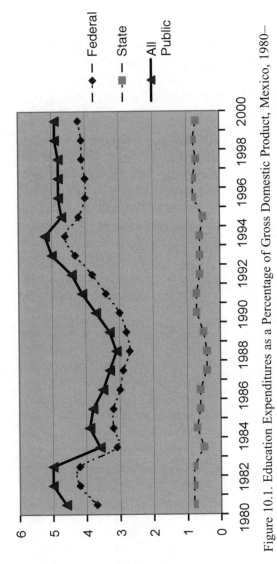

Figure 10.1. Education Expenditures as a Percentage of Gross Domestic Product, Mexico, 1980–2000

Source: SEP (2000b, 173).

occurring at the school and classroom level. At the same time, it was the consequence of a restructured education system in which new conflicts often slowed or stymied efforts to achieve better schooling and in which responsibility for improved performance was difficult to pin down.

Thus, as the structure of education services changed, so too did the arenas of conflict and the actors who were important in education policy and performance. Before decentralization, all but six states had systems of education that existed side by side with the national system. Thus, decentralization meant that most states would have to find ways of incorporating two separate teachers' corps, two separate administrative systems, and two sets of educational infrastructure. Budgets for education automatically doubled, tripled, quadrupled, or more. It is no wonder that many states were ill prepared to take on these new responsibilities and that considerable chaos characterized the transfer of funds, personnel, students, and infrastructure.[30]

Governors now became central figures in determining education policies. And given the weight of education expenditures in state budgets, newly empowered education ministers or managers of independent educational agencies also became important players in state level politics. Now responsible for the education payroll and the administration of schools, they, and the governors they served, had significant new resources. If they wished, the governors could appoint personnel and distribute operating resources in ways that helped them politically; alternatively, they had an increased capacity to become known as "education governors" during their administrations.[31] Moreover, the leaders of SNTE locals increased in importance as they focused new energies on gaining advances for teachers at the state level (Ornelas n.d., 13). In some states, officials and union leaders managed to routinize a bargaining relationship; in others, they were at loggerheads; and in still others, the locals of the union demanded and received positions within the new ministry leadership structures (Ornelas n.d., 14).

In many states, conflict over the control of education involved governors, ministries, new education institutes, and union locals. In Guanajuato, for example, a new institute for education was created for the transfer of funds, personnel, and infrastructure. At the same time, the state-level ministry of education, which had managed about 27 percent of basic education in

30. Mendoza et al. (1997, 348).
31. While governor of the state of Guanajuato, Vicente Fox—elected president of Mexico in 2000—was known as the education governor.

the state, remained in control of this system. Eighteen months of intense conflict ensued between the two organizations (Fierro Evans and Tapia García 1999, 177–80).

Eventually, a group of reformers within the ministry gained power over education policy and managed to limit the capacity of SNTE to shape its content. This made it possible unify the two bureaucratic structures and introduce innovations at lower levels in the system. At the same time, by failing to incorporate important interests in their plans for improving education, the reformers were unable to sustain the initiative. Indeed, as one study concluded, "a school reform was designed without the school," including participation of the teachers, the school directors, the parents, or local officials (Fierro Evans and Tapia García 1999, 236).

A somewhat similar situation emerged in Nuevo Leon, where a new state ministry of education was established and a new minister was put in charge of a unified national and state system. Within a short period of time, two groups emerged within this organization. One, known for its commitment to innovation and reform confronted another, made up of older, politically oriented officials with links to the teachers' union, who sought to slow the process of change (Mejía Ayala 1999, 263). When the reformers were able to push forward with their agenda, "there was hardly an area of the administrative apparatus of the education sector that was not subjected—with different degrees of intensity—to important structural changes carried out with great innovativeness and in the context of real and radical restructuring of the state" (Mejía Ayala 1999, 297; author's translation). Nevertheless, by the end of the decade, the fusion of the two systems was very incomplete: Many teachers in both systems felt orphaned by the state's handling of reform; the problems of implementation were taken as evidence of the failure of decentralization as a reform objective (Mejía Ayala 1999, 298).

SNTE locals were often at the center of education conflicts at the state level. The state of Chihuahua, for example, was the site of serious conflicts between a government representing the Partido Acción Nacional (PAN) and SNTE over virtually all aspects of education and conflicts within SNTE about the integration of state and federal teachers. The union locals were united in their suspicion that PAN was intent on privatizing the public education system (Loera Varela and Sandoval Salinas 1999, 438–39).

In contrast, the state of Oaxaca was characterized by accommodation between the union and the government. At the time of the national agreement, the PRI governor met frequently with union leaders, provided a meeting place for retired teachers, increased retirement funds for some teachers, and promised to find land for a warehouse for teaching materials and for the normal school (Ruiz Cervantes 1999, 513). His successor built new schools and improved old ones, expanded the teacher corps, and built housing for teachers, but did little to improve the quality of education (Ruiz Cervantes 1999, 522–28). In Aguascalientes, the governor introduced new leadership and improved resource management and supported innovation and creativity in the decentralized institute in charge of education.[32] Initially, the local SNTE took to the streets to demand higher salaries and to protest against the changes, but the governor reached agreement on some issues and resisted other demands. His successor also moved ahead with a series of innovative reforms and invited union leaders to be part of these initiatives (Zorrilla Fierro 1999, 346–47).

Much of the variation among these states can be credited to the priorities of the governors, their perspectives about the importance of education, and their political party ties. In addition, however, the degree to which SNTE locals were powerful at the state level was important, as was the ability of governors to manage this difficult relationship. Thus, the tensions and opportunities for leadership in reform that characterized the national level were replicated at the state level in the new structure of the education system.

A recurring theme in studies of the implementation of decentralization—and one found in other chapters of this volume—is the failure of the reform to encourage more active community and parental engagement. The Mexican initiative included social participation councils that were to be established at the school level along with new municipal councils to bring together parents, local officials, teachers, administrators, and representatives of business and religious organizations to discuss issues of importance to the local education system. In fact, however, by the end of the decade, these councils had not resulted in effective involvement of parents and other citizens in the schools. The school councils, indicated one observer, "never had a chance in the face of the union and the power of the school professionals."[33] One official argued that "Traditionally, teachers have

32. Mendoza et al. (1997, 347). According to one study, the average years of schooling increased from 6.8 in 1990 to 8.4 in 1998, school attendance increased from 83 percent in 1992 to 95 percent in 1997, and the number of children finishing primary school increased from 86 percent of those beginning school in 1987 to 93 percent of those beginning in 1991 (Zorrilla Fierro 1999, 386–87).

33. Interview, July 2, 2001, Mexico City.

been very jealous of their rights in the classroom. . . . The Constitution says the role of parents is to see that their children get to school—that's all!"[34] According to others, "The teacher decides what happens in the school," and does not invite others to share in such decisions.

And, in fact, there was little that parents could do to influence the performance of local schools. Although state governments were now administering basic and normal education, and municipalities were given responsibility for the construction of schools at the end of the decade, most decisions were taken either in Mexico City or in state capitals. Local input was further limited by ambiguities in the decentralization initiative. As one observer noted, "If you go to the governor or the secretariat of education in the state and complain, they will say 'No, no, we don't have anything to do with that; you have to go to the federal government.' If you go to the federal government to complain, they will say 'No, no, that's the responsibility of the state.'"[35] Under the Vicente Fox administration, governors of two states, Tlaxcala and Oaxaca, declared that they were returning their education responsibilities to the central government because they did not have sufficient resources to operate the systems. Given the difficulty of assigning responsibilities, concerned citizens found it difficult to hold officials directly accountable for educational performance.

Conclusions

Education reform is replete with empirical evidence of strong losers and weak winners, and of institutions that privilege the status quo and constrain reformers. But the relative weight of winners and losers and the biases of institutions do not fully exhaust the political possibilities for change. The case of Mexico indicates that reform leaders are at times able to alter the conflict equations that surround such initiatives. They are able to do so when they can seize the reformist initiative; control the timing of its introduction, discussion, and approval; set the terms of debate; and use their positions within government to alter institutional biases against change.

This chapter has focused on a major reform episode that demonstrates the ways in which reform initiatives can be pursued even in the face of strong opposition to them. Mexico's 1992 Agreement for the Modernization of Basic and Normal Education was the culmination of a long-term

34. Interview, July 4, 2001, Mexico City.
35. Ibid.

effort to decentralize education to the state level. To be sure, there were
other aspects of the reform—the teachers' career, new curriculum and
textbooks, efforts to increase opportunities for teacher training. But these
initiatives were subplots in the larger story of decentralization, the defining
educational reform of the 1990s. The teachers' career, which was both a
success and a failure—many teachers joined the new scheme that provided
incentives for them to improve their qualifications, but the system was soon
captured by the clientelist politics of SNTE—was a bargaining chip the
government used to encourage the union to agree to decentralization. The
curriculum reform and the introduction of new textbooks were subject to
much controversy and proceeded slowly in subsequent years. Teacher-
training initiatives increased, but they were not a major focus of reformers'
attention.

After 1992, it was decentralization, and not the other aspects of the
reform, that drove the dynamics of education planning, administration, and
evaluation. And it was decentralization that was central to the objectives
and strategies of the reformers and their opponents. This episode, then,
captures much of the politics of reform in the education sector in the 1990s.

The story of the 1992 reform initiative is largely the story of the interaction of the government (represented by the president, the minister of education, and Ministry of Education negotiators) and the leadership of SNTE
between 1989 and 1992. In a pattern that is widely replicated in both the
health and education reforms that are explored in other chapter case studies
in the present volume, the Mexican reform was a top-down one. There was
little involvement of interest groups other than the union, parents were not
publicly pressing for reform, and even the state governors were peripheral
to the agreement that was forged (Ornelas n.d., 2–3).

Certainly much of the story about how the reform came about can be
credited to the importance of reform leadership. It was clearly through the
initiative of President Salinas that an effort to improve the education system
was put on the political agenda in 1989. More important, however, were the
strategic choices he made in attempting to alter the composition of opposition and changing institutional balances of power in favor of change. The
president, presented with an opportunity to alter the obstructionist leadership of SNTE through internal union discord and extensive public protests,
removed Jonguitud Barrios and replaced him with Gordillo. As a consequence, not only was there new leadership for the union; it was also one that
was beholden to the president and whose own political future was tied to
negotiating successfully with government. In addition, the teachers were

recognized through salary adjustments, and peace returned to the sector in late 1989 and 1990. Through these actions, the nature of the interests opposed to change were fundamentally altered.

Similarly, reformers were able to take advantage of the need for the new union leadership to attend to internal business and consolidate its power. While this was occurring, the minister of education had an opportune moment to alter the leadership ranks of the ministry by bringing in people who were committed to policy reform rather than to the SNTE. Later, Salinas emphasized the importance of the reform by replacing this minister with one who was strongly associated with his own vision of modernization and known to be part of the inner circle in Salinas's Cabinet. In this way, one of the key institutional constraints to change was altered. The agreement that was possible in 1992 would probably have failed unless the president had been able to take advantage of the authoritarian control over the system that traditionally characterized the Mexican presidency. Moving against some of the most powerful dinosaurs in the unions and removing state governors at will, he also improved his popularity with the PRO-NASOL program. The consolidation of his power was evident in 1991 elections and, at the same time, improvements in the economy further enhanced his position.

These actions suggest that the reformers controlled the timing of the reform and determined the principal actors who would be engaged in negotiating about it. Moreover, they determined the terms of the debate, replacing talk of decentralization with discussions of "federalization" and modernization, dealing with SNTE as an "interlocutor" for the teachers, and providing salary inducements for the union to go along with the change. That reform was on the agenda, that it got discussed, and that it got agreed upon was certainly largely a result of a series of leadership choices. In this, then, there was a clear "change team" in charge of the reform in Mexico, as was the case with most of the other reforms considered in this volume.

Indeed, one aspect of the Mexican case not dealt with above suggests the extent to which strategic decisions of reform proponents are central to the subsequent history of their initiatives. Although the teaching career issue was dealt with as part of the larger negotiation with SNTE, curriculum reform became the responsibility of a small team in the Ministry of Education. Its task was to develop new textbooks and materials that would modernize learning in classrooms throughout the country.

When Zedillo became minister of education in 1992, he selected a small group of young, well-educated technocrats to redesign the free textbooks that all students in Mexico received. These textbooks had last been fully revised in 1972. Twenty years later, students continued to learn about topics such as the importance of national sovereignty vis-à-vis the United States, hostility to international business, and the value of a statist approach to economic development—topics that were anathema to the goals of the Salinas economic modernization project. Most of those assigned responsibility to produce more up-to-date textbooks were imbued with the modernizing vision of the president and the minister, and they believed they could take risks because of the support they enjoyed from these two impressive sources of power. And, in early 1992, time was of the essence because the reformers wanted to have new materials in the classrooms by the beginning of the 1992–93 school year.

However, the ministry team did not allow for consultation about the content of new materials and made the critical choices about which texts—and particularly, about which interpretations of history—would be adopted. In the event, the introduction of the new books was met with a strong negative reaction that played out in daily newspapers, protests, and meetings. In particular, new history texts presented interpretations of the country's past that displeased many, including a former president who was offended by the way in which his administration was portrayed. Public furor left the minister exposed to considerable public criticism, and his resignation was called for. In the face of this protest, the government abandoned the distribution of the offending textbooks.

The following year, other materials were selected, but criticism of the new books was as strong as those in the previous year, in part because they sidestepped so many issues. In August 1993, echoing the previous year, the Ministry of Education announced that there would be no new history texts for the fourth, fifth, and sixth grades, leaving teachers confused and annoyed. Clearly, this political brouhaha could have been avoided had the ministry team thought strategically and politically about the task they were undertaking. In not doing so, they made the government look uncertain and ineffective, and they also dimmed, at least for a while, the presidential ambitions of the minister. The textbook case signals the importance of strategic choices in introducing and pursuing reform.

Nevertheless, part of the Mexican case suggests that reform leadership operates within constrained arenas, however strategic it is. SNTE could certainly not be ignored in pursuing reform, and although the option of confronting the union rather than negotiating with it existed, prior experience had suggested that this would be a losing strategy. In Mexico, then, reformers settled for less than they wanted in their negotiations with the union. The relationship between the union and the then-dominant political party, the PRI, made this the wisest course of action. In addition, as education sector reform was implemented, the impact of the policy was altered by new conflicts at the state level and the variable ability of reform proponents to manage that conflict.

It is significant that the reform in Mexico was initiated, planned, negotiated, and carried out among a very small group of government and SNTE officials. Although some citizens became involved in the 1989 CNTE protests, this case replicates the reform initiatives in other cases surveyed here in its absence of public demands or support for educational change. Although the reform emerged at a time of increasing pressures for democratization in Mexico and increasing skepticism of the PRI regime, education did not figure among the demands being made by mobilized interests or citizen groups more generally.

CNTE's demands for union democracy were important, of course, but the long-cemented corporatist relationship among SNTE, the PRI, and the government meant little opportunity for broader participation in policy-making. Moreover, CNTE was not demanding better education; it was demanding a better deal for teachers and a more responsive union. Moreover, after the reform was put into practice, there were few spaces in which parents and communities could become active in encouraging and monitoring its implementation.

In comparative perspective, the 1992 agreement was modest in comparison with what other countries in Latin America were putting in place at about the same time. Some countries, such as Chile and Colombia, were decentralizing to the municipal level. Others, such as Nicaragua and some states in Brazil, were placing the main responsibility for the management of education at the school level in radical efforts to increase accountability and performance. In Argentina and Venezuela, reformers sought to devolve more federal responsibilities to the state level.

Yet Mexico's reform was significant, given education's highly centralized prereform condition and the failure of earlier efforts to alter this structure. Decentralization was thus the lynchpin for all subsequent reforms in the sector. The designers of Mexico's reform were adamant that the quality of education in the country would not improve until the system was decentralized and the hold of the union over education policy was weakened. With the 1992 reform, however, the capacity to improve education ceased to be a central government prerogative; governors and other state-level actors became central figures in explaining advances or retreats in the quality of schooling in Mexico. Indeed, any future education reforms would face a very different structure of power in the sector; reformers would have to address not only the national Ministry of Education and SNTE but also governors, state ministries, and SNTE locals.

Thus the 1992 reform multiplied the number of actors who would be engaged in subsequent reform initiatives and expanded the institutional sites where conflict over change could emerge. Nevertheless, although the potential for national reform may have become more complex and difficult, at the state level reformers had new opportunities to launch quality-enhancing reforms. Some of them took up this challenge, while others shied away from it. The capacity to enhance the quality of Mexico's education system in the future, then, will have much to do with the quality of state leadership and commitment to change.

References

Alvarez Béjar, Alejandro. 1991. Economic Crisis and the Labor Movement in Mexico. In *Unions, Workers, and the State in Mexico,* ed. Kevin J. Middlebrook. La Jolla: Center for U.S.–Mexican Studies, University of California, San Diego.

Arnaut, Alberto. 1998. *La federalización educativa en México.* Mexico City: Centro de Investigación y Docencia Económicas, Colegio de México.

Cabrero Mendoza, Enrique, Laura Flamand Gómez, Claudia Santizo Rodall, and Alejandro Vega Godínez. 1997. Claroscuros del neuvo federalismo mexicano: Estratégias en la decentralización y capacidades en gestión local. *Gestión y política pública* 6, no. 2.

Cominetti, Rossella, and Emanuela de Gropello. 1998. Descentralización de la educación y la salud: Un análisis comparativo. In *La descentralización de la educación y la salud: Un análisis comparativo de la experiencia latinoamericana,* ed. Emanuela de Gropello and Rossella Cominetti. Santiago: Comisión Económica para América Latina y el Caribe.

Cook, Maria Lorena. 1996. *Organizing Dissent: Unions, the State, and the Democratic Teachers' Movement in Mexico.* University Park: Pennsylvania State University Press.

Cornelius, Wayne, Ann Craig, and Jonathan Fox, eds. 1994. *Transforming State–Society Relations in Mexico: The National Solidarity Strategy.* La Jolla: Center for U.S.-Mexican Studies, University of California, San Diego.

de la Garza, Enrique. 1991. Independent Trade Unionism in Mexico: Past Developments and Future Perspectives. In *Unions, Workers, and the State in Mexico,* ed. Kevin J. Middlebrook. La Jolla: Center for U.S.-Mexican Studies, University of California, San Diego.

Duarte, Jesús, 1999. Política y educación: Las tentaciones particularistas en la educación latinoamericana. Paper prepared for a conference on education reform in Latin America, Santiago, January.

Fierro Evans, María Cecilia, and Guillermo Tapia García. 1999. Decentralización educative e innovación: Una Mirada desde Guanajuato. In *Federalización e innovación educativa en México,* ed. María del Carmen Pardo. Mexico City: Colegio de Mexico.

Fiske, Edward B. 1996. *Decentralization of Education: Politics and Consensus.* Washington, D.C.: World Bank.

Gershberg, Alec Ian. 1999. Fostering Effective Parental Participation in Education: Lessons from a Comparison of Reform Processes in Nicaragua and Mexico. *World Development* 27, no. 4.

Gordillo, Elba Ester. 1992. El SNTE ante la modernización de la educación básica. *El Cotidiano* 51, November–December.

Grindle, Merilee S. 1996. *Challenging the State: Crisis and Innovation in Latin America and Africa.* Cambridge: Cambridge University Press.

———. 2004. *Despite the Odds: Education Reform in Latin America.* Princeton, N.J.: Princeton University Press.

Laboratorio Latinoamericano de Evaluación de la Calidad de la Educación. 1998. *Primer estudio internacional coparativo.* Santiago: UNESCO.

Larmer, Brook. 1989. Mexico Teacher Strike Tests Salinas. *Christian Science Monitor,* April 21, 4.

Loera Varela, Armando, and Fernando Sandoval Salinas. 1999. La innovación educativa en el proceso de descentralización en el estado de Chihuahua. In *Federalización e innovación educativa en México,* ed. María del Carmen Pardo. Mexico: Colegio de Mexico.

Loyo, Aurora. 1992. Actores y tiempos politicos en la modernización educative. *El Cotidiano* 51, November–December.

Martin, Chris. 1993. "UPE" on the Cheap: Educational Modernization at School Level in Mexico. *Oxford Studies in Comparative Education* 3, no. 2.

Mejía Ayala, José Antonio. 1999. Federalismo e innovación educative en México: El caso de Neuvo León. In *Federalización e innovación educativa en México,* ed. María del Carmen Pardo. Mexico: Colegio de Mexico.

Merino Juárez, Gustavo. 1999. Decentralization of Education and Institutional Change: A Look at Mexico. *DRCLAS News* (Cambridge, Mass., Harvard University), spring.

Muñiz M., Patricia E. 2000. The Schooling Situation of Children in Highly Underprivileged Rural Localities in Mexico. In *Unequal Schools, Unequal Chances: The Challenges to Equal Opportunity in the Americas,* ed. Fernando Reimers. Cambridge, Mass.: Harvard University Press for David Rockefeller Center on Latin American Studies.

Murillo, Maria Victoria. 1999. Recovering Political Dynamics: Teachers' Unions and the Decentralization of Education in Argentina and Mexico. *Journal of Interamerican Studies and World Affairs* 41, no. 1.

Ornelas, Carlos. No date. The Politics of the Educational decentralization in Mexico. Autonomous Metropolitan University of Mexico, Mexico City (unpublished).

Ornelas, Carlos. 1988. The Decentralization of Education in Mexico. *Prospects* 18, no. 1.

Pescador Osuna, José Angel. 1992. Acuerdo Nacional para la Modernización de la Educación Básica: Una vision integral. *El Cotidiano* 51, November–December.

Reimers, Fernando. 2000. Educational Opportunity and Policy in Latin America. In *Unequal Schools, Unequal Chances: The Challenges to Equal Opportunity in the Americas,* ed. Fernando Reimers. Cambridge, Mass.: Harvard University Press.

Rohter, Larry. 1989. Mexican Labor Chiefs Feel the Heat. *New York Times,* February 27, 2.

Ruiz Cervantes, Francisco José. 1999. El proceso de federalización educativa en Oaxaca. In *Federalización e innovación educativa en México,* ed. María del Carmen Pardo. Mexico: Colegio de Mexico.

Salinas de Gortari, Carlos. 2002. *Mexico: The Policy and Politics of Modernization.* Barcelona: Plaza y Janés.

Schmelkes, Sylvia. 2000. Education and Indian Peoples in Mexico: An Example of Policy Failure. In *Unequal Schools, Unequal Chances: The Challenges to Equal Opportunity in the Americas,* ed. Fernando Reimers. Cambridge, Mass.: Harvard University Press.

SEP (Secretaría de Educación Pública, Mexico). 2000a. *Memoria del quehacer educativo, 1999–2000.* 2 vols. Mexico City: SEP.

———. 2000b. *Perfil de la educación en México.* Mexico City: SEP.

Street, Susan. 1998. *El sindicalismo docente en México: Fuerza institucional o sujeto social?* FLACSO/PREAL Boletín 2. Buenos Aires: Proyecto Sindicalismo Docente y Reforma Educativa en América Latina.

Tatto, Maria Teresa. 1999. Education Reform and State Power in Mexico: The Paradoxes of Decentralization. *Comparative Education Review* 43, no. 3.

UNDP (United Nations Development Program). 2001. *Human Development Report 2001.* New York: Oxford University Press.

UNESCO (United Nations Educational, Scientific, and Cultural Organization). 1998. *World Education Report 1998: Teachers and Teaching in a Changing World.* Paris: UNESCO.

———. 2000. *World Education Report 2000: The Right to Education—Towards Education for All Throughout Life.* Paris: UNESCO.

Zorrilla Fierro, Margarita María. 1999. Federalismo e innovación educative en Aguascalientes, 1992–1998: De un modelo armado a un modelo para armar. In *Federalización e innovación educativa en México,* ed. María del Carmen Pardo. Mexico: Colegio de Mexico.

Chapter 11

Multiple Preferences, Variable Strengths: The Politics of Education Reform in Argentina

Javier Corrales

Why do social policy reforms generate uneven and often contradictory outcomes, even when enacted under the same administration? In Argentina, the education reforms by two-term president Carlos Menem (1989–95, 1995–99) yielded inconsistent outcomes. Some areas of education were profoundly revamped; others were left untouched. Some reforms decentralized power away from the central ministry; others concentrated power in the ministry. Some decisions were made in consultation with non-state groups; others were made unilaterally.

The author was privileged to count on the research assistance of Milagros Nores. He is also grateful to Ricardo Kirschbaum for granting access to *Clarín* archives, and to Ministers Antonio Salonia, Jorge Rodríguez, and Susana Decibe for agreeing to be interviewed. The author received valuable comments from Esteban Cocorda, Tulia Falleti, Merilee Grindle, Robert Kaufman, M. Victoria Murillo, Mariano Narodowski, Joan Nelson, Joseph Tulchin, Laurence Wolff, and two anonymous reviewers.

This chapter offers an explanation for uneven outcomes in social policy reform, using the case of education reform in Argentina in the 1990s. Inconsistencies in reform outcomes reflect, first and foremost, reformers' multiple motives. Rather than pursue one single preference, as some theorists posit, reformers embrace multiple preferences at once. Consequently, they can accept different, contradictory outcomes because those outcomes can still be consistent with their multiple preferences.

Second, inconsistencies also reflect the shifts in the bargaining power of affected actors. Whether state reformers abandon their initial preferences and accept secondary results depends on the strength of opposing actors. Institutions and structures (e.g., economic conditions, structure of the party system, levels of presidentialism and federalism, size of unions, electoral rules) may not vary much, and yet affected actors may experience wide variations in their bargaining leverage, even from one year to the next. This chapter identifies factors that generate sudden changes in the bargaining power of affected actors.

The chapter begins with a brief explanation of the overall argument about multiple preferences and variable strengths, followed by a brief review of the state of education in Argentina before the reforms. It then examines three cases, or rounds, of reforms: a case of ministerial unilateralism (the 1991 Decentralization Law), a case of successful negotiations between the government and various nonstate groups (the 1993 Federal Law of Education), and a case of failed negotiations (the 1997–99 Carpa Blanca conflict).

Multiple Preferences

Many theorists of the state—as diverse as Edmund Burke, James Madison, Karl Marx, Max Weber, Charles Tilly, and James Scott—assume that state reformers pursue a unitary overriding objective. These thinkers differ on what constitutes the primary objective of state reformers (e.g., preserving the status quo, frustrating factions, advancing bourgeoisie interests, maximizing bureaucratic rationality, accommodating civil society, making society more legible), but they nonetheless agree in seeing the state reformer as single-minded.

However, more recent scholarship on reform experiences shows instead that reformers seek not one but multiple goals simultaneously.[1] In his study

1. Many contemporary rational-choice theorists see the reformer as equally single-

of reforms within the U.S. Congress in the twentieth century, for instance, Schicker (2001) found that the only way to explain the abundance of "disjointed" reform outcomes is to posit that reformers and reform coalitions are motivated by multiple interests. Reelection is one of those interests, but there are others, such as promoting the status of the majority party, the power of Congress vis-à-vis the executive branch, the institutional power bases of legislators, or a specific policy interest. Most reform acts in Congress satisfy any combination of these multiple preferences; seldom do they satisfy only one.

The perspective of the multiple-preference reformer helps to explain why reform policies are often incoherent, not just within the U.S. Congress but in other arenas as well. Weiler (1990), for instance, has found that state reformers in education indeed pursue conflicting goals simultaneously (see also Carnoy 1999, 37–46). Following this line of thought, I will show that state reformers in education are willing to accept any of these goals:

1. Solve short-term fiscal problems of the state ("savings").
2. Promote personal political careers and those of their colleagues (privilege political allies, engage in spending to benefit constituents).
3. Expand the prestige of their political party.
4. Signal commitment to change (engage in huge, symbolic political fights).
5. Eschew political traps (avoid huge political fights).
6. Unburden their office as a way to free themselves of responsibilities (decentralize).
7. Retain control over other actors (concentrate power).

Some of these goals are mutually compatible. But many are not. State reformers accept policy compromises that allow them to balance these multiple, often clashing, preferences.

Fluctuating Strengths

Policy outcomes also reflect the "political strength" of opponents. Although we know that the professional background or ideological commitments of reformers lead them to prefer certain policies over others (Blyth 2003;

---

minded, interested mostly in advancing personal political career goals, whether to maximize votes in elections or simply to prolong their stay in power. For a summary and critique of these views, see Weyland (2002).

Domínguez 1997; Centeno and Silva 1998; Lauglo 1995), we also know
that interactions with opponents lead them to accept outcomes that depart
from their starting preference. The more powerful the adversarial forces,
the more likely the reformer is to accept a compromise. The key question
then is: What determines actors' strength, that is, the capacity to influence
policy?

Most studies on determinants of political strength focus on prevailing
institutions and economic conditions: whether actors succeed in shaping
policy on behalf of their preferences depends on the institutional and economic resources at their disposal. Yet entrenched institutions and structures
are not the only factors that matter—they are not deterministic. The political ingenuity of actors also matters. For instance, actors can figure out how
to take advantage of the very same institutional and structural resources that
in a previous round proved unfavorable. As Shepsle (2003) argues in a
review of the work of William Riker, the level of ingenuity of actors varies
depending on whether they are winners or losers. Losers face an enormous
incentive to resuscitate: "They are the desperate ones; they are the ones
whose survival is at stake; they are the ones driven by their despair to seek
ways to triumph; they are, therefore, inventors" (2003, 310). Given another
opportunity to play the game, losers will "invent new actions," "reframe
issues," and avail themselves of any existing institutional opportunity.
Losers can be expected to restrategize and perhaps even make smarter use
of the very same institutional resources of the past.

I argue that actors, especially losers in one round of reform, can regain
strength in a second round by developing:

1. well-defined policy preferences, including a tangible reform counterproposal;
2. the internal cohesion of the organization or group; and
3. coalitions with other groups.

One way to show this capacity to regain strength is to focus precisely on
a reform experience that takes place in a short span of time, where there was
minimum variation in institutional and structural conditions but significant
fluctuation in the bargaining power of actors. Hence, this chapter focuses
on reforms in a brief nine-year period (1991–99). The key actors were the
same throughout: state officials under the same administration (the minister
of education and the minister of the economy), provincial governors and
ministers of education, both chambers of the national Congress, political

parties, the national teachers' union (Confederación Nacional de Trabajadores de la Educación, CTERA), some civic groups, and to a lesser extent, the church (compare Willis, Garman, and Haggard 1999). In a relatively short period, the political strength of these actors fluctuated significantly. Sometimes, state reformers had the upper hand; other times, the losers had the upper hand.

The Context before the Reforms: Argentina's Education and Economic Deficit

Relative to Latin America, Argentina's education system was well-advanced before the reforms of the 1990s (table 11.1). Since the 1853 Constitution, the state has assumed the responsibility of providing free compulsory education. By the late nineteenth century, the Argentine state was not only building schools but also subsidizing the efforts by provincial governments, and even private schools, to deliver education services. In the 1940s and 1950s, major strides were made in achieving universal primary education. By the 1980s, the system was large and fairly all-encompassing. Enrollments in primary education were nearly universal, with mostly uniform coverage across provinces (Parrado 1998). As a middle-income country, Argentina could afford to spend more on education than many other Latin American countries. In the early 1990s, Argentina ranked among the top in Latin America in terms of basic adult literacy, enrollments at all levels, and average years of schooling among adults (PREAL 2001).

Table 11.1

Basic Indicators for Argentina's Education System, circa 1990

Indicator	Measure
Percentage of students in public schools[a]	78.2
Public spending on education as a percentage of gross domestic product[b]	3.3
Public spending on education as a percentage of public expenditures[b]	11.6
Public spending on education (and science and technology) by the federal government (as a percentage of total)[b]	36.0
Public spending on education by the provinces (as a percentage of total)[b]	61.9
Net schooling rate (primary/secondary education; percent)[c]	95.7/53.7
Teachers' real wages in 1992 (1980 = 100)[d]	45

[a]Data are from Morduchowicz (2002).
[b]Data are from Nicolini, Sanguinetti, and Sanguinetti (2000).
[c]Data are from Llach, Montoya, and Roldán (1999).
[d]Data are from Tiramonti (2001).

In addition, the system was semidecentralized: In 1978, the provinces were given the responsibility to finance and deliver primary school services. This major structural reform took place under a military regime (1976–83) with very little consultation with nonstate actors (Hanson 1996; Falleti 2003).

Nevertheless, the education system faced numerous challenges in the late 1980s. Despite the transfer of primary schools, the system remained fairly centralized. The national government was responsible for financing and administering secondary and tertiary education, and for setting all policy guidelines. Yet its capacity to carry out these functions was collapsing. Education was a major casualty of Argentina's chronic economic decline starting in the 1950s and state bankruptcy in the 1980s.

A good indicator of the deterioration of the school system was the extent of exit, that is, the decline in the proportion of students attending public schools. Approximately 78 percent of total students attended public schools in 1990, down from approximately 90 percent in the 1960s (Morduchowicz 2002). That private school enrollment increased in a context of economic contraction is evidence of declining quality of public sector; even an increasingly impoverished society was opting for private schooling.

The most comprehensive study of Argentina's education system is that by Llach, Montoya, and Roldán (1999). It uses econometric tools to assess Argentina's education performance in comparison with countries of similar levels of economic development. Despite some positive findings,[2] the report uncovered serious problems: (1) inefficiency of invested resources (too much money was spent covering repetition and desertion rates), (2) low accountability of actors in the sector, and (3) inequity of access and outputs (see also World Bank 1994, 17; Aguerrondo 2000). Others would add the problem of declining real wages for teachers (Tiramonti 2001; Parrado 1998).

The transition to democracy in the 1980s did not bring any major improvements, but it did propel one of the most comprehensive debates about education reform ever witnessed in Argentina (MCE 1999). In 1984, the new administration of Raúl Alfonsín summoned a National Pedagogical

2. For instance, Argentina did not face a problem of insufficient coverage, relative to countries of similar development levels. Spending levels in education (both total and per student) were commensurate to what countries with similar GDP per capita spend. Also, coverage of primary and education levels, i.e., the number of students enrolled, was higher than expected for countries of similar GDP per capita (approximately 95 percent and 69 percent).

Congress (Congreso Pedagógico Nacional). The idea was to have leading figures in education—teachers from different grades, school authorities, philosophers, intellectuals, university deans, politicians, civic leaders, economists, church leaders, business representatives, and the like—debate possible reforms. The congress met throughout most of 1987 (preceded by multiple smaller meetings of working groups throughout the country). This was the largest consultative effort about policy ever undertaken in Argentina.

Although no major policy change resulted, the Pedagogical Congress issued a national document embracing major goals, such as extending the number of compulsory years, enhancing teacher training, improving student evaluation, increasing investments in infrastructure, and further decentralizing education (MCE 1999). These proposals had solid support; only those proposals that obtained 71 percent of the votes of the delegates (rather than 51) made it into the list of final recommendations. The Alfonsín administration was too overwhelmed by economic problems to pursue any of these proposals. But the Menem administration surprised many when, a few years later, it embraced one of the most profound recommendations of the Pedagogical Congress, the full decentralization of education.

Round One: Decentralization
The Transference Law, December 1991

The first round of education reforms under Menem was the decentralization of education—that is, transferring secondary education to the provinces, essentially completing the job begun by the military. The outcome of the reforms reflected, almost faithfully, the predominant preference of the executive branch. This occurred because of a unique set of political conditions that would not recur in Argentina in the rest of the decade: (1) the executive branch enjoyed enormous popularity, and (2) the affected parties were politically isolated and disorganized at the time that the reform was launched.

One of the most "sweeping" recommendations of the Pedagogical Congress was the full decentralization of education. This policy sounded very unobjectionable—very democratic—and in principle, most provinces welcomed it. But the provinces worried about a number of possible complications (see Eaton 2002, 203–33). They feared receiving this responsibility without sufficient funding and technical capacity, as had happened in 1978, when the military regime transferred primary schools (Falleti 2003). Furthermore, the provinces worried about the uneven levels of preparedness

(Salonia 1996, 41). Argentine provinces varied enormously in enrollment levels, demographic trends (i.e., whether the school population was stagnant or rising), financial resources, teacher and personnel costs, number and conditions of schools, technical capacity, and so on. Equalizing these differences would be contentious.

Thus, when Menem announced as early as August 1989 that decentralization would indeed be the centerpiece of his first education reform, most actors were shocked, even incredulous. There is disagreement as to whose initiative this was. The minister of education at the time, Antonio Salonia (1989–92), claims credit, arguing that he agreed to join the administration on condition that he be allowed to decentralize the system (interview with author).[3] In fact, Salonia was responsible for the first education-transfer bill project submitted by the national government to the Legislature (February 1990). Yet this first bill remained dormant in Congress, pushed by neither the government nor the legislators (Falleti 2003).

This changed when Domingo F. Cavallo became minister of the economy in February 1991. He soon decided to relaunch the decentralization idea. Cavallo was motivated mostly by fiscal concerns. He wanted to use the transfer of social policy responsibility as a way to force provinces to adjust their finances. He believed that much provincial spending was wasteful. By forcing them to spend more on social services, rather than on other less useful programs, he figured that he could force provinces to channel resources (which had increased in the previous years) into more productive uses.[4] Others argue that instead of pushing for an adjustment at the provincial level, all that Cavallo cared about was unburdening the federal government—hence, the little effort that he invested in ensuring that provincial spending become more streamlined.

Cavallo's decentralization proposal of 1991 represents the most unilateral attempt at education reform in Argentina in the 1990s.[5] Cavallo ignored the bill that was dormant in Congress. Instead, he inserted his reform within the massive budget bill for the 1992 fiscal year, hoping that

3. Salonia belonged to the MID Party, a splinter group of the UCR known locally as the *desarrollistas* and associated with the administration of Arturo Frondizi (1958–62), the first to try to decentralize primary education.

4. Revenues raised by provinces through taxes increased from 1.9 percent of GDP in 1989 to 3.2 percent in 1992 (Repetto 2001).

5. For a comparison of Salonia's and Cavallo's decentralization projects, see Repetto (2001).

this would ensure a rapid approval.[6] Legislators noticed this insertion almost by accident.[7] The provinces were shocked to see that the proposal did not include additional monies. They began to negotiate with Cavallo—secretively and outside Congress.[8] In the end, all they got was an agreement whereby the federal government guaranteed minimum financing in the event of revenue shortfalls.[9]

Despite this concession, the basic outcome (Law 24,049, which decentralized education services, some food programs, and several hospitals) reflected mostly the starting preferences of the state reformer, in this case, the Ministry of the Economy, to the exclusion of almost everyone else. The provinces' preference for gradualism was summarily ignored. Negotiations included few actors, took place behind closed doors, and did not result in any new federal monies for the provinces.

Provinces came out of the negotiations frustrated, harboring political and policy complaints. Their political complaint focused on the unilateral handling of the reform. Their policy complaint focused on the fact that neither sufficient cash nor much help to bolster institutional capacity was offered.

6. Two articles in the massive 1992 budget bill established that the provinces would be in charge of delivering secondary education, effective January 1, 1992.

7. Susana Decibe, at the time a staff aid for Deputy Jorge Rodríguez, discovered the measure, reading the budget bill (Falleti 2003).

8. In Argentina, the financing structure of the provinces is highly centralized. The federal government maintains control of the majority of revenue tools, leaving very few revenue-collecting instruments in the hands of the provinces. In return, the federal government agrees to distribute to the provinces a given share of the taxes it collects. This tax revenue-sharing system, known as the *coparticipación,* became law in 1988 (Law 23, 548). In 1991, the provinces initially wanted the federal government to increase the amount of money (i.e., the percentage of tax revenues) transferred to the provinces as a condition for accepting the responsibility of delivering secondary education. They did not get this. Cavallo argued that because of the successful stabilization package of 1991 (the Convertibility Law), the economy was booming and thus revenues for both the central government and the provinces were rising and would continue to rise, generating sufficient funds to finance decentralization and making it unnecessary to increase the percentage of revenues channeled to the provinces.

9. The provinces were only able to obtain from Cavallo a financial guarantee clause: Any time that revenues would fall below the levels registered in the April–December 1991 period (the peak of revenues collected so far), the federal government would cover the shortfall (Article 15). Furthermore, in August 1992, Cavallo even obtained consent by the provinces to lower the percentage of tax revenue sharing, from 57.7 percent of all revenues to 49 percent, in order to fund the social security system (the Fiscal Pact of 1992). For a thorough discussion of these negotiations, see Falleti (2003).

Despite these frustrations, the provinces were unable to mount an effective resistance for a number of reasons. First, the executive was enjoying a delayed honeymoon in the second half of 1991, due to the success and popularity of the April 1991 Convertibility Law, which killed inflation and reignited economic growth. Moreover, most political actors that could have served as allies of the provinces in 1991 were too distracted, focusing on the executive branch's massive privatization drive, which also gained momentum under Cavallo. Thus, the provinces could not easily find many suitable allies in 1991.

Furthermore, demonstrating too much opposition to a policy that was agreed upon by the Pedagogical Congress seemed politically indecorous. The provinces could not even make a compelling case for their plight (lack of institutional capacity), because they were already delivering primary education and substantial secondary education, administering many more schools than the federal government (Falleti 2003). Finally, the administration succeeded in preventing unity among the provinces themselves by offering to negotiate individually with each province the terms of the transfer (e.g., the exact day of the transfer, personnel issues such as teachers' health insurance, and infrastructure issues).

The leading teachers' union, CTERA, was also relatively fragmented and politically unimportant in 1991. Although it claimed to have many affiliates (approximately 120,000 members), CTERA was a federation of some (not all) teachers' unions from the provinces. It did not hold a monopoly of representation, as did its counterpart in Mexico. This lessened its bargaining leverage (see Murillo 1999). It did not have strong links with any party at this point either. Instead it was loosely affiliated with the faction of the labor union confederation that had broken ranks with the executive branch (the Dissident General Confederation of Labor, or Confederación General del Trabajo–Disidente). This alliance did not add much strength to CTERA. Furthermore, decentralization did not displease many teachers, because it entailed salary raises for many teachers, given that many provinces paid higher wages than the national government (Repetto 2001).

Because of the weakness of the opposition and the heightened popularity of state reformers, the outcome that prevailed was the primary policy preference of technical experts at the state. And because policy was driven by the Ministry of the Economy rather than the Ministry of Education, the standard of technical correctness that prevailed was that of a fiscally conscious economist: unburdening the federal government (i.e., transfer salary and school maintenance to the provinces without new monies). Even though tax revenues for the national government increased by 152 percent between 1991 and 1995, revenue transfers to the provinces remained constant (Eaton 2002, 227).

The result was a major transformation in education. Provinces acquired responsibility for 2,000 national schools, 72,000 teachers, and 700,000 students (Faletti 2002). Primary and secondary education became the most decentralized of all social services in Argentina (see table 11.2). The national ministry withdrew completely from delivery and financing of schools, adopting the nickname of "ministry without schools" (*ministerio sin escuelas*). Provinces and municipalities had to boost spending on education, doubling it from $3.9 billion in 1991 (2.18 percent of gross domestic product, or GDP) to $8.0 billion in 1994 (2.81 percent of GDP) (World Bank 1994, 72). No other sector experienced this degree of federal retreat in Argentina.

At the same time, little effort was made at this point to improve the quality of education; no provision was made to reform the curriculum, train educators, improve the infrastructure of schools, build institutional capacity of service delivery, or assess performance of students—all major recom-

Table 11.2

Expenditure Allocations of Federal, Provincial, and Municipal Governments in Argentina, 1999

Expenditure	Delivery of Service	Financing	Regulatory Powers
Environment	FPM	FPM	FPM
Education			
Primary	PM	PM	FPM
Secondary	P	P	FPM
University	F	F	F
Health	FPM	FPM	FP
Health insurance	FP	FPM	FP
Immigration	F	F	F
Justice	FPM	FPM	FPM
Public safety			
Prisons	FP	FP	FP
Police	FP	FP	FP
Social housing	P	FP	
Social welfare	FP	FP	FP
Unemployment insurance	F	..	FP

Note: F = federal government, P = provincial government, M = municipal government.
Source: Based on Tommasi (2002).

mendations of the Pedagogical Congress. This infuriated many provinces, and also of course teachers.

The unilateralism of the Transference Law would not recur in the 1990s. One of the unintended consequences of this first round of reforms was to ignite affected actors. From this point on, education reformers in Argentina confronted more serious political obstacles, leading to a reform process that involved more negotiations and setbacks, and to outcomes that departed from the starting preferences of state reformers.

Round Two: Negotiating State Guarantees
The Federal Education Law, 1993

The next round in the reform process was to decide which services and resources the federal government would "guarantee." Provinces were keen on maximum federal guarantees; the Ministry of the Economy was keen on minimum guarantees. Everything was up for negotiation: the number of mandatory years of schooling, the levels of investment, the mix of public–private education, the future of free-tuition universities, the extent of school autonomy to hire or fire personnel, the allocation of responsibility for measuring the performance of schools and students, and so on. This was the largest opportunity in the Menem era to negotiate a profound rewriting of the rules governing education.

However, the political context in 1992, when this debate was launched, was considerably different from the year before, when decentralization was legislated. Both the reformers and the targeted sectors became politically stronger. Consequently, a bargaining process ensued that led to reforms that departed significantly from the initial objectives of state reformers.

The executive branch became even stronger politically in 1992 because of the increased prestige of Menem's economic program. Having suc- cessfully eliminated inflation, and restored economic growth, the admin- istration seemed invincible in 1992. This was the administration's belated honeymoon, permitting it to approach the education sector with bravado. The executive was interested mostly in (1) "savings," that is, spending as little as possible; (2) ensuring that the provinces, not the federal government, finance most of the reforms (*provincialización*); (3) relaxing the free-tuition system of universities; (4) increasing the flexibility of the teachers' labor market (i.e., reducing the stronghold of unions on the labor market for teachers, permitting merit-based promotions); and (5) avoiding "shackles" (i.e., agreements that would commit the state to any fixed level of spending).

But at the same time, the main target groups—the provinces, CTERA, and certain civic groups—had become politically stronger as well. Their capacity to fight back increased because of three factors. The first was a well-defined policy position: Both the provinces and CTERA developed a very coherent, easy-to-summarize policy position, in opposition to the designs of the executive branch. They wanted to "shackle" the federal government, that is, get it to commit to high levels of investment in education. The provinces were proposing 6 percent of GDP; the teachers' union wanted 8 percent. Although the numbers differed, there was unity of purpose: guaranteeing a strong federal presence in the finance of education.

The second factor was internal cohesion. Both the provinces and the unions avoided major divisions within their ranks. The provinces did their best to avoid bilateral negotiations with the administration (as happened with the Transference Law in 1991). And CTERA learned to avoid the splits that plagued other labor unions in 1989–91. By 1992, CTERA emerged as one of the most united forces opposed to Menem.

The third factor was coalitions. Both the provinces and CTERA were able to create important coalitions, not just with each other but also with various civic groups. Specifically, several citizen groups emerged in 1992 to protest against the education reforms. These were citizens who had become alarmed at the extent of privatizations of state-owned enterprises under Menem. They feared that the executive branch would privatize education as well (i.e., charge for all services, privilege private ownership and management of schools) (Decibe 2001). This was a misinterpretation of the executive's intention, since at no point did the executive ever suggest privatizing schooling. Yet the antiprivatization sentiment of these groups was so strong that they could not help suspecting the worst. This is one negative consequence of bundling education reforms with a program of economic structural adjustment. The opportunity for cooperation between market-reform enemies and teachers' unions and provinces increases.

Table 11.3 lists the different actors involved in the debate about the Federal Education Law, their starting policy preferences, and political power in 1992. The executive was enjoying enormous political prestige and determination. The opposition was enjoying internal unity, cohesive strategy, and cross-sectoral coalitions. The minister of education was caught between several titans: a powerful savings-oriented minister of the economy, who did not want to be tied down financially; the internal views of its own technocrats, who were pushing for expansion of schooling and reform of the curriculum (which required investments); and powerful opposing

Table 11.3

Main Actors in the Conflict over the Argentine Federal Education Law,
mid-1992

Actor	Starting Position	Political Strength
Minister of the economy	Savings (*provincialización*); encourage flexible personnel policies; avoid fiscal shackles.	High
Minister of education	Improve technical standards; expand schooling; empower ministry to monitor performance.	Weak
Provinces	Expand and guarantee federal financing.	High
CTERA	Expand and guarantee federal financing; keep personnel policies intact.	Medium
Public opinion	Prevent the privatization of education.	High

Note: CTERA = Confederación de Trabajadores de la Educación de la República Argentina.

interest groups, who were more unified than ever. The stage was set for a huge confrontation.

The battleground of this confrontation turned out to be the Legislature, which in Argentina was gradually replacing "the street" and "visits to ministries" as the crucial site of political fights. Previously, the Legislature played a minor, even negligible, role in education reform. This changed in 1992, for several reasons. First, the executive branch displayed a strong preference to engage the Legislature in the reform process, in part because it had confident expectations that its own party would cooperate (see Corrales 2002b; Eaton 2002). Second, governors, who had a strong stake in the education reform process, also began to use the Legislature to advance their interest, in part because they exercised strong influence over senators (often controlling the nomination process for Senate seats) (Tommasi 2002; Jones et al. 2001; Gibson and Calvo 2000).

A third reason that the Legislature became a key actor had to do with the nature of relations between the executive branch and the political parties—a seldom discussed but nonetheless crucial issue in the politics of education reforms. At the risk of simplifying, one can posit three possible executive–party relations: (1) a dominant ruling party willing to cooperate with the executive; (2) a dominant ruling party unwilling to cooperate; and (3) a dominant opposition party unwilling to cooperate (divided government). Under conditions 2 or 3, the chances that the Legislature would become involved in negotiating reforms are minimal because the interested parties have no desire to negotiate but rather seek to block change (see Corrales

2002a). Rather than negotiation, the likely outcome is a political stalemate, in which the targeted sectors (teachers' unions and governors) side with the uncooperative parties against the reformers. In Argentina after 1991, condition 1 prevailed: the Peronist, or Justicialist, Party (PJ) was dominant (with winning majorities in Congress and in provincial governorships) and cooperative (see Corrales 2002b). Large factions of the PJ were willing to negotiate with the executive in shaping reforms. The setting was right for the Legislature to emerge as a principal locus of negotiation.

The negotiation began with the Senate issuing a counterproposal to the executive's bill, essentially acting on behalf of the mostly Peronist provinces in tacit alliance with the unions. The two proposals were in many ways incompatible with each other (see table 11.4).

For a while, the opposing senators had the upper hand; their bill was well received by the press and had the backing of the provinces, CTERA, and even opposition parties. The Senate passed the bill unanimously. Appalled,

Table 11.4

Key Features of Competing Proposals for the Argentine Federal Education Law, Mid-1992

Issue	Ministry of Education's Proposal	Senate's Proposal
School fees	Ambiguous. The federal government and the provinces must only guarantee "access." Did not mention the concept of free schooling (*gratuidad*)	Free schooling (*gratuidad*)
Who attends	Seven years of compulsory schooling (i.e., leave system as is). Expansion of compulsory schooling to be considered in the future	Ten years of compulsory schooling
Financing	Contingent on budget laws negotiated each year between the executive branch and the Legislature. If anything, it should be the provinces, not the federal government, that ought to guarantee levels of investment (*provincialización*)	To be determined by a separate law; the executive branch must commit at least 6 percent of gross domestic product (GDP), up from 3.3 percent of GDP
Universities	No stated preference, but signaled desire to relax the free-tuition system	Change little; any changes to be discussed in a separate bill

Note: This table gives only representative highlights. Each proposal contained many more sections.
Source: Página/12, July 4, 1992.

the executive threatened to veto this bill (*Página/12,* July 4, 1992), but CTERA mobilized protests by parents and students (sometimes reaching 70,000 participants) to deter the executive (*Clarín,* July 9, 1992).

At this point, the Chamber of Deputies joined the fight. Specifically, the head of the Education Commission in the Chamber of Deputies, Jorge Rodríguez, of the ruling party (PJ), stepped in to try to resolve the stalemate between the Senate and the executive branch (interview with author). Rodríguez was motivated by several goals. The first was to help his own party solve this difference so that the party could still take credit for a major reform and avoid the image of inaction (i.e., partisan interest). Second, he was also interested in becoming better known in political circles (i.e., maximize his political career). Third, he wanted to "Peronize" the administration (i.e., policy interest). Rodríguez was part of those members of the ruling party who supported the overall reforms of the government but who also wanted the government to adopt a more "human face," that is, counterbalance the government's neoliberal economic program with more center-left Peronist social policies featuring a strong state role in social service delivery. As he said: "We did not agree with the idea that the national government should disengage from education" (*Clarín,* special supplement, December 30, 1993, 4). The Federal Law of Education provided an opportunity to Peronize the administration.

Thus, Rodríguez (acting on behalf of deputies) made a counterproposal to both the Senate's and the executive's projects. It incorporated the Senate's call for the state to guarantee the *"gratuidad"* of public school, as well as the executive's position to soften some shackles on the federal government. Rather than commit the federal government to invest 6 to 8 percent of GDP on education, Rodríguez proposed to double the amount of investment in a period of five years. Given that the Ministry of the Economy was predicting growth rates of 6 percent for the next several years, as well as major increases in tax collection, this doubling did not appear overly optimistic, even to the austere minister of the economy (Rodríguez interview). In addition, Rodríguez introduced the idea that universities could find "alternative sources" of financing. This was perhaps the only legal window through which the free-tuition system could be modified without generating political turmoil.

Having a coherent policy in mind was not enough. After all, Rodríguez was an inconsequential deputy fighting two juggernauts—the Senate and the executive branch. To rise in stature, Rodríguez needed to become less isolated. He accomplished this by emulating the provinces and CTERA, that is, through coalition building, starting first with civil society groups.

Unusual for Argentine legislators, Rodríguez and his staff visited more than seventy civil society institutions of different political persuasions throughout the country in early 1992, for a total of approximately 260 meetings (*rondas consultivas*) (Decibe interview). The idea was to explain the proposal and calm the rising civil protests. An explicit effort was made to talk to church officials and allay their fears that state subsidies would end (Rodríguez interview). Later in 1993, he focused on another set of actors: provincial ministers of education (more on this below).

The coalition-building strategy worked. Protests subsided gradually. This gained Rodríguez prestige in the Chamber of Deputies. Witnessing this political effect, most members of the ruling party, all provincial parties, and all members of the Ucedé voted for the bill, for a total of 129 votes; the main opposition party, the Radical Civic Union (Union Cívica Radical, or UCR), tried to prevent a quorum, but failed (*Clarín,* September 3, 1992).

The result was that the Chamber of Deputies, under the leadership of Rodríguez, emerged as a leading actor in the reform process, as a conciliating agency rather than an opponent. The intensity of preferences of state reformers and senators galvanized an until-then inactive deputy into action. Motivated by multiple motives, this deputy galvanized the until-then dormant Chamber of Deputies into action. Like the provinces and CTERA, the Chamber of Deputies amassed sufficient political resources to become consequential: a coherent policy preference (a proposed bill), significant support within its institutional base (majority votes in the chamber), and coalitions across civil society (the *rondas consultivas*).

Facing two formidable contenders (the Senate and Chamber of Deputies), the executive branch needed to make a decision: whether to ignore both bills (and jeopardize the chance of enacting reform) or to side with one of them (and compromise its starting preferences). Impressed by Rodríguez's rescue efforts, Menem sided with the Chamber of Deputies. Even more momentously, he appointed Rodríguez as minister of education in December 1992.

With the blessing of the executive branch (including the Ministry of the Economy), various civic groups and the ruling party in the Chamber of Deputies, the Ministry of Education thus emerged as a powerful political actor in 1993—for the first time in decades. At this point, the Senate had no option but to accept this new political reality and endorse the bill of the Chamber of Deputies (i.e., "Rodríguez's" bill) with very few modifications. The final version, passed in April 1993, was closer to the original bill of the Chamber of Deputies than to either the Senate's or the executive's original proposal (see table 11.5).

Table 11.5
Representative Provisions of the Argentine Federal Education Law (April 1993) and the Preferences of the Federal Government

Issue	Stipulation	Federal Government's Preference Violated	Federal Government's Preference Supported
School fees	*Gratuidad*: All school services would be free	Flexibility	Accommodate the ruling party, which wanted to reaffirm a strong state presence in education
Who attends	Ten years of compulsory schooling	Go easy on poor, peripheral provinces, which did not want to have onerous burdens	Accommodate technical experts and center-left groups, who demanded more schooling
Financing	Double federal spending in five years	"Savings"	Accommodate the provinces, which wanted investment guarantees
Universities	Free tuition, supported by the state; expanded autonomy to design curriculum and expand finance sources	"Savings" (no savings occurred because the financing structure remained unchanged)	Accommodate the opposition parties, which had strong links with university deans and student groups and did not want to lose federal guarantees[a]
Evaluation	Performed by technical experts in the ministry; issue annual report to Congress	Minimize accountability to other political bodies	Power concentration: all aspects of governance and evaluation remained centralized under the ministry; large sums are invested to bolster the institutional capacity of the ministry to carry out this function
Federal Council of Ministers	Provincial ministers and national minister of education charged with coordinating education guidelines and curriculum	Minimize number of actors involved in decision making	Maximize the number of political allies, by forming territorially-based (federal government and provinces) and epistemic-based coalitions (coalitions of education officials)

[a]The Ministry of the Economy did obtain the provision that universities can seek alternative sources of financing.
Source: Federal Law of Education, 1993.

The resulting law shows how the rise in the political strength of affected actors changes the position of the executive branch, away from its starting preference for unilateralism and savings, but still conforming to its various and partly conflicting secondary goals. When pushed politically, state reformers accepted a number of compromises, in part because they embraced multiple preferences to begin with.

Reform Implementation, 1993–1997

Between 1993 and 1997, the education sector experienced relative political tranquility. Having obtained an Education Law, the Ministry of Education enjoyed political and institutional space to focus on implementation. Why was there political peace between 1993 and 1997, despite all the major changes taking place? What exactly did the reformers accomplish?

Why Stability?

Several factors explain the relative political tranquility in the education sector between 1993 and 1997. In part, this tranquility was a consequence of the comfortable political status of the administration as a whole. Menem became politically secure in office, enjoying the reliable support of a "new coalition" that included the traditional core of Peronism, most provincial governors, and many business leaders. The government won the 1995 presidential elections comfortably, and for the most part, ruling party leaders and the provinces remained cooperative with the administration.

This, however, was not the whole story. Important intrasectoral political factors also explain the political tranquility of this period. First, there was relative stability and continuity with regard to ministry leadership. Rodríguez's tenure in office lasted 1,221 days, the second-longest-lasting minister of education in decades (table 11.6). He resigned in 1996 not because of political wear and tear but to accept a political promotion—Chief of Cabinet. He was succeeded by his second in command, Susana Decibe, signifying policy continuity. Decibe also had a long stay in office—1,118 days. These terms contrasted sharply with the high ministerial turnover of the 1980s and after 1999.

Second, the Ministry of Education secured crucial political allies at the cabinet, provincial, and international levels. The key cabinet ally was none other than the minister of the economy, Domingo Cavallo, who remained in

Table 11.6

Education Ministers of Argentina, 1983–2002

Minister	Administration	Entry	Days in Office
R. S. Alconada Aramburu	Alfonsín	Dec. 1983	934
J. Rajneri		July 1986	442
J. F. Sábato		Sept. 1987	618
J. G. Dumón		May 1989	43
A. F. Salonia	Menem	July 1989	1,245
J. A. Rodríguez		Dec. 1992	1,221
S. B. Decibe		April 1996	1,118
M. García Solá		May 1999	214
J. J. Llach	De la Rúa	Dec. 1999	275
H. Juri		Sept. 2000	181
A. G. Delich		March 2001	294

Source: Centro de Políticas Educativas, Fundación Gobierno y Sociedad.

office until 1996. Although initially skeptical about the ministry's penchant for spending, Cavallo came around. Both Rodríguez and Decibe recognized the importance of always meeting Cavallo's approval, going out of their way to demonstrate that spending, though substantial, was done under criteria of efficiency. Rodríguez and Decibe did all they could to open their activities to the scrutiny of Cavallo, often inviting him to tour the new and rehabilitated schools. This earned them Cavallo's blessing.

The other political allies of the Ministry of Education were the provincial ministers of education. One of the most politically savvy decisions by Rodríguez was to activate the Consejo Federal Educativo, a consultative body composed of provincial ministers of education. Created in 1972, the Consejo remained fairly inactive until the Rodríguez tenure. The Federal Law of Education specifically stipulated, by petition of Rodríguez, that the Consejo be engaged in policymaking. Elevating the political standing of provincial ministers—giving them a seat at the policymaking table at the national level, even bypassing provincial governors—was a smart political move. It earned the Ministry of Education important allies in the provinces.

The political ally at the international level was the World Bank, which had been an absentee actor in Argentina's education sector since 1980.[10] Now, however, the World Bank—impressed by the reform impetus of the

10. The last World-Bank–supported education project was a small loan approved in 1980. It was never implemented (World Bank 1994). Bank assistance to Argentina as a whole was interrupted in 1988, due to the economic crisis, and resumed in 1990, with a focus on assisting the government stabilize and restructure the economy.

new Ministry of Education after 1993—approved a $190 million loan project to fund decentralization in 1994. Thereafter, the ministry was able to negotiate (rather effortlessly) a series of new loans to help finance the reform effort, for a total of $1.3 billion in loans from 1994 to 1999.[11] The Inter-American Development Bank supplemented these efforts with a total of $600 million in education loans (Decibe 1999). The alliance between the ministry and multilateral aid agencies was politically useful. The World Bank provided the ministry not only with money and advice but also the opportunity to offer subloans to the provinces on the condition of implementing reform at the provincial level.

Finally, the opposing CTERA, while angry, returned to its pre-1992 levels of political isolation. In terms of policy preference, CTERA clung to three demands: (1) opposing the Menem administration, to the point of consistently refusing to negotiate; (2) revoking the Federal Law of Education; and (3) obtaining higher salaries. The first two demands hurt CTERA politically. Its refusal to negotiate with the Menem administration gave it an image of intransigence. And its insistence on revoking the law was simply unviable, given that the law was approved by Congress, with support from the provinces and the church.[12]

CTERA's third demand (salaries), however, did elicit more sympathy across the population. The problem was that there was no strong enough political actor available to align with CTERA on this issue during this period. The provinces were unwilling to side with a call for more wages, because they would have had to shoulder any increase. And the opposition parties did not have much institutional power to lend much help either. Between 1989 and 1997, the UCR underwent a serious electoral decline, losing ground in Congress. The other opposition party, the Front for a Country in Solidarity (Frente País Solidario, or FREPASO), was making some inroads, but its power was too small (confined mostly to Buenos Aires) to serve as a powerful ally.

The combination of a politically strong administration, a stable Ministry of Education with two crucial pillars of support (the provinces and multilaterals), and an isolated CTERA explain the relative peace of 1993–97. State reformers enjoyed the legal, institutional, and political space to implement change.

11. This is based on the list of education loans to Argentina at www.worldbank.org (click the link for Policies, Projects, and Strategies).
12. Argentina's bishops reiterated their support for the Law in 1997, right after CTERA launched a major protest in Buenos Aires (*Clarín,* August 7, 1997).

What Did the Reformers Implement?

The Federal Law of Education established the parameters of what the reformers could do. It provided the mandate (that which the state was obliged to do), the possibilities (that which the state was not banned from doing), and the restrictions (that which the state was banned from doing). The mandate included: more investments, especially in infrastructure and school supplies, curricular reform and expansion of school years, teacher training, and evaluations. The possibilities included offering financial aid for students, helping universities develop alternative sources of finance, developing the institutional capacities of provincial governments to deliver better education services, providing more investments for teachers' salaries, and promoting further decentralization, such as transferring more responsibilities to municipalities and school boards. Among the most important restrictions was moving to a merit-based system of teacher promotion. This would have required changing the teachers' labor code, or *estatuto docente,* which essentially banned firing of teachers and merit pay.

The Ministry of Education devoted most of its energy to implementing the mandate, less energy on the possibilities, and almost no energy on trying to ease the restrictions. Among the mandates, one of the most salient areas of focus was the reform of the curriculum (see Gvirtz 2002). This consisted not only of expanding the mandatory years of schooling (see table 11.7), but also of agreeing on new subjects to be taught in the classroom.[13] Reforming the curriculum, especially in social sciences and the humanities, tends to be polemical. To the ministry's credit, this reform was implemented in relative peace. The reason is that the deliberations were both participative and decentralized. They were participative in that input was sought from the provinces (the Consejo Federal Educativo), as well as academics and representatives from civil society. They were decentralized in that the reform was broken down into three types of curricular changes, intended to incorporate input from three levels of the education system: (1) a federally mandated set of subjects to be taught in all schools ("basic common contents)"; (2) provincially mandated contents, to be decided by each province ("provincial curricular design"); and (3) school-decided contents.

In 1994, the government negotiated the Pacto Federal Educativo, an agreement with the provinces to invest almost $3 billion in school in-

---

13. Curricular reform of preschool was approved in September 1994 (updated in 1995), of the *polimodal* (equivalent to high school) in 1997, and of middle school in 1998.

Table 11.7

Argentina's Expansion of Obligatory Schooling, Pre- and Post-1993 Structures

Pre-1993 Structure		Age (years)	Post-1993 Structure		
Level	Grade		Grade	Cycle	Level
Initial	1st	3	1st		Initial
	2nd	4	2nd		
	3rd	5	3rd		
Primary	1st	6	1st	1	EGB1
	2nd	7	2nd	1	
	3rd	8	3rd	1	
	4th	9	4th	2	EGB2
	5th	10	5th	2	
	6th	11	6th	2	
	7th	12	7th	3	EGB3
Middle	1st	13	8th	3	
	2nd	14	9th	3	
	3rd	15	1st		Polimodal
	4th	16	2nd		
	5th	17	3rd		

Note: Shaded areas indicate compulsory schooling. EGB = Educación General Básica (Basic General Education).
Source: MCE (1999).

frastructure.[14] Table 11.8 shows the increase in education spending between 1992 and 1999. The sector was showered with resources to a degree unprecedented in Argentina in decades, resulting in enrollment expansion, most notably in preprimary programs and middle and secondary schools, but also in primary education, where coverage was extensive to begin with (see table 11.9). More than 2,500 "ranch" and "precarious" schools were eradicated. A total of 1.5 million square meters of school facilities were built, and 2.3 million square meters were refurbished (MCE 1999, 46). By 1998, more than $120.2 million and $123 million had been invested in infrastructure and student scholarships, respectively.

Another accomplishment was an innovative program to generate education-related statistics, including evaluations of student performance, with substantial World Bank support (Narodowski, Nores, and Andrada 2002).[15]

14. Many provinces and CTERA wanted the money to be used for salaries, but the government argued that provinces should use their own savings to finance salaries (see *Clarín,* August 31, 1994).

15. Starting in 1993, Argentina launched a comprehensive system of student testing.

Table 11.8

Public Expenditures on Education, Culture, Science, and Technology in Argentina, 1980 and 1990s

Year	Amount (billions of dollars)	Percentage of Gross Domestic Product	Percentage of Public Expenditures
1980	8.0	3.3	10.3
1991	8.0	3.3	11.6
1992	9.3	3.5	12.1
1993	10.7	4.1	12.9
1994	11.5	4.2	13.1
1995	11.3	4.3	13.2
1996	11.4	4.2	13.7
1997	12.7	4.3	14.3
1998	13.2	4.4	14.2
1999	13.9	4.8	14.3

Source: Nicolini, Sanguinetti, and Sanguinetti (2000).

Table 11.9

School Enrollment in Argentina, 1991–98

Level	1991	1998	Percentage Increase
Preschool/initial	483,029	684,878	42
Primary	4,816,004	5,272,828	10
Middle/secondary	2,033,198	2,548,634	25
Total	7,333,231	8,506,340	16

Source: MCE (1999).

Because there was relative stability within the ministry (both at the level of ministers and at the level of lower-tier technical experts),[16] these programs experienced continuity, avoiding the short life span typical of government programs.

The implementation stage had shortcomings. One was the failure to push provinces to go beyond the minimum mandated by the Federal Law of

---

By 1999, Argentina was evaluating students in third year (mathematics, language, social sciences, natural sciences), sixth year (for the same subjects), seventh year (math and language), and ninth year (math and language). The number of students evaluated increased from 23,500 in 1993 to 411,000 in 1999 (Narodowski, Nores, and Andrada 2002, 31–35).

16. The office in charge of evaluations (the Subsecretaría de Programación y Evaluación Educativa) exhibited remarkable stability, with only two changes of undersecretaries: Horacio Santángelo, from January 1993 to January 1995, and Hilda Lanza, from January 1995 to May 1999) (Narodowski, Nores, and Andrada 2002, 69).

Education. Very few provinces did more than implement "access" reforms (expand infrastructure, raise salaries, introduce the new mandatory school years, and expand coverage). Innovative "quality" programs were rare. The Federal Law, for instance, permitted provinces to go much farther in decentralization (e.g., transferring responsibilities to municipalities, and increasing school autonomy to hire and fire teachers). Only the medium-sized province of San Luis took advantage of these provisions, launching an innovative program of charter schools, the so-called *escuelas autogestionadas* (see Corrales 2003).

The national government's failure to push for more school autonomy contrasts with its insistent efforts to reform *obras sociales* (see chapter 4 of the present volume). School autonomy consists of authorizing school authorities to hire and fire teachers and to make budget decisions. Although school autonomy is not the same type of reform as introducing competition in *obras sociales* (the equivalent in education would be giving parents more school choice by introducing vouchers), it makes sense to compare them because they reflect different state attitudes—more desire to introduce neoliberalism (competition) in health than in education.

When asked to explain why the government held back on education, Decibe argued that she knew that school autonomy "would have involved changing the teachers' labor code, which we knew we couldn't do" (interview with the author). Clearly, the government did not want to pick another fight with CTERA. But perhaps the most important reason has more to do with fiscal priorities. The Menem administration developed a very strong interest in reducing labor costs in general. Health reform could contribute to this goal if it facilitated reductions in the extremely high employers' social security contributions. School autonomy, conversely, generated few fiscal and or business savings, and so the government had fewer incentives to push it (see Murillo 1997; Murillo and Maceira 2002). This shows that one consequence of decentralization (i.e., of unburdening the central government) is that it lessens the government's desire to persevere with major reforms. Once spending was transferred to the provinces, the state lost interest in deepening reforms.

The central Ministry of Education did not achieve uniform implementation of the law either (see Cocorda 2003). By 1999, only five provinces were fully compliant with the legal requirement to offer the mandatory nine years of schooling.[17] Provinces differed in the degree to which

17. Buenos Aires Province, Córdoba, La Pampa, San Luis, and Santa Cruz (Decibe 2001).

they built the necessary schools to accommodate the new mandatory grades, improved efficiency, diminished repetition rates, raised teacher salaries, obtained necessary financing, and adopted consistent evaluation methods.

Whether this lack of uniformity in provincial performance was mostly the fault of the central Ministry of Education (lack of trying) or the provinces (lack of trying, different starting points and obstacles) is hard to ascertain. However, there is no question that part of the problem was the ministry's lack of a sanctioning mechanism. The financing structure of education in Argentina confers on the federal government almost no leverage vis-à-vis the provinces. The federal government cannot establish conditionalities in the *coparticipación* (block grant) funds. Provinces are essentially free to use these funds as they see fit. Furthermore, most of the revenue coming from the federal government is absorbed by teachers' salaries—the largest component of education spending in the provinces—leaving little for anything else.

The federal government tried to compensate for this leverage weakness through two mechanisms: using monies from multilateral agencies, which did permit conditionalities,[18] and creating the Social Education Plan (Plan Social Educativo), a pool of funds available to the provinces on a competitive basis. Neither mechanism, however, solved the problem of leverage weakness. Total external aid amounted to no more than 2 percent of the total spending on education (Decibe 2001), and its impact at the provincial budgets was also too modest to make much difference.[19] The Social Education Plan was a bit more effective. The ministry invited applications from the provinces to finance programs designed to "fight educational inequalities." The financing structure of this program (competitive-based funding) granted the federal government some leverage in persuading provinces to generate innovative proposals. Yet its effects were limited as well.

18. For instance, the seminal 1994 World Bank loan stipulated conditions for granting loans to provinces, tightened after 1996, such as (1) introducing "significant structural reforms," including deficit reduction and privatizations; (2) accepting the transfer of the provincial pension funds to the national system; and (3) demonstrating "political commitment to further reforms" (World Bank 2001, 2).

19. An analysis of one of the largest Bank loans for education reforms (totaling $115.5 million) showed that the highest impact on the provinces would be to increase the local budget by no more than 3.7 percent in Corrientes. In the other provinces, the impact was more modest (3.4 percent in Salta, 3.0 percent in Chaco, 2.1 percent in Entre Ríos, and 0.1 percent in Buenos Aires). After the first two years of the loan, the impact on each province declined significantly (World Bank 1995).

Most of the funds were used for infrastructure development.[20] And once the funds were distributed to the winning applicants, the federal government could do little to sanction misuse of funds.

Another problem was the return of old ministerial vices, such as the penchant for power concentration. In part, this was the result of the manner in which the reforms were designed, that is, with the explicit objective of transforming the ministry into a regulator (rather than a provider) of services. Enormous investments were made to bolster the technical and supervisory capacity of the ministry. The result was an enormous asymmetry in capabilities. The central ministry became highly technical, far surpassing most provincial ministries.[21] This asymmetry—what Rodríguez (1993) called "the new centrality"—led to a concentration of power in the hands of the more technically developed entity—the central ministry. Soon, the ministry found itself making policy decisions without much consultation, in contradiction of its ideology of decentralizing power. Provincial ministers of education were consulted,[22] and this was a constructive step, but almost no one else, sometimes not even the schools themselves. The result was the gradual reemergence of a unilateral, detached Ministry of Education. It was typical, for example, for schools to receive books that they did not request, need, or know what to do with—and still leave many of their other real needs unmet. This eroded the ties between the ministry and the schools. Technocratic development interfered with inclusiveness.

Another vice was lax commitment to doubling investment. Despite the increase in resources overall, the government did not achieve the promised doubling of investments (see table 11.8). The Ministry of Education became liable to accusations of "breach of contract."

In short, in the implementation phase, the reformers pushed for some goals and not others. Furthering decentralization, carrying out more struc-

---

20. More than 11,820 schools benefited from these funds (Decibe 2001).

21. World Bank support contributed inadvertently to this. The seminal 1994 loan, designed to support the ministry and seven provinces in implementing decentralization, was heavily geared toward strengthening the technical capacity of the central ministry. The loan assigned 15 percent of total project costs to the ministry. This included the creation of an office of national management and information system, in charge of generating statistics; an office of student assessment, in charge of creating student tests; and the training of approximately 11,500 managers, planners, operators, and surveyors, in addition to providing technical support for 4,000 staff (World Bank 1994, 40).

22. Between 1992 and 2001, the Consejo Federal de Cultura y Educación issued 150 resolutions (Narodowski, Nores, and Andrada 2002, 56), denoting a high degree of engagement.

tural changes, committing to doubling investments—all strong preferences of the central Ministry of Education in the early 1990s—were relaxed or replaced by other goals, such as concentrating decision-making power on central technocrats and privileging infrastructure development.

Round Three: The Carpa Blanca Conflict, 1997–1999

The third major round in the politics of education under Menem was a conflict with teachers regarding wages. In the previous two rounds, the central Ministry of Education prevailed, obtaining its primary preference (the 1991 Law of Decentralization) or its second-best options (the 1993 Federal Law of Education). In this third round, the ministry was defeated. The reason was that the factors that led to political tranquility in the education sector after 1993 changed in 1997.

Three major political changes took place in 1997 that marked a turning point in the strength of the opposition. First, CTERA made the strategic decision to focus on demand 3 (salary increases) and downplay demand 2 (revoke the Federal Law of Education). Always the most popular policy preference in the eyes of public opinion, CTERA's demand for higher salaries became all the more justifiable in 1997 given the country's spectacular economic growth of 1996 and 1997. By 1999, some studies placed the average salary for a teacher with fifteen years of experience at $8,025, significantly lower than historical levels and in comparison with workers in the formal sector (Llach, Montoya, and Roldán 1999, 222).[23] Wide sectors of the population sided with CTERA on the salary issue. Teachers became a symbol of the dark side of neoliberalism—the neglect of the neediest. Furthermore, the focus on salary served to reunify CTERA's rank and file, a demand that resonated with all teachers nationwide.

Second, the political parties with which CTERA could form an alliance became stronger in 1997. Early that year, the two opposition parties, the UCR and FREPASO, increased their electoral momentum, with most polls suggesting excellent prospects for the upcoming midterm congressional elections. They formed an electoral alliance, the so-called Alianza. CTERA decided to reinforce ties with these parties.

23. How low was this salary depends on the standard of comparison. Llach, Montoya, and Roldán (1999, 218–26) show it was low compared with (1) the average teachers' salary in Chile, (2) the average salary of a typical worker in Argentina's formal sector, and (3) the average salary of Argentine teachers at the beginning of the twentieth century. Yet, if measured in terms of hours worked, teachers' salaries in Argentina in 1999 were comparable to those of workers in the formal sector.

These two new political resources (unity and coalition with reinvigorated opposition parties) permitted CTERA to flex its muscle. In April 1997, a group of teachers fully backed by CTERA started a sleep-in vigil in front of the National Congress, installing a huge white tent (*carpa blanca*) and taking turns fasting.[24] The protest was an instant public relations success. Labor unions, politicians, the media, university students, and public opinion in general became fascinated with the image of poor teachers, mostly women, traveling from the provinces to camp outside the Congress demanding better wages. No other claimant since the pensioners' protest of the early 1990s had captured the fascination of Argentines to the same degree. CTERA capitalized on this support by organizing a series of national strikes—four in 1997 alone. By September, another labor union gave CTERA $12,000 to purchase the tent (saving money on tent rental fees), an example of the expansion of CTERA's alliances with groups outside of the education sector. The tent became a local attraction in Buenos Aires, with parents taking their children to visit it on their weekend walks through the city. Artists and entertainers offered free performances and exhibits on the site of the tent. Teachers who could not travel to participate of the sleep-in vigil held their own fasting vigils at their local schools. This became the most headline-catching political protest of the entire Menem era.

The third and final political change of 1997 was a cabinet split between the Ministries of the Economy and Education. The Ministry of the Economy instantly rejected CTERA's demand for higher wages, due to concerns about the nagging fiscal deficit. Because Menem lost interest in securing much needed fiscal reforms, such as cutting spending and raising revenues, the minister of the economy, Roque Fernández (1996–99), had to adopt an intense "savings" preference. Fernández refused to consider any discussion of increasing spending, not even to pay salaries. He continued to reiterate the legally correct but politically incorrect position that teachers' salaries were a provincial issue, to be negotiated between governors and local unions—not between the national government and the national union.[25]

At this point, the Ministry of Education resorted to another of its multiple preferences. The minister reasoned: If she could not please the Ministry of the Economy, why not try to please the unions? As soon as Decibe

24. For a detailed discussion of this protest, see Behrend (2000).
25. Furthermore, Fernández insulted the teachers by declaring that most teachers were *ñoquis,* an Argentinism for civil servants who collect a salary but who do not report to work. "For every teacher in a classroom, there are three other teachers collecting a paycheck" (*Clarín,* September 13, 1997).

Javier Corrales

detected the renewed strength of the teachers in 1997, she endorsed their claim. "The teachers in this country are poorly paid," she declared (*Clarín*, September 12, 1997),[26] and she proposed raising salaries by 20 percent—the first time that someone at the executive-branch level departed from the government's position that salaries were a provincial issue. This cabinet split dominated the press in the middle of September 1997.

Given the rising strength of the opposition and the split at the cabinet level, there was very little hope that the Ministry of Education would prevail politically. Decibe did her best to regain her political strength. For instance, she convinced Menem to promise a salary raise. In another example of shifting preferences, in 1988 Decibe also negotiated with Alianza legislators a proposal to raise salaries (*Clarín*, August 20, 1998). The preference for defending cabinet unity, and even privileging negotiations with members of the one's own party, was relaxed.

But CTERA was too politically strong at this point to accept any peace settlement. The cash needed for salaries, even if it had been secured, would have done little to mollify CTERA. First, the division within the cabinet eroded the credibility of the executive. The government was offering a salary increase without the backing of the Ministry of the Economy and without any real plan to raise revenues, which made the offer virtually noncredible. Second, CTERA was at the peak of its political strength (in terms of unity, policy coherence, and allies). This was no time to capitulate. And because the true political objective of CTERA was to weaken the administration, CTERA simply had no incentive to negotiate. For CTERA, maintaining an open conflict with the government was both feasible and desirable.

The Carpa Blanca protest lasted the remainder of the Menem administration, for a total of 1,000 days. More than 1,400 teachers and 86 civic groups participated; more than 475 cultural events took place, including 46 radio shows and 29 television shows. An estimated 2.8 million Argentines physically visited the tent. CTERA organized 12 national strikes during the duration of the Carpa Blanca protest (*Clarín*, December 31, 1999). The conflict overwhelmed the minister of education. She was trapped by an intransigent opposition and an unsupportive minister of the economy. Decibe resigned in May 1999, unable to conclude the last seven months of the Menem administration.

26. She also openly criticized Fernández for using the word *ñoqui*, arguing that there are many teachers with legitimate reasons to be on leave.

Conclusion

The story of education reform in Argentina in the 1990s shows that the range of outcomes of social policy reform can be wide and often internally contradictory, for several reasons. First, state reformers embrace multiple preferences. They might start out with one main objective in mind, but they end up accepting different policy results because those also can conform to their alternative, secondary preferences. Many of these alternative preferences need not be in harmony with each other. For instance, reformers may want to unburden their responsibilities and simultaneously concentrate power, preserve cabinet unity and simultaneously maintain cordial relations with constituents, save money to please the minister of the economy and simultaneously spend money as a way to exercise control over agents, and engage in huge political battles to gain publicity and simultaneously avoid political conflicts to avoid bad press. An internally coherent policy outcome is thus unlikely, because it would probably satisfy only one preference of the reformer. Instead, the reformer seeks to satisfy multiple preferences at once, and this leads to internally inconsistent reform outcomes.

The extent to which a state reformer will relax initial preferences and accept secondary outcomes also depends on the evolving strength of the two sides of the conflict—the state reformers themselves and affected actors. Education reforms occur in stages. At every stage, actors have an opportunity to restrategize, and thus to gain or lose strength. Hence, different rounds of reforms may result in different outcomes.

This chapter has identified several factors that determine the relative strength of each. For state reformers, the factors include (1) the relative popularity of the government as a whole (strong in 1991–95); (2) unity at the cabinet level (strong in 1991–97); (3) stability and expertise at the ministerial level (strong in 1992–99); (4) cooperation from Congress, especially the ruling party (1992–97); (5) alliances with provincial actors, especially in federalist systems (strong in 1993–99); and (6) ties with multilateral organizations (strong 1994–99). For the opposition, the crucial factors include (1) a well-defined policy preference, (2) internal cohesion, and (3) coalitions with actors both within the sector and outside the sector.

The political strength of actors is thus less fixed than one would imagine. In Argentina, it changed sometimes in as short a time span as a matter of months. Between 1991 and 1992, for instance, the strength of the opposition increased substantially, which explains the difference in the politics of the Transference Law and the Federal Law of Education. In the latter, the government was forced to accept the input of the opposition. And between 1996 and 1998, the strength of the opposition also increased, whereas the strength of reformers declined, which explains the difference between the relative peace of 1993–97 and the Carpa Blanca turmoil and reform paralysis of 1997–99.

Finally, several generalizations emerge concerning the different political conditions that shape the outcome of education reforms (figure 11.1). When the state comes forward with a reform proposal, the first relevant condition is the strength of the executive branch. If the executive is weak (e.g., Alfonsín in 1988, or Menem in 1990), reforms will not occur because the

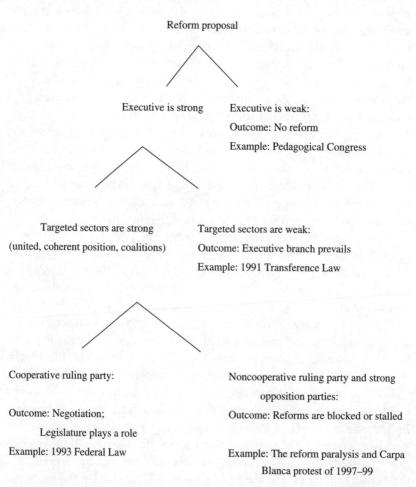

Figure 11.1. Political Conditions and Reform Outcomes in Argentina

executive will not invest political energy. If the executive is strong and willing to push the reforms (e.g., Menem and Cavallo in 1991), the next set of conditions relates to the political strength of targeted sectors. If the targeted sectors are weak, the reforms will be unilateral and reflect the primary preferences of the executive (e.g., the Transference Law of 1991). If, however, the targeted sectors are strong, the next set of conditions depends on the nature of executive–party relations. If the opposition parties have the upper hand or the ruling party is uncooperative, the reforms will probably be blocked or lead to enormous political turmoil (the Carpa Blanca conflict, 1997–99). If, however, the ruling party is dominant and cooperative, a process of negotiation will ensue, which is likely to involve the Legislature. It will also result in a reform outcome that reflects the secondary and often-conflicting preferences, not just of the executive but also of other actors in the system.

References

Aguerrondo, Inés. 2000. Can Education Measure Up to Poverty in Argentina? In *Unequal Schools, Unequal Chances,* ed. Fernando Reimers. Cambridge, Mass.: David Rockefeller Center for Latin American Studies, Harvard University.

Behrend, Jacqueline. 2000. The Carpa Blanca: Civil Society and Democratic Process. A Study of Teachers' Protest and Political Response in Argentina. M. Phil. thesis, Saint Anthony's College, University of Oxford, Oxford.

Blyth, Mark. 2003. Structures Do Not Come with an Instruction Sheet: Interests, Ideas, and Progress in Political Science. *Perspectives on Politics* 1, 4 (December): 695–706.

Carnoy, Martin. 1999. *Globalization and Educational Reform: What Planners Need to Know.* Paris: UNESCO.

Centeno, Miguel A., and Patricio Silva, eds. 1998. *The Politics of Expertise in Latin America.* New York: St. Martin's Press.

Cocorda, Esteban. 2003. ¿Es posible hacer un seguimiento y evaluación de las reformas educativas? Paper presented at the colloquium, The Federal Law of Education Ten Years Later, University of Córdoba, Córdoba, Argentina, no date.

Corrales, Javier. 1999. *The Politics of Education Reform: Bolstering the Supply and Demand; Overcoming Institutional Blocks.* Education Reform and Management Series. Washington, D.C.: World Bank.

———. 2002a. Political Parties and Legislative Oversight. Paper presented at the 2002 Meeting of the Midwest Political Science Association, Chicago, April.

———. 2002b. *Presidents without Parties: The Politics of Economic Reforms in Argentina and Venezuela in the 1990s.* University Park: Pennsylvania State University Press.

———. 2003. The Conflict between Technocracy and Participation: Education Reforms in Argentina. Paper presented at the Latin American Studies Association Congress, Dallas, March.

Decibe, Susana. 2001. Argentina: Una década sólo alcanzó para comenzar una reforma estructural de la educación. In *Economía política de las reformas educativas en*

América Latina, ed. Sergio Martinic and Marcela Pardo. Santiago: Centro de Investigación y Desarrollo de la Educación and Partnership for Educational Revitalization in the Americas.

Domínguez, Jorge I., ed. 1997. *Technopols.* University Park: Pennsylvania State University Press.

Eaton, Kent. 2002. *Politicians and Economic Reform in New Democracies: Argentina and the Philippines in the 1990s.* University Park: Pennsylvania State University Press.

Falleti, Tulia. 2001. Federalism and Decentralization of Education in Argentina. Brown University, Providence (unpublished).

———. 2003. Governing Governors: Coalitions and Sequences of Decentralization in Argentina, Colombia, and Mexico. Ph.D. thesis, Department of Political Science, Northwestern University, Evanston, Ill.

Gibson, Edward L., and Ernesto Calvo. 2000. Federalism and Low-Maintenance Constituencies: Territorial Dimensions of Economic Reform in Argentina. *Studies in Comparative International Studies* 35, no. 3 (fall): 32–55.

Gvirtz, Silvina. 2002. Curricular Reforms in Latin America with Special Emphasis on the Argentine Case. *Comparative Education* 38, 4: 543–69.

Hanson, E. Mark. 1996. Educational Change under Autocratic and Democratic Governments: The Case of Argentina. *Comparative Education* 32, no. 3: 303–17.

Jones, Mark P., Sebastián Saiegh, Pablo T. Spiller, and Mariano Tommasi. 2001. Amateur Legislators—Professional Politicians: The Consequences of Party-Centered Electoral Rules in a Federal System. *American Journal of Political Science* 46, no. 3 (July): 656–69.

Lauglo, Jon. 1995. Forms of Decentralisation and Their Implication for Education. *Comparative Education* 31, no. 1 (1995): 5–29.

Llach, Juan José, Silvia Montoya, and Flavia Roldán. 1999. *Educación para todos.* Buenos Aires: Instituto de Estudios sobre la Realidad Argentina y Latinoamericana.

MCE (Ministerio de Cultura y Educación, Argentina). 1999. *Enseñar el futuro: Diez años de transformación educativa en la Argentina.* Buenos Aires: MCE.

Morduchowicz, Alejandro. 2002. (Des)Regulación y financiamiento de la educación privada en la Argentina. In *Educación privada y política pública en América Latina,* ed. Laurence Wolff, Pablo González, and Juan Carlos Navarro. Santiago: Partnership for Educational Revitalization in the Americas and Inter-American Development Bank.

Murillo, M. Victoria. 1997. *Latin American Unions and the Reform of Social Service Delivery Systems.* Office of the Chief Economist, Working Paper 332. Washington, D.C.: Inter-American Development Bank.

———. 1999. Recovering Political Dynamics: Teachers' Unions and the Decentralization of Education in Argentina and Mexico. *Journal of Interamerican Studies and World Affairs* 41, no. 1 (spring): 31–58.

Murillo, M. Victoria, and Daniel Maceira. 2002. Markets, Organizations, and Politics: Social Sector Reform and Labor in Latin America. Inter-American Development Bank, Washington, D.C. (unpublished).

Narodowski, Mariano, Milagros Nores, and Myrian Andrada. 2002. *La evaluación educativa en la Argentina.* Buenos Aires: Promoteo 3010.

Nelson, Joan M. 1999. *Reforming Health and Education: The World Bank, the IDB, and Complex Institutional Change.* Policy Essay 26. Washington, D.C.: Overseas Development Council.

Nicolini, J. P., P. Sanguinetti, and J. Sanguinetti. 2000. *Análisis de alternativas de financiamiento de la educación básica en el marco de las instituciones fiscales federales.* Buenos Aires: Universidad Torcuato di Tella.

Nores, Milagros. 2002. El Sistema Nacional de Evaluación de Calidad (SINEC). Un análisis del marco del programa, su implementación y su desarrollo. Fundación Gobierno y Sociedad, Buenos Aires (unpublished).

Parrado, Emilio A. 1998. Expansion of Schooling, Economic Growth, and Regional Inequalities in Argentina. *Comparative Education Review* 42, no. 3 (August): 338–64.

PREAL (Partnership for Educational Revitalization in the Americas). 2001. *Lagging Behind: A Report Card on Education in Latin America.* Washington, D.C. and Santiago, Chile: PREAL.

Repetto, Fabián. 2001. *Transferencia educativa hacia las provincias en los años 90: Un estudio comparado.* Buenos Aires: Centro de Estudios para el Desarrollo Institucional, Fundación Grupo Sophia.

Rodríguez, Jorge. 1993. La educación en la Argentina: Una nueva centralidad. Transcript of speech by the minister of education, Jorge Rodríguez, at a conference, the Business Firm and Education, Buenos Aires, November.

Salonia, Antonio F. 1996. *Descentralización educativa, participación y democracia.* Estudio 10. Buenos Aires: Academia Nacional de Educación.

Shepsle, Kenneth A. 2003. Losers in Politics (and How They Sometimes Become Winners): William Riker's Heresthetic. *Perspectives on Politics* 1, no. 2 (June): 307–15.

Schicker, Eric. 2001. *Disjointed Pluralism: Institutional Innovation and the Development of the U.S. Congress.* Princeton, N.J.: Princeton University Press.

Tiramonti, Guillermina. 2001. Sindicalismo docente y reforma educativa en la América Latina de los 90. In *Sindicalismo docente y reforma educativa en América Latina,* ed. Guillermina Tiramonti and Daniel Filmus. Buenos Aires: FLACSO / Grupo Editorial Temas.

Tommasi, Mariano. 2002. Federalism in Argentina and the Reforms of the 1990s. Documento 69, Centro de Estudios para el Desarrollo Institucional, Buenos Aires, (unpublished).

Weiler, Hans. 1990. Comparative Perspectives on Educational Decentralization: An Exercise in Contradictions? *Educational Evaluation and Policy Analysis* 12, no. 4 (winter): 433–48.

Weyland, Kurt. 2002. Limitations of Rational-Choice Institutionalism for the Study of Latin American Politics. *Studies in Comparative International Development* 37, no. 1 (spring): 57–85.

Willis, Eliza, Chistopher Garman, and Stephan Haggard. 1999. The Politics of Decentralization in Latin America. *Latin American Research Review* 34, no. 1: 7–56.

World Bank. 1994. *Argentina: Decentralization and Improvement of Education Project.* Staff Appraisal Report 12993-AR. Washington D.C.: World Bank.

———. 1995. *Decentralization and Improvement of Secondary Education and Polymodal Education Development Project (DISEPED).* Staff Appraisal Report 14559-AR. Washington, D.C.: World Bank.

———. 2001. *Argentina—Santa Fe Provincial Reform Loan.* Report PID10004. Washington, D.C.: World Bank.

Chapter 12

Education Reform in Colombia: The Elusive Quest for Effectiveness

Pamela S. Lowden

The story of education reform in Colombia during the past decade is largely a story of reform failure. That applies, at least, up until mid-2001, when the very crisis of the reform process led to a further overhaul of the system, the implementation of which is still in its early stages at the time of writing. By 2001, it was clear that decentralization had not achieved the goal of establishing an efficient division of responsibilities and resources among the different levels of the state. Issues of equity, quality, and efficiency had been subordinated to political expediencies. In short, the reforms had failed to make an effective public education system.

There was, to be sure, some important progress. Coverage of primary education rose from 61.5 percent in 1985 to 83.5 percent in 1997; secondary levels rose from 37.7 to 61.1 percent in the same period (National Planning Department 1998).[1] Yet although these quantitative gains were

---

1. The proportion represented by private education is relatively high by regional

substantial, they started from a low threshold, fell far short of what was needed, and belied tremendous inefficiencies. When Alvaro Uribe took over the presidency in July 2002, his education reform program estimated the number of children excluded from those levels of basic education to be 3 million out of a population of about 16.5 million under eighteen years of age. Indeed, extending basic education coverage was the number one priority of the program.

Quality gains were second on Uribe's education agenda. Quality reforms had also tended to fall by the wayside during the 1990s, in large part because the vacuum-like black hole of teachers' pay had tended, relentlessly, to suck in all available funds. When the preceding government of Andres Pastrana (1998–2002) began to undertake the revamping of the education reform process, in mid-2001, it noted, "It is clear that the problem of education in Colombia is not the lack of financial resources. Rather, what leaps to the eye is that, in spite of the magnitude of resources, Colombia faces problems in their inappropriate use, reflected in inequitable distribution, low efficiency and inadequate funding of investment in quality and equipment." The reasons further cited were poor distribution of functions and regulation of the system by the state, and the inflexible nature of costs in the sector. These last were rather euphemistic references to the core problems that have dogged education in Colombia: its clientelist use as a source of patronage by political leaders, and the political leverage of the Federation of Colombian Teachers (FECODE), which has successfully defended those spending "rigidities."

Decentralization of education was the principal component of the reform process. Part of the reason why it had failed, by 2001, to deliver the hoped-for results lay in the widely divergent interests in play in formulating just what kind and degree of decentralization would be pursued, the often self-contradictory bargaining processes this entailed, and the resulting legislative confusion. Confusion, of course, tends to serve the status quo.

The resistance of the education system to reform reflected that of the Colombian political system as whole: the process of political decentralization (the direct election of mayors from 1988 and departmental governors from 1992), was hoped in many quarters to lead to a kind of Colombian "perestroika." Greater accountability of the lower levels of government,

---

standards, standing at 20 percent for primary levels, 35 percent for secondary, and 65 percent for higher. Public spending by level is as follows: 40 percent on primary, 30 percent on secondary, and 16 percent on higher, with the remainder going to administrative costs.

together with greater space for participation in decision-making processes, was intended—certainly by the terms of the 1991 Constitution—to guarantee not only better public service provision but also a more democratic polity. There undoubtedly were advances in those directions, more noticeable in some parts of the country than in others, but change remained uneven and, at best, incremental. That is not surprising given the conditions and the weight of vested interests in play. These conditions suggest interesting themes of comparison with the generally more positive story of health reform in Colombia, a subject to which this chapter will also return in its conclusions.

The Education System in Colombia by 1991

Financing of primary and secondary education was quite decentralized up until the early 1970s, at which time the central government assumed greater responsibility in a drive to improve standards and coverage. From a mere 1.9 percent of gross domestic product (GDP) in 1973, education spending rose to 3.7 percent in 1984 (Sarmiento 2000). With economic adjustment, it declined once more from 1985 on, to 3.1 percent by 1991. Indeed, one of the concerns of the new Constitution was to ensure not only that levels of social spending should be raised but also that increases should be protected against any future cyclical cuts.

The spending impetus of the 1970s was also linked to the eventual success of the teachers' movement, in 1978, in establishing their own national labor regime, the Estatuto Docente. This unified the system of promotions, wages, and Social Security. As such, it was a major and historic victory for the teaching profession, and a necessary step at the time for social development in the country as a whole; moreover, it had been hard won. Under the previous regime, wherein the departments were largely responsible for paying teachers, the situation had been chaotic. For example, there were reported to be occasions when teachers were paid in crates of rum (one assumes for resale), spirit production being a department monopoly. However, there were aspects of the Estatuto that were to have far-reaching and highly negative consequences for future developments. Promotion in the career ladder was automatic, being dependent merely on years of service and nominal attendance of courses, and/or production of publications, and not any actual performance-related criteria. Not only that, security of tenure was also virtually guaranteed and dismissal from the payroll practically nonexistent.

The consolidation of the political power of FECODE as a united national federation negotiating directly with central government cemented these rigidities in place. Its membership by 1991 was more than 300,000. Its leaders established considerable influence over successive education ministers, as well as national and regional politicians. They enjoyed long-term stability and control of the organization, despite being highly ideological (and Marxist), in complete contrast to the vast majority of the membership. Factors accounting for their longevity in office included their effective concentration on improving the labor conditions of that membership, together with the authoritarian and hierarchical nature of the organization. As well as adamantly defending the Estatuto, they equally consistently opposed decentralization as a threat to their national-level bargaining power. Their arguments combine a constant harping on "the bad old days", with a rhetoric of anti-neoliberalism. This was also leveled at other types of reform such as school autonomy, parental participation, and mechanisms for private–public cooperation. There was a group within the teachers' movement concerned with the improvement of learning skills and school performance, called the Pedagogic Movement. In contrast to the FECODE leadership, this movement tended to favor school autonomy, as well as being more open to other innovations—but its leaders were not in control of the union.

Although funding became more centralized in the 1970s, the administration of the greater part of teachers, and the distribution of resources to the municipalities, remained largely in the hands of the departments. There were laws in place stipulating the appointment of teachers by open competition, but these were seldom applied in anything but the most token fashion. Teachers were hired en masse at election time, with little or no regard to the availability of funding (far less actual need), because protests from subsequently unpaid new teachers could be referred to central government and the latter obliged to pay. More blatant outright corruption was also widespread. Brokers in a position to obtain teaching posts would simply sell them and distribute earnings among the members of that brokerage chain. The same applied to transfer of teachers to different posts, because there was always a good market for the more attractive, city-based jobs. For both financial and political reasons, then, there has traditionally been strong competition among local officials and political brokers to hold education posts: They were the honey pot.

These features of the education system are not only common knowledge within the country but also well documented, notably by Duarte (1998). Equally well documented is that when more administrative responsibilities began to be devolved from the departments to the municipalities, there was no noticeable change. The same basic political logic continued in play, regardless of the structure of the state. The process of municipalization began in 1986, when more resources were given to the municipalities and one attendant responsibility was the provision of school buildings. This accompanied the legislation that paved the way for the election of mayors in 1988. Law 29 of 1989 passed the management of the majority of teachers to the municipalities. It passed into law before FECODE could organize a national strike (as it subsequently did), but it was never pressed by the government or welcomed by the municipalities. In the case of the latter, the fear that funding would not, in fact, make its way down the system in sufficient quantities to make wholesale management an attractive proposition (as opposed to the piecemeal existing system) seems to have been the key factor. As a result, it was only very partially implemented by a few of the larger municipalities, and the bulk of the administration of teachers remained in the hands of the departmental education authorities—which at that stage were still deconcentrated units of the ministry.

The schools themselves were the forgotten elements of the equation, given the structures in place. Teachers were often transitory and appointed by the channels described. Heads had no say in the appointment or dismissal of staff, nor control over more than the most insignificant funds. Raising these was virtually the only activity of parents' associations. The lack of a national examination system, other than at the end of the secondary stage (which most students never reached), meant limited means to assess, and still less control, school performance.

The 1991 Constitution

The 1991 Constitution was the product of a unique set of political circumstances. The perceived crisis of legitimacy of the political system, registered in increasing electoral abstention and civil unrest, had already led the governments of Belisario Betancur (1982–86) and Virgilio Barco (1986–90) to adopt measures aimed at addressing the structural causes of political, social, and economic exclusion. One such was the introduction of direct elections of mayors, which was finally brought into effect in 1988, after a political struggle of four years. This was accompanied by some fiscal strengthening of the municipalities, updating their tax base and raising their share of the value-added tax from 30.5 percent in 1986 to 50 percent in 1992.

Nonetheless, violence both by guerrilla and by drug cartel activity continued to mount, with events such as the assassination of the important Liberal Party reformist Luis Carlos Galan in August 1989 underlining the extent of the national crisis. Galan's death not only stimulated a concerted offensive against drug interests but also gave new impetus and urgency to pursuing deeper, constitutional reform. The Barco government failed in its attempts to bring this about, due in large part to resistance on the part of Congress. In the end, the balance was tipped by a student-led civic movement that, in the course of the March 1990 congressional elections, garnered an unofficial ballot of about 2 million votes in favor of electing a Constituent Assembly. Bending to such pressure, the authorities allowed for an official vote on the issue in the May 1990 presidential elections, which won 5,236,863 votes, 86.6 percent of the total. This paved the way for the December election of the Assembly. Of seventy-four seats, nineteen were won by a formerly armed (non-Marxist) group known as the Democratic Alliance of the M-19, twenty-five by Liberals, twenty by Conservatives, and the remainder by diverse smaller groups and individuals. It appeared to be a major breakthrough in challenging the historic domination of the Liberals and Conservatives.

An opening clause of the Constitution declares Colombia to be a "socially orientated, decentralized, State." The emphasis on deepening decentralization, together with renewing and expanding social service delivery with a view to equity, were two of the defining characteristics of the new charter. The Constitution also sought to create a gamut of new mechanisms for popular participation in public decision-making processes, and to put curbs on the clientelist practices of the political parties, particularly the use of local constituencies as virtual fiefdoms by established national and regional leaders. One key measure was the direct election, from 1992, of department governors (the territorial equivalent of U.S. state governors) although the country remained a unitary state.

In the centralized system, which was enshrined in the 1886 Constitution, the president nominated the department governors, and they in turn appointed the mayors in their jurisdiction. Mayoral appointments in particular tended to be short-lived, because the discretionary powers of national political leaders were absolute. These national leaders, based in Congress, effectively controlled local life through their domination of municipal and departmental councils, and their brokerage of centrally controlled funds and favors. From 1958 to 1974, in the wake of a near civil war, Colombia functioned under what was known as the National Front system, which

enforced alternation in the presidency between Liberal and Conservative
leaders, and parity in the distribution of bureaucratic and legislative posts.
With the end of the National Front, the old-style party discipline under
supreme chiefs tended to erode and be replaced by a movable feast of
shifting alliances among regionally based leaders, based on calculations of
electoral advantage and the potential for patronage, as well described in
Leal and Dávila (1990). The parties thus became increasingly factionalized,
both at the national level, among contending would-be presidential figures,
and at the regional level, as new bosses and would-be bosses jockeyed for
position.

Moreover, the ideological differences between the parties (never great
on much beyond religion) eroded to little more than vestiges of past traditions. This partisan decline therefore also provided an opportunity for new,
reformist leaders to emerge under decentralization. There had not been
much sign of this, however, in the first two mayoral elections, of 1988 and
1990, where, whatever their relative weakness, the two main parties' official candidates won the overwhelming majority. Nevertheless, those wish-
ing to undermine clientelism (the emerging reformist political and civic
leaders, and those of technocratic bent) felt that the answer was more
decentralization, which they hoped would help the political system to become more pluralist. This lay behind the introduction of direct elections for
department governors, and the creation of various mechanisms for public
voice in local affairs.

The struggle between those seeking to defend the status quo and the
reformists came to the fore in one of the most contentious issues in the
Assembly: the question of whether to tip the balance of decentralization to
the departmental or the municipal level. There were diverse interests in
play, but the reformers tended to see the greatest hopes for making gains at
the municipal level. This applied particularly to education, where the division between the sides was underlined by FECODE's stringent opposition
to municipalization. FECODE was quite strongly represented in the Assembly by the presence of two of its former leaders. Its huge membership
was inevitably in the minds of the established political leaders who made up
the majority of the Assembly, especially because congressional elections
were looming on the horizon. Many of these leaders had cause to fear too
great a deepening of decentralization, with its potential to erode their own
power bases. The departments, even with elected governors, were easier to
keep under control, if only for reasons of simple arithmetic: There were
thirty-two of them, not a thousand. More than that, however, the tacit

understanding was that the governors themselves would come preponderantly from established political groups, because the parties' electoral machinery would play a determining role in their election.

In contrast, in its own national plan, the then-incumbent government of Cesar Gaviria (1990–94) had clearly opted for municipalization. The highly technocratic National Planning Department played a key role in shaping the government's views on this issue, and it strongly favored the principles of subsidiarity and local public choice, including greater autonomy for the schools themselves. With this also went the hope for greater private-sector involvement in service provision. Government officials worked closely with Assembly members on these issues (López 1998). Other voices heard in the Assembly were nongovernmental organizations, church groups, and private school associations. These, however, played a fairly minor role because the essentially fiscal issues at stake were beyond their competence. Political parties took virtually no part in the debates. Two new actors who might have been expected to take an active role were the Federation of Colombian Municipalities and the Association of Departments. They did not, perhaps because of their lack of institutional consolidation, which was compounded in the case of the municipalities by the immense diversity of interest of members (Montenegro 1995).

The outcome, enshrined in Articles 356 and 357, was something of a compromise, as was characteristic of the Assembly and a reflection of its composition. But the balance leant to the departments. They maintained their previous sources of income, but they were also assigned the *situado fiscal,* the primary fund for social spending. The municipalities were assigned an incrementally increasing share of current income, to be allocated according to criteria of equity and local fiscal effort. The details were left to be defined in subsequent legislation.

The debates on education in the Assembly were predominantly fiscal and administrative, not pedagogical. The issue of equity was also to the fore. There were, moreover, a few other items that the members felt it was important to have enshrined, because the opportunity might not come again. These included the affirmation of education as a right and the raising of obligatory schooling levels. The government successfully avoided an article calling for "free and mandatory education for all," which would have undermined its hopes for greater private participation. The stage was set for the continuing struggle to determine the design and implementation of education policy reform. The old guard had essentially won round one, albeit with important concessions as a result of the climate of desire for root-and-branch reform from those sectors that had successively pushed for the Assembly in the first place.

There was awareness at the time that these measures would entail considerable fiscal cost, as well as administrative effort. Thus the Assembly gave the government the power to pass tax reform by decree, as well as the authority to suppress agencies as necessary, the latter on the understanding that central spending would have to shrink to make the new decentralized system viable.

The Reforms of 1993–1994

The draft bill presented to Congress to regulate and detail the new educational policy framework was the work of the National Planning Department, and reflected the concerns already outlined, becoming known as the Decentralization Bill. FECODE quickly drafted what amounted to a counterproposal, opposing decentralization, school autonomy, and private participation. For instance, it proposed a key administrative role for departmental juntas, under the control of union representatives, thus undermining the authority of elected departmental and municipal governments. In this, the union had the tacit support of the Education Ministry. Congress was, in effect, presented with two competing visions of the future of education, each with the support of unreconciled branches of the government.

Unsurprisingly, the debate was once again long and arduous. The inevitable—and lengthy—national teachers' strike that formed its background came also at a time when pressures to respond to popular demands were high and other events distracted the government; there was a series of national power cuts, rationing, and telephone strikes. A further element was the escape from jail of drug baron Pablo Escobar, who had been responsible for the assassination of Galan.

Once more, the result was a series of compromises. Both laws were passed. The first, and more important, was Law 60 on Resources and Responsibilities; the Decentralization Law governing the fiscal and administrative management of the key social sectors. As eventually approved by Congress, its main features were as follows. The *situado fiscal,* in the hands of the departments and special districts (the latter being Bogotá and the three coastal cities of Cartagena, Santa Marta, and Barranquilla), was to rise from 22.1 percent of current central government revenues in 1993 to 24.5 percent in 1996; the municipal share of current income was to rise from 14 to 22 percent during the same period. A share totaling 60 percent of spending financed by the *situado* was designated for education, with 20 percent allocated for health and the remaining 20 percent being discretionary. For their part, municipalities were to allocate 30 percent of their share to education, 25 percent to health, 20 percent to basic infrastructure and sanitation, and the remaining 25 percent to a number of smaller rubrics. In terms of responsibilities, the basic regulatory and policy-setting role remained with the ministry; the departments were to administer and pay teachers and exert a supervisory role over the municipalities, which were basically left with the administration and provision of infrastructure.

The devolution process was to be gradual. The now politically independent departments had to receive the "certification" of the ministry to take over their functions and funds from the deconcentrated departmental authorities. To qualify, the department had to have an institutional structure, a development plan for education, and an information system. Municipalities with populations of more than 100,000 (in the 1985 census) could be "certified" (i.e., take over their relevant proportion of the *situado* and attendant responsibilities) once their departments had done so, and they complied with the same stipulations. Those wanting to promote decentralization had wanted this option to be available to municipalities of more than 50,000, but they were defeated. The distribution of these resources to each individual department, district, and municipality was set according to a complex formula, which was intended to combine criteria of regional equity with demands and rewards for local efficiency and fiscal effort (Coyuntura Económica 2001).

The second major piece of legislation, promoted by FECODE, became the General Education Law 115 of 1994. Law 115 paid lip service to the notion of school autonomy with the so-called Institutional Education Projects. These allowed schools to present pedagogic projects but gave them no financial or administrative authority. Vouchers for poor students were allowed, and there were incentives for building new public and private schools. A principal feature of the final law was that it enhanced the role of the departmental education secretariats (i.e., those to be created in conjunction with the certification process), leaving the proposed elected departmental *juntas* with a consultative rather than a decisive role in the administration of teachers. Yet in a quest for balance, Law 115 also allowed for the creation of municipal education secretariats. The actual functions of these remained vague, however, being left that they should fulfil "the role assigned to them by Law 60."

There is something of a sense of "legislative fatigue" in that last clause. It is important to bear in mind that while all these debates were going on, so was a great deal else, as the country entered a period of something like reform frenzy in the wake of the Constituent Assembly. Judicial reform was very high on the agenda, with the creation of a Fiscalía, or Public Prosecution Service, a system of ombudsmen, a constitutional court, and other measures designed to protect—or rescue—the rule of law. "Modernization of the state" was another crusade of the government, involving numerous pieces of legislation and regulation aimed at instilling professionalism and combating corruption in the public sector. A parallel economic process was also under way, aimed at undermining the often rather cozy relations between business and government. This change had begun in the late 1980s, but it was now strongly pursued. Tariff reductions and a gradual revaluation of the real exchange rate put firms under increasing pressure to become competitive.

Not for nothing had Gaviria called his government plan the "Peaceful Revolution." Of course, not everything was peaceful in the country. Conflicts with the drugs cartels grew, as did the various fronts of the guerrilla war. Between 1988 and 1995, for example, 29 mayors were assassinated and 102 kidnapped (Rangel 1998). Nonetheless, by the end of his government there was a sense, nationally, that the country had been put back on a path toward recovery and renovation, and Gaviria left office with approval ratings of about 70 percent (*Semana* magazine, August 2–9, 1994).

What was the legacy of his period in office for education policy reform? It is only too easy to be wise in hindsight and reflect that the signs were not propitious. Perhaps the clearest weakness was that no measures had been taken to curb the power of FECODE or rationalize the Estatuto Docente. Yet the balance of political forces at the time was against such action. A failing that could have been avoided, or lessened, was the administrative confusion attending the design of the decentralization process. But many of those difficulties could have been (but were not) ironed out during implementation, under the following government.

The other critical factor for the success of decentralization lay, essentially, out of the government's hands: the emergence of local and regional governments with the political will and capacity to take over the sector responsibly. The gamut of measures taken to promote professionalism, accountability, and participation were as much as the center could contribute; such is democracy. Indeed, worth reiterating is the amount of pluralism that had gone into the whole reform process, stemming as it did from the exceptional circumstances of the Constituent Assembly. However, this very pluralism, given the conflicting interests in play, was a cause of much of the incoherence in the reform agenda.

The determination to ensure adequate funding for a decentralized social policy, enshrined in the Constitution, was ironically to prove to be yet another—eventually fatal—stumbling block. Education had been high on the government's agenda, because it was certainly seen as a key component for modernizing the country as a whole and stimulating long-term sustainable development, under a liberal economic model. Yet it was one goal among many, during a period of considerable legislative ferment and with all the added distractions described.

The Reforms in Practice, 1994–2000

In 1994, Ernesto Samper was elected Colombia's new president on an essentially populist platform of seeking to redress or at least curb what were seen as the highly neoliberal dimensions of the previous government. His plan called for a great Social Leap, with renewed efforts to enhance social policy as its cornerstone. Yet the 1991 Constitution had sharply circumscribed the actual ability of the government to dictate the bulk of social policy; that agenda was confined to implementing the existing legislation. The new social policy regime, as dictated by Law 60, had a further critical flaw: It forced the central government to transfer escalating amounts of current revenues to subnational governments, regardless of prevailing economic conditions, its own finances, and *any actual results in the performance of the social sectors.* The annual rate of real growth in the value of the transfers (the *situado fiscal* and the municipal share of current income) from 1990 to 2000 was 10.5 percent, being especially high during periods of healthy national growth to 1996, at 14 percent on average, then dropping to 5.5 percent for the second period (Coyuntura Económica 2001). As a proportion of GDP, the transfers represented 2.4 percent in 1990, and 5.5 percent in 1999. Education spending in 1991 was 3.1 percent of GDP, and it rose by 1997 to 4.5 percent. Eighty-six percent of that figure represented national transfers (Borjas and Acosta 2000).

Naturally, the relatively higher proportions of GDP also reflected declining national growth rates. The greater vulnerability of the economy to external shocks under the new more liberal model, together with the rising cost of civil violence and an absence of effective economic management, set the parameters for the conditions of mounting recession from 1996. The specific factors in play were many. Accusations of use of drug money in Samper's presidential campaign dogged his entire period in office and undermined the country's trade relations with the United States as well as the legitimacy of the government and its concomitant ability to lead any peace process. Key commodity prices declined, and the Asian crisis also bit. Thus the background to the Samper period was one of constant pressures to control public spending, at the same time as the institutional framework demanded ever-increasing central transfers. Moreover, the weakness of the government made it particularly vulnerable to political expediencies in terms of its own, central spending.

A critical case in point was teachers' salary and pension levels. In 1995, bowing to pressure from FECODE, all teachers, including those working on a part-time basis, were incorporated into the formal career structure, thus obligating the payment of full salary rates and social security. Teachers enjoy a number of special pension privileges, which amount to a considerable liability to public finances, on the order of 30 percent of GDP in 1998. By the same calculation, the rest of public-sector workers (2.3 million, as opposed to 310,000 teachers) had liabilities representing 40 percent of GDP (Borjas and Acosta 2000). The system meant, moreover, that once in the career structure, there were no incentives for teachers voluntarily to leave it. As one key commentator put it, "It's like a thirty-five-year prison sentence with a glorious pension heaven at the end."[2]

To make things worse, the government also conceded an additional 8 percent pay rise, over the statutory increments dictated by the Estatuto Docente, for the period 1995–98. The combination of these factors, together with increased teacher enrollment (19,000 were enrolled into the *situado fiscal* during the period 1996–98), meant an increase in teachers' costs of 4 percent a year during the period in question. In 1993, central transfers covered 100 percent of the municipalities' and departments' current education costs, with sums left over for quality reforms and other investment. But by 1998, all the money only covered 90 percent of current costs, of which 99 percent was teachers, under the Estatuto Docente. In other words, in absolute terms, the funds were greater, but they still had not grown fast enough to meet teachers' pay rises.

This situation led to the creation of the Education Compensation Fund, known as the FEC. This fund enabled the departments to cover deficits to

2. Interview with Margarita Peña, vice minister of education, Bogotá, October 24, 2001.

teachers paid through the *situado fiscal.* In 2000, this fund amounted to about 1 billion pesos, meaning that the sum paid to education through the two sources (*situado* and FEC) rose from 2.2 billion pesos (at 1998 values) in 1994 to 3.2 billion pesos in 2000 (Coyuntura Económica 2001).

There is no question that the departments (and indeed the municipalities) faced real, structural problems in meeting their teachers' salary bills. Their difficulties, moreover, were compounded by the fact that their income, tied to transfers from central revenues, fluctuated wildly, while costs were fixed. Budgeting was a long-standing problem for subnational governments, and, time and again, it was the money assigned to quality improvements that went by the board. However, many departments have themselves aggravated the situation. On the whole, those departments that hired the largest number of teachers during the period 1995–99 were those where student coverage was either reduced or grew very little (Government of Colombia 2001).

To make matters worse, the distribution between departments of the *situado fiscal* had as a benchmark the teachers' payroll of 1993. In other words, funds were weighted toward the historic geographic preferences of the teachers, not where there were educational needs. The inequity in the system became such that some departments received five times more resources per capita than others. Intradepartmental inequities were equally serious, with teachers receiving payment through the *situado* tending to concentrate in larger urban centers. This meant that smaller and poorer municipalities were forced to pay teachers through their own resources, further diminishing their capacity for quality investments. Municipal spending on teachers' pay doubled between 1993 and 1998, and it accounted for 80 percent of their education outlays. Coverage for outlying rural areas remained poor at best.

The government tended to meet those municipal deficits, as a matter of political expediency. The FEC institutionalized this pattern. Thus, the incentives for the municipalities and departments to rationalize spending on teachers were nonexistent (indeed, negative), with all the results outlined. In response to this situation, the government created performance agreements (*convenios de desempeño*). In 2000, these were linked to provisions whereby departments agreed to meet increased coverage goals in return for the payment of the FEC. In 2001, the conditionality was dropped, and the effectiveness of the program was, inevitably, reduced. Nonetheless, it did achieve some results; coverage rose by about 240,000 with no additional hiring of teachers but rather redistribution of the existing staff within each department.

Law 60 had allowed for direct payment of the *situado fiscal to* municipalities with populations of more than 100,000, subject to their certification
by their department. By the end of 2001, *only one municipality,* Armenia,
had received certification. The reasons for such poor progress toward the
municipalization of education were political conflicts between FECODE
and the governors, between the governors and mayors, and also the reluctance of many municipalities to push for control of the system when the
department refused to cover Social Security deficits. The picture varied
from one department to another, but those were the reasons cited by key
actors. Underlying those reasons, however, is clearly the bureaucratic
weakness and incoherence of the education system as a whole. This
weakness began with the Education Ministry and its lack of adequate
information systems to evaluate both educational needs and the institutional capacity of the departments and municipalities. As a result, it
was unable effectively to monitor the subnational levels, far less guide
and supervise them. Staffing of the ministry had historically tended
to be poor, and this situation did not change. Well-trained staff, those
capable of leading the decentralization process, tended to be isolated
from the ministry as a whole, with little done to improve the ethos of the
institution.

Thus, although decentralization did proceed to the departmental level, it
never went beyond it. Moreover, potential gains in bureaucratic efficiency
thereby were not, on the whole, achieved. On the contrary, duplication of
functions and confusion have reigned, further adding to the breach between
education spending and results. Indicators of results were extremely worry-
ing, moreover. The national test of the Colombian Institute for the Promotion of Higher Education, applied at the end of the secondary level,
showed a 20 percent *drop* in results in 1998 compared with 1993. Tests
applied in some parts of the country at the third-grade level in 1997 and
1999 showed substandard reading levels in more than half the pupils;
tests of fifth- and ninth-grade students showed fewer than 20 percent of
pupils attaining adequate mathematics levels (Government of Colombia
2001).

The reasons for such a dismal panorama are multifaceted. In the first
instance, the institutional framework was confused and confusing, based as
it was on the series of compromises framed in the Constitution and the
subsequent legislation. The enforced rate of central transfers was economically unsound, a situation compounded by the country's financial difficulties. Yet the government itself made matters worse by deferring to

FECODE as well as to irresponsible municipalities and departments, thus still further escalating spending on teachers. This was particularly true of the Samper government, for reasons outlined, but did not alter greatly with his successor, Pastrana. Once more, indeed with even greater urgency, the priority of the government had become national security, with much of social policy essentially left in a holding pattern. The effort toward rationalization represented by the *convenios de desempeño* was a case of too little, too late. Only when the fiscal deficit reached proportions requiring intervention by the International Monetary Fund, in early 2001, was action finally taken.

The efficiency incentives in the decentralization process as it was implemented, then, were negative, and they also tended to work against quality gains. More funds brought poorer results—the worst possible outcome. The hope that local accountability would spur more responsible governance in the departments and municipalities proved, in general, unfounded. This picture begs the question of whether or not the decentralization of education is a flawed concept in itself, and thus inevitably doomed to failure. Here it is worth considering the counterfactual of what would have happened had the system remained centralized. All the evidence, based on the working of the previous system, indicates that the situation would have been at least as bad. True, without the enforced rise in transfers, the central government would have had greater freedom of action. However, that was a flaw of the design of the transfer system at the time of the Constituent Assembly, rather than an argument against decentralization itself. Moreover, given the weight of FECODE and the central government's political imperatives to ensure teachers' pay, together with the earlier working of the centralized political system, it is difficult to envisage better outcomes. The issue, at bottom, is what decentralization *can* deliver which the centralized system has proved itself incapable of doing.

Here a key issue is political will at the local level. Despite the bleak overall picture, a number of governors and mayors did lead innovative education reform efforts. These included the Department of Antioquia, and the cities of Cartagena, Manizales, Medellín, and Pasto, and involved various measures of public–private cooperation, mainly based on voucher schemes (Reyes 2001). On the whole, these local efforts were only partially successful, and they seldom addressed the overall system of management in education in their jurisdictions. The case of Bogotá, however, provides a clear instance of substantial systemic progress and innovation at the local level.

Education Reform in Bogotá

Bogotá, Colombia's capital city, has been a dramatic example of the potential of directly elected mayors to shake up the political process and improve
the performance of the local public sector. Reform-minded mayors during
the 1990s greatly improved public finance and energetically tackled problems of corruption, crime, and ineffective public services. In 1998, a new
mayor appointed Cecilia Maria Velez as secretary for education. Velez
came from a strong management background, and she promptly launched a
vigorous education reform effort guided by a clear strategy.

Better coverage and quality of education in the poorest areas of the city
were among her top priorities. By late 2001, places for an additional
200,000 students had been created, accompanied by gradually improving
performance in the system as a whole (measured, for the first time, by
comprehensive annual testing, rather than sample testing as earlier). Improved information regarding the system's capacity and performance was
one of the new secretary's earliest initiatives. Additional key routes to
improvement included strengthening the technical capacities of the Education Secretariat itself, careful attention to management of teachers, and an
innovative program of public–private cooperation to bring high-quality
schools to the poorest neighborhoods.

The basic strategy for management of teachers and their unions was
twofold: standing firm against confrontational behavior, coupled with a
strong effort to redress legitimate grievances. Prompt payment of salaries
and provision of operating funds for each school, plus as much improvement as possible in physical facilities, went a long way toward defusing
teachers' complaints. The Education Secretariat also refused to pay teachers for days on strike, and it verified who attended and who was absent on
strike days, thereby dramatically reducing strike participation. The secretariat successfully challenged the earlier practice of demanding automatic
union membership by teachers. At the same time, a series of workshops and
meetings sought to engage teachers and union leaders in new, more positive
approaches to teaching.

About 50,000 of the new student places created between 1998 and the
end of 2001 were located in new schools managed by a novel system of
public–private cooperation. The system, known as the *colegios en concesión,* leased new schools in the poorest areas of the city to private operators.
Initial funding drew on proceeds from the privatization of the city's electri-
cal company. The specially designed contracting system awarded contracts

through open, competitive bidding. In the initial round, a diverse set of six groups, including private schools, religious teaching organizations, and a private social enterprise, won contracts to manage sixteen schools. The groups were variously motivated, but all were attracted in part by the opportunity for social mission, educational experiment, and enhanced national reputation. Recognizing the long-term nature of the challenge of providing quality education to students from extremely poor backgrounds, the contracts ran for fourteen years, with guaranteed funds per student, subject to meeting agreed performance standards. The program has continued to expand, and interactions between the schools and the Education Secretariat have been constructive.

The schools provide support services, including doctors, nurses, social workers, and in some cases psychologists. They engage in a variety of outreach programs directed mainly to parents. All have emphasized special teacher training. Salaries are slightly above national equivalents. The schools provide an eight-hour day, including free lunches, at costs per student roughly a quarter higher than the traditional public schools in the city; however, the latter offer only a five-hour day. Although academic results remain poor, no one expected high performance during the schools' initial years. The program is widely regarded as promising; moreover, it sends a dramatic (and controversial) message regarding providing special attention and opportunities to the previously most neglected children in the city.

The system as a whole has also been improved by additional initiatives—four large new public libraries, again in poor areas; computerization; enhanced teacher training; and special support focused on the 100 worst-performing schools in the traditional system. An intangible but extremely important effect of these diverse efforts has been a gradual change in public opinion; the people of Bogotá are learning to be less fatalistic and more demanding about the state of public services in their city. This, and support within the city council, are perhaps the best guarantee of sustainability.

Moreover, if broader economic and political conditions permit, progress in Bogotá and in a handful of other enterprising municipalities may exercise demonstration effects elsewhere in the nation. Granted, Bogotá has important structural advantages over most of the rest of the country, primarily in the form of human and social capital resources. Outside the three major cities (Bogotá, Medellín, and Cartagena), there are few private-sector organizations like those managing the *colegios en concesión,* nor are

368   *Pamela S. Lowden*

high-quality technical staff available. The major cities are also magnets for teachers.

Yet Bogotá also faces disadvantages: high teaching costs, and the immense social problems of a continually swelling, poor immigrant population. In the past, the capital's problems were widely viewed as intractable. Now commentators tend to stress Bogotá's advantages, a telling sign of great progress that, in fact, took much effort to achieve. What became ever clearer was that a better national institutional framework might help to prompt other departments and municipalities to follow Bogotá's lead. And indeed, the national framework established by the 1991 Constitution and Laws 60 and 115 of 1994 was radically revised in 2001.

Reforming the Reform: Law 715 of 2001 and Beyond

By early 2001, Colombia's fiscal deficit had reached proportions requiring intervention by the International Monetary Fund. In June, in the face of a massive FECODE strike, the Pastrana government gained legislative approval for changes in the Constitution, paving the way for the annulment of Law 60. In December of the same year, Law 715 was passed, creating a new legal framework for the decentralized education and health sectors.

Law 715 did not challenge the 1991 Constitution's emphasis on decentralization. On the contrary, it sought to deepen it, at the same time that central capacities to regulate the decentralized system were strengthened—which are mutually reinforcing measures. With regard to funding, Law 715 attempted to rationalize the system of transfers from the central to subnational governments and to halt constantly increasing demands, while ensuring a stable and reliable flow of funds. The new law also addressed a range of other education issues, seeking above all to block perverse incentives and substitute more constructive ones.

Law 715 combined the several sources of finance for education and health—the *situado fiscal,* a share of the value-added tax, and the FEC—into a single fund called the Sistema General de Participaciones. This fund was delinked from increases or decreases in the level of central government revenues, and a ceiling was established on total transfers.[3] The new law

3. The funding provisions in Law 715 are complex. The law established an absolute amount for 2001. It created guidelines for increases after 2001, linked to the rate of inflation and the growth or decline in central government ordinary revenues over the previous four years. However, for 2002 to 2005, the fund was to increase by the rate of inflation plus 2 percent, and for three years thereafter (to 2008), by inflation plus 2.6 percent.

also broke away from the complex and essentially unworkable formulas in Law 60 for allocating funds among subnational governments (and from the de facto system in the education sector of allocating central funds on the basis of the number of teachers employed in different jurisdictions). The new system basically allocated central funds for education according to the number of students enrolled in public schools in each locality, with adjustments to reflect proportions of students in primary and secondary levels, in rural versus urban schools (a proxy for poverty levels), and other factors affecting costs per student. This "capitation" system is a fundamental gain in ensuring the long-run rationalization of costs.

Moreover, the departments and municipalities are no longer able to create teaching posts whose costs would exceed the sums assigned to them in the new combined transfer system. To further contain costs, teachers' ascent on the career ladder will be slowed, with enforcement of time periods for passing through each level. To reinforce this, the departments and municipalities may assign only very limited funds to real increases in teachers' payroll costs: 1 percent a year during the period 2002–5, and 1.25 percent for 2006–8. That represents half the amount of increases proposed in draft stages of the law, an indication of the climate of austerity that accompanied its passage.

In addition to restructuring the system for financing social services and constraining growth of payrolls, Law 715 established new rules to strengthen management and incentives. First, the Education Ministry has gained considerably greater control over the management of teachers, as indeed have the governors and mayors, under the oversight of the ministry. Teaching posts may be suppressed and teachers moved on its orders. They may now also be moved between departments, subject to mutual agreement between the departments. Rationalization goals for teachers can now be enforced. Enforcement, indeed, is a keynote of the new law. It applies also, for example, to establishing clear and accurate information from the departments and municipalities. There are carrots as well as sticks, inasmuch as the ministry can offer funds for the evaluation of results (subject to local contributions of 20 percent), and there will also be a further central Fund for Education Services, also on a cofinancing basis, to allow schools to make infrastructure improvements (a reintroduction of a previous system, but with tighter controls).

The law seeks to boost decentralization by facilitating certification (the assumption of control of funds and administration from the departments) for municipalities of more than 100,000 inhabitants; for the first time, municipalities under that size may also apply. Also for the first time, a quite high degree of autonomy is being given to school heads, including in the selection and management of teachers and school funds. They may, moreover, be demoted after two years of poor results, and they will be subject to annual evaluation. Again, the essential thrust of the reform is more decentralization, but with more central enforcement capacity. There is also greater room for municipalities and departments to work with private-sector service providers, though always with stipulations against rising costs. Finally, the Estatuto Docente itself is under fire. Although Law 715 did not address the teachers' code, decree powers were invested in the president to reform it. A commission was formed to design a new statute, with a target date of June 2002.

In short, Law 715 of 2001 radically revised the measures taken eight years earlier under the Gaviria government. Many forces converged to make the changes politically feasible. The shortcomings of the system set up by Law 60 had become increasingly obvious. The capitation system for allocating funds had been proposed in the debates leading to Law 60, and it had been considered again on at least two later occasions, during the Samper and early Pastrana periods. Each time, the idea had been defeated by FECODE, which claimed that capitation was a hidden form of privatization, and by politicians interested in maximizing patronage. By 2001, however, the increasingly severe economic crisis—virtually unprecedented in Colombia during the previous fifty years—established a new context. The key element in play was the sheer fiscal necessity of rationalizing the system, together with mounting awareness that spiraling spending for worsening results was a situation that simply had to be reversed for the good of the country as a whole. The minister of finance, Juan Manuel dos Santos, was powerful and respected. He was also affiliated with the party then in opposition, the Liberals, a point that helped attract considerable support from Liberal ranks within the Congress. While the Ministry of Education had played little role in earlier reform initiatives, by 2001 a new and vigorous minister of education, Francisco Jose Lloreda, joined the Ministry of Finance and the National Planning Department in pressing for far-reaching reforms. Law 715 was presented as an element in a broader package of reforms to stabilize and revitalize the economy as a whole.

The law was hard-fought in the Congress. In addition to the united front in the government, the Associations of Governors and Mayors lent its support to the reform, partly in the interests of stabilizing its revenues and clarifying its responsibilities, and partly simply because the current situation was no longer sustainable nor, therefore, in its political interests. The government also conducted a vigorous and well-designed publicity campaign explaining the need for and rationale of the reforms. The power of FECODE, moreover, was considerably curbed by the national context. The union had stood virtually alone in opposing the enabling reforms of the Constitution in June. At a time when unemployment was reaching more than 20 percent, public sympathy for the teachers was rather thin—of which Congress was no doubt quite aware. The government was determined to take the opportunity of reforming Law 60 to address the overall management and incentive structure of the education system. It got its way.

The government also kept to its deadline of reforming the Estatuto Docente, and it duly produced Decree 1278 in June 2002, entitled the Estatuto de Profesionalización Docente. This maintained the momentum of the new reform process by defining clear requisites for entrance to and ascent on the career ladder, as well as conditions for the reallocation and dismissal of teachers. It was complemented by Decree 230, which established norms for curricula setting and evaluation of pupil and school performance. It is particularly important that the new teachers' statute links their assessment to pupil performance.

By the end of the Pastrana government, then, the institutional framework for education reform had been radically adjusted to overcome the negative incentive structures set in place from 1991. Equally important, the political momentum behind this process has been maintained into the government of Uribe, who took office in 2002.

Uribe had taken a keen interest in education during his governorship of the Department of Antioquia in the mid-1990s, and he made education reform one of the key campaign issues of his election—second only to the inevitable priority attached to national security. What is more, his education minister is none other than Cecilia Maria Velez, whose reforms in Bogotá were the spearhead of the new performance driven approach to education, and a clear demonstration of the technical and intellectual capacity to deliver results. There is no doubt that the critical strengthening of the Education Ministry, so essential to effectively managing decentralization, will proceed apace under her supervision.[4] Such immediate indicators as there are, moreover, are encouraging. A year into office, in July 2003, the government announced that it had created 477,598 new pupil places, attributing its success in this regard to the new system of payment by student

4. A good demonstration of this may be had by visiting the revamped Web site of the ministry (www.mineducacion.gov.co), which is a model of clear and impressive information provision.

numbers and maximization of existing resources. The government's goal for its four years in office is the creation of 1.5 million new pupil places, together with quality reforms and other measures aimed at linking education to skills training. Inevitably, these ambitions will put severe strains on the ability of the new institutional framework to deliver results within budget restrictions. The capacity of the center to work constructively with subnational governments—and the teaching profession—will continue to face tremendous tests.

Conclusions

If this latest reform cycle does succeed over time in shaping a process that attains that elusive goal of an effective education system, it will certainly be a case whereby Colombia has had to learn the hard way. Yet, given the forces in play and the national political history, culture, and context, the hard way may well have been the only way possible. In other words, perhaps the very perverseness of the situation that had evolved by 2001 may prove to have been the best stimulus for achieving better educational results in the future. Up till now, those results have been in the minds of all too few leaders, and certainly not enough to offset the overall national picture. Too often, education reform has been seen as a means to other ends, namely, political capital in the short-term and often clientelist sense. Adding to the problems posed by the working of the political system has been the preponderant force of FECODE in resisting reforms aimed at real improvements in results. Although politically weakened, the influence of the union is not going to disappear.

There is also another, albeit intangible, factor working in favor of further reform gains, however. Key actors assert that the general public consciousness of the need to give greater opportunities to the nation's children, particularly the poor children among them, has grown as the national situation, particularly with regard to the rule of law, has worsened. Although such attitudes are difficult to define and measure, they can offer considerable positive impetus to reform within a rational institutional framework. Whether or not that framework is really now in place—and reforms can be effectively implemented within it—remains an unfolding story.

Education reform in Colombia has been presented here as a case of reform failure, with the lessons learned perhaps opening, at last, a new path for real progress. This begs the question of the sharp contrast between Colombia's experiences in the education and health sectors, and why the health reforms, albeit with slow starts and setbacks, proceeded more positively from the process set in motion from 1991. Clearly, the lack of a FECODE equivalent in the health sector was a key factor. The Health Ministry was more dynamic, better staffed and led, and more closely linked to the key "reform mongers" in the government and international community than was the case with the Education Ministry for the great majority of the period. Support for health reform was also certainly stronger with key members of Congress than it was for education. That in itself was a reflection of the different political natures of the two sectors. They are different "animals" for a number of obvious reasons, most notably the considerably greater patronage potential in teaching posts, as well as the markedly greater urgency in producing positive results in health than education. Badly educated students (particularly when no effective testing system is in place) can only too easily become the rule and not the exception.

Perhaps most important, though, through the linking of pension and health reforms (albeit in part as a matter of political expediency), a genuine root-and-branch process was set in motion, within a fairly coherent whole. That was not the case with education, despite the radical shift (or attempted shift) toward a decentralized model. The focus still remained on the administration and pay of teachers, not on education results—better educated students. This meant that the way remained open for "more of the same"; indeed, "still worse," with the negative incentives described. The present phase of education reform has been dubbed (admittedly by the government) an "education revolution." Not surprisingly, in a country that has seen all too many "peaceful" (as well as not peaceful) revolutions, there is much skepticism on that score.

However, the shift in emphasis toward the students themselves, for both funding and performance criteria, really does mark a significant break with the past. It may well be that the kind of sea change effect generated in health reforms in Colombia was an important factor in its more positive progress. The shift in education toward concentration on the students themselves is very much in consonance with the national mood of determination to work the country's way out of the cycles of violence in which it has become immersed. We can only hope that conditions are now in place, finally, for starting to meet those aspirations.

References

Borjas, George J., and Olga Lucia Acosta. 2000. *Education Reform in Colombia.* Working Papers 19. Bogotá: Fedesarrollo.

Coyuntura Económica. 2001. La reforma a las transferencias y la descentralización. *Fesdesarrollo coyuntura económica* 31, no. 2: 51–72.

Duarte, Jesús. 1998. State Weakness and Clientelism in Colombian Education. In *Colombia: The Politics of Reforming the State,* ed. Eduardo Posada Carbo. New York: St. Martin's Press.

Government of Colombia. 2001. Exposición de motivos al proyecto de Ley 120/01. Government of Colombia, Bogotá (unpublished).

Leal, Franciso, and Andres Dávila. 1990. *Clientelismo: El sistema político y su expresión regional.* Bogotá: Tercer Mundo / IEPRI.

López, Maria Margarita. 1998. *Pluridad en la manera de hacer política educativa: Reforma de descentralización de la edducación.* Bogotá: Fundación Corona.

Montenegro, Armando. 1995. *An Incomplete Educational Reform: The Case of Colombia.* Human Capital Development and Operations Policy Working Paper 60. Washington, D.C.: World Bank.

National Planning Department. 1998. *Informe de desarrollo humano para Colombia.* Social Mission. Bogotá: Tercer Mundo Editores.

Rangel, Alfredo. 1998. *Colombia: Guerra en el fin del siglo.* Bogotá: Tercer Mundo / Uniandes.

Reyes, Joel. 2001. *Colombia: Decentralized Education Management.* LSCHD Paper 68, Human Development Department. Washington D.C.: World Bank.

Sarmiento, G. Alfredo. 2000. Equity and Education in Colombia. In *Unequal Schools, Unequal Chances: the Challenges to Equal Opportunities in the Americas,* ed. Fernando Reimer. David Rockefeller Center Series in Latin American Studies. Cambridge, Mass.: Harvard University Press.

Chapter 13

Federal Leverage in a Decentralized System: Education Reform in Brazil

Sônia M. Draibe

At the onset of democratization in the early and middle 1980s, Brazil's educational indicators placed the country in the lowest ranks of Latin America; and a broad consensus had emerged that schooling needed to be improved, especially at the primary and secondary levels. By the second half of the 1980s, some states within the federal system had undertaken a variety of institutional innovations in their own educational systems, with largely positive results.[1] Nevertheless, at the national level, educational policy reform was slow to come. Although a reformist agenda did emerge during the democratization period of the 1980s, the first significant changes in the educational system did not occur until the 1990s, in a second reform

1. The states of Minas Gerais, São Paulo, Rio Grande do Sul, and Mato Grosso had introduced important innovations in their primary school systems in the 1980s. Innovations covered almost all aspects of school organization and practices: pedagogic planning, autonomy to make small expenditures, teachers' and parents' councils, the election of school principals, teacher training, etc.

cycle of social policies.[2] At that point, during President Fernando Henrique Cardoso's first term (1995–98), the Brazilian educational system experienced a radical change, in institutional and organizational terms, which contributed to better system performance and some positive results in educational indicators.

The main focus of these reforms was on primary schooling. The changes were partial in the sense that—with some exceptions, such as a new system of student evaluations—they generally did not affect higher education. At the primary level, however, the reforms introduced radical changes, including a constitutional amendment in 1996 that significantly altered the distribution of educational resources between states and municipalities. This measure, together with a number of other innovations, amounted to a "silent revolution" in the lower levels of the educational system.

How do we account for the timing and extent of these changes? We argue that to a considerable extent, political factors explain both the delay of reforms in the 1980s and its successful results in the 1990s. Unlike health and, in some measure, social welfare programs, the educational area was not characterized by the presence of strong and mobilized groups of policy advocates during the 1980s; there were no strong challenges to the conservative, pork-barrel politicians who had controlled the Ministry of Education since the onset of military rule (1964–85). The turning point came with the election of Fernando Henrique Cardoso in 1995 and the new governing coalition, headed by the Partido da Social Democracia Brasileira (PSDB, Brazilian Social Democratic Party). The new minister and his associates could draw both on close ties with Cardoso and the PSDB leadership, and extensive experience within the Brazilian educational system. These resources enabled them to engineer a reform from the top down, changing the ministry's political style and inducing state and municipal governments to undertake greater efforts in the area of primary education.

This chapter describes and analyzes these changes. The first section presents the main features of the Brazilian educational system, the diag-

2. In other studies of Brazilian social reform programs, I have adopted an analytical framework that examines social policies in association with two reform cycles. The first took place in the 1980s in a context of re-democratization and economic instability. The second began in the second half of the 1990s, under the aegis of a complex agenda of economic stabilization, institutional reform, and consolidation of democracy. Educational reform was undertaken only in the second cycle, whereas health policy began in the first cycle and completed its implementation process in the mid-1990s. *Path dependency* can be found between the two events, when the policy sector has experienced significant reform already in the first cycle. See Draibe (2001, 2002a, 2002b).

nosis before the reforms, and a brief identification of the crucial actors in the reform process. The second section analyzes two sets of educational reforms undertaken by Ministry of Education reformers in the second half of the 1990s. We first describe the Program for the Maintenance and Development of Teaching (PMDE) and the School Meals Program (PNAE), each of which involved a substantial decentralization of federal funding and programs supporting primary schools; and we then focus on the establishment of the Fundo para o Desenvolvimento da Educação Fundamental e de Valorização do Magistério (FUNDEF, Elementary Education Development and Teacher Valorization Fund), which set significant new conditions for the transfer of education funds to state and municipal governments. The final section of the chapter discusses the main results of the reforms.

The Brazilian Educational System and the Motivations for Reform

Brazil has more than 50 million students registered in all levels of the educational system, as shown by the figures on public and private enrollment in 2000 given in table 13.1. Primary education is compulsory and free. Middle education is also free, but not mandatory. Nursery and preschool education is not required for entry into the system, but it does serve some of the age group below seven years. Young and adult citizens who did not finish regular schooling may take supplementary examinations to obtain their degrees (*ensino supletivo*). The national education system is predominantly public at preschool, primary, and secondary levels (respectively 73, 91, and 85 percent of all enrollments in 2000), and predominantly private in higher education (67 percent of all enrollment, as of 2000).

Within the federal system, state and municipal governments share responsibility for primary and secondary schooling, and municipalities are the main providers of preschool education. The federal government, states, and municipalities also share educational funding. Public financing of education fundamentally relies on tax revenues—constitutionally allocated for education—and on the "education wage" (*salário educação*), a compulsory contribution of 2.5 percent of firms' payrolls, which is collected by the federal government.[3] A constitutional norm (Calmon Amendment,

3. Two-thirds of the resources obtained through this mechanism return to their states of origin (QESE, the state quota of the education wage). The remaining part (QFSE, the federal quota of the education wage) goes to the National Educational Development Fund (FNDE) and is used by the federal government to implement programs directed to improve teaching quality and school efficiency.

Table 13.1
Public and Private Enrollment by Education Level, Brazil, 2000

Educational Level	Total for Brazil		Private Sector		Public Sector				
	Number	Percent	Number	Percent	Total (number)	Total (percent)	Federal (percent)	States (percent)	Municipalities (percent)
Infant education	6,010,240	11.4	1,670,392	27.7	4,339,848	72.3	0.4	8.6	91
Primary education	35,717,948	68	3,189,241	9	32,528,707	91	0.1	4.9	51
Secondary education	8,192,948	15	1,153,419	24	7,039,529	86	1.7	94.6	3.7
Higher education	2,694,245	5.1	1,807,219	67	887,026	33	54.4	37.4	8.2
Total	52,615,381	100.0	7,820,271	14.8	44,795,110	85.2			

Note: The Brazilian educational system is organized in three hierarchical levels: (1) Primary education covers the age group 7–14 years, lasts eight years, and is divided into two cycles, first through fourth grades and fifth through eighth grades. (2) Secondary education lasts three years and serves the age group 15–17 years. (3) Higher education is divided into two levels, undergraduate (from four to six years) and graduate (master's and Ph.D. programs); it also includes specialization, and postgraduate and postdoctoral programs.
Source: MEC-INEP-SECC (2002).

1983) mandates that 18 percent of federal tax revenues and 25 percent of all state and municipal revenues, including federal transfers, must be allocated to the development and maintenance of primary and secondary schooling.

For a better understanding of the Brazilian education system, it is important to underline the complex picture of how power is distributed within the federal structure. On the one hand, Brazil is currently organized into 26 states, the Federal District, and 5,561 municipalities. From a cross-national perspective, the educational system is highly heterogeneous in its organization, content, and performance.[4] State and municipal governments have a high degree of autonomy to design their own systems and to legislate important aspects of education policy at both the primary and the secondary levels. Their sphere of responsibility includes curriculum design (within the limits of the National Curriculum Guidelines established by the Ministry of Education, MEC); setting the school term; staffing (in accordance with the constitutional norms that establish open examinations for government employment); and determining teachers' salaries and career progression.

Even so, the federal government has considerable regulatory and economic power, which makes for a high degree of dependence of state and municipal administrations, particularly in the poorer regions of the country. For example, a high-level ministry agency, the National Education Council (CNE), has traditionally exercised considerable influence over the National Education Plan, syllabus orientation, certification of higher education institutions, and integration of different levels and modalities of schooling. Consequently, the council is a central locus of political bargaining. In addition, the ministry has traditionally influenced negotiations over a variety of nonmandatory resource transfers to the states and municipalities. Although these did not constitute a large proportion of the funds allocated

---

4. Legislation is not clear with respect to the division of functions among the three levels of government. Basic legislation stipulates that the Union, through the Ministry of Education, MEC, and the National Council of Education, is responsible for the coordination of the design of National Education Plans; the provision of financial and technical assistance to the states, municipalities, and the Federal District (Brasília); the maintenance, administration, and development of its own technical and higher education systems; and the supervision of the network of private universities. Within their own jurisdictions, states and municipalities are responsible for similar functions through state and municipal secretariats of education and state and municipal councils of education. Municipal councils may also discharge functions delegated by state councils. Finally, functions may be delegated and partnerships established, through collaborative agreements, among levels of government and between those and the private sector.

within the federal system, they were valuable to mayors and governors who were free to spend them on "special" political projects.

These kinds of resources established the Ministry of Education as an important center of patronage and clientelism. During the military period (1964–84) and into the 1990s, it became an increasingly valuable political prize, and was usually dominated by conservative political forces. During the military period, the ministry belonged first to the promilitary Alliance for National Renovation (the ARENA Party) and, after the party reform of 1979, to the conservative Partido Democrático Social (PDS, Social Democratic Party). From 1985 until 1995, it was dominated by the Partido da Frente Liberal (PFL, Party of Liberal Front), the right-wing party established in the aftermath of military rule.

In addition to the upper echelons of the Ministry of Education, finally, it is also important to note that a great deal of decision-making power is held by regional branch offices of the ministry, as well as by secretariats of education controlled by the governors and mayors. In other words, historically, the school unit and the school directors have had a very low degree of autonomy. In the mid-1990s and after, the decentralization of educational policy—both to subnational governments and to school directors—has become one of the main tenets governing the reorganization of the system.

Education Funding and Expenditures

Several data tables can provide some perspective on how public funds are allocated to education in Brazil. Table 13.2 compares education spending in Brazil with that of a number of European and Latin American countries. In 1995, the portion of gross domestic product going to education in Brazil was estimated at 5.1 percent, above the average for the European Union, and for Mexico, Argentina, and Chile. (OECD 1998; Almeida 2001). However, spending per student on primary and secondary education ranked below all the other countries except Paraguay. Allocations to primary education were particularly low; almost one-third less than Mexico, the next lowest country.

Tables 13.3 and 13.4 show how funds are allocated within Brazil, according to the level of government and the level of education. While federal expenditures are concentrated in higher education, states and municipalities spend the largest part of their resources on primary and secondary education. Almost 59 percent of all funding went to primary education, but more than one-quarter of all spending went to higher education, a level with only a small fraction of the student population.

Table 13.2

International Comparisons of Education Spending, Selected Countries and European Union (EU), 1995–96

Education Expenditures (percentage of gross domestic product)		Annual Spending per Student (dollars)			
		Primary Education		Secondary Education	
Canada	5.8	EU	5,371	EU	6,812
France	5.8	Spain	2,628	Spain	3,455
Portugal	5.4	Chile	1,807	Chile	2,059
Brazil	5.1	Argentina	1,158	Mexico	1,798
EU	5.0	Mexico	1,015	Argentina	1,575
Spain	4.8	Brazil	709	Brazil	1,502
Mexico	4.6	Paraguay	343	Paraguay	492
Argentina	3.4				
Chile	3.0				

Note: Countries are ranked by education spending.
Sources: OECD (1998); Almeida (2001).

Table 13.3

Public Education Spending by School Level, Brazil, 1996 (percent)

School Level	Governmental Level			Total
	Federal	State	Municipal	
Infant education	0.0	0.6	18.5	5.6
Primary education	11.2	77.7	71.8	58.6
Secondary education	9.4	9.7	7.8	9.0
Higher education	79.4	12.0	1.9	26.8
Total	100.0	100.0	100.0	100.0

Source: Rodriguez and Herrán (2000, 77).

Table 13.4

Public Education Spending by Governmental Level, Brazil, 1996 (percent)

School Level	Governmental Level			Total
	Federal	State	Municipal	
Infant education	0.0	5.2	94.8	100.0
Primary education	5.1	59.7	35.3	100.0
Secondary education	27.3	48.0	24.6	100.0
Higher education	77.9	20.1	2.0	100.0
Total	20.2	49.1	30.8	100.0

Source: Rodriguez and Herrán (2000., 77).

The last row of table 13.3 shows that, even before the mid-1990s educational reform, there was substantial decentralization of Brazilian education spending. State and municipal governments accounted for almost 80 percent of all spending, while the federal government accounted for just over 20 percent. According to data not presented in the table, the federal government net transfers to subnational governments for education represented only 12 percent of total public expenditures in this area (Afonso 1996, 12).

Although states and municipalities played a large role in the distribution of educational funds, however, extreme inequalities in financial resources existed both among states and between states and municipalities. The provisions of the 1983 Calmon amendment, referred to above, substantially reinforced decentralization but did not define a minimum for expenditures per student or teachers' pay and lacked any mechanism to provide for an equalization of expenditures across states. Consequently, inequality across regions and subnational levels of government remained extremely high.

Another critical problem with the Calmon Amendment and its implementing legislation was a vague specification of how money was to be spent. This allowed local officials to divert funding into "para-educational" and noneducational programs, particularly in municipalities that did not provide primary and secondary schooling. As we will see below, the most important measure in recent primary education reform was the restructuring of primary education funding in ways intended to address these problems.

Before Reform: An Overview of the Educational System

For at least twenty years before the 1990s, there had been a mounting chorus of criticism about the inefficiency and low quality of public education. Such criticisms came from many different sectors: the media, academics, educational specialists, and local and state officials. Concerns focused on inadequate educational coverage at all levels of schooling; the absurdly high levels of dropout and repetition rates; the poor quality of teaching; and the distortions of higher education and the big gap between the new demands for workforce qualifications and the educational contents of school curriculums. Most education indicators supported such criticism. For example (MEC-INEP-SEC 2002):

- In 1991, the Brazilian illiteracy rate was still 21.3 percent, and the adult population had completed, on average, less than five years of schooling.

- In 1994, access to primary education reached only 83 percent of the age group (7–4 years) and less than 20 percent in the secondary level, one of the lowest rates of secondary coverage among Latin America countries.
- In the early 1990s, the combined repetition and dropout rates in primary education were about 50 percent.

The consequences in terms of inefficiencies of the school system were tremendous: in 1998, the gross rate of enrollment (as a percentage of children age 7–14 years enrolled in primary schools) was about 163 percent at the primary first cycle (first–fourth grades) and about 105 percent at the second cycle (fifth–eighth grades). Estimates for the same year indicated that only two in every three students who began could expect to complete the eighth grade. And those successful pupils took an average of fourteen years to complete eight school years at the primary schooling, and twenty-three years to complete the regular eleven years of primary and secondary education (Rodriguez and Herrán 2000, 13–15)! Also, a large number of students attended classes out of step with their age group (the age gap was more than four years).

A related problem, pointed out by almost all educational critics, was teacher qualifications. The difficulty was less quantitative—for the ratio of pupils to teachers was about 22:3 at the primary level in 1994—than qualitative. Although rates of teacher certification were relatively high—about 80 percent of primary teachers were certified at either the college or secondary level—only four or five states had teacher training programs. Teachers' salaries were low at the primary and secondary levels, and even more important, varied enormously across the regions and levels of government. In 1996, for example, monthly salaries of primary school teachers averaged about $70, but varied from $24 to $900. In general, states paid more than municipalities (Draibe 1998b). Most analyses of the educational situation during the first half of the 1990s pointed to the perverse relation—really a vicious circle—between low wages and low qualification of teachers. Solving this equation was one of the great concerns of the 1995 educational reform group.

Problems of inequality in access to education also cut across the social spectrum. There are sharp disparities in both access and performance among different income strata, although these have been reduced somewhat over time. There are no sharp gender differences, but the gap between white and Afro-Brazilian students remains as wide as it was forty years ago, despite improvement among members of both racial categories. At least until the mid-1990s, there were large regional differences between the poor North and Northeast and the wealthier South and Southeast, both in terms of efficiency indicators such as coverage and repetition rates and in terms of qualitative measures, such as teachers' certification or student performance on national exams. Recently, the quantitative indicators have shown improvement, as rates in the North and Northeast have approached the national mean. But, as expected, the education differences are present in the adult population, as the Southeast's population had an average of 5.7 years of school versus the Northeast's 3.3 years.

Finally, there are major differences in the quality of state and municipal public schools. Municipal schools are generally of lower quality and are located mainly in poorer neighborhoods and poorer regions. This tends to reinforce the other inequalities mentioned above, and it constitutes a major challenge to the ongoing municipalization of primary education.

The Social and Political Basis of Education Reform: Actors and Interests

The reforms in primary and secondary education initiated after 1995 did not result from the demands of social movements or interest groups. In this area of public policy, in contrast to the *movimento sanitarista* in the area of health care (see chapter 6 of the present volume), no collective societal actors of national scope were able to present a coherent reform agenda, a fact that accounts in part for the relative lag in efforts to reform the education system. In the education sector, the decisive actors came from within the government and political system: local and state officials, and ministry authorities and politicians, rather than members of teachers' unions, school officials, or members of parent or community organizations.[5]

The political weakness of educational interest groups—teachers, school principals, technicians, and bureaucrats—reflected the extreme fragmentation and the great heterogeneity of the educational system. Primary and secondary school teachers were never successful in organizing a strong national union. There were, however, significant differences between state and municipal teachers. State-level teachers in general were better educated and better paid and were recruited through meritocratic systems; they moved along a career track. In some states, they were (and still are) organized into relatively efficient unions for the defense of their corporate

5. The situation is different in higher education, where teachers have strong national unions and some support from the Congress and media.

interests, especially salaries. In contrast, municipal teachers were not organized except in the largest municipalities, like São Paulo, Rio de Janeiro, and other state capitals, because there are separate educational systems in each municipality.

Within the municipal school systems, moreover, the relations among mayors, local schools, and state and federal educational authorities were characterized by a traditional, clientelistic political style. The negotiation of particularistic favors, indifference to the quality of education services, and irresponsibility in the management of public resources were especially pronounced in poorer and relatively isolated small and medium-sized cities. Although such conditions have improved significantly in recent years, they still have an important effect on efforts to transfer responsibility to the municipalities. In particular, state-level teachers tend to react negatively to municipalization, which they fear would imply lower salaries and a weaker institutional infrastructure. In some states—for example, São Paulo—this has led to explicit, often successful, movements of resistance to municipal decentralization.

Regarding the main beneficiaries of educational policy—students and their parents—we note two characteristics of their organizational and political behavior. First, Brazil lacks a strong tradition of active school communities and associations. Parent–teacher associations, school councils, municipal councils of education, and other types of associations—with social, advisory, and decision-making functions—are mandated in legislation, but implementation was very limited until the mid-1990s or later. So these collective actors were not significant in the most recent round of reform.

A second characteristic of public school communities was the absence of families from the middle class. Since the 1970s, much of the middle class had exited from the system, seeking better quality in private schools. During the 1990s, the impoverishment of many middle-class families did force some of its children to reenter the public schools, especially in secondary education. For the most part, however, middle-class parents were not active in the contemporary politics of reform.

Given the relative weakness of the societal actors with interest in education, what other actors made reform possible during the late 1990s, and what kinds of political resources did they deploy? In the next section of this chapter, we try to answer this question. We argue that reform was led from the top down, by a small team of high-level Education Ministry officials who mobilized both formal and informal power resources. However, the success of the reform was also based to a considerable extent on prior state and municipal experiences and initiatives occurring mainly during the second half of the 1980s and the first half of the 1990s. Although these institutional legacies did not directly alter the structure of the national system, they provided an intellectual framework and expertise on which national reformers could draw. And they also promoted institutional administrative improvements, mainly in the state schools, that could anchor future measures of educational reform.

Primary Education Reform in the 1990s

In the mid-1990s, the contour of the Brazilian primary and secondary school system maintained the characteristics inherited from the previous reform undertaken in 1971, during the military regime. This was the institutional legacy that the primary education reform of the 1990s had to face, as the new Constitution of 1988 but also the first three civilian governments—those of José Sarney (1985–89), Fernando Collor de Mello (1990–93), and Itamar Franco (1993–94)—introduced few changes in the system.

The Policy Legacy

The Brazilian educational system underwent profound changes during the 1964–84 military regime. In fact, as in other aspects in the field of social policies, the educational system "matured" during this period, became institutionalized and acquired more definite contours, and also noticeably experienced a growth in enrollment and of the physical network. Such changes were implemented through an effective educational reform, as part of the more general effort to modernize the state, under the guidance of the conservative principles and technocratic rationalism in force during that period.

The first set of changes, introduced during the governments of Humberto de Alencar Castelo Branco (1964–67) and Artur da Costa e Silva (1967–69), consisted of a series of innovations introduced in the new educational legislation—the Lei de Diretrizes e Bases da Educação Nacional (National Educational Platform and Guidelines Act)—approved in 1961 and implemented in the following years. The change introduced by the military authorities, which would be of enormous significance later, was the creation of an additional source of revenue, the educational wage, paid by firms on the basis of 2.5 percent of their payrolls. The university reform of 1968 and the basic education reform (primary and secondary levels) of 1971 were significant and more clearly manifested the ideology of the military regime.

The university reform drastically changed the previous structure and had two fundamental objectives: creating human resources for economic development and, more immediate, suppressing the pressures and mobilization of the student movement, as well as the more progressive alternatives of restructuring and democratization of the university.[6] During the 1970s, a second and rather successful reform cycle strengthened the network of federal public universities, their national graduate programs, and the advancement and funding of research.[7]

During the Emílio Garrastazu Médici administration (1969–74), primary and secondary education reforms extended compulsory basic schooling from four to eight years and introduced a professional orientation in the curriculum of these levels, although this last, anachronistic measure was never really implemented. Later, during the João Baptista de Figueiredo administration (1980–84), a congressional initiative—the aforementioned Calmon Amendment—was approved.

In step with the broader political orientation of the military governments, centralization of power in the federal sphere became more pronounced. In the case of educational policies, the Ministry of Education and the National Council of Education concentrated practically all decision-making and political resources, reducing state and municipal autonomy in the definition of educational policies better suited to their characteristics, and thus introducing greater uniformity in the national system.

Throughout the twenty years of military governments, the Ministry of Education was headed by ministers within or close to the parties allied with the regime—ARENA first, and then the Democratic Social Party after the 1979 political reform. Although it is true that bureaucratic centralism was the golden rule organizing the educational system, as Durham (1993) indi-

6. The University Reform was rapidly formulated and had the support of the U.S. Agency for International Development, which collaborated with the Ministry of Education.

7. Among the measures enacted for the advancement of science and technology: the Plano Básico de Desenvolvimento Científico e Tecnológico (PBDCT, Basic Plan for Science and Technology); the Sistema Nacional de Ciencia e Tecnologia (SNDCT, National Science and Technology System), coordinated by FINEP (Research Financing Fund); the National Graduate Program and the Development Plans (Planos de Desenvolvimento, PEDs).

cates, the administration of educational policies was extremely politicized throughout the period, subject during the entire period to political bargaining, pork barrel deals, negotiated agreements, and privileges for all kinds of "clients" from the top down in states, municipalities, parties, and parliaments, and even involving renowned public figures. The National Council for Education—which held, and still holds, the power of granting licenses to private universities—was itself the stage for intense pork barrel negotiations and a target of the lobbies of private interest groups, especially those related to the supply of private higher education (Draibe 1994).

Although it permitted a renewal of discussions and greater transparency, the resumption of a democratization process and civilian governments in 1985 did not mean the introduction of many changes in the existing framework, whether with regard to federal centralization of power, right-wing control of the Ministry of Education or the pork-barrel style of government. From the perspective of educational reforms—our main focus—there were hardly any innovations until the following decade.

Educational reform undoubtedly occupied an important place in the democratization agenda that began with the civilian government in 1985 up to the new Brazilian Constitution of 1988. The period of the National Constitutional Assembly was marked by strong participation of civil society and a healthy confrontation of opinions and interests mobilized to exert influence in the committees, subcommittees and working groups receiving demands and elaborating the proposals for the new constitutional text. Education activists were able to mobilize close to thirty national associations, which organized a national education forum and participated in the public hearings of the Education Committee in the National Congress (NEPP 1989, 389–90).

However, unlike other social areas, this mobilization was not geared for change, nor did it present proposals for a real improvement in the educational system. The debates and confrontations of interests were practically limited to the issue of private versus public schools from the perspective of higher education. Except for the authorization of preschool as the first educational level, the new constitution did not introduce any changes in the principles and structure of the preexisting national educational system; it merely restated the principles already established in the previous constitution (NEPP 1989).

For the most part, federal education authorities also failed to introduce innovations at any other point during the 1985–95 decade. Although a good deal of change and experimentation did occur in some states and municipalities, the federal ministers continued to be drawn from right-wing political coalitions, especially the Partido da Frente Liberal (PFL, Liberal Front Party). Besides maintaining a high degree of centralization, the Ministry of Education continued to engage in pork-barrel politics, both through large national projects—such as the Projeto Nordeste (Northeast Project), funded by international donors—or through federal grants from the National Fund for Educational Development (FNDE) for the "special projects" of politicians, regional representatives, and others.

Two initiatives undertaken during this decade do deserve attention. The first was the decentralization of some federal programs to support primary and secondary education, hesitantly begun by the Sarney government (1985–90) and intensified by the Itamar Franco administration (1992–94). The best known example is the decentralization of the School Lunch Program, whose first steps were taken during the Franco administration. The second initiative, also taken in 1994 by the Franco government, was to dismantle the Federal Council on Education, which was suspected of irregular or corrupt behavior. This cleared the way for it to be reconstituted and reorganized as the National Council on Education during the first year of the Cardoso government. Although restricted to the federal level of government, such measures were relatively important for improving the credibility and rationality of the system. In general, however, the legacy faced by the government in 1995 was one of considerable institutional inertia in the federal sphere.

The Reform of the 1990s

The Cardoso government that came to office in 1995 considered education reform one of the major commitments of its political program. A small but committed team of reformers was appointed from outside the ministerial bureaucracy to assume the leadership of the Ministry of Education, and from 1995 to 2002, it was charged with expanding access to education and improving the efficiency and quality of the system. This marked the first time since the military regime that control of national education policy had been taken away from the conservative forces that had long dominated Brazilian educational politics. Dismantling the patronage networks and the bureaucratic resources that supported these forces was viewed as an essential step for increasing the efficiency, equity, and quality of the system, and was thus a major objective of the 1995 reformers.

To accomplish this objective, central education authorities systematically pursued two types of measures: first, the radical decentralization of the ministry programs, focusing on primary and secondary education; second, the introduction of general criteria that defined the amounts of transferable resources to states and municipalities (e.g., a value per student), and third and most important, through the passage of FUNDEF (discussed below).

The Ministerial Reformers of Cardoso's Government

The leader of the reform team was the new minister of education, Paulo Renato de Souza. Renato was a member of the historic nucleus of the president's party, the PSDB, and a former dean of a large public university. From 1983 to 1986, he had been the secretary of education for the State of São Paulo, under the first directly elected governor since the beginning of the military regime. Both as a dean and as a secretary of education, Renato had undertaken a number of institutional reforms, most important the decentralization of the budget and the reform of the teachers' code (Estatuto do Magistério). In the course of these reforms, the future minister acquired a reputation as a skillful negotiator.

Other members of Renato's reform team also drew on extensive experience in municipal and state educational management. Two of his three closest collaborators—all of them women—had worked with him in both the university and the state administration. The third, a university professor, was a former municipal secretary of education in Campinas, one of the largest and wealthiest Brazilian cities, also in the State of São Paulo.

Their long experience as educational administrators provided this group with important institutional and technical resources, but they had substantial political resources as well. First, in negotiating the formation of his congressional coalition, Cardoso reserved all of the "social ministries," except for Social Security, for members of the PSDB. All were generally oriented toward the political left, or were persons with recognized expertise in their respective policy areas, and this contributed to a high level of cohesion within the area of social policy. At least as important, Renato was part of Cardoso's inner circle within the federal government, and he exercised significant influence in political decision making.[8] Moreover, Renato also counted on the strong support of the first lady, Ruth Cardoso, a former anthropologist and professor at the University of São Paulo, who played a central role in social policy decision making.

8. In addition to being one of the founders of the PSDB, and president of the party, Renato resigned from a position at the Inter-American Development Bank to become the coordinator of Cardoso's campaign program.

These factors established an open channel from the minister of education to the president, and they served as an important source of leverage in cabinet negotiations over limited fiscal resources. Although such negotiations rarely involved open confrontations with the finance minister, Pedro Malan, there were inevitable tensions over the size of the education budget. In some important instances, Renato's close ties to Cardoso enabled him to win presidential backing for the "protection" of a variety of new education programs. Important examples include the School Meals Program and the free distribution of textbooks to primary schools. Renato was also able to prevail over the preferences of the finance minister in establishing a two-year fiscal commitment for FUNDEF.

On the other hand, it must be emphasized that—especially in times of difficult fiscal adjustment—Renato was compelled to accept severe limits on the Education Ministry's budget. Between 1996 and 2000, the economic authorities successfully vetoed repeated proposals to increase the per capita transfers of educational resources to the states and municipalities through FUNDEF. An even more dramatic veto came during a long university teachers' strike; the Finance Ministry blocked any concessions on salaries or other expenditures, seriously constraining the ability of the Education Ministry to negotiate a settlement.

The Strategy for Education Reform

Despite these limitations, Renato and his team did introduce significant changes, and some of the most important occurred in the area of funding. The education reform *strategy* was founded on a set of relatively integrated lines of action. Table 13.5 shows the main components of the educational system that were affected, and the content or guidelines of the changes.

Throughout Cardoso's eight-year term, a wide variety of laws and presidential or ministerial decrees and policy initiatives reflected the goals presented in the table, the most general being the establishment of achievement tests to evaluate schools at all educational levels. However, the most extensive changes were undertaken at the primary level, and they included the decentralization of resources, municipalization, syllabus modernization, and investment in teaching quality. In the following pages, I will limit my discussion to two of the most important sets of reform measures initiated by the ministry between 1995 and 1998. The first set is the extensive decentralization of federal resources and programs that support state and municipal primary schools. I focus in particular on two such programs: the

Table 13.5
Brazil's Recent Education Reforms: Dimensions and Content

Changed Dimensions	Content and Guidelines
Funding and spending	Redistribution of funds to benefit primary schooling
	Decentralization of spending
	Reinforcement of progressive and distributive impact of funds
	Reduction of regional inequality in resources allocation
Organizational structure and decision-making system	Decentralization
	(De)concentration of funds and posts
Public-private relations	Parent participation
	Partnerships with civil society
Didactic-pedagogical aspect	Modernization of syllabuses
	Diversification of careers
	Creation of national teacher training systems
Introduction of new programs	Cash program to poor families to support fundamental education (Bolsa-Escola)
Monitoring and quality control	Creation of an integrated national education evaluation system

Program for the Maintenance and Development of Teaching (PMDE), and the School Meals Program (PNAE). The second refers to a major change in the law regulating the transfer of educational funding to state and municipal governments: FUNDEF.

Decentralizing Federal Education Programs: PMDE and PNAE

The transfer of spending powers to states, municipalities, and schools themselves has been a guiding principle for the Education Ministry for virtually all federal programs to promote primary education. Decentralization conformed both to an ideological commitment to democratize the educational system, and to a conviction that it could serve as a powerful mechanism for reducing patronage, clientelism, and corruption, patterns that had characterized such programs as the distribution of school meals. At the same time, the team also viewed decentralization as an incentive to move away from state primary schools—which shared responsibility about equally with municipal schools—toward fuller municipalization. Finally, decentralization was also understood as a way to reinforce the ability of the school unit, including directors, parents, and community, to confront political interference from mayors, politicians, and higher-level educational bureaucrats.

In 1995, the Ministry of Education introduced the Program for the Maintenance and Development of Teaching (again, PMDE), later called the

Efficient Public School Management Program. The program had the dual purpose of strengthening the autonomy of school units, and encouraging parents and the community to take an active part in the running of schools.

PMDE is funded from a special earmarked source: the Ministry of Education's one-third share of the total amount of corporations' educational contribution (*salário educaço*). The program distributes approximately $250 million annually, disbursed to each municipal and state public primary school on a per student basis, and according to the size and regional location of the school. In the North and Northeast, sums range from about R$600 to about R$15,000; in most of the rest of the country, between R$500 and R$10,000. Those modest funds must be spent on small items of day-to-day expenditures and for physical maintenance of school buildings.[9]

The decree establishing the PMDE required that the funds be delivered directly to a school board, normally organized along the lines of parent–teacher associations. Because such associations have traditionally been nonexistent or inactive in Brazilian public schools, the PMDE permits municipal authorities or school directors to manage the funds until the boards are formed. However, the program has actively encouraged their formation, and it has had considerable success in reaching this goal. After two years of implementation, the program covered more than 90 percent of schools, and in most of these (87 percent) funds were managed by parents' councils and school authorities (Draibe 1998a).

As implied above, the PMDE was authorized by ministerial decree, rather than congressional legislation; and although the program was widely advertised and promoted, it was designed and implemented without negotiations with stakeholders or other actors. It is important to note, however, that by introducing the PMDE, the ministry relinquished an important component of its bargaining power with states and municipalities. Before 1995, the funds deployed under PMDE had been allocated to states and municipalities through special education projects that the ministry negotiated on a case-by-case basis. In contrast, the PMDE was designed with automatic criteria for resource allocation, thereby eliminating any negotiation about sums. The program proved highly popular with principals and teachers; in a survey of school principals, 95 percent supported greater

9. The program required that the money be spent on the following items: maintenance of the premises, purchase of teaching aids and materials, training and qualification of school staff, assessment of learning, implementation of the school's pedagogical project, and development of sundry educational activities. In 1997, schools were authorized to also spend this money on investments on school facilities.

autonomy for the school unit, and 86 percent agreed that the program had contributed to a reduction of red tape and increased their ability to solve priority problems (Draibe 1998a).

Decentralization of the School Meals Program (again, PNAE) likewise sought to promote greater autonomy for municipal and school authorities. Funds for school meals derive from taxation and are part of the Ministry of Education's budget. The program annually transfers federal funds for school meals in public elementary schools on a per capita basis, supplying one daily school meal to approximately 35 million school children. Between 1995 and 1998, the program covered about 95 percent of all public elementary schools and funding was extended from 180 to 200 days of attendance. Decentralization in the administration of this program has advanced substantially in recent years; between 1994 and 1998, coverage expanded from 1,532 to 4,123 municipal districts, roughly 80 percent of all such districts in the country. Decentralization directly to individual schools has been more limited, but still substantial. About 27 percent of Brazil's public primary schools now receive funds directly.

From the point of view of the actors' strategic and political behavior, the implementation of the PNAE shows some important differences with that of the PMDE. The PMDE, as noted, received strong support from actors at the school level. Even more interesting, however, was that mayors were generally willing to relinquish control over the program's resources and allow funds to flow directly to the schools. In fact, they did not seek to retain control over these funds even when schools had not established the required parent–teacher councils. The reason for this willingness was that the amount of funding available for the district was relatively small and was subdivided into a large number of even smaller sums allocated to individual schools. For the mayors, the administrative and accounting costs of such allocations apparently outweighed the advantages that might come from control over the funds (Draibe 1998a).

In contrast to the PMDE, the resources involved in the school lunch program were, and still are, very important components of total municipal revenues, at least in the vast majority of the municipalities, and an important source of patronage. The mayors must negotiate transfers with the ministry, but they also have wide discretion over the way the funds are spent, which affords them considerable bargaining power vis-à-vis suppliers. Unlike the PMDE, moreover, the school lunch program required formal acceptance by the states and municipalities, because of requirements for counterpart funding, supervision, and control. Such factors may explain why school lunch decentralization was characterized mainly by municipalization of resources, and why only a relatively small percentage involved the direct transfer to school units.

Evaluations of PMDE and Lunch School Program implementation (Draibe 1998a, 1999) provided sound empirical evidence of the positive effects of decentralization on program performance and on the schools' and municipalities' administrative capacities, autonomy, and institutional learning—results on which the ongoing decentralization processes can rely.

They also showed positive but more limited effects on equality. There is evidence that the decentralization process extends the programs' benefits to schools that were once excluded due their marginal position in the educational system. But evaluation research also shows that the decentralization results are strongly shaped by institutional factors—information and training processes, as well as institutional characteristics of schools, especially those related to the principals' professional profile (Draibe 1998a). The results of the decentralization process continue to reflect the inequalities and the heterogeneous nature of school and educational networks, especially the highly unfavorable situations of municipal schools, small schools, and local schools in the Northeast and North regions.

Financial Incentives for Municipalization: The New Law for Funding Primary Education, FUNDEF

FUNDEF was the most radical reform undertaken by the Ministry of Education. It was presented to the Congress and passed in September 1996, and the law went into effect in January 1998. The measure sought to change the distribution of educational resources to favor primary education, to address regional inequalities in funding, and to establish clear guidelines for state and municipal responsibilities.

As was already discussed, the constitution previously required states and municipalities to spend 25 percent of their revenues on education; but because economic conditions varied widely, this meant widespread inequalities in education funding. Soares estimates that, in 1995, expenditures per student varied from only a quarter of the national average (municipal schools in Maranhao State) to more than three and a half times the average (municipal schools in São Paulo State), and from about 66 percent of the national average in the Northeast to about 128 percent in the Southeast (Soares 1998, 6).

FUNDEF—devoted exclusively to primary education—addressed this inequality through the following mechanisms (Soares 1998, 14):

- A total of 15 percent of all tax collection and constitutionally required transfers to each state and each municipality were collected into a FUNDEF fund for each state, to be devoted exclusively to primary education. This would count toward the 25 percent of revenues that states were constitutionally required to spend on education.
- These funds were then divided by the number of students enrolled in grades one through eight of the state and municipal schools, and allocated to each school on a per capita basis.
- The per capita values were permitted to differ across states, depending on their wealth and available resources. But the FUNDEF law determined a national minimum per student. In 2002 reais, this came to R$418 per student in first through fourth grades, and R$438 in fifth through eighth grades. If a state fell short of that minimum, the federal government was required to make up the difference.
- States were allowed (but not required) to spend at least 60 percent of the fund on teachers' salaries, although the law did not establish a minimum salary.[10]

Figure 13.1 describes the FUNDEF organization and allocation mechanisms.

The law, which went into effect in January 1998, had several important consequences. One of them is a strong incentive to improve the quality of schooling. Because FUNDEF permits 60 percent of the fund to be used for teachers' salaries, the government is now able to establish standards for educational inputs, especially personnel. Such standards would include qualifications as well as wages, because no municipality would be able to claim that it lacked the funds to pay teachers with at least a secondary education (Soares 1998, 16). Thus, although the FUNDEF law does not establish a formal minimum for teachers' salaries, it has encouraged a

10. The FUNDEF Law defines only the minimum amount (60 percent of the total FUNDEF) that would be spent on primary teachers' salaries. But states and municipalities can spent more than this amount on salaries, using additional resources from their own sources outside of FUNDEF. Other items of spending, including teacher training, cannot be funded from this part of FUNDEF. The remaining 40 percent may be applied to all other educational items, including teacher training. See the FUNDEF legislation at www.mec.gov.br/sef/fundef/Legisla.shtm.

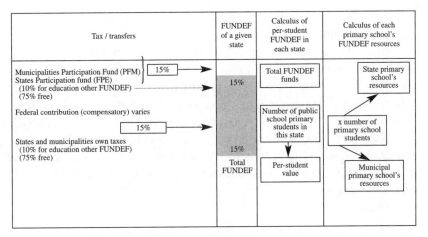

Figure 13.1. Brazil's Federal Law on Education Finance (FUNDEF)

substantial increase, especially in regions where they had previously been low relative to the national average.[11]

An even more important consequence was the incentive that the law provided for the municipalization of primary education. This was especially the case in the Southeast and South, where state school systems had predominated. The guarantee of a per capita minimum for each student meant that each student brings money. Municipal as well as state schools had an incentive to compete for students, and enrollments grew significantly in grades one through four.

FUNDEF also had an important redistributive impact. Within each state, resources were redistributed from relatively wealthy state-level schools to poorer municipal schools. At the same time, inequality between states was also reduced, because of the federal compensation provided to states that fell below minimum standards of expenditure. The magnitude of this redistributive effect is indicated by the fact that the resources transferred annually within states and through federal compensation to poorer states comes to about 1.5 percent of gross domestic product. In its first year, FUNDEF increased municipal revenues by R$664 million and state reve-

11. Since 1994, a proposal to set a minimum teacher's wage has been debated among federal and local officials and union representatives. The ministry team decided that it would be better to tie substantial funding exclusively to primary education, while leaving open their application to teachers' salaries. With this formula, it was also assumed that local officials could address not only teachers' salaries but other quality issues as well.

nues by R$370 million, benefiting mainly the poorest areas and those with the largest number of students.[12]

Finally, the new law also attempted to establish mechanisms of accountability and social control. It required that each state and municipality establish a FUNDEF council (Monitoring and Social Control FUNDEF' Council), which was to be composed of representatives of municipal or state authorities, parents, teachers, school directors, and administrative personal. The councils were charged with monitoring the expenditure of FUNDEF resources, on the basis of monthly reports from the municipal executive authority.[13] Currently, these councils are in operation in 98 percent of all municipalities and states.

Winning Legislative Approval for FUNDEF

The FUNDEF proposal was put forward as a constitutional amendment, and thus required the approval of three-fifths of the legislature. To rally support, the ministry team sought the backing of two important sets of stakeholders: the National Council of State Secretariats of Education (CONSED) and the National Union of Municipal Education Directors (UNDIME). These organizations played an important role in mediating the interests of local political and educational authorities within their respective states. One factor that facilitated their agreement was that a former UNDIME president was one of the members of the Education Ministry team.

As anticipated by the ministry strategists, there was some opposition from state and municipal political authorities, but this was relatively unorganized at the time the amendment was presented to the congress. Objections from one set of governors, particularly among the wealthier states, stemmed from the fact that their states would lose from FUNDEF because they already spent more than the minimum required amount on primary education. More important, they were concerned that the requirement that they spend 15 percent of their education funding at the primary level would

12. According to Ministry of Education estimates for 1998, twenty of Brazil's twenty-six states transferred funds to municipal administrations, while in six states (São Paulo, Roraima, Goiás, Espírito Santo, Minas Gerais, and Santa Catarina) the reverse occurred; i.e. municipal governments forfeited funds to the state schools system, if they failed to increase the number of places offered in municipal schools (MEC 1999).

13. The values distributed in each state can also be found on the FUNDEF Web page (www.mec.gov.br/sef/fundef/default.shtm).

jeopardize the funding available for secondary education. This was the case of São Paulo and Rio de Janeiro States.

Another group of states stood to lose resources for their municipalities, because they had failed to provide places in elementary schools proportional to 15 percent of their revenues. This was the situation of the most of the Northeastern and Northern states, both regions where the municipalities were the main suppliers of primary schooling. In some cases, there was also concern about the scarcity of resources for funding other levels of education, especially preschool facilities. This was the case of the mayors of state capitals and of largest cities.

To forestall the mobilization of this opposition and veto by potential losers, the Education Ministry team moved quickly to negotiate an agreement among members of the congressional committees on education policy. The proposal gained strong support from the legislators, including individual members of the opposition Workers' Party. With the committee backing, Cardoso's large governing majority passed the new bill in less than a month, before affected stakeholders had become fully aware of all of its fiscal consequences. The only concession made by the ministry was to postpone the implementation of the amendment until January 1, 1998.[14] In the final vote, the Worker's Party voted against the bill, in keeping with its principle of systematic opposition to government initiatives.

Active opposition did increase during 1997. Municipal associations and teachers' unions in São Paulo and several other states[15] organized demonstrations, often actively supported by opposition politicians in the city councils and the state legislatures and by some educational nongovernmental organizations. The new law was, to be sure, somewhat inflexible, inasmuch as it tied such a large portion of funding to primary schooling and limited allocations to other levels of education. To a certain extent, moreover, it reduced the autonomy of states and municipalities to structure their educational expenditures in other ways. However, the law also gave authorities greater discretion to allocate FUNDEF resources toward primary teachers' salaries, which provided the states and larger cities with more opportunity to define their wage policies. Despite the initial opposition to

14. According to a ministry team member, this delay was actually welcomed, because the ministry did not yet have the education statistics needed for the annual calculation of FUNDEF's value.

15. E.g., the Associação Paulista de Municípios, Associação Brasileira de Municípios, and teachers' state associations, such as APEOESP, Associação dos Professores do Estado de São Paulo.

the FUNDEF initiative, there was by the early 2000s a broad consensus about its positive results. The debate, in fact, is now directed toward demands that FUNDEF be extended to cover preschool and secondary education.

Improving the Schools: Main Results of Changes

Long-term changes in educational achievements are the result of many interrelated factors, and it is impossible to establish precise causal links between the reforms discussed in this chapter and overall educational outcomes. Indeed, many of the positive changes in the sector are attributable to developments occurring over a much longer period of time. With this caution in mind, however, a review of some important improvements can provide a useful perspective on the recent policy changes.

First, high rates of growth in enrollments confirm that primary education is becoming universal. Attendance in the age group seven to fourteen years, which was about 87 percent at 1991, reached 97 percent in 2000 (MEC-INEP-SEC 2002). Although secondary enrollments are still lower than in many Latin American countries, the increase in coverage is still impressive. Within the age group fifteen to seventeen years, enrollments grew from 17.6 to 32.6 percent between 1991 and 1999 (MEC-INEP-SEEC 2002).

The rate of adult illiteracy (among people 15 years or older) also fell sharply, from 21.3 to 13.3 percent, between 1991 and 2000. Differences among the regions remain very large, however, with the backward Northeast still recording adult illiteracy rates as high as 30 percent. Between 1990 and 1999, the average length of schooling among adults aged 15 years or more rose from 3.6 to 5.7 years but remained lower than in many countries at about the same level of economic development (IBGE 1992, 2001).

Between 1995 and 2000, there were indications of impressive improvement in the efficiency of the educational system. Table 13.6 shows a significant increase in the promotion rate and a decline in dropout and repetition rates.

A number of other indicators show changes that might plausibly be related more directly to the FUNDEF innovations:

- *Increase in coverage rates for primary schooling.* Between 1997 and 2000, enrollments increased more than 10 percent, and the coverage rate rose from 93 to 97 percent. The increase was strongest in municipal schools and in the Northeast and North.

Table 13.6

Primary Education Promotion, Repetition, Dropout, and Age–Grade Gap Rates, Brazil, 1995–96 and 1999–2000

Promotion Rate		Repetition Rate		Dropout Rate		Age–Grade Gap Rate	
1995–96	1999–2000	1995–96	1999–2000	1995–96	1999–2000	1996	2000
64.5	73.6	30.2	21.6	5.3	4.8	47	41.7

Source: MEC-INEP data; www.inep.gov.br.

- *Regional redistributive effects.* Gross transfers of FUNDEF funds in 1998 totaled R$13.3 billion (approximately $7.3 billion), or 1.5 percent of the Brazilian gross domestic product. More than 61 percent of this went to states, and more than 38 percent to municipalities. The eight states of the Northeast and North—the regions that had registered the lowest levels of spending per student—were net beneficiaries of these transfers.
- *An increase in public spending for primary education.* Between 1998 and 2001, federal transfers for primary education increased about 30 percent (from R$13.2 billion to R$19 billion). In the same period, the total FUNDEF expenditures increased from 1.5 to 1.7 percent of Brazilian gross domestic product (MEC 2003).
- *An increase in average spending per student.* The increase in per capita spending on schoolchildren was about 22.7 percent nationwide, and considerably higher (90 percent) in the Northeast. There was an increase of annual spending in 49 percent of Brazil's municipalities, which provided 34 percent of places available in elementary schools. Between 1997 and 1998, spending per student in these municipalities increased by almost 125 percent, from R$167 to R$375 (the minimum value set by FUNDEF was R$315). Between 1998 and 2000, annual spending per pupil grew 48,5 percent nationwide, and by 117.5 percent in Northeast, 90 percent in North, and 20 percent in Southwestern regions. Without the FUNDEF and with the same enrollment growth, spending would have increased by only 6 percent (Semeguini 2001).
- *Improvement of teachers' salaries.* The average increase nationwide was 13 percent between 1997 and 1998, while in municipal schools of Northeast region, the average increase was about 49 percent.[16] Between

16. The improvement in salaries was truly remarkable in some municipal districts: 270 percent in Girau de Ponciano (Alagoas State); 195 percent in Boa Viagem (Ceará);

mid-1997 and mid-2000, average teachers' salaries increased 29.5 percent nationwide, and by 54 percent in the Northeastern and 35 percent in the North.

* *Improvements in teachers' qualifications.* Between 1997 and 2000, the number of unqualified lay teachers was reduced by 46 percent, while the proportion of teachers who completed secondary education rose by 10.6 percent and the proportion with a higher education rose 12 percent.

The most impressive impact of the reform was on the municipalization of primary schooling. As was discussed above, the new law contained powerful incentives for decentralization to municipalities, because small municipalities would increase revenues if they expanded enrollment, and the large and medium-sized municipalities stood to lose resources if they failed to spend 15 percent of their revenues on elementary education. These incentives appeared to work as intended. Between 1990 and 2001, states' share of elementary school enrollment fell from 70 to 46 percent, while the share of municipalities increased from 30 to 54 percent. The growth of municipal schools, which had been relatively slow until 1997, accelerated sharply between 1998 and 2001 after the implementation of FUNDEF. The biggest increase was in the first cycle, grades one through four, where municipal schools reached almost 70 percent enrollment. In grades five through eight, municipal schools enrolled 30 percent of the students.

The FUNDEF effects on preschool enrollments are ambiguous. Enrollments fell during the first year of implementation. This may have been due to resource constraints, or to the fact that many mayors began to count literacy-course students as part of their primary enrollment—a step that enabled them to maximize FUNDEF resources. In any event, after the second year, preschool enrollments began to grow again, with municipal schools accounting for 91 percent of all public preschool enrollments in 2000.

Secondary schools remain without a specific funding mechanism. In response to the concentration of FUNDEF resources at the primary level, many governors and state-level education officials negotiated with mayors over a clearer division of labor, in which municipalities would assume full responsibility for preschool and grades one through four, while the states

---

180 percent in Coroatá (Maranhão); 175 percent in Itabaiana (Sergipe); 165 percent in Redenção (Ceará); 150 percent in Santo Antônio de Jesus (Bahia) and Barras (Piauí); 131 percent in Araci (Bahia); 125 percent in Anápolis (Goiás); and from 85 to 110 percent in Marapanim (Paraíba), Ceará-Mirim, and Macaíba (Rio Grande do Norte).

would retain responsibility for secondary education and, in some instances, grades five through eight. But the issue of how to fund secondary schools remains unresolved, at a time when enrollments at this level are increasing rapidly. The current debate points to the creation of a funding mechanism similar to FUNDEF to generate stable resources for secondary schooling.

Conclusions

As we have seen, during recent years, there have been extraordinary changes in traditional patterns of bureaucratic centralization within the Brazilian primary school system. To an important extent, these were consequences of the kinds of reforms we have examined here. After almost thirty years of only limited change in the way states and municipalities divided responsibilities, the incentives of the FUNDEF legislation stimulated rapid municipalization of primary education, especially in the early grades. Over time, the legislation won strong support from mayors and governors, who gained from enhanced fiscal resources.

FUNDEF has also contributed significantly to the reduction of regional inequalities, an increase in nationwide spending per student, and a significant improvement in the salaries of primary school teachers. As I have also emphasized, moreover, the reforms discussed here were only part of a much larger array of institutional innovations, which in conjunction have contributed to attaining near universal primary education coverage, reducing dropout and repetition rates, and improving teacher qualifications.

This analysis has also pointed to some interesting and paradoxical aspects of the conditions in which these developments occurred. The first is that the reforms were undertaken during a period of stringent fiscal adjustment. Nevertheless, although this adjustment did constrain spending in education as well as in other areas, the reforms I have described were not motivated by a concern for fiscal savings and did not suffer extraordinary cutbacks. In general, the educational innovations were aimed at reinforcing the public education system, reducing allocative inequalities, and enhancing average spending per student. Notwithstanding the fiscal adjustment, the education policies we have described in this chapter were far from what has sometimes been characterized as a "neoliberal" model of social reform.

How was this possible? Who were the actors that pushed this process forward, and what factors enabled them to accomplish their reform objectives? I have emphasized the crucial, "top-down" role of the reform team that dominated the Ministry of Education during the eight years of the Cardoso presidency (1995–2002). Both the policies and political influence of these reformers reflected a close connection between the education minister and the president, a connection based on their shared experiences as leaders of the PSDB. Along with their strong ideological commitment to reform, the members of this team could build on an institutional legacy of local and state-level reform originating during the second half of the 1980s, and on their own experiences as education leaders within their respective states and cities.

At the same time, other actors have lacked the organization and political resources that might have enabled them to promote or block policy changes in Brazil. The delay in education reform before the mid-1990s may in fact be attributed in part to the lack of strong, nationally organized advocates for change, as well as to the reluctance of stakeholders to support changes. Because of the dispersion of more than 5,000 municipalities, primary school teachers could never be organized as a national political force, even though some local associations have acquired visibility in recent years. State-level school teachers' unions have expressed opposition to municipal decentralization, out of concern that they would fare less well in dealing with municipal authorities. Nevertheless, they have typically limited their demands to issues of pay.

Municipal authorities, especially in the state capitals and larger cities, have also been reluctant to expand their own primary education systems. Apart from school construction, they had few political or electoral incentives to do so, and they have been reluctant for fiscal reasons to increase expenditures beyond constitutionally mandated obligations. As we have seen in this chapter, the educational reforms of the mid-1990s made an attempt to increase the involvement of parents and community councils. However, parents traditionally have not been crucial actors. Since the 1970s, much of the middle class had exited from the public school system. And although education laws in most states have mandated the formation of parent–teacher councils, these had not been active.

The success of top-down reformers, despite the absence of broader pressures for decentralization, owed a great deal to a strategy characterized by the following elements:

- strong financial incentives to states and municipalities concerning primary education level;

- the flexible implementation of at least three models of decentralization (to states, to municipalities, and to school units), which allowed Education Ministry authorities to negotiate different kinds of support with different state governors and mayors;
- the reformers' intensive use of three sets of political resources: the political support of the president and of the first lady for Education Ministry measures, and the strong regulatory capacity and political bargaining power of the Education Ministry and, in general, of the federal government, both to obtain congressional approval and to implement reforms; and
- the introduction of strong innovations in ministry's own educational programs, such as those used in the School Lunch Program and PMDE. Besides the decentralization objective, the ministry hoped these programs would have demonstration effects on the states' and municipalities' own education programs.

It is somewhat ironic that the Education Ministry's success in deploying its bargaining resources led to changes that fundamentally reduced its own discretionary power. In my opinion, this irony reflects two aspects of the reformers' motivations. One was their strong ideological commitment to decentralization, which they conceived as a necessary condition for democratizing and enhancing the efficiency of education policy. The other aspect was a political strategy that sought to capitalize on the momentum generated by the more general wave of institutional reform backed by the government coalition. By the end of Cardoso's term, the "silent revolution" in education—despite being focused mainly on the primary level—was widely understood as the most successful achievement of the government in the social policy domain.

References

Afonso, J. R. 1996. Um diagnóstico (breve e preliminar) do atual padrão de financiamento e gasto com educação no Brasil. Ministério da Educação, Brasília (unpublished).

Almeida, Ivan. C. 2001. A comparação internacional de indicadores de financiamento e gasto com educação. *Em Aberto* 74, no. 18: 121–35.

Croso Silva, Camila, I-Juca-Pirama Camargo Gil, and Maria Clara Di Pierro. 1999. *Política educacional no Brasil: Avaliando o primeiro ano do FUNDEF;* available at www.acaoeducativa.org/TEXTOS06.

Draibe, Sônia M. 1994. As políticas sociais do regime militar brasileiro. In *21 anos de Regime Militar,* ed. Gláucio A. Dillon Soares and Maria Celina D. Araújo. Rio de Janeiro: Fundação Getúlio Vargas.

―――, ed. 1998a. *Avaliação da descentralização de recursos do FNDE e da merenda escolar: Síntese dos resultados.* Brasília: INEP-MEC.

―――. 1998b. La reciente descentralización de la política Brasileña de ensensañaza básica y de salud. In *La descentralización de la educación y de la salud: Un análisis comparativo de la experiencia latinoamericana,* ed. Cominnetti e Gropello. Santiago de Chile: Comisión Económica para América Latina y el Caribe.

―――. 1999. A reforma da educação no Brasil: A experiência da descentralização de recursos no ensino fundamental estudos de casos. In *Reformas em educación y salud em América Latina y el Caribe,* ed. Sergio Martinic, Cristian Aedo, and Javier Corvalán. Santiago: CIDE-ILADES-BID-CIID.

―――. 2001. A experiência brasileira recente de reforma dos programas sociais. *Socialis* 5: 131–58.

―――. 2002a. The Brazilian Welfare State in Perspective: Old Issues, New Possibilities. In *The State of Social Welfare: The Twentieth Century in Cross-National Review,* ed. John P. Dixon and Robert Scheurell. Westport, Conn.: Greenwood-Praeger.

―――. 2002b. Social Policies in the Nineties. In *Brazil in the 1990s: An Economy in Transition,* ed. Renato Baumann. Saint Anthony's Series. London: Palgrave Publishers and Houndmills.

Durham, E. 1993 O sistema federal do ensino superior: problemas e alternativas. *Revista Brasileira de Ciencias Sociais* (ANPOCS) 23.

IBGE (Instituto Brasileiro de Geografia e Estatística). 1992. *Censo populacional, 1991.* Rio de Janeiro: IBGE.

―――. 2001. *Censo populacional, 2000.* Rio de Janeiro: IBGE.

MEC (Ministério da Educação). 1999. *Balanço do primeiro ano do FUNDEF;* available at www.mec.gov.br/sef/fundef/pdf/aval1998.pdf.

―――. 2003. FUNDEF: Relatório sintético 1998–2002; available at www.mec.gov.br/sef/fundef/pdf/balanco9802.pdf.

MEC-INEP-SEC (Ministério da Educação, Instituto Nacional de Estudos e Pesquisas Educacionais, and Serviço de Estatística da Educação e Cultura). 2002. *Números da educação no Brasil;* available at www.inep.gov.br/estatisticas/numeros/2001/.

NEPP (Núcleo de Estudos de Políticas Públicas). 1989. *Brasil 1987: Relatório sobre a situação social do país.* Campinas: Universidade Estadual de Campinas.

OECD (Organization for Economic Cooperation and Development). 1998. *Education at a Glance: OECD Indicators.* Paris: OECD.

Rodriguez, Alberto, and Carlos A. Herrán. 2000. *Educação secundária no Brasil: Chegou a Hora.* Washington, D.C.: Inter-American Development Bank and World Bank.

Semeguini, Ulisses C. 2001. Fundef: corrigindo distorções históricas. *Em Aberto* 74, no. 18: 43–57.

Soares, Serguei. 1998. *The Financing of Education in Brazil.* Human Development Department Paper 17. Washington, D.C.: World Bank.

Chapter 14

Empowering Parents while Making Them Pay: Autonomous Schools and Education Reform Processes in Nicaragua

Alec Ian Gershberg

Introduction: Philosophical and Political Underpinnings of Nicaraguan Education Reform

This chapter explores the benefits, pitfalls, and politics of the school reform process around the Nicaraguan Autonomous Schools Program (ASP). The ASP has transferred more power from the state *to* parents, while demanding more *from* parents, than any other school reform in the Americas. The ASP and the social movements behind it represent an important school governance reform on the world development stage, and especially in Latin America. School reform in Nicaragua exemplifies how market-oriented strategies are being incorporated into elementary and secondary school governance, and it raises a key question: Did Nicaragua go too far by charging fees for public schools, even if it greatly empowered parents at the same time?

In addition, Nicaragua followed a reform model that could be cate-
gorized as putting the reform cart before the legislative horse: Nearly ten
years passed between when the reform was first implemented and the very
recent passing of a law to support it. Thus, though the Nicaraguan reform
process was strategically risky, it also created space for learning by doing
despite the absence of initial legislative support, and indeed it created a
great deal of change in a short period of time. Whatever one thinks of the
merits of the reform, it is clear that the education reform process in Nicaragua was far more effective than most at implementing the changes
intended by its creators. This chapter seeks to shed light on that decade-
long progress.[1]

During the past decade, the multilateral development community has
strongly supported decentralization of education in Latin America. Too
little is known about the actual attributes of such policies, which often go
hand in hand with a call for increased parental and community involvement. Too little is also known about the nature of reform processes most
likely to prove successful in navigating difficult political waters and foster
beneficial educational outcomes. The origin of the call for increased participation is broad-based; it has been both top-down (e.g., from central
governments and/or the multilateral community) and more rarely bottom-
up (e.g., from grassroots organizations and nongovernmental organizations,
or NGOs). The ASP implemented a system of school-based management,
creating local school councils that (1) had a voting majority of parents and
(2) allocated resources that derived in part from fees charged to parents.
These councils had (and continue to have) broad powers including hiring
and firing school principals. Nowhere in the Americas have parents officially been given so much responsibility, and nowhere have they been
asked to provide directly such a large proportion of school resources.[2] In

1. This chapter relies significantly upon and updates Gershberg (1999a, 1999b,
1999c)—which were based on relevant interviews and fieldwork in 1996—and Winkler
and Gershberg (2000). Additional fieldwork and interviews were performed in 2000 and
2001.

2. Reforms in Chicago transferred a similar amount of power to parents but have not
required any cash or in-kind contributions from them. By far the most contentious and
controversial component of the ASP was the imposition upon parents of fees used, at
least in part, to augment teacher salaries. For example, for a poor family, the monthly
payments if fully collected could hardly be called inconsequential. Fees for a family
with six children could easily be 50 percent of household income. Naturally, the result
was that they did not pay some or all of the fees, or they discouraged their children from
attending.

addition, there are officially municipal-level councils that aggregate the school-site councils and bring in mayors and other municipal stakeholders. Table 14.1 summarizes the overall nature of the Nicaraguan reforms, including which factors and characteristics were decentralized and which remained (or became more) centralized.

Educational decentralization in Latin America (and elsewhere) has taken two basic forms: (1) the transfer of power from higher to lower levels of government, or from more centralized units of one government to more

Table 14.1

Framework for Analyzing Accountability in the Nicaraguan Autonomous Schools Program

Framework Aspect	Comment and Summary Judgment
I. Finance	*Significant transfer of central authority to schools.* Though the Education Ministry continues to finance the system centrally, contributions to schools from parents play a growing role in resources available to schools for the first five years. Now, their role appears to be diminishing. Schools have greater control on the expenditure side; principals and school councils have increased discretion over spending patterns. Councils altered centrally suggested levels of contribution; however, there is a strong, if nontransparent, central role in financially supporting poor autonomous schools over poor state schools. Regarding grants-in-aid, the ministry uses newly developed grants to autonomous schools to transfer resources for salaries, benefits, maintenance, and utilities based on capitation principles and average costs at the school before autonomy. But transfers are not truly formula driven.
II. Auditing and evaluation (financial, performance, operational, and program)	*Moderate transfer of central authority.* Very little change in central functions regarding financial audits, which rely on a small number of random audits and analysis of departmental performance reviews. Some increased vigilance on the part of parents and teachers due to interest in financial contributions to schools. School and municipal councils perform program evaluations but may be ineffective due to lack of sufficient training. Strong recentralization of evaluation as the central government began a new and much more comprehensive method of quantitative and qualitative evaluations concomitantly with the Nicaraguan Autonomous Schools Program.

continued

Table 14.1
Continued

Framework Aspect	Comment and Summary Judgment
III. Regulation and policy development	*Little change in central authority.* Norms, standards, textbooks, and basic curriculum still developed centrally. New centrally developed curriculum has proven popular. Local councils have some leeway in (1) developing curriculum, though they have done so little in practice; and (2) text selection, though the Education Ministry only pays for their own. Little or no attention by local actors to improving teaching methods.
IV. Demand-driven mechanisms (expression of demand)	*Significant change in some schools.* Required, voluntary, and (in some cases) extorted fees reflected and influenced parental demand for schooling, especially at the secondary level. Participation of parents in local councils provides community input to provision of services.
V. Democratic mechanisms (voting, citizen participation, and conflict resolution)	*Significant transfer of central authority de jure; varied results de facto.* Where school councils function according to norms, parents, through elected representatives, are given significant voice in school policy including budget, personnel, and curriculum. Principals are elected by the school councils.
VI. Service provider choice/mix (public, private, and nongovernmental organization provision)	*Little change.* Although autonomous schools represent a significant change in school administration, the public sector is still responsible for service provision. Parents do not have increased capacity to choose schools via vouchers or other mechanisms. Nongovernmental organizations and private organizations do not run autonomous schools.
VII. Civil service and management systems	*Very significant change in central authority.* Principals and the school councils gain considerable control over management of personnel and budget. Municipal-level Education Ministry delegates are the front line, having gained primary responsibility for recruiting and overseeing autonomous schools, training participants, and resolving disputes.

Source: Framework developed in Gershberg (1998a, 1998b).

decentralized units of the same government; and (2) the transfer of power to schools (as occurred in Nicaragua). As Winkler and Gershberg note (2000, 203):

The two types of education decentralization—to lower levels of government and to individual schools—have very different origins and aims.

The decentralization of education to lower levels of government has almost without exception been undertaken in the context of a more general decentralization of government, the causes of which vary widely. The decentralization of education to individual schools, on the other hand, has typically been motivated by concerns about poor school performance. Both types of education decentralization are well represented in Latin America.

In addition, while nearly all education decentralization in Latin America has taken place in a politically charged environment, the political and economic context in Nicaragua was particularly turbulent and ideologically conflictual. More than four decades of often violent and oppressive dictatorship under the Somoza family ended with a revolutionary war in 1979. The Cuban-inspired leftist government of Daniel Ortega and the Frente Sandinista de Liberación Nacional (FSLN) ruled during the 1980s, but it experienced nearly continuous threats from United States–backed counter-revolutionaries, commonly called the Contras. The FSLN submitted to democratic elections in 1990 and lost to a conservative-centrist government coalition—led by Violetta Chamorro and the National Opposition Union (UNO)—with many ties to expatriats who had lost property and fled the country during the FSLN rule.

Shortly after the election, the UNO coalition began to unravel under withering splits and attacks by the most conservative forces in its coalition. Chamorro was left in the difficult position of having to choose between making deals with radical conservatives on the one hand, and embittered Marxists on the other. Moreover, these fractious politics were also found in the divisions and battles between various teachers' unions, which left the union movement considerably weaker and less unified than in most Latin American countries attempting educational decentralization.

Finally, one must mention that mother nature has not been kind to Nicaragua either. An earthquake that devastated Managua in 1972 and Hurricane Mitch in 1998 (by some accounts the worst natural disaster of the century) are merely the two most prominent in a series of misfortunes that have helped make Nicaragua the second poorest country in the Americas (after Haiti). The country is often at the mercy of international aid organizations to provide even the most basic government services.

In this context, the confluence of transferring responsibilities to school councils and the charging of fees is not coincidental. Both derive from social movements solidly within the so-called "neoliberal" reform model espoused by both the multilateral development community and the conservative government that came to power in Nicaragua in 1990.[3] The layering of this philosophy over the famous 1980s Sandinista grassroots education movements provides an opportunity to examine how the government implemented, via its education policies, a new system of tenets and beliefs about the nature of the state and its role in providing social services.

In fact, the philosophical contrast could not be starker between the Sandinistas' socialist education philosophy and the market-orientation and religious bent of the government that came to power democratically in 1990. Both governments used education's power to indoctrinate a culture, but to very different ends.[4] Politically and financially, after 1990 it was advantageous for Nicaragua to align its reforms with the general models of decentralization actively supported by the World Bank and other international donors. Interestingly, the underlying philosophy of the ASP would appear to favor bringing many actors in civil society into the provision and support of education, but this has not been the case. Although the ministry in the 1990s often had a stated goal of bringing in and working with civil society (including both religious and nonreligious NGOs and mayors), it has not happened. In part, this may be due to the facts that NGOs are largely associated with the Sandinistas, and mayors were essentially cut out of the administrative power structure of the ASP.[5]

The reforms cut to the core purpose of public education. The implementation of fees, on the one hand, has raised questions about the privatization of public education and has exposed the Nicaraguan government to claims that it is sacrificing the public interest for the sake of economic stability. On the other hand, the high level of parental involvement and school autonomy

3. See Walker (1997, 16) for a summary of the common usage of the concept. I put the word "neoliberal" in quotation marks because I believe that its ubiquitous use has diluted and in some cases obfuscated its meaning. In addition, the word now carries nearly universally negative connotations, and I do not necessarily wish to imply such connotations.

4. In this sense, *both* governments could claim to be followers of Paolo Freire's *Pedagogy of the Oppressed* (1974). Freire certainly was prescient when he said "I am certain that Christians and Marxists, though they may disagree with me in part or whole, will continue reading to the end" (1974, 21). Both governments also prove Richard Shaull's assertion in the preface to the 1974 edition of Freire: "There is no such thing as a *neutral* education process" (p. 15).

5. In fieldwork performed in 2000, we looked specifically to interview actors from civil society (other than parents and parent associations) involved with autonomous schools. We had great difficulty even finding appropriate interviewees and little evidence of involvement from them. This was particularly surprising in the case of local priests and other religious leaders, given the nature and philosophy of the reforms.

hold promise for improved educational outcomes (Winkler and Gershberg 2000). In addition, the official tax system is so weak that any innovative means to channel more resources to schools deserves serious consideration. Nevertheless, questions about the equity of the reforms are paramount, and it is clear now that the program's benefits did not accrue to very poor people as much as to those in a better position to pay.

Background: Educational Outcomes and Investments in Nicaragua

Pre-Sandinista education was highly centralized. The Ministry of Public Education (MOE) governed national education at all levels, controlling central administration, supervision, planning, and extension and development (Arrien 1977, 176).[6] Education made up 15 percent of total government expenditure in 1976. There were, however, elements of community economic involvement within many of the schools. Most primary schools had an Economic Committee that organized fund-raising activities, such as raffles and food sales. These funds were used for buying school materials and for paying the equivalent of school custodians. Some primary schools also used a quota system, charging the equivalent of less than a dollar in 1974. This quota system was established by parents of students, to add to central funding.[7] Secondary school students also paid fees directly to their schools for matriculation, exams and diplomas. Registering students paid 35 córdobas (roughly five dollars) in 1974. Thus, there was an established history of parental monetary contributions under Somoza, before the Sandinistas and before the 1990s.

The state of education during the final years of the Somoza era was dire, in part because of the country's lack of recovery from the 1972 earthquake. Between 1970 and 1975, in rural communities only 5.3 percent of children made it past the sixth grade, and 83 percent of the school-age population (6–29) did not attend school. Dropout rates were less serious in urban communities, with 44 percent of children passing the sixth grade. Overcrowding of classrooms was a serious issue. Rural schools averaged 49 students per classroom and urban averaged 51. The MOE was, however, addressing this issue before the earthquake, and with international as-

6. University education was an exception; according to Arrien, university education operated autonomously in developing curriculum and administratively. Unless otherwise noted, the data in this paragraph and the text are taken from Arrien and Kauffman (1977).

7. Arrien points out this quota system disappeared after the 1973 earthquake.

sistance it constructed 303 schoolrooms between 1968 and 1972. Nationally, nearly half the total population was illiterate in 1975.

Despite touted improvements in educational outcomes under the FSLN, conditions improved little in many primary and secondary schools during the 1980s. The Chamorro government inherited a system in which official government estimates showed only 19 percent of students satisfactorily completed primary school; the yearly primary school dropout rate was also 19 percent; and the secondary school enrollment rate was 25 percent of the eligible population, with a 15 percent yearly dropout rate (Government of Nicaragua 1996). In fact, reliable data (comparable to that available for other countries) for the period of Sandinista rule are largely unavailable because many of the international organizations that compute such data were unable to request or receive them.

In general, the country made advances in primary school coverage in the 1990s, but rates of repetition, dropout, and primary school inefficiency remain high in comparison with the rest of Latin America and even other similar Central American neighbors. Overall educational expenditure was a respectable 3.9 percent of gross domestic product in 1997 (PREAL 2002), up very slightly from 3.5 percent in 1980. However, educational spending in Nicaragua is more skewed toward tertiary education than perhaps any other country in Latin America. The national constitution stipulates that 6 percent of central government spending must go to universities (traditionally a Sandinista stronghold). Although university students represent about 3 percent of the student population, about a third of education spending is targeted to them. Primary and secondary teachers are paid poorly, about $42 and $53 per month in basic salary, respectively. Four out of five students attend public (state) schools,[8] and the rest attend private schools, some of which receive government support.

Except for some funds raised locally by schools (discussed in detail below), all funds for public schools come from the central Education Ministry. In primary and secondary school, there are large gaps between urban and rural areas, especially because the latter often have schools that do not offer all years of primary school. Rural teachers and school directors have less training and experience and are often not graduates of normal schools or other certification programs. Nationally, about one-third of teachers are not certified correctly for the subject matter or level they are teaching, and this figure reaches about two-thirds in rural areas. Only about 7 percent of

8. This can be disaggregated to 84 percent of primary school students, 68 percent of secondary, and 42 percent of preschool (IDB 1999).

secondary school students are in rural areas, though about one-third of the national population is rural.[9]

By official counts, gross primary school coverage is 97 percent.[10] The largest problems stem from poor quality, which plays a key role in the facts that only 23 percent of primary students finish without repeating a grade and fewer than half ever finish sixth grade. More than 90 percent of students finishing sixth grade enroll in secondary school, but more than 18 percent drop out in the first year, and only half graduate. The 1998 literacy rate among those of age fifteen to twenty-four years is only 78 percent, and the adult literacy rate is only 67 percent, among the worst in the Americas and even poor in comparison with El Salvador, Guatemala, and Honduras (UNDP 2000; PREAL 2002).

Reform Carts and Legislative Horses

Most countries follow educational reform strategies that first create a legal and legislative framework for reform and then implement changes. Nicaragua was one of the very few that did the opposite, putting the reform cart before the legislative horse, so to speak. Here we examine how this was done and the implications for implementing successful reforms. We describe and analyze how the MOE at first created two decentralization programs but fully implemented only one. Next we examine how they did this, and in particular we focus on the fostering of school-based management, citizen participation, and the strategic dichotomy of having a ministry-led versus a legislature-led reform process.

Educational Decentralization Strategies: Autonomous Schools versus Municipalization

Under the FSLN regime, the Nicaraguan system of basic education was highly centralized, although during and after the 1979 revolutionary war, the tradition of local payments by parents to support secondary schools was solidified (Arnove 1994, 109). The most famous educational reform of the

9. The data in this paragraph and the next are drawn from IDB (1999) and UNDP (2000).

10. The 97 percent figure comes from IDB (1999). Note that UNDP (2000) reports that only 78.6 percent of the primary school age cohort was enrolled in 1997. PREAL (2002) reports *net* primary and secondary enrollment rates of about 83 and 24 percent, respectively.

revolutionary period was the literacy campaign, which has been well chronicled by Arnove (1994). Nicaragua's social revolution played out in a significant way through its education system. The literacy campaign itself was devised as a means to pull the country together through a system of voluntarism and education. Interestingly, this strategy required highly centralized bureaucratic control.[11]

With the change of government in 1990, decentralization arose as a goal of the new, in essence counterrevolutionary, government; education decentralization was thus a highly politicized and ideological component of the new conservative administration. But the attempt to use education as a principal means of effecting radical social change was still a characteristic of the government strategy in Nicaragua. Thus, after the 1990 elections brought Chamorro and the UNO to power, followed by the Liberal Party of Arnoldo Alemán in November 1996, there were policy efforts to transfer more responsibility and decision making to the subnational and school level.

As was mentioned, the system under the Sandinistas had been highly centralized, with a bloated central bureaucracy; in one of its first reform efforts, the Chamorro government reduced the staff of the central ministry by more than 50 percent by 1992 (Arnove 1994, 102), one year before the policy reform efforts in this study began. Although there is no proof that these cuts were politically driven, it is possible that these personnel moves were motivated by more than simply efficiency gains. The U.S. Agency for International Development (USAID) offered a severance plan of about $2,000 for MOE officials to leave the public sector, and Arnove points out that

> the leadership of ANDEN [the main teachers' union] notes that although teacher petitions to opt out of employment were not automatically granted by [MOE] administrators, in those cases involving ANDEN militants, the petition was always granted as part of a general move to diminish the influence of Sandinista-affiliated teachers' union.

Both the Chamorro and the Alemán administrations were relatively conservative and at least partial adherents to the "neoliberal model" (see

11. As Arnove and Torres (1995, 318) assert: "Nicaragua, during the period of Sandinista rule, 1979–1990, represents the case of a revolutionary society attempting to use education as a principal means of effecting radical social change and overcoming the historic traits of a 'conditioned state.'"

Walker 1997). On this background, the major post-1990 policy reform associated with education decentralization was the ASP. The second policy reform of the decade labeled as decentralization by the Education Ministry was La Municipalización de la Educación (the municipalization of education, or "municipalization"), a program through which municipalities received fiscal transfers to administer school payrolls and other limited powers. Post-1992 education reforms in Nicaragua also functioned in conjunction with an effort to establish municipal-level education councils intended to further involve municipal and other local stakeholders.[12]

The reforms were the brainchild of the minister of education, Humberto Belli, a dynamic, well-trained conservative (and an open advocate of Christian values) who garnered solid support from the development community (in particular the World Bank, the Inter-American Development Bank, and USAID).[13] Belli was the only minister from the UNO government to be reappointed by President Alemán, indicating that the new government considered the autonomous schools program, the most prominent educational reform fostered under the previous government, a success.[14]

As is often the case in smaller (and poorer) countries, international financial institutions played a strong role in both financing and providing technical support for Nicaraguan education reform, and in many ways, were the impetus behind decentralization. USAID played an essential role in funding the adoption and distribution of new textbooks in 1991 (Arnove 1994, 79). USAID also financed the aforementioned "occupational conversion," which encouraged officials in many parts of government to leave. Also, the market force logic and education research that was used for justifying and planning reform came directly from World Bank and USAID

12. Nicaragua has seventeen regional governmental units called departments that have hardly any own-source revenues and no elected head such as a governor, and are essentially regional administrative extensions of the central government. Within them, there are 143 municipalities that have more autonomy: municipal presidents are elected, and a significant number are from opposition parties including the Sandinistas. The Ministry of Education appoints a departmental director of education in each department and a municipal delegate in each municipality.

13. See Kampwirth (1997) for a concise summary of the Christian values and ideological framework of the education administration and teaching materials in the 1990s.

14. In addition, one should not underestimate Belli's personal skills in his ability to survive the change in government, as well as his U.S. academic credentials and his international stature. He was, for instance, asked to direct the reform of the Ecuadorian educational decentralization.

education research and policy. World Bank studies were frequently cited by
MOE officials in explaining allocation of funds and reform policies.

The ASP grew impressively rapidly after its inception in 1993. According to King and others (1996), about 100 secondary schools and more than
200 single primary schools had entered the program in three years. There
were approximately 250 secondary schools and 4,288 primary and pre-
schools nationally. Primary schools became eligible for autonomy only in
1995. In terms of scope, approximately 8,000 of the 32,000 primary and
secondary public school teachers in the country taught in autonomous
schools by the end of 1996. By 2000, more than 50 percent of primary
school students and approximately 80 percent of secondary students were
in autonomous schools.

The story with municipalization was significantly different. Many countries (e.g., Brazil and Chile) implemented policies that transfer some school
administration responsibilities to municipalities. Nicaragua, through the
Municipalization Program, was no exception. At the same time that the
Education Ministry first started developing and promoting the ASP as one
form of decentralization, it formulated and began to implement a municipalization process that transferred certain limited powers to municipalities
chosen to participate. Early publicity from the ministry touted the two
programs equally as efforts to "decentralize." Although the ASP grew
rapidly despite lacking a legislative base, municipalization—which was
started at the same time as the ASP, also by ministerial directives—was all
but abandoned as a national reform by 1996. Fewer than 10 percent of the
nation's municipalities had entered the program in the four years since its
inception. Because this seems to have occurred because of a policy decision
within the ministry to prioritize the ASP, it can certainly be counted as
beneficial that the Municipalization Program was not legislated.[15] Such a
process would have resulted in a large waste of administrative effort as well
as large expenditure of political capital. One interesting lesson learned is
that a central ministry can indeed set up two reforms, one more controversial than the other, as a way to hedge its administrative investments.

The basic components of school autonomy involved

15. One could argue that the municipalization program was not popular with the
central government because it could involve transferring power to Sandinista mayors
while both principals and MOE municipal delegates were generally considered *puestos
de confianza* (political appointments) of the the MOE. In any case, it is clear that the
ASP was the preferred program from the start.

- a monthly fiscal transfer to the school principal to pay for teacher salaries, benefits, and basic maintenance; teachers received their salary in cash rather than checks;
- the formation of a Consejo Directivo (Directive School Council), a school site council led by the school director, with a voting majority of parents, charged with powers over budget, personnel, and (officially) some curricular decisions and evaluation and planning functions; and
- the implementation of supposedly mandatory school fees for secondary school students and supposedly voluntary school fees for primary students; the fees—which could be for monthly attendance and/or exams, registration forms, and services such as diploma processing and library use (e.g., the use of a computer lab)—were used to augment teacher salaries or pay for other operations as deemed necessary.

Though it represented a fundamental change in the way that a significant portion of the national system of education was governed, the ASP was not established in national law. The ASP had not been ratified by the national legislature or approved by other elected officials, but rather was governed for nearly ten years by a series of Education Ministry internal directives, many of which were not in the public domain. The ministry officials proudly proclaimed that the reform process was one of "*hechos no de derechos*" (accomplishments, not laws). This provides an interesting alternative to the more common process in countries like Colombia and Mexico, where the decentralization legislation was well-established as a prerequisite to reform. This strategy provided some tangible benefits aside from the mere speed of the reform. The Nicaraguan government, and the ministry more specifically, learned a great deal from the early experiences of the ASP—and this knowledge undoubtedly positively affected the legal and administrative framework (as we explore below).

This tactic also played a role in a more general strategy for weakening the largest teachers' union, the Asociación Nacional de Educadores de Nicaragua (ANDEN, National Association of Nicaraguan Educators), which was still politically associated with the Sandinistas. Kampwirth (1997, 122) notes: "The new MOE sought to relate to a civil society that was organized from above—that is, by the MOE itself," and one could argue that the purging of the Ministry, the abandonment of muncipalization, and the strengthening of municipal delegates and school directors all played a role in wresting power in the education sector from Sandinista supporters. None of the participatory mechanisms examined in this study provides space for union participation. Four teachers' unions vie for power, and several ministry officials and even union representatives we interviewed stated that it was the fighting among them that had allowed the autonomous schools program to succeed, particularly because it had enabled the government to exclude them from the policy formation process. One sign of decreased union power was the declining willingness of teachers to participate in strikes. An implication that emerges is that weakened union power simplifies the fight to implement controversial decentralization reforms.

Kampwirth (1997, 122) adds that "there is an important difference between the Sandinista conception of civil society as comprised of *organizations,* albeit imperfectly autonomous organizations, and the Chamorro administration's conception of civil society as based on *individuals.*" Thus, the ministry's chosen strategy was part of an attempt to alter the power dynamics in the education sector inherited from the Sandinistas, including the inculcation of Christian values. The Nicaraguan strategy of relying on ministry directives rather than law avoided a very bitter legislative battle over the program. At the same time, it helped establish some of the merits of the program first, and this helped the reform survive years of bitter legislative negotiations.

The danger with this strategy is, of course, that the reform is more easily reversible until it is firmly and legally established. Luckily (for ministry officials and others in Nicaragua favoring the ASP), the results of the 1996 presidential election probably assured the program's short-run survival. The minister of education was the only minister from the Chamorro government to be reappointed by President Alemán. However, at the end of the Chamorro administration, uncertainty both imperiled the program's stability and put many participants in a "wait and see" mode.[16] Yet another pitfall with this process has been considerable confusion (or even purposeful manipulation) on the part of government officials and other participants over the precise rules governing the ASP, as is discussed below. For instance, the rules for school councils picking school directors have changed several times, as have the practices and policies concerned with the fees.

16. A new minister could have discarded the ASP with a wave of his or her pen. The number of schools entering autonomy ground to a near halt in the last six months of the Chamorro government.

The Process and Politics of Fostering Autonomous Schools

Secondary schools were targeted for autonomy first. The logic was that they were larger, fewer in number, generally run by more experienced principals, and more accustomed to charging fees than primary schools. Presumably, these characteristics contributed to the early success of the program. The size of the schools helped ensure that the fees imposed would generate significant additional income. Their smaller number allowed the program to have a quick and significant impact. Their more experienced principals provided much needed leadership, and their history of fees helped quell public outcry over the increased cost to parents. In addition, the ministry hand-picked the first twenty secondary schools for their strong, competent leadership and their capable and interested parents. The lesson here is obvious but worth stating: Determine the features that will make success most likely, start with a few model schools, and make sure they work.

From 1993 on, the autonomous schools program relied heavily on the municipal Ministry of Education delegates in each of the 143 municipalities. Mostly women and many of them former teachers, these officials were almost exclusively loyal to the ministry and not to the Sandinistas. Moreover, the education delegates create an important presence for the central government at the local level because they exist in each and every municipality.

The ministry recognized the need for a cadre of loyal local representatives to promote the program and make sure that its ideology was presented in the most attractive possible light. With support from USAID, it trained its delegates in the philosophy, goals, and components of the reform and the strategies for promoting it. This training took place in a central location, and it is clear from our interviews that it served its purposes well. In addition to the initial training, delegates received assistance in overcoming some of the obstacles encountered in the early stages. For instance, opponents of the autonomous schools program (most prominently ANDEN) publicly equated autonomy with privatization; the delegates we interviewed could all eloquently explain, from the ministry's point of view, the difference between the two concepts.[17]

---

17. The argument over the correctness of labeling the autonomous schools program as "privatization" is instructive. It is true that the program does not fit the traditional and popular definition of the term. Autonomous schools are not private schools independent of the state and its regulations. Public funds do not follow students to private institutions

The first step in the process of becoming an autonomous school was a request by the teachers, often after being urged by the municipal delegate. The teacher vote for autonomy was not, however, a secret ballot, and there were some accusations of teachers being treated differently or even fired depending upon how they voted (Fuller and Rivarola 1998). Because many of the teachers who voted against autonomy were members of ANDEN, the result was a political battle at the school level. It is not difficult for the teachers to perceive from the outset that autonomy is potentially disadvantageous. The delegates' primary selling point with the teachers in the early years was the promise of increased salaries supported by school fees. This was perhaps the most inventive, if controversial, aspect of the program. Teachers may have had substantial reason to oppose autonomy, particularly because of the new power it gave principals and parents to hire and fire them. The potential for increased pay was an incentive that compensated for the loss of the security often provided by a powerful union. One could argue that it was unnecessary to combine a fee policy with school autonomy, but the government clearly considered fees important to the success of the program. Local financial participation was seen as critical to the enhancement of accountability, and in any case there was a need to raise more money for the sector.

Of course, the long-term effectiveness of increased pay as a way of inducing teachers to participate depends upon the reality of increased pay, and this did not prove consistent. In fact, the monies collected have declined precipitously in many schools in the past three to four years, disappearing in many poor primary schools. Concomitantly, in recent fieldwork in twelve schools, we found a generally low level of participation of teachers in the councils compared with parents and directors.

After entering autonomy, a school was governed by the principal along with the school-site council, which always had a voting majority of par-

---

as a result of the program, and the autonomous schools continue to receive per-student allocations from the state. Private groups cannot set up their own schools and receive funds via the program; it is not a voucher program. Although the school-site councils have some power over personnel, budgeting, and curriculum, all their decisions are overseen by the ministry at both the local and the regional level. The fee system is a form of user charge, which, while unarguably within the neoliberal ideology, is not the same as privatization. Nevertheless, by some definitions (see Fox and Riew 1984), the increase in the proportion of funding received from parents constitutes at least a partial privatization of public school finance.

ents.[18] In practice, parent members are selected in a variety of manners, some more democratic than others. "More democratic" practices observed included the election of all parents in a general assembly and the election of all teachers, regardless of rank or seniority. "Less democratic" practices observed included the selection of all parents and/or teachers by the school principal, the mayor, and/or the ministry delegate. Thus, the vagueness in the rules or laxness in their enforcement—in part a result of the ministry's strategy of "accomplishments, not laws"—allowed school-site councils to be selected idiosyncratically. It is clear that, given such opportunity, local actors will interpret the rules of the game on their own and that principals, teachers, parents, municipal officials, and ministry delegates will compete for control of the organism that is granted considerable power over school governance.

In primary school, the fees were voluntary by constitutional law. However, in the early years of reform, instances of teachers refusing to administer exams to nonpaying primary school students were not rare, and even cases of teachers or principals refusing to admit students occurred. In these situations, the ministry delegates and the mayors played a key role in conflict resolution by "reminding" school staff that the fees were voluntary. But even if they were often successful in supporting the students, it is hard to escape the class-based social environment created within the institutions that are supposed to play an equalizing role. The ministry could have mollified this situation by firming up guidelines and by using what it learned in the early stages of the reform to incorporate these guidelines into law.

Schools exhibited a broad range of fee-collection strategies. In relation to the size of the monthly transfer received from the ministry, total fee collection ranged from zero to as much as 161 percent in a small sample of schools we examined in 1996. In other words, some schools derived nothing from fees, while others used them to more than double their available resources. Fee policy was set by the school councils, obviously based only loosely upon ministry guidelines. Councils allocated fee revenue according to the priorities they established.[19]

18. See Gershberg (1999a) for official rules for council membership.
19. Interviews revealed that if fee revenue was substantial, the councils typically allocated half to teacher remuneration and half to maintenance/repair; purchase of furniture or other amenities, e.g., computers or library books; and/or social events. However, if fee revenue was low, councils tended to cut the teacher remuneration first.

Table 14.2 shows more recent data for all autonomous schools. Though most schools in 1999 collected little or no fee revenue (less than 2 percent), the majority did collect at least some, and many schools collected significant revenues, more than 5 percent. Because the funds collected are discretionary, even 5 percent of total revenue could be nearly all discretionary spending.

Citizen Participation and Autonomous Schools

It is clear that the level of genuine citizen participation generated by the ASP was significant in many schools. School-site committees are given real powers and parents have a voting majority. The committees were constituted and functioning at every school we visited in both 1996 and 2000, and King and others (1996) presented preliminary results indicating that school governance improved and that most stakeholders supported the reform. We noted that the committees made important decisions, in several instances voting to replace the school principal and deciding how to allocate revenues from fees. This provides some support for the hypotheses (e.g., as developed by Esman and Uphoff 1984) that participatory groups perform better when given (1) more than advisory status and (2) the responsibility to raise and manage funds.[20]

In addition, it is clear that the reform strategy followed by the ministry played a helpful role in fostering effective school councils. The rules governing the councils changed form several times (e.g., size guidelines were revised to allow smaller councils), and the methods for selecting council members were reworked based on early experiences. Finally, the ministry was able to choose a few schools that were likely to succeed early and then to hold them up as examples for the rest of the country. The Nicaraguan reform strategy clearly created a space for learning by doing that supported the swift spread of the ASP.

In early February 2002, the Nicaraguan parliament approved the new Ley de Participación Educativa (LPE, Law of Educational Participation). After ten years, the reform now has legal backing. Significantly, the law

---

The salary bonus for teachers ranged from 0 to 50 percent of their monthly income for secondary school teachers and 0 to 30 percent for primary school teachers. Unfortunately, this is probably why we found morale to be particularly low among teachers in very poor, and particularly rural, communities, where autonomy has wrought none of the promised financial rewards for teachers.

20. The hypotheses are explored further in Gershberg (1999c).

Table 14.2

Basic Fees as a Proportion of Central Transfers, Primary and Secondary Schools, Nicaragua, 1998–99

Range of Fee or Type of School	Number of Schools	Percentage of All Schools
Range of fee (percent)		
0	311	42.78
1	106	14.58
2	58	7.98
3	33	4.54
4	21	2.89
5–10	80	11.00
10–15	59	8.12
15–20	32	4.40
20–25	13	1.79
25–30	8	1.10
More than 30	6	0.83
Total number of schools	727	100
Maximum percentage: 35		
Type of school		
Primary	582	80
Secondary	138	19
Primary and secondary	1	0
Not reported	6	1
Total	727	100

Note: Calculated as *aportes voluntarios* and *matriculas* as a percentage of *ingresos* for all schools (AV + MA)/(AV + MA + *transferencias corrientes*). Schools charge fees or encourage contributions for a wide range of activities and services, e.g., computer use, food, school supplies, uniforms, and even library use. Here we look at only *aportes voluntarios,* which are voluntary monthly contributions, and *matriculas,* which are funds solicited upon enrollment.

Source: Calculations made by the author from data provided by the Ministry of Education.

officially does away with autonomous schools (*colegios autónomos*) and replaces them with schools of educational participation (*colegios de participación educativo*). However, the law keeps most aspects of the ASP intact, including the school councils. The name change, at least at present, appears to be a political conciliation though it does provide an indication of how the reform might now proceed. The law, for instance, emphasizes that education must be free and restores the power of the school councils to hire principals. Most important, the law states that all autonomous schools are now schools of educational participation, and that all other schools must soon convert as well. So the spirit of the ASP will now become universal, albeit under a different name.

Table 14.3

Initial Strategic Dichotomy Faced in Education Reform Strategies

(1) *High legislative involvement:* Start with a comprehensive normative and legal framework (e.g., Mexico, Colombia). The Ministry of Education may play a role, perhaps even a leading role, in the development of policies and legislation, but these must pass through the politicized process of gaining approval from the national legislature.

Emphasizes	*Disadvantages*
Consistency	May maximize opposition
Comprehensiveness	Builds in unforeseen problems
Clean sense of final outcomes	Prevents learning by doing
	Enforces a one-size-fits-all approach
	Subsequent changes may be costly
	May emphasize pork-barrel politics

(2) *Low legislative involvement:* Start with de facto changes (e.g., Nicaragua). The Ministry of Education plays the lead role in the development of policies and implements them without gaining approval from the national legislature.

Emphasizes	*Disadvantages*
Operational viability	Reforms vulnerable to reversal or
Local responsiveness	abandonment
Learning by doing	May create confusion or lack of
Subsequent changes may be less costly	transparency
Putting reform in the hands of education	Scandals or mistakes can doom entire
officials	reform

The Initial Strategic Dichotomy Faced in Education Reform Strategies

Clearly, there are advantages and disadvantages to beginning a reform process with a series of changes via ministry directives without strong legal backing. Any reform process confronts an initial strategic dichotomy: (1) Start with a comprehensive normative framework, or (2) start with de facto changes. This dichotomy is summarized in table 14.3.

The first strategy will emphasize consistency, comprehensiveness and a clean sense of what the final outcomes should look like. It has the disadvantage that it can maximize opposition, build in unforeseen problems, and enforce a one-size-fits-all approach. It may also emphasize pork-barrel politics. The second will emphasize operational viability, local responsiveness, and a sense that doing is the best way of learning. It also has the potential advantage of giving education administrators, such as the minister of education—rather than governors or other politicians without specialized knowledge of the education sector—more direct control over policy development while providing an initial buffer to difficult political battles. However, it may yield reforms that are vulnerable to being reversed or abandoned, particularly if political battles are heated and sustained. It may also create confusion or a lack a transparency in the reform process, and scandals or mistakes may put the entire reform movement in jeopardy.

Nicaraguan School Reform in Comparative Perspective

As was described in detail above, the Nicaraguan reforms relate to trends worldwide to bring free-market concepts into school governance. They also fit into the growing trend toward school- based management—or decentralization to schools rather than governments. The World Bank evaluated a range of outcomes of the ASP and was rather positive and supportive.[21] My own work on Nicaragua, while not entirely critical, has been less sanguine.[22]

Conversely, Winkler and Gershberg (2000) show that the trend toward school autonomy (in the absence of charging fees for attendance) does show promising results in Latin America and a few U.S. cities with primarily poor public school populations. They also assert that other forms of decentralization, more akin to municipalization, have yet to show clear-cut success, although there are cases of clear-cut failure. In addition, there is a growing qualitative and quantitative research literature on the characteristics of high-performing or effective schools that mirrors the much larger literature on successful organizations.[23] These intellectual trends dovetail with work on participatory development, empowerment as alternative development, and parental participation.[24] They suggest that high-performing schools are characterized by strong leadership, highly qualified and committed staff, a focus on learning, responsibility for results, and (perhaps) effective parental participation in school governance. For example, Dalin

21. See (1) King et al. (1996); (2) King and Özler (1998); and (3) Fuller and Rivarola (1998).
22. See Gershberg (1999a, 1999c); and Kaestner and Gershberg (2002).
23. See (1) Wohlstetter (1994); (2) Creemers (1994); (3) Darling-Hammond (1997); and (4) Savedoff (1998). For literature on successful organizations, see (1) Barzelay (1992); and (2) Lawler (1992). See also PREAL (2002), which recommends that teacher salaries be linked to performance and that both pre- and in-service training be improved.
24. See (1) Shaeffer (1994); (2) Friedmann (1992); (3) Esman and Uphoff (1984); and (4) Dimmock, Donoghue, and Robb (1996).

(1994) concludes that the essential ingredients in successful reforms are a sustained commitment to quality improvement, local empowerment to adapt programs to local conditions, strong emphasis on school and classroom practice, and strong support linkage between education authorities and the school "via information, assistance, pressure and rewards."

Many analysts (e.g., Esman and Uphoff 1984; Marc 1992; Carrol 1992) have hypothesized and to some extent shown the links between stakeholder participation and improved efficiency, effectiveness, or other outcomes. Table 14.4 presents a summary judgment of the potential factors for improved effectiveness of government services from stakeholder participation in Nicaragua, and overall these judgments suggest that the potential for improvement was very high.

The Organization for Economic Cooperation and Development develops a methodology for measuring the degree of education decentralization, and groups educational functions into four categories: the organization of instruction, personnel management, planning and structures, and resources (OECD 1998). The content of each group is given in table 14.5, along with a summary judgment about the results of the ASP thus far.

Given the difficulty of isolating the effects of such complex reforms on learning and educational attainment, table 14.5 examines how the Nicaraguan reforms have changed factors known to be related to learning. Ultimately, the goal is determining the right mix, for any given country's institutional context, of centralized and decentralized arrangements for the sets of decisions listed in table 14.5. This, not a massive push to decentralize all decisions, holds the most promise for improving outcomes.

No decentralization reform can, of course, convert school principals who are accustomed to passively following ministerial orders into dynamic leaders overnight. However, reform can provide a transparent, competitive selection process for school principals that selects, in part, for leaders. To the extent that the ASP has achieved this, we would expect an environment conducive to more effective schools. Decentralization can contribute to excellent teaching in a variety of ways. When decisions on significant pedagogic matters are transferred to schools, teachers are empowered and motivated to work collectively to improve the services delivered to students. When school principals are given the authority to carry out meaningful evaluations of teaching staff, teachers can focus their training on what they need to improve. When resources for training and training decisions are given to the school, teachers and principals can purchase the training

Table 14.4

Nicaraguan Autonomous Schools Program: Effectiveness Gains from Participation

Potential Factors for Improved Effectiveness from Participation	Conditions Observed in Nicaragua via the Program's School Councils
1. More accurate fit of services to recipient demand.	Council power over personnel leads to better fit between principals and teachers and the populations they serve. Councils have more flexibility to change school calendar to account for parental work seasons. Fee revenues invested in areas prioritized by parents. Some adaptation of curriculum to account for parental interests and concerns.
2. Adaptation of standardized government programs to local conditions.	Councils have altered centrally suggested fee policies to account for local socioeconomic conditions. Some evidence of other adaptations.
3. Reduced costs of communication with poor and rural populations on issues involving other government programs.	Some evidence that school construction has improved in rural areas and that existing World Bank projects function better because they rely on community participation promoted by the reform.
4. Increased sectoral resources through local resource mobilization, based on either self-help, user charges, or matching grant basis.	School fees have greatly increased the resources available in some schools. Municipalities have also been goaded into contributing some modest additional resources.
5. Gains in technical knowledge, both from and to local populations.	Clearly, parents serving on councils receive training and gain knowledge and expertise that last beyond their time of service to the council. In addition, the central government has learned more about the priorities for and needs of the sector.
6. Better accountability and performance, derived particularly from factors 1 and 4, as well as stakeholders acting as watchdog entity.	Many stakeholders indicate that accountability and performance have improved. Fuller assessment is still needed.
7. Lower costs through cooperation.	Little evidence of such an effect.

Sources: Potential factors for effectiveness adapted from Esman and Uphoff (1984). Results reported from Gershberg (1999c).

Table 14.5

Types of Decisions That Can Potentially Be Decentralized and Those That Have Been Decentralized in Nicaragua

Decision Type	Examples of Decisions	Nicaraguan Case
Organization of instruction	Instruction time	Yes
	Choice of textbooks	No
	Curriculum content	No, or little
	Teaching methods	No
	School attended by student (choice)	No
Personnel management	Hire and fire school principal	Yes
	Recruit and hire teachers	Yes, but limited
	Set or augment teacher pay scale	Yes
	Assign teaching responsibilities	Yes, but variable
	Determine provision of in-service training	Unknown
Planning and structures	Create or close a school	No
	Selection of programs offered in a school	Unknown
	Definition of course content	No, or little
	Set examinations to monitor school performance	No
Resources	Develop school improvement plan	Yes
	Allocate personnel budget	Yes, with center
	Allocate nonpersonnel budget	Yes
	Allocate resources for in-service teacher training	Mixed

they need, which thus is demand-driven, rather than the supply-driven training provided by the Education Ministry. Table 14.5 indicates that in the areas of personnel management the Nicaraguan reform holds promise.

Good information on student learning, and on the value added of the school, is essential to the diagnosis of learning problems that is an important part of the school improvement plan. Good information is also essential to monitoring progress toward attaining learning goals. The devolution of appropriate pedagogic decisions is critical to the local design of solutions to local learning problems. Table 14.5 shows that decisions concerning resources have been significantly decentralized in Nicaragua. Far less has been decentralized in the area of the organization of instruction, though it is not clear that doing so would improve outcomes. Fuller and Rivarola (1998), for instance, document that while the Education Ministry was promoting autonomous schools, it also developed and implemented centrally a new, John Dewey–inspired curriculum and method of instruction that proved highly popular with teachers. This has augmented key political tensions, because many radical groups, having seen that the school-level control and decision making wrought by the ASP are likely to remain, have lobbied to have curricular decisions decentralized to schools as well.

King and Özler (1998) find that the degree of decision making actually exercised by autonomous schools varies greatly, and there is a positive and statistically significant relationship between the degree of decision making exercised and student achievement. Furthermore, the strongest positive relationship to learning was found for variables measuring decision making by the school-site councils on teacher staffing and monitoring of teacher activities. Again, in the areas of personnel management and resources, the goals in Nicaragua may be in line with achieving the right mix of centralized and decentralized decision making.[25]

The "Central" in Decentralization

Thus, the study of decentralization requires an examination of the continued and important role of central government in such decentralization policies, a role that has too often been ignored (Tendler and Freedheim 1994). It also likely requires some centralized action and support. Three main central functions are paramount in any effort to foster parental participation: (1) establishing a supportive legal and bureaucratic environment within which the participation will take place (we call this "creating the space for participation"), (2) compensatory financing and the promotion of equity, and (3) technical support and training.

The central government's support for the autonomous schools during the reform process went well beyond the explicit programs mentioned above, and the financial support supplementing the transfers, at least in the first four years, went well beyond the fees that schools were encouraged to collect. To some extent, this additional financial support was hidden in the system or at least not well publicized by central Education Ministry officials.[26] One might also point out here that if the fees were intended to be

25. See Gershberg (1998a, 1998b) for a discussion of getting the mix of decentralization and centralization right, as well as for an application to Nicaragua. In addition, King's results face a number of serious methodological hurdles, and should be taken as purely suggestive.

26. One obvious subvention was the subsidy for each student exempted from fees. Students qualified for the exemption if they were poor, high-achieving, or children of teachers. As stated in the co-management agreements between the school director and the minister, the ministry provided C$5 for each exempted student. While this transfer is

truly voluntary there would have been no need for the ministry to lay out guidelines for exemptions. In any case, this policy resulted in direct central government financial support of autonomous over traditional schools.

Furthermore, though the central government established transfers to the autonomous schools on a capitation basis, there was no set rule or formula for doing so. They were essentially negotiated or unilaterally determined by the ministry in a less than transparent manner. One high-level official revealed that there were direct instructions from the minister to compute higher transfers to autonomous schools in poor communities.[27] In theory, the new education law will make the process of fiscal transfers to schools and compensatory policies more transparent.

Taken together, this systematization of financial preferences for primarily poor autonomous schools served as the de facto compensatory policy, making up in part for their limited capacity to collect fees. The lack of transparency in this "compensatory program" could certainly have been cleared up, though perhaps this more clandestine subsidization of poor autonomous schools helped mute accusations of favoritism or abandonment of the state system. And this extra support may have been helpful for

---

less than the fee received by paying students, not only did traditional schools not receive this subvention but in fact they were bound by an old agreement to transfer 25 percent of the fees they collect to the Ministry of Education. These schools had never collected primary school fees, but did collect secondary school fees, even under the Sandinistas, and continued to collect fees, or voluntary contributions, for primary schools as well. The government did not provide the transfer for exempted students if the total per student transfer to the school exceeds C$30. This policy was redistributive, because it targeted resources to schools with the lowest per-student transfers.

27. The ministry claimed that the transfers are computed via a formula, but this was not entirely true. Initially, it had considered using a formula developed by the World Bank, but—having determined that the transfers would have been too small for its objectives—it developed a "Nicaraguan formula." Although this formula is largely based on the number of teachers and their characteristics, this same official stated, "Here, we do not have rigid formulas, not like steel, but neither like butter . . . under the instructions of the minister not to be too hard or too soft." School-site interviews revealed that central payment of substitute teachers were much more complete and effective under autonomy and ministry officials told us that the Ministry of Finance has provided extra funds to support this policy. There was clearly a perception on the part of local officials that World Bank support, for instance, through a teacher incentive program, was targeted to autonomous schools. Whether or not this was the case, the perception was significant because it provided added incentives for teachers to accept autonomy lest they lose out on still more opportunities to supplement their salaries and improve their schools. Delegates expressed fear that they would lose out on World Bank money if they failed to bring schools into autonomy.

its success. However, as more and more schools entered into autonomy, the ministry's fiscal capacity to subsidize was taxed, and this too led to a decrease in school-level revenues and an increase in fiscal problems for autonomous schools.

One compensatory policy not explored by the ministry was a poverty-based match of parental contributions and other funds raised locally by schools. Autonomous schools in poor communities could receive matching funds for all local funds collected. This would produce multiple benefits and should be acceptable for four reasons. First, it would maintain the sense of local financial involvement that in theory makes parents more dedicated to participating in school affairs. Second, it would also maintain the increased accountability and citizen oversight that come when people feel that they are paying directly for a service. Third, it would increase the likelihood that compensatory funds are targeted to supporting teachers' salaries. And fourth, it would combat the inequity that results from throwing schools more at the mercy of the endowments of their communities. In short, a matching mechanism would preserve the ideological base upon which the ministry built the program while also addressing dire compensatory issues.

In addition to compensatory funds and the aforementioned Dewey-inspired pedagogy, the ministry made a concerted effort to improve central evaluation during the school reform process. With significant support (both financial and technical) from the World Bank, the central ministry began testing larger and larger representative samples of students and augmenting their ability to improve accountability. Student assessment measures that were used to help the World Bank evaluate the ASP were adapted and implemented by the ministry as national policy in 1997.[28]

Conclusions and Lessons Learned

The Nicaraguan case provides valuable insight into educational reform processes labeled as decentralization. The Nicaraguan reform has been a top-down process solidly within the so-called "neoliberal model." The ASP's solid political and ideological support from an anti-Sandinista government in the early 1990s, along with the backing of the international finance institutions and donor communities, played a large role in the

28. See PREAL (2002) for a discussion of Nicaragua's student assessment system in the context of other systems in Central America.

effective implementation of the program. The lack of a unified opposition and infighting among teachers' unions also played facilitating roles politically. Because this kind of reform is on the rise in Latin America (in part because of support from the development community), it is important to understand the benefits and pitfalls of its implementation. Although the lessons given here focus primarily on issues of process, they also hold insights for policymakers and policy analysts.

One can put the reform cart before the legislative horse. Decentralization was achieved not through legislation but through ministerial directives. This allowed an extended period of experimentation and learning by doing in both the administrative and political arenas of the reform. The ministry likely would not have achieved as much if it had tried to pass the appropriate laws first. The moment to turn from experimentation to consolidation is difficult to discern, however, and harder to achieve. Waiting too long undermines the confidence key actors have in the future of the program and endangers the survival of the reform itself.

Where money is involved, take with one hand but give with the other. Charging fees and augmenting other school revenue potentially bought the loyalty of the teachers, who otherwise could have been the primary losers in the reform. But when the promise to augment their salaries was not fulfilled, low morale threatened the reform. To achieve this goal without sacrificing equity, compensatory programs and policies must be clearly thought out and effectively implemented. Now that the new education law will apparently lead to a greater diminution of school-level fees, new strategies should be explored for supporting schools centrally to mobilize local support and help improve working conditions for teachers.

Both the central and the local levels must be made stronger and more inclusive. School-based management programs in Nicaragua relied heavily on a cadre of well-trained local representatives of the central government. The importance of the ministry delegate training cannot be overemphasized, nor can central training of parents and other actors. The Nicaraguan reforms have not necessarily helped reduce central administration. In fact, there is little reason to believe that they *should* reduce central bureaucracy. To the contrary, they necessitated an expansion of key offices such as budgeting and finance, which had to manage entirely separate and in some ways more challenging budgeting systems for different categories of schools.

Pick the schools and other participants, but at the same time let them pick themselves. On the one hand, school-based management in a context in which such practices are new to the stakeholders needs to start small and selectively. On the other hand, it is important that key stakeholders be allowed to "buy in" to the reforms, at least in the early stages. The fact that teachers to some extent choose to make their schools autonomous has been important.

Overall, the Nicaraguan decentralization reforms provide a very interesting and innovative example from which to learn. Of course, it remains to be seen if positive results will be generated in the most important aspect, student outcomes. At least, as Fuller and Rivarola (1998) point out, the program has made student achievement a more clearly defined goal for more stakeholders than before. And King and Özler (1998) suggest that the kind of school-level decision making advocated (though not necessarily achieved) by the autonomous schools program might improve student outcomes. However, the new legislation has the potential to reduce community financial support on the one hand or fail to address equity issues on the other. If these issues remain unresolved, the reform is likely to fail for political reasons. Nevertheless, the unique characteristic of the reform is the extensive role of the school-site council in setting policy for school governance, and the initial results indicate that this arrangement is at least achievable and potentially beneficial. Finally, among Latin American school reforms, there is no other example in which the parental contributions were so sizable while being controlled by the councils themselves. Whether or not the program proves successful, development institutions and education analysts are sure to learn a great deal more from the experience.

References

Arrien, Juan B., and Rafael Kauffman. 1977. *Nicaragua en la educacíon.* Managua: Universidad Centroamericana.

Arnove, Robert F. 1994. *Education as Contested Terrain: Nicaragua, 1979–1993.* Boulder, Colo.: Westview Press.

Arnove, R., and C. A. Torres. Adult Education and State Politics in Latin America: The Contrasting Cases of Mexico and Nicaragua. *Comparative Education* 31, no. 3: 311–26.

Barzelay, Michael. 1992. *Breaking through Bureaucracy: A New Vision for Managing in Government.* Berkeley: University of California Press.

Bryk, A. S., Y. M. Thum, J. Q. Easton, and S. Luppescu. 1997. Assessing School Productivity Using Student Achievement: The Chicago Public Elementary Schools. Consortium on Chicago School Research, Chicago (unpublished).

———. 1998. Examining Productivity: Ten-Year Trends in the Chicago Public Schools. Consortium on Chicago School Research, Chicago (unpublished).

Carrol, Thomas F. 1992. Capacity Building for Participatory Organizations. In *Participatory Development and the World Bank: Potential Directions for Change,* ed.

Buvan Bhatnagar and Aubrey Williams. World Bank Discussion Paper 183. Washington, D.C.: World Bank.

Chubb, John E., and Terry M. Moe. 1990. *Politics, Markets, and America's Schools.* Washington, D.C.: Brookings Institution Press.

Creemers, Bert P. M. 1994. *The Effective Classroom.* New York: Cassell.

Dalin, Per, with Tekle Ayono, Anbesu Biazen, Birhanu Dibaba, Mumtaz Jahan, Matthew B. Miles and Carlos Rojas. 1994. *How Schools Improve: An International Report.* New York: Cassell.

Darling-Hammond, Linda. 1997. *The Right to Learn: A Blueprint for Creating Schools That Work.* San Francisco: Jossey-Bass.

Dimmock, Clive, Thomas A. Donoghue, and Allison A. Robb. 1996. Parental Involvement in Schooling: An Emerging Research Agenda. *Compare* 26: 5–20.

Esman, Milton J., and Norman T. Uphoff. 1984. *Local Organizations: Intermediaries in Rural Development.* Ithaca, N.Y., Cornell University Press.

Fox, Thomas G., and John Riew. 1984. Partial Privatization of Public School Finance. *Journal of Education Finance* 10: 108–20.

Freire, Paolo. 1974. *Pedagogy of the Oppressed.* New York: Seabury Press.

Friedmann, John. 1992. *Empowerment: The Politics of Alternative Development.* Cambridge, Mass.: Blackwell.

Fuller, Bruce, and Magdalena Rivarola. 1998. *Nicaragua's Experiment to Decentralize Schools: Views of Parents, Teachers, and Directors.* Development Economics Research Group, Impact Evaluation of Education Reforms Working Paper 5. Washington, D.C.: World Bank.

Gershberg, Alec Ian. 1998a. *Decentralization and Re-Centralization: Lessons from the Social Sectors in Mexico and Nicaragua.* Office of the Chief Economist, Working Paper 379. Washington, D.C.: Inter-American Development Bank.

———. 1998b. Decentralization, Re-Centralization, and Performance Accountability: Building an Operationally Useful Framework for Analysis. *Development Policy Review* 16, no. 4: 405–31.

———. 1999a. Decentralization, Citizen Participation, and the Role of the State: The Autonomous Schools Program in Nicaragua. *Latin American Perspectives* 26, no. 4: 8–38.

———. 1999b. Education "Decentralization" Processes in Mexico and Nicaragua: Legislative versus Ministry-Led Reform Strategies. *Comparative Education* 35, no. 1: 63–80.

———. 1999c. Fostering Effective Parental Participation in Education: Lessons from a Comparison of Reform Processes in Nicaragua and Mexico. *World Development* 27, no. 4: 753–71.

Government of Nicaragua. 1996. *Plan nacional de desarrollo sostenible.* Managua: Government of Nicaragua.

Hanushek, Eric A. 1994. *Making Schools Work: Improving Performance and Controlling Costs.* Washington, D.C.: Brookings Institution Press.

IDB (Inter-American Development Bank). 1999. *Nicaragua: Preparacion del programa reforma educativa.* Washington, D.C.: IDB.

Kaestner, Robert, and Alec Gershberg. 2002. Lessons Learned from Nicaragua's School Autonomy Reform: A Review of Research by the Nicaragua Reform Evaluation Team of the World Bank. Available at www.newschool.edu/milano/cdrc/schoolreport/index.html.

Kampwirth, Karen. 1997. Social Policy. In *Nicaragua without Illusions: Regime Transition and Structural Adjustment in the 1990s,* ed. T. W. Walker. Wilmington, Del.: Scholarly Resources.

King, Elizabeth, and Berk Özler. 1998. *What's Decentralization Got to Do with Learning: The Case of Nicaragua's School Autonomy Reform.* Impact Evaluation of Education Reforms Working Paper 9. Washington, D.C.: World Bank.

King, Elizabeth, Laura Rawlings, Berk Özler, Patricia Callejas, Nora Gordon, and Nora Mayorga. 1996. *Nicaragua's School Autonomy Reform: A First Look.* Impact Evaluation of Education Reforms Working Paper 1. Washington, D.C.: World Bank.

Lawler, Edward E. 1992. *The Ultimate Advantage: Creating the High-Involvement Organization.* San Francisco: Jossey-Bass.

Marc, Alexander. 1992. Funding Mechanisms and Participation: A Brief Review of World Bank Experience and Related Issues. In *Participatory Development and the World Bank: Potential Directions for Change,* ed. Buvan Bhatnagar and Aubrey Williams. World Bank Discussion Paper 183. Washington, D.C.: World Bank.

OECD (Organization for Economic Cooperation and Development). 1998. *Education at a Glance—OECD Indicators.* Paris: OECD.

PREAL (Partnership for Educational Revitalization in the Americas). 1998. *The Future at Stake: Report of the Task Force on Education, Equity, and Economic Competitiveness in Latin America and the Caribbean.* Santiago: PREAL.

———. 2002. *Tomorrow Is Too Late: Report of the Task Force on Education Reform in Central America.* Santiago: PREAL.

Ross, Steven M., William L. Sanders, S. Paul Wright, and Samuel Stringfield. 1998. The Memphis Restructuring Initiative: Achievement Results for Years 1 and 2 on the Tennessee Value-Added Assessment System (TVAAS). Center for Research in Educational Policy, University of Memphis, Memphis (unpublished).

Savedoff, William, ed. 1998. *Organization Matters: Agency Problems in Health and Education.* Washington, D.C.: Inter-American Development Bank.

Shaeffer, Sheldon. 1994. *Participation for Educational Change: A Synthesis of Experience.* Paris: International Institute for Educational Planning, UNESCO.

Tendler, Judith, and Sara Freedheim. 1994. Trust in a Rent-Seeking World: Health and Government Transformed in Northeast Brazil. *World Development* 22, no. 12: 1771–91.

UNDP (United Nations Development Program). 2000. *Human Development Report 2000.* New York: Oxford University Press.

Walker, Thomas W. 1997. Introduction: Historical Setting and Important Issues. In *Nicaragua without Illusions: Regime Transition and Structural Adjustment in the 1990s,* ed. T. W. Walker. Wilmington, Del.: Scholarly Resources.

Winkler, Donald R., and Alec Ian Gershberg. 2000. Education Decentralization in Latin America: The Effects on the Quality of Schooling. In *Decentralization and Accountability of the Public Sector: Proceedings of the Annual World Bank Conference on Development in Latin America and the Caribbean 1999,* ed. S. Javed Burki and G. Perry. Washington, D.C.: World Bank.

Wohlstetter, Priscilla. 1994. New Boundaries for School-Based Management: The High Involvement Model. *Educational Evaluation and Policy Analysis* 16, no. 3: 268–86.

World Bank. 1996. *World Development Report 1996: From Plan to Market.* New York: Oxford University Press.

Chapter 15

Innovation and Frustration: Education Reform in Venezuela

Josefina Bruni Celli

Venezuela's education reform initiatives in the 1990s occurred in an increasingly turbulent context. In the aftermath of the debt crisis, the 1980s had featured continuous economic decline and cutbacks in public spending, as well as mounting political discontent due to excessive centralization of the political system and the perception that the state apparatus lacked operational capacity. During the 1990s, there was added commotion as tightening public budget restrictions and a stagnating economy led to various policy experiments geared at improving economic competitiveness and public-sector efficiency, experiments that respectively hit poor people and traditional structures of political patronage. In this context of weakened support for the established government, the leaders of two coup d'état attempts in 1992, who attributed increasing poverty to corruption and the established party system, gained popular approval.

The main educational reform initiatives in the 1990s responded primarily to issues raised in the 1980s. Efforts to formulate a merit-based career statute for teachers and to decentralize the educational system and empower school communities were sectoral expressions of a more general push for modernization of the state and political inclusion, which sought to boost political legitimacy in the context of economic decline. Similarly, initiatives to establish mechanisms for private provision of public education were intended to increase quality and cost-efficiency in the context of public budget downsizing. Nonetheless, certain reform programs emerged out of circumstances that were particular to the 1990s. Full-school-day pilot programs, aimed at reversing decreasing quality, were an initiative of regional governments that had been selected for the first time, and thus a result of the more general process of political decentralization occurring in the 1990s. In addition, an unforeseen grand initiative in curricular reform in the middle to late 1990s resulted from an opportunity provided by a set of loosely framed multilateral-bank funding agreements.

Despite a great deal of debate and experimentation, most reform efforts in the decade failed to come off as intended. With regard to private provision with public funding, church-administered schools catering to poor people succeeded in obtaining stable subsidies, but attempts at chartering out existing public schools and giving schools greater managerial autonomy were firmly obstructed by teachers' unions. Decentralization efforts backed by multilateral banks served to improve regional administrative capacities but failed to definitively transfer responsibility and authority to the states. A merit-based teacher career statute was enacted, but its contents, reflecting the negotiating power of teachers' unions, set the stage for serious difficulties in teacher workforce management; and subsequent efforts to solve this problem were effectively blocked by the unions. An ambitious new curriculum was partially developed and implemented during the administration of Rafael Caldera, but the effort was discontinued when Hugo Chávez came to power. Efforts to expand coverage of full-school-day programs are still under way at the time of writing, but they have been seriously set back by lack of public funds.

Formation of the Reform Agenda in the Late 1980s

The agenda for education reform for the 1990s emerged out of two public questions that surfaced in the preceding decade. The first was a broad concern with the need to both democratize the political system and rationalize public administration, which led to initiatives in general state reform that in turn had important spillovers in the education sector. The second involved sectoral concerns with the quality and inefficiency of the public education system.

The push for general state reform began when President Jaime Lusinchi (1984–88) won the elections with the support of the middle class, who were attracted by his promise for a social pact and the modernization of the state. The initiative for a social pact came from the intellectual wing of the Acción Democrática (AD) Party, which was primarily concerned with democratizing the highly centralized party structure. Its proposal aimed to open the party to the participation of the middle classes, as well as to the entrepreneurial and professional elites who were pressing to modernize the state apparatus, which they viewed as excessively centralized and weakened by patronage and partisan control.

Keeping to his electoral promise, President Lusinchi created the Presidential Commission for State Reform (Comisión Presidencial para la Reforma del Estado, COPRE) in 1984, just a few months after winning the presidency. As we will see below, this commission was to play a very important role in setting the agenda for education reform in the mid-1990s. In the late 1980s, the commission pushed for decentralization of the political system, which it hoped would simultaneously address the problems of insufficient participation and inefficiency of the state (COPRE 1989, 9–11). In 1989 (in the first year of Carlos Andres Pérez's administration), the National Congress passed a decentralization bill sponsored by COPRE, which established direct elections of state and local governments and sketched out a procedure for the gradual transfer of social services to the regions. This law framed all efforts to achieve decentralization of the education system in the early and middle 1990s.

Concurrent with the broader efforts at state reform, policy specialists within the educational sector began to express concern about the decline in the quality of public education in the aftermath of the debt crisis of 1983. The most important result was the report of a presidential commission appointed by Lusinchi in 1985 (National Education Project Presidential Commission, or Comisión Presidencial para el estudio del Proyecto Educativo Nacional, COPEN), which was composed of some of the most distinguished figures in the educational system. The report pointed out that the explosive expansion of the school system had successfully eradicated illiteracy but had "led to quality reduction because measures were not taken to preserve and promote excellence in the schools." It also indicated that liberal budget growth for education until 1983 had "hidden the inefficacy of the system" and added that contraction in fiscal funds "imposes today the need for a more efficient and effective use of resources, which should be allocated in areas that are relevant to the educational process rather than in the hypertrophic upper end" of the bureaucracy or in the service of patronage (COPEN 1986, 44). Together, these considerations placed *improved quality at a lower cost* at the forefront stage of the reform agenda.

The report was not well received by top officials in the Ministry of Education, who at the time were members of AD Party education sector cadres. In their view, the report gave insufficient recognition to accomplishments in reducing illiteracy and expanding coverage, understated the financial constraints, and disregarded improvements then under way in curriculum and administration. To counter, the AD Party cadres organized the First National Education Congress (FNEC), assembled in 1989, for the purpose of engaging fairer analysis and developing a policy agenda. Recommendations stemming from the congress placed greater emphasis than COPEN on improving coverage of preschool education, and on the need for more community participation, self-management, and empowerment. They also deemphasized the question of efficiency, instead pressing the need for budget expansion. The COPEN recommendation of restoring the full-day school schedule was completely omitted. Nevertheless, many FNEC policy suggestions were in line with those of COPEN: establishing a meritocratic statute for the teaching career that would put an end to patronage; improving school supervision; decentralization; and increasing investment in infrastructure, school materials, and teacher training.

Education policy and reform efforts in the 1990s reflected various themes stemming from the work of COPEN, the FNEC, and COPRE. COPEN's concern with efficiency and quality surfaced in efforts at establishing private provision of public education and the full school day as well as in curriculum reform, while attention placed in the FNEC to community empowerment obtained increasing support as the decade drew on. Common concerns with participation and modernization of the state showed up in efforts to bring about a teaching career statute and decentralization of the school system.

It must be pointed out that both COPEN and the FNEC conceived decentralization differently from the way this reform was actually undertaken in the 1990s. The FNEC emphasized curricular decentralization and the transfer of power for self-management to school communities. COPEN recommended curricular decentralization and deeper administrative "deconcentration": transferring certain administrative competencies to ministerial divisions (Zonas Educativas) in the provinces. This process was already under way in the 1980s. The focus was either on deconcentration or school autonomy, rather than on transference of school administration to state governments, as was conceived in the decentralization law of 1989.

Reform Efforts under Carlos Andres Pérez, 1989–1993

During his electoral campaign, Carlos Andres Pérez projected a modernizing image that won him the massive vote of the middle class. Once in power, he put into place a program of deep reforms known as El Gran Viraje, which included radical macroeconomic adjustments that had not been explicitly announced during his campaign, as well as a set of institutional reforms aimed at improving the quality, efficiency, and accountability of public services.

In his approach to economic policy, Pérez made the controversial decision (which contributed to his later impeachment) to rely on a team of progressive entrepreneurs and a younger generation of technocrats, rather than members of his own AD party. Education sector appointments, however, generated less conflict because a greater balance was reached. Pérez appointed Gustavo Roosen, an upper-level manager of a large corporate group, as minister of education. Roosen focused on an initiative for the private provision of public schooling, and on dealing with the multilateral banks. Hans Neumann, the head of another corporate group, was named special commissioner for technical education. As vice minister, and to establish a political balance, Pérez appointed Francisco Castillo, a young AD Party activist and member of the party's education secretariat. Castillo focused on negotiating with teachers unions over the terms of a statute that was to provide teachers with a framework for career development based on merit.

Reform measures in the Pérez period included negotiating terms of decentralization with the regions, bringing to life the teacher career statute, developing a legal framework for private provision of public education, and signing the first such agreement. The period also featured a regional "integral school" pilot program that would gain force in the reform agenda later on in the decade.

However, the reform efforts were in some cases futile and in others only partially successful from the perspective of their promoters. Despite the initial enthusiasm of the governors over decentralization, no transfer agreements were signed. Negotiations stalled over differences about which level of government would bear the financial burden of accounts payable and collective contract differences, bureaucratic resistance, and reduced attention to the issue in the context of increasing internal security problems. A well-designed norm framing the transfer of public funds to private schools was enacted, but teachers' unions effectively blocked efforts to delegate the administration of existing public technical high schools to independent civil associations connected to the industrial sectors. A teacher career statute was effectively negotiated and enacted, but its final union-approved contents set the stage for increased anarchy and indiscipline of the teacher workforce. Finally, the proposal of expanding the "integral school" pilot program was dismissed by the Council of Ministers and National Congress as excessively expensive and unrealistic.

Official Statute of the Teaching Profession

Hopes for the establishment of a merit system derived in part from the perception that teachers were unhappy with the discretionary system of appointments associated with party patronage. Teachers were organized into seven competing federations, each with different links to the competing political parties. This meant that some of them were bound to suffer discrimination whenever "their" party lost ground. Moreover, unions were highly interested in achieving a "legal definition of their profession." Upgrading the definition of the profession as one requiring university degrees in pedagogical studies meant that the teaching profession would be elevated in prestige and wages to levels similar to those of other professionals.

Notwithstanding these incentives, however, union opposition repeatedly frustrated government efforts to negotiate a merit system. The first steps toward the development of a norm framing teachers' careers on the basis of merit were actually taken in the mid-1980s. In 1986, the vice minister of education, Laura de Gurfinkel, established a commission of all top members of the ministerial hierarchy to begin drafting a statute regulating the teaching profession and invited the teachers' unions to draft their own proposal. However, the response, according to Gurfinkel, was a project that "looked more like a collective contract than a norm framing teachers' careers."

In 1989, Francisco Castillo took up the work that Gurfinkel had begun. As he recalled, "I had the political will to make this a reality, and refused to be overcome by the growing fear that the process was going to get out of hand and end up responding to union interests only." Castillo set up a commission comprised of seven union and seven ministerial representatives. He recalls inviting the unions and reminding them "that the objective of the instrument was to assure the entrance, appointments and promotions of teachers would be based on merit." In 1990, the president and his cabinet approved the statute.

According to Castillo, "The most difficult points in the negotiation were the qualifications required for appointments and promotions." But upon reading the statute, one of its most striking characteristics is that it provided for costly and complex "due process" rules that made sanctions for worker offenses both lenient and very difficult to apply. When asked about this, Castillo admitted, "That is the bad part of unions. . . . They seek to protect their members unconditionally . . . and they tend to be adamant about this." On that point, the unions clearly had their way, and this was to deepen rather than solve the ungovernability of the teacher workforce.

Decentralization

As indicated above, up until the late 1980s, decentralization in the educational sector had been conceived as administrative "deconcentration," school autonomy, or increased flexibility of curricula. But the line of events leading to the first popular elections of state and local governments changed the decentralization reform agenda. The Decentralization Law established that governors could apply for the transfer of certain services to their regions, and soon many governors stepped forward to express their interest in having the educational services transferred to their regions.

To understand the initial enthusiasm of the governors, one must point out that state governments were not totally unfamiliar with school administration. Though the majority of schools in Venezuela were (and still are) administered directly by the Ministry of Education, 30 percent of the students enrolled in public schools attended state-administered institutions. Coverage expansion in the previous twenty years had occurred in the "national school system," but the states continued managing the state school systems they had administered since earlier times.

Though there were many initiatives to negotiate a full transfer of educational services, no transfer agreements were signed during the Pérez period. This was due to various obstacles. The first had to do with the transfer of the teacher payrolls to the states. The most complicated point was which level of government would acquire the burden of the accounts payable that according to Venezuelan labor law employers accumulate with worker seniority (*pasivos laborales*).[1] The national government wanted the states to absorb the whole burden, while states expected the opposite.

The second obstacle stemmed from differences in collective contracts. Teachers in the state school systems were subject to better collective contracts than teachers on the "national" payroll.[2] The central government wanted to transfer only the funds associated with the national collective contract and expected the states to cover the difference between the national contract and the better state contract, but the states claimed they did not have the funds to finance this difference.

Third, the students enrolled in the state schools appeared to do less well than those enrolled in national schools on a pilot achievement test administered in the early 1990s. The officials in the deconcentrated national bureaucracy (Zonas Educativas) made a big issue of this finding because they did not want to become state workers and lose the power associated with being "national supervisors."

Finally, decentralization was not a priority for the minister of the interior, who was overburdened with security problems stemming from the increasing social unrest catapulted by the macroeconomic adjustment program. This minister was a key actor in decentralization because he was in charge of relations between the national executive and the state governors. Intergovernmental grants were and are still channeled through this ministry, which was also responsible for negotiating and drafting the transfer agreements to be introduced and approved by the National Congress.

The complexities of the negotiations over education was soon compounded by the fact that governors were very quickly overwhelmed with the challenge of administering services such as health, roads, and state police that had been effectively transferred. Thus, as the presidential term wore on, governors began to lose interest in the decentralization of the educational service.

1. According to Venezuelan labor law, whenever the employer pays an employee, he or she incurs a current liability (account payable) equivalent to five wage-days a month. The employee has the right to claim cash payments from this account for special purposes (e.g., house repair and medical expenses) that cannot exceed 75 percent of the net value of the account. The employer must pay interest to the employee on a yearly basis on the net value of the account.

2. Up to this day, the "national" collective contract is a starting or floor reference in state collective contracts.

Private Provision of Public Education

A third area of reform involved an effort to provide public funding to private education. In 1990, the Ministry of Education signed an agreement whereby the Venezuelan Association of Catholic Schools (AVEC) was endowed with a block grant to funnel to 500 of its affiliated schools. For a number of reasons, this agreement marked a milestone for publicly funded private education. First, up to that point, each school had to negotiate subsidies individually with officials in the Department of Socio-Educational Matters; now 500 schools would receive funds under the umbrella of a single negotiation. Second, a bill that introduced the concept of "permanent subsidies" for qualifying private institutions framed the agreement. A "permanent commission," made up of three members of AVEC and three ministerial representatives, was set up to oversee the agreement. Finally, the agreement established that at the end of every fiscal year AVEC would present the permanent commission with a budget plan for the next year that permitted increments of up to 2 percent of student enrollment. Note that even though the agreement amounted to a one-year contract, the concepts of "permanent subsidies" and incremental annual budget plans, along with the creation of the permanent commission, institutionalized a more stable funding mechanism for Catholic education than had ever existed before.

This agreement materialized thanks the timely coincidence of an aggressive AVEC crusade for more stable public funding and the presence of Roosen in the Ministry of Education. AVEC had been lobbying for an agreement along those lines for six long years. Since 1978, AVEC-affiliated schools had been receiving individual subsidies. In the aftermath of the 1983 debt crisis, however, funding became so unstable that the large number of schools catering to the poor faced the possibility of a full closing. Moreover, the transaction costs for obtaining yearly subsidies had increased sharply in the context of repeated budget cutbacks.

In response to these difficulties, the AVEC board of directors began to lobby intensively among all the political parties. On the eve of the 1988 presidential elections, the group held meetings with all presidential candidates to present their case and obtain "the nonobjection of their parties." Pérez received them a few days before his victory, saying "don't worry, this problem will be solved," and soon thereafter asked Roosen to attend to it.

Roosen liked the idea of developing an agreement with AVEC, not because of his Catholic beliefs but because he firmly believed in the virtues of "creating competition" in the educational sector. To him, providing a stable flow of funds to popular Catholic education meant, "creating a war of comparisons . . . a benchmark in cost and quality for the public schools."

It is important to point out in this regard that Roosen had on various occasions headed the Caracas Chamber of Commerce, which had engaged in sustained promotional activities in favor of "free market" ideas. Roosen proceeded to call his contacts in the business sector to obtain funding and technical assistance for the purpose of developing an "impeccable design that would be invulnerable to changes of government." Various large corporations donated funds to pay topnotch lawyers and consulting companies in the development of the institutional framework. A decree (later Decree 722) framing the funding relationship between the state and nonprofit organizations such as AVEC was drafted. AVEC was asked to make changes in its charter, and an annual agreement with AVEC was negotiated and drafted.

Pérez cared about how this initiative "would look." Rather than signing right away, he gave the draft of the decree to two AD members of Congress who supported the idea. According to Roosen, "the idea was to make it look as if the initiative had come from Congress and not from the presidency." On January 11, 1990, President Pérez signed Decree 722, and on January 26 the first AVEC agreement was signed. The 242,198 students enrolled in popular Catholic schools would be the beneficiaries.

Another initiative to fund private education was less successful. This was a project to improve technical education led by Hans Neumann, an industrialist who had been named high commissioner for technical education. Neumann argued that stronger technical schools would reduce excessive demand for university education, but that as currently constituted, these schools were ungovernable and insufficiently linked to industry. In 1991, he tried to solve both problems with a decree that established that civil associations composed of public officials and industry representatives, rather than the Ministry of Education, would run selected technical high schools. As with charter schools today, these were to be free from many bureaucratic requirements. The Ministry of Education would subsidize them by "lending" them teachers that were ministry employees; but given their private character, civil associations would also be allowed to hire and fire teachers that were not on the "national" payroll.

Excited with the idea, the business sector began to organize for the purpose of participating in civil association boards. For example, the Civil Association for Technical Education in Informatics, Telecommunications, Electronics and Electrotechnics, a telecommunications-chamber-sponsored

organization, was created in 1992 under the leadership of the president of
Siemens of Venezuela, with the purpose of taking over the administration of
a technical high school that was to specialize in the fields of electronics and
telecommunications. But the "takeover" of technical school administrations never occurred because it was violently rejected by teachers' unions
who saw it as a first step toward the deunionization of public schools.
Visiting industrialists were received with rocks and tomatoes at the doors of
one technical high school in 1992, and though the decree was never revoked, the plan was not carried out.

The Escuelas Integrales Demonstration Program

The enthusiasm of the governors after their first popular election led to
important experiments in ways to improve quality in state administered
schools. For example, Governor Andrés Velásquez of the State of Bolivar
hired Maestro Marrero, a man of great experience in education, for the
purpose of developing a strategy for quality enhancement. Governor
Nucete of the State of Mérida called Antonio Luis Cárdenas for this same
purpose.

Antonio Luis Cárdenas had been a member of COPEN. Trained as a
teacher in the *escuelas normales* (teacher training schools) of the first half
of the twentieth century, he firmly believed in the need to direct schools at
the grassroots rather than through a top-down bureaucratic strategy of
resource distribution. Inspired by the work of Darcy Ribeiro in Brazil and
the Educo Schools of El Salvador, Cárdenas developed a program for
improving preschool and basic education featuring the "integral school," a
concept that simultaneously sought to bring together several components:
teacher training and updating, pedagogical assistance in the classroom for
teachers, extension of the school day, infrastructure improvement, procurement of classroom libraries, free school lunches, computer laboratories, and
the promotion of community participation in infrastructure maintenance
and the making and serving of the school lunch. A 1991 state decree
established the creation of twenty-two integral schools. Soon thereafter,
Cárdenas began to negotiate with various rural schools regarding entrance
into the program. Not all schools volunteered, because a central condition
for eligibility was the willingness of teachers to extend their workday from
five to eight hours.

The initiative was not without its political challenges. Unions demanded
doubling the wages of teachers entering the program, while Cárdenas's

offer was a 30 percent increase in the form of a bonus, rather than wage raises.[3] The unions campaigned in favor of their proposal among teachers, but Cárdenas did the same in school communities at large. As part of his strategy, Cárdenas conducted a survey among the teachers in the volunteering schools and results showed that 70 percent of them were willing to take the bonus. Thus, unions backed off from their hard-line position and agreed to the arrangement (Navarro 1995).

Though associated with different political parties, national Vice Minister Castillo and Cárdenas were good friends who had worked together in the education bureaucracy in the 1980s. Because of this, Castillo took careful note of what Cárdenas was doing in Mérida. He visited the integral schools and then invited Cárdenas to present his project in Caracas. Enamored with the project, Castillo set out to "sell" the concept, talking about its virtues through the national media and presenting it in the Council of Ministers and the National Congress for nationwide replication. As a consequence, the Mérida experience began to receive national (and very soon international) attention.

Castillo, however, failed to obtain support for the project in the Council of Ministers and the National Congress. In an interview with the author, he explained:[4]

3. Wage increases were subject to the accumulation of accounts payable, whereas bonuses were not.
4. The author conducted a number of interviews in researching this chapter. The people interviewed included Ruth Lerner de Almea, minister of education during the Jaime Lusinchi presidency and Acción Democrática Party leader; Laura Castillo de Gurfinkel, vice minister of education during the Jaime Lusinchi presidency and Acción Democrática Party leader; Gustavo Roosen, minister of education during the second Carlos Andrés Pérez presidency; Francisco Castillo, vice minister of education during the second Carlos Andrés Pérez presidency; Antonio Luis Cárdenas, minister of education during the Rafael Caldera presidency; Norma Odremán, director general of teaching during the Rafael Caldera presidency; Luis Manuel Peñalver, minister of education during the first Carlos Andrés Pérez presidency, Acción Democrática Party leader, and head of Consejo Nacional de Educación during the Jaime Lusinchi and Carlos Andrés Pérez presidencies; Isabel Mosqueda, staff member of the Consejo Nacional de Educación under Luis Manuel Peñalver; Leonardo Carvajal, head of Consejo Nacional de Educación during the Rafael Caldera presidency; Maritza Izaguirre, Inter-American Development Bank career official and minister of finance during the Rafael Caldera presidency; Jesús Orbegozo, head of Fé y Alegría; Joseba Lascane, leading staff member of Fé y Alegría; Ramón Piñango, professor at the Instituto de Estudios Superiores de Administración (IESA), education policy specialist María Elena Jaén, professor at IESA, health policy specialist, COPRE consultant during the Carlos Andrés Pérez presidency, and head of World Bank Health Project during the Rafael Caldera presi-

My argument was that the "integral schools" would not double expenses in education. First, because the full school day did not necessarily mean teachers had to work both morning and afternoon in the same school. The afternoons would be dedicated to sports, cultural activities, and guided homework, with a smaller number of monitors per child. Second, because the idea was to substitute the Beca Alimentaria Escolar[5] with school lunches, which was better because families were not necessarily using the Beca Alimentaria to feed their children. According to my numbers, the school lunch would be cheaper and we would be saving a lot of money. Thus I told them, give me 10 billion bolívares from the Beca Alimentaria to build a thousand integral schools because the difference between the Beca Alimentaria budget and the investment in infrastructure is sufficient to cover an equal amount of school lunches.

But members of the Council of Ministers and the National Congress were not convinced, and teachers' unions soon began to demand that if the school day was to be extended, salaries had to be doubled. Castillo concluded, "For all these reasons the proposal did not make it into the government's working agenda."

Obtaining Funding for Future Reform Efforts: Negotiations with Multilateral Banks

The World Bank and the Inter-American Development Bank (IDB) approached the Ministry of Education soon after the initiation of Pérez's effort at macroeconomic adjustment. Early in the presidential term, the IDB had provided a modest loan for the construction of preschool infrastructure, but it also held out the possibility of large funding for school quality improvement. However, as Venezuela had historically made little use of multilateral loans, lack of local know-how in dealing with these institutions generated serious strains and difficulties that delayed the signing of these funding agreements until the end of the presidential term.

dency; Rosa Amelia González, professor at IESA, education policy specialist, and COPRE consultant during the Carlos Andrés Pérez presidency; Marco Tulio Bruni Celli, member of Congress during the Luis Herrera, Jaime Lusinchi, and Carlos Andrés Pérez presidencies, founding member of COPRE, and Acción Democrática Party leader; and Franca Afilli, head of the Pedagogical School Project Office during the Rafael Caldera presidency.

5. The Beca Alimentaria Escolar was a compensatory program that accompanied the International Monetary Fund's macroeconomic adjustment program. Families received direct subsidies for every child they enrolled in the public school system.

The first source of strain stemmed from the antipathy of local officials toward "bank consultants," all from other parts of Latin America, who were hired for feasibility studies. In Roosen's view, these consultants knew and cared little about Venezuela, recklessly introduced recipes that had not been adapted to Venezuelan conditions, and charged extravagant amounts of money for low-quality "feasibility studies whose only beneficiaries were the consultants themselves." The second source of strain stemmed from the Venezuelan public officials' lack of experience in the procedures for dealing with the banks. This created critical delays.

To facilitate negotiations, Roosen hired Tania Miquelena, one of the few Venezuelans who had any experience with the multilateral banks. However, as Roosen recalled, "she knew nothing about education, only about multilateral banks." Loan agreements were signed with both the World Bank and the IDB in November of 1993, just three month before president-elect Rafael Caldera (1994–98) took office. As shall be seen in the next section, Caldera's minister of education disliked the agreements, which he viewed as an unintegrated set of individual initiatives. He was to spend a year renegotiating them to fit his own reform agenda.

The Caldera Administration, 1994–1998

To understand the composition of the education team assembled by the incoming Caldera administration, it is important to note that Caldera had created a new party, Convergencia, after having been denied the nomination for the presidency by the Social Christian Party, which he had founded fifty years earlier. Convergencia was not a party in the traditional sense but rather (as its name implied) an electoral coalition of various political tendencies. Its main components were disaffected "Calderists" of the Social Christian Party, and traditional leftist parties such as the Movimiento al Socialismo and the Partido Comunista de Venezuela.

Future vice minister of education Cesar Briceño, a university professor, public servant, and Social Christian, was Caldera's education program chief during the presidential campaign, and he took charge of forming an executive team. Briceño had been a participant in the activities of COPRE. In the early 1990s, COPRE had undertaken feasibility studies for the decentralization of various sectors, including education, and had organized workshops on educational reform in collaboration with professors from CENDES, a social science research institute that had long been an important center for the leftist intellectual establishment. Thus, for Briceño it was natural to turn to the COPRE to recruit reformists whose orientations were consistent with the composition of the coalition.

It was through contacts at the COPRE that Briceño recruited Leonardo Carvajal to head the National Education Council, the advisory board of the minister of education. In this role, Carvajal would later lead the largest mobilization ever over the issue of reform. Carvajal had arrived at the COPRE through the Jesuit authorities of the Catholic University. Though he was a left-leaning professor at the Universidad Central de Venezuela, and in his youth he had attended the Jesuit seminary and later taught as a layperson in a popular Jesuit high school. More recently, he had been a central figure in a large weeklong event in May 1993 called Encuentro con la Sociedad Civil, which was organized by Catholic University and addressed education among a number of social concerns. Despite being new on the political scene, Carvajal's links to both the Jesuit world and the political left of the university sector made him an attractive candidate for an executive appointment.[6]

Cárdenas, the leader of the Mérida reforms, was the logical candidate for minister of education. He had worked with Briceño both in the Andean University and in the University Sector Planning Office, where both had served during the previous Social Christian administration. Moreover, Caldera had visited Cárdenas's integral schools while campaigning in the State of Mérida, where the governor was a "Calderist" Social Christian.

As soon as Cárdenas became education minister, he set up an advisory board to establish an action plan that would guide his administration. The board included the people recruited through contacts at the COPRE as well as a number of Jesuits and professors from the Universidad Central de Venezuela's School of Education.

A few months into the administration, the board issued a Plan of Action, which was published and widely distributed through the national newspapers. The plan set the stage for reform efforts in decentralization, school empowerment, and the introduction of a new approach to curriculum design called "constructivism." Other reform episodes in the period, such as those involving the teacher career statute and private provision with public funding, were not a part of this initial agenda, but were instead the continuation of processes initiated in the previous presidential period. Inter-

6. In the early days of the Caldera administration, he received calls from both the Ministry of the Family and the Ministry of Education. Caldera and many "Calderists" had been schooled by the Jesuits and had close connections with them.

estingly, in the face of severe restrictions on fiscal resources, Cárdenas did not pursue the integral school program he had initiated in Mérida.

As we shall see below, reform initiatives in this period had very limited success. Though better planned, funded, and staffed than in the previous presidential period, efforts to transfer schools to the regions continued to stall because of disagreements and uncertainties over financing of the transferred services. An initiative promoting parental involvement in school management was blocked by a legal motion prepared by union representatives who feared privatization of public school administration. Curriculum reform had only been partially formulated and implemented by the time the presidential period was over. The capacity of unions to block threats to their corporate interests, finally, was made evident by the violent controversy that erupted over an attempt by a Catholic group to assume the administration of two public schools, and by the government's inability to remove provisions in the recently enacted teachers' statute that impeded more effective management of human resources.

Decentralization, School Empowerment, and the Constructivist Curriculum

The incoming administration centered its reform efforts on decentralization, school empowerment, and the introduction of a constructivist curriculum. This triad originated in the work of the COPRE in the early 1990s. The legitimacy crisis, made manifest in the two coup d'état attempts of 1992, had raised concerns about how to deepen participatory democracy and pave the way for a new social pact through education reform. In addressing this issue, COPRE participants concluded that the curriculum had to be redesigned to encourage the production of culture and the construction of knowledge in local communities; and that school communities, now envisioned as profoundly participatory and at the center of the decentralization process, should be given ample power over school management, curriculum development, and local community building.

Multilateral funding fueled reform efforts in these three areas, but Cárdenas had to renegotiate the terms of the funding agreements signed in the previous administration before this could occur. Cárdenas had been very upset by the original terms of the agreements with the World Bank and IDB, both because they were not integrated into a coherent plan and because he strongly objected to a number of specific measures that had been pushed by foreign bank consultants. For example, one measure encouraged by an international consultant was to use bank funds for the production and distribution of textbooks. Cárdenas disliked the concept of textbooks; in his view, every classroom needed a library that would allow teachers and students to explore and construct knowledge in a dynamic and critical way.

Cárdenas hired Norma Odremán, a reputed pedagogue and national supervisor, to develop a coherent working agenda, which would build on the ideas of decentralization, a flexible curriculum, and community empowerment. According to Cárdenas, renegotiating with the multilateral banks turned out to be long and tedious, but in the end was successful. During an interview he emphasized, "This shows that if one knows what one wants, all goes well. Many people like to blame the multilateral banks for the bad things that happen in this country, forgetting we are partners rather than subjects of the multilaterals. When one shows serious things to the banks, they accept, understand and don't try to impose."

Curriculum Reform

Despite discussion about curriculum reform in COPRE, a fresh initiative in this area seemed unlikely in the 1990s, because the educational bureaucracy was still trying to implement a new curriculum formulated just six years earlier. However, a new initiative did result from the opportunity provided by renegotiation of the existing multilateral loan agreement.

Odreman formulated curricular reform along constructivist lines, incorporating the pedagogical ideas of left-wing collaborators into the general scheme. Institutional Pedagogical Projects (IPP) and class projects were to be at the center of this more open, flexible, and decentralized curriculum. Multilateral funds were used to pave the way for the implementation of the new curriculum as it was being formulated. Teachers and supervisors were trained in the application of constructivist principles in the classrooms, school communities were "animated" into participating in the development of IPPs, and classroom settings were recast to serve constructivist teaching principles: tables were substituted for one-sided desks, classroom libraries were acquired, and CENAMEC[7] selected teaching materials and trained teachers in their use. In the meantime, dozens of curriculum experts, hired as consultants with loan funds, worked intensively in the formulation of the new national curriculum.

Just a few months before the new presidential elections, the new curricu-

7. CENAMEC is Venezuela's Center for the Improvement in Science Education.

lum was made official for the first six grades of the school system. Because most primary level teachers, supervisors, and school communities had by then been mobilized for the new scheme, the "constructivist" movement took hold. Success was nonetheless superficial. Most teachers made only token use of the new curriculum, given the serious difficulties they faced in its application. The reform, moreover, was incomplete, for Odremán and her team did not have time to develop the new curriculum for the middle and high school levels of the system. After Chávez won the presidency, Odremán sought to use her left-wing connections to keep her job, but she did not succeed.

Decentralization

The decentralization effort in the Caldera administration differed from the previous one in two ways. First, under the leadership of Elena Estaba, COPRE had by now developed a series of technical studies establishing guidelines for preparing and negotiating the transfer of services. Second, a new staff, financed by multilateral banks, had been established to implement the decentralization effort, removing responsibility from the Ministry of the Interior. Despite these steps, however, education services again failed to be transferred in this period.

As soon as the multilateral bank agreements had been renegotiated, Elena Estaba established Proredes, a multilateral-bank-funded ad hoc unit that was supposed to prepare the regions to assume the responsibility of school administration and negotiate the terms of transfer with the regions. In the area of preparation, a good deal was accomplished; regional cadres received training in school system administration, inventories were made of school infrastructure and equipment and their owners identified, and regional payrolls were audited and cleaned of irregularities. Moreover, many governors signed pre-transfer agreements, and transitory joint school administrations were set up that placed both the national deconcentrated units (Zonas Educativas) and the regional "education secretariats" under a single individual (an *autoridad única*) who was designated by the governor. This official was in turn charged with designing a strategy for the fusion of the two organizations.

The *autoridad única,* however, often faced considerable controversy within the states. The two national and regional bureaucratic structures were not easy to merge, and competition soon became evident. Moreover, the ministerial authorities in Caracas did not want to lose control of the deconcentrated regional bureaucracy, which was in charge of introducing the new curriculum reform into the schools. In one state, conflict over these issues became so severe that the governor abolished the position of the *autoridad única* and separated the two administrations once again.

Estaba did manage to get two states to sign the final payroll transfer agreements but was in fact unable to complete any transfer. The reasons were the same that had impeded transfer in the previous presidential period: disagreements about which level of government would take on the burden of accumulated payroll liabilities, problems of reconciling differences in state and national teachers' contracts, and a lack of clarity about annual central government financing for the regional system. The problem of financing stemmed from the wording of the decentralization law, which stated vaguely that the regions would receive the annual funds that had previously gone to the Ministry of Education for the management of the transferred schools. However, the ministry had not maintained the accounts needed to specify these amounts, and there were no legal provisions that determined how they would be adjusted for inflation or demographic change. For the governors, this implied that they would have to engage annually in risky and time-consuming lobbying in the National Congress for their education budget.

Community Empowerment

Decentralization to the school level was a guiding principle for the Cárdenas executive team, which believed that school accountability depended on parental involvement and participation in school affairs. Consequently, efforts were made to encourage school autonomy and community empowerment with the use of multilateral funds. Like Castillo in the previous administration, Cárdenas wanted to substitute a free school lunch program for the existing practice of providing direct subsidies to mothers who enrolled their children in grades one through six. In a memorandum, he asked school communities to register as Civil Associations, which would entitle them to receive and administer public funds destined for school lunches, minor repairs, and the procurement of school materials. Though many school communities did register, the plan did not take hold. Opposition from the unions proved a major impediment. They saw the formation of the associations as a first step toward the "privatization" of public school management, and they filed a suit challenging the right of "private" associations to manage public funds in public premises.

A Note on Bank Funding and Bureaucratic Politics

Multilateral bank funding for curriculum reform, decentralization, and community empowerment created many tensions in the public bureaucracy, both at the central level and in the regions. Central-level bureaucrats resented the bank-financed ad hoc units that had been set up in their premises. In their view, local consultants hired with bank resources were grossly overpaid. Moreover, they felt that these consultants were no more competent than they were, and were thus unqualified to tell them what to do or change. The fact that consultants often displaced them by taking over their regular tasks made them even more resentful. Bureaucratic efforts to sabotage the work of the consultants contributed to a slowing of reform efforts during this period.

Tensions also arose in the regions. To administer bank funds, the Ministry of Education created a structure that had a central unit in Caracas (UCEP) and a regional unit (UCER) in each state. It was through the latter that bank funds were funneled to the regions. The UCERs began to acquire power in the regions because they "had the money" and a certain amount of discretion in deciding where the money would be allocated. Soon the two regular educational authorities in the regions (Jefes de Zona and Secretarios de Educación) began to see the UCER heads as a competing authority.

Central bureaucracy resentment and resistance, and regional conflicts stemming from the parallel structure set up with multilateral bank funding, embittered the work of all involved and slowed down initiatives. However, these were not ultimately the fundamental obstacles to the reform efforts of Cárdenas's executive team. Decentralization efforts failed because the central and state levels of government did not reach an agreement as to who would bear the costs of transferring the payroll, and because governors felt future budget allocations for transferred services were insufficiently guaranteed. Curriculum reform was incomplete because time was too short for the magnitude of this ambitious endeavor. Efforts to construct the institutional framework for school self-management were interrupted by union leaders fearing the creeping privatization of public schools.

Private Provision of Public Education

Unlike Roosen and Neumann in the previous presidential period, Cárdenas did not make explicit efforts to institute models of private provision of public education. But the apparent success of the model under the AVEC subsidy agreement reached during the previous period did encourage pressure from the Catholic school sector to charter public schools. This in turn led to an episode of violent conflict with teachers' unions over the question of "privatization."

The episode originated in the attempt made by Fe y Alegría,[8] a beneficiary of the AVEC umbrella subsidy agreement, to take over the management of a group of public schools. In 1993, at the request of then–minister of education Elizabeth Caldera, the organization had already taken over one public school that was "out of control," and in 1998, it tried its luck in "acquiring" a pair of schools in the west-end of Caracas for the purpose of developing a project it called Educational Complex of the West. The public high school and primary school to be "acquired" were located around an ample green area that was endowed with two basketball courts and bordered by a municipal theater and a public library. Nearby was a prestigious "popular" Jesuit high school. The plan was to create an educational complex that ranged from basic school through "higher technical education" (equivalent to an associate degree) for the working-class poor people of the city's west end.

The state of the public schools that Fe y Alegría wanted provided a good argument in favor of chartering the schools to the Jesuit organization. The infrastructure was in a disgraceful state, the schools were overstaffed with teachers who rarely showed up at work, student enrollment was well below capacity, and the dropout rate was very high. So in 1998, the head of Fe y Alegría, Father Jesus Orbegozo, presented Minister Cárdenas with his Educational Complex of the West project and requested the administration of the two schools.

Though Cárdenas liked the project, he worried about the political consequences of the school takeover, and he told Orbegozo that his backing was contingent on acceptance by the local community. Orbegozo initiated a campaign to build this support, and reports having obtained 6,000 signatures and the backing of sixty organizations in the area. But union leaders reacted against the proposal for a takeover, and they began their own campaign of opposition. They formed a Conflict Committee with teachers from both schools and accused Fe y Alegría of trying to "privatize" public schools. Soon Orbegozo was receiving calls from Venezuelan Workers Central (CTV, the national union umbrella organization) leadership, re-

8. Fe y Alegría is an AVEC-affiliated Jesuit-run organization administering about 350 "popular" schools. These schools run at a very low cost, contrasting sharply with the public ones "next door" in appearance, order, and absence of teacher strikes. When registration comes around, the length of the queues at the front Fe y Alegría and public schools in the poor neighborhoods show parental preference for the former.

questing that he "respect" the schools. Members of Congress and a number of community organizations were also mobilized against the measure. As tensions increased, there were flare-ups of physical violence in the streets surrounding the schools.

In the end, Fe y Alegría obtained the primary school, but not the high school. According to Orbegozo, there were two reasons that Fe y Alegría managed to get the primary school. First, the most militant union leadership belonged to the high school teachers' union (Colegio de Profesores) and was less interested in preventing a transfer of the primary school. Second, the school principal and even some teachers of the primary school wanted to work under the administration of Fe y Alegría, and they helped out in the process. After Fe y Alegría took over, the principal and a number of teachers continued to hold their jobs in the school.

The episode, however, also shows the power of unions to prevent the introduction of the charter-school model in Venezuela. Though their central argument during the controversy focused on the "threat" of privatization, their central concern was the deunionization of educational institutions. This concern may have been exaggerated, because Fe y Alegría had some unionized teachers in most of its schools; but union representatives knew that Fe y Alegría had a practice of keeping troublesome unionized staff to a minimum and of replacing them with AVEC-funded nonunion teachers. In this regard, chartering public schools directly challenged the labor contract of teachers in the public school system.

Attempts to Reform the Teachers' Career Statute

For the new administration, the teacher career statute that had been enacted in the previous presidential period proved problematic for two reasons. First, because it narrowed the pool of "licensed" teachers to those holding a university degree in pedagogical studies, it had created a serious shortage of qualified teachers. Second, the statute contained a vague and unworkable disciplinary regime that made it impossible for the administration to manage the teacher workforce. As we shall see below, resistance from the unions blocked the administration's attempts to solve these problems.

Resolution No. 1

To deal with the shortage of qualified teachers, Cárdenas passed Resolution No. 1 as soon as he took over the Education Ministry. Resolution No. 1 established that any university graduate could obtain a teaching license after taking complementary courses in the area of pedagogy. He aimed in part to relieve a critical scarcity of licensed high school teachers in the sciences by attracting unemployed engineers and scientists into the educational system. A second objective was to increase the supply of licensed primary school teachers by offering graduates in other specialties the chance to obtain teaching positions without having to go through five years in a pedagogical program.

The teachers' unions did not like this measure because they wanted to strengthen the status of pedagogy as an area of specialization. Allowing graduates of other professions to be titled as pedagogues upon approval of a set of courses implied, from their point of view, that pedagogy was not being valued as a true profession. Though the resolution was not revoked, union pressure prevented it from being implemented in the pedagogical universities and schools of education.

Revising the Disciplinary Regime of the Teachers' Statute

Vice Minister Briceño had been assigned the task of making school administration more efficient; and a central part of this challenge was to rationalize the national teacher payroll, which was overflowing with a costly staff of irregular workers. To deal with this problem, he appointed a unionist affiliated with a small party to head the human resources unit. The appointee knew the intricacies of union culture and tactics, but he valued meritocracy because he resented majority party union leaders who had historically been the beneficiaries of political patronage.

Though Briceño and his partner managed to clear the system of many irregular workers, the lengthy, vague due-process provisions of the existing teacher career statute made it practically impossible to get at the source of the problem: the administration's inability to constrain teacher misbehavior. Therefore, he established a commission of lawyers, small party union members, and university professors to draft a reformed version of the statute that simplified and clarified disciplinary procedures. With one of their members heading the Education Commission in Congress, AD Party—affiliated union leaders of the Colegio de Profesores responded, however, by drafting a legislative initiative of their own, which was introduced in the Congress just as Briceño was introducing his proposals in the Council of Ministers. The union bill, which was much in line with the statute that the executive wanted to change, was approved "in first discussion" and had a serious chance of passage, because the president lacked a majority to block it. This caused major concern within the executive branch; because if the legislature approved the union version, it would have superseded any statute designed in the Council of Ministers. Briceño and his team was "saved by the bell," however, because Caldera's presidential term ended soon afterward.

Resolution No. 1 and statute reform episodes demonstrate the political supremacy of the unions and the weakness of the ministerial administration in the case of Venezuela. Unions commanded greater power than the executive in the National Congress and exerted greater influence in the pedagogical universities and schools of education.

The Chávez Administration, 1999–2002

Chávez won the presidency with the promise of a "Bolivarian revolution" that would feature true social justice and a profound cleansing of corrupt parties and public institutions. Upon taking office, he appointed Hector Navarro, a little-known university professor, to head the Ministry of Education. Navarro was a member of a leftist university-based circle called the Garibaldi Group. Chávez approved a policy program developed by the group, and he placed some of its members in the Finance Ministry and the Central Planning Ministry as well as in the Ministry of Education. But not all who were appointed to the Ministry of Education were Navarro's men. Some came from the Pedagogical University of Caracas, and they would later form an "officialist" faction that opposed the executive branch within the Education Commission of the National Congress.

Reform policy drew selectively on a number of ideas that had been put forward by Leonardo Carvajal, who had been arguing since the early 1990s for (among other things) more funding for primary education, decentralization, greater community involvement, a full school day, and a longer year. In 1998, as president of the National Education Council, he had set out to mobilize the educational establishment and other organizations of "civil society" to support what he called "the transformation" of education. The mobilization took the form of fifty large regional and national assemblies, which were attended by thousands of people over a period of about six months, leading to an ambitious reform agenda published as *Proposals of the National Education Assembly.*

Though Chávez supporters opposed some of these proposals, the new administration did focus on two important themes advanced by Carvajal:

(1) implementing the "integral school" scheme; and (2) investing 7 percent of the gross national product in education (Carvajal 1999, 18–21). In pursuit of the first measure, Chávez soon announced the creation of the Bolivarian School program. In the first year, 500 public schools were to be made "Bolivarian," meaning that they would offer a free school lunch and the full school day; moreover, their infrastructure would be revamped for the occasion. Public opinion applauded the measure; for Chávez was showing the political will to carry out a scheme that Cárdenas had promoted but failed take beyond his demonstration program in Mérida.

Fear of Totalitarianism and the Formation of New Coalitions

Although the Bolivarian School program has continued to have support from both the "opposition" and the general public, sharp hostility to the government has surfaced over the perceived politicization of the educational system. Controversies centered on the appointment and policies of Carlos Lanz, who had been a guerilla during the 1960s and the mastermind of an infamous political kidnapping in the 1970s.[9] From his position as adviser to the minister of education, Lanz developed a plan for the educational system that was widely condemned as "totalitarian," and he encouraged actors who had previously been antagonists to form a single front against the government.

There are various reasons why organized civil society began to fear the initiatives undertaken under Navarro and Lanz. First, although Lanz's ideas bore some resemblance to those of the Cárdenas team (empowerment of school communities through community organization and participation), Lanz took this a step further. School communities would include all the surrounding community, not just parents and teachers; these communities would have ample power to hire and fire, and they would be given resources to provide other social and cultural services. They would act as the hubs of a wider network of community organizations that would include "land committees, health committees, sports and cultural clubs and popular assemblies" (Lanz 2000a, 20). Even more broadly, school communities were to become centers for the "formulation, planning and execution of policies, programs and local projects . . . a space for the exercise of social control, for citizen education and decision-making" (Ministerio de Educación 2000, 4) a center of "popular local power . . . revolutionary power,"

9. Niheous, a manager for Owens Illinois, had been kidnapped for a ransom by Lanz's cell.

and a "space of cultural resistance against the counter hegemony . . . of confrontation with foreign values and knowledge" (Lanz 2000a, 24). Lanz added that the main task of schooling institutions would be to "shape the social fabric required for producing and assuring the revolutionary process," and that the objective of education was "the construction of a new political culture that will guarantee the irreversibility of the revolutionary process" (Ministerio de Educación 2000, 4–5). Lanz's conception of the school community reminded many of Cuba's Committees for Defense of the Revolution; and they were alarmed when the word spread that committees along these lines were being formed in a number of secondary schools.

Second, Navarro took another initiative that looked to many like an attempt at taking political control of the education system. Decree 1011 established that the executive branch could appoint itinerant supervisors with ample powers, which opened the way to place Bolivarian militants in supervisory positions. Unions reacted against this, arguing that this was a step back from progress made through the Statute of the Teaching Profession in assuring appointment by qualifying merit tests. The organized middle class, and particularly parents of children attending private schools, also felt menaced by the ample powers of the itinerant supervisor who, according to the decree, could intervene schools, oust school staffs, and name transitional authorities who would administer schools until further notice. It was this measure that sparked the most fervent mobilization of the urban middle class against the Chávez regime.

Third, Chávez was making aggressive moves to take political control of labor unions, including education unions. The unions viewed Decree 1011 as one such attempt. But moves for political control also came through the Bolivarian Labor Movement, which had been created for the purpose of overthrowing traditional union leaderships. Traditional leaderships of all political orientations soon reacted against this. Unions had been bastions of democratic "resistance" against the dirigisme of dictatorships in the first half of the twentieth century. They were proud of this tradition, and they defended labor independence as "part of the meaning of democracy."

Soon after Chávez took office, union leaders began to attend meetings and conferences organized by Carvajal with the support of the Jesuits. During the previous government, unions had always questioned Carvajal and his proposals for reform, and many of them had refused to participate on amicable terms with the Asamblea Nacional de Educación. With the ascent of Chávez, however, Carvajal became the lesser evil, and even an ally in the defense of independent unionism.

The estranged urban middle class and teachers' unions soon joined Carvajal in a coalition that was to introduce an Education Law bill in the National Congress in January 2000. Carvajal drafted the bill from his position as head of the Asociación Civil Asamblea de Educación. This was a civic association created in 1999 which included many of Carvajal's collaborators from his days in the National Education Council, and it used office space provided by the Jesuit order. When Decree 1011 was issued, Carvajal gave talks to audiences of angry parents in private schools, and he used this platform to promote his own legislative proposal. The unions did not like the proposal, because it eliminated entitlements they deemed "conquests of the labor movement." But under the circumstances, a number of unions gave their support to Carvajal and joined him in a march to the National Congress on the day the bill was introduced.

A group of members of Congress of the progovernment Movimiento Quinta República Party began to write their own bill as soon as the news came out that Carvajal was drafting one, and they defiantly introduced it in the Congress on the same day as Carvajal. But this initial antagonism was soon to end, because these members were also on bad terms with key actors in the Ministry of Education. Among other things, they considered Lanz's ideas anarchistic and contrary to the principle of the "teacher state." These objections, coupled with their desire to make the government look inclusive and democratic, led them to open the congressional Education Commission to civil society; they began to draft a "consensus" bill, working closely with Carvajal.

The consensus bill differed from Carvajal's original one in its more conservative conception of the role of school communities in managing daily school affairs; for example, communities were not to be given the power to fire and hire teachers, as Carvajal had first proposed. And Carvajal agreed, for as he reported, "upon visiting a public school to discuss my bill, I was hit in the face by a teacher who said, 'parents should not have that kind of power because they could try to oust us for political reasons rather than for motives having to do with our competence and responsibility as teachers. Parents could be easily manipulated by government activists.' The Bolivarian Circles whose creation Chávez is promoting and supporting are an example of the kind of organization the teacher was talking about, and the prospects are scary."

The education bill episode was to widen the split between the Ministry of Education and the government party members of the congressional Education Commission. Given Chávez's continued support for Lanz's project, some of these members of Congress were soon to defect from the government coalition in the Congress.

In sum, unlikely bedfellows formed a single front in opposition to Lanz's radical National Education Project, governmental maneuvers for gaining control of teachers' unions, perceived threats to private school autonomy, and the government's effort to form revolutionary committees and Bolivarian Circles in schools and neighborhoods. It is interesting to note that in the light of the new circumstances, the unions made once "unthinkable" concessions to the members of the previous administration's executive team who drafted the education bill. It remains to be seen whether such concessions will hold over time.

The Status of Earlier Reform Initiatives during the Chávez Administration

In light of the revolutionary goals of the Chávez administration, what has been the fate of reform projects initiated earlier in the 1990s? Interestingly, these reform initiatives have not been drastically affected by ideological conflicts. Cash-flow problems and circumstantial political alliances appear to have been much more important.

During the transition from Caldera to Chávez, Orbegozo continued to press to gain control of the secondary school sought by Fe y Alegría. However, he remained unsuccessful for two reasons. First, one of the factions taking office at the Ministry of Education adamantly defended public education in its traditional form: The state had to administer public schools. Second, the union leader who had mobilized resources against the earlier Fe y Alegría initiative was at the head of the Bolivarian Teachers Movement. Orbegozo reported making repeated attempts to get Navarro's approval but never received either a "no" or a "yes." The technical assistance that Fe y Alegría had provided during the ministry's literacy campaign was of no help in this regard.

The AVEC agreement has been respected until now by the Chávez administration; however, from the beginning of 2002, AVEC schools began to encounter serious difficulties because the transfer of government funds fell grossly behind schedule and teacher salaries were not being paid with needed regularity. According to Orbegozo, "I don't think this was done with any kind of bad intention. It is mainly that the National Treasury is very low in liquid funds and unfortunately the government has had other priorities." By late 2002, the problem had been partially solved.

Decentralization as conceived by Estaba lost ground for two reasons. First, it did not receive the support of the ministerial executive staff, which believed in decentralization to the schools, rather than the regions, in keeping with the ideas of Lanz. The unit that Estaba had set up to promote decentralization was dissolved. Second, in recent years, the governors of various regions have considered turning their state school systems over to the national school administration. This is because increasing budgetary restrictions in the regions have induced ever more unpopular teacher strikes affecting the governors' own popularity.

The constructivist curriculum that was formulated during the Cárdenas administration continues to hold. This is partly because the pedagogical universities and schools of education have tended to abide by the international trend toward constructivism. Presently, it is these institutions (rather than the Education Ministry), along with regional education secretariats, that are making the most active efforts to assure implementation of the curriculum in the classrooms. Another factor explaining the continued acceptance of the curriculum is that incumbent ideologues and pedagogues also abide by constructivist philosophies, even if from the more extreme position of the neo-Marxist "radical critique."

A Review of Sources of Frustration to Innovation

In the 1990s, Venezuela was rich in education reform initiatives serving a variety of motives, including both a general push for modernization of the state and political inclusion, and the desire to increase both the quality and cost-efficiency of educational services. But most reform projects were never fully carried out. Patterns of reform failure throughout the period point to budgetary constraints and teacher union resistance as the most critical obstacles in this regard.

Legislation leading toward gradual decentralization of the school system was initially welcomed by first time elected governors who were eager to expand their scope of authority. During the Pérez administration, factors associated with the central bureaucracy (other priorities in the troubled Ministry of the Interior and bureaucratic resistance in the Ministry of Education) may have contributed to lack of progress in service transfer; but the large investments made during the Caldera government in building administrative procedures and structures to facilitate the transferal of the service suggest that the reluctance of the central bureaucracy to move forward was not a sufficient factor. The obstacle that persisted over both presidential periods and finally led the governors to lose interest in obtaining the educational service was budgetary. There was disagreement over which level of government would carry the burden of payroll accounts payable and the more expensive regional collective contracts; and the governors felt uncertain about the future annual budget allocations to their state education systems in the National Congress.

Efforts to establish mechanisms for the private provision of public education were persistently blocked by the unions throughout the period. Initial progress was made when church-administered schools serving poor people succeeded in obtaining stable subsidies (i.e., the AVEC agreement). But this initial success rested on the fact that unions perceived the AVEC agreement as affecting only private schools and thus lay outside their scope of action. All ensuing attempts at chartering out existing public schools or giving them greater managerial autonomy were firmly obstructed by the teachers' unions, which feared the creeping privatization of public schools. During the Chávez administration, the fear of Bolivarian Circle control of schools led sectors that had previously pushed for school autonomy to join the unions in the fight against this line of reform.

During the Pérez administration, two first-time elected governors took on full-school-day demonstration programs to show their capacity to reverse decreasing quality. Even though President Caldera's minister of education had been at the head of one of these demonstration programs in the previous presidential period, however, the full-school-day scheme was not expanded by any level of government during Caldera's term, because of increasing budget constraints and decreasing oil prices. Chávez has given new impulse to this initiative with his Bolivarian School banner program. Though efforts to expand coverage of full- school-day programs are still under way at the time of writing, these have been seriously set back by a lack of sufficient public funds.

In line with its promise to "modernize" public administration, the Pérez government negotiated and enacted a merit-based teacher career statute. Nevertheless, the contents of the statute, reflecting the negotiating power of teachers' unions, set the stage for subsequent difficulties in teacher workforce management. Succeeding efforts to solve this problem have been effectively blocked by teacher unions.

The lack of progress in curricular reform is exceptional, in the sense that its slowdown cannot be traced back to budgetary constraints and union resistance. The grand yet incomplete reform initiative that took place in the middle to late 1990s has not been discarded by the Chávez administration, because its constructivist approach has been accepted by the incumbent ideologues. Yet though this reform is still under way, its full implementation has slowed down simply because ministerial authorities are allocating efforts and resources toward what they view as more urgent matters.

References

Asamblea Nacional de Educación. 1998a. *Compromiso educativo nacional: Calidad para todos*. Caracas: Consejo Nacional de Educación.

———. 1998b. *Propuestas para transformar la educación*. Caracas: Fundación Polar.

Carvajal, Leonardo. 1994. Apuntes para la transformación educativa. In *Encuentro y alternativas*. Encuentro Nacional de la Sociedad Civil. Caracas: Universidad Católica Andrés Bello.

———. 1999. *La Asamblea Nacional de Educación ante el país y el nuevo gobierno*. Caracas: UCAB. .

CERPE (Centro de Reflexión y Planificación Educativa). 1986. *La educación católica en Venezuela, 1889–1986*. Caracas: CERPE.

COPEN (Comisión Presidencial para el estudio del Proyecto Educativo Nacional). 1986. *Educación en Venezuela: Problemas y soluciones*. Caracas: Fondo Editorial IPASME.

COPRE (Comisión Presidencial para la Reforma del Estado). 1989. *La descentralización: Una oportunidad para la democracia*. Caracas: COPRE.

———. 1990. *Proyecto educativo para la modernización y la democratización*. Caracas: COPRE.

———. 1992. *Descentralización de la educación*. Caracas: COPRE.

———. 1994. *Reforma educativa: La prioridad nacional*. Caracas: CINTERPLAN.

Conferencia Episcopal. 2001. *10 documentos en el marco actual del debate educativo*. Caracas: Departamento de Educación, Conferencia Episcopal.

Consejo Nacional de Educación. 1989. *Informe final, Congreso Nacional de Educación, expresión pluralista del pensamiento pedagógico venezolano: La educación venezolana hacia el año 2000*. Caracas: Consejo Nacional de Educación.

Gobierno del Estado Aragua, Descentralización y modernización del Estado en Venezuela. 1993. *II jornada de la procuraduría general del estado Aragua*. Maracay: Gobierno de Aragua.

González Deluca, María Elena. 1996. La cámara de comercio de Caracas en el debate sobre lo público y lo privado. *Economía y Ciencias Sociales* 2–3.

González de Pacheco, Rosa Amelia. 1995. Una rebelión cívica por la educación. Inter-American Development Bank, Washington, D.C. (unpublished).

———. 2001. Estudio sobre nuevas formas de organización escolar en escuelas con financiamiento público en Venezuela. Inter-American Development Bank, Washington, D.C. (unpublished).

Lanz Rodríguez, Carlos 2000a. *Aspectos propositivos del Proyecto Educativo Nacional*. Caracas: Ministerio de Educación, Cultura y Deporte.

———. 2000b. *Propuestas para el ensamblaje de la Asamblea de Ciudadanos, las redes sociales y la nueva resolución de comunidades educativas*. Caracas: Cultura y Deporte, Ministerio de Educación.

————. 2001. *Invedecor y el aprendizaje significativo por descubrimiento.* Maracay: Zona Educativa del Estado Aragua, Cultura y Deportes, Ministerio de Educación.

Ministerio de Educación. 1995. *Plan de acción.* Caracas: Ministerio de Educación.

————. 2000. *Propuesta de la nueva resolución para las Comunidades Educativas.* Caracas: Cultura y Deportes, Ministerio de Educación.

Naim, Moisés. 1993. *Paper Tigers & Minotaurs.* Washington, D.C.: Carnegie Endowment for International Peace.

Navarro, Juan Carlos. 1992. *Descentralización: Una alternativa de política educativa.* Caracas: Cinterplan.

————. 1995. La gerencia de la reforma educativa en Venezuela: En caso de las escuelas integrales en el Estado Mérida. In *Ruta a la eficiencia,* ed. Rafael de la Cruz. Caracas: Ediciones IESA.

Rey, Juan Carlos. 2001. Estado, sociedad y educación en Venezuela. In *10 documentos en el marco actual del debate educativo.* Caracas: Departamento de Educación, Conferencia Episcopal.

Rodríguez, Nacarid. 1997. Las tres décadas de la democracia, 1958–1989. In *Temas de historia de la educación en Venezuela desde finales del siglo XVIII hasta el presente,* ed. Rodríguez Nacarid. Caracas: Fundación Gran Mariscal de Ayacucho.

Part Three

Conclusions

Chapter 16

Conclusions: The Political Dynamics of Reform

Robert R. Kaufman and Joan M. Nelson

In chapters 2 and 9, we focused on the actors and institutions that shaped cross-national patterns of reform of health and education services. One point to emerge from these chapters was the difficulty that reformers faced in maneuvering around strong opposition from a variety of stakeholders within the existing systems—including teachers and health workers' unions, patronage politicians, and in the case of the health sector, private insurers and providers. Indeed, the cases provided considerable evidence to support the conventional wisdom that there is an asymmetry of power between well-organized groups who stand to lose from the reform process, and prospective "winners" who face serious collective action problems.

At the same time, however, it was also clear that changes were occurring

---

The authors thank Javier Corrales, Christina Ewig, Alejandra González Rossetti, Merilee Grindle, Pamela Lowden, James McGuire, Maria Victoria Murillo, Michael Reich, Juan Carlos Navarro, and Patricia Ramírez for their helpful comments on this chapter.

in many countries, and that some of these involved quite substantial reorganizations of financing and lines of accountability within the social sectors. In part, not surprisingly, these reforms tended to be most extensive in countries where stakeholder groups—particularly, the providers' unions—were relatively weak. But this dimension of interest-group politics tells only part of the story in any of the countries we have examined. Reforms were shaped as well by the broader international context, by links between social service reforms and broader goals and issues, and by political contingencies and strategies that sometimes opened new windows of opportunity for policy changes.

In this concluding chapter, we take a step back from the specificities of the health and education sectors and examine the *processes* through which reforms have been shaped and implemented. Reform in any aspect of public policy is never just a single event, and social service reforms tend to be particularly long, drawn-out processes, played out in multiple arenas and involving different challenges at each stage. We distinguish analytically between four phases. In the first phase, reforms become *part of a policy agenda;* decision makers begin to seriously consider the need to fix perceived problems in the social sectors. The second is an initiation phase in which a *concrete proposal is designed* and advanced as a proposal of the executive branch. A third is *formal authorization,* either through legislation or decree. The fourth is an *implementation* phase, which engages additional actors and interests, and which may take years to unfold. The distinction among these phases, although somewhat artificial, offers a more dynamic view of the factors that shape reform over time. A reform may die, or become so watered down as to be pointless, at any point in this process.

Highlighted here are six general observations on which we will elaborate in the rest of this concluding chapter. *First, with regard to how reforms move onto government agendas: Although it is impossible to map a direct link between specific reforms and either globalization or democratization, general trends toward more open polities and more globalized economies have created a new context in which reforms have moved onto the political agenda of debate in most countries of the region.* Sector specialists had advocated reforms for decades, but democratization and exposure to international markets have tended to increase the political salience of these issues for government decision makers. External agencies such as the World Bank have often encouraged and supported reforms, although they have seldom been the primary initiators of successful efforts.

Second, top government officials, presidents, and their closest associates generally have regarded social sector reforms as less urgent than other policy goals and political objectives. Yet their sustained support has often been pivotal throughout the reform process. Whether or not they backed such reforms depended on whether and how they were linked to these other goals. Top-level support for health or education reform was generally strongest when presidential decision makers felt it would advance the pursuit of other objectives; reforms were generally trimmed down or shelved when they were seen to jeopardize these other goals.

Third, with regard to the design phase: Officials within the executive bureaucracy have predominated in the design phases of reform. Specific proposals have generally been designed from the top, by reform or "change" teams within or among the ministries. Stakeholders were consulted early in only a few cases, and broader public debate was even more rare. In that respect, social sector reforms have resembled earlier first-generation reforms.

Fourth, with regard to authorization: Officials within the executive bureaucracy and stakeholder groups have also been the main actors in the authorization phases of reform. With few exceptions (most notably, both sector reforms in Colombia and the education reform in Argentina), party politicians and congressional politics have played little part in reshaping the reform initiatives coming from the executive branch. The narrow array of actors reflected collective action problems faced by prospective beneficiaries of reform; as with first-generation reforms, the costs of social sector reforms were prompt, clear, and concentrated on well-organized interests, while gains were usually delayed, uncertain, and diffused across much of the public. The top-down approach may also reflect the relative lack of traditions of citizen involvement in public policymaking.

Fifth, implementation is normally by far the longest phase in the reform process, and involves the broadest set of actors. It is profoundly "political" and—perhaps more than in first-generation reforms—carrying out social service reform is riddled with risks that can abort, delay, or fundamentally distort the reformers' intent. Sustaining the momentum of reform during this phase has depended not only on the emergence of new stakeholders, a well-established point in the literature, but also on continuing support from national policy elites.

Sixth, different kinds of reforms entail markedly different political challenges. Not surprisingly, measures that generate prompt, visible, and widespread benefits attract support; measures that impose costs (in income, status, security, or convenience) on providers provoke resistance; so do measures that reallocate significant resources. Less obviously, value judgments affect the politics of reforms. Measures *perceived* as increasing equity or quality are likely to attract support and inhibit opposition; measures viewed as mainly concerned with efficiency are often regarded as undesirable by providers and the public. Integrated and comprehensive reform programs usually prompt more opposition than narrower measures.

These six generalizations help to explain why some kinds of reforms are much more frequently launched and carried through than other types of measures.

Politically Noncontroversial versus Contentious Reforms

The sixth point above cuts across all phases of reform, and we will examine it before we turn directly to each phase in the political process. In both the health and education sectors, the reforms that came onto the political agenda in the 1990s encompassed a wide array of policies, programs, and actions. Distinctions among these programs are important, because they generate very different patterns of benefits and costs that affect political support and opposition. Although some kinds of measures are extremely contentious, others may be relatively noncontroversial or actually popular. Stated more precisely, reforms vary with respect to

- the extent, speed, and transparency of benefits to users; "transparency" means the degree to which users—parents of schoolchildren, patients in hospitals or clinics—recognize the connection between specific reforms and improvement in the services they receive; equity-oriented measures are usually more transparent in this sense than reforms focused on efficiency;
- the costs—monetary and nonmonetary—imposed on vested sector interests; and
- perceived financial and other costs or benefits for agencies and interests outside the sector, including ministries of finance and political parties or leaders.

Some reforms, such as the extension of services or the creation of new programs, generate quick benefits to users. Others, such as restructuring the national ministry or decentralizing authority, may initially have little impact on students or patients, or may even cause administrative confusion that delays or impairs service. Still others, for example, creating health care payers' organizations, may have little discernible effect on services in the short run but nonetheless create new stakeholders that will defend the reform.

Whether or not they generate rapid and transparent users' benefits, some reforms, like expanded services, impose few costs. Vested interests object to measures that reduce their control over resources including funds and personnel, threaten their security or independence, or alter established status, relationships, and standard operating procedures. Most reforms do shift control and change procedures to some degree, but they often can be bundled with "sweeteners" that partly compensate the losers.

Reforms also impinge to different degrees on agencies and interests outside of the sector. Expensive measures require the approval or cooperation of the Ministry of Finance; reforms that alter patronage patterns may have to be approved by the Ministry of the Interior or by party leaders; state and local politicians and officials are keenly interested in programs that shift responsibility or alter financing patterns among levels of government.

Goals, Values, and Politics

In addition to their varied costs and benefits, proposed social service reforms trigger value judgments. Social values such as individual self-reliance versus solidarity, equity, the responsibilities of the state to its citizens, and religious or secular orientations are built into and reflected by education and health systems. Proposed changes are defended and attacked not only for their expected impact on material, professional, organizational and status interests but also for their perceived effects on social values. In particular, we posit that support for or opposition to specific reforms is shaped, in addition to the costs and benefits noted above, by public and stakeholder perceptions of dominant goals—especially the balance between equity and efficiency goals.

In practice, efficiency and equity objectives are intertwined in many kinds of reforms, as we discussed in chapter 2. Targeting expenditures on primary schools or clinics, for example, is motivated by equity concerns. However, targeting may also increase efficiency, because modest expenditures can yield larger improvements in health or education at primary levels than in universities or specialized hospitals. Nonetheless, certain measures are largely driven by equity goals; for instance, Costa Rica's primary health care teams, EBAIS, were introduced earliest in the poorest districts of the country. Other measures may have mixed goals but offer unusually obvious and quick improvements in equity; for example, the subsidized insurance component of the Colombian health reforms that rapidly expanded access to medical care for poor people. Other measures are (or appear to be) mainly aimed at increased efficiency. One example is the unsuccessful effort to introduce competition among the Argentine unions' health services (although one intended effect of that reform would have been to permit workers to escape poor-quality programs and seek better ones). Reforms promoting hospital autonomy and associated changes in funding principles are also generally viewed as efficiency focused.

What is key to political responses are perceptions and interpretations of goals and values, rather than reformers' intentions or the probable or actual effects of reforms under way. Measures that are viewed as equity oriented tend to attract support in principle by politicians and much of the public—though that support may be counterbalanced if the measures entail shifts in resources away from vocal interest groups. Or politicians may simply view such measures as less high priority than other issues. In contrast, social service reforms that focus mainly on efficiency tend to be viewed with indifference or hostility by service providers and other vested interests. Perhaps more important, much of the public (including intended beneficiaries), oppose efficiency reforms because they assume cost cutting means reduced quality or quantity. Some incentives intended to increase efficiency, such as altered payment mechanisms for doctors, also tend to be perceived as "privatization"—interpreted as gains for the few, at the expense of the public, prompting wide resistance.

It is striking that most of the aborted or stalled initiatives described in the health section of this volume were directed mainly to efficiency goals. These included the effort to introduce competition among union-based health organizations (*obras sociales*) in Argentina; the even less effective attempt to reform PAMI (the Argentine organization providing health and other services to the elderly); several of the proposed innovations in health care that were removed from Mexico's 1995 social security law; and the very-slow-moving efforts to increase hospital autonomy in Costa Rica and in the Argentine provinces. Decentralization reforms in the education sector were more likely to include important equity components, in the form of funding formulas designed to increase funds allocated to poorer districts and regions. In Argentina, however, the initial attempt to decentralize secondary education was widely regarded as motivated mainly by fiscal concerns, and it quickly encountered strong opposition from both unions and a public sympathetic to the unions. Moreover, "quality" reforms related to the use of testing or merit criteria to assess the performance of teachers or schools gained little political traction in any of the countries.

Categories of Reform: A Spectrum

The array of reforms listed here reflects the points discussed above. The list moves from measures that are relatively noncontroversial in political terms to those that are most contentious. In general, reforms provoke less controversy if they generate prompt and visible benefits to users, do not require providers to make painful adjustments or impose significant costs on other important stakeholders, and/or are perceived as improving equity. Note that "easy" reforms are by no means insignificant; they can make important contributions to improved services. Conversely, "hard" reforms do not necessarily produce big improvements in performance. The array from easy to hard runs as follows:

- Expanding capacity and improving existing facilities and materials (school libraries, equipment for clinics) are easy and popular, benefiting users, providers and their unions, contractors, and politicians. Building schools, clinics and hospitals is especially appealing to politicians, because a one-time outlay creates a visible and durable benefit; in contrast, expanding staff and ensuring supplies require ongoing expenditures. The main constraint is cost, and the fiscal implications of large and rapid spending increases. Especially in small countries, external aid may temporarily ease funding difficulties. Somewhat harder (because they often entail obvious reallocations of funds), but still relatively noncontroversial, are expansions and improvements targeted to under-served areas or groups. Costa Rica's EBAIS primary health care teams fit this description.
- Add-on programs (targeted or universal) that do not demand change in existing programs are also relatively easy, especially if funding is provided by external sources. Examples include early childhood (prekindergarten) education, and "categorical" or "vertical" initiatives in health like immunization campaigns or campaigns focused on specific diseases.

Social funds established in many countries also fit this description.[1] Such programs avoid major changes in the core of the system. Usually they can be handled through ministerial decrees, rather than through more controversial and difficult legislation.

- Creating new organizations is somewhat more difficult but has been a prominent feature of reforms in several countries, even when the new entities imply some changes in modes of operation of established parts of the system. Examples include the new health care purchasing organizations (quasi–health maintenance organizations) in Colombia and, on a limited scale, Peru; or the broadly representative National Health Council created to provide policy guidance to Colombia's Ministry of Health. Often, however, establishing the new structures turns out to be easier than integrating their operations with those of established organizations: Form is comparatively easy; function is harder.
- Changes in rules governing financial flows among different levels of government can be intensely controversial, but once authorized can be put into effect fairly rapidly. Examples: Brazil's restructuring of federal funding for education channeled to states and municipalities (FUNDEF); and Brazil's health care finance.

Changes in structure and function within the administrative core of the system—reforms requiring substantial changes in the standard operating procedures of established ministries, schools, and hospitals—are much more difficult politically. They entail shifts in control over staff and budget, and changes in working relations and relative status. They are also likely to be, or appear to be, focused mainly on efficiency objectives (though some are also promoted as ways to deepen democracy). Such changes can take many forms. Among the more common are:

- Decentralization of operating authority over schools or hospitals to state and local governments. As many of the chapters above have made clear,

1. Social funds were established in several Latin American countries (as well as outside the region) at the end of the 1980s and during the 1990s, in part to buffer the effects of austerity and structural adjustment measures on vulnerable groups. They provide money for modest socially oriented projects selected by the community, such as expansion or repair of schools, clinics, potable water, or feeder roads. Social funds are usually managed by a small autonomous agency outside of the established ministries, and are permitted to set aside the normal bureaucratic rules regulating personnel, procurement, and other procedures.

decentralization appeals to the left on grounds of deepened democracy, and to the right on grounds of increased efficiency; it has been widely adopted despite being a far-reaching structural change. But shifts in the locus of control over personnel decisions and labor policies have been bitterly, and usually successfully, opposed. The details of implementation vary tremendously across localities, and often leave a great deal to be desired.

- Major reorganization of the national ministry, often to heighten attention to some functions and to reduce emphasis on others, to increase efficiency, or in conjunction with decentralization.
- Creating and empowering parents' or community councils to oversee important aspects of the operations of schools or clinics. This is now almost an article of faith in international circles, and it is a widespread formal feature of reforms. There have been some striking cases of success, mainly in the education sector and especially where school councils have been given significant control over financial and personnel resources. Such control, however, is usually resisted, and councils mostly remain a paper provision or are quite ineffectual.
- Monitoring performance and establishing links between performance and reward: for instance, using national testing to assess not only individual students' progress, but also the effectiveness of individual teachers and schools; altering salary and promotion policies to give greater weight to assessed performance. As we have noted again and again, reforms of this kind are resisted more tenaciously than almost any other category.

The relatively noncontroversial or contentious nature of reforms helps to explain why certain kinds of changes are widely attempted and often implemented more or less as planned, while others are less often attempted and much less often carried out successfully. However, as momentum for social service reforms mounted in the 1990s, many countries attempted reforms toward the more difficult end of the scale. Our cases suggest very mixed results. Yet it is encouraging that some Latin American governments increasingly recognize the need for, and are tackling, the tougher challenges—including changes in basic definitions of goals and incentives at the core of their systems. We now turn to the processes through which these reforms are initiated and implemented.

Getting onto the Agenda: Democratization, Markets, and International Financial Institutions

Throughout Latin America, the 1990s inaugurated a period of electoral democracy and increasing exposure to international market forces and the influence of international financial institutions. The impact of these trends varied from country to country, but in most they created a new context that increased the political salience of social sector reforms. Although proposals and initiatives for reforms were not new, the momentum increased palpably as high-level politicians increasingly saw such reforms not only as important to improve sector performance but also as major components of broader agendas of modernizing the state, opening the economy, and deepening democratic legitimacy. In this section, we examine more closely the scope and limits of these influences, and the mechanisms through which they were transmitted.

Democratization

There is some evidence that the turn or return to electoral democracy in most of Latin America in the 1980s has, on balance, increased incentives to improve social services. But it is important to emphasize as well that the effects are complex and often indirect. An important limit to the effects of democratization is that it empowers a wide variety of groups that *oppose* certain aspects of social service reform. Politicians and political parties regard building schools and clinics as vote-getters, but fear that more contentious or slow-acting reforms may lose more votes than they gain. Citizens and organizations concerned with better education and health services often focus on local providers rather than on national policies and programs. Many middle-class voters, who might be expected to be particularly vocal on these issues, cope with their concerns by choosing exit over voice; they put their children in private schools and seek private medical attention for all except the most costly procedures.

At the same time, teachers and health care workers are often the largest groups of public-sector workers, are highly organized, and may be linked through patronage or tradition to particular parties or politicians. Especially where turnouts are low, politicians may be loath to risk alienating such large blocs of voters. Moreover, more open political systems create pressures for a wide array of policies and programs. Democracy may increase demands for social services but prompt even more strident calls for action on other issues. In other words, the relative priority of better education and health services may not increase.

Conversely, there are also a number of reasons why democratization has encouraged governments to undertake improvements in the social sectors. It has opened the way to the rapid multiplication of nongovernmental organizations that are deeply concerned with education and/or health services; some are working closely with local or national governments in these sectors. The more open political environment also encourages policy debate within and beyond sector circles, and facilitates emergence of reformist networks like Brazil's Sanitaristas. Shortly after the transition in Argentina, for example, the newly elected president, Raul Alfonsín, convoked a National Education Congress, which gathered a wide spectrum of teachers, business groups, and church and civic leaders who debated education policy initiatives throughout most of 1987. As Corrales observes in chapter 11 above, "The transition to democracy did not bring any major changes in the education system, but it did propel one of the most comprehensive debates about education reform ever witnessed in Argentina." Similar conferences considered education reforms in Venezuela and Chile, and health reforms in Brazil and Colombia. Though these conferences did not always lead directly to reforms, they helped to define and publicize key issues and options for change.

Opinion surveys show a somewhat mixed picture regarding popular support for social sector reform (see tables 9.2 through 9.4 in the present volume). As was discussed in chapter 9, labor market issues—particularly employment—often rank well above social sector reforms as a major concern of the general public, especially during periods of economic crisis such as the one in 2002. Yet in 1998 and 2000, significant proportions of the general public did regard education as the most important issue facing their country—in all eight nations discussed in this volume, and in half a dozen others covered by the survey. Concerns about health reform ranked much lower than education in all three survey years. Nevertheless, it is quite probable that improvement in the delivery of health services can be a highly popular undertaking, particularly among sectors of the population that had previously had only limited access.

Popular concerns, especially regarding education, may therefore have encouraged electoral politicians to take up the call for reform, and there is some evidence that this is more than rhetorical. Recent statistical studies have shown that democracies in Latin America have tended to spend more on health and education in recent decades (Kaufman and Segura-Ubiergo

2001). More important, indicators of service provision such as school enrollments and prenatal care tend to improve under democratic regimes, as
do certain indicators of health and education status such as infant mortality
and literacy (McGuire 2001a, 2001c, 2002; Brown 1999; Lake and Baum
2001).

The significance of the electoral connection, we might note, is evident
even in some authoritarian or only semidemocratic systems, where heightened electoral competition has increased politicians' interest in providing
those kinds of social service that are immediately popular. For example,
Peruvian president Alberto Fujimori launched a vigorous school construction program targeted to poor areas to build electoral support for the elections of 1995 (Graham 1998, 93, 99).

Democratization trends throughout the region also contributed to social
service reforms through an additional route: substantially deepened decentralization, enhancing the autonomy and powers of local and provincial
governments and transferring to them responsibility for a range of government functions. In five of our six cases of education reform, and three of
those in health, decentralization restructured important aspects of service
delivery. As was noted above, decentralization appealed to groups across
the political spectrum. Groups concerned with democracy and social justice
saw decentralization as a means to make government more accessible and
responsive to the public, to permit more citizen participation in decision-
making, and to break the domination of private or partisan political interests
within national ministries. For instance, as Weyland (1996) and Arretche
(chapter 6 above) argue, Brazilian health reformers in the 1980s viewed the
alliance between the centralized social security health services and private
hospitals and suppliers as a key obstacle to more efficient and pro-poor
sector policies. Draibe makes a similar point regarding the Brazilian education reforms. Meanwhile, more conservative or market-oriented groups
increasingly viewed decentralization as a means to increase government
efficiency, by providing more accurate and timely information about local
conditions, and tailoring services to local needs.

As things turned out, in many countries decentralization was mandated
and carried out in haste, without adequate preparation of local authorities or
appropriate adjustment of national regulations and procedures. The results
were often immense confusion and uncertainty, deterioration of services,
and waste or diversion of funds (Rojas 1999, 9–10). Among the cases in
this volume, the story of decentralization of education services in Colombia
is illustrative. Decentralization also sometimes empowered local *caudillos*

far more interested in patronage than better public services. But as the discussion of decentralization of education in Mexico makes clear, outcomes varied tremendously from one state or locality to another, depending largely on the leadership, capacities, and politics of each. Decentralization did open space for local or provincial initiatives. A promising program with charter schools in Bogotá is discussed in chapter 12 of this volume; an expanded list would include large-scale reforms in Minas Gerais, Brazil (Grindle 2004) and more limited programs in other Brazilian states and in the province of San Luis, Argentina.

Electoral incentives to promote better social services may be more salient for state and local than national political leaders, because social services comprise a larger share of local than national government responsibilities. National leaders may hope to attract support through their policies and programs on trade, labor regulations, or foreign policy; governors and mayors have narrower portfolios and may therefore give more attention to education and health reforms. Thus, for example, financial and other support for social services increased in a number of Venezuelan states in the early 1990s, after the introduction of direct elections for governors and mayors, but *before* increased central transfers to the subnational governments were in effect (Navarro 2000).

In a few cases, finally, broad efforts to establish or "deepen" democracy opened the way to very ambitious attempts to restructure the health sector. New constitutions in Brazil (1988) and Colombia (1991)—each intended to consolidate or revive democratic institutions—included mandates for extensive social sector reforms. In Brazil, the 1988 constitution called for a unified national health system with universal access, whereas the new Colombian constitution laid out a framework for decentralization of education and health services supported by growing shares of central revenues. These measures were, of course, only the beginning of long complicated processes of legislating and implementing more specific proposals. Nevertheless, the mandates were important first steps in what turned out to be far-reaching changes in the Colombian and Brazilian health sectors.

To sum up: the effects of democracy are important, but complex and often indirect. On the one hand, as just implied, neither the incentives of electoral politics nor pressures from civil society can fully account for whether reforms are initiated, or the specific course that they take. Democratic processes can even initially strengthen the relative power of stakeholders opposed to reforms. On the other hand, there is considerable evidence from our cases and from other studies that democratization did increase the salience of social sector issues and helped to focus attention on measures such as decentralization that were perceived as ways to improve services.

Integration into International Markets

The effects of international markets on social sector reform are even more ambiguous. Critics of "globalization" have argued that cutthroat international competition will stimulate a destructive "race to the bottom," in which governments are forced to cut social benefits to the level of their least generous rivals. A more optimistic perspective, drawing on postwar experience in Western Europe, suggests that governments in open economies face strong incentives to increase economic competitiveness and political stability by investing in human capital and broadening social safety nets (Cameron 1978; Garrett 1999; Huber and Stephens 2001; Hurrell and Woods 1999; Pierson 2001; Rodrik 1998b; Swank 2002).

The cases in this volume suggest that, although each perspective contains an element of truth, each seriously overstates the general impact of these constraints on domestic political choices. On the one hand, structural adjustment has indeed limited politicians' control over important economic levers, and heightened concern for ongoing fiscal responsibility imposes tight limits on increased spending. Fiscal concerns motivated the transfer to provincial control of secondary education and certain federal hospitals in Argentina in the early 1990s. Economists have been concerned that high payroll taxes for social security pension and health programs discourage investment; Argentina did lower employers' contributions in the mid-1990s, and Mexico similarly lowered business quotas, while increasing support from general revenues for social security programs. Yet in most of Latin America, including Argentina, social sector expenditures during the 1990s rebounded significantly from the disastrous lows of the 1980s (ECLAC 1999). In Colombia, the legislature approved a significant increase in social security contributions to subsidize health insurance for poorer citizens. More broadly, there is little evidence of a general drive to reduce social benefits as a means to improve international competitiveness.

During the past decade, economic volatility, rather than a deliberate squeeze on social sectors to meet international competition, appears to have had the most damaging effect on social policies. The periodic financial crises that have rocked the region since the mid-1990s have put pressure on funding and sometimes diverted attention from medium-term measures to improve sector performance to short-run social safety-net programs. The history of economic volatility in Latin America, however, began long before the current era of market reforms, and it is unclear whether periodic macroeconomic crises are linked to economic integration per se, to the overly rapid liberalization of capital accounts, or to poor macroeconomic management (Rodrik 1998a; Stiglitz 2002; Baghwati 2002).

As in Europe in the post–World War II era, on the other hand, the opening of Latin American economies has increased concern about the need to construct social safety nets that would cushion the dislocations of economic adjustment. The concern with "adjustment with a human face" at the end of the 1980s rapidly evolved into renewed emphasis on better governance, pro-poor policies, and human resource development: some of the reforms described in this book reflect that evolution. However, one does not find in contemporary Latin America the types of strong, centralized labor and business associations that negotiated new social contracts in much of Western Europe (Katzenstein 1985; Lehmbruch 1984; Wallerstein 1990; Hicks 1999); indeed, labor associations have generally eroded in the face of economic crisis and market-oriented reforms.

Ideas as well as market incentives are mechanisms through which economic integration can exert influence on policy, and the global diffusion of market ideology has shaped approaches to social service reforms examined here (Weyland 2003). A substantial number of reform initiatives sought to encourage efficiency by redesigning providers' incentives. Specific proposals included efforts (largely unsuccessful) to link service providers' pay and promotion to their performance or (somewhat more successfully) to have funding follow patients or students rather than be allocated on the basis of past budgets or number of teachers. Collecting and publicizing information on performance (e.g., school test scores), and giving clients wider choice of doctors or schools are additional proposals based on desire to reorient sector incentives. However, in contrast to the area of pension reform, the privatization of public education and health services was not a theme pressed by reformers, other than some limited local experiments with contracting out specific functions and with charter schools.

In short, international economic integration and the wave of market ideology that swept the region in the 1990s changed the broad context for and ideas regarding health and education reforms, but in ways more complex than the fairly simple conventional theories suggest. New social contracts to replace older understandings have yet to emerge, yet there is indisputably increased priority for more equitable, efficient, and high-quality social services. There is no evidence of a systematic race to the bottom, but increased emphasis on fiscal responsibility and limited government intervention in the economy alters the context in which social policy is devised. Market ideology has not captured public policy in health and education, but it has injected some new thinking.

The Role of International Financial Institutions

International organizations such as the International Monetary Fund, World Bank, and Inter-American Development Bank constitute important channels of financial assistance and advice from the international economic system to Latin American countries. During the 1990s, these organizations greatly expanded their attention and support for health and education services. It is widely assumed that they exerted a strong influence on the politics of social sector reform.

However, recent statistical evidence casts doubt on that assumption (Hunter and Brown 2000). Qualitative evidence from our cases also suggests that international agencies' attempts to directly influence reforms often were ineffective, unless they coincided with domestic priorities. In Argentina, the World Bank pushed hard for increased competition among union-based health insurance funds, and sought to clean up PAMI, the notoriously patronage-ridden and corrupt agency providing health and other services to the elderly. The first endeavor was never effectively implemented; the second died stillborn. Costa Rica reluctantly accepted World Bank advice regarding increased hospital autonomy and altered payment systems, but implementation has been extremely slow. World Bank and Inter-American Development Bank health sector initiatives in Peru at the end of the 1990s foundered. Efforts to introduce improved data systems in Venezuela's Ministry of Education met sullen resistance. Conversely, several of the more successful reforms—Colombia's sweeping restructuring of its health sector; unification of Brazil's health system and financial incentives for state and local reforms in both health and education; Costa Rica's expanded primary health care teams; and Peru's restructured clinic systems—were almost entirely internal initiatives.

The World Bank, the Inter-American Development Bank, and other international agencies did play important roles in many cases, perhaps particularly in smaller and poorer countries. They helped to sustain some reform efforts at key moments, including Peru's innovative primary health care program (CLAS). They provided substantial funds and technical support for implementation of some reforms, for instance, Argentine education and Mexican health sector programs. Such support can be crucial, despite the fact that even quite large grants or loans comprise only a small fraction of total sector outlays in all but the smallest countries. Because internal education and health sector budgets often are almost entirely precommitted for salaries and other legally required outlays, external aid often provides the main source of funds available for new undertakings. Perhaps equally important, international agencies contributed substantially to the general climate of heightened priority and altered ideas regarding social services. For instance, the World Bank's *World Development Report 1993,* which focused on the health sector, influenced thinking throughout the region. The Inter-American Development Bank's 1996 report "Making Social Services Work" was also highly influential. In short, in many cases the international agencies supported reforms with vital information, advice, and financing. But most effective reform *initiatives* were primarily homegrown. External pressures for specific social sector measures have a poor track record.

National Politics, Institutions, and the Reform Process

Although international trends contributed, albeit in complex ways, to the surge of sector reforms, the scope and character of the reforms have been mainly shaped by specific features of national and sector politics and institutions.[2] Health and education sectors are deeply embedded in domestic social structures. Social service workers are usually by far the largest categories of state employees, and their services directly touch the lives of very large portions of the population. Therefore, domestic power relations and political institutions have had a decisive impact. Whether and how reforms in these sectors move forward depends on internal bureaucratic and coalition politics, on the constraints and opportunities offered by specific aspects of the constitutional or party systems, and on the strategic choices of reformers.

The Design of Reform Initiatives: The Role of Bureaucratic Politics

Reform proposals that rose to the surface of political life in the early 1990s often grew out of years or decades of debate and earlier initiatives and came

2. In this and later sections of this chapter, specific information regarding any of the countries featured in case studies in this volume is based on those chapters, unless otherwise noted.

from varied sources both inside and outside the executive branch: local sector specialists, individual politicians, international experts, high-level cabinet officials, and presidents themselves. Whether reform initiatives come from inside or outside of the executive branch, however, the bureaucracy was typically the central—indeed, virtually the only—arena during the initial phase of designing reform proposals. The detailed design of reforms was almost always the work of fairly small teams, sometimes entirely within the ministry (as in the Peruvian health reforms), and sometimes including a network across several key agencies.[3] In most of our cases, there was little or no consultation beyond the executive at the design stage (see tables 16.1 and 16.2).

For reform to move forward, a concrete proposal that commands sufficient agreement within the executive branch is crucial. Failure to gain adequate consensus within the executive temporarily killed health reforms in Colombia, although Senate pressures for reform and a cabinet shuffle later revived the process. But how much agreement is essential? The answer depends in large degree on the scope and character of the reform proposal itself. The responsible agency (Ministry of Health or Education, or the Social Security Institute) acting alone can launch measures with modest costs and few repercussions beyond itself, as long as the president and Ministry of Finance do not oppose the measure. In Peru, for example, separate small groups within the Ministry of Health designed substantial reforms in the administration of basic health care services (the CLAS and PSBT programs), with little discussion within the ministry and virtually none outside of it. The programs impinged on the interests of no other bureaucratic sector except (to some degree) regional units of the ministry itself. Broader and more complex measures, such as the structural health sector reforms adopted in Brazil and Colombia, demand agreement and active cooperation from top political leadership and a wider range of ministries.

In Latin America, most health sectors include a major segment linked to the social security system. As a result, the bureaucratic politics of health reforms is likely to involve bargaining among a broader range of interests and agencies than education reform. Reforms entail untangling complex cross-flows of budgetary resources between the health and social security sectors, and redefining the responsibilities of the Social Security

3. Weyland (1996, 158) reached a similar conclusion regarding Brazilian experience: "Experts . . . remained decisive in designing projects for redistributive health reform."

Table 16.1

Leadership, Process, and Tactics in Health Sector Reform

Leadership, Process, and Tactics	Argentina	Brazil	Colombia	Mexico	Costa Rica	Peru
Main source of initiative	Minister of finance; World Bank regarding *obras sociales*, PAMI	Sanitaristas' network initially; Ministry of Health later	Minister of Health and team; key senators	Economic team, working through change team placed within IMSS	CCSS division head (EBAIS); World Bank (reform hospital finance)	Small committees in Ministry of Health (PSBT, CLAS). Fujimori initiated insurance for school children
President's role and motives	Menem indifferent	Collor hostile. Cardoso supportive, priority higher in second term, but little direct role	Gaviria initially skeptical; became active supporter to promote pension reform, improve equity, modernize	Salinas, Zedillo supportive but no direct role	Calderon, Figueres supportive, but little direct role	Fujimori indifferent, except regarding school children's insurance: motive to gain political support
Authorization process	Decrees, except for law authorizing provinces to give increased hospital autonomy	1988 Constitution mandated unified system.. Laws implemented mandate. Ministry norms and control over funding main tools for influencing state and city governments	1993 laws 60 and 100 decentralized and restructured the sector. Substantial revisions by Congress	Legislation largely rubber-stamped agreements reached with IMSS union	Legislation (required because measures supported by foreign—World Bank—loan)	Presidential and ministerial decrees

continued

Table 16.1
Continued

Leadership, Process, and Tactics	Argentina	Brazil	Colombia	Mexico	Costa Rica	Peru
Negotiations with and concessions to stakeholders	Protracted negotiations with union federation regarding *obras*; became bargaining chip in larger labor relations struggle	Negotiations with private health interests in Constituent Assembly. Later, ongoing negotiations with state and municipal governments regarding regulations and finance	Negotiations during legislative process with unions, private insurers. Teachers' and oil unions exempted, other concessions	Negotiations before legislation with IMSS union greatly weakened measures focused on efficiency and incentives	Negotiations with Ministry of Health medical staff on merger into CCSS; wages increased	Virtually no negotiations
Public relations efforts reaching beyond main actors	Little effort	Little effort; most negotiations were between central and subnational authorities	Nationwide workshops, presentations to concerned groups, while Congress was considering the bill	Little or no effort	Substantial effort to persuade concerned groups, after agreement with World Bank concluded	No public relations effort

Implementation progress and tactics	Nineteen federal hospitals transferred to provinces and Buenos Aires. Little progress on other measures, though some *obras* used World Bank funds to modernize operations	Poorer states and municipalities gained from changed criteria for allocating federal funds. Many states and cities took increased responsibilities; improved primary and preventive programs	Dramatic increase in insurance coverage for poorer citizens. Purchasers' organizations rapidly established. Gradual shift in hospital funding and procedures	Dramatic increase in funding of IMSS health services from national budget. Very limited changes in other respects	EBAIS program improved quality of clinics nationwide. Much slower, limited progress on reform of hospital finance and autonomy	Major improvement in primary health care in much of nation. Effective community management of CLAS clinics
Notes on context	Health workers' unions mostly not strong, but union federation powerful. Provincial governors powerful. Menem government power eroded late in decade	Health workers' unions not strong; state governors powerful. Changes in government in first half of decade complicated reform efforts; much more influential minister of health at end of decade promoted efforts	Health workers' (ISS) union fairly strong. New president and turnover in ministers of health after 1994 disrupted reform, as did broader economic and political decline	Extremely strong IMSS union. Substantial political continuity	Union moderately strong. Change of government in mid-decade but continuity in support for reforms	Virtually no unions. Continuity in government; early problems with internal security and devastated economy eased by mid-decade

Note: CCSS = Costa Rican Social Security Fund; CLAS = Local Health Administration Committees; EBAIS = Equipos Básicos de Atención Integral de Salud; IMSS = Mexican Institute of Social Security; ISS = Institute of Social Security; PAMI = Programa de Atención Médica Integral; PSBT = Basic Health for All Program.

Table 16.2
Leadership, Process, and Tactics in Education Sector Reform

Leadership, Process, and Tactics	Argentina	Brazil	Colombia	Mexico	Nicaragua	Venezuela
Main source of initiative	Decentralization: Minister of the Economy Cavallo; 1993 law on coverage and quality: key legislators	Minister of Education Renato de Souza and his team	Decentralization: Constituent Assembly. Little reform leadership thereafter	President Salinas; ministers of education	Minister of Education Belli	Varies under different governments
President's role and motives	Menem uninvolved	Cardoso supportive, backed minister of education in some funding disputes; better education seen as vital for state modernization and equity	Gaviria uninvolved, preoccupied with other reforms	Salinas played major direct role; viewed reform as major element in modernizing state and economy; also sought to calm teachers' disputes	Chamarro backed Belli; both sought reduced Sandinista influence in sector. Aleman reappointed Belli	

Authorization process	Transfer of secondary schools originally buried in budget bill. 1993 Law in large part legislative initiative; shaped by Senate, Chamber of Deputies, and the executive	Important decentralization programs established by ministry decree. Major reforms in formula for federal funding to states/cities (FUNDEF) a constitutional law (required 3/5 majority)	Struggle in Congress over reforms; competing bills from Planning Agency and union (backed by Ministry of Education); both passed; result was confusing inconsistencies	Reforms approved by, but not much influenced in legislature	Autonomous Schools Program authorized by Ministry decree; endorsed in legislature ten years later
Negotiations and concessions to stakeholders	Decentralization: Provinces won guarantee of financial floor but no funding increase. 1993 Law: compromises from all parties	FUNDEF: discussed with federations of state and city authorities before submitted to Congress. Government agreed to delay effective date to January 1998	Rival bills drafted with little consultation. Teachers' union blocked almost all changes in incentives, and other reforms	Old leader of teacher's union forced to resign. Extensive negotiations with new leader; concessions on pay, career ladder, etc.	No negotiations
Public relations efforts reaching beyond main actors	Reform leader in Chamber of Deputies conducted hundreds of meetings with civic groups	Substantial publicity effort for school autonomy program	Virtually none	Virtually none	Ministry agents in each municipality trained to explain reforms

continued

Table 16.2
Continued

Leadership, Process, and Tactics	Argentina	Brazil	Colombia	Mexico	Nicaragua	Venezuela
National ministry reorganized?	No	Ministry patronage networks dismantled	No	Yes; big cuts in staff, for efficiency and to reduce union influence	Yes; big cuts in staff to erase Sandinista influence	No
Implementation progress and tactics	Secondary schools transferred to provinces. 1993 law selectively pursued: funds, enrollment, facilities expanded; also curriculum reform and statistics. Central ministry reactivated council of provincial education ministries; introduced competitive programs to reduce inequalities	Primary enrollment, teachers' pay and quality, spending per student all up, particularly in poor states. Much primary education shifted to municipalities. Modest increases in school autonomy. Financial incentives were main instrument	Primary and secondary education largely shifted to departments, but mostly not to municipalities. Steep rise in funds absorbed by teachers' wages. Severe financial problems by late 1990s. Tests suggest reduced student achievement	Primary and secondary education shifted to states. Detailed implementation varied widely among states	By 2000, ASP covered half of primary and 80% of secondary students. School councils active. Targeted secondary schools first, handpicked initial 20, schools self-selected. Well-trained ministry delegates in every municipality. Regulations flexible, fine-tuned over time. Special subsidies for poorer ASP schools	

Notes on context	Teachers' union initially fragmented and lacked allies; later united regarding salaries. Broader political context evolved: government initially strong, gradually eroded in late 1990s	Teachers' unions fragmented; few unions at municipal level	Very strong teachers' union, controlled Ministry of Education. Gaviria government preoccupied with other reforms; Samper government distracted by economic and political problems	Strong teachers' union but challenged by dissidents. State governors not consulted but became responsible for implementing decentralization	Rivalry among four teachers' unions eased reforms. Minister Belli spanned two governments, providing continuity at sector level	Teachers' unions fragmented. Three governments in 1990s, each with different goals and priorities: great discontinuity

Note: ASP = Nicaraguan Autonomous Schools Program; FUNDEF = Elementary Education Development and Teacher Valorization Fund, Brazil bureaucracy and the Ministry of Health, issues of considerable concern to the Ministry of Finance. In Colombia, comprehensive health and pension reforms were bundled in the same legislation; in Mexico, reforms in the social security segment of the health sector were packaged with pension reforms. The Social Security bureaucracy was also directly and deeply involved in health reform in Costa Rica and Brazil. That bureaucracy often reflects strong status quo interests and wields powerful patronage resources. In contrast, education sector reforms were less likely to engage other strong bureaucratic players in the central government.

In both sectors, entrenched attitudes and interests within the key agencies themselves can pose formidable obstacles, as Grindle describes vividly in her discussion of education reforms in Mexico in chapter 10 above. In that case, as well as in Nicaragua (education), and Peru (health), reforms were preceded or accompanied by strategic changes in ministry personnel.

Where key agencies disagree, or there is powerful opposition to reform from within a single ministry (often deeply entangled with union and party interests), active backing from the president often determines whether and when a reform goes forward. Typically, as was suggested above, such decisions turn on how education or health reforms are linked to other, higher-priority issues. In Colombia, President Gaviria was persuaded to reopen the drive for major health reforms when key senators made this the price of support for pension reform. In Mexico, President Zedillo dropped most plans for structural reforms in IMSS health services to ensure legislative approval of partial pension privatization. His predecessor, President Salinas, strongly favored education reforms for their own sake, but was also motivated early in the process by the need to calm divisions and escalating civil disorder within the massive teachers' union. In Brazil, President Cardoso failed to back the Ministry of Health in funding disputes during his first term, when stabilization was the overriding priority, but he appointed and backed a far stronger minister of health in his second term, when modernization of the state had become a major goal.

Presidential support for social sector reforms is influenced not only by links to more urgent policy and program goals but also by the requirements of maintaining a governing coalition in the cabinet and legislature. For instance, the capacity of Brazil's minister of social security to withhold funds from the minister of health in late 1992 was in large degree a result of the need to maintain cohesion within the congressional coalition. Conversely, when the ex-guerrilla M19 withdrew from Colombia's Cabinet in 1993, President Gaviria had a freer hand to empower a cohesive reform team to design a health proposal. Coalition calculations also influence presidents' choices of cabinet appointments. In Mexico, for instance, a strong legislative majority gave President Salinas leeway in his choice of reform-oriented Cabinet officials. In Brazil, President Cardoso assigned all but one social sector Cabinet position to members of his own Social Democratic Party.

Legal Authorization: Legislative, Party, and Interest-Group Politics

After a proposal has gained sufficient support within the executive branch, it must be authorized. Depending on the scope of the reform and on a country's institutional and legal requirements, the necessary measures may be authorized by ministerial order, presidential decree, or legislation.

In most democracies, at the authorization stage the reform must "go public," or, if there was already some public discussion during the design phase, debate and negotiations must now be considerably broadened. In principle, the main arena of action shifts to the legislature, and to the key groups that will influence legislative action: political parties, unions and other interest groups, and public opinion. In Colombia and Costa Rica, reform teams launched intensive campaigns to explain the proposed reforms to a wide array of stakeholders, holding dozens, perhaps hundreds of meetings, workshops, and conferences. Yet in most of our cases, consultation and publicity regarding reforms remained rather restricted in the authorization phase, and the direct role of legislatures was relatively modest.

In some instances, either the political context or a more autocratic institutional framework permitted a significant reform to be authorized in a low-key manner, with little or no public debate or interest-group involvement. In Nicaragua, the minister of education took a strategic decision to initiate his reforms by decree, avoiding confrontation with a predictably hostile legislature. That choice was risky, since policies authorized by ministerial decree can be reversed by the same process. Nevertheless, the Autonomous Schools Program operated for a decade on the basis of ministerial directives, before it was finally approved in Congress in 2002. There was virtually no public discussion regarding the two primary health initiatives undertaken under Peru's semiauthoritarian Fujimori government, and unions and doctors' associations associated with the Ministry of Health were too weak to protest the radical changes in personnel policy embedded in the programs. Neither of the two primary health care initiatives required legislative action, other than budget authorization; both were funded through one article buried in the sweeping 1994 budget bill submitted to the Congress in 1993. The CLAS program was established through a presidential decree.

In other instances, legislatures did play a more direct, deliberative role. The Brazilian Congress not only passed measures to unify the health sector in accord with the 1988 Constitution; it also approved new measures to overcome President Collor's attempt to block implementation. In Argentina's education reform, the Senate provided an important venue through which both provincial governors and the teachers' union exerted influence, and the Peronist leadership in the Chamber of Deputies was the architect of a compromise eventually forged with the Finance Ministry. However, the Argentine Congress played the reverse role regarding health reforms, refusing to enact laws to reform the union-based health insurance system. President Menem was forced to resort to decrees; ultimately, the reform bogged down. In Colombia, during President Gaviria's administration, key senators insisted on broad and radical reforms in the health sector. The Congress as a whole debated education and health sector reforms at length and in detail, and they introduced substantial changes in both programs.

The authorization process was often shaped by bargains struck in advance of formal legislative initiatives, either within the executive branch, or between the executive and key interest groups—usually providers' unions or organizations representing state and local governments. In most of our cases, reformers negotiated directly with powerful stakeholders before reform bills reached the floor of the legislature, and either gained their acquiescence (often by offering wage increases or other sweeteners) or watered down the proposed reforms. Major components of sector reforms in Brazil (education) and Mexico (education and health) were approved by compliant legislatures after such negotiations. In Costa Rica, congressional approval was required for the World Bank loan supporting health sector reforms; the leader of the reform team consulted closely with the then-leader of the opposition party and presumptive next president, José Figueres, and the program was approved unanimously. Often authorizing legislation was kept broad and vague, to minimize opposition. As a result, reform teams in the executive branch retained a great deal of control over crucial details, which were spelled out in later enabling regulations that did not require legislative approval.

Like legislative politicians, "leftist" or reformist parties and the broader union movement (as distinct from teachers' or health workers unions) generally did not have a consistent influence on social service reforms. Moderate left-wing groups did play an important role in the constitutional assemblies in Brazil in 1988 and Colombia in 1991, and the long Social Democratic tradition in Costa Rica was reflected in the Figueres's government's vigorous equity-oriented primary health care reforms. But major, partly equity-oriented, reforms in primary health care were also pursued in Peru under the conservative and semiauthoritarian Fujimori regime. And while the new Colombian constitution called for decentralizing and expanding the reach of health services, the radical restructuring embodied in Law 100 was substantially inspired by the centrist Gaviria government's concern for improved state efficiency.

The role of reformist parties also had some significance in Brazil. The drive for education reform gained momentum only after the mid-1990s, when the newly elected president, Fernando Henrique Cardoso, named one of his closest associates in the Social Democratic Party of Brazil (PSDB) as minister of education. Somewhat later, the appointment of another PSDB associate, José Serra, as minister of health also gave a significant impetus to health reform. Nevertheless, policies in both social sectors were generally managed within the bureaucracy, with little sustained consultation or input from the party leadership outside the executive branch. Throughout his two terms in office, moreover, President Cardoso relied on a center-right legislative coalition and generally attached his highest priority to maintaining macroeconomic stability. The Workers' Party, conversely, generally voted against Cardoso's reform initiatives, although individual members did support the FUNDEF legislation within congressional committees.

Labor unions were in retreat throughout the region, weakened by the economic debacle of the 1980s and by aspects of neoliberal policies. The labor movement in general was barely visible in most of the reform cases we have examined. Unions were preoccupied with preventing further erosion of earlier victories embedded in labor relations codes, and (in some countries) resisting privatization of state industries. Argentine unions bitterly fought efforts to introduce competition among their separate health insurance systems; however, their concern was not the quality of health care but the retention of social security health contributions that were their main source of finance.

In contrast to the union movement in general, teachers' and health workers' unions were major players in most of the cases examined here, and they often managed to dilute reforms or win concessions. Providers' unions were best positioned to block aspects of reforms that they did not like where they were organized at the national level, unified, and had close links with the government and the ministry or agency responsible for reforms. Some might expect political alignment to increase trust and communication, and facilitate bargaining and cooperation between government and union. However, in our cases close ties between unions and government strengthened the unions' bargaining position. In contrast, where unions were affiliated with opposition parties, governments with fairly strong political support from other sources felt free to ignore or confront union demands.

In Mexico, the social security union was able to kill or greatly dilute virtually all the proposed reforms to the IMSS health services in the draft 1995 bill, except the provision for sharply increased central government budget support to compensate for reduced transfers from pension funds—a provision obviously in the union's interests.[4] The Mexican teachers' union agreed not to block decentralization, but only after winning major wage and career concessions and ensuring that much authority over personnel matters remained centralized. Both unions are extremely large, powerful, and influential in their respective agencies, and they were intimately entwined with the dominant political party and government at the time of reform. In contrast, Brazil's teachers' and health workers' unions are fragmented by the federal system and the decentralized structure of both sectors; they played little role in the national politics of sector reform in the 1990s. In Nicaragua, the largest teachers' union was strongly Sandinista and therefore at loggerheads with the post1990 governments. Despite its size and cohesion, it could not block the spread of the Autonomous Schools Program, which was designed in part as a deliberate device to appeal to teachers' self-interest and weaken union ties.

Reformers often used wage or benefit increases to win over providers' unions. Pay increases were packaged with health or education reforms not only in Mexico but also in Argentina, Colombia, and Peru, and for health workers transferred from Costa Rica's Ministry of Health to the Social Security Institute as part of the EBAIS program. This tactic, of course, may purchase acquiescence at the price of mortgaging the future. In Colombia, public expenditures on health increased by more than 21 percent annually between 1993 and 1996, but much of that dramatic increase was absorbed by increased salaries and wages (in accord with a provision inserted into

---

4. The increased budget support was also necessary to compensate for reduced social security contributions from employers, and to provide fresh resources.

Law 100, and later decisions under the Samper government), without requirements for improved services.

Aside from service providers' unions, reformers most frequently had to negotiate with governors of states or provinces, municipal mayors, and their organizations. In Argentina, shifting secondary schools and certain hospitals to provincial control required extensive negotiations with governors, who sought and got guarantees that increased responsibilities would be matched by increased funding from the central government. Brazilian education reforms relied on changes in the rules for transferring federal funds to state and local authorities; the ministry consulted with the major associations of state and local officials before sending the FUNDEF law to Congress. It is worth noting that in both Argentina and Brazil, governors have considerable political power vis-à-vis presidents and members of Congress (Jones 1995; Mainwaring 1999). In contrast, Mexico's governors traditionally have had little independent political power vis-à-vis the president, and they were largely ignored in the negotiations paving the way for the new school decentralization law.

Private-sector interests played surprisingly little role in the authorization phase of most of the cases we examine. Exceptions include Colombia, where private health insurance groups actively lobbied Congress regarding provisions in Law 100 affecting their interests, and Brazil, where powerful associations representing private hospital and related interests bitterly but unsuccessfully fought the merger of the social security health program into the Ministry of Health. In Venezuela, some business groups played a more positive role, contributing to Foro Educativo, an advocacy group seeking education reforms (Navarro, communication to the authors). In general, however, broader business and industrial associations outside of the health and education sectors were not engaged, even though in principle they have a stake in more efficient and effective education and health systems. This pattern may reflect the period on which we focus, the 1990s. However, the evidence is mixed. On the one hand, there are some indications that business interest may be growing; in parts of Brazil there has recently been business support for public opinion campaigns to support education initiatives.[5] On the other hand, there is also evidence that many parts of the

---

5. A different form of business support for social service reforms is direct business sponsorship of private projects or programs. E.g., in Brazil the Fundacão Roberto Marinho, the grant arm of TV Globo, created and runs telecurso 2000, a TV preparatory course for young adults who have dropped out of the formal education system. The program is estimated to have benefited hundreds of thousands.

business sector prefer to rely on an unskilled, but "docile" labor force (Tendler 2002).

In short, common strands in many of our cases are the limited extent of consultation not only in the design phase but also during the authorization process, and the modest role of legislatures. While the executive branch was usually under no legal or constitutional obligation to consult a wide array of interests, recent literature on social sector reforms has asserted that such consultations are advisable, and sometimes imperative, to ensure that reforms are authorized and implemented (e.g., see Orenstein 2000; Nelson 2000; Navia and Velasco 2003). Yet with notable exceptions (most clearly Colombia and Costa Rica), our reformers focused their discussions and negotiations on stakeholders whose acquiescence or cooperation would be crucial for implementing the new policies, above all providers' unions and representatives of state and local governments. Even these groups tended to be bypassed or consulted only in a pro forma manner in those countries where unions were fragmented or tied to opposition parties, or where governors were weak relative to the president.

Implementation: From Policy to Reality

Implementation is in many respects the most problematic phase of the reform process, and it is probably at this point that social sector reforms differ most notably from "first-phase" adjustments. Presidents and other high-level officials whose support may have been crucial in earlier phases are likely to turn their attention to other issues. Others whose cooperation is essential—middle-level bureaucrats within the initiating agency itself; state and local politicians and health and education authorities; school, hospital, and clinic directors; and ultimately the teachers, doctors, and nurses—are likely to be skeptical or hostile. Their tendency is to wait, hoping that the reforms will be delayed or reversed. Sometimes key opponents such as providers' unions hold their fire until after reform decrees or laws are in place, judging that they will be in a better position to block or reshape the measures in the course of implementation (González-Rossetti 2001, 234–35).[6]

6. Derick Brinkerhoff and Benjamin Crosby provide a useful perspective on implementation in terms of tasks to be addressed: policy legitimation, constituency building (mobilizing winners), resource accumulation, organizational design and modification (introducing new tasks and goals, and developing acceptance and capacity), mobilizing resources and actions, and monitoring progress and impact (Brinkerhoff and Crosby 2002, chap. 2).

Whether a reform is authorized by presidential or ministerial decree or by law, a first step in implementation is the development of detailed regulations, procedures, and administrative guidance. Often the authorizing law or decree is deliberately broad and vague; the implementing regulations substantially shape the reform. Some regulations are at least intended to be semipermanent, for instance, the rules for establishing health care payers' organizations in reforms such as those in Colombia or Peru. Other rules and regulations, such as the norms periodically issued by Brazil's Ministry of Health, become part of an ongoing struggle by reformers to impel their own staffs, and state and local officials in decentralized systems, to pursue desired objectives.

Implementation therefore shifts the arena of politics back to the sector bureaucracies, national and subnational, and opens up the micropolitics of change at the level of individual schools, hospitals, and clinics. At the center, reformers usually face a lengthy struggle to persuade, isolate, or replace their own skeptical or hostile staffs. The problem was particularly acute in Brazil's Ministry of Health, because the first step in the 1990s reforms was the transfer into the ministry of a large number of former Social Security staff bitterly opposed to unification. In this struggle, dedicated and stable leadership is a great asset: Nicaragua's education reforms prospered in part because the same committed minister held office across two administrations. In contrast, Colombia's health reforms stalled during the first two years after Law 100 passed, under a hostile new president and minister of health.

Where state and local bureaucracies carry the main burden of implementing centrally mandated initiatives, reformers often confront not only professional disagreements but also limited capabilities (especially in poor regions), resistance to central "meddling," and entrenched patronage networks linking local bureaucracies to unions and parties. Moreover, national ministries typically lack detailed and timely information on state and local systems, nor do they have effective arrangements to monitor and evaluate reforms. Poor information and communication, patronage and politics, and misaligned incentives extend all the way to the individual schools, hospitals, and clinics where teachers', health workers', and administrators' actions ultimately determine the quality and efficiency of service. In short, education and health sector reforms confront monumental principal-agent challenges (Castaneda, Beeharry, and Griffin 1999).

Our cases suggest some of the instruments and strategies reformers use to address these challenges (see tables 16.1 and 16.2). Where reforms permit "quick wins," that tactic can both create new constituencies and influence public opinion, promoting implementation and consolidation. Among our cases, Colombia's rapid expansion of insurance coverage is a dramatic example of rapid benefits, not only to poor people needing medical attention but also (and less benignly) to mayors suddenly provided with a new source of patronage (by manipulating the SISBEN system used to identify those eligible for subsidized health care). It seems likely that any effort to roll back the expanded coverage would provoke fierce resistance. In Costa Rica, after a number of EBAIS teams had been installed during the first years of the program, communities that had not yet received a team were clamoring for attention.

Reformers can choose among a range of options regarding the process of decentralization. The transfer of responsibilities can be mandatory or voluntary: in Venezuela, for instance, state governments were offered the opportunity to take control of specific services but were not required to do so. Arrangements can be uniform for all states or municipalities, or can be negotiated wholly or partly one-to-one. In Argentina, the 1991 transfer of federal hospitals to three provinces entailed separate bargaining with each, in the larger context of an attempted fiscal pact. Decentralization can also be implemented rapidly or gradually, and it may involve a complex certification process that substantially slows the process, as in Colombia.

Financial inducements linked to reform requirements are the main instrument reformers at the center can use to alter behavior in decentralized systems. The chapters in this volume on Brazil's education and health sectors are in large part stories about the design and redesign of financial transfers conditional on specific measures by state or municipal governments. Over time, financial inducements accompanied by close monitoring can have powerful effects.

However, institutional contexts—more precisely, the rules governing the flow of central revenues to subnational governments—vary among countries and determine to what extent reformers have control over financial inducements. In Brazil, federal funds for health and education are channeled to state and local governments through the respective ministries. In Argentina, in contrast, provinces receive predetermined revenue transfers from the federal government without specifying the share to be directed to health, education, or any other sector. The national ministries therefore have virtually no financial leverage over provincial policies and programs, except with regard to special programs funded with supplementary federal funds or foreign assistance channeled through those ministries. Reformers at the national level in Colombia, Venezuela, and to some degree

Mexico are or were similarly handicapped by the rules governing financial transfers to subnational governments. In Colombia in 2001, a constitutional amendment and new legislation changed these rules. In short, the precise mechanisms and rules of fiscal federalism are crucial in constraining or facilitating central government influence in decentralized systems. Those mechanisms deserve closer attention from reformers contemplating new measures, and from analysts seeking to understand the effects of past measures.

Changes in the national economic or political context may affect implementation even more strongly than the struggles within the sector between reformers and their opponents. Reform can be put at risk by changes in government. In Colombia, as has been noted, a new administration appointed a hostile minister of health a few months after Law 100 was approved. Serious efforts at implementing the law were delayed for roughly two years. In Venezuela in the 1990s, three different governments followed in rapid succession, each pursuing different goals and designs for education reform. Even an ongoing government must continually reassess its priorities. In Argentina, control of secondary schools was shifted to the provinces early in President Menem's first term. Further measures to improve quality and equity were then planned and partly implemented, but weakened support and mounting political difficulties in Menem's second term left the minister of education without effective higher-level backing.

Like changes in the political setting, economic downturns can undercut reforms. In Colombia, health insurance coverage more than doubled in the three years following the adoption of Law 100, despite slow progress in other aspects of the reform package. But deepening economic difficulties then led to growing unemployment and evasion, cutting the social security collections used in part to subsidize the expanded system. Central government contributions and other funding sources also shrank. By late 2000, coverage dwindled from 57 to 53 percent. In Brazil, the Health Ministry's struggle throughout the mid-1990s for adequate funding (and therefore for leverage to influence state and municipal health programs) reflected the imperatives imposed by the ongoing struggle for macroeconomic stabilization. Mexico's mid-decade economic crisis caused a sharp scaling back of plans for social service initiatives.

For all these reasons, implementing social service reforms is often a long and hazardous process. The history of education and health sector initiatives is littered with abandoned or discredited initiatives. Nevertheless, our exploration of reform attempts in eight countries include several that appear to be substantially successful in overcoming political obstacles and achieving their objectives, including Costa Rica's EBAIS health teams, Peru's two primary health care programs, and Nicaragua's Autonomous School Programs. Others, like Colombia's radical restructuring of the health sector and Brazil's altered systems of financial incentives for state and local education and health programs, have clearly changed their sectors' paradigms; they continue to evolve while drawing both criticism and praise.

Consolidating Social Service Reforms

Indeed, social sectors are and should be constantly evolving. Reform efforts are ongoing; reforms do not and cannot "fix the system" and remove the need for further change. What does it mean, then, to describe a reform as "consolidated?" We suggest, as a working definition, that an initiative is consolidated when it is accepted and valued by many stakeholders and parts of the public, and efforts to reverse it would be politically difficult. Stated slightly more precisely, a measure may be viewed as consolidated when the political costs of reversal are higher than the gains of reversal. A consolidated reform is likely to persist until broader demographic, technological, or other trends make the arrangement no longer appropriate to sector and national needs and resources, prompting a new cycle of debate, conflict, and experimentation.

Many of the reforms discussed in this volume fall well short of that point. For an innovation to be consolidated, three key groups of stakeholders—users, providers, and politicians—must come to accept or approve it.

Users must come to regard the new policy or arrangement as expanding access or improving the quality of service. Several of the reforms we review have substantially expanded services to poor groups and regions.

Most *providers* must become convinced that the innovation does not seriously damage, or may even promote, their pocketbook and professional interests. This is a difficult hurdle, because efficiency reforms usually do demand greater effort and sometimes reduce perquisites, while equity reforms push teachers and doctors to serve in poor urban neighborhoods and remote rural districts. Yet a reform cannot be firmly consolidated if most service providers remain deeply dissatisfied. Pay increases, clearer (and less political) career ladders, training, supportive supervision, improved materials and facilities, and evidence of increased status can all contribute to that outcome. Some teachers, doctors, or health workers, perhaps especially older ones, will remain disgruntled, as will union leaders who see reforms undermining their influence. However, over time new recruits into the system may be more likely to accept new arrangements, gradually deepening their consolidation.

Politicians must come to accept the limitations on patronage implied by the reforms, not because of moral renewal but because alternative channels for winning support become more readily available and effective. Of course, not all reforms reduce patronage; indeed, some (e.g., the screening system used in Colombia to identify those qualified for subsidized health insurance) may be perverted to increase local patronage opportunities. But to the extent that politicians and parties have relied on appointments and promotions of teachers and health workers and administrators as a rich pool of patronage, either clientelism must be reduced or the reforms will be eroded or destroyed. Chapter 9 briefly noted the experience in the Brazilian state of Minas Gerais, where a large-scale and broadly successful program of school autonomy and community participation was partly reversed by a new governor, who was motivated in part by the desire to reclaim control over patronage. In the medium and long runs, politicians' desire to use social services as patronage pools will be curbed by some combination of legal and institutional constraints, and the emergence of alternative means for parties and individual politicians to build and maintain their constituencies. It is possible that as more citizens vote, and to the degree that they judge candidates by their policy and program appeals, responsive politicians will find policy proposals a better route to power than patronage. The politics of sector reforms, in short, is embedded in highly specific ways in broader local and national, and formal and informal, political institutions and practices.

Strategies, Prospects, and Process

Education and health sector reformers cannot control the larger political context, but they can often find ways to maneuver within it. Our cases and others' descriptions suggest a wide array of strategies, tactics, and instruments. Gathering and analyzing new data (including survey data), and utilizing established forums and creating new ones (e.g., task forces and blue ribbon commissions) are likely to be particularly useful during the effort to put social service reforms on the policy agenda, as well as during the next stage of designing a concrete proposal that can win substantial commitment within the executive branch itself. Political mapping and network analysis can assist design decisions; change teams, cross-ministerial committees, and the bundling of issues are among the tactics and instruments that can help to build coalitions within the government. Within legal and institutional constraints, reformers can choose to authorize decisions through ministerial or presidential decrees or to pursue more difficult but probably more enduring legislative approval; log rolling and bundling of issues are among the tactics available to ease reforms through congress. From the outset, reformers have strategic and tactical options regarding when and how widely to consult stakeholders, and what combinations of persuasion, compensation, and pressures are most likely to permit reform to move ahead without being gutted. The implementation stage requires a somewhat different but still wider array of choices regarding timing, tactics, and instruments.[7]

When we consider the wide array of tactics and instruments available, and the tremendous variety of contexts and circumstances in different cases, it is hardly surprising that no neat generalizations emerge regarding the best options for generating commitment and consensus, overcoming political obstacles, and maintaining reform momentum. Evidence from our and others' case analyses can suggest conditions under which particular approaches proved helpful or ineffective, but fall far short of delineating "best practice." Indeed, we believe the search for formulas is a chimera. However, case evidence and comparative analysis does suggest some themes that may help inform reformers' strategies regarding design and process.

A key dimension of *design* is the scope of attempted reform. The reforms examined in this volume vary in scope from the near-total reengineering of an entire sector (as in Colombia's health reforms) to modest experiments or pilot projects. The most ambitious reforms usually reflect a comprehensive vision of a future sector operating on different principles than in the past. This was clearly true of Brazilian and Colombian health sector reforms. However, most reforms were undertaken "piecemeal"— that is, they tried to put in place specific measures to improve some segment or aspect of the existing system, without a comprehensive vision for change. Not infrequently, several partial reforms were introduced more or

---

7. For a detailed and excellent analysis of implementation tasks, strategies and instruments, see Brinkerhoff and Crosby (2002, chap. 2). For a discussion of political mapping, see Reich (1994b).

less at the same time, but were quite independent of each other. Initiatives in the health sector in Argentina and Peru are clear examples.

With so few cases of systemic reform in our "sample," we can suggest some of the factors at work but cannot offer a convincing set of propositions explaining why Brazil, Colombia, and Nicaragua launched such broad-gauged efforts, while most other countries pursued more partial changes. Top-level backing does not, we would note, distinguish these cases from others; though Mexico's school decentralization was vigorously pushed by President Salinas, in both Brazil and Colombia systemic health reforms received only episodic presidential support (and in Brazil in the early 1990s, President Collor sought to block the measures). Nor do broad reforms require weak unions; though Brazil's reforms were indeed eased by fragmented and comparatively weak providers' unions, in Colombia, relatively powerful health workers' unions failed to block the region's most ambitious reform.

On the basis of these cases, however, we can speculate that the scope of changes in the social sectors is related to broader efforts to restructure the institutional foundations of the political system. Post-Sandinista politics created the space for Nicaragua's bold education reform. In Brazil and Colombia, new constitutions were driven in good part by a desire to restructure relations between state and citizens and included broad mandates for changes in the social services. It is important to emphasize, however, that such mandates were not self-executing. Indeed, though some ambitious reforms may mobilize broad support, they are highly likely to galvanize a wide array of opponents. Thus Colombia's far-reaching health sector reforms prompted strong stakeholder resistance during authorization and especially implementation stages. By comparison, narrower though still significant measures to improve primary health care in both Costa Rica and Peru provoked little resistance.

Major decentralizations of responsibility for education and health services are also certainly broad reforms, because they alter the basic sector structure and incentives. We have argued that most of the decentralizations of the 1990s were driven not only (and sometimes not mainly) by the goal of better services but also by broader objectives including modernization of the state, deepening of democracy, and fiscal restructuring. The general vision of decentralization and its presumed benefits was seldom supported by more detailed programs to improve equity, efficiency, and quality through decentralized channels, or even measures to create capacity to pursue those goals. Thus what was envisaged as a broad systemic reform has often turned out to generate partial and reactive change within states and municipalities—a piecemeal approach triggered not by a vision but by an unavoidable mandate from above.

With this partial caveat regarding decentralization, our cases and additional evidence (see chapter 10 above; and Berman and Bossert 2000) suggest that the specific combinations of circumstances, institutions, and leadership that produced broad systemic reforms are rare, and differ across cases. More modest, piecemeal changes are the norm. In some countries, as in Argentina, that pattern reflects comparatively low priority for social sector improvements. Elsewhere, commitment may be stronger, but reforms may be designed from the beginning to take account of powerful political constraints, or they are cut back in scope or depth or speed during the difficult process of winning agreement within the government, passage in the legislature, and cooperation from the multiple agencies and groups that must actually put measures into effect. Or reformers may opt for gradual and experimental approaches to reform precisely because they are aware of multiple, competing models and disagreements about what measures will work best in their specific circumstances.

Partial and modest reforms are the rule rather than the exception, but they are by no means simple or likely to succeed (Berman and Bossert 2000). Key strategic questions are how they can be sustained, integrated with each other, and made to spread. There has been surprisingly little analysis of these questions, and reform designs often neglect them.[8] For example, pilot projects are widely used, but often there is little planning for how to make reasonably successful pilots spread. Decentralization of education and health sectors in much of Latin America will multiply de facto "pilots," as more progressive localities are given greater leeway to innovate. A number of promising examples are mentioned in this volume. (See also Grindle 2002 regarding Minas Gerais; Tendler 1997 regarding health delivery reforms in Ceará, Brazil; and McGuire 2001b regarding health care reforms in Neuquen, Argentina.)

It is probably easier to encourage the geographic spread of a reform than to use a specific functional change to prompt further change. Geographic spread entails copying, with or without modification for local conditions. From a political perspective, being able to point to successful experience elsewhere may help reformers overcome doubts and opposition in their

8. However, see Uvin 1999 for useful concepts and analysis and additional references focused on how nongovernmental organizations scale up their activities.

own jurisdiction. Sometimes a spirit of competition with other states or cities may also help prompt action.

Analysts interested in the politics of education and health sector reforms could usefully give more attention not only to how innovations spread geographically but also how specific narrow reforms can be used to trigger additional policy or structural changes in a sector.[9] For example, after some years in which educational testing was out of favor in much of Latin America, the 1990s saw the gradual introduction or reintroduction of standardized tests. Although most countries do not use tests as diagnostic tools for schools and school systems as well as for individual students, Chile uses scores on its national assessment test to identify the weakest schools; the P900 program then directs special assistance and inducements to those schools. In other words, the information generated by the tests has helped to focus and energize further reform efforts (PREAL 2001, 15). Strategies of gradual, cumulative reform should be high on the research agenda of those who seek to accelerate progress toward more equitable, efficient, and effective health and education systems in Latin America.

Case and comparative analyses suggest general political considerations not only regarding the *scope,* but also regarding the *combination of goals* embedded in reform designs. We argued earlier in this chapter that reforms regarded as enhancing equity are more likely to win political support (and to soften political opposition) than reforms perceived to focus mainly on efficiency. That pattern suggests that it may be good strategy to package efficiency-oriented measures with other reform components that more obviously improve equity or quality. The Colombian health reforms are a good example of this bundling strategy. The pattern also raises intriguing questions regarding the politics of targeting. Financial and technical specialists and economists in general have long emphasized the need for policies and programs targeted to disadvantaged groups, to improve the equity of services within limited budgets. Political scientists have long countered that tightly targeted programs may be less sustainable politically than programs offering broader or universal benefits (Goodin and Le Grand 1987; Gelbach and Pritchett 1997; Nelson 1992, xxx, 243–44; Reich 1994a, 429; Skocpol 1991).

The partial evidence offered by our cases suggests a nuanced version of this latter argument: Tight targeting was not a feature of any of the reforms

9. Uvin (1999, 77–86) draws a similar distinction between quantitative and functional scaling up of grassroots organizations, and he identifies additional political and organizational dimensions of development.

examined, but broadly pro-poor-people targeting (e.g., Colombia's expanded health insurance, or the Costa Rican and Peruvian primary health care reforms) proved to have considerable appeal. Finally, case evidence of resistance to measures viewed as focused solely on efficiency underscores the need for extensive and energetic education campaigns directed to stakeholders and the public at large regarding why such measures are needed, how they are expected to work, and how they can improve equity and quality.

Reformers must make strategic choices not only regarding design but also regarding the *process* of reform. Their decisions regarding timing, the extent and character of consultation, how the measures should be presented and explained to the public, whether and how to submit the initiative to the legislature, and how best to launch and sustain implementation powerfully shape the trajectory of reform. Choices early in the process may have repercussions in later stages. But at any stage, unexpected opportunities or obstacles may call for quick and flexible decisions.

Much recent commentary on social sector reforms urges an open and democratic process with broad consultation from the earliest stages forward—in sharp contrast to the top-down, closed door approach characteristic of first-wave macroeconomic stabilization and structural adjustment measures (Orenstein 2000; Nelson 2000). Yet case evidence from our and others' research (Grindle 2004) strongly suggests that early consultation can be problematic. Where unions or other stakeholders are strong, have ties with the government, and adamantly oppose reform, consultation may well cripple or kill reform—as in Mexico's abortive social security—funded health sector reforms, or during certain chapters of Bolivia's long-drawn-out struggle for education reforms (Grindle 2004). In Colombia, consultation and bargaining with the teachers' union undermined the coherence of the reform.

Often, reformers are operating within tight time limits; extensive consultation takes time and permits opposition groups to mobilize. Moreover, organized stakeholders are not necessarily representative. Union leaders' concerns, for instance, often differ from those of many members. Important interests (e.g., those of patients) remain without representation. One careful analysis of previous social sector reform efforts in Brazil, from the early 1980s to the early 1990s, concluded that equity-oriented reforms could move forward only if consultation with established interests was sharply limited (Weyland 1996).

Nevertheless, the fact remains that effective implementation of many education and health sector reforms requires the acquiescence or active cooperation of a wide array of agencies and groups. Antagonistic unions or state or local officials can often block implementation. So can rank-and-file teachers and health workers who feel marginalized and disadvantaged by the changes in their respective sectors (Grindle 2004). The broader the consensus on the general direction of reform, the less difficult will be the implementation process. The cases in this volume suggest that there may be many routes to the emergence of partial consensus. Early consultation with moderate unions can be helpful; case examples include teachers' unions in Minas Gerais in Brazil (Grindle 2004) and Mexico—though in the Mexican case earlier changes in union leadership, direct interventions from the president himself, and generous concessions were also crucial ingredients in the story.

Colombian and Costa Rican health reformers followed a different strategy: closely held design, followed by extensive efforts to explain the measures to all interested stakeholders (and, in Colombia's case, modest compromises). The Brazilian health reforms pursued still a third approach: an initial major structural change through constitutional and legislative channels, followed by arrangements to give state and local health authorities a direct voice in the design of follow-up measures. (The arrangements for ongoing consultation were themselves the focus of an ongoing tug-of-war.)

There are also multiple routes to engaging the cooperation of the providers themselves, even if their unions oppose change. In Nicaragua, education reforms ignored the hostile teachers' union but were designed to appeal to teachers' self-interest in augmented salaries. In Chile, efforts to improve the weakest schools sought the cooperation of teachers and principals through technical and material support and incentives channeled directly to the schools. There and in the state of Mérida, in Venezuela, special teams periodically visited and worked with individual schools. In short, conventional wisdom regarding consultation is too sweeping. Where major organized stakeholders can be induced to accept reforms, that course is highly desirable. But it is not always possible, or the price in terms of diluted reforms or fiscal costs may be too high. However, successful *implementation* of reforms will almost certainly require more effective forms of recruitment, incentives, and communication to enlist the cooperation of providers themselves—the teachers, doctors, and nurses who ultimately determine the quality of education and health services.

A central theme of this volume has been that education and health sector reforms are embedded in broader national and local political systems and contexts. The settings both constrain and offer opportunities for reform. There is reason to believe that in much of Latin America, political contexts are gradually becoming somewhat more supportive of reforms. We argued above that while electoral competition and more open democratic systems rarely generate social sector reforms in a direct way, they do create a more receptive political climate. Decentralization has had mixed effects, but it does alter incentives for local political leaders and open the way for local innovation; promising approaches may then spread.

Moreover, though international agencies cannot effectively promote reforms in the absence of strong domestic commitment, the crescendo of international emphasis on poverty reduction and social sector reform strengthens the hands of domestic reformers. The cross-national case comparisons in this volume highlight the choices and processes of reform. But they are semi-static snapshots, capturing at best the trajectory of a decade or so. They cannot adequately reflect the dynamic forces at work. The evidence cautions against expecting rapid or radical change, save in rare instances. But the next decades may well see quickened tempo and momentum.

References

Baghwati, Jagdish. 2002. Coping with Antiglobalization. *Foreign Affairs* 81, no. 1 (January/February): 1–7.

Berman, P., and Thomas Bossert. 2000. *A Decade of Health Sector Reform in Developing Countries: What Have We Learned?* Data for Decision-Making Report 81. Cambridge, Mass.: School of Public Health, Harvard University.

Brinkerhoff, Derick W., and Benjamin L. Crosby. 2002. *Managing Policy Reform.* Bloomfield, Conn.: Kumarian Press.

Brown, David S. 1999. Reading, Writing, and Regime Type: Democracy's Impact on Primary School Enrollment. *Political Research Quarterly* 52, no. 4: 681–707.

Cameron, David. 1978. The Expansion of the Public Economy: A Comparative Analysis. *American Political Science Review* 72 (December): 1243–61.

Castaneda, Tarsicio, Girindre Beeharry, and Charles Griffin. 1999. Decentralization of Health Services in Latin American Countries: Issues and Some Lessons. In *Decentralization and Accountability of the Public Sector: Proceedings of the Annual World Bank Conference on Development in Latin America and the Caribbean 1999,* ed. S. Javed Burki and G. Perry. Washington, D.C.: World Bank.

ECLAC (Economic Commission for Latin America and the Caribbean). 1999. *Social Panorama of Latin America 1998.*

Garrett, Jeffry 1999. Globalization and Government Spending around the World. Paper presented at the annual meeting of the American Political Science Association, Atlanta, September 1–5.

Gauri, Varun, and Peyvand Khaleghian. 2002. Immunization in Developing Countries: Its Political and Organizational Determinants. *World Development* 30, no. 12: 2109–32.

Gelbach, Jonah B., and Lant H. Pritchett. 1997. *More for the Poor Is Less for the Poor: The Politics of Targeting.* Policy Research Working Paper 1523. Washington, D.C.: World Bank.

González Rossetti, Alejandra. 2001. The Political Dimension of Health Reform: The Case of Mexico and Colombia. Ph.D. thesis, Department of Public Health Policy, London School of Hygiene and Tropical Medicine, University of London.

Goodin, Robert E., and Julian Le Grand. 1987. *Not Only the Poor: The Middle Classes and the Welfare State.* London: Allen and Unwin.

Graham, Carol. 1998. *Private Markets for Public Goods: Raising the Stakes in Economic Reform.* Washington, D.C.: Brookings Institution Press.

Grindle, Merilee S. 2004. *Despite the Odds: Contentious Politics and Education Reform.* Princeton, N.J.: Princeton University Press.

Hicks, Alexander 1999. *Social Democracy and Welfare Capitalism,* Ithaca, N.Y.: Cornell University Press,

Huber, Evelyne, and John Stephens. 2001. *Development and Crisis of the Welfare State.* Chicago: University of Chicago Press.

Hunter, Wendy, and David S. Brown. 2000. World Bank Directives, Domestic Interests, and the Politics of Human Capital Investment in Latin America. *Comparative Political Studies* 33, no. 1: 113–43.

Hurrell, Andrew, and Ngaire Woods, eds. 1999. *Inequality, Globalization, and World Politics.* Oxford: Oxford University Press.

Inter-American Development Bank. 1996. Making Social Services Work. In *Economic and Social Progress in Latin America.* Washington, D.C.: Inter-American Development Bank.

Jones, Mark. 1995. *Electoral Laws and the Survival of Presidential Democracies.* Notre Dame, Ind.: University of Notre Dame Press.

Katzenstein, Peter. 1985. *Small States in World Markets: Industrial Policy in Europe* Ithaca, N.Y.: Cornell University Press.

Kaufman, Robert R., and Alex Segura-Ubiergo. 2001. Globalization, Domestic Politics, and Social Spending in Latin America: A Cross-Sectional Time Series Analysis, 1973–1997. *World Politics* 53, no. 4: 553–88.

Lake, David, and Matthew A. Baum. 2001. The Invisible Hand of Democracy: Political Control and the Provision of Public Services. *Comparative Political Studies* 34, no. 6: 587–621.

Lehmbruch, Gerhard. 1984. Concertation and the Structure of Corporatist Networks. In *Order and Conflict in Contemporary Capitalism,* ed. John H. Goldthorpe. Oxford: Clarenden Press.

Lowden, Pamela. 1996. The Escuelas Integrales Reform Program in Venezuela. In *Implementing Policy Innovations in Latin America: Politics, Economics and Techniques,* ed. A. Silva. Washington, D.C.: Inter-American Development Bank.

Maceira, Daniel, and Maria Victoria Murillo. 2001. *Social Sector Reform in Latin America and the Role of Unions.* Working Paper 456. Washington, D.C.: Inter-American Development Bank.

Mainwaring, Scott. 1999. *Rethinking Party Systems in the Third Wave of Democratization: The Case of Brazil.* Stanford, Calif.: Stanford University Press.

McGuire, James W. 2001a. Democracy, Social Policy, and Mortality Decline in Brazil. Paper prepared for delivery at the 23rd International Congress of the Latin American Studies Association, Washington, September 6–8.

————. 2001b. Health Policy and Mortality Decline in the Province of Neuquen, Argentina. Wesleyan University, Middletown, Conn. (unpublished).

————. 2001c. Social Policy and Mortality Decline in East Asia and Latin America. *World Development* 29, no. 10: 1673–97.

————. 2002. Democracy, Social Provisioning, and Under-5 Mortality: A Cross-National Analysis. Paper prepared for delivery at the 2002 Annual Meeting of the American Political Science Association, Boston, August 29–September 1.

Navarro, Juan Carlos. 2000. The Social Consequences of Political Reforms: Decentral-ization and Social Policy in Venezuela. In *Social Development in Latin America: The Politics of Reform,* ed. Joseph S. Tulchin and Allison M. Garland. Boulder, Colo.: Lynne Rienner Publishers for the Latin American Program of the Woodrow Wilson International Center for Scholars.

Navia, Patricio and Andrés Velasco. 2003. The Politics of Second-Generation Reforms. In *After the Washington Consensus: Restarting Growth in Latin America,* ed. Pedro-Pablo Kuczynski and John Williamson. Washington, D.C. Institute for International Economics.

Nelson, Joan M. 1992. Poverty, Equity, and the Politics of Adjustment. In *The Politics of Economic Adjustment,* ed. Stephan Haggard and Robert Kaufman. Princeton, N.J.: Princeton University Press.

————. 2000. Reforming Social Sector Governance: A Political Perspective. In *Social Development in Latin America: The Politics of Reform,* ed. Joseph S. Tulchin and Allison M. Garland. Boulder, Colo.: Lynne Rienner Publishers for the Latin Ameri-can Program of the Woodrow Wilson International Center for Scholars.

Nelson, Joan M. 2003. Grounds for Alliance? Overlapping Interests of Poor and Not-So-Poor. In *Changing Paths: International Development and the New Politics of Inclusion,* ed. Peter P. Houtzager and Mick Moore. Ann Arbor: University of Michi-gan Press.

Orenstein, Mitchell A. 2000. *How Politics and Institutions Affect Pension Reform in Three Postcommunist Countries.* Policy Research Working Paper 2310. Washington, D.C., World Bank.

Pierson, Paul, ed. 2001. *The New Politics of the Welfare State* Oxford: Oxford Univer-sity Press.

PREAL (Partnership for Educational Revitalization in the Americas). Lagging Behind: A Report Card on Education in Latin America. Washington, D.C.: Inter-American Dialogue.

Reich, Michael R. 1994a. The Political Economy of Health Transitions in the Third World. In *Health and Social Change in International Perspective,* ed. Lincoln Chen, A. Kleinman, and N.C. Ware. Cambridge, Mass.: School of Public Health, Harvard University.

————. 1994b. Political Mapping of Health Policy: A Guide for Managing the Political Dimensions of Health Policy. Cambridge, Mass.: School of Public Health, Harvard University.

Rodrik, Dani. 1998a. Who Needs Capital Account Convertibility? Harvard University, Cambridge, Mass. (unpublished).

————. 1998b. Why Do More Open Economies Have Bigger Governments? *Journal of Political Economy* 106, no. 6: 997–1032.

Rojas, Fernando. 1999. The Political Context of Decentralization in Latin America. In *Development in Latin America and the Caribbean: Decentralization and Accounta-*

bility of the Public Sector, ed. Shahid Javed Burki and Guillermo Perry. Proceedings of a conference held in Valdivia, Chile. Washington, D.C.: World Bank.

Skocpol, Theda. 1991. Universal Appeal: Politically Viable Policies to Combat Poverty. *Brookings Review* 9, no. 3: 29–33.

Stiglitz, Joseph E. 2002. *Globalization and Its Discontents.* New York: W. W. Norton.

Swank, Duane. 2002. *Global Capital, Political Institutions, and Policy Change in Developed Welfare States.* Cambridge: Cambridge University Press.

Tendler, Judith. 1997. Preventive Health: The Case of the Unskilled Meritocracy. In *Good Government in the Tropics,* ed. J. Tendler. Baltimore: Johns Hopkins University Press.

———. 2002. Fear of Education. Massachusetts Institute of Technology, Cambridge, Mass. (unpublished).

Uvin, Peter. 1999. Scaling Up, Scaling Down: NGO Paths to Overcoming Hunger. In *Scaling Up, Scaling Down: Overcoming Malnutrition in Developing Countries,* ed. Thomas J. Marchione. Amsterdam: Gordon and Breach Publishers for the Overseas Publishers Association.

Wallerstein, Michael. 1990. Centralized Bargaining and Wage Restraint. *American Journal of Political Science* 34, no. 4: 982–1004.

Weyland, Kurt, 1996. *Democracy without Equity: Failures of Reform in Brazil.* Pittsburgh: University of Pittsburgh Press.

———. 2003. *Learning from Foreign Models in Latin American Policy Reform.* Baltimore and Washington, D.C.: Johns Hopkins University Press and Woodrow Wilson Center Press.

Contributors

Marta Arretche is a professor of political science at the University of São Paulo and a researcher at the Centro Brasileiro de Análise e Planejamento. Her research interests are primarily comparative politics, particularly federalism, intergovernmental relations, and social policies. Her most recent book is *Estado Federativo e Políticas Sociais*.

Josefina Bruni Celli is an aggregate professor at the Center for Public Policy of the Instituto de Estudios Superiores de Administración in Caracas. She holds a Ph.D. in public administration from New York University's Wagner School of Public Service and is currently studying the politics of violence in Venezuelan public high schools.

Mary A. Clark is an associate professor of political science at Tulane University. She is the author of *Gradual Economic Reform in Latin America: The Costa Rican Experience*. Her current research is on the medical profession's response to health reform in Chile and Costa Rica.

Javier Corrales is an assistant professor of political science at Amherst College in Massachusetts. He is the author of *Presidents without Parties: The Politics of Economic Reform in Argentina and Venezuela in the 1990s*. His research on the politics of economic and second-generation reforms has been published in several edited volumes and academic journals. He was a fellow at the Woodrow Wilson International Center for Scholars in Washington in 2000 and 2001.

Sônia M. Draibe is an associate professor at the Economics Institute at UNICAMP and former director of the Núcleo de Políticas Públicas da UNICAMP. She is an international consultant with expertise in design and evaluation of public policies and social programs and is currently the general secretary of the Brazilian Political Science Association (2000–4). She has published a number of articles and books on Brazilian social protection systems, policies, and programs.

Christina Ewig is an assistant professor of political science and women's studies at the University of Wisconsin—Milwaukee. Her research interests include feminist comparative policy and social policy in Latin America. She is currently working on a book on the impact of Latin American health sector reforms on gender equity.

Alec Ian Gershberg is an associate professor at the Milano Graduate School of Management and Urban Policy at the New School University. He is a research associate at the National Bureau of Economic Research and has done extensive research on school reform in Latin America. His forthcoming book *Beyond Bilingual Education* examines school policies for immigrant students in the United States.

Alejandra González Rossetti is a public policy consultant with international experience in the field of social sector reform. She has acted as an adviser to the governments of Mexico, Honduras, the Dominican Republic, El Salvador, and the Samara Oblast in Russia, as well as to numerous multilateral organizations. Most recently her work has focused on structuring financial and institutional incentives in multilateral loans to increase the political feasibility of social sector reforms. She has published widely on the political economy of social sector reforms.

Merilee S. Grindle is the Edward S. Mason Professor of International Development at the Kennedy School of Government at Harvard University.

She is a specialist on the comparative analysis of policymaking, implementation, and public management in developing countries. Her two most recent books are *Despite the Odds: The Contentious Politics of Education Reform* and *Audacious Reforms: Institutional Invention and Democracy in Latin America,* both of which deal with the politics of reform.

Robert R. Kaufman is a professor of political science at Rutgers University. He is the author and editor of numerous books and articles on economic reform, democratization, and, more recently, social policy. His publications include *The Political Economy of Democratic Transitions* and *Reforming the State: Fiscal and Welfare Reform in Transition Economies.*

Peter Lloyd-Sherlock is a senior lecturer in social development at the School of Development Studies, University of East Anglia, United Kingdom. His main interests are population aging in developing countries and the political economy of sectoral reform in Argentina. His publications include two edited volumes, *Living Longer: Ageing, Development and Social Protection* and *Healthcare Reform and Poverty in Latin America.*

Pamela S. Lowden has worked as a research officer at the Queen Elizabeth House International Development Center, Oxford University, and was the coauthor of *Decentralizing Development: The Political Economy of Institutional Change in Colombia and Chile.* She was a long-term consultant with the Economic Development Institute of the World Bank and has also done a number of consultancy assignments for the Inter-American Development Bank, working on the politics of social reform in various countries of the region.

Joan M. Nelson is a senior scholar at the Woodrow Wilson International Center for Scholars and a scholar in residence at the School of International Service at American University. She is the author or editor of several books and many articles on the politics of economic reforms. Most recently, she has focused on the politics of social sector reforms and the role of external agencies in promoting those reforms, publishing *Reforming Health and Education: The World Bank, the Inter-American Development Bank, and Complex Institutional Change.*

Patricia Ramírez is a consultant on health and social policy. She is a graduate of Universidad de los Andes, Colombia, where she studied economics and anthropology, and holds a master's degree in social policy and planning in developing countries from the London School of Economics. She began her career in the National Planning Department of Colombia, working on the design, implementation, and evaluation of social policies and projects, and has been a consultant for the United Nations Development Program, UNICEF, the Harvard University School of Public Health, and the Colombian President's Office for Social Policy.

Index

Carvajal, Leonardo, 452, 461–62, 463–64

Castillo, Francisco, 442, 443–44, 449–50

Cavallo, Domingo F., 265, 273, 322–23, 323*n*

CCSS. *See* Costa Rican Social Security Fund

CEDESS (Mexico). *See* Centro de Desarrollo Estratégico para la Seguridad Social

centralization, 288–89, 301

Centro de Desarrollo Estratégico para la Seguridad Social (CEDESS) (Mexico), 79, 81, 87–88

Chamorro, Violeta, 411, 416, 420

change teams, Brazilian education reform, 390–91, 403–4; Colombia, 131, 137–38; Costa Rica health reform, 190, 200, 201, 201*n*, 202, 204–5, 207, 214; Mexico education reform, 298, 305, 309, 311; Mexico health reform, 79, 80, 82, 83–84, 86–88; Peru, 226, 234, 235, 236, 241, 242; *See also* Bogotá, Colombia, education reform

charter schools, 458–59, 467

Chávez, Hugo, 461–66

Chile, 12, 198, 258

civil society, Brazilian constitution, 388; Colombian constitution, 357; Nicaragua, 412, 412*n*, 420; Peru, 242

CLAS (Peru). *See* Local Health Administration committees

clientelism, Brazil, 380, 385, 388, 389; Colombia, 137, 150, 356; municipal schools, 385. *See also* patronage

CNE (Brazil). *See* National Education Plan

CNTE (Mexico). *See* Coordinadora Nacional de Trabajadores de la Educación

Colegio de Médicos (Costa Rica), 199, 235–36

Colegio de Profesores (Venezuela), 459, 460

Collor de Mello, Fernando, 50, 159, 168–69, 170–71

Colombia, 23, 28, 41; 2001 reform revisions 368–71; decentralization, 55; economic indicators, 7*t*, 125; educational reform compared, 261*t;* educational system, 352–54; education indicators, 8*t*, 9, 350; education patronage, 265; health care system, 128; health indicators, 7*t*–8*t*, 9; health workers' unions, 134–5; scope and vision, 41, 42*t*, 44–46; teachers' unions, 268; *vinculados,* 148, 148*n*. *See also* Federation of Colombian Teachers; Institute of Social Security (ISS)

Colombian Institute for the Promotion of Higher Education, 364

Colombian Medical Federation (ASCOFAME), 132, 133

Colombian Medical School Association, 132

community participation, education. *See* school councils

community participation, health, Costa Rica *juntas de salud,* 208–9; Peru, 227, 234, 242

competition, 143, 278, 478

CONSED (Brazil). *See* National Council of State Secretariats of Education

Constituent Assembly, Brazil, 157, 158–59; civil society, 388; described, 168

Constituent Assembly, Colombia, civic pressures, 355; debates, 355–58; education reform, 271; equity, 355; transfer system design, 365

Constitution, Brazil, 28, 29, 44; decentralization, 158; education activists, 388; education reform, 271; health care mandates, 44, 45; national health laws, 166–70; unified health system, 156

Constitution, Colombia, 28, 29, 44, 127; described, 354–55; health care mandates, 44–45; political participation, 352; revised, 368; social policy, 361

Constitution, Colombia (*continued*)
consultation with stakeholders, in design phase, 475; Argentine citizen participation, 327; assessed, 514–15;
Colombian health reform, 128,131–32;
135; Costa Rican health reform, 197
contracting-out of services, Argentine
health, 115; Brazilian health, 182;
Costa Rican health, 212; education reform in Colombia, 366–67; Mexican
health reforms, 78, 85, 86
Contras in Nicaragua, 411
Convertibility Law (Argentina, 1991),
323*n*, 324
Coordinadora Nacional de Trabajadores
de la Educación (CNTE) (Mexico),
292–93, 311
COPEN (Venezuela). *See* National Education Project Presidential
Commission
COPRE (Venezuela). *See* Presidential
Commission for State Reform
corporatism, 65, 66–68, 69, 72, 289
corruption, 114–15, 353
Costa Bauer, Marino, 238
Costa Rica, 10, 25, 28, 44, 58; economic
indicators, 7*t;* education indicators, 8*t,*
9; health care reform, 197–215; health
indicators, 9; health reform themes,
190; health care outcomes, 44*n;* health
indicators, 7*t*–8*t;* public health systems, 25; scope and vision, 44
Costa Rican Social Security Fund
(CCSS), board of directors, 192,
192*n;* described, 191–93; domination
by, 189, 191; positive view, 50; reforms, 36
coverage, education, Bogotá, 366; Brazil, 383, 400; Colombia, 350, 350*n*–
51*n*, 363, 371–72; Mexico, 306*n;*
Nicaragua, 414, 415; school enrollments, Argentina, 319, 319*t;* Venezuela, 444
coverage, health care, Brazil, 180, 184;
Colombia, 141, 142–43, 149, 151;
Costa Rica, 191, 195, 205; family

coverage, 142; Mexico, 70–71, 86;
Peru, 222, 223*f,* 237, 239. *See also*
uninsured, health care
CTERA (Confederation of Education
Workers of the Argentine Republic),
319, 324, 327
Cuba, 23, 44; health care system, 25,
44*n*
curriculum reform, Mexico, 309–10;
Nicaragua, 430–31; Venezuela, 439,
454–55, 457, 467–68
curriculum and textbook issues, summarized, 258

decentralization, 355, 356–57; and
democratization 484–85; failings, 38;
federal system, Brazil, 158, 169;
federalization, Mexico, 297, 298;
meanings of, 441–42; mixed effects,
511, 516; options, 506–7; organization of instruction, 428, 430*t;* outcomes summarized, 52, 53*t,* 55–57;
patronage, 39; personnel management, 428, 430*t;* planning and structures, 428, 430*t;* pluralism, 360–61;
political, 351–52; political parties,
272–73; progress, 52; resources, 428,
430*t;* role of central government,
431–33; rules and channels, 51; via
ministerial decrees, 434. *See also* fiscal transfers
decentralization, education reforms, Argentina, 321–26; benefits analyzed,
279, 392; Brazil, 382, 384,389, 390,
392; 395, 400, Colombia, 264, 350,
351, 360–61, 369–70; compared, 259,
260*t,* 261; design, 272–73; destabilizing effects, 279; emphasis, 269; implementation, 273–75; initiation of,
270–72; Latin America, 409–11; local officials, 266; Mexico, 284, 285,
288, 297–307; outcomes, 279; politics
summarized, 270–75; School Meals
program (PNAE), 276; two types,
409–11; Venezuela, 439, 440, 441–
42, 444–45